Lecture Notes in Computer Science   13478

More information about this series at https://link.springer.com/bookseries/558

Adrian Riesco · Min Zhang (Eds.)

Formal Methods and Software Engineering

23rd International Conference
on Formal Engineering Methods, ICFEM 2022
Madrid, Spain, October 24–27, 2022
Proceedings

Editors
Adrian Riesco ⓘ
Complutense University of Madrid
Madrid, Spain

Min Zhang ⓘ
East China University of Science
and Technology
Shanghai, China

ISSN 0302-9743 ISSN 1611-3349 (electronic)
Lecture Notes in Computer Science
ISBN 978-3-031-17243-4 ISBN 978-3-031-17244-1 (eBook)
https://doi.org/10.1007/978-3-031-17244-1

This Springer imprint is published by the registered company Springer Nature Switzerland AG
The registered company address is: Gewerbestrasse 11, 6330 Cham, Switzerland

Preface

The International Conference on Formal Engineering Methods (ICFEM) is a premier conference for research in all areas related to formal engineering methods, such as verification and validation, software engineering, formal specification and modeling, software security, and software reliability. Since 1997, ICFEM has been serving as an international forum for researchers and practitioners who have been seriously applying formal methods to practical applications. Researchers and practitioners, from industry, academia, and government, are encouraged to attend, present their research, and help advance the state of the art. We are interested in the work that has been incorporated into real production systems, and in the theoretical work that promises to bring practical and tangible benefit.

In recent years, ICFEM has taken place in Singapore (2021, corresponding to ICFEM 2020, postponed due to the COVID-19 pandemic), Shenzhen, China (2019), Gold Coast, Australia (2018), Xi'an, China (2017), Tokyo, Japan (2016), and Paris, France (2015). The 23rd edition of ICFEM physically took place in Madrid, Spain, during October 25–27, 2022. The Program Committee (PC) received 61 full research papers. Each submission was reviewed by at least three Program Committee members. The committee decided to accept 23 papers. The program also included three invited talks by Xiaowei Huang from the University of Liverpool, Santiago Escobar from the Universitat Politècnica de València, and Yuan Feng from the University of Technology Sydney. The main event was preceded by the 11th International Workshop on SOFL + MSVL for Reliability and Security, SOFL + MSVL 2022, and the 1st International Workshop on Formal Analysis and Verification of Post-Quantum Cryptographic Protocols, FAVPQC 2022. ICFEM 2022 was organized and supported by the Facultad de Informática of the Universidad Complutense de Madrid.

We would like to thank the numerous people who contributed to the success of ICFEM 2022: the Steering Committee members, the PC members, and the additional reviewers for their support in selecting papers and composing the conference program, and the authors and the invited speakers for their contributions without which, of course, these proceedings would not exist. We would also like to thank Springer for their help during the production of this proceedings volume and the EasyChair team for their excellent conference system. We also thank the Local Organizing Committee for their hard work in making ICFEM 2022 a successful and exciting event.

August 2022   Min Zhang
                                                                                                    Adrian Riesco

Organization

Program Committee

Yamine Ait Ameur	IRIT, INP-ENSEEIHT, France
Étienne André	Université de Lorraine, CNRS, Inria, LORIA, Nancy, France
Cyrille Valentin Artho	KTH Royal Institute of Technology, Sweden
Christian Attiogbe	L2N - Université de Nantes, France
Guangdong Bai	University of Queensland, Australia
Christel Baier	TU Dresden, Germany
Richard Banach	University of Manchester, UK
Luís Soares Barbosa	University of Minho, Portugal
Christiano Braga	Universidade Federal Fluminense, Brazil
Hadrien Bride	Griffith University, Australia
Ana Cavalcanti	University of York, UK
Yean-Ru Chen	National Cheng Kung University, Taiwan
Yu-Fang Chen	Academia Sinica, Taiwan
Yuting Chen	Shanghai Jiao Tong University, China
Yunja Choi	Kyungpook National University, South Korea
Ranald Clouston	Aarhus University, Denmark
Sylvain Conchon	Université Paris-Saclay, France
Florin Craciun	Babes-Bolyai University, Romania
Frank De Boer	Centrum Wiskunde & Informatica, The Netherlands
Yuxin Deng	East China Normal University, China
Thi Thu Ha Doan	Freiburg University, Germany
Naipeng Dong	National University of Singapore, Singapore
Flavio Ferrarotti	Software Competence Centre Hagenberg, Austria
Marc Frappier	Université de Sherbrooke, Canada
Lindsay Groves	Victoria University of Wellington, New Zealand
Xudong He	Florida International University, USA
Zhe Hou	Griffith University, Australia
Pao-Ann Hsiung	National Chung Cheng University, Taiwan
Fuyuki Ishikawa	National Institute of Informatics, Japan
Eun-Young Kang	University of Southern Denmark, Denmark
Tsutomu Kobayashi	Japan Aerospace Exploration Agency, Japan
Xuandong Li	Nanjing University, China
Yi Li	Nanyang Technological University, Singapore
Shang-Wei Lin	Nanyang Technological University, Singapore

Si Liu	ETH Zurich, Switzerland
Yang Liu	Nanyang Technological University, Singapore
Zhiming Liu	Southwest University, China
Brendan Mahony	DSTO, Australia
Frederic Mallet	Université Nice Sophia-Antipolis, France
Dominique Mery	Université de Lorraine, Loria, France
Stephan Merz	Inria Nancy, France
Shin Nakajima	National Institute of Informatics, Japan
Masaki Nakamura	Toyama Prefectural University, Japan
Peter Ölveczky	University of Oslo, Norway
Jun Pang	University of Luxembourg, Luxembourg
Yu Pei	The Hong Kong Polytechnic University, Hong Kong, China
Shengchao Qin	Teesside University, UK
Silvio Ranise	University of Trento and Fondazione Bruno Kessler, Trento, Italy
Elvinia Riccobene	Computer Science Dept., University of Milan, Italy
Adrian Riesco (Chair)	Universidad Complutense de Madrid, Spain
Rubén Rubio	Universidad Complutense de Madrid, Spain
David Sanan	Singapore Institute of Technology, Singapore
Jing Sun	University of Auckland, New Zealand
Meng Sun	Peking University, China
Alwen Tiu	Australian National University, Australia
Elena Troubitsyna	KTH Royal Institute of Technology, Sweden
Ionut Tutu	Simion Stoilow Institute of Mathematics of the Romanian Academy, Romania
Bow-Yaw Wang	Academia Sinica, Taiwan
Hai H. Wang	University of Aston, UK
Ji Wang	National University of Defense Technology, China
Virginie Wiels	ONERA/DTIM, France
Naijun Zhan	Institute of Software, Chinese Academy of Sciences, China
Min Zhang (Chair)	East China Normal University, China

Additional Reviewers

Bodeveix, Jean-Paul	Chen, Xin
Bu, Hao	Cheng, Zheng
Cai, Chenghao	Chondamrongkul, Nacha
Cao, Qinxiang	Feng, Shenghua
Carbone, Roberto	Iyoda, Juliano

Jhou, Yan-Ru
Jiao, Jiao
Kaufmann, Daniela
Li, Yong
Liu, Peizun
Mitsch, Stefan
Pan, Minxue
Rademaker, Alexandre
Shen, Bo
Tsai, Wei-Lun

Wen, Cheng
Wu, Peng
Xiong, Jiawen
Xu, Xiong
Yatapanage, Nisansala
Zhang, Xiyue
Zhang, Yuanrui
Zhao, Jianhua
Zhao, Liang

Model Checking Quantum Markov Chains (Abstract)

Yuan Feng

University of Technology Sydney

Abstract. Quantum software will play an important role in harnessing the superpower of quantum computing. However, it is extremely difficult to guarantee its correctness. Model checking has been shown to be effective in the verification of classical programs, but a fundamental difficulty arises when it is applied to quantum systems: the state space of a quantum system is always a continuum even if its dimension is finite. To overcome this difficulty, we introduce a novel concept of quantum Markov chains, in which quantum effects are encoded as super-operators labelling transitions, keeping the location information (nodes) classical. We define a quantum extension of Probabilistic Computation Tree Logic called QCTL for the new model and develop algorithms to verify properties expressed in this logic. It is worth noting that in this framework, model checking is performed symbolically at the super-operator level, without resorting to the underlying quantum states, thus avoiding the difficulties brought about by the continuity of the (quantum) state space. To verify omega-regular (e.g. Linear Temporal Logic) properties, we transform the product of the quantum Markov chain and the property automaton into a single super-operator and show that the BSCC subspace decomposition of the associated state space provides a solution to the model checking problem.

Contents

Bridging Formal Methods and Machine Learning with Global Optimisation

Xiaowei Huang[1]([✉]), Wenjie Ruan[2], Qiyi Tang[1], and Xingyu Zhao[1]

[1] Department of Computer Science, University of Liverpool, Liverpool, UK
{xiaowei.huang,qiyi.tang,xingyu.zhao}@liverpool.ac.uk
[2] Department of Computer Science, University of Exeter, Exeter, UK
w.ruan@exeter.ac.uk

Abstract. Formal methods and machine learning are two research fields with drastically different foundations and philosophies. Formal methods utilise mathematically rigorous techniques for the specification, development and verification of software and hardware systems. Machine learning focuses on pragmatic approaches to gradually improve a parameterised model by observing a training data set. While historically the two fields lack communication, this trend has changed in the past few years with an outburst of research interest in the robustness verification of neural networks. This paper will briefly review these works, and focus on the urgent need for broader, and more in-depth, communication between the two fields, with the ultimate goal of developing learning-enabled systems with not only excellent performance but also acceptable safety and security. We present a specification language, MLS^2, and show that it can express a set of known safety and security properties, including generalisation, uncertainty, robustness, data poisoning, backdoor, model stealing, membership inference, model inversion, interpretability, and fairness. To verify MLS^2 properties, we promote the global optimisation based methods, which have provable guarantees on the convergence to the optimal solution. Many of them have theoretical bounds on the gap between current solutions and the optimal solution.

Keywords: Formal methods · Machine learning · Global optimisation

1 Introduction

Recent advances in machine learning have enabled the development of complex, intelligent software systems with human-level performance. A notable example is image classification, among many others. However, the machine learning systems (or models) are not rigorously engineered, even if many of them have been successfully applied to industrial applications. Instead, their design and implementation are based on developers' experience, and have been frequently referred to as "dark art". Compounded with the intensively discussed safety and security issues discovered through various adversarial attacks such as [6,22,32,38] and the clear expectation that machine learning models will be applied to safety-critical applications, it is clear that rigorous engineering methods are urgently needed.

© Springer Nature Switzerland AG 2022
A. Riesco and M. Zhang (Eds.): ICFEM 2022, LNCS 13478, pp. 1–19, 2022.
https://doi.org/10.1007/978-3-031-17244-1_1

Successful experience from industrial software engineering, which produced software currently applied in, e.g., automotive and avionic applications, suggests that, to develop high-quality and low-cost software in a limited production time, a software development life cycle (SDLC) process is required. Considering the V-model of an SDLC, as shown in the left diagram of Fig. 1, the development of a software system starts from the understanding and documentation of the operational concepts, the development of the requirement and architecture, and the conduction of detailed design before its actual implementation (i.e., coding). Once coded, the software must pass unit-level testing and system-level verification and validation before deployment. After the deployment, maintenance is still required throughout the life of the software. It should be noted that, during the execution of the V-model, feedback from a later stage may often trigger the modification to an earlier stage. Therefore the development is an iterative process rather than a sequential process.

Fig. 1. V-models for software (Left) and machine learning (Right) development

For machine learning software, the current V-model is not suitable anymore, because the machine learning models are over-parameterised with complex, fixed structures and, due to the lack of operational semantics, there is no explainable way of decomposing the architecture and parameters. A new V-model, as shown in the right diagram of Fig. 1, can still be considered, and we will discuss its details in Sect. 3.

Formal methods are essential tools throughout software development (e.g., by following the V-model) as they provide mathematical rigour (and therefore provable guarantees) to the performance, safety, and security of the final software products. However, unlike software systems where formal methods have been developed on the specification, development, and verification of a system, formal methods are only developed on the robustness verification of neural networks [12, 17]. That is, only local robustness defects of a neural network can be dealt with. This paper argues that, to support the new V-model, more formal method based techniques are needed to deal with various safety and security defects of neural networks.

While compelling, the development of formal methods for neural networks is non-trivial, because the machine learning community currently deals with safety and security defects in an ad-hoc way. That is, dedicated algorithms are developed for specific defects. In this paper, we first attempt to use a common specification language, named MLS^2, to specify a set of safety and security properties. Based on the specification language, the verification of MLS^2 properties can be reduced to the computation of a few constructs, including the data distribution, the posterior distribution, the distance between distributions, and the quantification over a set of inputs.

For the verification algorithms, we consider global optimisation (GO) methods to compute the language constructs. GO methods can not only make efficient computation but also converge to the optimal results. Many GO methods have a provable bound on the error between the obtained solution and the optimal one. For example, for the computation of the posterior distribution, we may consider Markov Chain Monte Carlo (MCMC), which approximates the distribution with a Markov chain, or Variational Inference, which finds the best-known distribution that approximates the unknown distribution. For the universal quantification over a set of inputs, we may consider Lipschitzian optimisation [15,16] as we did for the robustness verification [24].

2   Preliminaries

We use $f_\mathbf{w}$ to denote a neural network with weight matrix $\mathbf{w}$. We use $\mathbf{x}$ to range over the input domain $\mathbb{R}^n$, and y to range over the labels C. Given $f_\mathbf{w}$ and $\mathbf{x}$, we write $f_\mathbf{w}(\mathbf{x})$ for the probability distribution of classifying $\mathbf{x}$, such that $f_\mathbf{w}(\mathbf{x})(c)$ for $c \in C$ is the probability of classifying $\mathbf{x}$ with label c. Moreover, we write $\hat{y} = arg\,max f_\mathbf{w}(\mathbf{x})$ for the predictive label. Given a label y, we write $\mathbf{y}$ for its one-hot encoding. An one-hot encoding can be seen as a probability distribution.

3   V-Model for Machine Learning

In this section, we explain the phases in the new V-model as shown in the right diagram of Fig. 1.

Operational Profile and Data Collection. A neural network $f_\mathbf{w} : \mathbb{R}^n \to [0,1]^{|C|}$ is to simulate a target function $h : \mathbb{R}^n \to \{1, ..., |C|\}$. For real world function h, the appearance of an input $\mathbf{x}$ in the space $\mathbb{R}^n$ is not uniform. We assume there is a probability density function $\mathcal{D} : \mathbb{R}^n \to [0,1]$, which returns the probability $\mathcal{D}(\mathbf{x})$ for each input $\mathbf{x}$. We may also abuse the notation and write $\mathcal{D}((\mathbf{x},y))$, with the assumption that $\mathcal{D}((\mathbf{x},y)) = \mathcal{D}(\mathbf{x})$ because h is a deterministic function. The distribution $\mathcal{D}$ is called *data distribution*. It is usually required that the training data includes a set of inputs sampled i.i.d. from the data distribution.

When designing a neural network for some critical application, we may need to consider the environment where it will be deployed. In the operational environment, we also have a distribution $\mathcal{O} : \mathbb{R}^m \to [0,1]$, which we call *operational profile* by inheriting the terminology from the reliability engineering area [21]. In [39,40], methods have been proposed to learn an approximate operational profile

$\hat{\mathcal{O}}$ through a set of data collected from the operational environment. The main challenges are on the accurate estimation for high-dimensional input space and how to provide provable guarantees on the gap between $\hat{\mathcal{O}}$ and $\mathcal{O}$.

Requirement and Specification. Usually, the target function h is unlikely to correctly and precisely specify. The training data can be seen as partial specification, with positive and negative examples. Beyond training data, we may need other requirements that cannot be explicitly expressed with the training data, such as robustness, privacy, and security properties that we will discuss in Sect. 5. A common practice in formal methods is to design a specification language (as we will do in Sect. 4), show that it can express desirable properties (Sect. 5), and design verification algorithms that can work with any specification expressible with the language (Sect. 6).

Architecture and Hyperparameter. The detailed design of a neural network is based on its architecture and hyper-parameters. Various criteria have been utilised to determine the quality of a trained model, and generalisation is the most popular one. We write G_f^{0-1} for the 0-1 generalisation error of neural network f, and $\mathcal{F}$ for the set of neural networks. Then, G_f^{0-1} can be decomposed as follows:

$$G_f^{0-1} = \underbrace{G_f^{0-1} - \inf_{f \in \mathcal{F}} G_f^{0-1}}_{\text{Estimation error of } f} + \underbrace{\inf_{f \in \mathcal{F}} G_f^{0-1} - G_{\mathbf{d}_{train}}^{0-1,*}}_{\text{Approximation error of } \mathcal{F}} + \underbrace{G_{\mathbf{d}_{train}}^{0-1,*}}_{\text{Bayes error}} \quad (1)$$

where $G_{\mathbf{d}_{train}}^{0-1,*}$ is the 0-1 generalisation error of the Optimal Bayes classifier over the training dataset $\mathbf{d}_{train}$. The *Bayes error* is the lowest and irreducible error over all possible classifiers for the given classification problem [9]. It is non-zero if the true labels are not deterministic (e.g., an image being labelled as y_1 by one person but as y_2 by others), thus intuitively it captures the uncertainties in the dataset $\mathbf{d}_{train}$ and the true distribution $\mathcal{D}$ when aiming to solve a real-world problem with machine learning. The *approximation error of $\mathcal{F}$* measures how far the best classifier in $\mathcal{F}$ is from the overall optimal classifier, after isolating the Bayes error. The set $\mathcal{F}$ is determined by the architecture of the machine learning model. Thus the activities at this stage are to minimise this error with optimised architecture and hyper-parameters.

Model Training. Once the architecture and the hyper-parameters are selected, the training is an optimisation process to reduce the estimation error. The *estimation error of f* measures how far the learned classifier f is from the best classifier in $\mathcal{F}$. Lifecycle activities at the **model training** stage essentially aim to reduce this error.

Both the approximation and estimation errors are reducible. The *ultimate goal* of all lifecycle activities is to reduce the two errors to 0. This is analogous to the "possible perfection" notion of traditional software as pointed to by Rushby and Littlewood [19,26]. That is, assurance activities, e.g., performed in support of DO-178C, can be best understood as developing evidence of possible perfection. Similarly, for a safety-critical machine learning model, we believe its lifecycle activities should be considered as aiming to train a "possibly perfect" model in terms of the two *reducible* errors. Thus, we may have some confidence that the two errors are both 0 (equivalently, prior confidence in the *irreducible* Bayes error since the other two are 0), which indeed is supported by ongoing research into finding globally optimised DNNs [7]. When GO is not achievable, heuristic methods to achieve estimation errors as small as possible should also be considered, for example, the adversarial training methods such as [13,14,20].

Testing and Empirical Evaluation. It has been a common practice in machine learning that some empirical evaluation methods, such as test accuracy and ROC curve, are taken to roughly understand the performance of a trained model. This step is still required to efficiently rule out some poorly performed architecture and hyperparameters. Besides, the testing methods, such as [11,29–31], are also developed to utilise automatically generated test cases to estimate the performance of the trained model. When using a testing method, we need to evaluate test adequacy, i.e., when to terminate the test case generation process. There are mainly two approaches that can be utilised, including the behaviours of a machine learning model in the inference stage and the data instances that might appear in the operational stage, respectively. For these approaches, objective metrics are needed to determine the extent to which an analysis technique has been conducted, as discussed in the later ALARP principle.

Verification and Validation. Neither empirical evaluation nor testing methods can have a provable guarantee of the result. For safety-critical applications, formal verification may be needed. Formal verification requires mathematically rigorous proof to argue for or against the satisfiability of a property on a given neural network. Existing verification algorithms are mainly focused on point-wise robustness, i.e., the robustness of the model over a given input. The algorithms can be roughly categorised into constraint-solving based methods [17], abstract interpretation based methods [10,18], GO based methods [12,24,25], and game-based methods [33,35]. The first two categories treat deep learning as a white box, with the computation needed on all neurons. This results in the scalability issue due to the complexity of the problem and the size of the deep learning. The latter two categories can work with real-world deep learning models, but are still subject to the curse of dimensionality. Currently, the verification is focused on the robustness problem, and we will discuss how to work with other properties in Sect. 6.

Operational Reliability Assessment. In [39,40], we have known that it is possible to compute the reliability in a given operational profile $\mathcal{O}$. However, the deployment environment may change, rendering the reliability assessment inappropriate. Nevertheless, experience may be learned from the reliability engineering for conventional software, where techniques have been developed to monitor the changes between different software versions to ensure the maintenance and improvement of reliability [5,23,28]. For the machine learning models, it is suggested that we may monitor two data distributions (or operational profiles), one for the original environment and the other for the new environment. Since the reliability result is on the original environment, and we can measure the distance between two data distributions, techniques can be developed to conservatively predict the reliability in the new environment.

4   Specification Language

We introduce a specification language MLS^2, abbreviated for Machine Learning Safety and Security, which will be used in the next section to specify a number of known properties.

Definition 1. *The syntax of the language MLS^2 is*

$$
\begin{aligned}
\mu &:= P(W|\boldsymbol{d}) \mid P(Y|\boldsymbol{x},\boldsymbol{w}) \mid P(\hat{Y}|\boldsymbol{d},\boldsymbol{w}) \mid \boldsymbol{y} \\
u &:= (\boldsymbol{x},y) \sim \mathcal{D} \mid \boldsymbol{w} \sim P(W|\boldsymbol{d}) \\
v &:= y \in C \mid (\boldsymbol{x},y) \in \boldsymbol{d} \mid \boldsymbol{x} \in Mut(\boldsymbol{x}) \\
\gamma &:= c \mid \mu(c) \mid D_{KL}(\mu,\mu) \mid ||\mu - \mu||_p \mid \mathbb{E}_u(\gamma) \mid \mathbb{V}_u(\gamma) \mid \mathbb{V}_v(\gamma) \mid \\
&\quad \mathbb{A}_v(\gamma) \mid \gamma + \gamma \mid \gamma - \gamma \mid |\gamma| \\
\phi &:= \gamma \leq c \mid \neg\phi \mid \phi \vee \phi \mid \exists \boldsymbol{t}: \phi
\end{aligned}
\tag{2}
$$

*where the **bold** lower capital letters $\boldsymbol{x}$, $\boldsymbol{w}$, $\boldsymbol{d}$, and $\boldsymbol{y}$ denote an input, a weight matrix, a set of data instances, and a probability distribution, respectively. We use $\boldsymbol{t}$ to range over $\{\boldsymbol{x}, \boldsymbol{d}, \boldsymbol{y}\}$. Capital letters W and Y denote random variables for the weight matrix and the label, respectively. Moreover, we use c to express either a constant value or some concrete value of a random variable. We use variable u to range over the support of a distribution (i.e., $(\boldsymbol{x},y) \sim \mathcal{D}$ or $\boldsymbol{w} \sim P(W|\boldsymbol{d})$), and use variable v to range over the instances in a known set (i.e., $(\boldsymbol{x},y) \in \boldsymbol{d}$ or $y \in C$ or $\boldsymbol{x} \in Mut(\boldsymbol{x})$), where Mut is a set of mutations that maps an input instance $\boldsymbol{x}$ into a set of new input instances.*

Intuitively, $P(W|\mathbf{d})$ expresses the posterior distribution of the models parameterised with W, when they are trained on a dataset $\mathbf{d}$. The expression $P(Y|\mathbf{x},\mathbf{w})$ is the predictive distribution when the model is parameterised with known $\mathbf{w}$ and the input instance is $\mathbf{x}$, and $P(\hat{Y}|\mathbf{d},\mathbf{w})$ denotes the probability distribution of predictive labels $\hat{Y}$ over a set of data $\mathbf{d}$. These three distributions serve as the most fundamental elements of the properties. We can also have the distributions from the one-hot encoding $\mathbf{y}$ of the labels.

The formulas γ return real values. Specifically, $\mu(c)$ is the probability density of the distribution μ on c. For example, we can write $P(Y|\mathbf{x},\mathbf{w})(y)$ for some $y \in C$ to denote the probability of predicting $\mathbf{x}$ as label y when the model is parameterised with $\mathbf{w}$. The formulas $D_{KL}(\mu,\mu)$ and $||\mu - \mu||_p$, for $p \geq 0$, expresses the distance between two distributions with the KL divergence[1] and

---

[1] There are different measurements to measure the distance between two distributions. In this paper, we take KL divergence as an example and believe the formalism can be extended to other measurements.

the norm distance, respectively. The formulas $\mathbb{E}_u(\gamma)$ and $\mathbb{V}_u(\gamma)$ return the mean and the variance, respectively, of γ. If, instead of having the distribution μ, we have a dataset $\mathbf{d}$, the average value and the variance of γ over $\mathbf{d}$ can be expressed with the formulas $\mathbb{A}_{(\mathbf{x},y)\in\mathbf{d}}(\gamma)$ and $\mathbb{V}_{(\mathbf{x},y)\in\mathbf{d}}(\gamma)$, respectively. Moreover, we may use the linear combination of γ, i.e., $\gamma+\gamma$ and $\gamma-\gamma$, and the absolute value $|\gamma|$.

Once having γ, the formula ϕ can be formed by firstly asserting relational relations between γ and a constant c, then composing a Boolean formula with Boolean operators. In the definition, we only write the relational operation $\leq$ and a minimum set of Boolean operators, i.e., $\{\neg, \vee\}$, and it is straightforward to extend them to other relational operators $\{<, \geq, >\}$ and other Boolean operators $\{\wedge, \Rightarrow, \iff\}$. Similarly, we only write the existence quantifier $\exists$ in the definition, but will use $\forall$ in the following.

The semantics of the language can be obtained by first having the standard semantics for the language constructs and then following the syntax. We omit the details.

5 Properties

This section formalises several safety and security properties with the specification language described in the previous section.

5.1 Generalisation

Generalisation concerns the performance of the machine learning model on unseen data (or on the underlying data distribution). The following formula ϕ^1_{gen} expresses that the expected loss, measured over the difference between the prediction $P(Y|\mathbf{x}, \mathbf{w})$ and the ground truth y on the data distribution $\mathcal{D}$, is lower than a pre-specified threshold. Formally,

$$\phi^1_{gen} \triangleq \mathbb{E}_{(\mathbf{x},y)\sim\mathcal{D}}(||P(Y|\mathbf{x}, \mathbf{w}) - \mathbf{y}||_2) < \epsilon^1_{gen} \tag{3}$$

where $\mathbf{y}$ is the one-hot encoding of the label y and $\epsilon^1_{gen} > 0$ is a small constant.

Moreover, generalisation is a concept close to overfitting, which suggests that a model may perform (much) better on the training data than on the test data (i.e., the data distribution). We can specify this view – generalisation gap – with the following formula

$$\phi^2_{gen} \triangleq |\mathbb{E}_{(\mathbf{x},y)\sim\mathcal{D}}(||P(Y|\mathbf{x}, \mathbf{w}) - \mathbf{y}||_2) - \\ \mathbb{A}_{(\mathbf{x},y)\in\mathbf{d}_{train}}(||P(Y|\mathbf{x}, \mathbf{w}) - \mathbf{y}||_2)| < \epsilon^2_{gen} \tag{4}$$

where $\mathbf{d}_{train}$ is the set of training data and $\epsilon^2_{gen} > 0$ is a pre-specified small constant. Intuitively, ϕ^2_{gen} requires that the gap between the performance on the data distribution, i.e., $\mathbb{E}_{(\mathbf{x},y)\sim\mathcal{D}}(||P(Y|\mathbf{x}, \mathbf{w}) - \mathbf{y}||_2)$, and the performance on the training dataset, i.e., $\mathbb{A}_{(\mathbf{x},y)\in\mathbf{d}_{train}}(||P(Y|\mathbf{x}, \mathbf{w}) - \mathbf{y}||_2)$, is bounded and insignificant.

Finally, since a model with good generalisation ability may refer to either of the above cases, we use the following formula

$$\phi_{gen} \triangleq \phi_{gen}^1 \vee \phi_{gen}^2 \tag{5}$$

to ensure that the model has a good generalisation ability.

5.2   Uncertainty

While a neural network may output a prediction, it is desirable to understand its confidence in making such a prediction. The ability to output not only a prediction but also the confidence is key to downstream tasks. For example, when the neural network is for a perception task, a planning module may consider the confidence (to understand if the result from the perception module is trustable) when determining the actions to be taken in the following steps.

Assume we have a model with weight matrix $\mathbf{w}$ and an input $\mathbf{x}$. First of all, we may ascertain the data uncertainty through the predictive probability, i.e.,

$$\phi_{unc}^1 \triangleq \mathbb{V}_{y \in C}(P(Y|\mathbf{x}, \mathbf{w})(y)) > \epsilon_{unc}^1 \tag{6}$$

which requires the variance of the output probability to be greater than a positive constant ϵ_{unc}^1. We note that, a small variance may suggest that the predictive probability values of different classes are close to each other [36,37]. Therefore, a greater variance can represent a lower uncertainty in this case.

Moreover, we may work with the total uncertainty, i.e., both the data and the model uncertainties. In this case, the following formula may be considered:

$$\phi_{unc}^2 \triangleq \mathbb{V}_{\mathbf{w} \sim P(W|\mathbf{d})}(P(Y|\mathbf{x}, \mathbf{w})(\hat{y})) < \epsilon_{unc}^2 \tag{7}$$

where $\hat{y}$ is the predicted label of $\mathbf{x}$ with the model parameterised with $\mathbf{w}$. Intuitively, it is to determine if the variance of the prediction on $\hat{y}$ over the posterior distribution is smaller than a positive constant ϵ_{unc}^2.

Finally, we may use the following formula:

$$\phi_{unc} \triangleq \phi_{unc}^1 \wedge \phi_{unc}^2 \tag{8}$$

to ensure that the uncertainty over the prediction of $\mathbf{x}$ on the model $\mathbf{w}$ is low.

5.3   Robustness

Robustness concerns whether or not a perturbation may lead to a drastic change in the output. Simply speaking, a model with weight matrix $\mathbf{w}$ is robust over an input $\mathbf{x}$ can be expressed as

$$\phi_{rob} \triangleq \forall \mathbf{r} : ||\mathbf{r}||_2 \leq c \Rightarrow |P(Y|\mathbf{x} + \mathbf{r}, \mathbf{w})(\hat{y}) - P(Y|\mathbf{x}, \mathbf{w})(\hat{y})| \leq \epsilon_{rob} \tag{9}$$

where $\mathbf{r} \in \mathbb{R}^n$ denotes the perturbation. Intuitively, it says that as long as the perturbation is within a range, the predictive probability on $\hat{y}$ is bounded by ϵ_{rob}. Note that, $||\mathbf{r}||_2$ is not in the syntax, but is a syntax sugar for $||\mathbf{r} - \mathbf{0}||_2$, where $\mathbf{0}$ is an all-zero vector of the same shape with $\mathbf{r}$.

5.4   Data Poisoning

Data poisoning suggests that by adding a set $\mathbf{d}'$ of poisoning data to the training dataset $\mathbf{d}$, it is able to make the model predict a specific input $\mathbf{x}_{adv}$ as a target label y_{adv}. Formally, we can write the following formula

$$\phi_{poi}^1 \triangleq \forall y : \mathbb{E}_{\mathbf{w} \sim P(W|\mathbf{d} \cup \mathbf{d}')}(P(Y|\mathbf{x}_{adv}, \mathbf{w})(y_{adv})) \geq \\ \mathbb{E}_{\mathbf{w} \sim P(W|\mathbf{d} \cup \mathbf{d}')}(P(Y|\mathbf{x}_{adv}, \mathbf{w})(y)) \tag{10}$$

where $\mathbb{E}_{\mathbf{w} \sim P(W|\mathbf{d} \cup \mathbf{d}')}P(Y|\mathbf{x}_{adv}, \mathbf{w})(y_{adv})$ returns the probability of labelling $\mathbf{x}_{adv}$ with y_{adv} after poisoning. Intuitively, ϕ_{poi}^1 suggests that y_{adv} is the predictive label. We remark that, this expression is stronger than the usual definition of data poisoning as we utilise the Bayesian view and obtain the prediction for $\mathbf{x}_{adv}$ after considering the posterior distribution.

While the targeted action is required, we may also need to ensure that the poisoning does not affect the performance on the training data, i.e.,

$$\phi_{poi}^2 \triangleq (\mathbb{E}_{\mathbf{w} \sim P(W|\mathbf{d} \cup \mathbf{d}')}(\mathbb{A}_{(\mathbf{x},y) \in \mathbf{d}}(||P(Y|\mathbf{x}, \mathbf{w}) - \mathbf{y}||_2))) \leq \epsilon_{poi}^2 \tag{11}$$

Intuitively, the average loss on the training data, when weighted over the posterior distribution, is no greater than a positive constant ϵ_{poi}^2.

Now, to ensure the resistance to the data poisoning attacks, we require the non-existence of a poisoning dataset $\mathbf{d}'$ of size no more than k to make the above two formulas hold, i.e.,

$$\phi_{poi}(k) \triangleq \neg \exists \mathbf{d}' : |\mathbf{d}'| \leq k \wedge \phi_{poi}^1 \wedge \phi_{poi}^2 \tag{12}$$

Finally, the ability to resist the data poisoning attack can be evaluated, and compared, with the smallest k, written as k^*, which makes the formula $\phi_{poi}(k)$ hold. A model with smaller k^* is more vulnerable than a model with greater k^*.

5.5   Backdoor

Backdoor attack is to determine the existence of a trigger $\mathbf{r}$, by which all inputs $\mathbf{x}$ will be classified as a specific label y_{adv}. Formally, we have the following formula

$$\phi_{bac}^1 \triangleq \neg \exists \mathbf{r} \forall \mathbf{x} \forall y : P(Y|\mathbf{x} + \mathbf{r}, \mathbf{w})(y_{adv}) \geq P(Y|\mathbf{x} + \mathbf{r}, \mathbf{w})(y) \tag{13}$$

to express the resistance to the backdoor attack. We can also take the Bayesian view, and write

$$\phi_{bac}^2 \triangleq \neg \exists \mathbf{r} \forall \mathbf{x} \forall y : \mathbb{E}_{\mathbf{w} \sim P(W|\mathbf{d})}(P(Y|\mathbf{x} + \mathbf{r}, \mathbf{w})(y_{adv})) \geq \\ \mathbb{E}_{\mathbf{w} \sim P(W|\mathbf{d})}(P(Y|\mathbf{x} + \mathbf{r}, \mathbf{w})(y)) \tag{14}$$

5.6   Model Stealing

Model stealing is reconstructing a model that is functionally equivalent to the original model. The reconstruction can be conducted by first querying a set of data instances and then training a surrogate model with the data instances.

First of all, we define the following formula

$$\phi_{ste}^1 \triangleq D_{KL}(P(W|\mathbf{d}_1), P(W|\mathbf{d}_2)) < \epsilon_{ste}^1 \tag{15}$$

to express that the two posterior distributions trained on two different datasets $\mathbf{d}_1$ and $\mathbf{d}_2$, i.e., $P(W|\mathbf{d}_1)$ and $P(W|\mathbf{d}_2)$, are similar. Second, the following formula expresses that the dataset $\mathbf{d}$ is classified well by the original model whose weight matrix is $\mathbf{w}$, i.e.,

$$\phi_{ste}^2(\mathbf{d}) \triangleq \mathbb{A}_{(\mathbf{x},y)\in\mathbf{d}}(1 - P(Y|\mathbf{x},\mathbf{w})(y)) < \epsilon_{ste}^2 \tag{16}$$

where ϵ_{ste}^2 is a small positive constant. Actually, we can use $\phi_{ste}^2(\mathbf{d})$ to express that $\mathbf{d}$ is from the same distribution as the underlying data distribution.

Based on them, we have the following formula

$$\phi_{ste}^3(k) = \forall\mathbf{d}_1\forall\mathbf{d}_2 : (|\mathbf{d}_1| = |\mathbf{d}_2| = k \wedge \phi_{ste}^2(\mathbf{d}_1) \wedge \phi_{ste}^2(\mathbf{d}_2)) \Rightarrow \phi_{ste}^1 \tag{17}$$

which expresses that for any two datasets $\mathbf{d}_1$ and $\mathbf{d}_2$ of size k, if they are both on the underlying data distribution, the posterior distributions resulted from them are similar. That is, it is indistinguishable for either $\mathbf{d}_1$ or $\mathbf{d}_2$ to be used for the reconstruction of the original model.

Finally, the resistance to the model stealing is to find the largest k such that the following formula holds:

$$\phi_{ste} = \neg\phi_{ste}^3(k) \tag{18}$$

We remark that, once we find the largest k, for any dataset $\mathbf{d}$ of size greater than k and the formula $\phi_{ste}^2(\mathbf{d})$ holds, the model can be stolen.

5.7   Membership Inference

Membership inference is to determine if an instance $(\mathbf{x}_{adv}, y_{adv})$ is in the training dataset or not. Formally, we use

$$\phi_{mem}^1(\mathbf{x}, y, \mathbf{d}) \triangleq \mathbb{E}_{\mathbf{w}\sim P(W|\mathbf{d})}(P(Y|\mathbf{x},\mathbf{w})(y)) > \epsilon_{mem}^{1,e} \wedge \\ \mathbb{V}_{\mathbf{w}\sim P(W|\mathbf{d})}(P(Y|\mathbf{x},\mathbf{w})(y)) < \epsilon_{mem}^{1,v} \tag{19}$$

to express that the data instance $(\mathbf{x}, y)$ is on the same distribution as $\mathbf{d}$. Technically, $\mathbb{E}_{\mathbf{w}\sim P(W|\mathbf{d})}(P(Y|\mathbf{x},\mathbf{w})(y)) > \epsilon_{mem}^{1,e}$ says that, once a model is trained with dataset $\mathbf{d}$, the expected predictive probability of labelling $\mathbf{x}$ with y is higher than $\epsilon_{mem}^{1,e}$. If the constant $\epsilon_{mem}^{1,e}$ is close to 1, the satisfiability of formula $\phi_{mem}^1(\mathbf{x}, y, \mathbf{d})$ suggests that the instance $(\mathbf{x}, y)$ is on the same distribution with $\mathbf{d}$. The other expression $\mathbb{V}_{\mathbf{w}\sim P(W|\mathbf{d})}(P(Y|\mathbf{x},\mathbf{w})(y)) < \epsilon_{mem}^{1,v}$ imposes a stronger condition that the variance needs to be small, when the positive constant $\epsilon_{mem}^{1,v}$ is close to 0.

Based on the above, we have the following formula

$$\phi^2_{mem}(k) \triangleq \forall \mathbf{d}_1 \forall \mathbf{d}_2 : (|\mathbf{d}_1| = |\mathbf{d}_2| = k \wedge \phi^2_{ste}(\mathbf{d}_1) \wedge \phi^2_{ste}(\mathbf{d}_2)) \Rightarrow \\ (\phi^1_{mem}(\mathbf{x}_{adv}, y_{adv}, \mathbf{d}_1) \iff \phi^1_{mem}(\mathbf{x}_{adv}, y_{adv}, \mathbf{d}_2)) \tag{20}$$

which expresses that for any two datasets $\mathbf{d}_1$ and $\mathbf{d}_2$ of size k, if they are both on the underlying data distribution, the decision on whether the sample $(\mathbf{x}_{adv}, y_{adv})$ is in the training data is unambiguous.

Finally, the resistance to the membership inference is to determine the largest k such that the following formula holds:

$$\phi_{mem} \triangleq \neg \phi^2_{mem}(k) \tag{21}$$

Once found the largest k, for any dataset $\mathbf{d}$ of size greater than k, if the formula $\phi^2_{ste}(\mathbf{d})$ holds, we can determine the membership of $(\mathbf{x}_{adv}, y_{adv})$ correctly. Also, a model is more vulnerable to the membership inference attack, if the largest k as defined above is smaller.

5.8   Model Inversion

During the inference phase, a model inversion attack infers sensitive information about an instance. Without loss of generality, we assume that each data instance includes m features $X_1, ..., X_m$, and X_1 is the sensitive feature to be inferred. Then, given partial information about a data instance $\mathbf{x}$ (e.g., values of features $X_2, ..., X_n$), and its predictive label $\hat{y}$ by a machine learning model f, it is to infer the value for sensitive feature X_1.

We write x_i as the i-th element of $\mathbf{x}$. The following formula expresses that the input $\mathbf{x}$, with the feature X_1 being x_1, is on the data distribution, i.e.,

$$\phi^1_{inv}(\mathbf{x}[X_1 \leftarrow x_1], \mathbf{d}) \triangleq \exists y : \phi^1_{mem}(\mathbf{x}[X_1 \leftarrow x_1], y, \mathbf{d}) \tag{22}$$

Note that, we quantify away the label y because any label y satisfying $\phi^1_{mem}(\mathbf{x}[X_1 \leftarrow x_1], y, \mathbf{d})$ will be sufficient.

Now, assume that we have two datasets $\mathbf{d}_1$ and $\mathbf{d}_2$, and two input instances $\mathbf{x}$ and $\mathbf{x}'$ whose only difference is on the feature X_1, we define

$$\phi^2_{inv} \triangleq D_{KL}(P(W|\mathbf{d}_1), P(W|\mathbf{d}_2)) < \epsilon^{2,l}_{inv} \Rightarrow |x_1 - x'_1| < \epsilon^{2,r}_{inv} \tag{23}$$

which expresses that, as long as the posterior distributions are close to each other, the values of the sensitive feature X_1 are also close to each other.

Finally, the resistance to the model inversion is to find the smallest number k such that the following formula $\phi_{inv}(k)$ holds:

$$\phi^3_{inv}(k) \triangleq \forall \mathbf{d}_1 \forall \mathbf{d}_2 : ((|\mathbf{d}_1| = |\mathbf{d}_2| = k \wedge \phi^2_{ste}(\mathbf{d}_1) \wedge \phi^2_{ste}(\mathbf{d}_2)) \Rightarrow \\ \forall x_1 \forall x_2 : ((\phi^1_{inv}(\mathbf{x}[X_1 \leftarrow x_1], \mathbf{d}_1) \wedge \\ \phi^1_{inv}(\mathbf{x}[X_1 \leftarrow x'_1], \mathbf{d}_2)) \Rightarrow \phi^2_{inv})) \tag{24}$$

Intuitively, the second line of Eq. (24) says that, as long as $\mathbf{x}[X_1 \leftarrow x_1]$ is on the same distribution with $\mathbf{d}_1$, and $\mathbf{x}[X_1 \leftarrow x'_1]$ is on the same distribution with $\mathbf{d}_2$, the similarity of two posterior distributions (i.e., $D_{KL}(P(W|\mathbf{d}_1), P(W|\mathbf{d}_2)) < \epsilon_{inv}^{2,l}$) will lead to the requirement that the two values of feature X_1, i.e., x_1 and x_1', are very close. In other words, the obtaining of any dataset of size k will lead to unambiguous inference of the feature X_1.

Finally, the resistance to the model inversion attack is to determine the largest k such that the following formula holds:

$$\phi_{inv} \triangleq \neg\phi_{inv}^3(k) \tag{25}$$

That is, once found the largest k, for any dataset $\mathbf{d}$ of size greater than k, if the formula $\phi_{ste}^2(\mathbf{d})$ holds, we can use any x_1 such that $\phi_{inv}^1(\mathbf{x}[X_1 \leftarrow x_1], \mathbf{d}_1)$ for the model inversion. Also, a model is more vulnerable to the model inversion attack, if the largest k as defined above is smaller.

5.9   Interpretability

There are many different definitions of interpretability. Here, we follow a popular definition that maps an n-dimensional instance $\mathbf{x}$ into a weighted map $exp(\mathbf{x})$: $\{1, ..., n\} \rightarrow [0, 1]$ on the input features. The weighted map $exp(\mathbf{x})$ can then be displayed as a saliency map, as the explanation of the decision made by the machine learning model on $\mathbf{x}$. The weighted map can be normalised into a probability distribution, and we assume so in the following discussion.

First, we may require as a criterion of a good explanation that the output of the neural network does not have a major change (expressed as the L_∞ norm distance less than a constant ϵ_{int}^1) when masking less important input features according to the weighted map $\mathbf{x}$. Formally, we let

$$\phi_{int}^1(\mathbf{x}) \triangleq \mathbb{V}_{\mathbf{x}' \in Mut_{exp(\mathbf{x})}(\mathbf{x})}(||P(Y|\mathbf{x}', \mathbf{w}) - \mathbf{y}||_\infty) < \epsilon_{int}^1 \tag{26}$$

where $Mut_{exp(\mathbf{x})}(\mathbf{x})$ is a set of mutations that mask less important input features from $\mathbf{x}$ according to the weighted map $exp(\mathbf{x})$. We may require the masking of important features leads to significant change on the predictive output, and we omit the details for the limitation of space.

Beyond the correctness criterion as set up in Eq. (26), there are also research on requiring the robustness of explanations, i.e.,

$$\phi_{int}^2(\mathbf{x}) \triangleq \forall \mathbf{r} : ||\mathbf{r}||_2 \leq c \Rightarrow D_{KL}(exp(\mathbf{x} + \mathbf{r}), exp(\mathbf{x})) < \epsilon_{int}^2 \tag{27}$$

which states that the explanation, expressed as a probability distribution $exp(\mathbf{x})$, does not change significantly when subject to perturbations.

Finally, a specification for the interpretability of an instance $\mathbf{x}$ by a weighted map $exp(\mathbf{x})$ can be expressed as follows:

$$\phi_{int}(\mathbf{x}) \triangleq \phi_{int}^1(\mathbf{x}) \wedge \phi_{int}^2(\mathbf{x}) \tag{28}$$

5.10   Fairness

Fairness concerns whether certain sensitive features may have a causality relation with the decision-making. Without loss of generality, we assume X_1 is the sensitive feature. Then, the fairness can somewhat be re-stated as that the predictive distribution of letting the sensitive feature X_1 have the value x_1 be the same as the predictive distribution of letting the sensitive feature X_1 have the value x_1', i.e.,

$$\phi_{fai}(\mathbf{x}) \triangleq \forall x_1, x_1' : D_{KL}(P(\hat{Y}|\mathbf{x}[X_1 \leftarrow x_1], \mathbf{w}), P(\hat{Y}|\mathbf{x}[X_1 \leftarrow x_1'], \mathbf{w})) < \epsilon_{fai} \tag{29}$$

for ϵ_{fai} a small constant.

6   Verification of Properties

From the language MLS^2, we can see that most of the constructs can be easily evaluated. For example, $P(Y|\mathbf{x}, \mathbf{w})$ can be obtained by simply querying the model of wight matrix $\mathbf{w}$ with the input $\mathbf{x}$, and $\mathbb{A}_v(\gamma)$ can be obtained by enumerating over all elements in the finite set if we know how to evaluate γ. Nevertheless, a few constructs might require significant computational effort to evaluate, which we will discuss below.

6.1   Estimation of Posterior Distribution $P(W|\mathbf{d})$ Through MCMC

MCMC refers to a family of algorithms to sample a probability distribution usually defined in a high-dimensional space. These algorithms perform Monte Carlo estimates by constructing a Markov chain with the desired distribution as its stationary distribution. The more samples we draw, the more closely the distribution of the samples matches the desired distribution.

Given an unknown distribution $P(W|\mathbf{d})$, different MCMC algorithms will construct Markov chains with different probability transition matrices. In the following, we briefly describe the Metropolis-Hastings algorithm, the most common MCMC algorithm, and the Markov chain constructed by this algorithm.

A Markov chain is a tuple $M(W|\mathbf{d}) = (S, \mathbf{w}_0, T, L)$, where S is a set of states, $\mathbf{w}_0 \in S$ is an initial state, $T : S \times S \to [0, 1]$ is a probability transition matrix, and L is a labelling function. The construction of $M(W|\mathbf{d})$ proceeds by first sampling $\mathbf{w}_0$ from $P(W|\mathbf{d})$ as the initial state, and then gradually adding states $\mathbf{w}_{n+1}$ to S and updating the transition matrix T until it converges. Let H be a transition matrix for any irreducible Markov chain, whose state space contains the support of $P(W|\mathbf{d})$. Suppose the last sample we draw is $\mathbf{w}_n$. We generate a new sample $\mathbf{w}_{n+1}$ as follows:

1. Choose a proposal state $\mathbf{w}'$ according to the probability distribution given by $H(\mathbf{w}'|\mathbf{w}_n)$.

2. Calculate the acceptance probability of the proposal $\mathbf{w}'$ as

$$A(\mathbf{w}'|\mathbf{w}_n) = \min\left(1, \frac{P(\mathbf{w}'|\mathbf{d})H(\mathbf{w}_n|\mathbf{w}')}{P(\mathbf{w}_n|\mathbf{d})H(\mathbf{w}'|\mathbf{w}_n)}\right)$$

3. Let $u \sim \text{Uniform}([0,1])$. Accept the proposed value as the new sample if $u \leq A(\mathbf{w}'|\mathbf{w}_n)$, that is, let $\mathbf{w}_{n+1} = \mathbf{w}'$. Reject the proposed value otherwise, that is, let $\mathbf{w}_{n+1} = \mathbf{w}_n$.

The probability transition matrix T of the Markov chain constructed by the Metropolis-Hastings algorithm has the following probability transition matrix:

$$T(\mathbf{w}'|\mathbf{w}) = \begin{cases} H(\mathbf{w}'|\mathbf{w})A(\mathbf{w}'|\mathbf{w}) & \text{if } \mathbf{w} \neq \mathbf{w}' \\ 1 - \sum_{\mathbf{w} \neq \mathbf{w}'} H(\mathbf{w}'|\mathbf{w})A(\mathbf{w}'|\mathbf{w}) & \text{otherwise} \end{cases}$$

This Markov chain satisfies (1) the uniqueness of the stationary distribution and (2) the detailed balance with respect to the desired distribution $P(W|\mathbf{d})$, that is, $T(\mathbf{w}'|\mathbf{w})P(\mathbf{w}|\mathbf{d}) = T(\mathbf{w}|\mathbf{w}')P(\mathbf{w}'|\mathbf{d})$. These conditions guarantee that the constructed Markov chain has the desired distribution $P(W|\mathbf{d})$ as its stationary distribution. MCMC algorithms such as simulated annealing can converge to global optimum.

6.2   Estimation of Posterior Distribution $P(W|\mathbf{d})$ Through Variational Inference

MCMC can be computationally expensive when dealing with large dimensional problems. In this case, we may consider an alternative approach, i.e., variational inference (VI), which casts the computation of the distribution $P(W|\mathbf{d})$ as an optimisation problem. VI assumes a class of tractable distributions $\mathcal{Q}$ and intends to finds a $q(W) \in \mathcal{Q}$ that is closest to $P(W|\mathbf{d})$. Apparently, once we have the distribution $q(W)$, we can use it for any computation that involves $P(W|\mathbf{d})$.

We use the KL divergence to measure the distance between $q(W)$ and $P(W|\mathbf{d})$. Formally, we have the following:

$$
\begin{aligned}
&D_{KL}(q(W)||P(W|\mathbf{d})) \\
&= \int q(W) \log \frac{q(W)}{P(W|\mathbf{d})} dW \\
&= \mathbb{E}_{q(W)}(\log \frac{q(W)}{P(W|\mathbf{d})}) \\
&= \mathbb{E}_{q(W)}(\log \frac{q(W)}{P(\mathbf{d}|W)P(W)} P(\mathbf{d})) \\
&= \mathbb{E}_{q(W)}(\log \frac{q(W)}{P(\mathbf{d}|W)P(W)}) + \log P(\mathbf{d}) \\
&= D_{KL}(q(W)||P(W)) - \mathbb{E}_{q(W)}(\log P(\mathbf{d}|W)) + \log P(\mathbf{d})
\end{aligned}
\tag{30}
$$

To minimise this, we can minimise the negative log evidence lower bound

$$\mathcal{L}_{VI} = D_{KL}(q(W)||P(W)) - \mathbb{E}_{q(W)}(\log P(\mathbf{d}|W)) \tag{31}$$

The expectation value $\mathbb{E}_{q(W)}(\log P(\mathbf{d}|W))$ can be approximated with Monte Carlo integration. Therefore, the optimisation

$$\hat{q}(\mathbf{W}) \triangleq arg\,min_{q(W)\in\mathcal{Q}}\mathcal{L}_{VI} \tag{32}$$

can be conducted by iteratively improving a candidate $q(W)$ until convergence. There are GO algorithms for VI, such as [27], which guarantees to converge to the ϵ-global variational lower bound on the log-likelihood.

The computational complexity of VI depends on the distribution class $\mathcal{Q}$. For example, if it is mean field approximation, the complexity is in polynomial time with respect to the number of input features, and if it is Gaussian processes, the complexity is exponential with respect to the number of input features.

6.3 Estimation of Data Distribution $\mathcal{D}$ and Distribution of Predictive Labels $P(\hat{Y}|\mathbf{d}, \mathbf{w})$

The estimation of data distribution $\mathcal{D}$ usually is based on a set of known data points $\{(\mathbf{x}_1, y_1), ..., (\mathbf{x}_n, y_n)\}$. This can be done through e.g., Kernel density estimation. Actually, we have

$$\hat{\mathcal{D}}(\mathbf{x}) = \frac{1}{nh} \sum_{i=1}^{n} K(\frac{\mathbf{x} - \mathbf{x}_i}{h}) \tag{33}$$

where K is a non-negative function called the kernel, and $h > 0$ is a smoothing parameter called the bandwidth. The normal kernel, where $K(x)$ is the standard normal density function, is often used. In this case, the obtained estimation $\hat{\mathcal{D}}(\mathbf{x})$ is a multivariate Gaussian mixture model. There are GO methods for KDE such as [34] that can converge to global optimum.

The distribution $P(\hat{Y}|\mathbf{d}, \mathbf{w})$ of predictive labels can also be estimated in this way as having the known data points $\{\hat{y}|(\mathbf{x}, y) \in \mathbf{d}\}$, where $\hat{y}$ is the predictive label of $\mathbf{x}$ over network parameterised with $\mathbf{w}$.

6.4 $\mathbb{E}_u(\gamma)$ or $\mathbb{V}_u(\gamma)$

Given u can be either $\mathbf{w} \sim P(W|\mathbf{d})$ or $(\mathbf{x}, y) \sim \mathcal{D}$, and we have suggested in Sects. 6.1, 6.2, and 6.3 a few methods to estimate distributions $P(W|\mathbf{d})$ and $\mathcal{D}$ with error bounds, the expressions $\mathbb{E}_u(\gamma)$ and $\mathbb{V}_u(\gamma)$ can be evaluated.

6.5 $D_{KL}(\mu, \mu)$ or $||\mu - \mu||_p$

A direct computation of the KL divergence or the norm distance of two unknown high-dimensional distributions, such as the posterior distributions, will be hard. However, we can apply VI to estimate two distributions $q_1(\mathbf{W})$ and $q_2(\mathbf{W})$, one for each of the distributions. Then, because $q_1(\mathbf{W})$ and $q_2(\mathbf{W})$ are known, we can compute KL divergence analytically. Alternatively, we can compute two Markov chains M_1 and M_2 with MCMC and then compute their distance.

6.6 ∃t and ∀t

The quantifiers ∃t and ∀t will cause significant increase in computational complexity, when they are alternating and when **t** represents a high-dimensional variable for either an input **x** or a set of inputs **d**. We note that, the properties in the previous section require at most one alternating between ∃ and ∀.

In robustness verification, GO has been applied in e.g., [24,33,35], but it is mainly for **t** to represent an input **x**. For the cases where **t** represents the output y, for example Eq. (10), we can simply enumerate all possible values of y, as the classes C is usually fixed and finite. For the cases where **t** represents a set **d** of inputs, we can apply similar techniques as in [24,33,35], because the number of inputs in **d** is usually fixed as k in Eqs. (17), (20), and (24).

7 Related Works

We review some work that formalises the specification for learning-enabled autonomous systems. [4] introduces a specification language based on LTL which utilises event-based abstraction to hide the details of the neural network structure and parameters. [8] formalises requirements for the runtime verification of an autonomous unmanned aircraft system based on an extension of propositional LTL, where temporal operators are augmented with timing constraints. [2] proposes Timed Quality Temporal Logic (TQTL) to express monitorable [1] spatio-temporal quality properties of perception systems based on neural networks. In addition, the typed first-order logic [3] suggests the explicit typing of variables, functions and predicates to allow the reasoning about the domain of runtime control at the abstract level of types.

Different from previous attempts, our specification language for machine learning considers not only the functionality (i.e., the relation between input and output) of a trained model but also the training process (where objects such as training dataset, model parameters, and distance between posterior distributions are considered). With this, the language can express the safety and security properties that describe the attacks during the lifecycle stages.

8 Conclusions

This paper makes an attempt to use a formal specification language to describe ten different safety and security properties of machine learning models. The language can describe not only the input-output relations but also the relations between training data and trained models. For the verification of properties expressed with the language, we suggest global optimisation methods to deal with basic constructs like posterior distributions. We hope this forms a new step towards the communication between formal methods and machine learning.

Acknowledgment. ▓ This project has received funding from the European Union's Horizon 2020 research and innovation programme under grant agreement No 956123. Moreover, XH is also supported by the UK EPSRC under projects [EP/R026173/1, EP/T026995/1].

References

1. Balakrishnan, A., Deshmukh, J., Hoxha, B., Yamaguchi, T., Fainekos, G.: Perce-Mon: online monitoring for perception systems. In: Feng, L., Fisman, D. (eds.) RV 2021. LNCS, vol. 12974, pp. 297–308. Springer, Cham (2021). https://doi.org/10. 1007/978-3-030-88494-9_18
2. Balakrishnan, A., et al.: Specifying and evaluating quality metrics for vision-based perception systems. In: Design, Automation & Test in Europe Conference & Exhibition (DATE), pp. 1433–1438 (2019)
3. Beckert, B., Hähnle, R., Schmitt, P.H. (eds.): Verification of Object-Oriented Software. The KeY Approach - Foreword by K. Rustan M. Leino. LNCS (LNAI), vol. 4334. Springer, Heidelberg (2007). https://doi.org/10.1007/978-3-540-69061-0
4. Bensalem, S., et al.: Formal specification for learning-enabled autonomous systems (extended abstract). In: FoMLAS2022 (2022)
5. Bishop, P., Povyakalo, A.: Deriving a frequentist conservative confidence bound for probability of failure per demand for systems with different operational and test profiles. Reliab. Eng. Syst. Saf. **158**, 246–253 (2017)
6. Demontis, A., et al.: Why do adversarial attacks transfer? Explaining transferability of evasion and poisoning attacks. In: 28th USENIX Security Symposium (USENIX Security 2019), Santa Clara, CA, August 2019, pp. 321–338. USENIX Association (2019)
7. Du, S.S., Lee, J.D., Li, H., Wang, L., Zhai, X.: Gradient descent finds global minima of deep neural networks. arXiv e-prints, arXiv:1811.03804 (2018)
8. Dutle, A., et al.: From requirements to autonomous flight: an overview of the monitoring ICAROUS project. In: Proceedings of the 2nd Workshop on Formal Methods for Autonomous Systems. EPTCS, vol. 329, pp. 23–30 (2020)
9. Fukunaga, K.: Introduction to Statistical Pattern Recognition. Elsevier (2013)
10. Gehr, T., Mirman, M., Drachsler-Cohen, D., Tsankov, P., Chaudhuri, S., Vechev, M.: AI2: safety and robustness certification of neural networks with abstract interpretation. In: 2018 IEEE Symposium on Security and Privacy (SP) (2018)
11. Huang, W., et al.: Coverage-guided testing for recurrent neural networks. IEEE Trans. Reliab. 1–16 (2021)
12. Huang, X., Kwiatkowska, M., Wang, S., Wu, M.: Safety verification of deep neural networks. In: Majumdar, R., Kunčak, V. (eds.) CAV 2017. LNCS, vol. 10426, pp. 3–29. Springer, Cham (2017). https://doi.org/10.1007/978-3-319-63387-9_1
13. Jin, G., Yi, X., Huang, W., Schewe, S., Huang, X.: Enhancing adversarial training with second-order statistics of weights. In: CVPR 2022 (2022)
14. Jin, G., Yi, X., Zhang, L., Zhang, L., Schewe, S., Huang, X.: How does weight correlation affect the generalisation ability of deep neural networks. In: NeurIPS 2020 (2020)
15. Jones, D.R., Martins, J.R.R.A.: The DIRECT algorithm: 25 years later. J. Glob. Optim. **79**(3), 521–566 (2021)
16. Jones, D.R., Perttunen, C.D., Stuckman, B.E.: Lipschitzian optimization without the Lipschitz constant. J. Optim. Theory Appl. **79**, 157–181 (1993)
17. Katz, G., Barrett, C., Dill, D.L., Julian, K., Kochenderfer, M.J.: Reluplex: an efficient SMT solver for verifying deep neural networks. In: Majumdar, R., Kunčak, V. (eds.) CAV 2017. LNCS, vol. 10426, pp. 97–117. Springer, Cham (2017). https://doi.org/10.1007/978-3-319-63387-9_5

18. Li, J., Liu, J., Yang, P., Chen, L., Huang, X., Zhang, L.: Analyzing deep neural networks with symbolic propagation: towards higher precision and faster verification. In: Chang, B.-Y.E. (ed.) SAS 2019. LNCS, vol. 11822, pp. 296–319. Springer, Cham (2019). https://doi.org/10.1007/978-3-030-32304-2_15
19. Littlewood, B., Rushby, J.: Reasoning about the reliability of diverse two-channel systems in which one channel is "possibly perfect". IEEE Transa. Softw. Eng. **38**(5), 1178–1194 (2012)
20. Madry, A., Makelov, A., Schmidt, L., Tsipras, D., Vladu, A.: Towards deep learning models resistant to adversarial attacks. In: ICLR 2018 (2018)
21. Musa, J.: Operational profiles in software-reliability engineering. IEEE Softw. **10**(2), 14–32 (1993)
22. Orekondy, T., Schiele, B., Fritz, M.: Knockoff nets: stealing functionality of black-box models. In: IEEE Conference on Computer Vision and Pattern Recognition, CVPR 2019, Long Beach, CA, USA, 16–20 June 2019, pp. 4954–4963. Computer Vision Foundation/IEEE (2019)
23. Pietrantuono, R., Popov, P., Russo, S.: Reliability assessment of service-based software under operational profile uncertainty. Reliab. Eng. Syst. Saf. **204**, 107193 (2020)
24. Ruan, W., Huang, X., Kwiatkowska, M.: Reachability analysis of deep neural networks with provable guarantees. In: IJCAI, pp. 2651–2659 (2018)
25. Ruan, W., Wu, M., Sun, Y., Huang, X., Kroening, D., Kwiatkowska, M.: Global robustness evaluation of deep neural networks with provable guarantees for the hamming distance. In: IJCAI 2019, pp. 5944–5952 (2019)
26. Rushby, J.: Software verification and system assurance. In: 7th International Conference on Software Engineering and Formal Methods, Hanoi, Vietnam, pp. 3–10. IEEE (2009)
27. Saddiki, H., Trapp, A.C., Flaherty, P.: A deterministic global optimization method for variational inference (2017)
28. Salako, K., Strigini, L., Zhao, X.: Conservative confidence bounds in safety, from generalised claims of improvement & statistical evidence. In: 51st Annual IEEE/IFIP International Conference on Dependable Systems and Networks, DSN 2021, Taipei, Taiwan, pp. 451–462. IEEE/IFIP (2021)
29. Sun, Y., Huang, X., Kroening, D.: Testing deep neural networks. CoRR, abs/1803.04792 (2018)
30. Sun, Y., Wu, M., Ruan, W., Huang, X., Kwiatkowska, M., Kroening, D.: Concolic testing for deep neural networks. In: 33rd IEEE/ACM International Conference on Automated Software Engineering (ASE) (2018)
31. Sun, Y., Wu, M., Ruan, W., Huang, X., Kwiatkowska, M., Kroening, D.: Deep-Concolic: testing and debugging deep neural networks. In: 41st ACM/IEEE International Conference on Software Engineering (ICSE 2019) (2019)
32. Szegedy, C., et al.: Intriguing properties of neural networks. In: ICLR. Citeseer (2014)
33. Wicker, M., Huang, X., Kwiatkowska, M.: Feature-guided black-box safety testing of deep neural networks. In: Beyer, D., Huisman, M. (eds.) TACAS 2018. LNCS, vol. 10805, pp. 408–426. Springer, Cham (2018). https://doi.org/10.1007/978-3-319-89960-2_22
34. Wirjadi, O., Breuel, T.: A branch and bound algorithm for finding the modes in kernel density estimates. Int. J. Comput. Intell. Appl. **08**(01), 17–35 (2009)
35. Wu, M., Wicker, M., Ruan, W., Huang, X., Kwiatkowska, M.: A game-based approximate verification of deep neural networks with provable guarantees. Theor. Comput. Sci. **807**, 298–329 (2020)

36. Xu, P., Ruan, W., Huang, X.: Towards the quantification of safety risks in deep neural networks. CoRR, abs/2009.06114 (2020)
37. Xu, P., Ruan, W., Huang, X.: Quantifying safety risks of deep neural networks. Complex Intell. Syst. (2022)
38. Yang, Z., Zhang, J., Chang, E.-C., Liang, Z.: Neural network inversion in adversarial setting via background knowledge alignment. In: Proceedings of the 2019 ACM SIGSAC Conference on Computer and Communications Security, CCS 2019, pp. 225–240. ACM, New York (2019)
39. Zhao, X., et al.: Assessing reliability of deep learning through robustness evaluation and operational testing. In: AISafety2021 (2021)
40. Zhao, X., et al.: Reliability assessment and safety arguments for machine learning components in assuring learning-enabled autonomous systems. CoRR, abs/2112.00646 (2021)

Canonical Narrowing for Variant-Based Conditional Rewrite Theories

Raúl López-Rueda and Santiago Escobar[✉]

VRAIN, Universitat Politècnica de València, Valencia, Spain
{rloprue,sescobar}@upv.es

Abstract. Maude currently supports many symbolic reasoning features such as order-sorted equational unification and order-sorted narrowing-based symbolic reachability analysis. There have been many advances and new features added to improve narrowing in Maude but only at a theoretical level. In this paper, we provide a very elegant, transparent, and extremely pragmatic approach for conditional rewrite theories where the conditions are just equalities solved by equational unification. We show how two conditional theories, never executed before, are now executable with very good performance. We also show how real execution works better than the manually transformed version.

Keywords: Canonical narrowing · Conditional rules · Maude · Program transformation

1 Introduction

Maude is based on rewriting logic, a logic suited to specify and execute computational systems in a simple and natural way. Concurrent systems are of particular interest to rewriting logic, as it has been demonstrated in the literature: from a Petri net [32] to a process calculus [37], from an object-based system [26] to asynchronous hardware [20], from a mobile ad hoc network protocol [21] to a cloud-based storage system [8], from a web browser [10] to a programming language with threads [24], or from a distributed control system [7] to a model of mammalian cell pathways [14,33]. And all *without any encoding*: what you see and get is a direct definition of the system itself, without any artificial encoding.

Many symbolic reasoning features are currently supported by Maude, especially order-sorted equational unification and order-sorted narrowing-based symbolic reachability analysis. Nowadays, many application areas rely on unification and narrowing in Maude: from cryptographic protocol verification [9,15,23] to

This work has been partially supported by the EC H2020-EU grant agreement No. 952215 (TAILOR), by the grant PID2021-122830OB-C42 funded by MCIN/AEI/ 10.13039/501100011033 and ERDF "A way of making Europe", by the grant PROMETEO/2019/098 funded by Generalitat Valenciana, and by the grant PCI2020-120708-2 funded by MICIN/AEI/10.13039/501100011033 and by the European Union NextGenerationEU/PRTR.

A. Riesco and M. Zhang (Eds.): ICFEM 2022, LNCS 13478, pp. 20–35, 2022.
https://doi.org/10.1007/978-3-031-17244-1_2

logical LTL model checking [5,6,13,16], and from partial evaluation [3,4] to reachability logic theorem proving [35,36]; see [29,30] for further references.

On the other hand, there have been advances and new features added to improve narrowing in Maude. A transformational approach for symbolic reachability in conditional rewrite theories in [11]. A new narrowing calculus for conditional rewrite theories with multiple types of conditions, including memberships, in [1,2]. A more concise definition of narrowing using irreducibility conditions in [17]. A notion of generalized rewrite theory in [29] where symbolic executability conditions are clarified.

In this paper, we provide a very elegant, transparent, and extremely pragmatic approach for conditional rewrite theories where the conditions are just equalities. Given a simple conditional rewrite theory, with just one conditional rule and one variant equation of the following form

```
crl f(x) => a if x = b [narrowing] .
eq c = b [variant] .
```

where narrowing from the term f(x) returns a with the computed substitution x ↦ c. This theory is transformed into the following semantically equivalent theory

```
rl f(x) | x =:= b => a [narrowing] .
eq c = b [variant] .
eq x =:= x = tt [variant] .
eq x | tt = x [variant] .
```

where again narrowing from the term f(x) returns a with the computed substitution x ↦ c. The point is that the narrowable term f(x) and the left-hand side f(x) | x =:= b are equationally unifiable thanks to the two extra equations "x =:= x = tt" and "x | tt = x".

In Sect. 2, we provide some preliminaries. In Sect. 3, we describe our implementation. In Sect. 4, we present some experiments using two examples from [29] that were presented as conditional rewrite theories, transformed into unconditional rewrite theories but were never fully symbolically executed. In Sect. 5, we conclude and give some future work.

2   Preliminaries

We follow the classical notation and terminology from [34] for term rewriting, and from [25,29] for rewriting logic and order-sorted notions.

We assume an order-sorted signature Σ with a poset of sorts $(S, \leq)$. The poset $(S, \leq)$ of sorts for Σ is partitioned into equivalence classes, called *connected components*, by the equivalence relation $(\leq \cup \geq)^+$. We assume that each connected component [s] has a *top element* under $\leq$, denoted $\top_{[s]}$ and called the *top sort* of [s]. This involves no real loss of generality, since if [s] lacks a top sort, it can be easily added.

We assume an S-sorted family $X = \{X_s\}_{s \in S}$ of disjoint variable sets with each X_s countably infinite. $\mathcal{T}_\Sigma(X)_s$ is the set of terms of sort s, and $\mathcal{T}_{\Sigma,s}$ is the set of ground terms of sort s. We write $\mathcal{T}_\Sigma(X)$ and $\mathcal{T}_\Sigma$ for the corresponding order-sorted term algebras. Given a term t, $Var(t)$ denotes the set of variables in t.

A *substitution* $\sigma \in Subst(\Sigma, X)$ is a sorted mapping from a finite subset of X to $\mathcal{T}_\Sigma(X)$. Substitutions are written as $\sigma = \{X_1 \mapsto t_1, \ldots, X_n \mapsto t_n\}$ where the domain of σ is $Dom(\sigma) = \{X_1, \ldots, X_n\}$ and the set of variables introduced by terms $t_1, \ldots, t_n$ is written $Ran(\sigma)$. The identity substitution is id. Substitutions are homomorphically extended to $\mathcal{T}_\Sigma(X)$. The application of substitution σ to a term t is denoted by $t\sigma$ or $\sigma(t)$.

A Σ-*equation* is an unoriented pair $t = t'$, where $t, t' \in \mathcal{T}_\Sigma(X)_s$ for some sort $s \in S$. Given Σ and a set E of Σ-equations, order-sorted equational logic induces a congruence relation $=_E$ on terms $t, t' \in \mathcal{T}_\Sigma(X)$ (see [27]). Throughout this paper we assume that $\mathcal{T}_{\Sigma,s} \neq \emptyset$ for every sort s, because this affords a simpler deduction system. We write $\mathcal{T}_{\Sigma/E}(X)$ and $\mathcal{T}_{\Sigma/E}$ for the corresponding order-sorted term algebras modulo the congruence closure $=_E$, denoting the equivalence class of a term $t \in \mathcal{T}_\Sigma(X)$ as $[t]_E \in \mathcal{T}_{\Sigma/E}(X)$.

An *equational theory* (Σ, E) is a pair with Σ an order-sorted signature and E a set of Σ-equations. An equational theory (Σ, E) is *regular* if for each $t = t'$ in E, we have $Var(t) = Var(t')$. An equational theory (Σ, E) is *linear* if for each $t = t'$ in E, each variable occurs only once in t and in t'. An equational theory (Σ, E) is *sort-preserving* if for each $t = t'$ in E, each sort s, and each substitution σ, we have $t\sigma \in \mathcal{T}_\Sigma(X)_s$ iff $t'\sigma \in \mathcal{T}_\Sigma(X)_s$. An equational theory (Σ, E) is *defined using top sorts* if for each equation $t = t'$ in E, all variables in $Var(t)$ and $Var(t')$ have a top sort.

An *E-unifier* for a Σ-equation $t = t'$ is a substitution σ such that $t\sigma =_E t'\sigma$. For $Var(t) \cup Var(t') \subseteq W$, a set of substitutions $CSU_E^W(t = t')$ is said to be a *complete* set of unifiers for the equality $t = t'$ modulo E away from W iff: (i) each $\sigma \in CSU_E^W(t = t')$ is an E-unifier of $t = t'$; (ii) for any E-unifier ρ of $t = t'$ there is a $\sigma \in CSU_E^W(t = t')$ such that $\sigma|_W \sqsupseteq_E \rho|_W$ (i.e., there is a substitution η such that $(\sigma\eta)|_W =_E \rho|_W$); and (iii) for all $\sigma \in CSU_E^W(t = t')$, $Dom(\sigma) \subseteq (Var(t) \cup Var(t'))$ and $Ran(\sigma) \cap W = \emptyset$.

A *conditional rewrite rule* is an oriented pair $l \to r$ if φ, where $l \notin X$, φ is of the form $t_1 = t_1' \wedge \ldots \wedge t_n = t_n'$, and $l, r \in \mathcal{T}_\Sigma(X)_s$ for some sort $s \in S$. An unconditional rewrite rule is written $l \to r$. A *conditional order-sorted rewrite theory* is a triple (Σ, E, R, T) with Σ an order-sorted signature, E a set of Σ-equations, T is a background theory, and R a set of conditional rewrite rules. The set R of rules is *sort-decreasing* if for each $t \to t'$ (or $t \to t'$ if φ) in R, each $s \in S$, and each substitution σ, $t'\sigma \in \mathcal{T}_\Sigma(X)_s$ implies $t\sigma \in \mathcal{T}_\Sigma(X)_s$.

The rewriting relation on $\mathcal{T}_\Sigma(X)$, written $t \to_R t'$ or $t \to_{p,R} t'$ holds between t and t' iff there exist a $p \in Pos_\Sigma(t)$, $l \to r$ if $\varphi \in R$ and a substitution σ, such that $\varphi = (t_1 = t_1' \wedge \ldots \wedge t_n = t_n')$, $t_1\sigma =_E t_1'\sigma \wedge \ldots \wedge t_n\sigma =_E t_n'\sigma$, $t|_p = l\sigma$, and $t' = t[r\sigma]_p$. The relation $\to_{R/E}$ on $\mathcal{T}_\Sigma(X)$ is $=_E; \to_R; =_E$. The transitive (resp. transitive and reflexive) closure of $\to_{R/E}$ is denoted $\to_{R/E}^+$ (resp. $\to_{R/E}^*$).

A term t is called $\rightarrow_{R/E}$-irreducible (or just R/E-irreducible) if there is no term t' such that $t \rightarrow_{R/E} t'$. For $\rightarrow_{R/E}$ confluent and terminating, the irreducible version of a term t is denoted by $t\downarrow_{R/E}$.

A relation $\rightarrow_{R,E}$ on $\mathcal{T}_{\Sigma}(\mathcal{X})$ is defined as: $t \rightarrow_{p,R,E} t'$ (or just $t \rightarrow_{R,E} t'$) iff there are a position $p \in Pos_{\Sigma}(t)$, a rule $l \rightarrow r$ if φ in R, and a substitution σ such that $\varphi = (t_1 = t_1' \wedge \ldots \wedge t_n = t_n')$, $t_1\sigma =_E t_1'\sigma \wedge \ldots \wedge t_n\sigma =_E t_n'\sigma$, $t|_p =_E l\sigma$ and $t' = t[r\sigma]_p$. Reducibility of $\rightarrow_{R/E}$ is undecidable in general since E-congruence classes can be arbitrarily large. Therefore, R/E-rewriting is usually implemented [19] by R, E-rewriting under some conditions on R and E such as confluence, termination, and coherence.

We call (Σ, B, E) a *decomposition* of an order-sorted equational theory $(\Sigma, E \cup B)$ if B is regular, linear, sort-preserving, defined using top sorts, and has a finitary and complete unification algorithm, which implies that B-matching is decidable, and the equations E oriented into rewrite rules $\overrightarrow{E}$ are *convergent*, i.e., confluent, terminating, and strictly coherent [28] modulo B, and sort-decreasing.

Given a decomposition (Σ, B, E) of an equational theory, (t', θ) is an E, B-*variant* [12,18] (or just a variant) of term t if $t\theta\downarrow_{E,B} =_E t'$ and $\theta\downarrow_{E,B} =_E \theta$. A *complete set of E, B-variants* [18] (up to renaming) of a term t is a subset, denoted by $[\![t]\!]_{E,B}$, of the set of all E, B-variants of t such that, for each E, B-variant (t', σ) of t, there is an E, B-variant $(t'', \theta) \in [\![t]\!]_{E,B}$ such that $(t'', \theta) \sqsupseteq_{E,B} (t', \sigma)$, i.e., there is a substitution ρ such that $t' =_B t''\rho$ and $\sigma|_{Var(t)} =_B (\theta\rho)|_{Var(t)}$. A decomposition (Σ, B, E) has the *finite variant property* (FVP) [18] (also called a *finite variant decomposition*) iff for each Σ-term t, a complete set $[\![t]\!]_{E,B}$ of its most general variants is finite.

In what follows, the set G of equations will in practice be $G = E \uplus B$ and will have a decomposition (Σ, B, E).

Definition 1 (Reachability goal). *Given an order-sorted rewrite theory* (Σ, G, R), *a reachability goal is defined as a pair* $t \xrightarrow{?}{}^{*}_{R/G} t'$, *where* $t, t' \in \mathcal{T}_{\Sigma}(\mathcal{X})_s$. *It is abbreviated as* $t \xrightarrow{?}{}^{*} t'$ *when the theory is clear from the context;* t *is the source of the goal and* t' *is the target. A substitution* σ *is a R/G-solution of the reachability goal (or just a solution for short) iff there is a sequence* $\sigma(t) \rightarrow_{R/G} \sigma(u_1) \rightarrow_{R/G} \cdots \rightarrow_{R/G} \sigma(u_{k-1}) \rightarrow_{R/G} \sigma(t')$.

A set Γ *of substitutions is said to be a* complete set of solutions *of* $t \xrightarrow{?}{}^{*}_{R/G} t'$ *iff (i) every substitution* $\sigma \in \Gamma$ *is a solution of* $t \xrightarrow{?}{}^{*}_{R/G} t'$, *and (ii) for any solution* ρ *of* $t \xrightarrow{?}{}^{*}_{R/G} t'$, *there is a substitution* $\sigma \in \Gamma$ *more general than* ρ *modulo G, i.e.,* $\sigma|_{Var(t) \cup Var(t')} \sqsupseteq_G \rho|_{Var(t) \cup Var(t')}$.

This provides a tool-independent semantic framework for symbolic reachability analysis of protocols under algebraic properties. Note that we have removed the condition $Var(\varphi) \cup Var(r) \subseteq Var(l)$ for rewrite rules $l \rightarrow r$ if $\varphi \in R$ and thus a solution of a reachability goal must be applied to all terms in the rewrite sequence. If the terms t and t' in a goal $t \xrightarrow{?}{}^{*}_{T/G} t'$ are ground and rules have no extra variables in their right-hand sides, then goal solving becomes a standard rewriting reachability problem. However, since we allow terms t, t' with variables, we need a mechanism more general than standard rewriting to find solutions of reachability goals. *Narrowing* with R modulo G generalizes rewriting by performing *unification* at non-variable positions instead of the usual matching modulo G.

A relation $\rightsquigarrow_{R,G}$ on $\mathcal{T}_\Sigma(\mathcal{X})$ is defined as: $t \rightsquigarrow_{\sigma,R,G} t'$ (or $\stackrel{\sigma}{\rightsquigarrow}$ if R, G is understood) iff there is a $p \in Pos_\Sigma(t)$, a rule $l \rightarrow r$ if φ in R such that $Var(t) \cap (Var(l) \cup Var(r) \cup Var(\varphi)) = \emptyset$, $\varphi = (t_1 = t'_1 \wedge \ldots \wedge t_n = t'_n)$, and $\sigma \in CSU_G^V(t|_p = l \wedge t_1 = t'_1 \wedge \ldots \wedge t_n = t'_n)$ for a set V of variables containing $Var(t)$, $Var(l)$, $Var(r)$ and $Var(\varphi)$, such that $t' = \sigma(t[r]_p)$.

Soundness and completeness of narrowing for solving reachability goals are proved in [19,31] for unconditional rules R modulo an equational theory G and in [29] for conditional rules R modulo an equational theory G, both with the restriction of considering only order-sorted *topmost* rewrite theories, i.e., rewrite theories were all the rewrite steps happen at the top of the term.

3   Implementation

To implement conditional rules handling in the narrowing algorithm, we have used our implementation of standard/canonical narrowing [22] as a starting point. To do this, we use the features of the Maude meta-level, thus creating an extension of the previous meta-level command.

3.1   Our Previous Narrowing Command

The meta-level command we use as a starting point already allows us to choose between several narrowing algorithms to use. First of all, it allows to invoke the standard narrowing algorithm, with a behavior similar to the standard narrowing built-in in Maude. It also allows the canonical narrowing algorithm [22] to be invoked, in which irreducibility constraints are used to reduce the width of the computed reachability tree. To control the algorithm used along with other parameters, such as the maximum depth of the tree or the maximum number of solutions to search for, the command uses ten arguments:

```
narrowing(Module, Term, SearchArrow, Term, AlgorithmOptionSet, VariantOptionSet, TermList, Qid,
          Bound, Bound)
```

In the implementation of that command, we already prepared an adequate infrastructure to allow future extensions. Several data structures and substructures were defined to represent the reachability tree, its nodes, and the solutions found. Additionally, we divided the implementation into three main parts, which correspond to the main steps of the algorithm at a theoretical level: (i) the generation of nodes (terms) in the reachability tree, (ii) the attempt to unify each new term with the target term, and (iii) the computation of solutions in case the unification is successful. Those main parts are further broken down into highly distinguishable subparts, making it easy to make extensions or modifications to some parts without having to change the rest of the implementation.

3.2   Automatic Transformation of Conditional Rules

So far, narrowing in Maude is not capable of processing rewriting theories that contain conditional rules. Implementing a narrowing algorithm that achieves this is a great advance in the field, since there are a large number of theories that use this type of rules. The main objective of this work, therefore, is to allow our narrowing algorithms (both standard and canonical) to be able to process theory with conditional rules. To do this, we transform these rules into non-conditional rules, taking advantage of Maude's reflective level.

We base our transformation on adding the conditions of each of the rules to the left-hand side of these. In this way, if we have a conditional rule of the following form:

```
crl Lhs => Rhs if Condition .
```

the idea is to remove the condition, but add it to the left part of the rule using a new operator:

```
rl Lhs | Condition => Rhs .
```

Subsequently, the conditions will be processed within the left-hand side of the rule. This requires the addition of a new sort, new operators, and several variant equations. For example, considering that we have an initial module that contains sorts $S1, \ldots, Sn$, it would be necessary to add the following to the theory:

```
sort BoolT .

op tt : -> BoolT .
op _&_ : BoolT BoolT -> BoolT [assoc comm id: tt] .

op _=:=_ : [S1] [S1] -> BoolT .
eq X:[S1] =:= X:[S1] = tt [variant] .
...
op _=:=_ : [Sn] [Sn] -> BoolT .
eq X:[Sn] =:= X:[Sn] = tt [variant] .

op _|_ : S1 BoolT -> [S1] .
eq X:[S1] | tt = X:[S1] [variant] .
...
op _|_ : Sn BoolT -> [Sn] .
eq X:[Sn] | tt = X:[Sn] [variant] .
```

In other words, we define a new BoolT sort that will help us process the satis-fiability of the conditions, which will now be found on the left-hand side of the rule as a term. An operator & is also defined that will be used to concatenate several conditions, if any. A constant tt will be used as the identity symbol, representing the value *true*. We can also see how an operator =:=, which represents equational unification, is defined along with a variant equation that defines when two elements are equal. In addition, an operator | is defined, which is precisely what allows us to add the conditions to the left of the rules. With a variant equation, we define that the constant tt functions as the identity symbol for this operator.

As we have previously mentioned, at the coding level in Maude, it is necessary
to use the reflective level to perform these transformations. We have defined
this transformation both for normal modules and for theories, strategies, and
strategies with theories. However, to simplify the explanation, we will use as a
guide in this article only the transformation applied to normal modules, since it
is very similar in any of the cases. We define a `transformMod` operator that will
receive the user's module when the narrowing algorithm starts. An equation will
take care of starting the transformation, adding to the module, first of all, the
new sort `BoolT` and the necessary operators:

```
var ModId : Qid .   var Imports : ImportList .   var Sorts : SortSet .
var Subsorts : SubsortDeclSet .   var Ops : OpDeclSet .   var Membs : MembAxSet .
var Eqs : EquationSet .   vars Rls1 Rls2 : RuleSet .

eq transformMod(mod ModId is Imports sorts Sorts . Subsorts Ops Membs Eqs Rls1 endm)
            = mod ModId is Imports (protecting 'META-TERM .)
                  sorts Sorts ; 'BoolT . Subsorts
                  (Ops
                      (op 'tt : nil -> 'BoolT [ctor] .)
                      (op '_&_ : 'BoolT 'BoolT -> 'BoolT [assoc comm id('tt.BoolT)] .)
                      (op '_=:=_ : 'Universal 'Universal -> 'BoolT [ctor poly (1 2)] .)
                      (op '_|_ : 'Universal 'BoolT -> 'Universal [ctor poly (0 1)] .)
                  )
                  Membs
                  addEqs(Eqs,
                  getKinds(mod ModId is Imports sorts Sorts ;
                              'BoolT . Subsorts Ops Membs Eqs Rls1 endm))
                  transformRls(Rls1) endm .
```

Note that the `=:=` and `|` operators make use of the `Universal` sort. This is a
special sort of the Maude's meta-level that allows defining polymorphic operators. Subsequently, any sort of those belonging to the module can take the place
of that special sort. This allows us to define both operators for any sort of the
original module in an easy and efficient way.

Regarding the addition of the new equations, we see in the code above a
call to an `addEqs` operator, which receives the equations of the original module
and all the kinds of that module, using Maude's own `getKinds` operator. The
behavior of the `addEqs` operator is defined recursively, and will ultimately return
a set of equations containing the original equations alongside the new ones:

```
var K : Kind .   var KSet : KindSet .   vars TP V : Qid .

op addEqs : EquationSet KindSet -> EquationSet .
eq addEqs(Eqs, K ; KSet)
            = addEqs(
                (Eqs
                    eq '_=:=_[addTypeToVar(K,'X), addTypeToVar(K,'X)] = 'tt.BoolT [variant] .
                    eq '_|_[addTypeToVar(K,'X), 'tt.BoolT] = addTypeToVar(K,'X) [variant] .),
                KSet) .
eq addEqs(Eqs, KSet) = Eqs [owise] .

op addTypeToVar : Type Qid -> Variable [memo] .
eq addTypeToVar(TP:Qid, V:Qid)
            = qid(string(V:Qid) + ":" + string(TP:Qid)) .
```

Recursion allows us to iterate over the set of Kinds received, managing to define
both equations for each of the Kinds contained in that set. You can see the use of

an auxiliary operator **addTypeToVar**, which allows us to define variables at run-time using each of the sorts over which we iterate. For the correct operation of this operator, it is necessary to have previously imported the module **META-TERM**.

Finally, it is necessary to transform the conditional rules of the original module into non-conditional rules, which make use of the previously defined operators to keep the conditions. It is done by calling the **transformRls** operator, which receives the set of rules from the original module:

```
vars Rls1 Rls2 : RuleSet .

op transformRls : RuleSet -> RuleSet .
eq transformRls(Rls1 (crl Lhs => Rhs if nil [Attrs] .) Rls2)
        = transformRls(Rls1 Rls2) (rl Lhs => Rhs [Attrs narrowing] .) .
eq transformRls(Rls1 (crl Lhs => Rhs if Cond1 /\ (T1 = T2) /\ Cond2 [Attrs] .) Rls2)
        = transformRls(Rls1 Rls2) transformConditions(crl '_|_[Lhs,'_=:=_[T1,T2]]
                                => Rhs if Cond1 /\ Cond2 [Attrs] .) .
eq transformRls(Rls1) = Rls1 [owise] .

op transformConditions : Rule -> Rule .
eq transformConditions(crl (Lhs) => Rhs if nil [Attrs] .)
        =  (rl (Lhs) => Rhs [Attrs narrowing] .) .
eq transformConditions(crl '_|_[Lhs,T1] => Rhs if Cond1 /\ (T2 = T3) /\ Cond2 [Attrs] .)
        = transformConditions(crl '_|_[Lhs,'_&_[T1,'_=:=_[T2,T3]]]
                => Rhs if Cond1 /\ Cond2 [Attrs] .)
```

Once again, we make use of recursion, in this case to iterate over the set of rules. We will go rule by rule looking for those that are conditional, and leaving intact those that are not. When we find a conditional rule, we process its conditions one by one, using a **transformConditions** auxiliary operator that receives a rule and iterates over its conditions. This operator is responsible for collecting each of the conditions of the rule and attaching them to the left part of it, using the operator | defined above. The & operator is also used to concatenate conditions within the left-hand side, in case the rule contains several. The operator =:= is now in charge of representing and processing the equality condition found in the rule conditions. Once all the conditions of the rule have been processed, the **narrowing** attribute is added to it, which originally will not be there since Maude does not allow it to be used when defining conditional rules. After this, another conditional rule is searched for in the set of rules, and the same process is repeated. When there are no conditional rules left to process, the transformed set is returned.

All the previous transformations will allow the narrowing to be able to process the received theory, regardless of the number of conditional rules it contains. At run-time, the conditions in the left parts of the rules will be processed. When the conditions are fulfilled, the term in which we find ourselves at each moment will be able to unify with the left part of the rule, thus achieving a rewriting step. When they are not met, the term will not be able to unify with any of the left parts, so it will not be possible to take a rewrite step, thus terminating the execution of a branch when one or more of the conditions are unsatisfiable.

4   Experiments

The experiments carried out in this work are about two rewrite theories with conditional rules (defined as modules in Maude) that come from [29]. In that work, the manual transformation of both modules is proposed in order to eliminate the conditional rules, defining the same behavior only with non-conditional rules, and also eliminating the use of variant equations along the way. Thanks to this transformation, the new modules allow the use of new operations, such as narrowing, on them. However, the transformation of one of these modules is incomplete, so narrowing cannot be executed on it.

First, we have expanded those two rewrite theories to be fully conditional, since the specifications in [29] where somehow altered. Second, our proposal consists of transforming the modules with conditional rules into modules with non-conditional rules automatically and transparently for the user. This is an important advancement in expressivity, since one will be able to write the modules with conditional rules without worrying about carrying out any kind of manual transformation.

The purpose of the experiments is to test the correct functioning of the new transparent transformation, including the application of narrowing to the module after transforming it. In addition, we perform comparisons between (i) the standard narrowing on the manually transformed module without variants of [29], (ii) the standard narrowing on our transparently transformed modules, and (iii) the canonical narrowing on our transparently transformed modules. All the experiments carried out, as well as the files necessary to execute them and the results, can be viewed and downloaded from the following link: https://github.com/ralorueda/conditional-narrowing.

4.1   Model of a Bank Account

The first rewrite theory used consists of a simple model of a bank account expressed with conditional rules in Maude. Since the original implementation is already detailed in the cited article, both for this module and for the one that we will see in Sect. 4.2, here we focus on this example was expanded to be fully conditional, since the original was somehow altered. These improvements are simply to express modules more intuitively with conditional rules, instead of using an extra `Boolean` parameter as originally done to model transitions.

In the case of the bank account model, an extra operator is used that, depending on the evaluation of a Boolean condition, moves to one state or another of the bank account. This is simply a different way of defining behavior similar to that of conditional rules:

```
op [_,_,_] : Bool State State -> State . *** if-then-else

vars s s' : State .   vars n m x : Nat .   var msgs : MsgConf .

eq [true,s,s'] = s [variant] .
eq [false,s,s'] = s' [variant] .
```

```
*** actual withdrawing of money from account
rl [w] : < bal: n pend: x overdraft: false > # withdraw(m),msgs =>
            [ m > n ,
            < bal: n pend: x overdraft: true > # msgs ,
            < bal: (n - m) pend: (x - m) overdraft: false > # msgs ] .
```

It's not hard to see that we can eliminate that extra operator, as well as the two variant equations, by rewriting the above rule as two conditional rules. Originally, it is not specified that way because it would hinder the transformation process that is performed later:

```
*** actual withdrawing of money from account
crl [w1] :  < bal: n pend: x overdraft: false > # withdraw(m),msgs =>
              < bal: n pend: x overdraft: true > # msgs
                if m > n .

crl [w2] :  < bal: n pend: x overdraft: false > # withdraw(m),msgs =>
              < bal: (n - m) pend: (x - m) overdraft: false > # msgs
                if m <= n .
```

When we run our transparent transformation algorithm, those conditional rules will become two unconditional rules as follows:

```
rl [w1] : < bal: n pend: x overdraft: false > # withdraw(m),msgs | m > n =:= true =>
            < bal: n pend: x overdraft: true > # msgs [narrowing] .

rl [w2] : < bal: n pend: x overdraft: false > # withdraw(m),msgs | m <= n =:= true =>
            < bal: (n - m) pend: (x - m) overdraft: false > # msgs [narrowing] .
```

Once the transformation of the conditional rules has been carried out using the new defined operators (see Sect. 3), we can execute the narrowing algorithms on the new module, solving the specified reachability problem. Specifically, we have used the following reachability problem for experiments with this module:

$$< bal : 1 + 1 + 1 + 1\, pend : Pend1 : Natural\ overdraft : Over1 : Bool >$$
$$\#\, Msgs1 : MsgConf$$
$$\overset{?}{\rightsquigarrow}{}^{*}$$
$$< Bal2 : Natural\ pend : Pend2 : Natural\ overdraft : Over2 : Bool >$$
$$\#\, Msgs2 : MsgConf$$

The results obtained when executing the narrowing algorithms on the manual transformation presented in [29] and on the transparent transformation performed in this work are detailed in Table 1. We can see how narrowing on our transparent transformation (both standard and canonical) performs better than narrowing on the original manual transformation. This is common in program transformation techniques when the number of resulting rules is bigger than the original, since more rules means more rule application attempts. Also, as expected, when going deeper into the search tree, the canonical narrowing algorithm outperforms the standard narrowing algorithm, since it reduces the number of solutions thanks to the use of irreducibility constraints and therefore their computation time. For the number of solutions, our transparent transformation does not remove some auxiliary symbols used in the conditions whereas these symbols disappear in the manually transformation version. And, as expected, the canonical narrowing reduces the search space thanks to the use of irreducibility constraints.

Table 1. Results of (i) the standard narrowing and canonical narrowing algorithms when solving a reachability problem in the bank account module using the conditional narrowing that we have implemented and (ii) the standard narrowing algorithm when solving the same reachability problem in the bank account module after the manual transformation from [29].

Narrowing algorithm, module	Depth limit	Execution time	Solutions found
Manually transformed	2	238 ms	440
Conditional standard narrowing	2	220 ms	461
Conditional canonical narrowing	2	222 ms	461
Manually transformed	3	40829 ms	3713
Conditional standard narrowing	3	35566 ms	4644
Conditional canonical narrowing	3	29363 ms	4168

4.2   Model of a Communication Channel

The second rewriting theory used for the experiments is a model of a communications channel. In this case, once again, an extra operator is originally used that is responsible for modeling the behavior of conditional rules:

```
op [_,_,_] : Bool Channel Channel -> Channel [frozen] . *** if-then-else

vars N M J K : Nat .    vars L P : NatList .
var S : MsgSet .    vars CH CH' : Channel .

eq [true,CH,CH'] = CH [variant] .
eq [false,CH,CH'] = CH' [variant] .

rl [recv] : [L,N] {J,K} S [P,M] =>
                [(K ~ M),
                 [L,N] S ack(K) [P ; J, M + 1],
                 [L,N] S ack(K) [P,M]] .

rl [ack-recv] : [J ; L,N] ack(K) S [P,M] =>
                [(K ~ N),
                 [L,N + 1] S [P,M],
                 [J ; L,N] S [P,M]] .
```

In addition, in this module, we do originally find a conditional rule, which is precisely the one on which the original transformation is not performed, which means that narrowing cannot be used on the module transformed in this way:

```
crl [loss] : [L,N] S S' [P,M] => [L,N] S' [P,M] if S =/= null .
```

Once more, we expand these rules to be fully conditional, thus removing the extra operator and the two variant equations. We also slightly modify the original conditional rule, so that the condition is manageable by narrowing. To do this, it is necessary to define a new operator empty. Notice that two unintuitive operators, ~ and ~/~, appear in the conditions of the rules. They express equality and inequality respectively. The resulting rules are as follows:

```
crl [recv-1] : [L,N] {J,K} S [P,M] => [L,N] S ack(K) [P ; J, M + 1]
                   if K ~ M .

crl [recv-2] : [L,N] {J,K} S [P,M] => [L,N] S ack(K) [P,M]
                   if K ~/~ M .

crl [ack-recv-1] : [J ; L,N] ack(K) S [P,M] => [L,N + 1] S [P,M]
                   if K ~ N .

crl [ack-recv-2] : [J ; L,N] ack(K) S [P,M] => [J ; L,N] S [P,M]
                   if K ~/~ N .

op empty : MsgSet -> Bool .
var MSG : Msg .

eq empty(null) = true [variant] .
eq empty(MSG S) = false [variant] .

crl [loss] : [L,N] S S' [P,M] => [L,N] S' [P,M]
                   if empty(null) .
```

We can now run our transparent transformation algorithm, which will express the above conditional rules into unconditional rules using the newly introduced operators:

```
rl [recv-1] : [L,N] {J,K} S [P,M] | M ~ K =:= true
                   => [L,N] S ack(K) [P ; J, M + 1] [narrowing] .

rl [recv-2] : [L,N] {J,K} S [P,M] | K ~/~ M =:= true
                   => [L,N] S ack(K) [P,M] [narrowing] .

rl [ack-recv-1] : [J ; L,N] ack(K) S [P,M] | K ~ N =:= true
                   => [L,N + 1] S [P,M] [narrowing] .

rl [ack-recv-2] : [J ; L,N] ack(K) S [P,M] | K ~ N =:= true
                   => [J ; L,N] S [P,M] [narrowing] .

rl [ack-recv-2] : [L,N] S S' [P,M] | empty(null) =:= true
                   => [L,N] S' [P,M] [narrowing] .
```

Now that, thanks to be able to perform our transparent transformation, we can apply the standard and canonical narrowing algorithms to the new resulting module. In this case, because the original manual transformation is incomplete, we cannot perform narrowing comparisons on it, but we can perform experiments to compare the performance of standard narrowing and canonical narrowing with our transformation. The reachability problem used in this case is the following:

$$[NL1 : NaturalList, N1 : Natural]\ null\ [NL2 : NaturalList, N2 : Natural]$$
$$\overset{?}{\leadsto}^*$$
$$C2 : Channel$$

The results obtained in the experiments are detailed in Table 2. We can see how, again, the canonical narrowing outperforms the standard narrowing. This time it occurs in each of the tests, since from depth level 2, the canonical narrowing is able to reduce the number of solutions computed, thus reducing the computation time accordingly. In this case, because the use of the idempotence property for the message sets, the improvement of the canonical narrowing with respect to the standard narrowing is even greater, since it is a property in which this type of narrowing behaves especially well, as we showed in one of our earlier works

Table 2. Results of the standard narrowing and canonical narrowing algorithms when solving a reachability problem in the communication channel module using the conditional narrowing that we have implemented.

Narrowing algorithm	Depth limit	Execution time	Solutions found
Standard	2	164 ms	65
Canonical	2	132 ms	45
Standard	3	2515 ms	731
Canonical	3	1446 ms	479
Standard	4	211056 ms	8760
Canonical	4	37253 ms	4497

(see [22]). In this way, we can see how for depth level 4 in the search tree, there is an improvement of more than 500% in performance in computation time. In addition, canonical narrowing manages to reduce the number of solutions to almost half.

5   Conclusions and Future Work

Many symbolic reasoning features are currently supported by Maude, especially order-sorted equational unification and order-sorted narrowing-based symbolic reachability analysis. Many application areas rely nowadays on these unification and narrowing capabilities. Also, there have been many advances and new features added to improve narrowing in Maude but only at a theoretical level. In this paper, we provide a very elegant, transparent, and extremely pragmatic approach for conditional rewrite theories where the conditions are just equalities solved by equational unification.

We have shown how two conditional theories of [29] are now executable with very good performance. We have also shown how real execution works better than the manually transformed version of one of these two theories. And we ascertained, as expected, that canonical narrowing works much better than standard narrowing even in these more complex conditional theories, which have an extra equational unification overhead.

We plan to continue working on both adding new features to narrowing in Maude and improving the performance.

References

1. Aguirre, L., Martí-Oliet, N., Palomino, M., Pita, I.: Conditional narrowing modulo SMT and axioms. In: Vanhoof, W., Pientka, B. (eds.) Proceedings of the 19th International Symposium on Principles and Practice of Declarative Programming, Namur, Belgium, 09–11 October 2017, pp. 17–28. ACM (2017)

2. Aguirre, L., Martí-Oliet, N., Palomino, M., Pita, I.: Sentence-normalized conditional narrowing modulo in rewriting logic and Maude. J. Autom. Reason. **60**(4), 421–463 (2018)
3. Alpuente, M., Ballis, D., Escobar, S., Sapiña, J.: Optimization of rewrite theories by equational partial evaluation. J. Log. Algebraic Methods Program. **124**, 100729 (2022)
4. Alpuente, M., Cuenca-Ortega, A., Escobar, S., Meseguer, J.: A partial evaluation framework for order-sorted equational programs modulo axioms. J. Log. Algebraic Methods Program. **110** (2020)
5. Bae, K., Escobar, S., Meseguer, J.: Abstract logical model checking of infinite-state systems using narrowing. In: van Raamsdonk, F. (ed.) 24th International Conference on Rewriting Techniques and Applications, RTA 2013, Eindhoven, The Netherlands, 24–26 June 2013. LIPIcs, vol. 21, pp. 81–96. Schloss Dagstuhl - Leibniz-Zentrum für Informatik (2013)
6. Bae, K., Meseguer, J.: Infinite-state model checking of LTLR formulas using narrowing. In: Escobar, S. (ed.) WRLA 2014. LNCS, vol. 8663, pp. 113–129. Springer, Cham (2014). https://doi.org/10.1007/978-3-319-12904-4_6
7. Bae, K., Meseguer, J., Ölveczky, P.C.: Formal patterns for multirate distributed real-time systems. Sci. Comput. Program. **91**, 3–44 (2014)
8. Bobba, R., et al.: Design, formal modeling, and validation of cloud storage systems using Maude. In: Campbell, R.H., Kamhoua, C.A., Kwiat, K.A. (eds.) Assured Cloud Computing, chapter 2, pp. 10–48. Wiley (2018)
9. Chadha, R., Cheval, V., Ciobâcă, Ş., Kremer, S.: Automated verification of equivalence properties of cryptographic protocols. ACM Trans. Comput. Log. **17**(4), 23:1–23:32 (2016)
10. Chen, S., Meseguer, J., Sasse, R., Wang, H.J., Wang, Y.-M.: A systematic approach to uncover security flaws in GUI logic. In: 2007 IEEE Symposium on Security and Privacy (S&P 2007), Oakland, California, USA, 20–23 May 2007, pp. 71–85. IEEE Computer Society (2007)
11. Cholewa, A., Escobar, S., Meseguer, J.: Constrained narrowing for conditional equational theories modulo axioms. Sci. Comput. Program. **112**, 24–57 (2015)
12. Comon-Lundh, H., Delaune, S.: The finite variant property: how to get rid of some algebraic properties. In: Giesl, J. (ed.) RTA 2005. LNCS, vol. 3467, pp. 294–307. Springer, Heidelberg (2005). https://doi.org/10.1007/978-3-540-32033-3_22
13. Durán, F., et al.: Equational unification and matching, and symbolic reachability analysis in Maude 3.2 (system description). In: Blanchette, J., Kovács, L., Pattinson, D. (eds.) IJCAR 2022. LNCS, vol. 13385, pp. 529–540. Springer, Cham (2022). https://doi.org/10.1007/978-3-031-10769-6_31
14. Eker, S., Knapp, M., Laderoute, K., Lincoln, P., Meseguer, J., Sonmez, K.: Pathway logic: symbolic analysis of biological signaling. In: Altman, R.B., Keith Dunker, A., Hunter, L., Klein, T.E. (eds.) Proceedings of the 7th Pacific Symposium on Biocomputing, PSB 2002, Lihue, Hawaii, USA, 3–7 January 2002, pp. 400–412 (2002)
15. Escobar, S., Meadows, C., Meseguer, J.: Maude-NPA: cryptographic protocol analysis modulo equational properties. In: Aldini, A., Barthe, G., Gorrieri, R. (eds.) FOSAD 2007-2009. LNCS, vol. 5705, pp. 1–50. Springer, Heidelberg (2009). https://doi.org/10.1007/978-3-642-03829-7_1
16. Escobar, S., Meseguer, J.: Symbolic model checking of infinite-state systems using narrowing. In: Baader, F. (ed.) RTA 2007. LNCS, vol. 4533, pp. 153–168. Springer, Heidelberg (2007). https://doi.org/10.1007/978-3-540-73449-9_13

17. Escobar, S., Meseguer, J.: Canonical narrowing with irreducibility constraints as a symbolic protocol analysis method. In: Guttman, J.D., Landwehr, C.E., Meseguer, J., Pavlovic, D. (eds.) Foundations of Security, Protocols, and Equational Reasoning. LNCS, vol. 11565, pp. 15–38. Springer, Cham (2019). https://doi.org/10.1007/978-3-030-19052-1_4

18. Escobar, S., Sasse, R., Meseguer, J.: Folding variant narrowing and optimal variant termination. J. Log. Algebraic Program. **81**(7–8), 898–928 (2012)

19. Jouannaud, J.-P., Kirchner, H.: Completion of a set of rules modulo a set of equations. SIAM J. Comput. **15**(4), 1155–1194 (1986)

20. Katelman, M., Keller, S., Meseguer, J.: Rewriting semantics of production rule sets. J. Log. Algebraic Program. **81**(7–8), 929–956 (2012)

21. Liu, S., Ölveczky, P.C., Meseguer, J.: Modeling and analyzing mobile ad hoc networks in Real-Time Maude. J. Log. Algebraic Methods Program. **85**, 34–66 (2015)

22. López-Rueda, R., Escobar, S.: Canonical narrowing with irreducibility and SMT constraints as a generic symbolic protocol analysis method. In: Bae, K. (ed.) WRLA 2022. LNCS, vol. 13252, pp. 45–64. Springer, Cham (2022). https://doi.org/10.1007/978-3-031-12441-9_3

23. Meier, S., Schmidt, B., Cremers, C., Basin, D.: The TAMARIN prover for the symbolic analysis of security protocols. In: Sharygina, N., Veith, H. (eds.) CAV 2013. LNCS, vol. 8044, pp. 696–701. Springer, Heidelberg (2013). https://doi.org/10.1007/978-3-642-39799-8_48

24. Meseguer, J., Roşu, G.: The rewriting logic semantics project. Theor. Comput. Sci. **373**, 213–237 (2007)

25. Meseguer, J.: Conditioned rewriting logic as a united model of concurrency. Theor. Comput. Sci. **96**(1), 73–155 (1992)

26. Meseguer, J.: A logical theory of concurrent objects and its realization in the Maude language. In: Agha, G., Wegner, P., Yonezawa, A. (eds.) Research Directions in Concurrent Object-Oriented Programming, pp. 314–390. MIT Press (1993)

27. Meseguer, J.: Membership algebra as a logical framework for equational specification. In: Presicce, F.P. (ed.) WADT 1997. LNCS, vol. 1376, pp. 18–61. Springer, Heidelberg (1998). https://doi.org/10.1007/3-540-64299-4_26

28. Meseguer, J.: Strict coherence of conditional rewriting modulo axioms. Theor. Comput. Sci. **672**, 1–35 (2017)

29. Meseguer, J.: Generalized rewrite theories, coherence completion, and symbolic methods. J. Log. Algebraic Methods Program. **110** (2020)

30. Meseguer, J.: Symbolic computation in Maude: some tapas. In: Fernández, M. (ed.) LOPSTR 2020. LNCS, vol. 12561, pp. 3–36. Springer, Cham (2021). https://doi.org/10.1007/978-3-030-68446-4_1

31. Meseguer, J., Thati, P.: Symbolic reachability analysis using narrowing and its application to verification of cryptographic protocols. Higher-Order Symbolic Comput. **20**(1–2), 123–160 (2007)

32. Stehr, M.-O., Meseguer, J., Ölveczky, P.C.: Rewriting logic as a unifying framework for Petri nets. In: Ehrig, H., Padberg, J., Juhás, G., Rozenberg, G. (eds.) Unifying Petri Nets. LNCS, vol. 2128, pp. 250–303. Springer, Heidelberg (2001). https://doi.org/10.1007/3-540-45541-8_9

33. Talcott, C., Eker, S., Knapp, M., Lincoln, P., Laderoute, K.: Pathway logic modeling of protein functional domains in signal transduction. In: Altman, R.B., Keith Dunker, A., Hunter, L., Jung, T.A., Klein, T.E. (eds.) Biocomputing 2004, Proceedings of the Pacific Symposium, Hawaii, USA, 6–10 January 2004, pp. 568–580. World Scientific (2004)

34. TeReSe (ed.): Term Rewriting Systems (2003)
35. Ştefănescu, A., Ciobâcă, Ş, Mereuta, R., Moore, B.M., Şerbănută, T.F., Roşu, G.: All-path reachability logic. In: Dowek, G. (ed.) RTA 2014. LNCS, vol. 8560, pp. 425–440. Springer, Cham (2014). https://doi.org/10.1007/978-3-319-08918-8_29
36. Ştefănescu, A., Park, D., Yuwen, S., Li, Y., Roşu, G.: Semantics-based program verifiers for all languages. In: Visser, E., Smaragdakis, Y. (eds.) Proceedings of the 2016 ACM SIGPLAN International Conference on Object-Oriented Programming, Systems, Languages, and Applications, OOPSLA 2016, Part of SPLASH 2016, Amsterdam, The Netherlands, 30 October–4 November 2016, pp. 74–91. ACM (2016)
37. Verdejo, A., Martí-Oliet, N.: Implementing CCS in Maude. In: Bolognesi, T., Latella, D. (eds.) Formal Techniques for Distributed System Development, FORTE/PSTV 2000, IFIP TC6 WG6.1 Joint International Conference on Formal Description Techniques for Distributed Systems and Communication Protocols (FORTE XIII) and Protocol Specification, Testing and Verification (PSTV XX), Pisa, Italy, 10–13 October 2000 Proceedings. International Federation for Information Processing Conference Proceedings, vol. 183, pp. 351–366. Kluwer (2000)

Modular Analysis of Tree-Topology Models

Jaime Arias[1], Michał Knapik[2], Wojciech Penczek[2],
and Laure Petrucci[1(✉)]

[1] LIPN, CNRS UMR 7030, Université Sorbonne Paris Nord, 99 av. J-B. Clément,
93430 Villetaneuse, France
{jaime.arias,laure.petrucci}@lipn.univ-paris13.fr
[2] Institute of Computer Science, Polish Academy of Sciences,
Jana Kazimierza 5, 01-248 Warsaw, Poland
{michal.knapik,wojciech.penczek}@ipipan.waw.pl

Abstract. Networks of automata that synchronise over shared actions are organised according to a graph synchronisation topology. In this topology two automata are connected if they can jointly execute some action. We present a very effective reduction for networks with tree-like synchronisation topologies such that all automata after synchronising with their parents can execute only local (non-synchronising) actions: forever or until *resetting*, i.e. entering the initial state. We show that the reduction preserves reachability, but not liveness. This construction is extended to tree-like topologies of arbitrary automata and investigated experimentally.

Keywords: Model checking · Networks of synchronising automata · State space reduction · Tree-like synchronisation topologies

1 Introduction

Networks of various types of finite automata (or labelled transition systems, LTSs for short) [10,14] are a popular choice of formalism when modelling complex systems such as protocols. In this approach, the components of the system under investigation are abstracted as state machines and the behaviour of the entire system is captured by their synchronised product. However, the cost of computing the synchronised product can be prohibitive: in practice the size of the state space grows exponentially with the number of the sub-modules. This observation led to an extensive research into how to analyse and represent models that consist of interacting components without building the entire state space.

In this paper, we tackle the problem of computing a compact representation of the state space of the entire product of networks of LTSs that exhibit tree-like synchronisation topologies. Intuitively, this means a graph, whose edges

The authors acknowledge the support of CNRS and PAN, under the IEA project MoSART, and of NCBR Poland and FNR Luxembourg, under the PolLux/FNR-CORE project STV (POLLUX-VII/1/2019).

A. Riesco and M. Zhang (Eds.): ICFEM 2022, LNCS 13478, pp. 36–53, 2022.
https://doi.org/10.1007/978-3-031-17244-1_3

depict synchronisation between LTSs over common actions of a system, is a tree. Examples of systems having such a synchronisation topology are e.g. attack-defense trees (ADT) [6,7,9,17], hierarchical [4], broadcast [12], multimedia [8], and workflow models [3].

This structure of communication is quite natural also in the system design where circular dependencies are sometimes treated as anti-patterns and cause problems such as deadlocks.

We design algorithms that compute a compact representation of the synchronised product bottom-up, focusing at each level only on the synchronisations between the pairs consisting of a parent and one of its children. As it turns out, the notion of memory is crucial to the size of the constructed LTS (called here the *sum-of-squares product*). Namely, if every component resets (i.e. returns to its initial state) after synchronising with its parent or enters a deadlock, then no information about its post-synchronisation states needs to be preserved. In this case, the sum-of-squares product is quite small and can be computed efficiently. In case some LTSs do not reset after synchronising with their parents, an additional memory gadget is needed. Then, the general sum-of-squares product also preserves reachability, but a reduction or good performance is not guaranteed. The burden of recording the post-synchronisation state of the components can even lead to substantial blowup of the state space.

Outline of the Paper

In Sect. 2 we provide the basic definitions of synchronising LTSs, live-reset and sync-deadlock LTSs, and synchronisation topologies. A bottom-up reduction for the networks of live-reset and sync-deadlock LTSs is presented in Sect. 3. We show how to transform these networks in a reachability-preserving way into a new, smaller model called the sum-of-squares product. The key idea is that the new model traces the interactions between the components and their parents, followed by upstream synchronisations. This bottom-up reduction is extended in Sect. 4 to a wider case of tree-like synchronisation topologies with general LTSs. Section 5 investigates experimentally the effectiveness of the reductions on several scalable examples and many random cases using a novel open-source tool [2]. Section 6 draws conclusions and discusses future work.

2   Tree Synchronisation Systems

In this section we recall the notions of networks of Labelled Transition Systems and their synchronisation topologies. We also introduce and explain the restrictions on the models assumed in the next section. In what follows $\mathcal{PV}$ denotes the set of propositions.

Definiton 1 (Labelled Transition System). *A* Labelled Transition System *($\mathcal{LTS}$) is a tuple* $\mathcal{M} = \langle \mathcal{S}, s^I, Acts, \rightarrow, \mathcal{L} \rangle$ *where:*

1. $\mathcal{S}$ is a finite set of states and $s^I \in \mathcal{S}$ the initial state;

2. *Acts is a finite set of action names;*
3. $\rightarrow \subseteq \mathcal{S} \times Acts \times \mathcal{S}$ *is a transition relation;*
4. $\mathcal{L} \colon \mathcal{S} \rightarrow 2^{\mathcal{PV}}$ *is a labelling function.*

We usually write $s \xrightarrow{act} s'$ instead of $(s, act, s') \in \rightarrow$. We also denote $acts(\mathcal{M}) = Acts$ and $states(\mathcal{M}) = \mathcal{S}$. A *run* in $\mathcal{LTS}$ $\mathcal{M}$ is an infinite sequence of states and actions $\rho = s^0 act^0 s^1 act^1 \ldots$ s.t. $s^i \xrightarrow{act^i} s^{i+1}$ for all $i \geq 0$. By $Runs(\mathcal{M}, s)$ we denote the set of all the runs starting from state $s \in \mathcal{S}$. If s is the initial state, we write $Runs(\mathcal{M})$ instead of $Runs(\mathcal{M}, s^I)$.

2.1 $\mathcal{LTS}$ Networks and Synchronisation Topologies

Model checkers such as SPIN [13], UPPAAL [11], and IMITATOR [5] usually expect the systems to be described in a form of interacting modules. Synchronisation over common actions [10] (or *channels*) is a popular primitive that enables such an interaction.

Definiton 2 (Asynchronous Product). *Let* $\mathcal{M}_i = \langle \mathcal{S}_i, s_i^I, Acts_i, \rightarrow_i, \mathcal{L}_i \rangle$ *be* $\mathcal{LTS}$, *for* $i \in \{1, 2\}$. *The asynchronous product of* $\mathcal{M}_1$ *and* $\mathcal{M}_2$ *is the* $\mathcal{LTS}$ $\mathcal{M}_1 \| \mathcal{M}_2 = \langle \mathcal{S}_1 \times \mathcal{S}_2, (s_1^I, s_2^I), Acts_1 \cup Acts_2, \rightarrow, \mathcal{L}_{1,2} \rangle$ *s.t.* $\mathcal{L}_{1,2}((s_1, s_2)) = \mathcal{L}_1(s_1) \cup \mathcal{L}_2(s_2)$ *for all* $(s_1, s_2) \in \mathcal{S}_1 \times \mathcal{S}_2$ *and the transition rule is defined as follows:*

$$\frac{act \in Acts_1 \setminus Acts_2 \wedge s_1 \xrightarrow{act}_1 s_1'}{(s_1, s_2) \xrightarrow{act} (s_1', s_2)} \qquad \frac{act \in Acts_2 \setminus Acts_1 \wedge s_2 \xrightarrow{act}_2 s_2'}{(s_1, s_2) \xrightarrow{act} (s_1, s_2')}$$

$$\frac{act \in Acts_1 \cap Acts_2 \wedge s_1 \xrightarrow{act}_1 s_1' \wedge s_2 \xrightarrow{act}_2 s_2'}{(s_1, s_2) \xrightarrow{act} (s_1', s_2')}$$

The above definition is naturally extended to an arbitrary number of components. We sometimes write $\|_{i=1}^n \mathcal{M}_i$ instead of $\mathcal{M}_1 \| \ldots \| \mathcal{M}_n$. If s is a state of $\mathcal{M}_1 \| \ldots \| \mathcal{M}_n$, then by $s_{\mathcal{M}_i}$ we denote its component corresponding to $\mathcal{M}_i$.

The synchronisation topology [17] is an undirected graph that records how LTSs synchronise with one another.

Definiton 3 (Synchronisation Topology). *A* synchronisation topology *(ST) is a tuple* $\mathcal{G} = \langle Net, \mathcal{T} \rangle$, *where* $Net = \{\mathcal{M}_i\}_{i=1}^n$ *is a set of* $\mathcal{LTS}s$ *for* $1 \leq i \leq n$, *and* $\mathcal{T} \subseteq Net \times Net$ *is s.t.* $(\mathcal{M}_i, \mathcal{M}_j) \in \mathcal{T}$ *iff* $i \neq j$ *and* $Acts_i \cap Acts_j \neq \emptyset$.

Note that $\mathcal{T}$ is induced by *Net*. Thus, with a slight notational abuse we sometimes treat $\mathcal{G}$ as *Net*. Moreover, we write $acts(\mathcal{G}) = \bigcup_{i=1}^n acts(\mathcal{M}_i)$.

Definiton 4 (Tree Synchronisation Topology). *A synchronisation topology* $\mathcal{G}$ *s.t.* $\mathcal{T}$ *is a tree rooted in* $root(\mathcal{G})$ *is called* tree synchronisation topology.

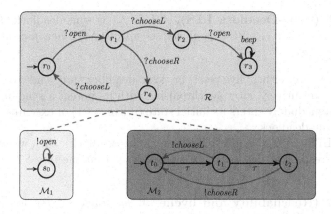

Fig. 1. A simple tree synchronisation topology $\mathcal{G}_x$.

It should be noted that $root(\mathcal{G})$ is not always uniquely induced by $\mathcal{G}$, the root is thus a part of the signature of tree synchronisation topology.

Let us fix a tree synchronisation topology $\mathcal{G} = \langle Net, \mathcal{T}, root(\mathcal{G}) \rangle$. For each $\mathcal{M} \in Net$ by $parent(\mathcal{M})$ we denote the parent of $\mathcal{M}$ in $\mathcal{T}$ (we assume that $parent(root(\mathcal{G})) = \emptyset$). By $children(\mathcal{M})$ we mean the set of the children of $\mathcal{M}$. By $upacts(\mathcal{M})$ (resp. $downacts(\mathcal{M})$) we denote the set of actions via which $\mathcal{M}$ synchronises with its parent (resp. children). For each $act \in downacts(\mathcal{M})$, $snd(\mathcal{M}, act)$ denotes the component $\mathcal{M}' \in children(\mathcal{M})$ s.t. $act \in upacts(\mathcal{M}')$. Thus, $snd(\mathcal{M}, act)$ is the child of $\mathcal{M}$ that synchronises with $\mathcal{M}$ over act. If $\mathcal{M}$ is clear from the context, we simply write $snd(act)$. The *local* unsynchronised actions of $\mathcal{M}$ are defined as $locacts(\mathcal{M}) = acts(\mathcal{M}) \setminus (downacts(\mathcal{M}) \cup upacts(\mathcal{M}))$.

For brevity, whenever we refer to a state, action label, transition, or state space of $\mathcal{G}$ we mean a state, action label, transition, or state space of $||_{i=1}^{n} \mathcal{M}_i$. We also extend the notion of runs to synchronisation topologies: $Runs(\mathcal{G}, s) = Runs(||_{i=1}^{n} \mathcal{M}_i, s)$ for each $s \in states(||_{i=1}^{n} \mathcal{M}_i)$. Moreover, for each $F \subseteq acts(\mathcal{G})$ we introduce the notion of *one-shot F* runs, $Runs_F(\mathcal{G}, s)$, as the set of all the runs in $Runs(\mathcal{G}, s)$ along which each action from F appears at most once.

Example 1. Figure 1 presents a small tree $\mathcal{ST}$ $\mathcal{G}_x$ with the root $\mathcal{R}$ and two children $\mathcal{M}_1$ and $\mathcal{M}_2$. The auxiliary symbols !/? are syntactic sugar, used to distinguish between $upacts$ and $downacts$. Here, $upacts(\mathcal{R}) = \emptyset$, $downacts(\mathcal{R}) = \{open, chooseL, chooseR\}$, and $locacts(\mathcal{R}) = \{beep\}$. Similarly, $upacts(\mathcal{M}_1) = \{open\}$, $upacts(\mathcal{M}_2) = \{chooseL, chooseR\}$, $downacts(\mathcal{M}_1) = locacts(\mathcal{M}_1) = downacts(\mathcal{M}_2) = \emptyset$, and $locacts(\mathcal{M}_2) = \tau$.

We start by dealing with networks whose components all share a similar, simple structure.

Definiton 5 (Live-Reset LTS). *A LTS $\mathcal{M}$ with initial state $s_{\mathcal{M}}^I$ is live-reset if for each run $\rho = s^0 act^0 s^1 act^1 \ldots$: $\forall i \in \mathbb{N}$ if $act^i \in upacts(\mathcal{M})$, then $s^{i+1} = s_{\mathcal{M}}^I$.*

Definiton 6 (Sync-Deadlock LTS). *A LTS $\mathcal{M}$ is sync-deadlock if for each run $\rho = s^0 act^0 s^1 act^1 \ldots$: $\forall i \in \mathbb{N}$ if $act^i \in upacts(\mathcal{M})$, then for each $j > i$, $act^j \in locacts(\mathcal{M})$.*

LTSs that are either live-reset or sync-deadlock are said to be *sync-memoryless*[1]. Intuitively, after synchronising with its parent a sync-memoryless LTS either immediately enters its initial state (if live-reset) or executes only local actions (if sync-deadlock).

If every LTS of $\mathcal{ST}$ $\mathcal{G}$ is live-reset (resp. sync-deadlock), then we say that $\mathcal{G}$ is live-reset (resp. sync-deadlock). It is easy to see that the tree $\mathcal{ST}$ in Fig. 1 is live-reset.

Definiton 7 (Reachability and liveness). *For each $p \in \mathcal{PV}$ we write $\mathcal{G} \models EFp$ (resp. $\mathcal{G} \models EGp$) iff there exists $\rho \in Runs(\mathcal{G})$ s.t. $\rho = s^0 act^0 s^1 act^1 \ldots$ and $p \in \mathcal{L}(s^i)$ for some (resp. for all) $i \in \mathbb{N}$.*

By replacing $\models$ with $\models_F$ and *Runs* with $Runs_F$ in Definition 7 we obtain the notion of *one-shot F-reachability* and the dual of liveness. Both *EF* and *EG* are Computation Tree Logic (*CTL*) modalities [10]. If $\mathcal{G} \models EFp$, then we say that p is reachable in $\mathcal{G}$ from the initial state.

Definiton 8. *Let $\mathcal{N} \subseteq Net$ and $\rho*$ be a prefix of some $\rho \in Runs(\mathcal{G})$ s.t. $\rho* = s^0 act^0 s^1 act^1 \ldots$ By $\rho* \downarrow (\mathcal{N})$ we denote the projection of $\rho*$ to the asynchronous product of LTSs in $\mathcal{N}$, i.e. the result of transforming $\rho*$ by (1) firstly, projecting each s^i on the LTSs in $\mathcal{N}$; (2) secondly, removing the actions that do not belong to $\bigcup_{\mathcal{M} \in \mathcal{N}} acts(\mathcal{M})$, together with their destinations.*

Intuitively, $\rho* \downarrow (\mathcal{N})$ contains the parts of the global states of $\rho*$ that belong to $||_{\mathcal{M} \in \mathcal{N}} \mathcal{M}$ and actions executed by some $\mathcal{M} \in \mathcal{N}$. It is not difficult to show that $\rho* \downarrow (\mathcal{N})$ does not need to be a valid run of $||_{\mathcal{M} \in \mathcal{N}} \mathcal{M}$.

Example 2. Consider a sequence: $\eta = (r_0, s_0, t_0)$ τ (r_0, s_0, t_1) τ (r_0, s_0, t_2) *open* (r_1, s_0, t_2) *chooseR* (r_4, s_0, t_0) τ (r_4, s_0, t_1) *chooseL* (r_0, s_0, t_0). Here, we have $\eta \downarrow (\{\mathcal{R}, \mathcal{M}_1\}) = (r_0, s_0) open(r_1, s_0) chooseR(r_4, s_0) chooseL(r_0, s_0)$.

3   Compact Representations of State Spaces of Live-Reset and Sync-Deadlock Trees

In this section we show how to generate compact representations of state spaces of sync-memoryless tree topologies preserving reachability. The procedure is presented in two steps. We start with the case of two-level trees. Then, we modify the construction to deal with trees of arbitrary height in a bottom-up manner.

---

[1] The family of sync-memoryless LTSs can in the future be extended beyond these two classes.

3.1   Constructions for Two-level Trees

Throughout this subsection let $\mathcal{G}$ be a sync-memoryless tree $\mathcal{ST}$ with components $Net = \{\mathcal{R}, \mathcal{M}_1, \ldots, \mathcal{M}_n\}$ s.t. $root(\mathcal{G}) = \mathcal{R}$ and $children(\mathcal{R}) = \{\mathcal{M}_1, \ldots, \mathcal{M}_n\}$. Moreover, let $\mathcal{R} = \langle \mathcal{S}_\mathcal{R}, s_\mathcal{R}^I, Acts_\mathcal{R}, \rightarrow_\mathcal{R}, \mathcal{L}_\mathcal{R} \rangle$ and $\mathcal{M}_i = \langle \mathcal{S}_i, s_i^I, Acts_i, \rightarrow_i, \mathcal{L}_i \rangle$, for $i \in \{1, \ldots, n\}$. We employ the observations on the nature of synchronisations with sync-memoryless components in the following definition.

Definiton 9 (Sum-of-squares Product). *Define* $SQ^u(\mathcal{G}) = \langle \mathcal{S}_{sq}^u, s_{sq}^I, Acts_{sq}, \rightarrow_{sq}, \mathcal{L}_{sq} \rangle$ *as an $\mathcal{LTS}$ s.t.:*

1. $\mathcal{S}_{sq}^u = \bigcup_{i=1}^n (\mathcal{S}_i \times \mathcal{S}_\mathcal{R}) \cup \{s_{sq}^I\}$.
2. $s_{sq}^I \notin \mathcal{S}_{sq}^u$ *is a fresh initial state.*
3. $Acts_{sq} = acts(\mathcal{G}) \cup \{\epsilon\}$, *where $\epsilon \notin acts(\mathcal{G})$ is a fresh, silent action.*
4. *The transition relation $\rightarrow_{sq}$ is defined as follows:*
    (a) $s_{sq}^I \xrightarrow{\epsilon}_{sq} (s_i^I, s_\mathcal{R}^I)$, *for all $i \in \{1, \ldots, n\}$;*
    (b) *if $(s_i, s_\mathcal{R}) \xrightarrow{act} (s_i', s_\mathcal{R}')$ is a transition in $\mathcal{M}_i \| \mathcal{R}$, then also $(s_i, s_\mathcal{R}) \xrightarrow{act}_{sq}$
    $(s_i', s_\mathcal{R}')$, for all $i \in \{1, \ldots, n\}$;*
    (c) *if $\mathcal{G}$ is live-reset and $(s_i, s_\mathcal{R}) \xrightarrow{act} (s_i^I, s_\mathcal{R}')$ is a transition in $\mathcal{M}_i \| \mathcal{R}$, then*
    $(s_i, s_\mathcal{R}) \xrightarrow{act}_{sq} (s_j^I, s_\mathcal{R}')$ *for all $j \in \{1, \ldots, n\} \setminus \{i\}$;*
    (d) *if $\mathcal{G}$ is sync-deadlock and $(s_i, s_\mathcal{R}) \xrightarrow{act} (s_i', s_\mathcal{R}')$ is a synchronised transition*
    in $\mathcal{M}_i \| \mathcal{R}$, then $(s_i, s_\mathcal{R}) \xrightarrow{act}_{sq} (s_j^I, s_\mathcal{R}')$, for all $j \in \{1, \ldots, n\} \setminus \{i\}$.
5. $\mathcal{L}_{sq}(s_i, s_\mathcal{R}) = \mathcal{L}_i(s_i) \cup \mathcal{L}_\mathcal{R}(s_\mathcal{R}) \cup \bigcup_{j \neq i} \mathcal{L}_j(s_j^I)$, *for each $(s_i, s_\mathcal{R}) \in \mathcal{S}_{sq}^u$.*

We call $SQ^u(\mathcal{G})$ the Sum-of-squares Product of $\mathcal{G}$.

Intuitively, $SQ^u(\mathcal{G})$ at any given moment traces only the interactions between the root and one of its children. Item 4a of Definition 9 introduces the new initial state connected via ϵ-transitions with the initial states of each square product $\mathcal{M}_i \| \mathcal{R}$. Item 4b ensures that the square product preserves the local and synchronised actions of the root and each child. Item 4c means that after resetting each component $\mathcal{M}_i$ can release control to another module, for live-reset topologies. Item 4d serves a similar purpose for sync-deadlock topologies.

Example 3. Figure 2 presents the sum-of-squares product $SQ^u(\mathcal{G}_x)$ for the small tree $\mathcal{ST}$ of Example 1. The fresh initial state s_{sq}^I is coloured green, the yellow box surrounds the square product $\mathcal{M}_1 \| \mathcal{R}$, and the pink box surrounds the square product $\mathcal{M}_2 \| \mathcal{R}$. The red colour of some states is explained in Sect. 3.2. The arcs that correspond to the transitions synchronised between a child and the root are coloured red if the control switches between components (according to Item 4c of Definition 9) and blue otherwise. The local transitions are black.

Theorem 1 (Sum-of-squares Product Preserves Reachability). *Let $\mathcal{G}$ be a sync-memoryless two-level tree $\mathcal{ST}$ with root $\mathcal{R}$ and $p \in \mathcal{PV}$. If $\mathcal{G}$ is live-reset, then $\mathcal{G} \models EFp$ iff $SQ^u(\mathcal{G}) \models EFp$. If $\mathcal{G}$ is sync-deadlock and $F = downacts(\mathcal{R})$, then $\mathcal{G} \models_F EFp$ iff $SQ^u(\mathcal{G}) \models_F EFp$.*

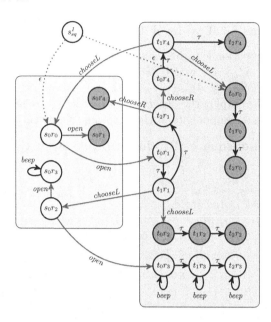

Fig. 2. The sum-of-squares product of the tree $\mathcal{ST}$ of Example 1. (Color figure online)

Proof. We only deal with the case of live-reset topology; the case of sync-deadlock follows similarly.

Recall that we assume $Net = \{\mathcal{R}, \mathcal{M}_1, \ldots, \mathcal{M}_n\}$ with root $\mathcal{R}$ and children $\{\mathcal{M}_i\}_{i=1}^n$. Let $\mathcal{G} \models EFp$ and $\rho = s^0 act^0 s^1 act^1 \ldots$ be a run of $\mathcal{G}$ s.t. $p \in \mathcal{L}(s^i)$ for some $i \in \mathbb{N}$. If ρ contains only local actions, then for any of the components $C \in Net$ each of its local states visited along ρ can be reached by executing in $\mathcal{SQ}^u(\mathcal{G})$ firstly the ϵ-action (cf. Item 4a of Definition 9) and then local actions of C found in ρ (cf. Item 4b of Definition 9). Moreover, consider a situation where a non-root component C synchronises with the root only a finite number of times. Now, each local state s of C that is reachable along ρ only after executing the final synchronising action of C can be reached in $\mathcal{SQ}^u(\mathcal{G})$ using only ϵ- and local actions. Such a run in $\mathcal{SQ}^u(\mathcal{G})$ reaching s can be built as described previously due to the fact that the final synchronisation resets the component. Also, let $\hat{\rho}$ be the result of iterative removal from ρ of all the local actions of any non-root component C that appear after its last synchronising action together with their targets, and replacing along the run all the further local states of C with s_C^I. It is not difficult to see that $\hat{\rho}$ visits the same local states of the root that are visited along ρ and all the local states of each non-root component C visited before the final synchronising action of C is executed.

We can therefore further assume ($\star$) that ρ contains at least one synchronising action and can be represented as $\rho = \alpha_1 F_1 \alpha_2 F_2 \ldots$, where for each $i \in \mathbb{N}$ there exist $j, k \in \mathbb{N}$ such that $\alpha_i = s^j act^j \ldots s^k act^k s^{k+1}$ and $act^j, \ldots, act^k \in locacts(\mathcal{R}) \cup \bigcup_{i=1}^n locacts(\mathcal{M}_i)$, $F_i \in downacts(\mathcal{R})$, and each local action of any component is eventually followed by some of its synchronising actions.

Actions are never synchronised between children, thus it can be proven by induction on the length of the run that the actions in ρ can be reordered to obtain a run $\rho' \in Runs(\mathcal{G}, s^0)$ that can be represented as $\rho' = \alpha'_1 F_1 \alpha'_2 F_2 \ldots$, such that:

1. For any $i \in \mathbb{N}$ there exist $j, k \in \mathbb{N}$ such that $\alpha'_i = s'^j \, act'^j \ldots s'^k \, act'^k \, s'^{k+1}$ and $act'^j, \ldots, act'^k \in locacts(\mathcal{R}) \cup locacts(snd(F_i))$.
2. For each $i \in \mathbb{N}$ we have $\alpha_i {\downarrow} (\{\mathcal{R}, snd(F_i)\}) = \alpha'_i {\downarrow} (\{\mathcal{R}, snd(F_i)\})$.
3. For each s'^j in α'_i, if 0 is the coordinate of root and k is the coordinate of $snd(F_i)$, then $s'^j = (s_0, s_1^I, \ldots, s_{k-1}^I, s_k, s_{k+1}^I, \ldots)$ for some $s_0 \in states(\mathcal{R})$, $s_k \in states(snd(F_i))$.

Intuitively, ρ' is built from ρ in such a way that firstly only the root and the component that synchronises with the root over F_1 are allowed to execute their local actions while all the other components stay in their initial states; then F_1 is fired; and then this scheme is repeated for F_2, F_3, etc. We can now project ρ' on spaces of squares of the root and components active in a given interval, to obtain $\rho'' = \alpha'_1 {\downarrow} (\{\mathcal{R}, snd(F_1)\}) F_1 \alpha'_2 {\downarrow} (\{\mathcal{R}, snd(F_2)\}) F_2 \ldots$ Notice that $\rho'' \in \mathcal{SQ}^u(\mathcal{G})$. We now show that ρ'' visits all the local states that appear along ρ. To this end firstly observe that ρ and ρ' contain the same local states. Moreover, if a local state of the root is visited in ρ' then it is also visited in ρ'', as we always project on squares of the root and some other component. If a local state of a non-root component is visited along ρ' before executing some synchronising action F_i then it will also be present before executing F_i along ρ''. This follows from the construction of ρ'' from ρ' and our assumption $(\star)$ of the structure of ρ. As we have shown that ρ'' visits each local state that appears along ρ, this part of the proof is concluded.

Let $\mathcal{SQ}^u(\mathcal{G}) \models EFp$ and $\rho \in Runs(\mathcal{SQ}^u(\mathcal{G}))$ visits a state labelled with p. Now, it suffices to replace in ρ each state (s_k, s_0) that belongs to the square $\mathcal{M}_k \times \mathcal{R}$ with the global state $(s_0, s_1^I, \ldots, s_{k-1}^I, s_k, s_{k+1}^I, \ldots)$ of $\mathcal{G}$. The result of this substitution is a run of $\mathcal{G}$ that visits p. $\qquad \square$

The next proposition shows that the sum-of-squares does not preserve EG.

Proposition 1 (Sum-of-squares Does Not Preserve EG). *There is a live-reset two-level tree $\mathcal{ST} \, \mathcal{G}$ s.t. for some $p \in \mathcal{PV}$, $\mathcal{G} \models EGp$ and $\mathcal{SQ}^u(\mathcal{G}) \not\models EGp$.*

Proof. Consider the tree $\mathcal{ST} \, \mathcal{G}_y$ in Fig. 3. Here, we have $\mathcal{G}_y \models EGp$, but each path ρ along which p holds globally starts with $\mathcal{M}_1^y$ executing τ followed by $\mathcal{M}_2^y$ executing τ and, consecutively, *chooseR*. Thus, it is not possible to partition ρ into intervals where one child and the root fire local actions until they synchronise and possibly release the control to another child. Hence, $\mathcal{SQ}^u(\mathcal{G}_y) \not\models EGp$. $\qquad \square$

As illustrated in Example 3, the size of the state space of the sum-of-squares product of a sync-memoryless $\mathcal{ST} \, \mathcal{G}$ can be equal to or greater than the size of the state space of $\mathcal{G}$. On the other hand, the size of a representation of a state will be smaller in the sum-of-squares product, as it records only local states of at most two components of the network. However, in less degenerate cases than

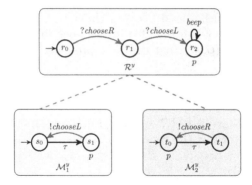

Fig. 3. The sum-of-squares does not preserve EG.

our toy model we can expect significant reductions. Let us consider a tree with a root and n children, each with a state space of size m. The number of states in the asynchronous product is m^{n+1}. In contrast, the size of the sum-of-squares product of such a topology is $n \cdot m^2 + 1$. Indeed we record pairs of states from a child and its root, i.e. m^2 possible states. This is done for all n children, and there is an added fresh initial state. To summarise, the sum-of-squares product has a size in $O(n \cdot m^2)$.

3.2 Reduced Sum-of-Squares for Any Tree Height

We now adapt the sum-of-squares product of two-level live-reset tree topologies to the general case. To this end we introduce the auxiliary operation $cmpl$ that transforms $\mathcal{SQ}^u(\mathcal{G})$ into a live-reset LTS. Intuitively, $cmpl$ redirects each transition that enters the initial state of the root to the fresh initial state s_{sq}^I. No additional operations are needed for sync-deadlock topologies.

Definiton 10. *Let $\mathcal{G}$ be a live-reset two-level tree $\mathcal{ST}$ with components $Net = \{\mathcal{R}, \mathcal{M}_1, \ldots, \mathcal{M}_n\}$. By $cmpl(\mathcal{SQ}^u(\mathcal{G}))$ we denote the result of replacing in $\mathcal{SQ}^u(\mathcal{G})$ every transition $((s_{\mathcal{M}_i}, s_{\mathcal{R}}), act, (s'_{\mathcal{M}_i}, s_{\mathcal{R}}^I))$ with $((s_{\mathcal{M}_i}, s_{\mathcal{R}}), act, s_{sq}^I)$.*

Algorithm 1 recursively performs reduction for two-level trees in a bottom-up manner. If the topology is live-reset, then each reduction is followed by applying $cmpl(\mathcal{SQ}^u(\cdot))$ to the computed sum-of-squares to ensure that the output is also live-reset. Note that $\mathcal{G}_{chld}$ denotes the subtree of $\mathcal{G}$ rooted in $chld$. The next theorem states soundness and correctness of Algorithm 1.

Theorem 2 (*reduceNet*($\mathcal{G}$) Preserves Reachability). *Let $\mathcal{G} = \langle Net, \mathcal{T} \rangle$, be a sync-memoryless tree $\mathcal{ST}$, $F = \bigcup_{\mathcal{M} \in Net} downacts(\mathcal{M})$, and $p \in \mathcal{PV}$. If $\mathcal{G}$ is live-reset, then $\mathcal{G} \models EFp$ iff reduceNet($\mathcal{G}$) $\models EFp$. If $\mathcal{G}$ is sync-deadlock, then $\mathcal{G} \models_F EFp$ iff reduceNet($\mathcal{G}$) $\models_F EFp$.*

Proof (Sketch) The proof follows via induction on the height of the tree $\mathcal{G}$. As we have Theorem 1, it suffices to prove that $cmpl(\mathcal{SQ}^u(\mathcal{G}))$ preserves reachability for any two-level live-reset $\mathcal{ST}$ $\mathcal{G}$. This, however, can be done in a way very similar to the proof of Theorem 1 and is omitted.

Algorithm 1. $reduceNet(\mathcal{G})$

Input: sync-memoryless tree sync. topology $\mathcal{G}$
Output: $\mathcal{LTS}$ M that preserves reachability of each proposition p in $\mathcal{G}$.

1: **if** $\mathcal{G}$ consists of a single LTS **then**
2:     **return** $\mathcal{G}$ (* $\mathcal{G}$ is a leaf *)
3: **end if**
4: **let** $redChdn := \emptyset$
5: **for** $chld \in children(root(\mathcal{G}))$ **do**
6:     $redChdn = redChdn \cup \{reduceNet(\mathcal{G}_{chld})\}$
7: **end for**
8: **let** $\mathcal{G}' := \{root(\mathcal{G})\} \cup redChdn$
9: **if** $\mathcal{G}$ is live-reset **then**
10:     **return** $cmpl(\mathcal{SQ}^u(\mathcal{G}'))$
11: **else**
12:     **return** $\mathcal{SQ}^u(\mathcal{G}')$
13: **end if**

In certain hierarchical systems such as attack-defense trees [17] we are interested only in the reachability of the root's locations. This enables for additional optimisations related to removing deadlocks and livelocks that halt the root's evolution.

Definiton 11 (Root-deadlock). *Let* $\mathcal{G}$ *be a* $\mathcal{ST}$ *with Net* $= \{\mathcal{R}, \mathcal{M}_1,$ $\ldots, \mathcal{M}_n\}$, $root(\mathcal{G}) = \mathcal{R}$ *and* $children(\mathcal{R}) = \{\mathcal{M}_1, \ldots, \mathcal{M}_n\}$. *We say that a state* s *of* $\mathcal{M}_i \in children(\mathcal{R})$ *is in a* root-deadlock *iff there is no run* $\rho \in Runs(\mathcal{M}_i, s)$ *s.t.* $\rho = s^0 act^0 s^1 act^1 \ldots$ *with* $act^i \in acts(\mathcal{R})$, *where* $s^0 = s$, *for some* $i \in \mathbb{N}$.

The set of root-deadlocked states of an $\mathcal{LTS}$ can be computed in polynomial time using either a model checker or conventional graph algorithms. These states can be removed without affecting the reachability of a location of the root.

Example 4. Let us consider the LTS $\mathcal{SQ}^u(\mathcal{G}_x)$ in Fig. 2. If it is a child of another LTS $parent(\mathcal{SQ}^u(\mathcal{G}_x))$ in a live-reset topology and $beep \in upacts(\mathcal{SQ}^u(\mathcal{G}_x))$, then all the states coloured red are root-deadlocked. Figure 4 displays the reduced sum-of-squares product of the topology.

Let us now evaluate the size of the state spaces for a tree of height h, considering each node has n children, each with a state space of size m. Such a tree has $\sum_{i=0}^{h} n^i$ nodes. Hence, the number of states in the asynchronous product is $m^{\sum_{i=0}^{h} n^i}$. The size of the sum-of-squares product of such a topology is $n^h \cdot m^{h+1} + \sum_{i=0}^{h-1} n^i \cdot m^i$. Indeed, for $h = 1$, this is exactly the size obtained for two-level trees in the previous section. The proof for any arbitrary

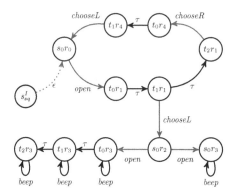

Fig. 4. The reduced sum-of-squares product of the tree $\mathcal{ST}$ of Example 4.

height is easily done by induction. To compute the increase from height h to height $h + 1$, the same arguments as for the computation in a two-level tree hold. This leads to the following maximal number of states for height $h + 1$: $1 + n \cdot (n^h \cdot m^{h+1} + \sum_{i=0}^{h-1} n^i \cdot m^i) \cdot m = n^{h+1} \cdot m^{h+2} + \sum_{i=0}^{h} n^i \cdot m^i$. To summarise, the sum-of-squares product has a size in $O(n^h \cdot m^{h+1})$.

4   The General Case and Local Products

The case of live-reset LTS tree networks entails substantial state space reductions due to the fact that children reset after synchronising with their root. Before resetting, only the local states of the root and one of its children need to be recorded; it can be assumed that all the children wait in their initial states. After single-level synchronisation, only the information about the root's state is relevant, as the synchronising child resets. In the general case of tree-like networks of synchronising LTSs, both the root's state and post-synchronisation state of its children have to be preserved.

In what follows let $\mathcal{G}$ be a two-level tree $\mathcal{ST}$ s.t. $Net = \{\mathcal{R}, \mathcal{M}_1, \ldots, \mathcal{M}_n\}$, where $root(\mathcal{G}) = \mathcal{R}$ and $children(\mathcal{R}) = \{\mathcal{M}_1, \ldots, \mathcal{M}_n\}$. Let $\mathcal{R} = \langle \mathcal{S}_\mathcal{R}, s_\mathcal{R}^I, Acts_\mathcal{R}, \rightarrow_\mathcal{R}, \mathcal{L}_\mathcal{R} \rangle$ and $\mathcal{M}_i = \langle \mathcal{S}_i, s_i^I, Acts_i, \rightarrow_i, \mathcal{L}_i \rangle$, for $i \in \{1, \ldots, n\}$. For each $i \in \{1, \ldots, n\}$ let $postSync(\mathcal{M}_i)$ denote the set of all the local states of $\mathcal{M}_i$ visited immediately after synchronising with $\mathcal{R}$. Formally:

$$postSync(\mathcal{M}_i) = \{s \in \mathcal{S}_i \mid \exists act \in Acts_\mathcal{R} \cap Acts_i \text{ s.t. } (s', r') \xrightarrow{act} (s, r) \text{ in } \mathcal{S}_i \times \mathcal{S}_\mathcal{R}\}.$$

The *memory unit*, defined as follows, is a collection of all the vectors of states of the components preserved after synchronisation.

Definiton 12 (Memory Unit). *The* post-synchronisation memory unit *of $\mathcal{G}$ is defined as:* $mem(\mathcal{M}_1, \ldots, \mathcal{M}_n) = \prod_{i=1}^{n}(\{s_i^I\} \cup postSync(\mathcal{M}_i))$.

Intuitively, Definition 13 generalises Definition 9 by extending the states of square products with the memory unit that is updated and consulted whenever a synchronisation takes place. This memory gadget can be implemented efficiently, but here we present it in an explicit way for the sake of readability.

Let $i \in \{1, \ldots, n\}$, $s_i \in \mathcal{S}_i$, and $m \in mem(\mathcal{M}_1, \ldots, \mathcal{M}_n)$. By $m[i/s_i]$ we denote the *memory update* of m defined as follows: $m[j] = m[j]$ for all $i \neq j$ and $m[i] = s_i$.

Definiton 13 (General Sum-of-squares Product). *Let* $\mathcal{GSQ}(\mathcal{G}) = \langle \mathcal{S}_{gsq}, s^I_{gsq}, Acts_{gsq}, \rightarrow_{gsq}, \mathcal{L}_{gsq} \rangle$ *be an* $\mathcal{LTS}$ *s.t.:*

1. $\mathcal{S}_{gsq} = \left(\bigcup_{i=1}^{n} (\mathcal{S}_i \times \mathcal{S}_\mathcal{R}) \times mem(\mathcal{M}_1, \ldots, \mathcal{M}_n) \right) \cup \{s^I_{gsq}\}$.
2. $s^I_{gsq} \notin \mathcal{S}_{gsq}$ *is a fresh initial state.*
3. $Acts_{gsq} = acts(\mathcal{G}) \cup \{\epsilon\}$, *where* $\epsilon \notin acts(\mathcal{G})$ *is a fresh, silent action.*
4. *The transition relation* $\rightarrow_{gsq}$ *is defined as follows:*
    (a) *For each* $i \in \{1, \ldots, n\}$, $s^I_{gsq} \xrightarrow{\epsilon}_{gsq} (s^I_i, s^I_\mathcal{R}, m_0)$, *where* $\forall_{i=1}^{n} m_0[i] = s^I_i$.
    (b) *If* $s_i \xrightarrow{act}_i s'_i$ *and* $act \in locacts(\mathcal{M}_i)$, *then* $(s_i, s_\mathcal{R}, m) \xrightarrow{act}_{sq} (s'_i, s_\mathcal{R}, m)$, *for each* $s_\mathcal{R} \in \mathcal{S}_\mathcal{R}$ *and* $m \in mem(\mathcal{M}_1, \ldots, \mathcal{M}_n)$; *similarly, if* $s_\mathcal{R} \xrightarrow{act}_\mathcal{R} s'_\mathcal{R}$ *and* $act \in locacts(\mathcal{R})$, *then* $(s_i, s_\mathcal{R}, m) \xrightarrow{act}_{sq} (s_i, s'_\mathcal{R}, m)$, *for each* $s_i \in \mathcal{S}_i$ *and* $m \in mem(\mathcal{M}_1, \ldots, \mathcal{M}_n)$.
    (c) *If* $act \in upacts(\mathcal{M}_i)$, $s_i \xrightarrow{act}_i s'_i$, *and* $s_\mathcal{R} \xrightarrow{act}_\mathcal{R} s'_\mathcal{R}$, *then* $(s_i, s_\mathcal{R}, m) \xrightarrow{act}_{sq} (s_j, s'_\mathcal{R}, m')$, *where* $m' = m[i/s'_i]$ *and* $s_j = m[j]$ *for some* $j \in \{1, \ldots, n\}$.
5. $\mathcal{L}_{gsq}(s_i, s_\mathcal{R}, m) = \mathcal{L}_i(s_i) \cup \mathcal{L}_\mathcal{R}(s_\mathcal{R}) \cup \bigcup_{j \neq i} \mathcal{L}_j(m[j])$, *for each* $(s_i, s_\mathcal{R}, m) \in \mathcal{S}_{gsq}$.

We call $\mathcal{GSQ}(\mathcal{G})$ *the General Sum-of-squares Product of* $\mathcal{G}$.

Item 4a of Definition 13 expresses that the new initial state enables ϵ-transitions to the initial state of any square product $\mathcal{M}_i \| \mathcal{R}$ with the memory unit set to the starting values. Similarly to the corresponding case in Definition 9, Item 4b ensures that the local actions are fully asynchronous and do not affect memory unit. The idea behind Item 4c is that in a state $(s_i, s_\mathcal{R}, m)$ executing a synchronised action act will require updating the outcome states, saving them into memory, and then moving all the values from memory to the current state tracker. The latter may mean switching to another component. The transition rule, as defined here, concatenates these three steps into one.

Example 5. Figure 5 presents a three-component $\mathcal{ST}$ $\mathcal{G}_z$. Note that the child $\mathcal{M}^z_2$ is not live-reset, as it does not reset after synchronising with $\mathcal{R}^z$ via *chooseF*. Figure 6 presents the general sum-of-squares product of $\mathcal{G}_z$.

The following analogues of Theorem 1 and Theorem 2 show that the general sum-of-squares preserves reachability. We omit the proofs of Theorem 3 and Theorem 4, as they follow via almost exactly the same techniques.

Theorem 3 (General sum-of-squares Preserves Reachability). *Let* $\mathcal{G}$ *be a two-level tree* $\mathcal{ST}$. *For each* $p \in \mathcal{PV}$ *we have* $\mathcal{G} \models EFp$ *iff* $\mathcal{GSQ}(\mathcal{G}) \models EFp$.

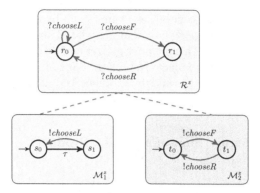

Fig. 5. A simple non live-reset tree synchronisation topology $\mathcal{G}_z$

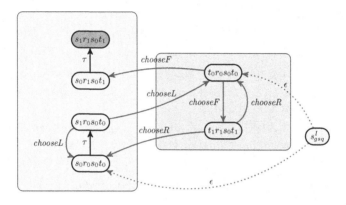

Fig. 6. The general sum-of-squares product of the non live-reset tree $\mathcal{ST}$ in Fig. 5 (Color figure online)

A two-level general sum-of-squares can be adapted to deal with tree topologies $\mathcal{G}$ of any height by using recursive construction. The appropriate algorithm, denoted by $reduceGenNet(\mathcal{G})$, is a slight modification of Algorithm 1 with recursive call in Line 6 replaced with $reduceGenNet(\mathcal{G}_{chld})$ and the if-else conditional in Line 9 substituted with **return** $\mathcal{GSQ}(\mathcal{G}')$.

Theorem 4 ($reduceGenNet(\mathcal{G})$ **Preserves Reachability**). *Let $\mathcal{G}$ be a tree $\mathcal{ST}$. For each $p \in \mathcal{PV}$, we have $\mathcal{G} \models EFp$ iff $reduceGenNet(\mathcal{G}) \models EFp$.*

It can be also easily observed that $\mathcal{GSQ}(.)$ does not preserve EG, by the same argument as in Theorem 1 and Fig. 3. Moreover, as previously, root-deadlocked states (e.g. the red location in Fig. 6) can be removed if only the reachability of a location in the root is to be preserved.

The general sum-of-squares does not guarantee a reduction of the statespace size. If $\mathcal{G}$ is a two-level tree $\mathcal{ST}$ with $Net = \{\mathcal{R}, \mathcal{M}_1, \ldots, \mathcal{M}_n\}$, then the size of the statespace of $reduceGenNet(\mathcal{G})$ can reach $\sum_{i=1}^{n} |\mathcal{S}_i| \cdot |\mathcal{S}_\mathcal{R}| \cdot \prod_{i=1}^{n} |\mathcal{S}_i|$, thus it crucially depends on the size of the memory unit. On the other hand, we conjecture that the memory needed to preserve the general sum-of-squares product is often much smaller than the memory needed to hold the asynchronous product of the entire network. This conjecture is based on the observation that the states of $\mathcal{GSQ}(\mathcal{G})$ are composed of two parts: the pair of local states of two interacting modules and the memory unit which can be shared when implemented efficiently.

5 Experiments

In this section we evaluate the implementation of reductions for sync-memoryless tree topologies. The files to reproduce our tests and figures can be found at https://depot.lipn.univ-paris13.fr/parties/publications/live-trees.

The theory presented in Sect. 3 has been implemented in the open-source tool LTR [2], written in C. LTR accepts LTSs networks in a *modgraph* format [16]. The size of the fully synchronised product is computed using a Binary Decision Diagrams-based open-source Python tool DD-Net-Checker [1].

Model Generators: Attack-Defence Trees. Attack-Defence Trees (*ADTs*) [15] are graphical models for representing possible scenarios of incoming risks and methods for their mitigation for complex systems. While descending from informal models, *ADTs* have been extended with various semantics. Here, we reuse the semantics based on translating the *ADTs* to networks of communicating LTSs [7,17]. These networks form tree-like synchronisation topologies with all the LTSs being sync-deadlock. An attack is deemed a success if a special location in the root of a network is reachable. For the purpose of this paper we implemented a simple translator from *ADTs* to modgraph format.

Comparing with *ADT* Reductions. In [17] we presented techniques for simplifying tree-like networks using *pattern-* and *layered* reductions. The former are similar to partial order reductions and the crux of latter is in the observation that it is sufficient to consider only runs where each level of a tree fully synchronises with its children before the execution proceeds to a higher level. In [17] these techniques are implemented using time parameter injection into LTSs networks and translation to timed LTSs networks.

The comparison with the results of reductions from [17] is included for reference, as the cited work is aimed at the full timed LTS-based semantics of *ADTs* which involves numeric attributes such as the time and cost of attack. Under this semantics the networks produce considerably larger fully synchronised models. Therefore, the comparison may be slightly unfair, favouring our approach.

***ADT* Experiments.** Table 1 shows the evaluation of the experiments on scalable models from [17]. Table 2 presents the results of running the experiments on security case studies, also taken from [17]. It should be noted that for the latter we used slightly simpler models than in [17], as contrary to the former paper our tool does not handle data variables such as cost, etc. The goal in each of these scenarios is reachability of a certain location in the root node and all

Table 1. Results for scalable models from [17].

model	no reductions |S|	no reductions |T|	sos reduction |S|	sos reduction |T|	pattern |S|	pattern |T|	pattern+layer |S|	pattern+layer |T|	pattern+sos |S|	pattern+sos |T|	reduced/original sos reduction %	pattern %	pattern+layer %	pattern+sos %
(2, 7, 2, 4)	185	432	111	310	72	123	54	69	45	62	68.233 %	31.605 %	19.935 %	17.342 %
(2, 9, 3, 4)	587	1,698	561	1,828	246	571	190	373	107	192	104.551 %	35.755 %	24.639 %	13.085 %
(2, 13, 3, 6)	8,823	35,602	861	2,800	2,405	7,584	883	1,802	176	306	8.241 %	22.485 %	6.044 %	1.085 %
(2, 13, 3, 8)	34,481	160,096	1,111	3,630	6,734	23,135	1,808	3,439	239	417	2.437 %	15.351 %	2.697 %	0.337 %
(2, 11, 4, 4)	1,825	6,332	2,811	10,498	840	2,458	652	1,680	231	513	163.16 %	40.432 %	28.589 %	9.121 %
(2, 15, 4, 6)	26,725	124,708	4,311	16,078	8,184	30,773	3,256	9,167	393	866	13.464 %	25.726 %	8.204 %	0.831 %
(2, 17, 4, 8)	103,955	549,762	5,561	20,828	22,854	92,393	6,606	17,615	541	1,203	4.037 %	17.629 %	3.705 %	0.267 %
(2, 23, 4, 10)	5,417,613	37,414,404	7,111	26,550	783,271	4,282,992	71,965	237,154	709	1,536	0.079 %	11.828 %	0.722 %	0.005 %
(2, 13, 5, 4)	5,603	22,774	14,061	59,248	2,868	10,124	2,228	7,088	480	1,281	258.34 %	45.784 %	32.829 %	6.206 %
(2, 17, 5, 6)	80,687	428,086	21,561	90,748	27,926	121,887	11,258	38,693	827	2,203	22.074 %	29.446 %	9.818 %	0.596 %
(2, 19, 5, 8)	312,889	1,858,220	27,811	117,498	77,948	362,276	22,808	74,986	1,144	3,075	6.693 %	20.276 %	4.504 %	0.194 %
(2, 25, 5, 10)	16,261,031	123,086,630	35,561	149,828	2,645,472	16,058,689	273,484	1,128,571	1,537	4,060	0.133 %	13.423 %	1.006 %	0.004 %
(2, 15, 6, 4)	17,065	79,784	TO	TO	9,792	40,476	7,608	28,796	979	3,067		51.903 %	37.588 %	4.178 %
(2, 19, 6, 6)	243,085	1,446,656	TO	TO	95,336	473,670	38,520	155,698	1,696	5,313		33.674 %	11.494 %	0.415 %
(2, 21, 6, 8)	940,715	6,202,486	TO	TO	266,084	1,397,360	78,020	303,724	2,351	7,425		23.287 %	5.344 %	0.137 %
(2, 27, 6, 10)	48,799,477	401,798,336	TO	TO	9,015,346	60,176,445	TO	TO	3,193	9,937		15.356 %		0.003 %
(2, 17, 7, 6)	51,707	273,994	TO	TO	33,432	158,372	25,976	113,996	1,978	7,139		58.89 %	42.976 %	2.799 %
(2, 21, 7, 6)	731,303	4,828,186	TO	TO	325,492	1,813,652	131,564	611,188	3,435	12,403		38.477 %	13.36 %	0.285 %
(2, 23, 7, 8)	2,826,241	20,492,984	TO	TO	908,440	5,319,108	266,464	1,198,156	4,766	17,333		26.706 %	6.281 %	0.095 %
(2, 19, 8, 4)	156,145	926,420	TO	TO	114,144	609,608	88,688	442,736	3,977	16,283		66.855 %	49.089 %	1.871 %
(2, 23, 8, 6)	2,198,005	15,951,260	TO	TO	1,111,296	6,862,916	449,216	2,357,964	6,914	28,323		43.937 %	15.467 %	0.194 %
(2, 21, 9, 4)	470,483	3,093,598	TO	TO	389,712	2,316,544	302,800	1,694,352	7,976	36,571		75.931 %	56.036 %	1.25 %
(2, 23, 10, 4)	1,415,545	10,225,856	TO	TO	1,330,560	8,712,240	TO	TO	15,975	81,147		86.268 %		0.834 %
(3, 13, 2, 6)	3,803	15,598	316	1,515	289	654	250	537	71	124	9.438 %	4.861 %	4.056 %	1.005 %
(3, 13, 2, 9)	43,387	228,362	463	2,226	1,283	3,424	653	1,192	104	183	0.99 %	1.732 %	0.679 %	0.106 %
(3, 13, 3, 6)	34,739	186,530	2,227	12,018	1,563	4,700	1,380	4,025	168	400	6.438 %	2.83 %	2.443 %	0.257 %
(3, 16, 3, 9)	392,531	2,577,950	3,256	17,625	6,771	23,024	3,846	10,667	246	602	0.703 %	1.003 %	0.489 %	0.029 %
(3, 16, 4, 6)	314,699	2,097,686	15,604	93,729	8,511	31,912	7,530	27,559	364	1,102	4.532 %	1.676 %	1.455 %	0.061 %
(3, 19, 4, 9)	3,540,971	27,920,114	22,807	137,388	36,777	152,390	21,117	74,504	531	1,655	0.509 %	0.601 %	0.304 %	0.007 %
(3, 19, 5, 6)	2,840,483	22,663,754	TO	TO	46,377	208,290	41,040	180,639	758	2,803		0.999 %	0.869 %	0.014 %
(3, 22, 5, 9)	31,901,507	293,805,446	TO	TO	200,349	978,834	115,164	491,799	1,103	4,193		0.362 %	0.186 %	0.002 %
(3, 22, 6, 6)	25,597,115	238,092,350	TO	TO	252,729	1,322,490	223,650	1,150,257	1,548	6,799		0.597 %	0.521 %	0.003 %
(3, 25, 6, 9)	287,244,635	3,027,198,170	TO	TO	1,091,763	6,143,676	TO	TO	2,249	10,130		0.218 %		0.0 %
(3, 25, 7, 6)	230,505,107	2,450,127,602	TO	TO	1,377,243	8,228,232	TO	TO	3,130	15,979		0.358 %		0.001 %

Table 2. Results for security case studies from [17].

model	no reductions |S|	no reductions |T|	sos reduction |S|	sos reduction |T|	pattern |S|	pattern |T|	pattern+layer |S|	pattern+layer |T|	pattern+sos |S|	pattern+sos |T|	reduced/original sos reduction %	pattern %	pattern+layer %	pattern+sos %
forestall	62,689	185,944	2,427	7,564	5,784	17,285	1,845	2,721	664	1,656	4.018 %	9.278 %	1.836 %	0.933 %
gain_admin	51,158,719	364,218,554	8,626	33,595	1,327,546	7,776,327	52,923	94,570	844	1,965	0.01 %	2.192 %	0.036 %	0.001 %
iot_dev	3,381	6,860	4,173	11,852	907	2,154	371	450	1,315	3,144	156.479 %	29.89 %	8.017 %	43.541 %
treasure_hunters	479	1,326	316	937	157	340	74	89	134	228	69.418 %	27.535 %	9.03 %	20.055 %

the networks are sync-deadlock. The timeout was set to 30 min (displayed as TO in the tables).

The model signature in the first column of Table 1 consists of the branching factor per an *ADT* node, the total number of nodes, the depth and the width of an *ADT* [17]. In both tables the second pair of columns collects the details of unreduced models, the third collects the results of applying the sum-of-squares (here, abbreviated to *sos*) construction to the unreduced models, the fourth of applying only pattern reduction, the fifth of pipelining the pattern and layer reductions, and the sixth of pipelining the pattern reduction and the sum-of-squares. The remaining columns collect the relative reduction/blowup rates.

The experimental data suggests that the reductions for sync-memoryless networks, proposed in this paper, are often comparable or exceeding [17]. This is especially evident when the sum-of-squares is applied to pattern-reduced models. The nature of the sum-of-squares construction can lead to statespace blowup, but this seems observable only for smaller networks. Moreover, larger networks enable more relative reductions.

To assess this further we conducted an independent series of scalable experiments on random live-reset tree networks. We generated 210 live-reset tree networks of depths 1–3 and computed their (reduced) sum-of-squares products. Figure 7 presents the scatterplot of the results. The red line denotes no reduction.

The same phenomenon as for sync-deadlock trees can be observed: the degree of reduction increases with the size of the network.

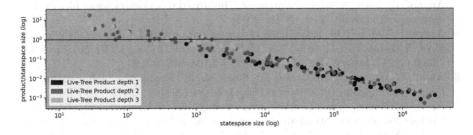

Fig. 7. Statespace sizes of sum-of-squares for live-reset tree networks.

6   Conclusion

In this paper we outlined how to simplify large tree networks of LTSs in which the components reset or deadlock after synchronising with their parents. We also proposed and investigated a similar construction for the general tree-like synchronisation topologies. It is shown that the constructions preserve a certain form of reachability, but do not preserve liveness. An experimental evaluation shows that the method yields extremely effective reductions for sync-memoryless networks.

We raise several questions to be explored as future work. Firstly, we only have a very rough theoretical estimate of the size of reductions for sync-memoryless networks. Stronger estimations can be obtained. Secondly, for general networks we only put a hypothesis that the state space of the general sum-of-squares may substantially grow as compared to the full asynchronous product (albeit with possibly smaller memory usage). This can be investigated experimentally. Moreover, the "vanilla" technique of general sum-of-squares is straightforward, thus surely enables many optimisations. Thirdly, the class of live-reset tree networks is probably one of many that do not need tracing what happens after synchronisation (sync-deadlock networks are slightly different, as one-shot transitions still need to be traced). Other such classes and topologies could probably be identified. Finally, the sum-of-squares for sync-deadlock LTS networks guarantees that a state is reachable before reduction iff it is *one-shot F*-reachable after (see Definition 7 and Theorem 1). We however do not know the complexity of verifying *one-shot F*-reachability; here we conjecture that it is NP-hard, which may make the reductions for this class of models less impressive than suggested by experimental results. All of these concerns can be addressed in further research.

References

1. DD-Net-Checker (2021). https://github.com/MichalKnapik/dd-net-checker
2. LTR (2021). https://github.com/MichalKnapik/automata-net-reduction-tool
3. van der Aalst, W.M.P., van Hee, K.M.: Workflow Management: Models, Methods, and Systems. Cooperative information systems . MIT Press (2002)
4. Aminof, B., Kupferman, O., Murano, A.: Improved model checking of hierarchical systems. Inf. Comput. **210**, 68–86 (2012)
5. André, É.: IMITATOR 3: synthesis of timing parameters beyond decidability. In: Silva, A., Leino, K.R.M. (eds.) CAV 2021. LNCS, vol. 12759, pp. 552–565. Springer, Cham (2021). https://doi.org/10.1007/978-3-030-81685-8_26
6. André, É., Lime, D., Ramparison, M., Stoelinga, M.: Parametric analyses of attack-fault trees. Fundam. Informaticae **182**(1), 69–94 (2021)
7. Arias, J., Budde, C.E., Penczek, W., Petrucci, L., Sidoruk, T., Stoelinga, M.: Hackers vs. security: attack-defence trees as asynchronous multi-agent systems. In: Lin, S.-W., Hou, Z., Mahony, B. (eds.) ICFEM 2020. LNCS, vol. 12531, pp. 3–19. Springer, Cham (2020). https://doi.org/10.1007/978-3-030-63406-3_1
8. Arias, J., Celerier, J.M., Desiante-Catherine, M.: Authoring and automatic verification of interactive multimedia scores. J. New Music Res. **46**(1), 15–33 (2016)
9. Arias, J., Petrucci, L., Masko, L., Penczek, W., Sidoruk, T.: Minimal schedule with minimal number of agents in attack-defence trees. In: ICECCS, pp. 1–10. IEEE (2022)
10. Baier, C., Katoen, J.: Principles of Model Checking. MIT Press, Cambridge (2008)
11. Behrmann, G., et al.: UPPAAL 4.0. In: QEST, pp. 125–126. IEEE Computer Society (2006)
12. Belardinelli, F., Lomuscio, A., Murano, A., Rubin, S.: Verification of broadcasting multi-agent systems against an epistemic strategy logic. In: IJCAI, pp. 91–97 (2017)
13. Holzmann, G.J.: The SPIN Model Checker - Primer and Reference Manual. Addison-Wesley (2004)

14. Knapik, M., Meski, A., Penczek, W.: Action synthesis for branching time logic: theory and applications. ACM Trans. Embed. Comput. Syst. **14**(4), 64:1-64:23 (2015)
15. Kordy, B., Mauw, S., Radomirovic, S., Schweitzer, P.: Attack-defense trees. J. Log. Comput. **24**(1), 55–87 (2014)
16. Lakos, C., Petrucci, L.: Modular analysis of systems composed of semiautonomous subsystems. In: ACSD, pp. 185–196. IEEE Computer Society (2004)
17. Petrucci, L., Knapik, M., Penczek, W., Sidoruk, T.: Squeezing state spaces of (attack-defence) trees. In: ICECCS, pp. 71–80. IEEE (2019)

Non-linear Optimization Methods for Learning Regular Distributions

Wenjing Chu[1(✉)], Shuo Chen[2], and Marcello Bonsangue[1]

[1] Leiden University, Leiden, The Netherlands
w.chu@liacs.leidenuniv.nl
[2] University of Amsterdam, Amsterdam, The Netherlands

Abstract. Probabilistic finite automata (PFA) are recognizers of regular distributions over finite strings, a model that is widely applied in speech recognition and biological systems, for example. While the underlying structure of a PFA is just that of a normal automaton, it is well known that PFA with a non-deterministic underlying structure is more powerful than deterministic one. In this paper, we concentrate on passive learning non-deterministic PFA from examples and counterexamples using a two steps procedure: first we learn the underlying structure using an algorithm for learning the underlying residual finite state automaton, then we learn the probabilities of states and transitions using three different optimization methods. We experimentally show with a set of random probabilistic finite automata that the ones learned using RFSA combined with genetic algorithm for optimizing the weight outperforms other existing methods greatly improving the distance to the automaton to be learned. We also apply our algorithm to model the behavior of an agent in a maze. Also here RFSA algorithms have better performance than existing automata learning methods and can model both positive and negative samples well.

Keywords: Probabilistic finite automata · Residual finite state automata · Learning automata · Passive learning · L_2 distance between discrete distributions

1 Introduction

Probabilistic Finite Automata (PFAs) [22] are non-deterministic automata where every state is allocated an initial and a final probability, and every transition is allocated a transition probability in addition to the alphabet symbol. PFAs are similar to Hidden Markov Models (HMM): HMMs and PFA with no final probabilities generate distributions over complete finite prefix-free sets. On the other hand, HMMs with final probabilities and probabilistic automata generate distributions over strings of finite length. In fact, a PFA can be converted into an HMM and vice-versa [12,28]. PFA and HMM are all in the same class of probabilistic models that are widely used for machine learning, such as in speech recognition [1,17,18] and biological modeling [2,13].

© Springer Nature Switzerland AG 2022
A. Riesco and M. Zhang (Eds.): ICFEM 2022, LNCS 13478, pp. 54–70, 2022.
https://doi.org/10.1007/978-3-031-17244-1_4

While nondeterministic finite automata (NFA) are equivalent to deterministic finite automata (DFA) [15], we have that PFAs are strictly more powerful than deterministic probabilistic finite automata (DPFAs) [12,16,28]. Consequently, a lot of effort has been paid to learning DPFAs from examples. The most famous algorithm is ALERGIA [6], based on merging and folding states guided only by a finite set of positive samples. In ALERGIA, the automaton's structure and probabilities are learned simultaneously. Later on, Carrasco et al. [6] provided a simpler version of ALERGIA, named RLIPS algorithm [7]. Ron et al. [24] developed an algorithm for learning only acyclic automata. As for learning full PFA, Baum et al. pioneered the Baum-Welch (BW) algorithm [3], which first constructs a fully connected graph and then assigns zero weight to unnecessary transitions. The approach is not practical as it has a vast number of parameters [21]. The Expectation-Maximization (EM) algorithm could learn the distribution of probabilistic automata [26]. However, how the resulting distribution could be adapted to fit into the structure of the automaton we learn is not fully clear. Another limitation of the EM algorithm is that each iteration can be slow when there are many parameters, meaning that the method can be computationally expensive [14,27].

In [9] we proposed a strategy to build a PFA using residual languages then assigning probabilities to the automaton by fairly distributing the values among the transitions. The advantage of this method is that we can learn the structure of a target automaton as an NFA. Unfortunately, the strategy used to assign probabilities is often not very effective, as in general probabilities are not fairly distributed in a PFA.

In this paper, we improve our previous work by using different strategies in learning the weight of a PFA. We focus on passive learning PFAs from examples and counterexamples and following two steps: first we learn the underlying structure of PFAs using residual languages, and then we use state of the art optimization methods to learn the probabilities labelling the states and transitions of the automaton. This boils down to defining a parametric PFA with unknown variables for probabilities that are then assigned to value by solving an appropriate optimization problem dictated by the sample and the structure of the automaton. We design two sets of experiments to compare our algorithm with flip-coin, ALERGIA, and k-testable [8]. First, we use a set of randomly generated PFAs. The results show that the numerical solution under constrained nonlinear optimization problems together with learning by residual learns automata generating a distribution very close to the target one, even in the case of non-deterministic distribution. In fact, our method based on genetic algorithm achieves improvements on existing learning algorithm up to 96%. Then we use all these algorithms to model an agent's behavior in a maze. Only the RFSA algorithm learns both positive and negative samples well. Since the target automata of traces are deterministic, RFSA with flip-coin, genetic algorithm, and sequential quadratic programming all have good performance.

2   Preliminaries

This section recalls some basic notions and facts of (probabilistic) automata and fixes the notation we use.

An alphabet Σ is a finite set of symbols and a string x over Σ is a finite sequence of alphabet symbols. We denote the empty string by λ and the set of all strings over Σ by Σ^*. A language L over Σ is a subset of Σ^*. For any language L and any string $u \in \Sigma^*$, the residual $u^{-1}L$ of a language L with respect to u is the language $u^{-1}L = \{v \in \Sigma^* | uv \in L\}$ and we call u the characterizing word of $u^{-1}L$.

A non-deterministic finite automaton (NFA) over an alphabet Σ is a tuple $A = \langle \Sigma, Q, I, F, \delta \rangle$, where Q is a finite set of states, $I : Q \to \{0, 1\}$ maps to 1 all states that are initial, $F : Q \to \{0, 1\}$ maps to 1 all states that are final, and $\delta : Q \times \Sigma \to \{0, 1\}^Q$ is a transition function. The extension δ^* of δ to strings instead of alphabet symbols is defined as usual by $\delta^*(q, \lambda)(q) = 1$ and $\delta^*(q, ax)(q'') = 1$ iff there exists q' such that $\delta(q, a)(q') = 1$ and $\delta^*(q', x)(q'') = 1$. Given an NFA A and a state $q \in Q$ the language $L(A, q)$ consist of all strings such that there exists q' such that $\delta(q, x)(q') = 1$, and $F(q') = 1$. The language $L(A)$ accepted by an NFA A is the union of all $L(A, q)$ for states q such that $I(q) = 1$. A language L is regular if it can be accepted by an NFA. An NFA A is said to be deterministic (DFA) if $I(q) = 1$ for at most one state, and for every q and a, $\delta_p(q, a)(q') = 1$ for at most one state.

Residual finite state automaton (RFSA) A is a non-deterministic automaton whose states correspond exactly to the residual languages of the language recognized by A, that is for each state $q \in Q$, there exists a string $u \in \Sigma^*$ such that $L(A, q) = u^{-1}L(A)$ [10]. In this case, every string from an initial state to q is a characteristic word for $L(A, q)$. For example, every minimal (no two states recognize the same language) and trimmed (every state is reachable from an initial one) automata is a residual automata with a finite set of characteristic strings.

A probabilistic language over Σ^* is a function $D : \Sigma^* \to [0, 1]$ that is also a discrete distribution, that is: $\sum_{x \in \Sigma^*} D(x) = 1$. An interesting class of probabilistic languages can be described by a generalization of non-deterministic automata with probabilities as weight on states and transitions. A probabilistic finite automaton (PFA) over a finite alphabet Σ is a tuple $A = \langle \Sigma, Q, I_p, F_p, \delta_p \rangle$, where: Q is a finite set of states, $I_p : Q \to (\mathbb{Q} \cap [0, 1])$ is the initial probability such that $\sum_{q \in Q} I_p(q) = 1$, $F_p : Q \to (\mathbb{Q} \cap [0, 1])$ determines the weight of the final states, and $\delta_p : Q \times \Sigma \to (\mathbb{Q} \cap [0, 1])^Q$ is the transition function such that $\forall q \in Q$,

$$F_p(q) + \sum_{a \in \Sigma, q' \in Q} \delta_p(q, a)(q') = 1.$$

We define the support of a PFA A as the NFA where the initial map, the final map and the transition function coincides with those of A when the value is 0 and otherwise maps everything else to 1. A PFA is said to be deterministic if its support is a DFA.

Given a string $x = a_1 \cdots a_n \in \Sigma^*$ of length n, an accepting (or valid) path π for x is a sequence of states $q_0 \cdots q_n$ such that: $I_p(q_0) > 0$, $\delta_p(q_i, a_{i+1})(q_{i+1}) > 0$ for all $0 \leq i < n$, and also $F_p(q_n) > 0$. We set $i_p(\pi) = I_p(q_0)$, $e_p(\pi) = F_p(q_n)$, and $\delta_p(\pi) = \Pi_{i=0}^{n-1} \delta_p(q_i, a_{i+1})(q_{i+1})$. Further, denote by $Paths_p(x)$ the set (necessarily finite) of all accepting paths for a string x. A PFA is said to be consistent if all its states appear in at least one accepting path. The probability of a path $\pi \in Paths_p(x)$ is given by $i_p(\pi) \cdot \delta_p(\pi) \cdot e_p(\pi)$, while the distribution of a string $x \in \Sigma^*$ is defined by:

$$D(A)(x) = \sum_{\pi \in Paths_p(x)} i_p(\pi) \cdot \delta_p(\pi) \cdot e_p(\pi). \tag{1}$$

If a PFA A is consistent then it is easy to show [12] that $D(A)$ is indeed a distribution on Σ^*, that is $\sum_{x \in \Sigma^*} D(A)(x) = 1$. We therefore call a distribution D on Σ^* regular if it is generated by a PFA A, that is $D = D(A)$.

The language $L(A)$ accepted by a probabilistic automaton A is the support of its distribution and is given by mapping an x to 1 if and only if $D(A)(x)$ a strictly positive. In other words, $L(A)$ is the language of the support of A. A language is regular if and only if it is accepted by a (deterministic) probabilistic finite automaton. However, differently, than for ordinary automata, the class of distributions characterized by deterministic PFAs is a proper subclass of the regular ones [12].

3 Learning a Regular Distribution from a Sample

Our strategy in learning a regular distribution on Σ^* from a sample will be to first learn the underlying non-deterministic RFSA automaton and then enrich its states and transitions with weights such that the resulting probabilistic automaton is consistent with the sample.

A *sample* (S, f) consists of a finite set of strings $S \subseteq \Sigma^*$ together with a frequency function $f : S \to \mathbb{N}$ assigning the number of occurrences of each string in the sample. The frequency function f partitions the strings in S into positive samples and negative ones. We denote by $S_+ = \{x \mid f(x) > 0\}$ the set of positive samples and by $S_- = \{x \mid f(x) = 0\}$ the set of negative samples. Obviously, one can convert a sample to a discrete distribution $D : S \to \mathbb{Q} \cap [0, 1]$ by mapping each x in the sample to its frequency divided by the total number of observations in the sample.

An NFA A is *consistent* with respect to a sample (S, f), if every positive sample is accepted by A and every negative sample is not, i.e. $S_+ \subseteq L(A)$ and $S_- \cap L(A) = \emptyset$. Learning a regular distribution D from a sample (S, f) of finite strings independently drawn with a frequency f according to the distribution D means building a probabilistic finite automaton A with a support consistent with respect to (S, f), and generating a distribution $D(A)$ that gets arbitrarily closer to D when the size of the sample (S, f) increases.

3.1 Learning the Structure

Assume given a regular distribution D and a sample (S, f) generated from D by counting the occurrence of independent draws. We build a RFSA from a sample (S, f) using the algorithm presented in [9]. The algorithm is similar to that presented in [11] but approximates the inclusion relation between residual languages by calculating on the fly the transitivity and right-invariant (with respect to concatenation) closure $\prec^{tr}$ of the $\prec$ relation, defined for $u, v \in Pref(S_+)$ by:

- $u \prec v$ if for all string x, $ux \notin S_+$ or $vx \notin S_-$,

Two strings u and v are indistinguishable with respect to a sample (S, f), denoted by $u \simeq v$, if both $u \prec v$ and $v \prec u$. This means that we can distinguish two strings u and v if we can extend them with a string x such that one of the resulting string belong to the positive sample and another to the negative sample.

We will use prefixes of strings in the positive samples as states of the learned RFSA, but we want to equate indistinguishable states with respect to the sample. Here $u \prec^{tr} v$ is an estimate for the inclusion between the residuals $L_u \subseteq L_v$. In fact, under some conditions on the sample with respect to language underlying the distribution D to be learned, this approximation will be exact [11].

Algorithm 1: Building a RFSA from a simple sample

Input: A simple sample (S, f)
Output: A RFSA $\langle \Sigma, Q, I, F, \delta \rangle$
1: Pref $:= Pref(S_+)$ ordered by length-lexicographic order
2: $Q := I := F := \delta := \emptyset$
3: $u := \varepsilon$
4: **loop**
5:      **if** $\exists u' \in Q$ such that $u \simeq^{tr} u'$ **then**
6:          Pref $:=$ Pref $\setminus u\Sigma^*$
7:      **else**
8:          $Q := Q \cup \{u\}$
9:          **if** $u \prec^{tr} \varepsilon$ **then**
10:             $I := I \cup \{u\}$
11:         **if** $u \in S_+$ **then**
12:             $F := F \cup \{u\}$
13:         **for** $u' \in Q$ and $a \in \Sigma$ **do**
14:             **if** $u'a \in$ Pref and $u \prec^{tr} u'a$ **then**
15:                 $\delta := \delta \cup \{\delta(u', a) = u\}$
16:             **if** $ua \in$ Pref and $u' \prec^{tr} ua$ **then**
17:                 $\delta := \delta \cup \{\delta(u, a) = u')\}$
18:     **if** u is the last string of Pref or $\langle \Sigma, Q, I, F, \delta \rangle$ is consistent with S **then**
19:         exit loop
20:     **else**
21:         $u :=$ next string in Pref
22: **return** $\langle \Sigma, Q, I, F, \delta \rangle$

The algorithm is shown in 1. Basically, given a sample (S, f) the algorithm starts with an empty set of states Q for the learned NFA. All prefixes of S_+ are explored, and only those which are distinguishable are added to the Q. States below λ with respect to $\prec$ are set to be initial states, while states that belong to S_+ are final ones. Finally, a transition $\delta(u, a)(v) = 1$ is added when $v \prec ua$, for u and v distinguishable prefixes of S_+ and $a \in \Sigma$. The algorithm ends either when all prefixes of S_+ are explored or earlier if the learned automaton is consistent with the sample. By construction the resulting automaton will be a (non-deterministic) RFSA consistent with respect to the sample. In general, the above schema will learn regular languages as NFA in the limit in polynomial time and space.

Example 1. Given a sample (S, f) with $f(\lambda) = 0.3$, $f(aa) = 0.03$, $f(ba) = 0.039$, $f(bb) = 0.036$, $f(abb) = 0.0045$, $f(a) = f(b) = f(ab) = 0$, so that $S_+ = \{\lambda, aa, ba, bb, abb\}$ and $S_- = \{a, b, ab\}$. Prefixes of strings in S_+ missing from S_+ are a, b, ab. Because $aa \in S_+$ and $\lambda a \in S_-$ it follows that $a \not\prec^{tr} \lambda$. Hence a is distinguishable from λ, it is not an initial state and is also not final. State λ instead is both initial and final. Finally, $\delta(\lambda, a)(a) = 1$ and $\delta(a, a)(\lambda) = 1$ since $a \prec^{tr} a$ and $\lambda \prec^{tr} aa$. Since the automata is not yet consistent with the sample, we add a new prefix of S_+ as state. String b is distinguishable from λ for similar reason as a, and again it is neither final nor initial. It is also distinguishable from a because $b \not\prec^{tr} a$ as they are both in S_-. Six transitions are added: $\delta(\lambda, b)(a) = 1$, $\delta(\lambda, b)(b) = 1$, $\delta(b, a)(\lambda) = 1$, $\delta(b, b)(\lambda) = 1$, $\delta(a, b)(b) = 1$ and $\delta(b, a)(b) = 1$. Now the automaton is consistent with the sample, and thus the algorithm terminates. See Fig. 1a.

3.2   Learning the Probabilities

Once we have learned the structure of the RFSA needed to represent the language underling the sample (S, f), we need to label it with weights representing the probabilities of a PFA. We will treat the probabilities for the initial states, the final states and the transitions as parameters, that will be used as variables in the solution of a non-linear optimization problem.

Given an NFA A, we first construct a system of equations depending on the structure of the automaton and the probabilities induced by the sample for each string in it. For each state $q \in Q$, we have variables i_q and e_q to denote the unknown values of $I(q)$ and $F(q)$, respectively. We also use variables $x^a_{q,q'}$ for denoting the unknown probability of the transition $\delta(q, a)(q')$. We add a few structural equations which are dictated by the structure PFA definition:

$$\sum_q i_q = 1, \quad \text{and} \quad \text{for all } q \in Q, \ f_q + \sum_{a,q'} x^a_{q,q'} = 1$$

Besides the above structural equations, we have equations depending on the sample and the automaton. For each string $u = a_0 \cdots a_n \in S$ we define $E(u)$ to be the polynomial equation:

$$\sum_{q_0 \cdots q_{n+1} \in Paths_p(u)} i_{q_0} \cdot x^{a_0}_{q_0,q_1} \cdots x^{a_n}_{q_n,q_{n+1}} \cdot e_{q_{n+1}}(\pi) = p(u).$$

where $p(u)$ is the probability of u induced by the frequency f in the sample. In other words, equations like $E(u)$ above represent the symbolic calculation of the probability of u in the automaton A with weights as parameters. In order to guarantee linear independence between the equations, we consider prime strings in S. A string u is said to be prime if there exists at least one path in $Path_p(u)$ without repeated loops, that is, without occurrence of the same part (at least two states) twice. If we have more prime strings in S than variable, we consider only prime strings u to build our equations $E(u)$. Otherwise, we consider strings from S_+, prioritizing them in lexicographic order. If we have a small sample with more variables than strings in S the result may be very poor, as expected.

We rewrite the system of equations as a function with some constraints. The function is derived from the structural equations while the constraints are stemming from the sample depending equations. We use three different methods to result optimization problem with constraints. The first one is via the solvers module in SymPy [19]. SymPy is a Python library for solving equations symbolically, trying to find algebraic solutions. In our experiments below, in most cases, SymPy is not able to find the exact algebraic solution, due to the fact that the structure of learned automaton is not always equal to the target one. The second method uses a genetic algorithm (GA). GAs are computational models simulating ideal for searching optimal solutions by imitating the natural evolutionary processes. GAs take individuals in a population and use randomization techniques to guide an efficient search of an encoded parameter space [20]. The third method is based on Sequential Quadratic Programming (SQP), one of the most widely-used methods for solving nonlinear constrained optimization problems [4]. It is an iteration method with a sound mathematical foundation that can be applied to large scale optimization problems.

The solutions from the GA and SQP methods are an approximation of the results, and in general will need a light adaptation via normalization to satisfy the structural rules of a PFA.

Example 2. Given the RFSA in Fig. 1a constructed from the sample (S, f) with $f(\lambda) = 0.3$, $f(aa) = 0.03$, $f(ba) = 0.039$, $f(bb) = 0.036$, $f(abb) = 0.0045$, $f(a) = f(b) = f(ab) = 0$, we obtain the PFA with variables as in Fig. 1b. From that we derive the system of equations

$$\begin{cases} i_\lambda & = 1 \\ f_\lambda + x^a_{\lambda,a} + x^b_{\lambda,a} + x^b_{\lambda,b} = 1 \\ x^a_{a,\lambda} + x^b_{a,b} = 1 \\ x^a_{b,\lambda} + x^b_{b,\lambda} + x^a_{b,b} = 1 \end{cases} \quad \begin{cases} i_\lambda f_\lambda & = 0.3 \\ i_\lambda x^a_{\lambda,a} x^a_{a,\lambda} f_\lambda & = 0.03 \\ i_\lambda x^b_{\lambda,a} x^a_{a,\lambda} f_\lambda + i_\lambda x^b_{\lambda,b} x^a_{b,\lambda} f_\lambda & = 0.039 \\ i_\lambda x^b_{\lambda,b} x^b_{b,\lambda} f_\lambda & = 0.036 \\ i_\lambda x^a_{\lambda,a} x^b_{a,b} x^b_{b,\lambda} f_\lambda & = 0.0045 \end{cases}$$

The corresponding function to be optimized is

$$(i_\lambda - 1)^2 + (f_\lambda + x^a_{\lambda,a} + x^b_{\lambda,a} + x^b_{\lambda,b} - 1)^2 + (x^a_{a,\lambda} + x^b_{a,b} - 1)^2 + (x^b_{b,\lambda} + x^b_{b,\lambda} + x^a_{b,b} - 1)^2 = 0$$

with as constraints all variables ranging between 0 and 1 and:

$$(i_\lambda f_\lambda - 0.3)^2 = 0 \qquad (i_\lambda x^b_{\lambda,b} x^b_{b,\lambda} f_\lambda - 0.036)^2 = 0$$
$$(i_\lambda x^a_{\lambda,a} x^a_{a,\lambda} f_\lambda - 0.03)^2 = 0 \qquad (i_\lambda x^a_{\lambda,a} x^b_{a,b} x^b_{b,\lambda} f_\lambda - 0.0045)^2 = 0$$
$$(i_\lambda x^b_{\lambda,a} x^a_{a,\lambda} f_\lambda + i_\lambda x^b_{\lambda,b} x^a_{b,\lambda} f_\lambda - 0.039)^2 = 0.$$

Then we use the GA and SQP to approximate the solution, the results are shown in Fig. 1c and Fig. 1d. The learned PFAs approximate to the given sample closely.

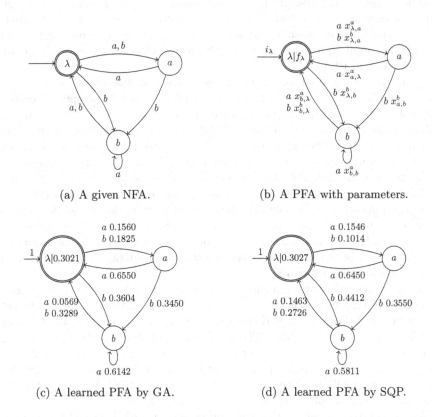

(a) A given NFA.

(b) A PFA with parameters.

(c) A learned PFA by GA.

(d) A learned PFA by SQP.

Fig. 1. The RFSA and PFA automata from Example 1.

4   Experimental Results

In this section, we summarize some experiments to compare the performance of our new learning method with other existing algorithms using some distributions generated from a random set of PFAs. In particular, we consider ALERGIA, the most well-known probabilistic languages learning algorithm, k-testable algorithm and RFSA algorithm with flip-coin distribution. ALERGIA and k-testable can identify only deterministic distributions. We use 999 different parameters setup for ALERGIA and 14 different values for k for the k-testable method. We avoid too large values for k to not make the learning model overfitting. In both cases we only consider the parameter achieving the best performance. For RFSA-GA and RFSA-SQP, we choose 1000 different start points at random. Also here we choose the start point with best result for each algorithm.

4.1   Learning Randomly Generated Probabilistic Automata

Target automata are generated by a PFA generator according to the number of states, symbols and transitions for each state. We generate three sets of 20 automata each with 3, 5 and 10 states. All automata are over a 2 symbols alphabet and with at most 3 transitions for each state. The probabilities of initial states, final states and of the transitions are chosen randomly. There are both DPFAs and PFAs.

From each of these 60 automata, we generate a sample of 248 strings over a two symbols alphabet uniformly and use the automaton to compute a probability for each string, including strings with probability 0. We generate samples with frequencies by scaling up the probabilities. For each sample, we learn an automaton with six different algorithms. We compute the L_2 distance between each learned automaton and the respective target PFA [9], considering the smallest L_2 distance for each algorithm. We repeat this experimental setup 20 times for different target automata, give the average variance of results, and then calculate the improvement between the best of our new methods and the best of the others. The results are reported in the table below. There are no results of RFSA with solver algorithm in this table since we cannot find the exact algebraic solutions in 75% of the cases for the set of 3-states automata. More experimental results are shown in Appendix.

For 3−states automata, our method combining RFSA learning with genetic algorithms (RFSA-GA) has on average the smallest distance from the target distribution and the smallest variance too, with an improvement on the learning via k-testable algorithm of 90%. The combination of RFSA with SQP scores as the second best on average. The average size of the automata learned by RFSA-GA is 3.05 states on average, a significant improvement compared to 12.95 for ALERGIA and 66.65 for k-testable. This means that RFSA learned automata structure is much simpler and closer to the target model.

As for 5-states automata, the situation is similar, with RFSA-GA scoring as the best, followed by RFSA-SQP and the k-testable algorithm. Our RFSA-GA algorithm learns 4.6 states on average, compared with 13.15 states by ALERGIA and 54.55 states by k-testable.

When the target automata have 10 states, the RFSA-GA still has the smallest average and variance with an improvement of 86% when compared to ALERGIA. The RFSA learns 8.1 states on average, while ALERGIA and k-testable get 20.1 and 59.4 states, respectively.

Only when the algebraic solver can find the solution, we have that the learned automaton is closer to the target one than RFSA-GA. In some cases the distance is even 0, meaning that the distribution learned is precisely the target one. In a few other cases, the distance is almost 0 due to the approximate structure given by the RFSA. In the table, we see the results of RFSA combined with a flip-coin method, assigning probabilities by equally distributing them among the transition. Clearly, this naive strategy has the largest distance on average from the target automata, but is not extremely far from ALERGIA and k-testable, underlying the importance of a simple and as close as the possible structure of the learned automata with respect to the target ones (Table 1).

Table 1. Averages, variances and improvements of L_2 distance between target 3-state, 5-state, 10-state automata and learned automata respectively.

Algorithms	3-states		5-states		10-states	
	Average	Variance	Average	Variance	Average	Variance
ALERGIA	0.1874	0.0208	0.1462	0.0238	0.2121	0.0310
k-testable	0.1729	0.0202	0.1065	0.0095	0.2128	0.0317
Flip-coin	0.2229	0.02147	0.1593	0.0112	0.2807	0.0324
RFSA-SQP	0.0213	0.0013	0.0348	0.0034	0.0301	0.0031
RFSA-GA	**0.0171**	**0.0006**	**0.0289**	**0.0017**	**0.0264**	**0.0007**
Improvement	90%↓	97%↓	67%↓	82%↓	86%↓	98%↓

4.2 Learning a Model of an Agent's Traces in a Maze

Next we compare our optimization-based approaches using a model for which we do not know a-priori the target regular distribution, but we only have a sample with frequency, as often happens in a real-world situation.

The idea is to build a model for an intelligent agent in two dimensional space with the goal of arriving to target end points. For simplicity, the space is represented as a matrix of possible positions, and the agent in any position can take four actions representing a move up, down, left or right to the current position. We model the agent as a PFA $A = \langle \Sigma, Q, I_p, F_p, \delta_p \rangle$. Here $\Sigma = \{U, D, L, R\}$ is the set of the four actions that the agent can perform, and strings over Σ represent possible consecutive actions taken by the agent. The set of states Q contains all possible positions of the agent in the space. I_p is the set of probabilities of being at a certain starting state, F_p is assigning 1 only to those states that are the target end points, and δ_p is the set of probabilities of executing one of the four actions in a state. We assume given a number of sequence of possible consecutive that are obtained, for example, in a training phase, when the agent uniformly select an action to try to find the target end point. Differently than ordinary reinforcement learning methods, we assume not known a-priory the size and shape of space, that, moreover, may have insurmountable obstacles.

Training an automaton from a sample is therefore to find the set of states Q, and right structure where the agent determine the probabilities of each transition $\delta(q, a)(q')$, the initial probabilities I_p and the final one F_p in accordance to the space structure.

We generated 20 different 10×10 rectangle maps of the space, all of them surrounded by obstacles (walls) that an agent cannot trespass. We differentiate those spaces randomly generating obstacles inside. For simplicity, for each map we choose only one start state (say with coordinates $(0,0)$) and only one target end state that is randomly chosen among the allowed positions. Here we show a simple example about the positive and negative samples under certain agent's moving memoryless strategy.

Example 3. Figure 2 is the illustration of a 3×3 maze, where 0 is available, 1 is an obstacle. $(0,0)$ is the start point, $(2,2)$ is the end point. The agent's moving strategy is $\{U : 0.1, D : 0.4, L : 0.1, R : 0.4\}$. The traces from start point to end point are positive samples. Otherwise, the traces hit the wall or the obstacle are negative samples. The following are few instances of traces in a sample (S, f): $f(DDLL) = 0.0256$, $f(DUDDLL) = 0.001024$, $f(DDLRLL) = 0.001024$, $f(DUDUDDLL) = 0.00004108$, $f(U) = 0$, $f(UUDD) = 0$, $f(DLRLU) = 0$ and $f(DRLDD) = 0$.

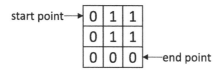

Fig. 2. A 3×3 maze, where 0 means available, 1 is an obstacle. $(0,0)$ is the start point, $(2,2)$ is the end point.

We simulate a training phase for the agent by using a uniform strategy, that is, we generate a trace by uniformly selecting the next action among the set of allowed one (thus avoiding obstacles). Note that this is a deterministic strategy and can therefore be approximated by all other methods for learning PFA we have considered in the previous section. The traces successfully reaching the target end point are our positive samples, with associated frequency (or probability) as calculated on the basis of the probability of each action taken.

In order to balance the data, we consider as negative samples all prefixes of the positive one (we assume that the agent once arriving to a target end state it stops) and concatenation of prefixes with suffixes that do not occurs as positive samples. We use 90% of the resulting traces for training, and 10% for evaluating the learned automaton and compare the performance with other PFA learning methods. As we do not have the full distribution to be learned in advance, to compare the different methods we use the F_1 score and optimized precision OP. Both methods are based on a probabilistic version of precision, sensitivity, specificity and accuracy, where the number of true positive TP and false negative FN is weighted by a the $L1$ distance between the finite sample (S, f_p) and the regular distribution $D(A)$ of the automaton A learned using one of the method we consider. In particular we consider

$$Precision = \frac{cTP}{|TP|+cFP} \qquad Sensitivity = \frac{cTP}{|TP|+cFN}$$
$$Accuracy = \frac{|TP|+|TN|}{|TP|+|TN|+|FP|+|FN|} \qquad Specificity = \frac{|TN|}{|TN|+cFP}$$

where $|TP|, |TN|, |FP|,$ and $|FN|$ are the number of true positive, true negative, false positive and false negative of the automaton A with respect to the sample, and $cTP = \sum_{x \in TP} 1 - |f(x) - D(A)(x)|$, $cFN = \sum_{x \in FN} f(x)$, and $cFP = \sum_{x \in FN} D(A)(x)$ (see [9] for a more extensive discussion). The F_1 score [25] is used to measure the method accuracy. It is computed in terms of both the precision and sensitivity, and basically is the harmonic average of them.

$$F_1 = 2 \cdot \frac{Precision \cdot Sensitivity}{Precision + Sensitivity} \tag{2}$$

The optimized precision OP [5,23] is a hybrid threshold metric combining accuracy, sensitivity and specificity, where the last two are used for stabilizing and optimizing the accuracy when dealing with possibly imbalanced data.

$$OP = Accuracy - \frac{|Specificity - Sensitivity|}{|Specificity + Sensitivity|} \tag{3}$$

When the distribution of the learned automaton coincides with that of the sample, precision, sensitivity and accuracy will all be 1, and thus both F_1 and OP will be equal to 1 too. However, the more the distribution of the learned automaton is distant from that of the sample, the more precision, sensitivity and accuracy will be closer to 0, setting both the scores F_1 and OP closer to 0 too.

Table 2 shows the summary of the results taking the average and the variance when learning with different methods the 20 mazes from the randomly generated samples. As in the case of learning the randomy generated automata, the RFSA method enhanced with an algebraic solver does not work in general because of the too many variables involved. RFSA-SQP is the most stable method as it has the lowest variance across the different mazes when compared using the F_1 score. In general, all algorithms perform well with respect to the F_1 score. However, when considering the OP score we see that RFSA-GA has the highest OP score on average and also has the lowest variance. This means that RFSA-GA has low probability of false positives and false negatives. When compared with the second best given by learning using the k-testable algorithm, we see that RFSA-GA has an improvement of 21% on the average OP score.

Table 2. Average, variance and improvement of F_1 and OP

Algorithms	F_1		OP	
	Average	Variance	Average	Variance
ALERGIA	0.9933	0.0003	0.3431	0.0107
k-testable	0.9997	1.68e−08	0.7990	0.0050
Flip-coin	0.9998	1.28e−08	0.9679	0.0005
RFSA-SQP	**0.9998**	**9.47e−09**	0.9586	0.0012
RFSA-GA	0.9998	9.94e−09	**0.9683**	**0.0004**
Improvement	0.003%↑	43%↑	21%↑	91%↑

5   Conclusion

In this paper, we learn regular distributions by combining the learning of the structure via RFSA with the learning of the probabilities using three different optimization methods: an algebraic solver, a genetic algorithm and sequential quadratic programming. We use some randomly generated PFAs and modeling an agent's traces in a maze for comparing these methods with existing ones. While theoretically the algebraic solver method is the best, in practice it often fails to provide a solution even for three states automata. The other two optimization methods are iterative and always find an approximate solution. In practice, we have seen that the solution is very close to the target distribution, order of magnitudes more than existing algorithms. Because the structure learned via RFSA is a non-deterministic automaton, our method behaves well even for regular distributions that are not deterministic, showing that one of the disadvantage of learning regular languages by RFSA has been actually turned into an advantage in the context of learning regular distribution. Besides, compared with k-testable and ALERGIA algorithm, which could only learn positive samples well, our method can model both positive and negative samples well. Important in learning the structure is the presence of both examples and counterexamples, i.e. strings with 0 frequency/probability, and to have a fair balance between them. The scalability of our algorithm depends very much on the scalability of the non-linearity optimization method used to solve the constrained equations. Algebraic solver becomes impractical already with 5 states automata. In contrast, GA and the SQP method seem to be more appropriate for larger one. Many works investigate concurrency to improve the scalability of the GA and SQP algorithms. Specifically, the evolutionary algorithm we used in our experiments is capable of learning in reasonable time automata up to 62 states and hundreds of transitions, resulting in a system with more than 110 variables. Our algorithm could be used for speech recognition, and biological modeling depending on how large the samples and target automata are. Next, we plan to investigate how our algorithm performs in these practical situations.

A   Appendix

(See Table 3).

Table 3. L_2 distance between target 3-states automata and learned automata.

Nb	RFSA-solver	RFSA-SQP	RFSA-GA	ALERGIA	k-testable
1	-	**0.0023**	0.0260	0.1962	0.1822
2	**3.73e−09**	0.0006	0.0033	0.1714	0.1314
3	-	2.33e−05	**1.23e−06**	0.2621	0.1847
4	**1.29e−08**	0.0054	2.91e−06	0.0593	0.0561
5	-	**0.0002**	0.0105	0.5255	0.5251
6	**0**	0.0045	3.39e−06	0.2798	0.1326
7	-	**0.0001**	0.0164	0.0365	0.0366
8	-	0.1021	0.1027	0.0064	**0.0046**
9	-	0.0006	0.0023	0.0491	0.0492
10	-	**7.94e−05**	0.0041	0.0152	0.0118
11	3.72e−05	0.0033	**3.05e−05**	0.0002	0.0002
12	-	**0.0123**	0.0131	0.1994	0.1989
13	-	**0.0265**	0.0279	0.1638	0.1634
14	-	0.0913	**0.0141**	0.5176	0.5172
15	-	**0.0290**	0.0296	0.2138	0.2101
16	-	0.0053	**1.49e−08**	0.3081	0.3080
17	-	0.1162	**0.0570**	0.2418	0.2417
18	-	0.0257	**0.0248**	0.1243	0.1928
19	-	**8.01e−05**	0.0101	0.1733	0.1732
20	**0**	1.22e−05	6.43e−05	0.2050	0.1388

From this table, we see that only 5 times the RFSA with algebraic solver found a solution, either approximate or precise. For all other automata no solution could be found, even if there were only at most 15 variables in the system of equations. Interestingly, the approximate solution resulted for automaton 11 with the algebraic solver is not better than the one found by a genetic algorithm.

B   Appendix

From Table 4, we see that RFSA-GA outperforms other algorithms in 19 out of 20 experiments, proving the stability and generality of our RFSA-GA method.

From the Table 5, we see that 15 times the RFSA with SQP algorithm out-performs. We also see all RFSA and k-testable work well since F_1 score only considers how well to learn the positive samples.

Table 4. OP of all learned automata.

Nb	RFSA-flip	RFSA-GA	RFSA-SQP	k-testable	ALERGIA
1	0.9684	**0.9684**	0.9684	0.8287	0.3732
2	0.9890	**0.9890**	0.9890	0.8287	0.3402
3	0.9802	**0.9802**	0.9802	0.9303	0.3672
4	0.9162	**0.9211**	0.9071	0.7261	0.2539
5	0.9589	**0.9589**	0.9589	0.7426	0.2119
6	0.9520	0.9521	**0.9522**	0.7471	0.1326
7	0.9909	**0.9909**	0.9909	0.7714	0.3403
8	0.9691	**0.9691**	0.9691	0.8445	0.3648
9	0.9725	**0.9725**	0.9725	0.7674	0.2765
10	0.9820	**0.9820**	0.9820	0.7604	0.3436
11	0.9381	**0.9401**	0.9381	0.7658	0.3646
12	0.9955	**0.9955**	0.9685	0.7299	0.4503
13	0.9877	**0.9877**	0.9877	0.8697	0.4878
14	0.9745	**0.9745**	0.9745	0.8124	0.5544
15	0.9342	**0.9351**	0.8741	0.8804	0.1451
16	0.9315	**0.9325**	0.9315	0.7880	0.5377
17	0.9651	**0.9651**	0.8755	0.7577	0.3898
18	0.9829	**0.9829**	0.9829	0.7810	0.2608
19	0.9850	**0.9850**	0.9850	0.6998	0.2499
20	0.9840	**0.9840**	0.9840	0.7890	0.2817

Table 5. F_1 of all learned automata.

Nb	RFSA-flip	RFSA-GA	RFSA-SQP	k-testable	ALERGIA
1	0.999432	**0.999498**	0.999497	0.999362	0.987498
2	0.999752	0.999751	**0.999775**	0.999706	0.923148
3	0.999783	0.999790	**0.999813**	0.999731	0.999541
4	0.999832	0.999846	**0.999848**	0.999826	0.999819
5	0.999801	0.999806	**0.999811**	0.999772	0.998079
6	0.999809	0.999807	**0.999816**	0.999785	0.998923
7	0.999823	0.999819	**0.999825**	0.999806	0.999560
8	**0.999824**	0.999809	0.999821	0.999807	0.999603
9	**0.999795**	0.999754	0.999769	0.999766	0.999331
10	0.999819	0.999814	**0.999831**	0.999866	0.966374
11	0.999817	0.999811	**0.999819**	0.999809	0.999786
12	0.999888	0.999896	**0.999898**	0.999857	0.999648
13	0.999882	0.999889	**0.999892**	0.999862	0.999849
14	0.999898	0.999899	**0.999902**	0.999877	0.999587
15	0.999721	**0.999733**	0.999732	0.999733	0.999033
16	0.999719	0.999723	**0.999733**	0.999738	0.999787
17	0.999700	0.999704	**0.999707**	0.999698	0.998969
18	0.999823	0.999824	**0.999849**	0.999749	0.999636
19	0.999518	0.999595	**0.999595**	0.999502	0.998340
20	0.999700	**0.999701**	0.999700	0.999499	0.998910

References

1. Bahl, L.R., Brown, P.F., de Souza, P.V., Mercer, R.L.: Estimating hidden Markov model parameters so as to maximize speech recognition accuracy. IEEE Trans. Speech Audio Process. **1**(1), 77–83 (1993)
2. Baldi, P., Brunak, S.: Bioinformatics: The Machine Learning Approach. MIT Press, Cambridge (2001)
3. Baum, L.E., Petrie, T., Soules, G., Weiss, N.: A maximization technique occurring in the statistical analysis of probabilistic functions of Markov chains. Ann. Math. Stat. **41**(1), 164–171 (1970)
4. Bonnans, J.F., Gilbert, J.C., Lemaréchal, C., Sagastizábal, C.A.: Numerical Optimization: Theoretical and Practical Aspects. Springer, Heidelberg (2006). https://doi.org/10.1007/978-3-540-35447-5
5. Branco, P., Torgo, L., Ribeiro, R.P.: A survey of predictive modeling on imbalanced domains. ACM Comput. Surv. (CSUR) **49**(2), 1–50 (2016)
6. Carrasco, R.C., Oncina, J.: Learning stochastic regular grammars by means of a state merging method. In: Carrasco, R.C., Oncina, J. (eds.) ICGI 1994. LNCS, vol. 862, pp. 139–152. Springer, Heidelberg (1994). https://doi.org/10.1007/3-540-58473-0_144
7. Carrasco, R.C., Oncina, J.: Learning deterministic regular grammars from stochastic samples in polynomial time. RAIRO-Theor. Inform. Appl. **33**(1), 1–19 (1999)
8. Chu, W., Bonsangue, M.: Learning probabilistic languages by k-testable machines. In: 2020 International Symposium on Theoretical Aspects of Software Engineering (TASE), pp. 129–136. IEEE (2020)
9. Chu, W., Chen, S., Bonsangue, M.: Learning probabilistic automata using residuals. In: Cerone, A., Ölveczky, P.C. (eds.) ICTAC 2021. LNCS, vol. 12819, pp. 295–313. Springer, Cham (2021). https://doi.org/10.1007/978-3-030-85315-0_17
10. De La Higuera, C.: Characteristic sets for polynomial grammatical inference. Mach. Learn. **27**(2), 125–138 (1997)
11. Denis, F., Lemay, A., Terlutte, A.: Learning regular languages using RFSAs. Theor. Comput. Sci. **313**(2), 267–294 (2004)
12. Dupont, P., Denis, F., Esposito, Y.: Links between probabilistic automata and hidden Markov models: probability distributions, learning models and induction algorithms. Pattern Recogn. **38**(9), 1349–1371 (2005)
13. Durbin, R., Eddy, S.R., Krogh, A., Mitchison, G.: Biological Sequence Analysis: Probabilistic Models of Proteins and Nucleic Acids. Cambridge University Press, Cambridge (1998)
14. Feldmann, A., Whitt, W.: Fitting mixtures of exponentials to long-tail distributions to analyze network performance models. Perform. Eval. **31**(3–4), 245–279 (1998)
15. De la Higuera, C.: Grammatical Inference: Learning Automata and Grammars. Cambridge University Press, Cambridge (2010)
16. de la Higuera, C., Thollard, F., Vidal, E., Casacuberta, F., Carrasco, R.C.: Probabilistic finite state automata-part ii. Rapport technique RR-0403, EURISE (2004)
17. Jelinek, F.: Statistical Methods for Speech Recognition. MIT Press, Cambridge (1998)
18. Lee, K.F.: On large-vocabulary speaker-independent continuous speech recognition. Speech Commun. **7**(4), 375–379 (1988)
19. Meurer, A., et al.: SymPy: symbolic computing in python. PeerJ Comput. Sci. **3**, e103 (2017)

20. Mitchell, M.: An Introduction to Genetic Algorithms. MIT Press, Cambridge (1998)
21. Murphy, K.P., et al.: Passively Learning Finite Automata. Citeseer (1995)
22. Paz, A.: Introduction to Probabilistic Automata. Academic Press, Cambridge (2014)
23. Ranawana, R., Palade, V.: Optimized precision-a new measure for classifier performance evaluation. In: 2006 IEEE International Conference on Evolutionary Computation, pp. 2254–2261. IEEE (2006)
24. Ron, D., Singer, Y., Tishby, N.: On the learnability and usage of acyclic probabilistic finite automata. J. Comput. Syst. Sci. **56**(2), 133–152 (1998)
25. Sammut, C., Webb, G.I.: Encyclopedia of Machine Learning. Springer, Heidelberg (2011). https://doi.org/10.1007/978-0-387-30164-8
26. Turin, W.: Fitting probabilistic automata via the EM algorithm. Stoch. Model. **12**(3), 405–424 (1996)
27. Turin, W., Van Nobelen, R.: Hidden Markov modeling of flat fading channels. IEEE J. Sel. Areas Commun. **16**(9), 1809–1817 (1998)
28. Vidal, E., Thollard, F., de la Higuera, C., Casacuberta, F., Carrasco, R.: Probabilistic finite state automata-part I. Pattern Anal. Mach. Intell. **27**(7), 1013–1025 (2005)

Separation of Concerning Things: A Simpler Basis for Defining and Programming with the C/C++ Memory Model

Robert J. Colvin[✉]

Defence Science and Technology Group, and The School of ITEE, The University of
Queensland, Brisbane, Australia
`r.colvin@uq.edu.au`

Abstract. The C/C++ memory model provides a range of mechanisms
that programmers of concurrent code can use to control accesses to
shared variables. The C standard describes the memory model in terms of
cross-thread relationships between events, making thread-local, compositional reasoning difficult. In this paper we define the C memory model
as a relationship between instructions, straightforwardly based on fundamental properties of data dependencies or artificially injected ordering
constraints. Reasoning comprises program transformation with respect
to potential instruction reorderings. In the best case one can then reuse
an existing result from standard imperative techniques, or failing that
employ standard techniques to the transformed program. Other formalisations typically involve complex semantic models, requiring the development of specialised inference systems and assertion languages. A key
aspect of our work is that the memory model definition is kept separate
to other considerations of a rich programming language such as C. The
formal framework is especially suitable for concise code targeting x86,
Arm, and RISC-V architectures.

1 Introduction

The C memory model provides an interface for instrumenting shared-variable
concurrency. It abstracts from the multitude of multicore architectures to which
C may be compiled – each of which has its own guarantees about accesses to
shared variables – and provides information to the compiler about what optimisations can be made. The C standard describes the memory model in terms of a
cross-thread "happens before" relationship and cross-thread "release sequences".
The fundamentals of this approach were established by Boehm & Adve [3] and
subsequently influenced by research works (e.g., [2,31]). However, because it is
cross-thread, verification techniques are often complex to apply, and the resulting formal semantics are often highly specialised involving global data structures
capturing a partial order on events, and rarely cover the full range of features
available in C [4,19].

© Springer Nature Switzerland AG 2022
A. Riesco and M. Zhang (Eds.): ICFEM 2022, LNCS 13478, pp. 71–89, 2022.
https://doi.org/10.1007/978-3-031-17244-1_5

In this paper we take a separation-of-concerns approach to specifying and reasoning about concurrent code in C, where the three fundamental principles involved in the ordering of execution of concurrent C code – data dependencies, fences, and memory ordering constraints – are specified separately and straightforwardly to other aspects. We cover a significant portion of the C weak memory model, including release/acquire synchronisation, sequentially consistent accesses, and fences. In our framework a program c whose behaviour may contain reorderings according to the C memory model is transformed (via refinement) into a "plain" command c^- in which the parallelisation/nondeterminism is made explicit in the structure of the program. From here, c^- can be treated as a standard imperative program and previous results or existing reasoning techniques can be applied, assuming it is to be compiled to x86, Arm, or RISC-V architectures (if the Power architecture is targeted then aspects specific to it also need to be addressed, as outlined in Sect. 5). The framework also allows other features of C – which are present with or without the memory model being considered – to be handled (with the unavoidable corresponding complicating affect on reasoning).

We highlight this separation in the diagram below: the compiler may transform concurrent code into assembler, where the atomicity of instructions is explicit and the code may have been restructured and expressions optimised. The execution of the generated assembler is then further impacted by instruction-level parallelism in the processor, and potentially other unrelated microarchitectural features (such as Power's cache coherency system). The programmer may "fight back" by injecting fences or ordering constraints to maintain order.

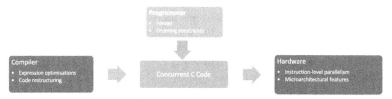

The combination of these factors creates a difficult environment for establishing correctness of the original code, however in the framework we provide standard techniques can be applied; this largely arises by keeping the memory model definition separate to compiler transformations and microarchitectural features.

We give an imperative language (with reordering via *parallelized sequential composition* [5]) in Sect. 2, and show how the C memory model is encoded in that language. We give a set of transformation rules for reasoning about the effects of the memory model in Sect. 3, and explain how standard reasoning techniques can be applied in Sect. 4. In Sect. 5 we briefly describe other aspects of C that can affect reasoning, and discuss related work in Sect. 6.

2   An Imperative Language with Instruction Reordering

The syntax of the language $\text{IMP}_{+\text{pseq}}$ is given in Fig. 1, which is as described in [5, 6,8] extended syntactically with some features specific to C. A *memory ordering*

$$\text{OC} ::= \text{RLX} \mid \text{REL} \mid \text{ACQ} \mid \text{CON} \mid \text{SC} \tag{1}$$

$$e ::= v \mid x^{ocs} \mid \ominus e \mid e_1 \oplus e_2 \tag{2}$$

$$f ::= \text{store}_\text{fnc} \mid \text{load}_\text{fnc} \mid \text{full}_\text{fnc} \tag{3}$$

$$\alpha ::= x^{ocs} := e \mid (\!| e |\!) \mid f^{ocs} \tag{4}$$

$$\mathbf{rel\_fence} \mathrel{\hat=} \text{store}_\text{fnc}{}^\text{REL} \qquad \mathbf{acq\_fence} \mathrel{\hat=} \text{load}_\text{fnc}{}^\text{ACQ} \qquad \mathbf{sc\_fence} \mathrel{\hat=} \text{full}_\text{fnc}{}^\text{SC} \tag{5}$$

$$c ::= \mathbf{nil} \mid \alpha \mid c_1 \overset{\text{M}}{;} c_2 \mid c_1 \sqcap c_2 \mid c_\text{M}^* \tag{6}$$

$$c_1 ; c_2 \mathrel{\hat=} c_1 \overset{\text{C}}{;} c_2 \qquad c_1 \centerdot c_2 \mathrel{\hat=} c_1 \overset{\text{SC}}{;} c_2 \qquad c_1 \parallel c_2 \mathrel{\hat=} c_1 \overset{\text{PAR}}{;} c_2 \tag{7}$$

$$\mathbf{if}^\text{M} \; b \; \mathbf{then} \; c_1 \; \mathbf{else} \; c_2 \mathrel{\hat=} (\!| b |\!) \overset{\text{M}}{;} c_1 \; \sqcap \; (\!| \neg b |\!) \overset{\text{M}}{;} c_2 \tag{8}$$

$$\mathbf{while}^\text{M} \; b \; \mathbf{do} \; c \mathrel{\hat=} ((\!| b |\!) \overset{\text{M}}{;} c)_\text{M}^* \overset{\text{M}}{;} (\!| \neg b |\!) \tag{9}$$

Fig. 1. Syntax of IMP$_\text{+pseq}$

constraint OC, used to control the ordering of variable accesses and fences, can be one of several types (1), which we discuss in Sect. 2.1. Expressions e can be base values v, variables x paired with a (possibly empty) set *ocs* of memory ordering constraints, or involve the usual unary ($\ominus$) or binary ($\oplus$) operators (2). A primitive fence f may be a store fence, load fence, or full fence (3). A primitive action α is either an assignment $x^{ocs} := e$ where x is a variable, *ocs* a set of ordering constraints, and e an expression; a guard c where e is an expression; or a fence f^{ocs}, where f is a primitive fence and *ocs* is a set of ordering constraints. For convenience we use the following abbreviations: for a variable r with an empty set of ordering constraints (i.e., a local variable) we let r abbreviate $r^\varnothing$; for a singleton set of ordering constraints we let x^{oc} abbreviate $x^{\{oc\}}$, and where appropriate we let x abbreviate x^RLX (i.e., by convention RLX is the default ordering constraint); and similarly for f a fence, f^{oc} abbreviates $f^{\{oc\}}$. We discuss C's fences (5) in Sect. 2.1.

Commands (6) include the terminated command, **nil**, an instruction, α (the extension to composite actions is straightforward), the parallelized sequential composition of two commands according to some memory model M, $c_1 \overset{\text{M}}{;} c_2$, a choice between two commands, $c_1 \sqcap c_2$, or a parallelized iteration of a command according to some memory model M, c_M^*.

The memory model paramaters M are relations on instructions (*reordering relations*), where, given $\alpha \overset{\text{M}}{;} \beta$, instruction α can be executed next as with standard sequential composition, *or* β can be executed next provided $(\alpha, \beta) \in \text{M}$. We define three memory models in this paper: C for C's memory model, defined in the next section; SC for sequential consistency; and PAR for parallelism. We define the latter two below where, here and throughout the paper, given a relation M we write $a \overset{\text{M}}{\Leftarrow} b$ for $(a, b) \in \text{M}$ and $a \overset{\text{M}}{\nLeftarrow} b$ for $\neg(a \overset{\text{M}}{\Leftarrow} b)$. For all instructions α, β,

$$\alpha \overset{\text{SC}}{\Leftarrow} \beta \; \Leftrightarrow \; \text{False} \qquad \alpha \overset{\text{PAR}}{\Leftarrow} \beta \; \Leftrightarrow \; \text{True} \tag{10}$$

We use . as an abbreviation for $\overset{\scriptscriptstyle{SC}}{;}$ and $\|$ for $\overset{\scriptscriptstyle{PAR}}{;}$ (7). As shown in [5], given the definitions in (10), '$\overset{\scriptscriptstyle{SC}}{;}$' and '$\overset{\scriptscriptstyle{PAR}}{;}$' correspond to the usual notions of sequential and parallel composition, respectively. For '$\overset{\scriptscriptstyle{C}}{;}$' we leave the C parameter implicit.

Conditionals (8) and while loops (9) are constructed in the usual way using guards and iteration, parameterised by a memory model. As is standard, if a guard evaluates to False this represents a behaviour that cannot occur. We define an empty False branch conditional, $\textbf{if}^{\scriptscriptstyle M}\ b\ \textbf{then}\ c$, as $\textbf{if}^{\scriptscriptstyle M}\ b\ \textbf{then}\ c\ \textbf{else nil}$. Treating a guard as a separate action is useful in breaking down allowed reorderings, and in understanding the interaction of conditionals with compiler optimisations as discussed in Sect. 4.1.

A small-step operational semantics for $\mathsf{IMP_{+pseq}}$ is outlined in Sect. A, adapted from [5], from which is derived trace-based and relational semantics.

2.1   Reordering in C

We now give the specifics of reordering in the C memory model, which considers three aspects: (i) variable (data) dependencies; (ii) fences; and (iii) "memory ordering constraints", that can be used to annotate variables or fences. We cover each of these three aspects in turn.

Respecting Data Dependencies/Sequential Semantics. A key concept underpinning both processor pipelines and compiler transformations is that of data dependencies. We write $\alpha \rightsquigarrow \beta$ if instruction β references a variable that instruction α writes to, and $\alpha \not\rightsquigarrow \beta$ if not. For instance, $x := 1 \rightsquigarrow r := x$ but $x := 1 \not\rightsquigarrow r := y$. The relevant definitions are given below.

$$\mathsf{wv}(.), \mathsf{rv}(.), \mathsf{fv}(.)\quad \text{Write, read and free variables, respectively} \tag{11}$$

$$\alpha \rightsquigarrow \beta\ \ \widehat{=}\ \ \mathsf{wv}(\alpha) \cap \mathsf{rv}(\beta) \neq \varnothing \tag{12}$$

$$\mathsf{wsv}(.), \mathsf{rsv}(.), \mathsf{sv}(.)\quad \text{As above, restricted to Shared} \tag{13}$$

The write and read variables of instructions are collected syntactically, and the free variables of an instruction are the union of the two (11) (for a full definition of these and other functions on the syntax see Sect. A). Then $\alpha \rightsquigarrow \beta$ if the set of write variables of α and read variables of β are disjoint (12). Shared and local variables have different requirements from a reordering perspective and so we introduce specialisations of write, read and free variables to just the shared variables (13). That is, the set Var is divided into two mutually exclusive and exhaustive sets of local (Local) and shared (Shared) variables. By convention we let x, y, z be shared variables and $r, r_1, r_2 \ldots$ be local variables.

We say β may be *reordered before* α with respect to data dependency concerns, captured in relation D, if there is no data dependence in either direction, they modify distinct variables, and if they read distinct *shared* variables; the latter constraint maintains "coherence" of loads. For convenience below we write $s_1 \not\between s_2$ to mean that sets s_1 and s_2 are mutually exclusive ($s_1 \cap s_2 = \varnothing$).

$$\alpha \overset{\scriptscriptstyle D}{\Leftarrow} \beta\ \ \widehat{=}\ \ \alpha \not\rightsquigarrow \beta \wedge \beta \not\rightsquigarrow \alpha \wedge \mathsf{wv}(\alpha) \not\between \mathsf{wv}(\beta) \wedge \mathsf{rsv}(\alpha) \not\between \mathsf{rsv}(\beta) \tag{14}$$

If $\alpha \stackrel{D}{\Leftarrow} \beta$ then, taking the usual interpretation of programs as relations on states, the effect of executing α then β is the same as executing β then α. The condition $\alpha \stackrel{D}{\Leftarrow} \beta$ can be checked syntactically (although semantic checks are also possible).

As examples of what D allows and disallows consider the following cases, where we assume $x, y \in$ Shared, $r, r_1, r_2 \in$ Local, and all are distinct, and $v, w \in$ Val. Firstly, independent stores can be reordered, but not stores to the same variable, i.e., $x := v \stackrel{D}{\Leftarrow} y := w$ but $x := v \stackrel{D}{\nLeftarrow} x := w$, and similarly independent stores and loads can be reordered, i.e., $x := v \stackrel{D}{\Leftarrow} r := y$ and $r_1 := x \stackrel{D}{\Leftarrow} r_2 := y$, but $x := v \stackrel{D}{\nLeftarrow} r := x$ and $r_1 := x \stackrel{D}{\nLeftarrow} r_2 := x$. Accesses of the same local variable, however, can be reordered since no interference is possible, i.e., $x := r \stackrel{D}{\Leftarrow} y := r$. Finally, stores can be reordered before (independent) guards, i.e., $(\!|r = v|\!) \stackrel{D}{\Leftarrow} x := w$ Since guards model branch points, this is a significant aspect of C as we explore in Sect. 4.1, and is the main point of difference with the hardware memory models defined in [5].

Respecting Fences. C's "fence" instructions are one way to enforce order on otherwise (data) independent instructions. Relation FNC relates primitive fences (3) and instructions.

$$\mathsf{store_{fnc}} \stackrel{FNC}{\nLeftarrow} \alpha \;\Leftrightarrow\; \mathsf{wsv}(\alpha) \neq \varnothing \qquad \mathsf{load_{fnc}} \stackrel{FNC}{\nLeftarrow} \alpha \;\Leftrightarrow\; \mathsf{rsv}(\alpha) \neq \varnothing$$
$$\mathsf{full_{fnc}} \stackrel{FNC}{\nLeftarrow} \alpha \quad \text{for all } \alpha$$

Hence a store fence blocks store instructions (those that write to a shared variable), while load fences block loads (those that read a shared variable) and a "full" fence blocks all instruction types. We lift this to instructions as follows.

$$\alpha \stackrel{FNC}{\Leftarrow} \beta \;\;\hat{=}\;\; (\forall f \in |\alpha| \bullet f \stackrel{FNC}{\Leftarrow} \beta) \;\wedge\; (\forall f \in |\beta| \bullet f \stackrel{FNC}{\Leftarrow} \alpha)$$

where $|\alpha|$ extracts the fences present in α, if any. Hence α and β can be reordered (considering fences only) if they each respect the others' fences. (Note that all C fences are defined symmetrically.) For example, $x := 1 \stackrel{FNC}{\nLeftarrow} \mathsf{store_{fnc}}$ but $\mathsf{store_{fnc}} \stackrel{FNC}{\Leftarrow} r := x$.

Respecting Memory Ordering Constraints. C introduces several types of "memory ordering constraints" (which we herewith call ordering constraints), used to tag loads and stores of variables declared to be "atomic" (e.g., type `atomic_int` for a shared integer). Similar to fences, these ordering constraints control how atomic variables interact.

Relaxed (RLX). A *relaxed* access is the simplest, not adding any extra constraints to the variable access, allowing both the hardware and compiler to potentially reorder independent relaxed accesses. For instance, given the code $x^{\mathrm{RLX}} := 1$; $flag^{\mathrm{RLX}} :=$ True, if the programmer's intention was that the $flag$ variable is set to True after the data x is set to 1, then they have erred: either the compiler or the hardware may reorder the independent stores to x and $flag$.

Release (REL). The *release* tag can be applied to stores, a typical use being to set a flag indicating the end of a set of shared accesses. For example, modifying the above code to $x^{\text{RLX}} := 1$; $\mathit{flag}^{\text{REL}} := \mathsf{True}$ now ensures that any other process that sees $\mathit{flag} = \mathsf{True}$ knows that the earlier update to x has taken effect.

Acquire (ACQ). The *acquire* tag can be applied to loads, and is the reciprocal of a release: any subsequent instructions will see everything the acquire can see. For example, continuing from above, a simple process that reads the flag in parallel with the above process may be written as follows: $f := \mathit{flag}^{\text{ACQ}}$; $r := x^{\text{RLX}}$. In this case the loads are kept in order by the acquire constraint, and hence at the end of the program, in the absence of any other interference, $f \Rightarrow r = 1$.

Sequentially Consistent (SC). The *sequentially consistent* constraint is the strongest, forcing order between SC-tagged instructions and any other instructions. For example, the snippet $x^{\text{SC}} := 1$; $\mathit{flag}^{\text{SC}} := \mathsf{True}$ ensures $\mathit{flag} \Rightarrow x = 1$ (in fact only one instruction needs the constraint for this to hold). This is considered a "heavyweight" method for enforcing order.

The standard also includes "consume" (CON) ordering constraints, which can be incorporated straightforwardly into the framework [7], and ACQREL constraints which combine an acquire and release component. Additionally shared data can be "non-atomic", i.e., shared variables that are not declared of type `atomic_*`, and as such cannot be directly associated with the ordering constraints above. Programs which attempt to concurrently access shared data without any ordering mechanisms have essentially no guarantees about their behaviour, and so we ignore such programs. For programs that include shared non-atomic variables which are correctly synchronised, i.e., are associated with some ordering mechanism (e.g., barriers or acquire/release flag variables) they can be treated as if *relaxed*, and are subject to the same potential reorderings and optimisations.

The relationship, OC, between ordering constraints is defined below.

$$\text{OC} \cong \{(\text{RLX}, \text{RLX}), (\text{RLX}, \text{ACQ}), (\text{REL}, \text{RLX}), (\text{REL}, \text{ACQ})\} \tag{15}$$

Expressing the relation as a negative is perhaps more intuitive, i.e., for all constraints OC, OC $\overset{\text{OC}}{\not\Longleftarrow}$ SC $\overset{\text{OC}}{\not\Longleftarrow}$ OC, OC $\overset{\text{OC}}{\not\Longleftarrow}$ REL, and ACQ $\overset{\text{OC}}{\not\Longleftarrow}$ OC.

We lift this to a relation on instructions, OCS.

$$\alpha \overset{\text{OCS}}{\Longleftarrow} \beta \cong \lceil\alpha\rceil \times \lceil\beta\rceil \subseteq \text{OC} \tag{16}$$

where the $\lceil.\rceil$ function extracts the ordering constraints from the expression and instructions syntax, e.g., $\lceil x^{\text{REL}} := y^{\text{ACQ}}\rceil = \{\text{REL}, \text{ACQ}\}$. Thus $\alpha \overset{\text{OCS}}{\Longleftarrow} \beta$ is checked by comparing point-wise each pair of ordering constraints in α and β.

The Complete Reordering Relation. We define the C memory model as the combination of the three aspects above.

$$\alpha \overset{\text{C}}{\Longleftarrow} \beta \;\; \cong \;\; \text{(i) } \alpha \overset{\text{D}}{\Longleftarrow} \beta, \;\; \text{(ii) } \alpha \overset{\text{FNC}}{\Longleftarrow} \beta, \;\; \text{and (iii) } \alpha \overset{\text{OCS}}{\Longleftarrow} \beta \tag{17}$$

Hence reordering of instructions within a C program can occur provided the data dependencies, fences, and ordering constraints are respected. The three reordering relations (on instructions) forming C lift straightforwardly to commands.

For example, for distinct $x, y \in$ Shared and $r, r_i \in$ Local, from D we can derive $x := 1 \overset{C}{\Leftarrow} y := 1$ and $r_1 := x \overset{C}{\Leftarrow} r_2 := y$. Taking relation OCS into account we have $y := 1 \overset{C}{\nLeftarrow} x^{\text{REL}} := 1$ but $x^{\text{REL}} := 1 \overset{C}{\Leftarrow} r := y$, and $r_1 := x^{\text{ACQ}} \overset{C}{\nLeftarrow} r_2 := y$ but $r_1 := y \overset{C}{\Leftarrow} r_2 := x^{\text{ACQ}}$.

Recall from (5) that we define C's fences (`atomic_thread_fence(.)`) as the combination of a primitive fence and an ordering constraint: a "release fence" **rel_fence** blocks stores and additionally operates as a REL action; similarly an "acquire fence" **acq_fence** acts as a load fence with an ACQ ordering; and a "sequentially consistent" fence **sc_fence** blocks all operations. We can therefore calculate, for all α, $\alpha \overset{C}{\nLeftarrow}$ **rel_fence** and **rel_fence** $\overset{C}{\Leftarrow} r := x$, and similarly **acq_fence** $\overset{C}{\nLeftarrow} \alpha$ and $x := 1 \overset{C}{\Leftarrow}$ **acq_fence**.

3 Transformation to Sequential or Parallel Form

The following properties have been derived and machine-checked for $\text{IMP}_{\text{+pseq}}$ [5]. Program c *refines to* c', written $c \sqsubseteq c'$, iff every behaviour of c' is a behaviour of c, and $c \sqsubseteq d$ is refinement in both directions. The standard operators of the language satisfy the usual properties of commutativity, associativity, etc.

$$c_1 \overset{M}{;} c_2 \sqsubseteq c_1 \bullet c_2 \tag{18}$$

$$c \sqcap d \sqsubseteq c \qquad c \sqcap d \sqsubseteq d \tag{19}$$

$$(\alpha \bullet c) \parallel d \sqsubseteq \alpha \bullet (c \parallel d) \tag{20}$$

$$c \parallel (\beta \bullet d) \sqsubseteq \beta \bullet (c \parallel d) \tag{21}$$

$$(c_1 \sqcap c_2) \parallel d \sqsubseteq (c_1 \parallel d) \sqcap (c_2 \parallel d) \tag{22}$$

$$(c_1 \overset{M}{;} c_2) \overset{M}{;} c_3 \sqsubseteq c_1 \overset{M}{;} (c_2 \overset{M}{;} c_3) \tag{23}$$

$$\alpha \overset{C}{\nLeftarrow} \beta \Rightarrow \alpha \, ; \beta \sqsubseteq \alpha \bullet \beta \tag{24}$$

$$\alpha \overset{C}{\Leftarrow} \beta \Rightarrow \alpha \, ; \beta \sqsubseteq \alpha \parallel \beta \tag{25}$$

$$\alpha \overset{C}{\Leftarrow} \beta \Rightarrow \alpha \, ; (\beta \bullet c) \sqsubseteq \beta \bullet (\alpha \, ; c) \tag{26}$$

Law 18 states that a parallelized sequential composition can always be refined to strict program (left-to-right) order. Law 19 states that a choice can be refined to either branch. Laws 20 and 21 state that the first instruction of either process in a parallel composition can be the first step of the composition as a whole. Such refinement rules are useful for elucidating specific reordering and interleavings of parallel processes that lead to particular behaviours. Law 22 is an equality, which states that if there is nondeterminism in a parallel process the effect can be understood by lifting the nondeterminism to the top level. Law 23 states that parallelized sequential composition is associative (provided the same model M is used on both instances). Laws 24 and 25 are special cases where, given two actions α and β, if they cannot reorder then they must be executed in program order, and if they can reorder it is as if they are executed in parallel, i.e., either order. Law 26 straightforwardly promotes action β of $\beta \bullet c$ before α, and depending on its structure further actions of c may be reordered before α. We can extend these rules to cover more complex program patterns.

$$c_1 \, ; \textbf{sc\_fence} \, ; c_2 \sqsubseteq c_1 \bullet \textbf{sc\_fence} \bullet c_2 \tag{27}$$

$$\textbf{if}^{\text{C}} \ y \geq 0 \ \textbf{then} \ x := y \sqsubseteq \textbf{if}^{\text{SC}} \ y \geq 0 \ \textbf{then} \ x := y \tag{28}$$

Law 27 shows that sequentially consistent fences enforce ordering on commands (lifted from the instruction level). Law 28 gives a special case of a conditional where the True branch depends on a shared variable in the condition, in which case the command is executed in-order.

Assuming $x \in$ Shared, $b \in$ Local, and that x is independent of commands c_1 and c_2 (i.e., $x \notin \mathsf{fv}(c_1) \cup \mathsf{fv}(c_2)$), we can derive the following.

$$(\mathbf{if}^c \ b \ \mathbf{then} \ c_1 \ \mathbf{else} \ c_2) \ ; \ x := v \ \sqsubseteq \ (\mathbf{if}^c \ b \ \mathbf{then} \ c_1 \ \mathbf{else} \ c_2) \ \| \ x := v$$

Loops can also be transformed, for example, consider a simple "await"-style loop, as used in lock implementations.

$$\mathsf{sv}(b) \neq \varnothing \ \Rightarrow \ \mathbf{while}^c \ b \ \mathbf{do} \ \mathbf{nil} \ \sqsubseteq \ \mathbf{while}^{sc} \ b \ \mathbf{do} \ \mathbf{nil} \tag{29}$$

Law 29 states that a spin-loop that polls a shared variable can be treated as if executed in strict order. These sort of structural rules help elucidate consequences of the memory model for programmers at a level that is easily understood.

4   Reasoning About Concurrent C

Assume that there is some program $c_{\mathtt{imp}}$, written in a standard concurrent imperative language (i.e., no weak memory model effects), which satisfies some property ϕ using method $\mathcal{M}$ (e.g., Owicki-Gries [27], rely/guarantee [15], linearisability [12], information flow security [28]). For convenience we will write this as $\mathcal{M} \vdash \phi(c)$. To port $c_{\mathtt{imp}}$ to concurrent C the programmer may write a new program c which has the same structure as $c_{\mathtt{imp}}$ but with injected fences and/or ordering constraints on accesses of global variables. In this scenario the question is whether $\phi(c)$ still holds, noting that in general $\mathcal{M}$ cannot be applied directly to c since its behaviours are different to $c_{\mathtt{imp}}$.

In our framework the C implementation c is encoded by (implicitly) replacing sequential composition in $c_{\mathtt{imp}}$ with parallelized sequential composition parameterised by C (17), and similarly for parallelized iteration. The semantics of $\mathtt{IMP}_{\mathtt{+pseq}}$ can be used to generate the behaviours (traces, i.e., sequences of actions) and perform trace-based, exhaustive analyses. However the semantics also supports program transformation, and in particular transforming c into some "plain" program c^- in which the extra behaviours due to reordering have been elaborated into a standard imperative form (e.g., using Laws 24 and 25), possibly containing nested parallelism or nondeterminism, and the memory model has been eliminated. We call this the "plain" subset of $\mathtt{IMP}_{\mathtt{+pseq}}$.

Definition 1 (Plain programs). *A command c of* $\mathtt{IMP}_{\mathtt{+pseq}}$ *is plain, i.e., in* $\mathtt{IMP}$, *if: (i) all instances of parallelized sequential composition in c are parameterised by either* SC *or* PAR, *and (ii) all parallelized iterations in c are parameterised by* SC.

A plain program c^- contains no instances of C, and as such any ordering constraints are ignored and fences can be treated as no-ops. We give some indicative scenarios for establishing a property of program c in $\text{IMP}_{+\text{pseq}}$ which is a C version of a structurally similar c_{imp} in an imperative language.

1. Proof reuse through order-preserving transformations. If the programmer-injected ordering constraints in c, in combination with the natural data dependencies, enforce an equivalence such that $c \,\square\, c^-$, where c^- in IMP is simply the original c with ';' becoming strict sequential, and hence c^- also has the same structure as c_{imp}, the original result $\mathcal{M} \vdash \phi(c_{\text{imp}})$ can be appealed to to derive $\phi(c^-)$ and as a result $\phi(c)$ as desired. The advantage in this situation is that the transformation to sequential form is straightforward – by appealing to the reordering relation – and a previous result is reused as-is.

2. Technique reuse for weaker behaviours. An alternative scenario is that the programmer-injected ordering constraints leave residual parallelism (nondeterminism) in the execution, and in this case the transformed c^-, while still being in IMP, can no longer reuse the proof of $\mathcal{M} \vdash \phi(c_{\text{imp}})$. However, one can still reuse the existing technique $\mathcal{M}$ to show $\phi(c^-)$ (or some other existing method), provided $\mathcal{M}$ can handle non-determinism or nested parallelism (such as rely/guarantee, or automata-based encodings, but not Owicki-Gries). If $\phi(c^-)$ is shown then $\phi(c)$ is immediate by assumption that $c \,\square\, c^-$.

3. Behaviours are too weak to establish ϕ. It is possible, however, that c has a behaviour that no longer satisfies ϕ, because the injected ordering constraints and/or fences are not sufficient. In this case one elucidates this problematic behaviour by refining $c \sqsubseteq c'$, where c' represents a particular interleaving and reordering such that $\phi(c')$ does not hold, which may again be shown using existing technique $\mathcal{M}$ or any other applicable method.

In the case where a novel program c in $\text{IMP}_{+\text{pseq}}$ is defined, with no earlier result $\mathcal{M} \vdash \phi(c_{\text{imp}})$, c is as above transformed into some c^- in IMP and then a suitable method is applied to show the desired property ϕ (or find an interleaving which contradicts it).

Alternative formalisations in the literature tend to keep the structure of c as-is, and define a specialised semantics where the nondeterminism due to potential reorderings is collected in a global data structure (often based around partial orders on events), and then specialised methods $\mathcal{M}^c$ along with specialised assertion languages that express some version ϕ^c of the original ϕ are defined, and applied directly to c (with no required transformation).

We note that the plain subset IMP of $\text{IMP}_{+\text{pseq}}$ has the standard semantics for an imperative language; it simply has ordering constraints on variables (which are ignored) and fences, which are also ignored and can be thought of as no-ops. For clarity we formalise this below.

Definition 2 (Imperative syntax equivalence). *Given a plain command c in $\text{IMP}_{+\text{pseq}}$, a command c_{imp} is imperative-syntax-equivalent to c if they are structurally and syntactically identical except that: (i) all variable references x^{ocs}*

in c appear in c_{imp} *as simply x; and (ii) no fence instructions are present in* c_{imp} *(they can be thought of as no-ops).*

We write $c \overset{plain}{\approx} c_{imp}$ if c is imperative-syntax-equivalent to c_{imp}, or if there exists a c' where $c \sqsubseteq c'$ and c' is imperative-syntax-equivalent to c_{imp}.

As an example, the following two programs are imperative-syntax-equivalent (where ';' in the program on the right should be interpreted as standard sequential composition).

$$x^{REL} := 1 \overset{SC}{;} y^{RLX} := 1 \overset{PAR}{;} r := z^{ACQ} \quad \overset{plain}{\approx} \quad x := 1 ; y := 1 \parallel r := z \tag{30}$$

The program on the left is plain because all instances of parallelized sequential composition correspond to sequential or parallel execution. As such the ordering constraints have no effect on behaviours, as they only influence reordering according to C (17) and are ignored by SC and PAR (10). A structurally typical case is the following, where **f** abbreviates an **sc_fence**. Note that the starting program is *not* plain, as it (implicitly) uses the C memory model, but the ordering mechanisms are enough to enforce strict order by Law 27.

$$(\alpha_1 ; \mathbf{f} ; \alpha_2) \parallel (\beta_1 ; \mathbf{f} ; \beta_2) \sqsubseteq (\alpha_1 . \mathbf{f} . \alpha_2) \parallel (\beta_1 . \mathbf{f} . \beta_2) \overset{plain}{\approx} (\mathsf{a_1} ; \mathsf{a_2}) \parallel (\mathsf{b_1} ; \mathsf{b_2}) \tag{31}$$

In the above $\mathsf{a}_i/\mathsf{b}_i$ are α_i/β_i with ordering constraints removed. For convenience we introduce notation for a program's plain interpretation.

Definition 3 (Plain interpretation). *Given a command c in* IMP$_{+pseq}$ *we let* c^- *be its plain interpretation, that is, c and* c^- *are syntactically and structurally identical except i) all instances of parallelized sequential composition and parallelized iteration in c are instantiated in* c^- *by* SC, *except for those instantiated by* PAR; *and ii) fences in c do not appear in* c^-.

4.1   Examples

In the following examples we use Hoare triples [13] to specify and prove properties of programs, as they most easily map to concurrent analysis via Owicki-Gries reasoning [27] or rely/guarantee [15] (several examples of this approach for Owicki-Gries appear in [5]). We use the following properties, where $\{p\} c \{q\}$ is a typical Hoare logic statement, and $\langle\!\langle p \rangle\!\rangle c \langle\!\langle q \rangle\!\rangle \mathrel{\hat{=}} \neg \{p\} c \{\neg q\}$ is the conjugate form [24] giving reachable/possible final states.

$$c \sqsubseteq c' \;\Rightarrow\; \{p\} c \{q\} \Leftrightarrow \{p\} c' \{q\} \tag{32}$$

$$c \sqsubseteq c' \wedge \{p\} c' \{\neg q\} \;\Rightarrow\; \neg \{p\} c \{q\} \tag{33}$$

$$c \sqsubseteq c' \wedge \{p\} c' \{q\} \;\Rightarrow\; \langle\!\langle p \rangle\!\rangle c \langle\!\langle q \rangle\!\rangle \quad \text{(Provided } \langle\!| p |\!\rangle . c' \text{ is feasible)} \tag{34}$$

Equation (32) allows properties of a transformed program to carry over to the original program. Alternatively by (33) if *any* behaviour is found to violate a property then that property cannot hold for the original. Finally by (34) if *any* behaviour is found to satisfy a property then it is a *possible* behaviour of the original (excluding miraculous cases which trivially reach any state).

Abstract Examples. Recall program (31): $(\alpha_1\,;\mathbf{f}\,;\alpha_2) \parallel (\beta_1\,;\mathbf{f}\,;\beta_2)$. To establish this program satisfies some Hoare triple one can use the Owicki-Gries method on the plain program $(\alpha_1 \cdot \alpha_2) \parallel (\beta_1 \cdot \beta_2)$. The fences enforce program order, and so whether the property holds for the program coded in C depends on whether it holds for the plain version, which can be determined using standard techniques.

Now consider the following slightly more complex case with nested parallelism, where one process uses a form of critical section. Assume $\alpha \overset{c}{\Leftarrow} \beta$, let $\mathbf{f}$ abbreviate **sc_fence**, and apply Laws 27 and 25.

$$(\gamma_1\,;\mathbf{f}\,;\alpha\,;\beta\,;\mathbf{f}\,;\gamma_2) \parallel (\gamma_3\,;\mathbf{f}\,;\gamma_4) \ \sqsubseteq\ (\gamma_1 \cdot \mathbf{f} \cdot (\alpha \parallel \beta) \cdot \mathbf{f} \cdot \gamma_2) \parallel (\gamma_3 \cdot \mathbf{f} \cdot \gamma_4)$$
$$\overset{plain}{\approx} (\gamma_1 \cdot (\alpha \parallel \beta) \cdot \gamma_2) \parallel (\gamma_3 \cdot \gamma_4)$$

The Owicki-Gries method is not directly applicable due to the nested parallelism (although in this case could be flattened out into nondeterministic choice), but the compositional rely/guarantee method can be used instead. Transformations can also make some sense out of otherwise complex relationships, for instance:

$$r_1 := x\,;\, z := 1\,;\, r_2 := y\,;\, z := 2\,;\, x := 3\,;\, y := 1$$
$$\sqsubseteq (r_1 := x \cdot x := 3) \parallel (z := 1 \cdot z := 2) \parallel (r_2 := y \cdot y := 1)$$

The derived structure shows exactly the way an Arm or RISC-V processor might execute this program – data-dependent instructions are kept in-order but data-independent instructions may execute in parallel.

We now give some more concrete examples. To save space we define $0_{x,y,\ldots} \,\hat{=}\, x = 0 \wedge y = 0 \wedge \ldots$ as an initialisation predicate for $x, y, \ldots$ a list of variables.

Message Passing. Consider the message-passing communication pattern.

$$\mathsf{mp} \,\hat{=}\, (x := 1\,;\, flag := 1) \parallel (f := flag\,;\, r := x) \tag{35}$$

The question is whether in the final state that $f = 1 \Rightarrow r = 1$, i.e., if the "flag" is observed to have been set, can one assume that the "data" (x) has been transferred? This is of course expected under a plain interpretation (Definition (3)).

$$\{0_{x,y,r,f}\}\,\mathsf{mp}^- \{f = 1 \Rightarrow r = 1\} \tag{36}$$

This can be proved using rely/guarantee inference: the key part of the proof is the left process guarantees $x = 0 \Rightarrow flag = 0$ and $flag = 1 \Rightarrow x = 1$.

If we naively code this pattern in C, however, where variable accesses are (implicitly) relaxed, the property no longer holds, i.e., $\neg\{0_{x,y,r,f}\}\,\mathsf{mp}\,\{f = 1 \Rightarrow r = 1\}$. This is because by definition both $(x := 1) \overset{c}{\Leftarrow} (flag := 1)$ and $(f := flag) \overset{c}{\Leftarrow} (r := x)$, and as a consequence, all instructions effectively execute in parallel, i.e., by Law 25, $(x := 1\,;\, flag := 1) \parallel (f := flag\,;\, r := x) \sqsubseteq x := 1 \parallel flag := 1 \parallel f := flag \parallel r := x$. We can pick a particular execution order (using Laws 20 and 21) that violates the postcondition, for instance, $\{0_{x,y,r,f}\}\,flag := 1 \cdot f := flag \cdot r := x \cdot x := 1\{\neg(f = 1 \Rightarrow r = 1)\}$. By (33) the naive encoding violates the desired property.

Release/acquire atomics are the recommended way to instrument message passing as made explicit below on *flag* (leaving x relaxed).

$$\mathsf{mp}^{RA} \mathrel{\widehat{=}} (x := 1 \,;\, flag^{\mathrm{REL}} := 1) \parallel (f := flag^{\mathrm{ACQ}} \,;\, r := x) \tag{37}$$

The new constraints prevent reordering in each branch and therefore the expected outcome is reached, that is, $\{0_{x,y,r_1,r_2}\}\,\mathsf{mp}^{RA}\,\{f = 1 \Rightarrow r = 1\}$, because by the definition of C (17) we have both $(x := 1) \mathrel{\not\overset{C}{\leftarrow}} (y^{\mathrm{REL}} := 1)$ and $(r_1 := y^{\mathrm{ACQ}}) \mathrel{\not\overset{C}{\leftarrow}}$ $(r := x)$, and hence $\mathsf{mp}^{RA} \mathrel{\sqsubseteq} (x := 1 \boldsymbol{.} y^{\mathrm{REL}} := 1) \parallel (r_1 := y^{\mathrm{ACQ}} \boldsymbol{.} r := x) \overset{plain}{\approx} \mathsf{mp}^{-}$. The proof now follows immediately from (36).

An alternative approach to restoring order is to insert fences as shown below, which also trivially transform to mp^{-}.

$$(x := 1 \,;\, \mathbf{sc\_fence} \,;\, flag := 1) \parallel (f := flag \,;\, \mathbf{sc\_fence} \,;\, r := x)$$
$$(x := 1 \,;\, \mathbf{rel\_fence} \,;\, flag := 1) \parallel (f := flag \,;\, \mathbf{acq\_fence} \,;\, r := x)$$

Out-of-Thin-Air Behaviours. We now turn our attention to the "out of thin air" problem [4], which arises in some memory model specifications, where values may be assigned even though those values do not appear in the program. Firstly consider the following program, oota, which appears in the C standard.

$$r_1 := x \,;\, (\mathbf{if}^C \ r_1 = 42 \ \mathbf{then} \ y := 42) \parallel r_2 := y \,;\, (\mathbf{if}^C \ r_2 = 42 \ \mathbf{then} \ x := 42) \tag{38}$$

Under a plain interpretation neither store ever happens: one of the loads must occur, and the subsequent test fail, first, preventing the condition in the other process from succeeding, i.e., $\{0_{x,y,r_1,r_2}\}\,\mathsf{oota}^{-}\,\{x = 0 \land y = 0\}$. However, under the C memory model, both local variables may receive the value 42 (although compiler writers are discouraged from allowing this). In our framework this behaviour occurs straightforwardly because (unlike hardware memory models [5]) stores may be reordered before guards via the $\overset{D}{\leftarrow}$ relation (14), that is,

$$\langle\!\langle 0_{x,y,r_1,r_2} \rangle\!\rangle \ \mathsf{oota} \ \langle\!\langle x = 42 \land y = 42 \rangle\!\rangle$$

Proof. Focus on the left process of oota (38).

$\quad r_1 := x \,;\, (\mathbf{if}^C \ r_1 = 42 \ \mathbf{then} \ y := 42)$
$\square\quad$ Defn. (8)
$\quad r_1 := x \,;\, ((\!(r_1 = 42)\!) \,;\, y := 42) \sqcap (\!(r_1 \neq 42)\!)$
$\sqsubseteq\quad$ Law 19
$\quad r_1 := x \,;\, (\!(r_1 = 42)\!) \,;\, y := 42$
$\square\quad$ Law 25 from $(\!(r_1 = 42)\!) \overset{C}{\leftarrow} y := 42$
$\quad r_1 := x \,;\, ((\!(r_1 = 42)\!) \parallel y := 42)$
$\sqsubseteq\quad$ By $\alpha \parallel \beta \sqsubseteq \beta \boldsymbol{.} \alpha$ (cf., Law 21)
$\quad r_1 := x \,;\, (y := 42 \boldsymbol{.} (\!(r_1 = 42)\!))$
$\sqsubseteq\quad$ Law 26 from $r_1 := x \overset{C}{\leftarrow} y := 42$; Law 18
$\quad y := 42 \boldsymbol{.} r_1 := x \boldsymbol{.} (\!(r_1 = 42)\!)$

The second process transforms similarly to $x := 42 . r_2 := y . (\!|r_2 = 42|\!)$. Interleaving the two processes (Laws 20 and 21) gives the following transformation to a particular execution.

$$\textsf{oota} \sqsubseteq (y := 42 . r_1 := x . (\!|r_1 = 42|\!)) \parallel (x := 42 . r_2 := y . (\!|r_2 = 42|\!))$$
$$\sqsubseteq y := 42 . x := 42 . r_1 := x . r_2 := y . (\!|r_1 = 42|\!) . (\!|r_2 = 42|\!)$$

Straightforward sequential reasoning gives the following.

$$\{0_{x,y,r_1,r_2}\} \, y := 42 . x := 42 . r_1 := x . r_2 := y . (\!|r_1 = 42|\!) . (\!|r_2 = 42|\!) \, \{x = 42 \wedge y = 42\}$$

The final state is therefore possible by (34).   □

Under *hardware* memory models (the observable effects of) writes cannot happen before branch points, and so dependency cycles and out-of-thin-air behaviours are not possible.

Consider the following variant of oota, which we call $\textsf{oota}_\textsf{D}$.

$$r_1 := x \,;\, (\textbf{if}^\textsf{c} \; r_1 = 42 \; \textbf{then} \; y := r_1) \quad \parallel \quad r_2 := y \,;\, (\textbf{if}^\textsf{c} \; r_2 = 42 \; \textbf{then} \; x := r_2) \quad (39)$$

The inner assignments have changed from $y := 42$ (resp. $x := 42$) to $y := r_1$ (resp. $x := r_2$). Arguably the compiler knows that within the true branch of the conditional it must be the case that $r_1 = 42$, and thus the assignment $y := r_1$ can be treated as $y := 42$, transforming to the original oota. But this outcome is expressly disallowed, by both the standard and naturally in our framework.

$$\{0_{x,y,r_1,r_2}\} \, \textsf{oota}_\textsf{D} \, \{x = 0 \wedge y = 0\} \quad (40)$$

Proof. The initial load into r_1 creates a dependency with the rest of the code, i.e., $r_1 := x \not\overset{\mathscr{L}}{=} (\textbf{if}^\textsf{c} \; r_1 = 42 \; \textbf{then} \; y := r_1 \; \textbf{else})$. Hence we can sequence the initial load of x (into r_1) with the remaining code.

$$r_1 := x \,;\, (\textbf{if}^\textsf{c} \; r_1 = 42 \; \textbf{then} \; y := r_1) \quad \sqsubseteq \quad r_1 := x . (\textbf{if}^\textsf{c} \; r_1 = 42 \; \textbf{then} \; y := r_1)$$

Although the guard and the assignment in the conditional may be reordered with each other (i.e., $(\!|r_1 = 42|\!) \overset{\mathscr{C}}{\Leftarrow} y := r_1$), the fact that the initial load must happen first means that, similarly to the plain case of oota, there is no execution of $\textsf{oota}_\textsf{D}$ in which a non-zero value is written to any variable.   □

Note that the C standard allows the behaviour of oota and forbids the behaviour of $\textsf{oota}_\textsf{D}$, and both results arise naturally in our framework.

5   Further Extensions

In this section we discuss some other extensions to the language and semantics that may be relevant to some programs; however we emphasise that the definition of the memory model does not need to change, we simply make the language and its execution model richer. All of these, with the exception of *forwarding*, remove the link between the syntax of the program as-written and the underlying indivisible steps the program may take.

Definition 4. *We say a program is* atomically-structured *if all basic building blocks (conditions, assignments) are evaluated/ executed atomically, and execution proceeds in program-order.*

Note that the *plain* (Definition (1)) subset of IMP$_{+pseq}$ is atomically-structured. Most inference systems for concurrent code apply only to atomically-structured code, and it is non-trivial to apply syntax-based approaches if the syntax does not directly map to execution (although many other approaches are still applicable to non-atomically-structured code, for instance, model checking). We emphasise that C programs are in general not atomically-structured, and this complicates analysis by some techniques, regardless of whether or not the C memory model is taken into account. An advantage of our framework is that any previously developed technique can be applied after the possible behaviours are elaborated via transformation.

Several relevant aspects of C are outlined below (see [7] for more detail).

Incremental Evaluation of Expressions. In C and other languages expressions involving more than one shared variable may be evaluated in several steps, possibly admitting interference during the evaluation (for instance, $x = x$ can theoretically evaluate to False). Incremental evaluation, including optimisation steps (see below), is straightforward to add to the semantics, as is the addition of composite actions (e.g., read-modify-writes) which allow the combination of guards and updates into a single indivisible step.

Expression Optimisation. Compilers will typically optimise expressions to improve efficiency, for instance, as a simple case, $x * 0$ can be optimised to just 0, saving an access of main memory. Such optimisations are more fraught in the presence of ordering constraints, as the optimisation of $r := x^{\text{ACQ}} * 0$ to $r := 0$ removes an acquire constraint which may now allow more behaviours than were possible before by the OCS relation, and similarly optimising away variable references may allow further reorderings by the D relation. Such concerns can be used as the basis to allow or discard optimisation strategies, of which several options and their consequences are discussed in [7].

Forwarding. Processor pipelines will often allow the transfer of calculated values from one instruction to a later one, possibly before the earlier instruction has "committed", a mechanism called "forwarding" (e.g., in $x := 1; r := x$ immediately assigning 1 to local r saves waiting for $x := 1$ to propagate to main memory). This aspect of weak memory models is straightforward to incorporate into the framework, as shown in [5,6].

Incorporating Compiler Transformations. Compiler transformations can be incorporated straightforwardly into our framework, for instance, if *pattern* is some code pattern that can be transformed into *pattern'* then this can become a transformation *pattern* $\sqsubseteq$ *pattern'* (an example of such a transformation might be to refactor a loop). Of course, depending on the complexity of transformation, this complicates reasoning. It is infeasible for the definition of C memory model to address every possible transformation of every possible compiler; however our framework allows the consequences of a particular transformation to be relatively straightforwardly assessed, separately to the specification of the memory model.

Self-fulfilling Prophecies. The out-of-thin-air example (4.1) is an example of an apparent "dependency cycle" [1]. A related but more complex issue is the "read-from-untaken-branch" behaviour [22]. This behaviour can be explained by extending forwarding (as outlined above) to allow conditions (guards) to affect later instructions, creating "self-fulfilling prophecies". While the exact definition of what should be allowed remains vexed, it can be addressed in our framework.

Power and Non-multicopy Atomicity. IBM's multicore Power architecture [29] has, in addition to processor pipeline reorderings, a cache coherence system that provides weaker guarantees than that of Arm (and x86): (cached) memory operations can appear in different orders to different processes (sometimes called non-multicopy atomicity). A formalisation of the Power cache system, separate from the processor-level reordering, and compatible with the framework in this paper, is given in [8] (based on [29]).

6   Related Work

The development of the C (and C++) memory model is ongoing and governed by an ISO committee (but heavily influenced by compiler writers [23]), covering the vast range of features of the language itself and including a semi-formal description of the memory model. Boehm and Adve [3] were highly influential initially, building on earlier work on memory model specifications e.g., [11,20]. Since then many formal approaches have been taken to further understand the implications of the model and tighten its specification, e.g., [2,17,31]. The C model abstracts away from the various hardware models on which C is designed to run, and is described with respect to a cross-thread "happens-before" order, which is influenced by so called "release sequences" of events within the system as a whole. As a formalism this is difficult to reason about – formally or informally – and removes the ability to think thread-locally: whether or not enough fences or constraints have been placed in a thread requires an analysis of all other events in the system, even though, with the exception of the Power architecture (see Sect. 5), weak behaviours are typically due to local compiler transformations or instruction-level parallelisation at the assembler level.

To handle this the typical approach in the literature is to design semantic models where the potential reordering of instructions is maintained in some global data structure(s) [4,14,16,25,26], and then specialised inference systems and assertion languages are developed to reason about that structure [18,34]. In comparison, as explained in Sect. 4, we have a relatively straightforward semantics where potential reordering manifests in the traces of the system, facilitating a program transformation approach to eliminating references to the memory model. At this point standard techniques for reasoning may be employed, saving the need to develop specialised inference systems and assertion languages for the property in question [32] and potentially allowing the reuse of results.

7   Conclusions

We have given a definition of the C memory model which keeps the fundamental concepts involved (data dependencies, fences, and memory ordering constraints) separate from other aspects of the language such as incremental expression evaluation and optimisations, which are present regardless of whether or not the memory model is considered. Reasoning in this framework comprises the transformation of the program with respect to potential reorderings of instructions (as in process-algebraic frameworks) and then applying already established techniques. We argue this is a more straightforward and intuitive approach to understanding the effects of the C memory model in comparison to formalisations in the literature, and indeed is a simpler definition of the relevant concepts than currently given in the C standard reference. The C language is rich in features and any claim to a full semantics of arbitrary C code with concurrency requires a full semantics of C in general, and as far as we are aware this has not been fully realised as yet; but we intend that our approach can be relatively straightforwardly incorporated into such by virtue of its *separation of concerns* - the fundamental properties of the memory model are universal and consistent even in the presence of complicating factors.

The reordering framework we present here is based on earlier work [5,6,8], which provides a model checker and machine-checked refinement rules for the language in Sect. 2. We straightforwardly encoded the definition of the C memory model (17) in the model checker and used it on the examples in this paper as well as those provided by the Cerberus project [21]. The framework has provided the basis for other analyses including security [9,10,30,33].

A   Syntax and Semantics Definitions

Functions over the Syntax. Write and read variables can be extracted from instructions (11) as follows.

$$\mathsf{wv}(x := e) \;=\; \{x\} \qquad \mathsf{wv}((\!|e|\!)) = \varnothing \qquad \mathsf{wv}(\mathsf{f}) \;=\; \varnothing$$
$$\mathsf{rv}(x := e) \;=\; \mathsf{fv}(e) \qquad \mathsf{rv}((\!|e|\!)) = \mathsf{fv}(e) \qquad \mathsf{rv}(\mathsf{f}) \;=\; \varnothing$$

We set $\mathsf{fv}(\alpha) = \mathsf{wv}(\alpha) \cup \mathsf{rv}(\alpha)$. The fences of an instruction α, $|\alpha|$, underpinning relation FNC, are given by $|x := e| = \varnothing$, $|(\!|e|\!)| = \varnothing$, and $|\mathsf{f}| = \{\mathsf{f}\}$. Memory order constraints from instructions and expressions, underpinning relation OCS, are extracted as follows.

$$\lceil v \rceil = \varnothing \qquad \lceil x^{ocs} \rceil = ocs \qquad \lceil \oplus e \rceil = \lceil e \rceil \qquad \lceil e_1 \oplus e_2 \rceil = \lceil e_1 \rceil \cup \lceil e_2 \rceil$$
$$\lceil x^{ocs} := e \rceil = ocs \cup \lceil e \rceil \qquad \lceil (\!|e|\!) \rceil = \lceil e \rceil \qquad \lceil \mathsf{f}^{ocs} \rceil = ocs$$

Any of the functions ($\mathsf{fn}(.)$) defined above can be straightforwardly lifted to commands in the following generic pattern.

$$\mathsf{fn}(\mathbf{nil}) = \varnothing \qquad \mathsf{fn}(c_1 \sqcap c_2) = \mathsf{fn}(c_1 \overset{\text{\tiny M}}{;} c_2) = \mathsf{fn}(c_1) \cup \mathsf{fn}(c_2) \qquad \mathsf{fn}(c_{\text{\tiny M}}^*) = \mathsf{fn}(c)$$

Operational Semantics. The main rules of the operational semantics for the language in (6) are below [5]. An action α executes as a single step and terminates, i.e., $\alpha \xrightarrow{\alpha} \textbf{nil}$. The composite commands execute as follows, where τ is a silent (unobservable) step and c_{M}^n is n-fold iteration of c wrt. M.

$$\frac{c_1 \xrightarrow{\alpha} c_1'}{c_1 \overset{\text{M}}{;} c_2 \xrightarrow{\alpha} c_1' \overset{\text{M}}{;} c_2} \qquad \frac{c_2 \xrightarrow{\beta} c_2' \quad c_1 \overset{c}{\Leftarrow} \beta}{c_1 \overset{\text{M}}{;} c_2 \xrightarrow{\beta} c_1 \overset{\text{M}}{;} c_2'} \qquad \frac{}{c_1 \sqcap c_2 \xrightarrow{\tau} c_1} \qquad \frac{}{c_1 \sqcap c_2 \xrightarrow{\tau} c_2} \qquad c_{\text{M}}^* \xrightarrow{\tau} c_{\text{M}}^n$$

These rules are standard, except for the rule for $c_1 \overset{\text{M}}{;} c_2$ that allows an action β of c_2 to proceed before c_1 provided β can be reordered with c_1 according to M.

References

1. Batty, M., Dodds, M., Gotsman, A.: Library abstraction for C/C++ concurrency. In: POPL 2013, pp. 235–248. ACM (2013)
2. Batty, M., Owens, S., Sarkar, S., Sewell, P., Weber, T.: Mathematizing C++ concurrency. In: POPL 2011, pp. 55–66. ACM (2011)
3. Boehm, H.-J., Adve, S.V.: Foundations of the C++ concurrency memory model. In: PLDI 2008, pp. 68–78. ACM (2008)
4. Chakraborty, S., Vafeiadis, V.: Grounding thin-air reads with event structures. Proc. ACM Program. Lang. **3**(POPL), 1–28 (2019)
5. Colvin, R.J.: Parallelized sequential composition and hardware weak memory models. In: Calinescu, R., Păsăreanu, C.S. (eds.) SEFM 2021. LNCS, vol. 13085, pp. 201–221. Springer, Cham (2021). https://doi.org/10.1007/978-3-030-92124-8_12
6. Colvin, R.J.: Parallelized sequential composition, pipelines, and hardware weak memory models. CoRR, abs/2105.02444 (2021)
7. Colvin, R.J.: Separation of concerning things: a simpler basis for defining and programming with the C/C++ memory model (extended version) (2022). https://arxiv.org/abs/2204.03189
8. Colvin, R.J., Smith, G.: A wide-spectrum language for verification of programs on weak memory models. In: Havelund, K., Peleska, J., Roscoe, B., de Vink, E. (eds.) FM 2018. LNCS, vol. 10951, pp. 240–257. Springer, Cham (2018). https://doi.org/10.1007/978-3-319-95582-7_14
9. Colvin, R.J., Winter, K.: An abstract semantics of speculative execution for reasoning about security vulnerabilities. In: Sekerinski, E., et al. (eds.) FM 2019. LNCS, vol. 12233, pp. 323–341. Springer, Cham (2020). https://doi.org/10.1007/978-3-030-54997-8_21
10. Coughlin, N., Winter, K., Smith, G.: Rely/guarantee reasoning for multicopy atomic weak memory models. In: Huisman, M., Păsăreanu, C., Zhan, N. (eds.) FM 2021. LNCS, vol. 13047, pp. 292–310. Springer, Cham (2021). https://doi.org/10.1007/978-3-030-90870-6_16
11. Gharachorloo, K., Lenoski, D., Laudon, J., Gibbons, P., Gupta, A., Hennessy, J.: Memory consistency and event ordering in scalable shared-memory multiprocessors. In: ISCA 1990, pp. 15–26. ACM (1990)
12. Herlihy, M.P., Wing, J.M.: Linearizability: a correctness condition for concurrent objects. TOPLAS **12**(3), 463–492 (1990)

13. Hoare, C.A.R.: An axiomatic basis for computer programming. Commun. ACM **12**(10), 576–580 (1969)
14. Jeffrey, A., Riely, J., Batty, M., Cooksey, S., Kaysin, I., Podkopaev, A.: The leaky semicolon: compositional semantic dependencies for relaxed-memory concurrency. Proc. ACM Program. Lang. **6**(POPL), 1–30 (2022)
15. Jones, C.B.: Specification and design of (parallel) programs. In: IFIP Congress, pp. 321–332 (1983)
16. Kang, J., Hur, C.-K., Lahav, O., Vafeiadis, V., Dreyer, D.: A promising semantics for relaxed-memory concurrency. In: POPL 2017, pp. 175–189. ACM (2017)
17. Lahav, O., Giannarakis, N., Vafeiadis, V.: Taming release-acquire consistency. In: POPL 2016, pp. 649–662. Association for Computing Machinery (2016)
18. Lahav, O., Vafeiadis, V.: Owicki-Gries reasoning for weak memory models. In: Halldórsson, M.M., Iwama, K., Kobayashi, N., Speckmann, B. (eds.) ICALP 2015. LNCS, vol. 9135, pp. 311–323. Springer, Heidelberg (2015). https://doi.org/10.1007/978-3-662-47666-6_25
19. Lahav, O., Vafeiadis, V., Kang, J., Hur, C.-K., Dreyer, D.: Repairing sequential consistency in C/C++11. In: Programming Language Design and Implementation (PLDI 2017), pp. 618–632. ACM (2017)
20. Lamport, L.: How to make a multiprocessor computer that correctly executes multiprocess programs. IEEE Trans. Comput. **C–28**(9), 690–691 (1979)
21. Lau, S., Gomes, V.B.F., Memarian, K., Pichon-Pharabod, J., Sewell, P.: Cerberus-BMC: a principled reference semantics and exploration tool for concurrent and sequential C. In: Dillig, I., Tasiran, S. (eds.) CAV 2019. LNCS, vol. 11561, pp. 387–397. Springer, Cham (2019). https://doi.org/10.1007/978-3-030-25540-4_22
22. Lee, S.-H., et al.: Promising 2.0: global optimizations in relaxed memory concurrency. In: PLDI 2020, pp. 362–376. ACM (2020)
23. Memarian, K., et al.: Into the depths of C: elaborating the de facto standards. SIGPLAN Not. **51**(6), 1–15 (2016)
24. Morgan, C.: Of wp and CSP. In: Feijen, W.H.J., van Gasteren, A.J.M., Gries, D., Misra, J. (eds.) Beauty Is Our Business: A Birthday Salute to Edsger W. Dijkstra. Texts and Monographs in Computer Science, pp. 319–326. Springer, New York (1990). https://doi.org/10.1007/978-1-4612-4476-9_37
25. Nienhuis, K., Memarian, K., Sewell, P.: An operational semantics for C/C++11 concurrency. In: OOPSLA 2016, pp. 111–128. ACM (2016)
26. Ou, P., Demsky, B.: Towards understanding the costs of avoiding out-of-thin-air results. Proc. ACM Program. Lang. **2**(OOPSLA), 1–29 (2018)
27. Owicki, S., Gries, D.: An axiomatic proof technique for parallel programs I. Acta Inf. **6**(4), 319–340 (1976)
28. Sabelfeld, A., Myers, A.C.: Language-based information-flow security. IEEE J. Sel. Areas Commun. **21**(1), 5–19 (2003)
29. Sarkar, S., Sewell, P., Alglave, J., Maranget, L., Williams, D.: Understanding POWER multiprocessors. In: Programming Language Design and Implementation (PLDI 2011), pp. 175–186. ACM (2011)
30. Smith, G., Coughlin, N., Murray, T.: Value-dependent information-flow security on weak memory models. In: ter Beek, M.H., McIver, A., Oliveira, J.N. (eds.) FM 2019. LNCS, vol. 11800, pp. 539–555. Springer, Cham (2019). https://doi.org/10.1007/978-3-030-30942-8_32
31. Vafeiadis, V., Balabonski, T., Chakraborty, S., Morisset, R., Nardelli, F.: Common compiler optimisations are invalid in the C11 memory model and what we can do about it. In: POPL 2015, pp. 209–220. ACM (2015)

32. Wehrheim, H., Travkin, O.: TSO to SC via symbolic execution. In: Piterman, N. (ed.) HVC 2015. LNCS, vol. 9434, pp. 104–119. Springer, Cham (2015). https://doi.org/10.1007/978-3-319-26287-1_7

33. Winter, K., Coughlin, N., Smith, G.: Backwards-directed information flow analysis for concurrent programs. In: 2021 IEEE 34th Computer Security Foundations Symposium (CSF), pp. 1–16 (2021)

34. Wright, D., Batty, M., Dongol, B.: Owicki-Gries reasoning for C11 programs with relaxed dependencies. In: Huisman, M., Păsăreanu, C., Zhan, N. (eds.) FM 2021. LNCS, vol. 13047, pp. 237–254. Springer, Cham (2021). https://doi.org/10.1007/978-3-030-90870-6_13

CREUSOT: A Foundry for the Deductive Verification of Rust Programs

Xavier Denis[1] , Jacques-Henri Jourdan[2] , and Claude Marché[1(✉)]

[1] Université Paris-Saclay, CNRS, ENS Paris-Saclay, INRIA, Laboratoire Méthodes
Formelles, 91405 Gif-sur-Yvette, France
`Claude.Marche@inria.fr`
[2] Université Paris-Saclay, CNRS, ENS Paris-Saclay, Laboratoire Méthodes Formelles,
91405 Gif-sur-Yvette, France

Abstract. Rust is a fairly recent programming language for system programming, bringing static guarantees of memory safety through a strict *ownership* policy. The strong guarantees brought by this feature opens promising progress for *deductive verification*, which aims at proving the conformity of Rust code with respect to a specification of its intended behavior. We present the foundations of CREUSOT, a tool for the formal specification and deductive verification of Rust code. A first originality comes from CREUSOT's specification language, which features a notion of *prophecy* to reason about memory mutation, working in harmony with Rust's ownership system. A second originality is how CREUSOT builds upon Rust *trait* system to provide several advanced abstraction features.

Keywords: Rust programming language · Deductive program verification · Aliasing and ownership · Prophecies · Traits

1 Introduction

Critical services like transportation, energy or medicine are nowadays controlled by software, and thus verifying the correctness of such software is highly important. However, *systems software* is often written in low-level, pointer-manipulating languages such as C/C++ which make verification challenging. The pitfalls and traps of C-family languages are well-known; a common thread among them is the unrestricted usage of *mutable pointers*, which allow *aliasing*. When two pointers are aliased, a write through one will silently change the value pointed by the other, wreaking havoc on the programmer and verification tool's understanding of the program. Much effort has been spent trying to control and reason about aliasing. Specialized logics like *separation logic* or *dynamic frames* [20] give a vocabulary to express these challenges. On the other side, language features like the *region typing* of WHY3 [9] or the *ownership typing* of the Rust programming language prevent mutable aliasing altogether. Indeed, Rust promises the performance and flexibility of C with none of the memory safety issues. To make good on this promise, its ownership type system guarantees

© Springer Nature Switzerland AG 2022
A. Riesco and M. Zhang (Eds.): ICFEM 2022, LNCS 13478, pp. 90–105, 2022.
https://doi.org/10.1007/978-3-031-17244-1_6

that pointers are always valid and that mutable ones are unique. The ownership discipline of Rust is enforced by a static analysis called *borrow checking*, which infers the *lifetime* of every borrow (temporary pointer), and ensures that, when mutating, only one pointer can be used to access the data, which is essential for memory safety. Once a variable is mutably borrowed, a second borrow cannot be created until the lifetime expires. Alternatively, immutable borrows can be duplicated, as one cannot modify the memory they point to. This combination of features, memory safety and low-level control, has led to Rust's exploding popularity. As Rust finds usage in key systems like Firefox and the Linux kernel, it becomes important to move beyond the safety guarantees of the language.

In 2020, Matsushita *et al.* [16] proposed a notion of *prophecies* to reason about the functional behavior of mutable borrows of Rust. Roughly speaking, a prophecy denotes the future value a borrow will have when its lifetime ends. Matsushita *et al.* developed a proof-of-concept tool RUSTHORN translating Rust code to *Constrained Horn Clauses*, making it possible to check the validity of code assertions using automated solvers. Our tool CREUSOT[1] allows for auto-active deductive verification of Rust code. CREUSOT uses a prophetic translation in the lineage of RUSTHORN, but aims to verify real-world programs, pushing the size, scope and features of programs far beyond RUSTHORN. Unlike RUSTHORN, CREUSOT has a specification language, PEARLITE[2], which allows users to write function contracts and loop invariants, where logic formulas can make use of a novel operator ˆ (pronounced *final*) to denote prophecies. CREUSOT has the ambition of going beyond a proof-of-concept verification tool. To support a large subset of Rust, including its standard library, it is mandatory to support the notion of *traits* which are a key mechanism for *abstraction* in Rust. CREUSOT not only supports the verification of Rust code involving traits, but it also builds upon the trait system to provide important features: first, the concept of *resolution* of prophecies is expressed as a `Resolve` trait; second, logical abstraction of concrete data is provided through a `Model` trait which is used pervasively in our case studies.

1.1 Example: A Polymorphic Sorting Function

As a motivating example, let's consider a simple *generic* sorting routine. We use the "Gnome Sort" algorithm, using a single loop that *swaps* out of order elements successively. We provide an implementation in Fig. 1. To verify this we face two primary challenges. The first is *genericity*: to compare values of a generic type in Rust we need to use the *trait* `Ord`. The traits of Rust are like the *typeclasses* of Haskell: here they allow us to constrain `T` to have an *ordering relation*. In Creusot, we can add the necessary logical specifications to the `Ord` trait, formalizing its documentation [21] stating that it *must* implement a total order. The second challenge is the need to handle the library `Vec` for vectors, providing a *safe* interface to resizeable arrays, despite being implemented using *unsafe code*. CREUSOT does not permit the verification of unsafe code but allows

---

[1] *Le Creusot* is an industrial town in the eastern France, whose economy is dominated by metallurgical companies, *cf.* https://en.wikipedia.org/wiki/Le_Creusot.

[2] Pearlite is a structure occurring in common grades of steels, cf https://en.wikipedia.org/wiki/Pearlite.

```
1    #[ensures(sorted_range(@^v, 0, (@^v).len()))]
2    #[ensures((@^v).permutation_of(@*v))]
3    fn gnome_sort<T: Ord>(v: &mut Vec<T>) {
4        let old_v = Ghost::record(&v);
5        let mut i = 0;
6        #[invariant(sorted_range(@*v, 0, @i))]
7        #[invariant((@*v).permutation_of(@*@old_v))]
8        while i < v.len() {
9            if i == 0 || v[i - 1] <= v[i] {
10               i += 1;
11           } else {
12               v.swap(i - 1, i);
13               i -= 1;
14           }
15       }
16   }
```

Fig. 1. Gnome sort and its specification.

the specification of *safe abstractions* like `Vec`: we choose a *model* for such types, representing vectors as *mathematical sequences*.

Now, we can finally specify what it means to *sort* a vector. We do this using two `ensures` clauses which establish the postconditions of the function. The first uses a helper *logical predicate* `sorted_range` to define what it means for a sequence to be sorted according to a generic order on `T`.

```
#[predicate]
fn sorted_range<T: Ord>(s: Seq<T>, l: Int, u: Int) -> bool {
    pearlite! { forall<i: Int, j : Int>
      l <= i && i < j && j < u ==> s[i] <= s[j] }
}
```

This definition is written using PEARLITE, the specification language of CREUSOT. While PEARLITE has a Rust inspired syntax, it adds several constructs like quantification `forall<..>`, or implication `==>`. Using these we can say a sequence is sorted if for any ordered pair of indices the values at those indices respect the order on `T`. On line 1 of Fig. 1, we use this definition with two more PEARLITE operators: the model operator (`@`) (syntactic sugar for the `Model` trait), and the prophetic operator *final* (`^`). The final operator provides access to the value of a mutable borrow at the end of its lifetime; here we use it to talk about the value the vector pointed by `v` has after the function call. The second postcondition on line 2 makes use of a similar helper predicate `permutation_of` to require that the final value of `v` is a permutation of its initial value. To prove these postconditions we provide two *loop invariants* (lines 6–7). The first states that the segment of the vector before `i` is sorted, while the second states that the vector at each iteration is a permutation of the input. To state this invariant about permutations we make use of the `Ghost` type, to record a *ghost value* which does not exist at runtime but does during proof, allowing us to remember the original value of `v`. The annotated program is fed through CREUSOT, which translates it to WHY3. In turn, WHY3 generates and discharges the verification conditions in under 2 s using automated provers including Z3 [19], CVC4 [2] and Alt-Ergo [6].

1.2 Contributions

Our contributions, and the structure of this paper, are summarized as follows. In Sect. 2 we give an introduction through the PEARLITE specification language and the verification process of CREUSOT. This section illustrates how prophecies are integrated in PEARLITE. In Sect. 3, we explain how CREUSOT translate Rust functions into WHY3 functions, this section explains how we generate the verification conditions for mutable borrows. In Sect. 4 we first present in deeper details how Rust traits are interpreted by CREUSOT, and in a second step we discuss the specific CREUSOT traits used in borrow resolution and in data abstraction. In Sect. 5 we present an overview of the implementation of CREUSOT and an experimental evaluation of the tool on a set of benchmarks. We discuss related work in Sect. 6. Notice that due to space limitations, we focus here on the original features of CREUSOT and refer to an extended research report [8] for more details.

2 Specifying and Proving Programs Using Prophecies

To formally specify the intended behavior of programs, one can use so-called *Behavioral Interface Specification Languages* [10], such as JML for Java [5], ACSL for C [3] or Spark for Ada [17]. CREUSOT follows this tradition by introducing the PEARLITE specification language, where Rust functions are given *contracts* which specify *pre-* and *postconditions*: logic formulas which respectively hold at the entrance and exit of a function call.

Traditionally, specification languages introduce specific contract clauses to specify the behavior of pointers such as the `assignable` or `assigns` in ACSL and JML. PEARLITE has no equivalent clause. Instead specifications can refer not only to the value of a borrow at function entry but also to its value at the end of its lifetime: this is the notion of *prophecies* that we detail in Sect. 2.2.

2.1 Background Logic

The background logic of PEARLITE is a classical, first-order, multi-sorted logic. Each Rust type corresponds to a sort in this logic. The logic connectives denoted by `&&`, `||` and `!` mirror their Rust counterparts, but Pearlite also introduces `==>` for implication, and the quantifiers `forall<v:t> formula` and `exists<v:t> formula`. Atomic predicates can be built using custom *logic functions and predicates*, constant literals, variables and built-in symbols, a central case being the logical equality denoted by a tripled equal sign (`===`) and defined on any sort. This logical equality is the symbol interpreted to the set-theoretic equality in a set-based semantics. This distinguishes it from the *program equal-*

ity of Rust, ==, which is sugar for `PartialEq::eq`. Finally, PEARLITE has support for logical sorts which do not exist in Rust, like `Int`, the unbounded mathematical integers, or like `Seq<T>` the generic sort of mathematical sequences. A syntactically valid formula is thus for example:

```
forall<x: Int> x >= 0 ==> exists<y: Int> y >= 0 && x * x === x + 2 * y
```

See [8] for more technical details on the background logic. PEARLITE formulas are type-checked by the front-end of the Rust compiler, but they are not borrow-checked. Hence values can be used in logic functions or predicates, even if the Rust ownership rules would forbid copying them.

A useful feature of PEARLITE is the introduction of user lemmas using the so-called *lemma function* construction. To achieve this, one provides a contract to a logical function returning (). By proving the contract valid, one obtains a lemma stating that for all values of arguments, the preconditions imply the postconditions. This construction is even able to prove lemmas by induction. Here is an example (detailed in [8]):

```
#[logic]
#[requires(x >= 0)]
#[variant(x)]
#[ensures(sum_of_odd(x) === sqr(x))]
fn sum_of_odd_is_sqr(x:Int) { if x > 0 { sum_of_odd_is_sqr(x-1) } }
```

This code is automatically proved conforming to its contract. Any call to this function would then add the hypothesis $\forall x, x \geq 0 \Rightarrow$ `sum_of_odd`$(x) = x^2$ in the current proof context.

2.2   Borrows and Prophecies

We illustrate the use of prophecies to specify mutable borrows in Fig. 2. The function `pick` returns, depending on its first boolean parameter, either its second or third argument. We wish to show that the client `pick_test` returns 42. For that purpose, `pick` must be given an appropriate contract: namely the postcondition of lines 1 and 2. The first part of the postcondition states that the result of `pick` (denoted by the identifier `result`) is either `x` or `y`, depending on the value of `t`. Importantly, when we say `result` === `x` (*i.e.,* when `t` === `true`), we are stating that the *borrow* `result`, which is a pointer, is equal to the *borrow* `x`, not merely the values being pointed. In particular, this captures that writing through the returned pointer affect the variable pointed to by `x`. In `pick_test`, this entails that the final value of `a` is 6. The second part of the post-condition is needed to state that the other borrow parameter (`y` when `t` === `true`) is released so the caller knows the value it points to can no longer change until the lifetime `'a` ends. This is specified using a *prophecy*. For any mutable borrow `b`, one can write `^b` in PEARLITE to denote its *final value*, the value the variable it points to will have when the lifetime expires. Prophecies act like a bridge between the lender and borrower, when a borrow is released we recover information which allows us to update the value of the lender. Releasing a mutable borrow is equivalent to

```
1   #[ensures(if t { result === x && ^y === *y }
2              else { result === y && ^x === *x })]
3   fn pick<'a>(t: bool, x: &'a mut i32, y: &'a mut i32) -> &'a mut i32 {
4     if t { x } else { y }
5   }
6
7   #[ensures(result === 42)]
8   fn pick_test() {
9       let (mut a, mut b) = (4, 7);
10      let x = pick(true, &mut a, &mut b);
11      *x += 2; return a * b;
12  }
```

Fig. 2. A toy example illustrating prophecies in the specification language.

stating that the current value of the borrow, *b, equals its final value, ^b. We refer to this process as the *resolution* of the borrow. Thanks to the resolution, we can prove the postcondition of pick and deduce in pick_test that the value of b at line 11 is its original value 7. The final value of a borrow is a logical artifact: it is not necessarily known at runtime when the specification mentions it, but one can prove [15,16] that it is sound to *prophesize* it in the logic. Note that the first equality (*i.e.*, result === x when t === true) actually implies the equality ^result === ^x, as we are asserting that result and x are completely indistinguishable. This explains why the first equality is enough to specify that a mutation through the borrow result causes a mutation of the variable pointed to by the argument x (when t === true). Since they both have the same prophecy, modifications to the memory pointed to by result will affect the lender of x. The approach is detailed and validated in prior work [15,16].

3   Handling Rust Function Bodies

CREUSOT translates Rust programs into WhyML, the programming language of WHY3. Rather than starting from source level Rust, translation begins from the Mid-Level Intermediate Representation (MIR) of the Rust compiler. MIR is a key language in the compilation of Rust and is the final result of desugaring and type checking Rust code. Many tools that wish to consume Rust code target MIR. There are rich APIs to access, extract and manipulate MIR code. Furthermore, MIR is created *after* type checking and is the representation on which Rust's flagship static analysis *borrow checking* is formulated. MIR is also the language modeled in RUSTHORNBELT [15] to prove the correctness of prophetic translation. Thus, we want to design our translation from MIR to WHY3 so the generated verification conditions are as close as possible to those proved sound in RUSTHORNBELT. MIR programs are unstructured: they are represented as a control-flow graph (CFG) whose nodes are basic blocks composed of atomic instructions (borrowing, arithmetic, dereferencing, etc.) each terminated by a function call, a goto, a switch, an abort or a return. To verify a MIR program, we find ourselves needing to calculate the *weakest-precondition (WP) of a function represented as a CFG*. We achieve this using a dedicated Why3 input front-end called MLCFG, that reconstructs a structured WhyML code from a control flow graph, and then use Why3's carefully designed WP computation algorithms.

3.1 Translating Owned Pointers

The ownership discipline of Rust makes a simple translation of (mutable) owned pointers possible. Consider the case of a local variable x containing an owned pointer to the heap (*i.e.*, of type Box<T> for some type T). Then, we know that mutating memory through x can only be observed by a read using variable x. Therefore, if t is the translation of type T, then we can translate type Box<T> to type t as well. An assignment through the pointer *x = e is simply translated to the assignment: x = e', where e' is the translation of e.

3.2 Translating Borrows to Prophecies in WHY3

Just like in RUSTHORNBELT, borrows are translated into pairs of a current value and a final value. Hence, we introduce a new polymorphic record type in WHY3:

```
type borrow 'a = { current : 'a ; final : 'a }
```

A Rust variable of type &mut T is translated by CREUSOT as an object of type borrow t, where t is the translation of T. The PEARLITE notations *x and ^x are translated into x.current and x.final.

Using the pattern of prophecies for encoding mutable borrows into a functional language poses a difficulty: when we create a borrow, we obtain a new *prophetized* value which comes out of thin air. We won't know anything concrete about this prophecy until the borrow is *resolved* at the moment it is dropped, and then at the lifetime's end the lender will have the value of this same prophecy. In between these points there can be arbitrary control flow, ownership changes, or *reborrowing*. We may no longer know who the lender of a borrow was at its lifetime's end, and therefore have no way to propagate the prophecy to the lender. Our solution may be surprising: we update the lender with the prophecy at the moment of the borrow's creation, foreseeing all the mutations that will occur. This is valid because the value of the lender cannot be observed before the lifetime's end. As a result, the creation of a borrow

```
let y : &mut T = &mut x;
```

is translated into

```
y : borrow t <- { current = x ; final = any t };
x : t <- y.final;
```

where any t is the WhyML non-deterministic construct which returns an arbitrary value of type t. It encodes the fact that the final value is not yet known, it is thus *prophetized*. The second line gives to x the final future value of y.

An important other case occurs when a borrow is *dropped*, where we insert a *resolution statement*:

```
1   val pick (t: bool) (a: borrow int32) (b: borrow int32) : borrow int32
2     ensures { if t then result = a /\ b.final = b.current
3       else result = b /\ a.final = a.current }
4
5   let cfg pick_test () =
6     ensures { result = 42 }
7     var a, b : int; var bor_a, bor_b, x : borrow int;
8     { a <- 4; a <- 7;
9     (* let x = pick(true, &mut a, &mut b); *)
10    bor_a <- { current = a ; final = any int32 }; a <- bor_a.final;
11    bor_b <- { current = b ; final = any int32 }; b <- bor_b.final;
12    x <- pick true bor_a bor_b;
13    (* *x += 2; *)
14    x <- { current = x.current + 2; final = x.final };
15    assume { x.final = x.current };
16    (* return a * b *)
17    return a * b }
```

Fig. 3. Simplified translation of the projection pick example in MLCFG.

```
assume { y.final = y.current };
```

The contents of a WhyML `assume` clause states a fact as a trusted hypothesis for subsequent statements. Resolution corresponds to the fact that at this point the value pointed to by the borrow will not change, and therefore its prophecy has been fulfilled.

The simplified translation of the `pick` example, from Fig. 2, is given in Fig. 3. See [8] for more details. The postcondition of `pick_test` and `pick` are proven using Why3 and SMT solvers.

4   Support for Rust Traits

Rust makes heavy use of a *trait system* to implement abstractions. Like type-classes in Haskell, traits allow functions, types or constants to be associated to specific types, and can automatically select the correct instance at each call-site. The trait system enables ecosystem-wide modularity and many common operations are expressed using traits, such as equality in the `PartialEq` and `Eq` traits, order relations in `PartialOrd` and `Ord`, and accessing collections in the `Index` and `IndexMut` traits. Supporting Rust's trait system is necessary for a verification tool, they manifest themselves in even the most basic programs, like Fig. 1. In this section, we explain how traits can be used in CREUSOT to modularly verify programs. But CREUSOT not only verifies programs using traits, it also *uses* traits for some of its core features: the `Resolve` and `Model` traits.

```
1   trait Ord {
2       #[logic] fn cmp_log(self, o: Self) -> Ordering;
3
4       #[ensures(result === self.cmp_log(*o))]
5       fn cmp(&self, o: &Self) -> Ordering;
6
7       #[law]
8       #[requires(a.cmp_log(*b) === o && b.cmp_log(*c) === o)]
9       #[ensures(a.cmp_log(*c) === o)]
10      fn trans(a: &Self, b: &Self, c: &Self, o: Ordering);
11      ...
12  }
```

Fig. 4. A simplified Ord trait with specifications

4.1   Specifying Trait Behavior

The trait PartialOrd implements a *heterogenous partial order*: instances must provide implementations for all of lt, gt, le, ge, and partial_cmp. Additionally, the official documentation [21] requires that these definitions are mutually compatible, for example: if a.le(b) then a.lt(b) || a.eq(b). This is an example of a *law* for PartialOrd. In CREUSOT, laws can be included in traits using the #[law] annotation and written in the style of *lemma functions* (see Sect. 2.1). A particularity of trait laws is their *auto-loading*: whenever we use *any* associated item of a trait or implementation, we will bring into scope any laws from that trait.

Traits can be arranged into a hierarchy, with *sub-traits* refining or expanding upon their super-traits. The *sub-trait* Ord strengthens the specification of PartialOrd, requiring the order to be *total* and *homogeneous*. The laws of Ord constrain the behavior of functions defined in the super-trait PartialOrd. In Fig. 4 we present a simplified version of our specifications for Ord (see [8] for more details). We require a definition of cmp_log and a proof of transitivity. Each time a user makes use of a comparison operation, CREUSOT will load the laws of Ord, allowing us to leverage the transitivity of our order.

Every implementation of a trait for a specific type must *refine* the contract of the trait. It must weaken preconditions and strengthen postconditions. This possibility of refinement allows implementations to provide stronger contracts which leverage specific knowledge of the type the trait is being implemented for. Whenever a trait method is used, CREUSOT will use the most specific contract possible. Performing the translation to Why3 of all such different usage of traits is indeed highly non-trivial: it relies on algorithms for construction of specific dependency graphs which are detailed in our research report [8].

4.2   The Resolve Trait

We use traits to generalize the notion of *resolution* discussed in Sect. 3.2, as follows.

```
#[trusted] trait Resolve {
    #[predicate] fn resolve(self) -> bool;
}
```

Much like how Rust's Drop trait allows types to customize their program destructors, we use the Resolve trait to define the knowledge gained from resolving a specific type. Following discussion of Sect. 3.2, the Resolve trait is given the following implementation for mutable borrows:

```
unsafe impl<T> Resolve for &mut T {
    #[predicate]
    fn resolve(self) -> bool { pearlite! { ^self === *self } }
}
```

so indeed, when a mutable borrow r is resolved, instead of assuming ^r === *r, CREUSOT will assume the equivalent assertion r.resolve().

Because Resolve represents information that is *assumed* about a type, an incorrect implementation can introduce unsoundness to CREUSOT, for this reason we mark the trait as #[trusted], and require all implementations to do the same. This mirrors the notion of unsafe trait in Rust for those traits where a malicious implementation could introduce undefined behavior in safe code.

The Resolve trait makes it possible to generalize the resolution mechanism to data structures containing mutable borrows, like vectors of borrows, pairs of pairs of borrows, etc. For example, when we resolve a pair p of mutable borrows, we wish to learn that both components of p are resolved, that is, *p.0 === ^p.0 && *p.1 === ^p.1. To achieve this goal, we give the following implementation of the Resolve trait for pairs:

```
unsafe impl<T1: Resolve, T2: Resolve> Resolve for (T1, T2) {
    #[predicate]
    fn resolve(self) -> bool {
        pearlite! { self.0.resolve() && self.1.resolve() }
    }
}
```

Then, resolving x: (&mut T, &mut T) would expand into the resolution of each component of the pair.

Like Drop, we need to be able to resolve a value of *any* type, but we don't have the benefit of being a first-class language feature of Rust. We solve this using a cutting-edge feature of Rust, *specialization*. This allows us to provide a generic implementation for every type T, and then provide more specific instances which specialize resolution. In practice, this means users can write x.resolve() for any value, and never need to constrain generic parameters to implement Resolve.

4.3 Specifying with Models: The Model Trait

Traits provide a convenient mechanism for abstracting specifications, just like in programs. When working with complex data structures we wish to treat their specifications in terms of a *model* which abstracts away implementation details.

For example, we may wish to view a `HashMap` as a mathematical map between two types, or a `Vec` as a sequence of values. To do this, we provide a function which shows how to interpret concrete values as members of the *model*. In certain cases (like `Vec` in CREUSOT), we may even take the existence of this function as an axiom. This *design pattern* is common enough that we can capture it in a trait.

```
trait Model {
    type ModelTy;
    #[logic] fn model(self) -> Self::ModelTy;
}
```

Each implementation of the `Model` trait specifies the type of the model and a function to interpret itself as a value of that type. By making this a trait, we can provide convenience instances that improve ergonomics. CREUSOT goes further and provides syntactic sugar for this trait. Rather than using `x.model()`, users can write `@x` where appropriate. Apart from this small sugar, models purely are a *library concern*, CREUSOT as a tool has no specific awareness of them.

5   Experimentation and Evaluation

We evaluated the performance of CREUSOT on a wide range of benchmarks. These benchmarks make heavy use of polymorphism and traits. Additionally, we improved on the benchmarks of other tools by proving additional functional properties. The evaluation shows that CREUSOT's approach scales well, with verification times remaining low even in complex examples. Furthermore, it provides evidence that our prophetic specifications are well-suited and concise.

Implementation. Like many other Rust verification tools, CREUSOT is implemented as an extension of the Rust compiler, and integrates easily into standard Rust workflows. The total implementation including the 'verification standard library' of Creusot totals 14 k lines of code, published under an LGPL license, available at https://github.com/xldenis/creusot/. During execution CREUSOT translates Rust libraries into MLCFG and outputs the result to a file. The resulting file can then be loaded in WHY3 and verified using either its IDE or command line.

Language Support. CREUSOT supports a large subset of *safe* Rust, including structs and enums, all forms of borrowing, loops and recursions. As we discussed in this paper, we also support polymorphism and traits, including associated types and functions, and super traits. Furthermore, we extend Rust with both logic functions and predicates, which can be used in the specifications of functions and traits. CREUSOT also allows types like `Vec` to be axiomatized so their safe clients can still be verified.

Table 1. Selected results of our evaluation. The column "LOC" indicates the lines of program code (excluding blank lines) we verify. The column "Spec. LOC" measures the lines of specifications (excluding blank) used. "# of VCs" measures the number of verification conditions that are sent as proof tasks to CVC4 or Z3. "Time (s)" measures the time WHY3 takes to run the provers. The "Has traits?" measures whether the test case has a function with a generic parameter constrained by a trait. Tests marked with † required a few manual proof steps in Why3 IDE [7].

Name	Has generics?	Has traits?	LOC	Spec. LOC	# of VCs	Time (s)	Additional properties
Inc some list	✗	✗	25	22	4	0.98	Func. correctness
Inc max	✗	✗	12	3	2	0.53	Func. correctness
Inc max many	✗	✗	13	3	2	0.74	Func. correctness
Binary search	✓	✓	21	20	31	2.15	Func. correctness
Knapsack 0/1	✓	✗	32	52	81	3.94	–
Knapsack 0/1	✓	✗	32	106	113	5.96	Func. correctness
Knuth shuffle	✓	✗	9	11	1	0.30	Permutation
100 doors	✗	✗	18	6	3	1.08	—
Heap Sort	✓	✓	30	71	125	14.6	Func. correctness
Selection Sort	✓	✓	15	27	30	2.14	Func. correctness
Gnome sort	✓	✓	11	17	31	2.06	Func. correctness
Filter Vector	✓	✗	21	39	6	0.98	–
Sparse array†	✓	✗	47	75	37	4.86	Func. behavior
In place List Rev.	✓	✗	12	10	1	0.55	Func. correctness
All zero list	✓	✗	11	10	1	0.64	Func. correctness
Swap pair	✓	✗	9	3	2	0.48	–
HashMap	✓	✓	50	111	71	5.43	Func. correctness

Evaluation. We measure the verification performance for programs translated with CREUSOT. We adapted and generalized programs from the PRUSTI [1] benchmark suite, additionally strengthening the verified properties. Other examples were inspired from the WHY3 gallery [4], Rosetta Code [18] or RUSTHORN [16].

Note that WHY3 has support for a wide range of manual proof tactics that allow users to setup proof structure before handing off obligations to provers. As these can dramatically help verification, we avoid them in our evaluation and instead apply a standard proof strategy to all examples. Each example is proved using WHY3's "Auto Level 2" strategy, a common first step when verifying programs with WHY3. One benchmark required a small number of additional manual proof steps, "Sparse Array", to prove a complex lemma about injections between sequences.

Our evaluation was performed using a 2016 Macbook Pro running macOS 11.6 installation with a Intel Core i7-7920 HQ CPU and 16 GB of RAM. We relied on a combination of Alt-Ergo 2.4.1, Z3 4.8.17 and CVC4 1.8 as back-ends to WHY3.

Discussion. The selected results are presented in Table 1, where benchmarks are grouped by origin. The first group come RUSTHORN's evaluation [16, §4.3], where we added specifications of the intended functional behavior. The second group of benchmarks are adapted from PRUSTI's evaluation [1, §7.2]. The third group are novel examples contributed as part of CREUSOT's test suite. "Filter Vector" is a challenging example regarding reasoning on memory separation [12]. "Sparse Array" is an example from the VACID-0 benchmarks [14]. The proof involves a mathematical lemma with a few steps of manual proof [7] before sending the sub-goals to SMT solvers. "In Place List Rev." is the in-place linked-list reversal procedure, classically used as an illustration of reasoning in separation logic. It is remarkable that the Rust code for that can be verified without the need for separation logic.

Our RUSTHORN tests show that we maintain the verification performance of RUSTHORN, as these examples are rapidly verified by our provers. While some manual annotation is required, even for safety, the overhead is low, and mostly consists of stating the properties we wanted to prove in the first place.

The PRUSTI examples listed here are derived from their introductory paper in 2019 [1]. In their paper they provide two versions for their functions, the first proving only safety while the second proves portions of functional correctness.

The difference in verification performance is made evident by the "Knapsack 0/1" example of PRUSTI. This example solves the 0/1-Knapsack problem using the traditional dynamic programming approach. PRUSTI takes over 2 min to verify the safety of the problem, whereas our proof of safety passes in approximately 4 s. This difference in performance helps us go further, being able to rapidly check proofs allows for faster iteration, which enabled us to extend this example with a complete proof of functional correctness. Our version of the Knapsack Problem with functional correctness takes longer to verify, with the proof passing in approximately 6 s.

6   Related Work

RUSTHORN [16] laid the foundations for CREUSOT by developing a prophetic encoding of mutable borrows and applying it to Rust. It translates MIR programs directly to Constrained Horn Clauses where existing dedicated automated solvers can be thrown at the task. CREUSOT on the other hand introduces an intermediate step: we translate first to an intermediate language which is then lowered to first-order logic (FOL) by calculating weakest-preconditions. As a tool RUSTHORN remains a proof-of-concept, it supports a core fragment of Rust: algebraic data types, borrows, simple loops and arithmetic and polymorphism. There is no support for unsafe types like Vec or for traits like Eq. Moreover, RUSTHORN has no specification language, it is limited to the verification of program assertions, which are by essence limited to executable boolean expressions on program variables, without any way to relate them with an abstract model. It relies entirely on automation to infer both function postconditions and loop invariants, meaning a seemingly small change can cause verification times to spiral out of control or fail unpredictably. While not an automated verifier, RUSTHORNBELT mechanizes a proof of soundness for prophetic verification of Rust [15], by extending the prior RustBelt proof. The proof shows that the uniqueness and lifetimes of mutable borrows enables prophetizing their final values, placing CREUSOT's approach on solid theoretical grounds. However, there remains a gap between an implementation like CREUSOT and the mechanization. In particular, the language of RUSTHORNBELT λRust makes a number of simplifying assumptions when compared to MIR, like boxing function parameters or using a CPS structure for the programs. Furthermore, RUSTHORNBELT establishes the soundness of the final verification conditions directly but CREUSOT introduces an intermediate step by targeting a functional language.

PRUSTI [1] is another deductive verifier for Rust, based on the Viper separation logic platform. It does not use a prophetic encoding, instead modeling ownership using *permissions*. Like CREUSOT, PRUSTI has a specification language which can be used to give contracts and invariants. Because PRUSTI has no notion of prophecy, it does not use the *final* operator (ˆ) to specify mutable borrows, instead using *pledges*. A pledge is an assertion that is guaranteed to hold at the time when the borrow expires, which is not necessarily in the body of the function. In contrast, the *final* operator of CREUSOT brings prophecies as first-class objects in the specification language, to specify the future values of borrows. The semantics of PRUSTI specifications were designed to preserve the behavior of program assertions when lifted into pure contracts. In particular, arithmetic in PRUSTI's specifications is machine arithmetic and has to be checked for overflow. CREUSOT takes a different approach by using a more abstract specifications language (PEARLITE), which is usually easier to reason with. A consequence of this difference is that PEARLITE logical functions cannot be executed, while PRUSTI's pure functions can be used in programs. While PRUSTI's permission system supports the common borrowing patterns of Rust, it struggles with patterns like *reborrowing in a loop* (*e.g.,* "All Zeros List" 5), with data structures *containing borrows* like pairs of mutable borrows 5, or with *nested borrows*. In contrast, CREUSOT's translation of Rust types using prophecies for mutable borrows is general and *compositional*: we place no restrictions on the usage of mutable borrows or their position within types. Another noticeable difference with PRUSTI lies in the choice of the underlying logic. PRUSTI encodes specifications into separation logic and delegates verification to Viper, whereas CREUSOT encodes them into FOL and delegates verification to SMT solvers via WHY3. PRUSTI chooses to verify Rust's ownership discipline with Viper, while CREUSOT depends on Rust's borrow checker for that, which means CREUSOT relies on the soundness of Rust's type system and of its implementation. We believe this difference explains the significant blow-up in verification times: on simple examples verification takes an order of magnitude more time than with CREUSOT. The simpler underlying logic in CREUSOT, allows it to benefit from WHY3's mature infrastructure to manage a herd of automated provers and a tactic system to provide guidance when they go astray. Both PRUSTI and CREUSOT support traits and polymorphism. However, because mutable borrows need special care in PRUSTI, a generic Rust function cannot be instantiated with a mutable borrow, which causes no problem in CREUSOT. Moreover, properties of traits in PRUSTI are specified using only pre- and postconditions; we use *laws* for specifying such properties, which we find more flexible.

AENEAS [11] is a novel verifier for Rust targeting interactive verification of programs in established proof assistants like F* or Coq. To achieve this they also translate Rust programs to functional programs in a State-Error Monad. Instead of using prophecies they use *backwards functions* to reconstruct the value of a lender has after the borrows expiry. This approach appears to have a deep and close link to prophecies as used by CREUSOT, instead of using non-determinism to pull the value out of thin air, AENEAS constructs the actual *witness* of this value. The constructive approach that AENEAS takes may very well be better suited to interactive provers which traditionally prefer constructive logics. AENEAS also makes the choice of using so called *extrinsic proofs*, all specification and proof work is done in the prover, with no annotations present in Rust. While this allows them to leverage all the existing tools in the underlying prover, the proof engineer must manually sync these proofs and specifications with the Rust code as it evolves. This attests to the different audiences targeted by the tools, AENEAS seeks to enable the users of existing advanced verification tools to perform more ergonomic verification using their traditional toolkits, while CREUSOT seeks to bring verification to regular engineers. In terms of language support, AENEAS is currently more limited than CREUSOT, it has no support for *loops, nested borrows* or *traits*.

Beyond the Rust ecosystem, Spark/Ada is a tool suite for deductive verification of Ada programs. For a long-time, it was restricted to a subset of Ada without pointers. Support for pointers was added in 2020 [13], based on an ownership policy similar to Rust's. At the start Spark used a notion of pledges similar to PRUSTI's, but they have now replaced it with prophecies. Similarly to CREUSOT, Spark/Ada makes use of the ownership information computed by the compiler to encode specifications and code into a first-order logic, instead of relying on a separation logic.

References

1. Astrauskas, V., Müller, P., Poli, F., Summers, A.J.: Leveraging rust types for modular specification and verification. Proc. ACM Program. Lang. **3**, 147:1–147:30 (2019). https://doi.org/10.1145/3360573
2. Barrett, C., et al.: CVC4. In: Gopalakrishnan, G., Qadeer, S. (eds.) CAV 2011. LNCS, vol. 6806, pp. 171–177. Springer, Heidelberg (2011). https://doi.org/10.1007/978-3-642-22110-1_14
3. Baudin, P., et al.: ACSL: ANSI/ISO C Specification Language, version 1.16 (2020), https://frama-c.com/html/acsl.html
4. Bobot, F., Filliâtre, J.-C., Marché, C., Paskevich, A.: Let's verify this with Why3. Int. J. Softw. Tools Technol. Transfer **17**(6), 709–727 (2014). https://doi.org/10.1007/s10009-014-0314-5

5. Cok, D.R.: OpenJML: software verification for java 7 using JML, OpenJDK, and Eclipse. Formal Integr. Dev. Env. **149**, 79–92 (2014). https://doi.org/10.4204/EPTCS.149.8

6. Conchon, S., Coquereau, A., Iguernlala, M., Mebsout, A.: Alt-Ergo 2.2. In: Satisfiability Modulo Theories (2018). https://hal.inria.fr/hal-01960203

7. Dailler, S., Marché, C., Moy, Y.: Lightweight interactive proving inside an automatic program verifier. In: Formal Integrated Development Environment (2018). https://doi.org/10.4204/EPTCS.284.1

8. Denis, X., Jourdan, J.H., Marché, C.: The Creusot environment for the deductive verification of rust programs. Research report 9448, Inria Saclay - Île de France (2021). https://hal.inria.fr/hal-03526634

9. Filliâtre, J.C., Gondelman, L., Paskevich, A.: A pragmatic type system for deductive verification. Research report, Université Paris Sud (2016). https://hal.archives-ouvertes.fr/hal-01256434v3

10. Hatcliff, J., Leavens, G.T., Leino, K.R.M., Müller, P., Parkinson, M.: Behavioral interface specification languages. ACM Comput. Surv. **44**(3), 1–58 (2012). https://doi.org/10.1145/2187671.2187678

11. Ho, S., Protzenko, J.: Aeneas: rust verification by functional translation (2022). https://doi.org/10.48550/ARXIV.2206.07185

12. Hubert, T., Marché, C.: Separation analysis for deductive verification. In: Heap Analysis and Verification, pp. 81–93 (2007). https://hal.inria.fr/hal-03630177

13. Jaloyan, G.-A., Dross, C., Maalej, M., Moy, Y., Paskevich, A.: Verification of programs with pointers in SPARK. In: Lin, S.-W., Hou, Z., Mahony, B. (eds.) ICFEM 2020. LNCS, vol. 12531, pp. 55–72. Springer, Cham (2020). https://doi.org/10.1007/978-3-030-63406-3_4

14. Leino, K.R.M., Moskal, M.: VACID-0: verification of ample correctness of invariants of data-structures, edition 0. In: Verified Software, Tools, Techniques and Experiments (2010)

15. Matsushita, Y., Denis, X., Jacques-Henri, J., Dreyer, D.: RustHornBelt: a semantic foundation for functional verification of rust programs with unsafe code. In: Programming Language Design and Implementation (2022). https://doi.org/10.1145/3519939.3523704

16. Matsushita, Y., Tsukada, T., Kobayashi, N.: RustHorn: CHC-based verification for rust programs. ACM Trans. Progr. Lang. Syst. **43**(4), 15:1–15:54 (2021). https://doi.org/10.1145/3462205

17. McCormick, J.W., Chapin, P.C.: Building High Integrity Applications with SPARK. Cambridge University Press, Cambridge (2015)

18. Mol, M., other contributors: The Rosetta Code chrestomathy of programs, https://rosettacode.org

19. de Moura, L., Bjørner, N.: Z3: an efficient SMT solver. In: Ramakrishnan, C.R., Rehof, J. (eds.) TACAS 2008. LNCS, vol. 4963, pp. 337–340. Springer, Heidelberg (2008). https://doi.org/10.1007/978-3-540-78800-3_24

20. Smans, J., Jacobs, B., Piessens, F.: Implicit dynamic frames: combining dynamic frames and separation logic. In: Drossopoulou, S. (ed.) ECOOP 2009. LNCS, vol. 5653, pp. 148–172. Springer, Heidelberg (2009). https://doi.org/10.1007/978-3-642-03013-0_8

21. The rust community: The `std::cmp::Ord` trait of Rust. https://doc.rust-lang.org/std/cmp/trait.Ord.html

Generation of a Reversible Semantics for Erlang in Maude

Giovanni Fabbretti[1]([✉]) [iD], Ivan Lanese[2]([✉]) [iD], and Jean-Bernard Stefani[1]([✉]) [iD]

[1] Univ. Grenoble Alpes, INRIA, CNRS, Grenoble INP, LIG, 38000 Grenoble, France
{giovanni.fabbretti,jean-bernard.stefani}@inria.fr
[2] Focus Team, University of Bologna, INRIA, 40137 Bologna, Italy
ivan.lanese@gmail.com

Abstract. In recent years, reversibility in concurrent settings has attracted interest thanks to its diverse applications in areas such as error recovery, debugging, and biological modeling. Also, it has been studied in many formalisms, including Petri nets, process algebras, and programming languages like Erlang. However, most attempts made so far suffer from the same limitation: they define the reversible semantics in an ad-hoc fashion. To address this limit, Lanese et al. have recently proposed a novel general method to derive a concurrent reversible semantics from a non-reversible one. However, in most interesting instances the method relies on infinite sets of reductions, making doubtful its practical applicability. We bridge the gap between theory and practice by implementing the above method in Maude. The key insight is that infinite sets of reductions can be captured by a small number of schemas in many relevant cases. This happens indeed for our application: the functional and concurrent fragment of Erlang. We extend the framework with a general rollback operator, allowing one to undo an action far in the past, including all and only its consequences. We can thus use our tool, e.g., as an oracle against which to test the reversible debugger CauDEr for Erlang, or as an executable specification for new reversible debuggers.

1 Introduction

Reversible computing studies computational models which have both (standard) forward and backward notions of execution. Reversibility has attracted interest thanks to its diverse applications in areas such as debugging [5,7,9,19], robotics [21], biological modeling [4], and error-recovery [26]. In sequential systems reversibility is well understood: intuitively it corresponds to undo actions in reverse order of execution. In concurrent settings, more care is needed. In 2004,

The work has been partially supported by French ANR project DCore ANR-18-CE25-0007. We thank the anonymous referees for their helpful comments and suggestions. We also thank Roberto Bruni for the useful comments and discussions provided. The second author also thanks INdAM-GNCS Project CUP_E55F22000270001 "Proprietà qualitative e quantitative di sistemi reversibili".

© Springer Nature Switzerland AG 2022
A. Riesco and M. Zhang (Eds.): ICFEM 2022, LNCS 13478, pp. 106–122, 2022.
https://doi.org/10.1007/978-3-031-17244-1_7

Danos and Krivine proposed the notion of *causal-consistent reversibility* [3], tailored for concurrent systems. In a concurrent execution, to undo an action causal consistency only requires to undo its causal consequences first. Actions which have been temporally interleaved with such consequences, but are causally independent, can be left untouched. Thus, causal consistency undoes events only if strictly necessary, which is useful to explore concurrent programs that can be prone to state explosion. Causal-consistent reversibility has been studied in several formalisms such as process calculi [2,3,17,28], Petri nets [23,27], and the Erlang programming language [5,9,12,19]. It also led to interesting practical applications, the most prominent example being as a debugging technique as proposed in [7] and then implemented in the CauDEr debugger for Erlang [5,9,19].

Most of the reversible semantics above have been devised ad-hoc for a specific formalism. The process is usually composed of three phases: i) definition of causal dependencies between events; ii) extension of the non-reversible semantics so that enough information is kept while going forward; iii) creation of a backward semantics that allows one to undo actions in a causal-consistent manner and restore past states. Performing this process manually is time-consuming, error-prone and lacks generality.

Recently Lanese and Medić proposed a general method to automate the production of reversible semantics [14]. The method generalizes the ad-hoc approaches above and works as follows. First, causal dependencies are defined in terms of resources *consumed* and *produced*. Without focusing on the details, let us consider the following Erlang example.

$$\langle p_1, \theta, p_2 \ ! \ hello, me \rangle \rightarrow \langle p_1, \theta, hello, me \rangle \mid \langle p_1, p_2, hello \rangle \tag{1}$$

On the left, a process p_1 is ready to send a message *hello* (! denotes message send). When the reduction is executed the process is consumed to produce the message $\langle p_1, p_2, hello \rangle$ and the evolution of the process itself after the send. We say that the reduction consumes the process and produces the continuation and the message. Then, the non-reversible semantics taken in input is extended so that each entity is tagged with a *unique key*, and *memories* are produced each time a forward step is performed. Memories are the extra pieces of information required to restore past states of the system and together with keys they also keep track of the causal dependencies. Finally, a causal-consistent backward semantics, symmetric to the forward one, is generated.

Contributions. The general method in [14] was only described theoretically. It takes in input a semantics described as a, possibly infinite, set of ground rules, making it not immediately clear that an implementation could exist. In this paper we provide such an implementation in Maude, by using schemas to capture (possibly infinite) sets of ground rules. As a case study, we use our tool to derive a causal-consistent reversible semantics for the functional and concurrent fragment of the Erlang programming language, which matches the one previously produced by hand [9].

Finally, we extend Lanese et al. approach by defining a causal-consistent rollback operator, allowing one to undo a past action including all and only its consequences, on top of the reversible semantics. Rollback is a key primitive for a concurrent causal-consistent debugger as described in [7]. In the literature, examples of causal-consistent rollback operators abound [5,9,19]. Nonetheless these operators were always designed in an ad-hoc fashion, suffering from the same limits as the ad-hoc reversible semantics. In contrast, our definition is able to cope with all the reversible semantics we produce, thanks to their uniformity. This is beneficial and desirable, as one can change or update the underlying semantics without the need to redefine the rollback operator.

To sum up, the main contributions of this work are:

- a novel formalization of Erlang in Maude (Sect. 3);
- a tool to derive a causal-consistent reversible semantics from a non-reversible one (Sect. 4) together with a proof of correctness of the approach (Sect. 5);
- a general definition of a causal-consistent rollback operator, built on top of the reversible semantics (Sect. 6).

All the code discussed in this paper is publicly available at [29].

2 Background

2.1 The Erlang Language

Erlang is a functional and concurrent programming language, it is widely used and appreciated because it is easy to learn, provides useful abstractions for concurrent and distributed programming, and because of its support for highly-available systems. Erlang implements the actor model [10], a concurrency model based on message passing. In the actor model, each process is an actor that can interact with other actors only through the exchange of messages, no memory is shared. Actors are identified by a unique pid (process identifier) and have a queue of messages which have arrived but have not yet been processed. An actor evaluates an expression, and has an environment to store variable bindings. Due to space constraints, here we only briefly describe the main concurrent primitives of Erlang, send, receive, spawn, and self, more details on the language can be found in the technical report [6].

The send primitive is written as $e_1 \ ! \ e_2$, where e_1 must evaluate to the pid of the receiver process and e_2 must evaluate to the payload, say v, of the message. The expression itself evaluates to v and, as a side-effect, the message is sent.

The receive $pat_1 \rightarrow exprs_1; \ldots; pat_n \rightarrow exprs_n$ end construct explores the queue of messages looking for one mathcing one of the patterns, say pat_i. If found, the corresponding branch $exprs_i$ is executed.

The spawn primitive creates a new process; it takes as argument the function f that the new process will execute, together with the parameters for f - if any. The spawn returns the (fresh) pid of the newly created process and, as a side effect, the new process is created.

Finally, function self returns the pid of the process who invoked it.

```
fmod BOOL is                                    var A : Bool .
   sort Bool .                                  eq true and A = A .
   op true : -> Bool [ctor] .                   eq false and A = false .
   op false : -> Bool [ctor] .                  eq A and A = A .
   op _and_ : Bool Bool -> Bool [assoc ..] .
endfm
```

Fig. 1. Maude module for Booleans (Due to space reason we represented the module on two columns, usually Maude modules are single-columned.)

2.2   Maude

Maude [22] is a programming language that efficiently implements rewriting logic [24]. Formally, a rewriting theory is a tuple (Σ, E, R), where Σ represents a collection of typed operators, E a set of equations $t = t'$, and R a set of semantic rules $t \rightarrow t'$. In both cases, t, t' are terms built from the operators in Σ.

The equational side of rewriting logic is well-suited to define the deterministic part of the model, where we define equivalence classes over terms. Equations can also be conditional, and conditions can be either the membership of the term to some kind or other equations.

Rewriting rules define the concurrent (non-deterministic) part of the programming language semantics. The set of rules R specifies how to rewrite a (parameterized) term t to another term t'. Rewriting rules can be conditional too, and conditions can be equations, as well as other rewriting conditions.

In other words the equational theory specifies which terms define the same states of a system, only using different syntactical elements, while the rewriting rules define how the system can evolve and transit from one state to another.

Let us now consider the module in Fig. 1, a sample Maude module that implements Booleans together with the **and** operation.

First, the sort `Bool` is declared. Then, the values `true` and `false` are declared as two constant operators of sort `Bool`. Successively, the **and** operation is defined as a function that takes in input some `Bool`s and produces a `Bool` as a result. Finally, the semantics of **and** is given by the equational theory defined on the right of the module. Equations are used from left to right to normalize terms. For instance, the first equation, `eq true and A = A`, is used to evaluate the **and** operator when the first argument has been normalized to `true`. For simplicity, this example does not include rewriting rules, memberships nor conditional equations.

As an additional example, we show a rewriting rule generating the Erlang reduction (1) from the Introduction:

```
< 1 | exp: 2 ! 'hello', env: {}, me: _ > =>
    < 1 | exp : 'hello', env: {}, me: _ > ||
       < sender: 1, receiver: 2, payload: 'hello' >
```

Labels exp (for the expression under evaluation), env (for the environment) and me (for the module environment, containing function definitions), and similarly for messages, give names to fields. Also, the first argument in each process is the pid (pids are integers in our implementation), the special notation highlights that it can be used as identifier for the tuple. Character _ means that the actual value is not shown.

We will define the generation of the reversible semantics as a program that, given the modules of the non-reversible semantics, produces new modules, which define the reversible semantics.

2.3 Derivation of the Reversible Semantics

The rest of this section summarizes the methodology to automatically derive a causal-consistent reversible semantics starting from a non-reversible one [14] that we will use as starting point. The approach requires that the latter is modeled as a reduction semantics that satisfies some syntactic conditions.

Format of the Input Reduction Semantics. We now describe the shape that the reduction semantics taken in input must have.

The syntax must be divided in two levels: a lower level of entities on which there are no restrictions, and an upper level of systems of the following form:

$$S ::= P \mid op_n(S_1, \ldots, S_n) \mid \mathbf{0}$$

where $\mathbf{0}$ is the empty system, P any entity of the lower level and $op_n(S_1, \ldots, S_n)$ any n-ary operator to compose entities. An entity of the lower level could be, for example, a process of the system or a message traveling the network. Among the operators we always assume a binary parallel operator $\mid$.

The rules defining the operational semantics must fit the format in Fig. 2, where $\rightarrowtail$ denotes the relation defining the reduction semantics taken in input. The format contains rules to: i) allow entities to interact with each other (S-ACT); ii) exploit a structural congruence (EQV); iii) allow single entities to execute inside a context (S-OPN); iv) execute two systems in parallel (PAR). While (EQV) and (PAR) are rules that must belong to the semantics, (S-ACT) and (S-OPN) are schemas, and the semantics may contain any number of instances of them. In the schema (S-ACT), the term $T[Q_1, \ldots, Q_m]$ denotes a context composed by operators. Actually, rule (PAR) is an instance of schema (S-OPN), highlighting that such an instance is required. Also, reduction (1) from the Introduction is an instance of schema (S-ACT). Moreover, notice that a notion of structural congruence on systems is assumed. We refer to [14] for more details on the definition of structural congruence. This is of limited relevance here, since the only structural congruence needed for Erlang is that parallel composition forms a commutative monoid, which translates to the same property in the reversible semantics.

$$(\text{S-Act}) \ \frac{}{P_1 \mid \ldots \mid P_n \rightarrowtail T[Q_1, \ldots, Q_m]}$$

$$(\text{Eqv}) \ \frac{S \equiv S' \quad S \rightarrowtail S_1 \quad S_1 \equiv S_1'}{S' \rightarrowtail S_1'}$$

$$(\text{S-Opn}) \ \frac{S_i \rightarrowtail S_i'}{op_n(S_0, \ldots, S_i, \ldots, S_n) \rightarrowtail op_n(S_0, \ldots, S_i', \ldots, S_n)}$$

$$(\text{Par}) \ \frac{S \rightarrowtail S'}{S \mid S_1 \rightarrowtail S' \mid S_1}$$

Fig. 2. Required structure of the semantics in input; S- rules are schemas

Methodology. To obtain a forward reversible semantics, we need to track enough history and causality information to allow one to define a backward semantics exploiting it. First, the syntax of systems is updated as follows:

$$R ::= k : P \mid op_n(R_1, \ldots, R_n) \mid \mathbf{0} \mid [R \, ; C]$$
$$C ::= T[k_1 : \bullet_1, \ldots, k_m : \bullet_m]$$

Two modifications have been done. First, each entity of the system is tagged with a key k. Keys are used to distinguish identical entities with a different history. Second, the syntax is updated with another production: memories. Memories have the shape $\mu = [R; C]$, where R is the configuration of the system that gave rise to a forward step and C is a context describing the structure of the system resulting from the forward step. C acts as a link between R and the actual final configuration. In other words, memories link different states of the entities and keep track of past states of the system so that they can be restored.

Then, the forward reversible semantics is defined by decorating the rules of the non-reversible reduction semantics as depicted in Fig. 3, where $\rightarrowtail$ is the relation defining the forward reversible semantics. Now each time a forward step is performed each resulting entity is tagged with a fresh key, and a memory, connecting the old configuration with the new one, is produced. E.g., the forward rule corresponding to reduction (1) from the Introduction is:

$$k : \langle p_1, \theta, p_2 \; ! \; hello, me \rangle \rightarrowtail k_1 : \langle p_1, \theta, hello, me \rangle \mid k_2 : \langle p_1, p_2, hello \rangle \mid$$
$$[k : \langle p_1, \theta, p_2 \; ! \; hello, me \rangle \, ; k_1 : \bullet_1 \mid k_2 : \bullet_2]$$

Notice that the approach allows one to manage different rules since the transformation is defined in terms of the schema they must fit.

The backward rules, depicted in Fig. 4, where $\rightsquigarrow$ is the relation defining the backward reversible semantics, are symmetric to the forward ones: if a memory $\mu = [R \, ; C]$ and the entities tagged with the keys in C are both available then a backward step can be performed and the old configuration R can be restored. E.g., the backward rule undoing the reduction (1) from the Introduction is:

$$k_1 : \langle p_1, \theta, hello, me \rangle \mid k_2 : \langle p_1, p_2, hello \rangle \mid$$
$$[k : \langle p_1, \theta, p_2 \; ! \; hello, me \rangle \, ; k_1 : \bullet_1 \mid k_2 : \bullet_2] \rightsquigarrow k : \langle p_1, \theta, p_2 \; ! \; hello, me \rangle$$

$$(\text{F-S-Act}) \; \frac{j_1,\ldots,j_m \text{ are fresh keys}}{k_1 : P_1 \mid \ldots \mid k_n : P_n \twoheadrightarrow T[j_1 : Q_1,\ldots,j_m : Q_m] \mid [k_1 : P_1 \mid \ldots \mid k_n : P_n \; ; T[j_1 : \bullet_1,\ldots,j_m : \bullet_m]]}$$

$$(\text{F-S-Opn}) \; \frac{R_i \twoheadrightarrow R_i' \quad (\text{keys}(R_i') \setminus \text{keys}(R_i)) \cap (\text{keys}(R_0,\ldots,R_{i-1},R_{i+1},\ldots,R_n)) = \emptyset}{op_n(R_0,\ldots,R_i,\ldots,R_n) \twoheadrightarrow op_n(R_0,\ldots,R_i',\ldots,R_n)}$$

Fig. 3. Forward rules of the uncontrolled reversible semantics

$$(\text{B-S-Act}) \; \frac{\mu = [k_1 : P_1 \mid \ldots \mid k_n : P_n \; ; T[j_1 : \bullet_1,\ldots,j_m : \bullet_m]]}{T[j_1 : Q_1,\ldots,j_m : Q_m] \mid \mu \rightsquigarrow k_1 : P_1 \mid \ldots \mid k_n : P_n}$$

$$(\text{B-S-Opn}) \; \frac{R_i' \rightsquigarrow R_i}{op_n(R_0,\ldots,R_i',\ldots,R_n) \rightsquigarrow op_n(R_0,\ldots,R_i,\ldots,R_n)}$$

Fig. 4. Backward rules of the uncontrolled reversible semantics

The reversible semantics produced by this approach captures causal dependencies in terms of resources produced and consumed, since, thanks to the memory, a causal link is created each time some entities are rewritten. We refer to [14] for the formal proof of the causal-consistency and of other relevant properties of the reversible semantics. We also remark that the semantics produced is uncontrolled [16], i.e., if multiple (forward and/or backward) steps are enabled at the same time there is no policy on which one to choose. Both in Fig. 3 and in Fig. 4 we omitted the rule for structural congruence as it is similar to the one in Fig. 2.

3   Formalizing Erlang in Maude

In this section we present the formalization of the semantics of the functional and concurrent fragment of Erlang in Maude. We mostly follow the semantics defined in [9]. Technically, we used as starting point the formalization of Core Erlang [1] in Maude presented in [25], which was aimed at model checking. While our formalization is quite different from theirs (e.g., we formalize a fragment of Erlang instead of one of Core Erlang), we were still able to re-use some of their modules, like the parsing module, and some of their ideas which greatly simplified the formalization task.

As in [9], our semantics of Erlang has two layers: one for expressions and one for systems. This division is quite convenient for the formalization in Maude, as we can formalize the expression level as an equational theory and then use rewriting rules to describe the system level.

The system level comprises a rewriting rule for each concurrent construct of the language and a few rules τ for sequential operations. We could define the sequential operations as an equational theory also at the system level, however equations are applied in a fixed order, hence only one possible interleaving of sequential steps would have been considered. For rewriting rules instead all possible orders can be considered, thus enabling all possible interleavings. Notably, also a different semantics where sequential steps are defined as equations could be made reversible using the approach we describe in the next section.

Before presenting the rewriting logic, let us discuss the entities that compose an Erlang system. Processes are defined as tuples of the form:

$$\langle p, \theta, e, me \rangle$$

where p is the process pid, θ is the environment binding variables to values[1], e is the expression currently under evaluation and me is the module environment, which contains the definitions of the functions declared in the module, that p can invoke or spawn. Messages instead are defined as tuples of the form:

$$\langle p, p', v \rangle$$

where p is the pid of the sender, p' is the pid of the receiver and v is the payload. In this work, processes and messages are entities in the lower level of the semantics, denoted as P in Sect. 2.3.

A system is composed of messages and processes, using the parallel operator.

Now, let us analyze in detail the shape of the corresponding rewriting logic by first analyzing the equational theory for expressions.

3.1 Equational Theory

The theory is defined as a set of conditional (i.e., with an if clause) and unconditional equations, represented as follow

eq : $[equation\text{-}name]$	ceq : $[conditional\text{-}equation\text{-}name]$
$\langle l, \theta, e \rangle = \langle l', \theta', e' \rangle$	$\langle l, \theta, e \rangle = \langle l'', \theta'', e'' \rangle$
	if $\langle l', \theta', e' \rangle := op(l, \theta, e) \wedge \langle l'', \theta'', e'' \rangle := \langle l', \theta', e' \rangle$

In the equations, to evaluate an expression e we also need two additional items: an environment θ and a label l. The environment binds each variable to its value, if any. The label communicates both i) the kind of side effect performed by the expression, if any; and ii) information on the details of the side effect back and forth between the expression level and the system level. An example of this mechanism is presented below.

Example 1 (Equation for self). The unconditional equation below describes the behavior of `self` at the expression level.

```
eq [self] : < self(pid(N)), ENV, atom("self")() > = < tau, ENV, int(N) > .
```

It reads roughly as follows: if the system level asks to check whether a `self` can be performed, communicating that the pid of the current process is N (via `self(pid(N))`) and the expression is actually a self (`atom("self")()`) then the expression reduces to the pid (`int(N)`) and the label becomes `tau`, denoting successful evaluation of a sequential step.   ◇

---

[1] In truth, θ is a stack of environments, such design choice is discussed in Sect. 3.2.

Conditional equations can: either define a single step that requires some side condition (e.g., binding a variable to its value), or perform some intermediate operation (e.g., selecting an inner expression to evaluate) and then use recursively other equations (with the clause $\langle l'', \theta'', e'' \rangle := \langle l', \theta', e' \rangle$) to reach a canonical form. Examples of conditional equations can be found in the technical report [6].

3.2 Expression Management

One of the difficulties of formalizing Erlang lies in the manipulation of expressions. In fact, a naive management could produce unwanted results or illegal expressions.

Consider the invocation below of function

$$pow\_and\_sub(N, M) \;\rightarrow\; Z = N * N, Z - M$$

which computes the difference between the power of N and M.

$$X = pow\_and\_sub(N, M) \quad\rightarrow\quad X = Z = N * N, Z - M. \tag{2}$$

By naively replacing the function with its body, we get a syntactically correct Erlang expression, but it would not have the desired effect, as the variable X would assume the value $N * N$ instead of $Z - M$, as desired.

Similarly, constructs that produce a sequence of expressions, like case, may also produce illegal terms. Consider, e.g., the following Erlang expression:

$$\text{case } pow\_and\_sub(N, M) \text{ of} \ldots \quad\rightarrow\quad \text{case } Z = N * N, Z - M \text{ of} \ldots \tag{3}$$

In this case the obtained expression is illegal, as case expects a single expression and not a sequence, and would be refused by an Erlang compiler.

The solution that we adopt to solve both problems consists in wrapping the produced sequence of expressions with the construct begin_end (the Erlang equivalent for parentheses), which turns a sequence of expressions into a single expression.

For instance, in (2) the produced expression would be

$$X = \text{begin } Z = N * N, Z - M \text{ end}.$$

and in this case X is correctly bound to the result of $Z - M$. This solution indeed produces the desired effect also in a real Erlang environment.

For this reason, θ, within a process tuple, is a stack of environments. Each time that a sequence of expressions is wrapped a new environment with the appropriate bindings (e.g., the function parameters) is pushed on θ. Then, each time the sequence of expression is fully evaluated, i.e., the expression looks like begin v end, then v replaces the expression and an environment is popped from θ.

```
crl [sys-send] :
    < P | exp: EXSEQ, env-stack: ENV, ASET > =>
    < P | exp: EXSEQ', env-stack: ENV', ASET > ||
    < sender: P, receiver: DEST, payload: GVALUE >
    if < DEST ! GVALUE, ENV', EXSEQ' > := < req-gen, ENV, EXSEQ > .
```

Fig. 5. System rule send

3.3   Rewriting Rules

Let us now focus on rewriting rules, which have the following general shape

$$\textsf{crl} : [\textit{conditional-rule-name}]$$
$$\langle p, \theta, e, me \rangle \mid E => \langle p, \theta', e', me \rangle \mid op(l', \langle p, \theta, e, me \rangle, E)$$
$$\textsf{if } \langle l', \theta', e' \rangle := \langle l, \theta, e \rangle$$

Here, E captures other entities of the system, if any, that may have an impact on the reduction, in particular a message that may be received. Rewriting rules are always conditional, as we always rely on the expression semantics to understand which action the selected process is ready to perform. Finally, we use op to apply side effects to E, determined by the label l' produced by the expression level. Example 2 below discusses the rewriting rule for send , additional examples can be found in the technical report [6].

Example 2. The rule in Fig. 5 is used to send a message. The **if** clause of the rule uses the equational theory to check if the current expression, EXSEQ, can perform a send of GVALUE to DEST. This exemplifies how the labels **req-gen** (a generic request about which step can be taken, more complex requests are used, e.g., for self, see Example 1) and DEST ! GVALUE serve to pass information between the system and the expression level. Using this information, side effects (in this case the send of a message) are performed at the system level. If the send can be performed, then the process evolves to evaluate the new expression EXSEQ' in the new environment ENV', and the new message is added to the system. Here, ASET includes other elements of the process which are not relevant (currently, only the module environment). W.r.t. the general schema described above, here E on the left-hand side is empty, and on the right-hand side op will add the message to E.

Note that the rewriting rule in Sect. 2.2 is an instance of the one above.   ◇

4   Generating the Reversible Semantics

We choose Maude to define the generation of the reversible semantics for two main reasons. First, Maude is well-suited to define program transformations thanks to its META-LEVEL module, which contains facilities to meta-represent a module and to manipulate it. Second, since we defined Erlang's semantics in Maude, we do not need to define a parser for it as it can be easily loaded and meta-represented by taking advantage of Maude's facilities.

```
mod SYSTEM is
 ...
  sort Sys .                        op #empty-system : -> Sys [ctor] .
  subsort Entity < Sys .            op _||_ : Sys Sys -> Sys [ctor ... ] .
endm
```

Fig. 6. Extract of the system module for Erlang.

4.1 Format of the Non-reversible Semantics

As in [14], the input semantics must follow a given format so that the approach can be applied. Let us describe such format. First, the formalization must include a module named SYSTEM which defines the system level. As an example, Fig. 6 depicts the system module for the Erlang language. We omit elements that are not interesting in this context (namely the import of other modules).

The module defines the operators of the system level, as discussed in Sect. 2.3. For Erlang, we just have parallel composition || and the empty system.

All the operators in the module SYSTEM must take in input and produce elements of sort Sys. The subsort relation Entity < Sys must be declared as well, to specify that entities of the lower level are systems. To this end, sorts of the lower level (in Erlang, messages and processes) must be subsorts of Entity.

Rules of the rewriting theory that define the single steps of the reduction semantics (like in Fig. 5) must be defined under the module TRANSITIONS.

4.2 Transformation to the Syntax

We describe here how to transform a non-reversible syntax as described above into a reversible one, as recalled in Sect. 2.3. Roughly, we add keys and memories.

Key is the sort generated by the operator key_ and EntityWithKey is the sort generated by the operator _*_, that composes an entity and a key.

To define memories, first we declare a new sort Context (which corresponds to C in the reversible syntax presented in Sect. 2.3), together with an operator @:_ to create a Context from a key. Then, memories are added by defining the sort Memory and by defining an operator that builds a memory by combining the interacting entities with keys with the final configuration of sort Context. E.g., the memory created by the reversible version of the reduction in Sect. 2.2 is:

```
[ < 1 | exp: 2 ! 'hello', ASET> * key(0) ; @: key(0 0) || @: key:(1 0) ]
```

Here, with the variable ASET, we hide the process environment and the module environment since they are not interesting. EntityWithKey, Context and Memory are all declared as subsorts of Sys so that system operators can be applied to them.

4.3 Generating the Reversible Semantics

The transformation to be performed over the rewriting rules is the one described in Sect. 2.3, rephrased in Maude notation. Rules must be extended to deal with

```
crl [label sys-send]:
   < P | ASET, exp: EXSEQ, env-stack: ENV > * key(L)
   => < sender: P, receiver: DEST, payload: GVALUE > * key(0 L) ||
       < P | exp: EXSEQ', env-stack: ENV', ASET > * key(1 L) ||
       [< P | ASET, exp: EXSEQ, env-stack: ENV > *
        key(L) ; @: key(0 L) || @: key(1 L)]
   if < DEST ! GVALUE, ENV', EXSEQ' > := < req-gen, ENV, EXSEQ > .

rl [label sys-send]:
   < sender: P, receiver: DEST,payload: GVALUE > * key(0 L) ||
   < P | exp: EXSEQ', env-stack: ENV', ASET > * key(1 L) ||
   [< P | ASET, exp: EXSEQ, env-stack: ENV > *
   key L ; @: key(0 L) || @: key(1 L)]
   => < P | ASET, exp: EXSEQ, env-stack: ENV > * key L
```

Fig. 7. Reversible rules: send.

entities with key, and each time a forward step is taken the resulting entities must be tagged with fresh keys and the appropriate memory must be created.

The transformation is mostly straightforward, the only tricky part concerns the generation of fresh keys. Indeed, we need a 'distributed' way to compute them, as passing around a key generator would produce spurious causal dependencies. We solved the problem as follows. Keys are lists of integers. Each time we need to produce a fresh key, to tag a new entity on the right-hand side of a rule, we take the key L of the first entity on the left-hand side of the rule, and we tag each of the new entities with L prefixed with an integer corresponding to the position of the entity on the right-hand side. Furthermore, we create the required memory.

Figure 7 shows the reversible rules -forward and backward- for the send rule depicted in Fig. 5. In the forward rule, on the left-hand side, the process is initially tagged with a key key(L), then the new entities on the right-hand side are tagged with fresh keys key(0 L) and key(1 L), built from key(L). Moreover, the rule also produces a memory binding the old and the new states.

The generation of the backward semantics is easy: a backward rule is obtained from the forward one by swapping the left- with the right-hand side and dropping the conditional branch. Indeed, the latter is not required any more because if the process has performed the forward step, as proved by the existence of a memory for it, then it can always perform the backward one. One has only to check that all the consequences of the action have been already undone. This is ensured by the presence of the entities whose keys are in the context inside the memory.

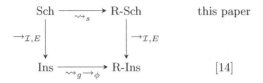

Fig. 8. Schema of the proof of correctness.

5   Correctness

This section is dedicated to prove the correctness of the generated reversible semantics. This requires to close the gap between the format of the rules expected by the general method from [14] and the actual format of the rules provided in input. In fact, the schema of the general method allows for an arbitrary number of rules, potentially infinitely many, describing the system evolution. Obviously, to efficiently describe a system, we cannot exploit infinitely many rules. Thus, in the formalization of the semantics we resorted to schemas, and we used the expression level semantics so to select only a subset of the possible instances.

For example, let us consider the following processes:

$$\langle p, \theta, 2\,!\,'hello', \_\rangle \qquad \langle p', \theta', \text{case } 2\,!\,'hello' \text{ of } \dots, \_\rangle \qquad \langle p'', \theta'', X = 2\,!\,'hello', \_\rangle$$

The three processes above are all ready to perform the same send action, even though they have a different shape, nonetheless thanks to the expression level semantics we are able to formalize their behavior in one single rewriting rule.

However, we need to prove that the instances of the corresponding reversible rules coincide with the set of reversible instances defined by the approach in [14]. That is, we need to show that the diagram in Fig. 8 commutes.

This result is needed also to ensure that our reversible semantics, defined over schemas, by construction enjoys the same desirable properties, e.g., loop lemma, as the reversible semantics defined over ground rules following [14].

Let us begin by discussing the functions on the sides of the square. First, function $\leadsto_s$ takes in input a set of non-reversible rule schemas of the form $t \to t'$ if C and generates the corresponding set of reversible (forward and backward) rule schemas. Then, $\to_{\mathcal{I},E}$ takes in input a set of (reversible or non-reversible) rule schemas and generates all possible instances using substitutions in $\mathcal{I}$, providing all the possible values for variables, and an equational theory E, allowing one to check whether the side condition C is satisfied. The side condition is then dropped. Notably, substitutions $i \in \mathcal{I}$ instantiate also key variables to lists of integers. Function $\to_{\mathcal{I},E}$ is undefined if there is some $i \in \mathcal{I}$ which is not defined on some variables of the schemas. Also, we expect the substitution to produce well-typed rules (however, we do not discuss typing here). Function $\leadsto_g$ models the general approach defined in [14]. Intuitively, $\leadsto_g$ works like $\leadsto_s$, but it takes only instances of rule schemas. Also, it adds concrete keys instead of key

$$\mathsf{dep}(S, k) \text{ when } M := \mathsf{getMem}(S, k) \rightarrow$$
$$K_c := \mathsf{contextKeys}(M), R = \{k\}$$
$$\text{for } k_i \text{ in } K_c \qquad\qquad\qquad \mathsf{dep}(S, k) \rightarrow$$
$$R := R \cup \mathsf{dep}(S, k_i) \qquad\qquad\qquad \emptyset$$

Fig. 9. Dependencies operator

variables. Function $\rightarrow_\phi$ is a function mapping keys in [14], which are taken from an arbitrary set, to keys in our approach, which are lists of integers.

These functions are formally defined in the technical report [6].

The proof of our main result below can be found in [6] as well.

Theorem 1 (Correctness). *Given functions* $\rightsquigarrow_g$, $\rightsquigarrow_s$ *and* $\rightarrow_{\mathcal{I},E}$ *in Fig. 8 such that each* $i \in \mathcal{I}$ *is injective on key variables, there exists a total function* $\rightarrow_\phi$, *injective on key variables belonging to the same rule, s.t. the square in Fig. 8 commutes, i.e.,* $\rightsquigarrow_s \rightarrow_{\mathcal{I},E} = \rightarrow_{\mathcal{I},E} \rightsquigarrow_g \rightarrow_\phi$.

6 Rollback Semantics

In this section we introduce a novel general causal-consistent rollback semantics built on top of the reversible backward semantics. Although general rollback semantics have been discussed in the literature [13], to the best of our knowledge this is the first general causal-consistent rollback semantics which is executable.

Causal-consistent rollback is a key primitive in causal-consistent debugging [7], which undoes a reduction of the system, possibly far in the past, including *all and only* its consequences. Intuitively it performs the smallest amount of backward steps allowing one to undo the selected action [8]. The workflow is the following: the user selects a past reduction by means of one of its unique keys (each key uniquely identifies the reduction consuming it); the set of consequences is computed; all the consequences are undone in a causal-consistent order.

Let us now describe the workflow in more detail. Given a key k in input, we want to undo the action that gave rise to the unique memory whose initial configuration contains k. First, we compute the set of keys $\mathsf{dep}(S, k)$, which contains keys identifying all the consequences of k. The dep operator, depicted in Fig. 9, recursively adds to set R the consequences of the current key, say k_1. A key k_2 is a consequence of k_1 if it occurs in the context part of the memory identified by k_1, and there exists a memory where k_2 occurs in the initial configuration. The code in Fig. 9 relies on two auxiliary functions, $\mathsf{getMem}(S, k)$ and $\mathsf{contextKeys}(M)$. The former, given a system configuration S and a key k, returns the unique memory in S containing k in its initial configuration, if any, while the latter returns the set of keys used in the context part of memory M. Notably, function $\mathsf{getMem}(S, k)$ is used as a guard: if no such memory is found, we apply the base clause on the right of the figure, returning $\emptyset$.

In the second step we need to perform backward steps to undo the computed dependencies. To this end we need to specify which backward ground rule needs to be applied. Fortunately, Maude provides a way to rewrite systems that fits our needs: the `MetaXApply` function. `MetaXApply` given a theory $\mathcal{R}$, a term t, a rule label l and a substitution σ applies the substitution to rule l (found inside $\mathcal{R}$) and then tries to apply it anywhere possible inside t.[2] Operatively, to undo a transition it suffices to feed to `MetaXApply` the backward rules theory ($\mathcal{R}$), the current system (t), the appropriate backward rule (l), and the selected key that has to be instantiated in the rule ($\sigma = [k/K]$ where k is the concrete key and K the corresponding variable; for simplicity in the implementation we always use the leftmost key in the rule).

If `MetaXApply` can perform a rewrite for some key k then its causal consequences have already been undone. Thus, it is enough to apply `MetaXApply` to all the keys in $\mathsf{dep}(S, k)$, removing a key when the corresponding reduction is performed. When the set is emptied we have reached the desired configuration.

7   Conclusion, Related and Future Work

We defined a new executable semantics of Erlang using Maude. We also implemented a program able to transform a non-reversible semantics into a reversible one, providing an implementation of the general method described in [14]. Making the approach executable posed some challenges. E.g., [14] just declares that keys are generated fresh, while we had to provide a concrete and distributed algorithm to generate keys ensuring their freshness. Finally, we presented a causal-consistent rollback semantics build on top of the backward semantics.

This allows one to use the produced semantics as an oracle against which to test an implementation, while being confident that it correctly captures the formal specification given that it is closer to it. Indeed, we applied our framework to test the reversible debugger CauDEr [18] (forward, backward as well as rollback) on the case study described in [20], thus gaining confidence on the fact that it correctly follows the semantics in [9]. Our experiment showed no discrepancies.

Our semantics of Erlang builds on two starting points, the executable semantics of Core Erlang in Maude described in [25] as well as the reversible semantics for Erlang described in [9]. While our general approach is close to [25], moving from Core Erlang to Erlang required to update most of the code. We could have applied our approach to generate a reversible semantics for Core Erlang from the irreversible one in [25], however the resulting reversible semantics would be sequential since the semantics in [25] relies on some global data structures to simplify the implementation of the model checking analysis, which would create fake causal dependencies. Notably, translating the semantics for Erlang in [9] into Maude directly is not trivial due to its high level of abstraction. E.g., the semantics in [9] resorts to the existence of suitable contexts to identify the redex inside an expression, while we need to explicitly give an inductive definition to find the redex. We could have started from [11] (formalized using the K framework for Maude) instead of [25], however the code in [25] was better documented.

---

[2] Technicalities have been omitted, we refer to [22] for further details.

Rollback semantics have been proved of interest for debugging techniques, we find examples in [5,7,9,19]. The rollback semantics presented here differs from the ones in [5,9,15,19] as it is agnostic of the underlying formalism, and from the ones in [7,8,13] as it is more concrete (to the point of being executable). We could combine generality and executability thanks to use of the Maude framework.

Let us now discuss possible future developments. First, one could apply the framework to other case studies or larger fragments of Erlang. In doing so one has to ensure that the causal-dependencies captured by the producer-consumer model used in [14] are appropriate - for example the model is not well-suited to capture causal dependencies due to shared memory. For the semantics of a larger fragment of Erlang, one could take inspiration from the one in [30].

As far as rollback is concerned, one would like to identify states by properties (e.g., when a given message has been sent), as in [5,9,19], instead of using keys.

References

1. Carlsson, R.: An introduction to core erlang. In: Erlang Workshop (2001)
2. Cristescu, I., Krivine, J., Varacca, D.: A compositional semantics for the reversible π-calculus. In: LICS, pp. 388–397 (2013)
3. Danos, V., Krivine, J.: Reversible communicating systems. In: Gardner, P., Yoshida, N. (eds.) CONCUR 2004. LNCS, vol. 3170, pp. 292–307. Springer, Heidelberg (2004). https://doi.org/10.1007/978-3-540-28644-8_19
4. Danos, V., Krivine, J.: Formal molecular biology done in CCS-R. LNCS **180**(3), 31–49 (2007)
5. Fabbretti, G., Lanese, I., Stefani, J.-B.: Causal-consistent debugging of distributed erlang programs. In: Yamashita, S., Yokoyama, T. (eds.) RC 2021. LNCS, vol. 12805, pp. 79–95. Springer, Cham (2021). https://doi.org/10.1007/978-3-030-79837-6_5
6. Fabbretti, G., Lanese, I., Stefani, JB.: Generation of a reversible semantics for Erlang in Maude. Research Report RR-9468, Inria (2022)
7. Giachino, E., Lanese, I., Mezzina, C.A.: Causal-consistent reversible debugging. In: Gnesi, S., Rensink, A. (eds.) FASE 2014. LNCS, vol. 8411, pp. 370–384. Springer, Heidelberg (2014). https://doi.org/10.1007/978-3-642-54804-8_26
8. Giachino, E., Lanese, I., Mezzina, C.A., Tiezzi, F.: Causal-consistent rollback in a tuple-based language. J. Log. Algebraic Methods Program. **88**, 99–120 (2017)
9. González-Abril, J.J., Vidal, G.: Causal-consistent reversible debugging: improving CauDEr. In: Morales, J.F., Orchard, D. (eds.) PADL 2021. LNCS, vol. 12548, pp. 145–160. Springer, Cham (2021). https://doi.org/10.1007/978-3-030-67438-0_9
10. Hewitt, C., Bishop, P., Steiger, R.: A universal modular actor formalism for artificial intelligence. In: IJCAI 1973 (1973)
11. Kőszegi, J.: KErl: Executable semantics for erlang. In: CEUR Workshop Proceedings, vol. 2046, pp. 144–166 (2018)
12. Lami, P., Lanese, I., Stefani, J., Coen, C.S., Fabbretti, G.: Reversibility in erlang: imperative constructs. In: Mezzina, C.A., Podlaski, K. (eds.) RC 2022. LNCS, vol. 13354, pp. 187–203. Springer, Cham (2022). https://doi.org/10.1007/978-3-031-09005-9_13
13. Lanese, I.: From reversible semantics to reversible debugging. In: Kari, J., Ulidowski, I. (eds.) RC 2018. LNCS, vol. 11106, pp. 34–46. Springer, Cham (2018). https://doi.org/10.1007/978-3-319-99498-7_2

14. Lanese, I., Medic, D.: A general approach to derive uncontrolled reversible semantics. In: CONCUR, vol. 171, pp. 33:1–33:24 (2020)
15. Lanese, I., Mezzina, C.A., Schmitt, A., Stefani, J.-B.: Controlling reversibility in higher-order Pi. In: Katoen, J.-P., König, B. (eds.) CONCUR 2011. LNCS, vol. 6901, pp. 297–311. Springer, Heidelberg (2011). https://doi.org/10.1007/978-3-642-23217-6_20
16. Lanese, I., Mezzina, C.A., Stefani, J.-B.: Controlled reversibility and compensations. In: Glück, R., Yokoyama, T. (eds.) RC 2012. LNCS, vol. 7581, pp. 233–240. Springer, Heidelberg (2013). https://doi.org/10.1007/978-3-642-36315-3_19
17. Lanese, I., Mezzina, C.A., Stefani, J.: Reversibility in the higher-order π-calculus. Theor. Comput. Sci. **625**, 25–84 (2016)
18. Lanese, I., Nishida, N., Palacios, A., Vidal, G.: CauDEr website (2018). https://github.com/mistupv/cauder-v2
19. Lanese, I., Nishida, N., Palacios, A., Vidal, G.: A theory of reversibility for Erlang. J. Log. Algebraic Methods Program. **100**, 71–97 (2018)
20. Lanese, I., Schultz, U.P., Ulidowski, I.: Reversible computing in debugging of Erlang programs. IT Prof. **24**(1), 74–80 (2022)
21. Laursen, J.S., Schultz, U.P., Ellekilde, L.-P.: Automatic error recovery in robot assembly operations using reverse execution. In: IROS, pp. 1785–1792 (2015)
22. All about maude (2007)
23. Melgratti, H.C., Mezzina, C.A., Ulidowski, I.: Reversing place transition nets. Log. Methods Comput. Sci. **16**(4) (2020)
24. Meseguer, J.: Rewriting logic as a semantic framework for concurrency: a progress report. In: Montanari, U., Sassone, V. (eds.) CONCUR 1996. LNCS, vol. 1119, pp. 331–372. Springer, Heidelberg (1996). https://doi.org/10.1007/3-540-61604-7_64
25. Neuhäußer, M., Noll, T.: Abstraction and model checking of Core Erlang programs in Maude. ENTCS **176**(4), 147–163 (2007)
26. Perumalla, K.S., Park, A.J.: Reverse computation for rollback-based fault tolerance in large parallel systems: evaluating the potential gains and systems effects. Clust. Comput. **17**(2), 303–313 (2014)
27. Philippou, A., Psara, K.: Reversible computation in petri nets. In: Kari, J., Ulidowski, I. (eds.) RC 2018. LNCS, vol. 11106, pp. 84–101. Springer, Cham (2018). https://doi.org/10.1007/978-3-319-99498-7_6
28. Phillips, I.C.C., Ulidowski, I.: Reversing algebraic process calculi. J. Log. Algebraic Methods Program. **73**(1–2), 70–96 (2007)
29. Automatic generation of reversible semantics in Maude. https://bit.ly/3RQgGsu
30. Svensson, H., Fredlund, L., Earle, C.B.: A unified semantics for future Erlang. In: ACM SIGPLAN Workshop on Erlang, pp. 23–32. ACM (2010)

Program Slicing Techniques with Support for Unconditional Jumps

Carlos Galindo⬛, Sergio Pérez$^{(\boxtimes)}$⬛, and Josep Silva⬛

VRAIN, Universitat Politècnica de València,
Camino de Vera s/n, 46022 Valencia, Spain
cargaji@vrain.upv.es, {serperu,jsilva}@dsic.upv.es

Abstract. The System Dependence Graph is a data structure often used in software analysis, and in particular in program slicing. Multiple optimizations and extensions have been created to give support to common language features, such as unconditional jumps (PPDG) and object-oriented features (JSysDG). In this paper we show that, unfortunately, the solutions proposed for different problems are incompatible when they are combined, producing incorrect results. We identify and showcase the incompatibilities generated by the combination of different techniques, and propose specific solutions for every incompatibility described. Finally, we present an implementation in which the issues found have been addressed, producing correct slices in all cases.

Keywords: Program slicing · Pseudo-predicate Program Dependence Graph · Control dependence · System Dependence Graph

1 Introduction

Program slicing [20,23] is a software analysis technique that extracts the subset of program instructions, the *program slice* [25], that affect or are affected by a specific program point called *slicing criterion*. Program slicing has a wide range of applications such as software maintenance [22], debugging [6], code obfuscation [18], program specialization [19], and even artificial intelligence [26]. Most program slicing techniques are based on a program graph representation called the System Dependence Graph (SDG). The SDG [11] is a directed graph that represents statements as nodes and their dependences as arcs. It builds upon and is composed of Program Dependence Graphs (PDG) [7], a similar intraprocedural graph.

This work has been partially supported by grant PID2019-104735RB-C41 funded by MCIN/AEI/10.13039/501100011033, by the *Generalitat Valenciana* under grant Prometeo/2019/098 (DeepTrust), and by TAILOR, a project funded by EU Horizon 2020 research and innovation programme under GA No 952215. Sergio Pérez was partially supported by *Universitat Politècnica de València* under FPI grant PAID-01-18. Carlos Galindo was partially supported by the Spanish *Ministerio de Universidades* under grant FPU20/03861.

© Springer Nature Switzerland AG 2022
A. Riesco and M. Zhang (Eds.): ICFEM 2022, LNCS 13478, pp. 123–139, 2022.
https://doi.org/10.1007/978-3-031-17244-1_8

```
1    min_max(int[] n) {          1    min_max(int[] n) {
2      min = n[0];               2      min = n[0];
3      max = n[0];               3      max = n[0];
4      i = 1;                    4      i = 1;
5      while (i < n.length) {    5      while (i < n.length) {
6        if (a[i] < min)         6        if (a[i] < min)
7          min = a[i];           7          min = a[i];
8        if (a[i] > max)         8        if (a[i] > max)
9          max = a[i];           9          max = a[i];
10       i++;                    10       i++;
11     }                         11     }
12     print(min);              12     print(min);
13     print(max);              13     print(max);
14   }                          14   }
```

(a) Program to compute min and max.   (b) Slice w.r.t. $\langle 12, min \rangle$.

Fig. 1. Example of program slicing. (Color figure online)

Example 1 (Program slicing). Consider the program in Fig. 1a. If we are interested in determining what parts of the program are needed to compute the value of variable min at line 12 we can define the slicing criterion $\langle 12, min \rangle$ (blue code in Fig. 1a). A program slicer will automatically generate the program representation (the SDG) and use the standard slicing algorithm (presented in [11]) to compute the slice shown in Fig. 1b, where all the statements that cannot influence the value of variable min have been removed from the program.

The original formulation of the SDG covered a simple imperative language with branches, loops, and calls; but later research have proposed extensions to cover different constructs of programming languages from all programming paradigms. Currently, there are versions of the SDG that cover most syntax constructs of some languages such as Java[1], C and C++[2], Erlang[3], or Javascript [21], among many others. Additionally, there are techniques that increase the precision of the slices generated, by removing or limiting the traversal of some dependences (see, e.g., [8,9,14,15]).

There are three important extensions of the SDG that we explore in this paper: (1) the extension of the SDG for object-oriented programs (the JSysDG [24]), the exception handling extension [9] (treatment for *try-catch, throws...*), and the unconditional jumps extension [15] (treatment for *break, continue, return...*). The three extensions have been implemented and work for different languages. Nevertheless, we are not aware of any implementation that combines all of them.

With the aim of developing a program slicer that is able to treat the whole Java language, we have implemented several extensions including those three. During the implementation and testing processes, we discovered a set of collisions between the extension of the PDG given to treat unconditional jumps (the

---

[1] Codesonar SAST: https://www.grammatech.com/codesonar-sast-java.
[2] Codesonar: https://www.grammatech.com/codesonar-cc.
[3] e-Knife: https://mist.dsic.upv.es/e-knife.

pseudo-predicate program dependence graph (PPDG) [15]) and the representation models used to solve other language features, leading, in several cases, to erroneous slices. In this paper, we showcase a set of identified incompatibilities generated by the combination of the PPDG representation used to treat unconditional jumps with other representation models used to solve orthogonal problems such as call representation, object-oriented features, or exception-handling. In most cases these incompatibilities produce an incorrect use of control-dependence arcs. For each detected conflict, we explain the rationale behind it, and propose a specific change in the model to solve it. This is valuable information for developers of program slicers and essential information for the definition of a more general theoretical program slicing model. From the practical perspective, we also provide an open-source implementation of a program slicer for a wide subset of Java.

The main contributions of this paper can be summarized as follows:

- The identification of several state-of-the-art program slicing techniques that cannot be implemented together. A counterexample is presented for each incompatible combination.
- The theoretical explanation about why each technique is incompatible with the PPDG and a solution proposed for each problem identified.
- The implementation of a public open-source program slicer for Java that implements all the techniques discussed in the paper with the solutions proposed, which makes them compatible.

The paper is structured as follows: Sect. 2 briefly explains how an SDG is built; Sect. 3 introduces the PPDG, a modification to the PDG to support unconditional jumps; Sect. 4 showcases the interference between the PPDG and techniques that handle calls, exceptions, and object-oriented programs; Sect. 5 describes the implementation where this interference has been corrected; Sect. 6 shows the related work; and Sect. 7 presents our conclusions.

2   Background

To keep this paper self-contained, in this section we introduce the necessary background on program slicing and the SDG. Readers familiar with program slicing can skip this section.

The SDG is built from a sequence of graphs: a control-flow graph (CFG) [1] is computed from the source code of each procedure in the program. Then, control and data dependences are computed in each CFG to create a series of Program Dependence Graphs (PDG); and, finally, the calls in the PDGs are connected to their corresponding procedures to create the System Dependence Graph (SDG). A slice can then be computed by traversing the SDG backwards from the node that represents the slicing criterion, producing the subset of nodes that affect it [11].

The CFG is a representation of the execution flow of a procedure in a program. Each statement is represented as a node (in a set N), and each arc (in a set A) represents the sequential execution of a pair of statements. In the CFG, statements only have one outgoing control-flow arc, and predicates, have a set of outgoing arcs. Additionally, the CFG contains two extra nodes, "Enter" and "Exit", which represent the source and sink of the graph. If a procedure has multiple `return` statements, then all of them are connected to the exit node.

The PDG [7] is built by computing control and data dependences (Definitions 2 and 3): given a CFG $G = (N, A)$, its corresponding PDG is $G' = (N \setminus \{Exit\}, A_c \cup A_d)$, where A_c and A_d are the set of control and data dependences, represented as directed arcs ($a \rightarrow b$ iff b is dependent on a).

Definition 1 (Postdominance [23]**).** *Given a CFG $G = (N, A)$, a node $m \in N$ postdominates a node $n \in N$ if and only if all paths from n to the "Exit" node in G contain m.*

Definition 2 (Control dependence [10]**).** *Given a CFG $G = (N, A)$, a node $b \in N$ is* control dependent *on a node $a \in N$ if and only if b postdominates some but not all of a's successors in G.*

Definition 3 (Data dependence [10]**).** *Given a CFG $G = (N, A)$, a node $n \in N$ is* data dependent *on a node $m \in N$ if and only if m defines (i.e., assigns a value to) a variable x, n uses variable x and there is a path in G from m to n where x is not redefined.*

The SDG [11] is the union of multiple PDGs, with the addition of new dependence arcs that connect procedure calls to their respective procedure definitions. Each node that contains a call is split into several nodes. For every call, there is a node that represents the call itself, and one node per input and output. These nodes are inserted in the graph, and connected to the node that contains the call via control dependence arcs. A similar structure is generated by the "Enter" node of each procedure definition: the inputs and outputs of a procedure are placed as nodes that are control dependent on the "Enter" node. When building the SDG, each call is connected to the "Enter" node of their target procedure, each input from a call is connected to a procedure's input, and each procedure's output is connected to the call's output via interprocedural arcs (input and output arcs, respectively).

Finally, summary arcs are added to method calls. Summary arcs join call inputs and call outputs when the value of the input is required inside the method definition to compute the output's value. The following example builds an SDG illustrating the whole process:

Example 2 (The creation of an SDG for a simple program). Consider the simple program shown in Fig. 2a. This program contains two procedures, f and g, where f calls g following the call-by-reference method. The computation of the CFG and the application of Definitions 2 and 3 for procedure f result in the PDG shown in Fig. 2b, where black arcs represent control dependences and red dashed arcs data dependences. Note that, for call nodes, inputs and outputs are separated from the call node and inserted in the PDG. Finally, the SDG is created by combining the PDG for each procedure and inserting interprocedural (blue and dotted) and summary (green, dashed and bold) arcs. The result is shown in Fig. 2c.

Given a SDG, a slice can be generated by traversing the arcs backwards, starting on the node that contains the slicing criterion. There are two phases: in the first, the arcs are traversed from the slicing criterion, ignoring output arcs (between output variables); and once no more arcs can be traversed, the second phase begins, starting with all the nodes reached in the first, but ignoring input arcs (between calls and definitions or input variables). The set of nodes reached at the end of the second phase is the slice.

Example 3 (Slicing the SDG in two phases). Consider the SDG in Fig. 2c. If node $x_{out} = x$ is picked as slicing criterion (it is shown in bold in the graph, and it represents the value of x at the end of $f(x)$, all the nodes from procedure f are included in the first phase (shown in grey). However, the nodes from g cannot be reached in this phase, as the $a_{out} = a \rightarrow x = a_{out}$ output arc (lower-right corner) cannot be traversed during the first phase. In the second phase it is traversed, and all the nodes that form g are added to the slice (shown in blue). The result is that all nodes are relevant to the value of x at the end of $f(x)$.

3   The Pseudo-predicate Program Dependence Graph

The *Pseudo-predicate Program Dependence Graph* (PPDG) [15] is an extension of the original PDG, which includes support for all kinds of unconditional jumps, such as *break*, *goto*, *return*, or *throw*. It minimizes the number of unconditional

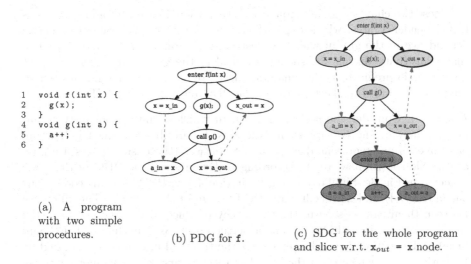

```
1   void f(int x) {
2      g(x);
3   }
4   void g(int a) {
5      a++;
6   }
```

(a) A program with two simple procedures.

(b) PDG for f.

(c) SDG for the whole program and slice w.r.t. $x_{out} = x$ node.

Fig. 2. The creation of the SDG for a small program with two procedures. (Color figure online)

jumps that are included in slices, with special effectiveness in structures like *switch*, as each case is typically terminated with a *break* or *return*.

The PPDG is built upon the Augmented Control-Flow Graph (ACFG) [2], which introduced a mechanism to correctly generate the control dependences caused by unconditional jumps. In the ACFG, unconditional jumps are not considered statements (which unconditionally execute the next instruction), neither predicates (which branch into multiple possible execution paths), they are classified as a new category of instruction called pseudo-predicate. As it happens with predicates, pseudo-predicates are represented as a node with two outgoing arcs: a true arc pointing to the destination of the unconditional jump and a false arc (called non-executable branch) pointing to the statement that would be executed if the statement failed to jump.

The PPDG's main contribution is two-fold: it modifies the definition of control dependence (replacing Definition 2 with Definition 4), and adds a traversal restriction to the slicing algorithm (see Definition 5) for control dependence arcs.

Definition 4 (Control dependence in the presence of pseudo-predicates [15]). *Let $G = (N, A)$ be a CFG, and let $G' = (N, A')$ with $A \subseteq A'$ be an ACFG, both representing the same procedure. A node $b \in N$ is control-dependent on node $a \in N$ if and only if b postdominates in G some but not all successors of a in G'.*

Definition 5 (PPDG traversal limitations [15]). *Given a PPDG $G = (N, A)$, a pseudo-predicate node $b \in N$ and a control dependence arc $(a, b) \in A$, if b is included in the slice, a should not be included in the slice if:*

1. *b is not the slicing criterion, and*
2. *b has only been reached via control dependence arcs.*

These two changes are interconnected: Definition 4 generates additional control dependence arcs, which explicitly represent part of the transitive control dependence in the graph; while the restriction of Definition 5 removes part of that transitivity during the slicing traversal of the graph. Together, they act upon pseudo-predicate nodes, maintaining or reducing the amount of pseudo-predicates included in slices (w.r.t. to the PDG built from the ACFG).

Example 4. Consider the code in Fig. 3a, in which a simple loop may terminate via any of the two **break** instructions. Figure 3b shows its CFG, where both **break**s are represented as pseudo-predicates (the dashed edges are non-executable control-flow arcs). According to Definition 2 the PDG of this code is shown in Fig. 3c. Similarly, using Definition 4, the PPDG of this code is the one in (Fig. 3d). In this specific case, the PDG and PPDG match. The difference between them can be seen in the slices they produce. If we pick $\langle 11, C \rangle$ as the slicing criterion, the PPDG obtains a better result, as it excludes **if (Z)** and break_A. The cause of this discrepancy is the traversal limitation established by Definition 5, by which once the slice has reached break_B, it cannot continue, as it is a pseudo-predicate, it is not the slicing criterion, and it has only been reached by control dependences.

```
1    void main() {
2        while (X) {
3            if (Y) {
4                if (Z) {
5                    log(A);
6                    break;
7                }
8                log(B);
9                break;
10           }
11           log(C);
12       }
13       log(D);
14   }
```

(a) A simple program with unconditional jumps.

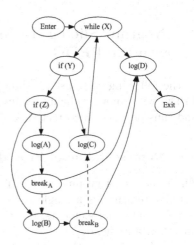

(b) The CFG.

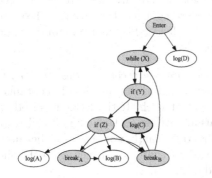

(c) The PDG with the slice shown in grey.

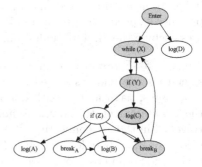

(d) The PPDG with the slice shown in grey.

Fig. 3. A comparison between the PDG and the PPDG.

Due to the increase in precision regarding unconditional jumps, the PPDG should be considered the baseline for adaptations of the PDG. However, the balance set by Definitions 4 and 5 is delicate, as it assumes that:

Assumption $\mathcal{A}$: all control dependence arcs in the SDG are generated according to Definition 4.

4   Program Slicing Techniques that Conflict with the PPDG

In the following sections, we showcase examples where the combination of the PPDG with another slicing technique results in Assumption $\mathcal{A}$ breaking down, and thus produces incorrect slices.

4.1   Representation of Procedure Calls

The sequence of graphs used in program slicing (CFG, PDG, SDG) represent most statements as a single node. Some extensions generate additional nodes to represent other elements, but the most common is the representation of calls and their arguments [11].

As described at the end of Sect. 2, calls are represented as an additional node in the PDG and SDG, connected to the node they belong to via a control dependence arc. It is precisely the insertion of that arc that breaks $\mathcal{A}$, because it has been hand-inserted instead of generated from Definition 4. Example 5 provides a specific counter-example, where these additional control dependence arcs exclude the "Enter" node from the slice.

Example 5 (Erroneous program slicing of procedure calls in the PPDG). Consider the code and associated SDG shown in Figs. 4a and 4b. It contains two procedures, `main` and `f`, with one statement each. If the SDG is sliced w.r.t. the `log` statement, the traversal limitation outlined in Definition 5 will stop the traversal in the arc connecting "Enter `main()`" and "`return f()`" because the second one is a pseudo-predicate. Thus, code that should belong to the slice is excluded and an erroneous slice is produced.

The source of the problem is the incorrect use of control arcs to connect nodes with a call (`return f()`) with the call node (`call f()`). This happens in most nodes that are split in order to improve precision: a control arc is used as a default kind of arc.

The solution would be to change the kind of arc used to connect these kinds of nodes (call nodes, argument and parameter input/output...) from control arc into any other kind. A data arc would not be semantically appropriate, so our proposal is the introduction of what we call *structural arcs*. Formally,

Definition 6 (Structural Arc). *Given two PDG nodes $n, n' \in N$, there exists a structural edge $n \dashrightarrow n'$ if and only if:*

```
1   int main() {
2      return f();
3   }
4   int f() {
5      log("ok");
6   }
```

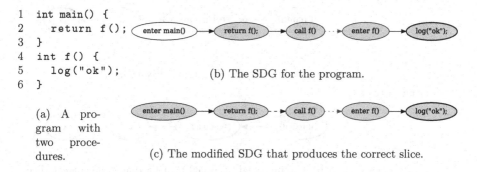

(a) A program with two procedures.

(b) The SDG for the program.

(c) The modified SDG that produces the correct slice.

Fig. 4. A simple SDG with two procedures (**main** and **f**), sliced w.r.t. the **log** statement. The slice is represented by grey nodes, the dotted blue arc is an interprocedural call arc, the black solid arcs represent control dependence arcs, and the dashed black arc is a structural arc. (Color figure online)

- n' contains a subexpression from n, and
- $\forall n'' \in N : if\ n\ \dashrightarrow n' \wedge n' \dashrightarrow n'' \Rightarrow n \not\dashrightarrow n''$ (structural edges define an intransitive relation).

Structural arcs have no restriction on their traversal, and otherwise behave as control arcs before the introduction of the PPDG's traversal restrictions.

An example of this solution has been applied to the erroneous Fig. 4b, producing Fig. 4c, a SDG where the traversal completes as expected.

4.2 Object-Oriented Program Slicing

Object-oriented programming languages are widely used, and there are program slicing techniques that adapt the SDG to include features such as polymorphism and inheritance [17]. An example is the *Java System Dependence Graph* (JSysDG), proposed by Walkinshaw et al. [24], an extension built upon the ClDG [16] (a previous attempt to include classes/objects in the SDG). Among other modifications, the JSysDG represents variables with fields as a tree of nodes. This allows the representation of polymorphism and increases its precision, allowing the selection of single fields.

Figure 5a showcases the structure of an object **a**, which contains a field **x**. As with procedure calls described in Sect. 4.1, the usage of control dependence arcs to represent the structure of the objects violates Assumption $\mathcal{A}$. The same solution can be applied here: using a different kind of arc to represent object structures.

Example 6 (Fixing the "JSysDG with unconditional jumps"). Consider again the graph in Fig. 5a, which has been transformed to produce Fig. 5b: some arcs have been turned into structural arcs (applying Definition 6). Now, the remaining control arc (between **if** and **return**) can be traversed by the standard algorithm and all the code is correctly included in the slice.

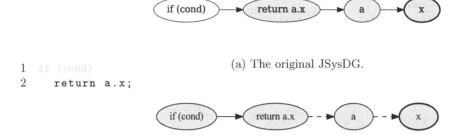

1 if (cond)
2   return a.x;

(a) The original JSysDG.

(b) The modified JSysDG that produces the correct slice.

Fig. 5. A segment of a JSysDG and its corresponding code snippet. A slice has been produced, w.r.t. variable `a.x` in the `return` statement.

4.3   Exception Handling and Conditional Control Dependence

The introduction of exception handling, including instructions like `throw`, `try`, `catch`, and `finally`, motivates the addition of a new kind of control dependence to increase the precision of `catch` statements: *conditional control dependence* [9].

Definition 7 (Conditional control dependence [9]**).** *Let* $P = (N, A)$ *be a PDG. We say that a node* $b \in N$ *is conditional control dependent on a pair of nodes* $a, c \in N$, *if:*

- *a is a pseudo-predicate,*
- *a controls b, and*
- *c is dependent on b.*

This definition is required to properly model the need for `catch` statements, as can be seen in the following example.

Example 7 (Conditional control dependence with `catch` *statements).* Consider three instructions a, b, and c where:

- a produces exceptions (e.g. `throw e`),
- b catches those exceptions (e.g. `catch (...) {}`) and
- c only executes if the exception is caught.

In this case, b is needed if and only if both a and c are present in the slice. Otherwise, either the exception is not thrown (a is not in the slice) or no instruction is affected (c is not in the slice).

Conditional control dependence (CCD) connects three nodes in a relationship where one of them controls the other two, but only if they are both present in the slice. Conditional control dependence is represented in the PPDG and SDG as a pair of arcs, named CC1 and CC2. CC1 and CC2 arcs are generated after the PDG has been built: some control dependence arcs are converted to CC1 arcs and CC2 arcs are inserted.

Similarly to the PPDG, the introduction of CCD requires some changes to the traversal algorithm, which are defined as follows:

Definition 8 (Traversal limitations of CCD). *A SDG that contains conditional control dependence must add the following limitations to its traversal algorithm:*

1. *A node that has only been reached via a CCD arc will not be included in the slice, unless it has been reached by both kinds (CC1 and CC2) of dependency.*
2. *If a node is added to the slice via the previous rule, no arcs are traversed from that node, unless it is reached via a non-CCD arc.*

The introduction of this new dependence and its corresponding arcs break Assumption $\mathcal{A}$ in two different ways: some control dependence arcs have been specialized (CC1), so they are no longer present in the graph; and some control dependence arcs have been inserted (CC2), so they do not follow Definition 4. The consequence is that the slicing traversal of the SDG is stopped too early, and some necessary nodes are left out. This can be in the form of "Enter" nodes, or even the structure that contains it (such as `if` or `for`). Figure 6a shows the described scenario, where the graph traversal stops before reaching the "Enter" node due to the pseudo-predicate nature of the `throw` and `try` nodes.

However, the solution to this situation is not so obvious, as changing the kind of arc does not solve the problem. Instead, one of the traversal restrictions imposed on control dependence arcs must be relaxed.

First, the difference between the PPDG and the PDG must be computed. Arcs that are only present in the PPDG and not in the PDG must be marked. Arcs that are marked are not considered control dependences for the purposes of traversal restrictions from the PPDG. This change solves the problem, and the traversal continues normally, reaching the "Enter" node.

Example 8 (Fixing slicing with exceptions and unconditional jumps). Consider Fig. 6a, obtained from Fig. 6b by marking the control arcs that are exclusive to the PPDG in bold blue. Then, when a slice is computed starting at "log", "try" would be reached via a marked arc, and the traversal would continue back to the "Enter" node, producing a correct slice.

5   Implementation

The incompatibility between different slicing models was detected during the implementation of a slicer that included all the described models. To solve the detected problems, the solutions proposed throughout this paper have been implemented as the base of a new Java slicer: JavaSlicer. It is publicly available at

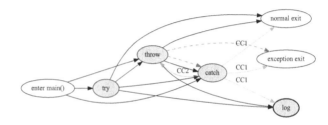

(a) The SDG with CCD produces an incorrect slice.

```
1  void main() {
2    try { throw e1; }
3    catch (T e2) {}
4    log(42);
5  }
```

(b) The SDG with CCD and marked arcs produces the correct slice.

Fig. 6. A simple program that throws an exception and two SDGs with CCD, sliced w.r.t. `log`. Black solid arcs are control dependence, red dashed arcs are data dependence, and green and orange solid arcs are conditional control dependence (labelled with their type). Marked control arcs are shown in bold blue. (Color figure online)

https://mist.dsic.upv.es/git/program-slicing/sdg, and contains and implements an SDG that covers parts of the Java programming language. It is a project with around 10K lines of code, and it contains a core module that contains the slicer, and a client module, with which users can interact (from the terminal, for now).

Due to space constraints, we have not included in this paper the description of the tests used to validate the proposal presented in this work. However, the interested reader has access to it in the URL: https://mist.dsic.upv.es/JavaSDGSlicer/evaluation. There, we describe the suite of tests, and the experiments performed with real programs, showing that all slices produced are equivalent to their associated original programs.

Solving the problems presented in Sect. 4 only requires changing the kind of arc used (see class `StructuralArc`). However, for Sect. 4.3 two changes are required. The first is computing the arcs that are present in the PPDG but not in the PDG, which is done in the `PPDG` class:

PPDG.java

```
47  /** Finds the CD arcs that are only present in the PPDG and marks
48  them as such. */ protected void
49  markPPDGExclusiveEdges(CallableDeclaration<?> declaration) {
50      APDG apdg = new APDG();
51      apdg.build(declaration);
52      Set<Arc> apdgArcs = new HashSet<>();
53      for (Arc arc : apgg.edgeSet())
54          if (arc.isUnconditionalControlDependencyArc())
55              apdgArcs.add(arc);
56      for (Arc arc : edgeSet())
57          if (arc.isUnconditionalControlDependencyArc()
58                  && !apdgArcs.contains(arc))
59                  arc.asControlDependencyArc().setPPDGExclusive();
60  }
```

Then, in the slicing algorithm, a check is included, to bypass the PPDG traversal condition when an arc is marked. This behaviour is defined in the Java class ExceptionSensitiveSlicingAlgoritm, specifically in lines 128–130:

ExceptionSensitiveSlicingAlgorithm.java

```
126  protected boolean essdgIgnore(Arc arc) {
127      GraphNode<?> target = graph.getEdgeTarget(arc);
128      if (arc.isUnconditionalControlDependencyArc() &&
129              arc.asControlDependencyArc().isPPDGExclusive())
130          return false;
131      return hasOnlyBeenReachedBy(target, ConditionalControlDependencyArc.class);
132  }
```

For any interested readers, the software repository contains instructions on how to run the slicer.

6 Related Work

There exist very few works that reason about the consequences of integrating different program slicing techniques in the same model. Unfortunately, the solutions proposed for the different slicing problems were mostly proposed in isolation of other problems and solutions. This means that every time a new challenging slicing problem is solved, the solution is presented as an evolution of a previous program representation used to solve the same problem (if there is a previous one) or from the original PDG/SDG representations. For example, this is the case of OO languages where the graph proposed by Larsen and Harrold in [16] was further extended by Liang and Harrold in [17], and lately used by Walkinsaw et al. in [24] to represent Java object-oriented programs. But none of them considered, e.g., exception handling; as they assumed that the standard solution to exception handling would not interfere with their solution to OO. The real world is however a continuous interference between problems and solutions. Any implementation for a real programming language must include different solutions and they will necessarily interfere.

Most solutions proposed in the literature are based on the original SDG and the original slicing algorithm proposed in [11]. Many proposals enhance the expressivity of the graph in different ways: adding modifications to the CFG used to generate the final graph ([9,15]) or including new program dependences ([4,5,8,27], and sometimes these new models come with some modifications to the slicing traversal algorithm to improve computed slices ([8,9,14,15]).

Since the initial graph of all these proposals is the original SDG, most of the solutions designed to slice other previously solved problems are not considered when designing a new program representation model. This is the case of several object-oriented program representations like [16,17], where the SDG is augmented to represent polymorphic method calls with the addition of new graph nodes that consider the statically undecidable method called. Another example is the one presented by Cheng [4,5,27] for program slicing of concurrent programs. Cheng's proposal starts from the PDG and defines a set of specialised dependences required in concurrent environments, building a representation called the *program dependence net* (PDN).

Taking a look at the literature, we consider whether a solution to a particular slicing problem can be classified as control dependence conservative (i.e. when all control arcs in the graph are computed over Definitions 2 and 4) or not. For example, the works presented by Krinke and Snelting [13], Cheda et al. [3], and the one presented by Kinloch and Munro [12] are all control dependence conservative. While Krinke and Snelting, and Cheda et al. define a new type of arc to represent what we call structural dependences, Kinloch and Munro construct the PDG by splitting assignments in different nodes (left-hand side and right-hand side) controlled by the same node. On the other hand, other approaches are not control dependence conservative, like the ones mentioned for object-oriented programs ([16,17,24]) because they arbitrarily represent the unfolding of object variables with the use of control arcs not computed by Definitions 2 and 4.

The concept of structural dependence was already noted by previous authors along the literature. Krinke and Snelting [14], in their fine-grained program representation, decomposed program statements and noted a new kind of dependence they called *immediate control dependence* which, in fact, is similar to our defined structural dependence. Unfortunately, the representation of Krinke and Snelting cannot be applied to the SDG because of its granularity level. Their fine-grained PDG split every single statement in a set of nodes and this immediate control dependence was only usable for connecting the different parts of the statement. Additionally, the main purpose of the immediate control dependence during the slicing phase was to avoid the appearance of loops by limiting the slicing traversal. Also Cheda et al. [3], in their approach to static slicing for first-order functional programs which are represented by means of rewrite systems, designed the *term dependence graph* (TDG), that includes a set of arcs labelled with S for being considered *Structural* when representing the dependence between method calls and their corresponding arguments. Their TDG is only usable for first-order functional programs which are represented by means of rewrite systems and is not a derivation of the PDG. The idea of considering structural arcs to connect calls and arguments is promising if applied to SDG program slicing, but it only solves one of the incompatibilities detected in this paper.

7   Conclusions

In this paper we identify an important problem in program slicing: various standard solutions to different well-known slicing problems can be incompatible when they are combined in the same model. In particular, we have identified, with a set of associated counterexamples, different combinations of SDG extensions (for the treatment of exception-handling, unconditional jumps, and OO programs) that are incompatible, as they may produce incorrect slices.

The root of these problems is that those techniques extended the original SDG to solve different slicing problems in an independent way, without considering that their restrictions imposed over the slicing traversal could not be satisfied by the algorithms proposed in other solutions. In this paper we take a different perspective: we consider different problems all together and try to integrate the solutions proposed. From the best of our knowledge, there does not exist any theoretical work that integrates the techniques discussed in this paper.

After having identified and explained the rationale of the incompatibilities that make it impossible to combine those techniques, we have also proposed a solution for each incompatibility. The technical reason in all the cases is the interpretation of control dependence. Control dependence preservation is a key factor to make a SDG model compatible with other models. We have joined and generalized the restrictions over control flow and control dependence that must be taken into account to make all the models compatible. This generalization should be considered in future proposals.

From our theoretical setting, we have been able to implement the first program slicer with support for all the Java constructs mentioned along the paper: object-oriented features (classes, objects, interfaces, inheritance, and polymorphism), exception handling (*try-catch, throw, throws*), and unconditional jumps (*break, continue, return...*).

References

1. Allen, F.E.: Control flow analysis. SIGPLAN Not. **5**(7), 1–19 (1970)
2. Ball, T., Horwitz, S.: Slicing programs with arbitrary control-flow. In: Fritzson, P.A. (ed.) AADEBUG 1993. LNCS, vol. 749, pp. 206–222. Springer, Heidelberg (1993). https://doi.org/10.1007/BFb0019410
3. Cheda, D., Silva, J., Vidal, G.: Static slicing of rewrite systems. In: Proceedings of the 15th International Workshop on Functional and (Constraint) Logic Programming (WFLP 2006), pp. 123–136. Elsevier ENTCS 177 (2007)
4. Cheng, J.: Slicing concurrent programs. In: Fritzson, P.A. (ed.) AADEBUG 1993. LNCS, vol. 749, pp. 223–240. Springer, Heidelberg (1993). https://doi.org/10.1007/BFb0019411
5. Cheng, J.: Dependence analysis of parallel and distributed programs and its applications. In: Proceedings of the Advances in Parallel and Distributed Computing, pp. 370–377 (1997). https://doi.org/10.1109/APDC.1997.574057

6. DeMillo, R.A., Pan, H., Spafford, E.H.: Critical slicing for software fault localization. SIGSOFT Softw. Eng. Notes **21**(3), 121–134 (1996). https://doi.org/10.1145/226295.226310. https://doi.acm.org/10.1145/226295.226310

7. Ferrante, J., Ottenstein, K.J., Warren, J.D.: The program dependence graph and its use in optimization. ACM Trans. Program. Lang. Syst. **9**(3), 319–349 (1987)

8. Galindo, C., Pérez, S., Silva, J.: Data dependencies in object-oriented programs. In: 11th Workshop on Tools for Automatic Program Analysis (2020)

9. Galindo, C., Pérez, S., Silva, J.: Program slicing with exception handling. In: 11th Workshop on Tools for Automatic Program Analysis (2020)

10. Horwitz, S., Reps, T., Binkley, D.: Interprocedural slicing using dependence graphs. In: Proceedings of the ACM SIGPLAN 1988 Conference on Programming Language Design and Implementation, PLDI 1988, New York, NY, USA, pp. 35–46. ACM (1988). https://doi.org/10.1145/53990.53994. https://doi.acm.org/10.1145/53990.53994

11. Horwitz, S., Reps, T., Binkley, D.: Interprocedural slicing using dependence graphs. ACM Trans. Program. Lang. Syst. **12**(1), 26–60 (1990)

12. Kinloch, D.A., Munro, M.: Understanding C programs using the combined C graph representation. In: Proceedings 1994 International Conference on Software Maintenance, pp. 172–180 (1994)

13. Krinke, J.: Static slicing of threaded programs. SIGPLAN Not. **33**(7), 35–42 (1998). https://doi.org/10.1145/277633.277638. https://doi.acm.org/10.1145/277633.277638

14. Krinke, J., Snelting, G.: Validation of measurement software as an application of slicing and constraint solving. Inf. Softw. Technol. **40**(11), 661–675 (1998). https://doi.org/10.1016/S0950-5849(98)00090-1. https://www.sciencedirect.com/science/article/pii/S0950584998000901

15. Kumar, S., Horwitz, S.: Better slicing of programs with jumps and switches. In: Kutsche, R.-D., Weber, H. (eds.) FASE 2002. LNCS, vol. 2306, pp. 96–112. Springer, Heidelberg (2002). https://doi.org/10.1007/3-540-45923-5_7

16. Larsen, L., Harrold, M.J.: Slicing object-oriented software. In: Proceedings of the 18th International Conference on Software Engineering, ICSE 1996, Washington, DC, USA, pp. 495–505. IEEE Computer Society (1996). https://dl.acm.org/citation.cfm?id=227726.227837

17. Liang, D., Harrold, M.J.: Slicing objects using system dependence graphs. In: Proceedings of the International Conference on Software Maintenance, ICSM 1998, Washington, DC, USA, pp. 358–367. IEEE Computer Society (1998). https://dl.acm.org/citation.cfm?id=850947.853342

18. Majumdar, A., Drape, S.J., Thomborson, C.D.: Slicing obfuscations: design, correctness, and evaluation. In: Proceedings of the 2007 ACM Workshop on Digital Rights Management, DRM 2007, New York, NY, USA, pp. 70–81. ACM (2007). https://doi.org/10.1145/1314276.1314290. https://doi.acm.org/10.1145/1314276.1314290

19. Ochoa, C., Silva, J., Vidal, G.: Lightweight program specialization via dynamic slicing. In: Proceedings of the 2005 ACM SIGPLAN Workshop on Curry and Functional Logic Programming, WCFLP 2005, New York, NY, USA, pp. 1–7. ACM (2005). https://doi.org/10.1145/1085099.1085101. https://doi.acm.org/10.1145/1085099.1085101

20. Silva, J.: A vocabulary of program slicing-based techniques. ACM Comput. Surv. **44**(3), 1–41 (2012)

21. Sintaha, M., Nashid, N., Mesbah, A.: Katana: dual slicing-based context for learning bug fixes (2022)

22. Soremekun, E., Kirschner, L., Böhme, M., Zeller, A.: Locating faults with program slicing: an empirical analysis. Empir. Softw. Eng. **26**(3), 1–45 (2021). https://doi.org/10.1007/s10664-020-09931-7

23. Tip, F.: A survey of program slicing techniques. J. Program. Lang. **3**(3), 121–189 (1995)

24. Walkinshaw, N., Roper, M., Wood, M.: The Java system dependence graph. In: Proceedings Third IEEE International Workshop on Source Code Analysis and Manipulation, pp. 55–64 (2003)

25. Weiser, M.: Program slicing. In: Proceedings of the 5th International Conference on Software Engineering (ICSE 1981), Piscataway, NJ, USA, pp. 439–449. IEEE Press (1981)

26. Zhang, Z., Li, Y., Guo, Y., Chen, X., Liu, Y.: Dynamic slicing for deep neural networks. In: Proceedings of the 28th ACM Joint Meeting on European Software Engineering Conference and Symposium on the Foundations of Software Engineering, ESEC/FSE 2020, New York, NY, USA, pp. 838–850. Association for Computing Machinery (2020). https://doi.org/10.1145/3368089.3409676

27. Zhao, J., Cheng, J., Ushijima, K.: Static slicing of concurrent object-oriented programs. In: Proceedings of 20th International Computer Software and Applications Conference: COMPSAC 1996, pp. 312–320 (1996). https://doi.org/10.1109/CMPSAC.1996.544182

Formal Verification of the Inter-core Synchronization of a Multi-core RTOS Kernel

Imane Haur[1,2(✉)], Jean-Luc Béchennec[1(✉)], and Olivier H. Roux[1(✉)]

[1] Nantes Université, Ecole Centrale Nantes, CNRS, LS2N UMR 6004, Nantes, France
{imane.haur,olivier-h.roux}@ec-nantes.fr, Jean-Luc.Bechennec@ls2n.fr
[2] Huawei, Paris Research Center, Paris, France

Abstract. Checking compliance of a Real-Time Operating System (RTOS) with the standard it is supposed to implement is usually achieved by executing a test suite. That is, for example, the case for OS conforming to the AUTOSAR standard. The task becomes complex for multi-core implementations because simultaneous executions are usually not tested and are, in any case, difficult to test generically as the possible interleaving depends on the execution speeds of the cores. In this paper, we propose to use model-checking to verify the communication and synchronization mechanisms involved in the concurrent execution of OS services: concurrent accesses to OS data structures, multi-core scheduling, and inter-core interrupt handling. The multi-core operating system and the application are modeled by a High-level Colored Time Petri Nets (HCTPN) reproducing the control flow graph and using the same variables as the actual implementation. This approach allows to verify compliance with some standards. This paper focuses on rare situations with simultaneous service calls in parallel on several cores that are almost impossible to test on real implementation but that we will be able to obtain by our model checking method. We applied our approach to an OSEK and AUTOSAR compliant RTOS called Trampoline.

Keywords: Real-Time Operating System (RTOS) · High-level Colored Time Petri Nets · Model-checking

1 Introduction

The presence of errors in the real-time software system can lead to severe incidents. It is, therefore, necessary to develop an error-free computer system. Testing is a standard approach to identifying errors in software programs. It does not guarantee the elimination of all errors because it is not exhaustive. Furthermore, it is not suitable alone for real-time critical systems where a failure could have unacceptable consequences. Formal verification is a solution to increase the system's implementation reliability and not negate testing. It has been recommended in various industry standards as a safety verification technique, as in the automotive industry standard ISO-26262 [12].

To prove the system's accuracy, one must verify that the system's specification properties are satisfied. The two essential types of these properties are safety

© Springer Nature Switzerland AG 2022
A. Riesco and M. Zhang (Eds.): ICFEM 2022, LNCS 13478, pp. 140–155, 2022.
https://doi.org/10.1007/978-3-031-17244-1_9

and liveness [14]. The safety property indicates that something unexpected will not happen, and the liveness property usually implies that finite parts of a program complete their execution if their input is correct. Model-checking allows the verification of the correctness of these significant properties on the entire execution path, exploring the whole state space of the system. The technique used in this work is based on model-checking of a real-time system. The reliability of the entire system depends on the operating system. Therefore, verifying that the operating system behaves as expected is essential and emphasizes the need for a formal treatment of safety systems.

1.1   Related Works

This section cites some modeling and verification work conducted on operating systems and based on formal methods.

The authors in [6, 8, 13] propose a formal verification of Real-Time Operating System with proof assistants. Gu et al. [8] develop a certified concurrent OS kernel mC2 using CertiKOS and Coq proof assistant. They verify its correctness and system-call specification. In [6], the Coq proof assistant is applied to the formalized specification description of FreeRTOS. The verification of seL4 microkernel in [13] is done inside Isabelle/HOL. However, for these works, the proofs cover neither application-specific properties nor the interaction of applications with the operating system.

The authors in [3, 5, 17] represent verification work done on the RTOS Trampoline [2]. Y. CHOI in [5] uses PROMELA to convert the kernel source code of the RTOS Trampoline into a formal model. However, the work focuses only on modeling the functions that verify five safety properties, not the entire RTOS. T. TIGORI et al. in [3, 17] propose a model-based approach to the RTOS Trampoline in its mono-core version using extended timed automata. They propose to check the conformity of the RTOS model to the OSEK/VDX standard through observers and the UPPAAL model checker.

1.2   Choice of the Model

We have a double objective: i) the verification of the RTOS behavior by stimulating it with application models such as those proposed for the conformance of the OSEK [16] and AUTOSAR [1] standards ii) the verification of application problems using this OS such as schedulability [10]. This second objective is not presented in this article.

We have mainly three challenges: i) The OS is subject to different kinds of stimuli and, in particular, real-time stimuli such as periodic interruptions generated by timers ii) Applications and code blocks of the OS are executed concurrently on several cores iii) Some parts of the OS code can be executed simultaneously by several cores (StartOS service, spin lock services).

As the RTOS we are dealing with is written in C, a model-checker running on concurrent C programs, such as [7], may seem to be usable, but the call to services goes through assembly code. Furthermore, the goal is not to check only the properties of a C program but to check behavioral properties against real-time stimuli and the management of the resulting interruptions. We, therefore, need a model-checker on timed models even if we do not take into account the execution times of the OS instruction blocks.

A product of timed automata as used in [17] can simulate concurrency and its interleaving but will not be able to model the simultaneous execution of a code sequence on several cores unless an artificial duplication of the model of this code sequence is done. We will therefore use time Petri nets for concurrency and time modeling. We will extend them with a particular notion of colors so that the same sequence of transitions can be traversed by several tokens, each with a different color modeling the core on which the code is executed.

1.3 Contribution and Outline

This study is part of the AUTOSAR compliance verification of a multi-core RTOS. Since the AUTOSAR test cases are synchronous and do not include concurrent situations, we are interested in verifying simultaneous service calls execution on cores for the safety analysis. Specifically, our approach formally verifies multi-core RTOS synchronization mechanisms and automatically identifies possible errors in the concurrent execution. We deal with the Trampoline RTOS, an OSEK/VDX, and AUTOSAR compliant OS. We use High-Level Colored Time Petri Nets (HCTPN) [9] to model both the multi-core RTOS and the real-time application. The application is modeled by a system call sequence of the RTOS. We then rely on the model-checking technique to verify the RTOS implementation: the scheduling performed by the cores, the inter-core interruption, and the shared data structures protection. The whole process is integrated into the ROMÉO tool [15] recently improved to support HCTPN.

The rest of this paper is organized as follows. Sections 2 and 3 present respectively the RTOS and the formalism used for its modeling. Section 4 describes the modeling rules for constructing the formal model of the application and RTOS. Section 5 presents the formal verification approach and the practical results of the conducted verification. Finally, Sect. 6 concludes the paper.

2   Trampoline RTOS

Trampoline is a free software implementation of the OSEK/VDX and AUTOSAR OS 4.2 standards. These two standards define a set of services and specifications for an RTOS with fixed priority scheduling. In addition, the AUTOSAR standard specifies a multi-core RTOS with a fixed priority partitioned scheduler where tasks are statically allocated to a computing core.

2.1 Calling Operating System Services

Both standards define a set of services, and AUTOSAR OS adds services to OSEK/VDX and also limits some configurations. As an example, here are some services grouped by category:

Tasks ActivateTask, TerminateTask, ChainTask, GetTaskState, GetTaskId;
Events synchronization services. WaitEvent, SetEvent, ClearEvent, GetEvent.
Resources for single-core critical sections. GetResource and ReleaseResource;
Spinlocks for multi-core critical sections. GetSpinlock and ReleaseSpinlock.

In Trampoline, the call to an OS service is made in an API function through a dedicated instruction of the microcontroller which, acting as a software interrupt, transfers the execution to a system call handler in supervisor mode. The latter is in charge of calling the corresponding kernel function. In the process, the interrupts are masked. This avoids that an interrupt routine calling the OS can run concurrently to prevent the OS's internal data structures from being corrupted.

On each core, two data structures are used to manage rescheduling and context switching: the list of ready tasks and the `tpl_kern` structure. `tpl_kern` gathers several pieces of information: the currently running task, the task that has been selected to replace the currently running task (if any) after a rescheduling, a flag indicating if a rescheduling shall be done (`need_schedule`), a flag indicating if a context switch shall be done (`need_switch`) and, finally, a flag indicating if a context save shall be done (`need_save`). In the call sequence of core 0 shown in Fig. 1, these flags are reset in the system call handler at the point labeled ①, before calling the kernel function. If the kernel function performs an operation that adds a task to the list of ready tasks or if the task being executed ends (TerminateTask or ChainTask services), `need_schedule` is set, and the kernel function ends by performing a rescheduling. If the rescheduling leads to a context switch, the `need_switch` flag is set, and the context switch is performed at the end of the system call handler just before returning to the newly scheduled task at the point labeled ② in Fig. 1.

2.2   Executing a Multi-core Service Call

In the multi-core implementation, interrupt masking is not enough. Indeed, it is necessary to prevent the OS kernel from running simultaneously on two or more cores if the called service can access the OS data structures common to the cores. For this purpose, a mutual exclusion mechanism operating in multi-core, such as spinlocks, is used. This lock is called *Biglock* in Trampoline. The entry in the multi-core critical section protected by the *Biglock*, is made at the beginning and then exit at the end of the system call handler. When a service is called and results in a rescheduling, for example, if one task activates another, the rescheduling is performed on the core where the service call occurs. However, the context switch must necessarily be performed on the core where the scheduled task is to be executed.

Having simultaneous service calls in parallel on several cores leads to a more complex scheme, especially if a core is the target of an inter-core interrupt while it is executing a service call that leads to a rescheduling. An example of this kind is shown in Fig. 1. Here, task τ_1 does a service call on core 1, e.g. `TerminateTask`, just after `ActivateTask(`τ_2`)` has been called by task τ_0 on core 0 and the task

τ_2 is assigned to core 1. In Ⓐ, a rescheduling is performed by core 0 for core 1 and in parallel, core 1 waits for the *Biglock* in Ⓑ. Then, an inter-core interrupt is sent in Ⓒ to notify core 1 that it must make a context switch, but since the interrupts are masked on core 1, it remains pending. Core 0 releases the *Biglock* by Ⓓ. The release of the *Biglock* allows core 1 to take it and to execute the `TerminateTask()` service. The context switch to the τ_2 task is then carried out, the *Biglock* is released, and core 1 returns to user mode to immediately take into account the inter-core interrupt by Ⓔ. The execution of this inter-core interrupt consists essentially in acknowledging the interrupt and does not lead to a context switch because τ_2 is the highest priority task on core 1, and we finally return to the execution of τ_2.

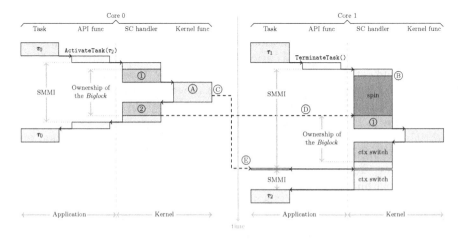

Fig. 1. The activation of a task τ_2 on core 1 by a task τ_0 running on core 0 in parallel with the termination of the task τ_1 on core 1. SMMI stands for *Supervised Mode, Masked Interrupts.*

We can see that it is probably not enough to protect access to the OS data structures (the list of ready tasks and the structure `tpl_kern`) through the *Biglock*. Indeed, the structure `tpl_kern` allows communication between the core where the rescheduling is performed and the core where the context switch is performed, and the example of the Fig. 1 suggests that a problem could occur when services are called concurrently on two or more cores.

Testing the situation presented in the Fig. 1 on a real target is not an easy thing because it requires synchronizing precisely the execution on the cores. However, since a precise model of Trampoline is available, it is possible to highlight this problem, thanks to model-checking, as we will see in what follows.

3   High-Level Colored Time Petri Nets

Petri nets are a mathematical formalism and a graphical modeling tool for describing distributed concurrent systems. A Petri net is a directed bipartite graph whose vertices are places and transitions. A place can contain any number of tokens. A marking M of a Petri Net is a vector representing the number of tokens of each place. A transition is enabled (it may fire) in M if there are enough tokens in its input places for the consumptions to be possible. Firing a transition from a marking M consumes token from each of its input places, and produces tokens in each of its output places.

High-level Petri nets [11] are proposed to model complex systems that handle different expressions and data structures. Time Petri nets extend the Petri nets formalism with the time notion. They associate to each transition an interval, indicating a minimum and maximum firing duration. The colored Petri nets allow distinguishing the tokens, so the marking M represents the number of tokens in each place and their colors. High-level colored time Petri nets encompass color, time, and high-level functionality. Multiple enableness is required for modeling true parallelism when multiple instances of code are executed [4]. It happens when many color combinations allow a transition at a particular time.

Notations: The sets $\mathbb{N}$, $\mathbb{Q}_{\geq 0}$, and $\mathbb{R}_{\geq 0}$ are respectively the sets of natural, non-negative rational, and non-negative real numbers. We denote by $\mathcal{I}(\mathbb{Q}_{\geq 0})$ the set of interval with endpoints in $\mathbb{Q}_{\geq 0}$. B^A stands for the set of mappings from A to B. If A is finite and $|A| = n$, an element of B^A is also a vector in B^n. The usual operators $+, -, <$ and $=$ are used on vectors of A^n with $A = \mathbb{N}, \mathbb{Q}, \mathbb{R}$ and are the point-wise extensions of their counterparts in A.

3.1   Definition of High-Level Colored Time Petri Nets

We now give the formal definition. An arc can be associated with a color of the set C or have a particular color called *any*.

Definition 1 (High-level Colored Time Petri Net). *A HCTPN is a tuple* $N = (P, T, X, C, \mathsf{pre}, \mathsf{post}, (m_0, x_0), guard, update, I)$ *where P is a finite non-empty set of* places, *T is a finite set of* transitions *such that $T \cap P = \emptyset$, X is a finite set of* variables *taking their value in the finite set $\mathbb{X}$ (such as bounded integer), C is a finite set of* colors *and $C_{any} = C \cup \{any\}$, $\mathsf{pre} : P \times T \to \mathbb{N}^{C_{any}}$ is the backward incidence mapping, $\mathsf{post} : P \times T \to \mathbb{N}^{C_{any}}$ is the forward incidence mapping, $guard : T \times \mathbb{X}^X \to \{true, false\}$ is the guard function, $update : T \times \mathbb{X}^X \to \mathbb{X}^X$ is the update function, $(m_0, x_0) \in \mathbb{N}^{P \times C} \times \mathbb{X}^X$ is the initial values m_0 of the marking and x_0 of the variables, $I : T \to \mathcal{I}(\mathbb{Q}_{\geq 0})$ is the* static firing interval *function.*

Discrete Behavior: For a marking $m \in \mathbb{N}^{P \times C}$, $m(p)$ is a vector in $\mathbb{N}^C$ and $m(p)[c]$ represents a number of *tokens* of color $c \in C$ in place $p \in P$. A valuation of the set of variables X is noted $x \in \mathbb{X}^X$. (m, x) is a discrete state of HCTPN.

Enabling of a Transition: An arc $\mathsf{pre}(p, t) \in \mathbb{N}^{C_{any}}$ is a vector of which at most one element is different from zero, such that $\mathsf{pre}(p, t)[c]$ is the number of token of color $c \in C$ in place p needed to enable the transition t and $\mathsf{pre}(p, t)[any] > 0$ represents the fact that any color can enable the transition. Let $T_{any} \in T$ the set of transitions that can be enabled by *any* color: i.e. $T_{any} = \{t \in T, \exists p \in P$, s.t. $\text{pre}(p, t)[any] > 0\ \}$. Moreover we define the set $T_{\overline{any}} = T \backslash T_{any}$.

A transition $t \in T$ is said to be *enabled* by a given marking $m \in \mathbb{N}^{P \times C}$ in two cases depending on whether $t \in T_{any}$ or not:

- if $t \in T_{\overline{any}}$, and $\forall p \in P$ and $\forall c \in C$, $m(p)[c] \geq \text{pre}(p, t)[c]$. We denote $\text{en}(m, t) \in \{true, false\}$, the true value of this condition.
- if $t \in T_{any}$, and $\exists c_a \in C$ such that $\forall p \in P$, $m(p)[c_a] \geq \text{pre}(p, t)[any]$ and $\forall c \in C$, $m(p)[c] \geq \text{pre}(p, t)[c]$. The corresponding set of color c_a is noted $\text{colorSet}_{any}(m, t) \subseteq C$

Finally, a transition $t \in T$ is said to be *enabled* by a given marking m and a valuation x if $\text{en}(m, t) = true$ or $\text{colorSet}_{any}(m, t) \neq \emptyset$ and $guard(t, x) = true$.

Firing of a Transition: An arc $\text{post}(p, t) \in \mathbb{N}^{C_{any}}$ is a vector such that $\text{post}(p, t)[c]$ is the number of token of color $c \in C$ produced in place p by the firing of the transition t and $\text{post}(p, t)[any]$ give the number of token produced in p with the color $c \in \text{colorSet}_{any}(m, t)$ used for the firing of t.

Firing an enabled transition $t \in T_{\overline{any}}$ from (m, x) such that $\text{en}(m, t) = true$ and $guard(t, x) = true$ leads to a new marking m' defined by $\forall c \in C, \forall p \in P$, $m'(p)[c] = m(p)[c] - \text{pre}(p, t)[c] + \text{post}(p, t)[c]$ and a new valuation $x' = update(t, x)$. This new marking is denoted $m' = \text{firing}(m, t, \bullet)$ where $\bullet$ denote the fact that no *any* color has to be instantiated for this firing.

Firing an enabled transition $t \in T_{any}$ from (m, x) with the *any* color $c_a \in \text{colorSet}_{any}(m, t)$ leads to a new marking defined by $\forall c \in C \backslash \{c_a\}, \forall p \in P$, $m'(p)[c] = m(p)[c] - \text{pre}(p, t)[c] + \text{post}(p, t)[c]$ and $\forall p \in P$, $m'(p)[c_a] = m(p)[c_a] - \text{pre}(p, t)[c_a] - \text{pre}(p, t)[any] + \text{post}(p, t)[c_a] + \text{post}(p, t)[any]$ and a new valuation $x' = update(t, x)$. This new marking is denoted $m' = \text{firing}(m, t, c_a)$.

Time Behavior: For any $t \in T_{any}$, $v(t, c)$ is the valuation of the clock associated with t and the color $c \in C$. i.e. it is the time elapsed since the transition t has been newly enabled by m with $c \in \text{colorSet}_{any}(m, t)$. For other transitions $t \in T_{\overline{any}}$, $v(t, \bullet)$ is the valuation of the clock associated with t. $\bar{0}$ is the initial valuation with $\forall t \in T, \forall c \in C \cup \{\bullet\}, \bar{0}(t, c) = 0$.

A *state* of the net $\mathcal{N}$ is a tuple (m, x, v) in $\mathbb{N}^{P \times C} \times \mathbb{X}^X \times \mathbb{R}_{\geq 0}^{T \times (C \cup \{\bullet\})}$. A run of $\mathcal{N}$ is a finite or infinite sequence of alternating delay and discrete transition.

3.2   Example of HCTPN

Figure 2 presents an HCTPN example with a set of 3 colors $C = \{blue, red, brown\}$ that illustrates the high-level functionalities, and the notion of color and multi-enableness. A firing of the transition $T_1 \in T_{any}$ produces a token in P_3 with the color ($\$any$) used for the firing. The $\$any$ variable represents the color used to fire the transition and is used in its precondition (guard) and the postcondition (update). Therefore, T_1 transition is not enabled by the blue token due to the guard $\$any \geq 1$. T_1 transition is multi-enabled and its interval is set to $[1, 1]$. Thus, it will be fired first twice with red and brown tokens leading to the execution of the update $cpt[\$any] = g(\$any, cpt)$ and producing the same tokens colors in P_3. Then the transition T_2 will be fired with the P_1 blue token and P_3 brown one, producing a red one in place P_2. The final value of cpt is $\{2, 4, 4\}$.

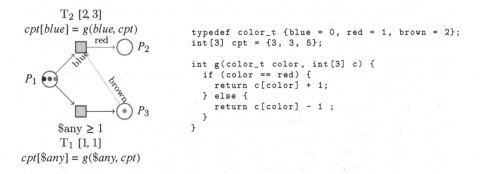

Fig. 2. HCTPN illustrating high-level functionalities and multi-enableness.

A *state* of the net $\mathcal{N}$ of Fig. 2 is a tuple (m, cpt, v). $T_1 \in T_{any}$ has a valuation for each color whereas $T_2 \in T_{\overline{any}}$ has only one valuation (column •).

The initial state is $s_0 = (m_0, cpt, v_0) =$

$$\left(\begin{pmatrix} & blue & red & brown \\ P_1 & 1 & 1 & 1 \\ P_2 & 0 & 0 & 0 \\ P_3 & 0 & 0 & 1 \end{pmatrix}, \{3,3,5\}, \begin{matrix} T_1 \\ T_2 \end{matrix} \begin{pmatrix} • & blue & red & brown \\ & 0 & 0 & 0 \\ 0 & & & \end{pmatrix} \right).$$

By elapsing 1 t.u. and then firing T_1 twice with colors red and then brown, elapsing 1.3 t.u. and then firing T_2 we have the following run:

$$s_0 \xrightarrow{1} \left(\left(\begin{smallmatrix} 1 & 1 & 1 \\ 0 & 0 & 0 \\ 0 & 0 & 1 \end{smallmatrix} \right), \{3,3,5\}, \left(\begin{smallmatrix} 0 & 1 & 1 \\ 1 & & \end{smallmatrix} \right) \right) \xrightarrow{T_1, red} \left(\left(\begin{smallmatrix} 1 & 0 & 1 \\ 0 & 0 & 0 \\ 0 & 1 & 1 \end{smallmatrix} \right), \{3,4,5\}, \left(\begin{smallmatrix} 0 & 0 & 1 \\ 1 & & \end{smallmatrix} \right) \right) \xrightarrow{T_1, brown} \left(\left(\begin{smallmatrix} 1 & 0 & 0 \\ 0 & 0 & 0 \\ 0 & 1 & 2 \end{smallmatrix} \right), \{3,4,4\}, \left(\begin{smallmatrix} 0 & 0 & 0 \\ 1 & & \end{smallmatrix} \right) \right)$$

$$\xrightarrow{1.3} \left(\left(\begin{smallmatrix} 1 & 0 & 0 \\ 0 & 0 & 0 \\ 0 & 1 & 2 \end{smallmatrix} \right), \{3,4,4\}, \left(\begin{smallmatrix} 0 & 0 & 0 \\ 2.3 & & \end{smallmatrix} \right) \right) \xrightarrow{T_2, blue} \left(\left(\begin{smallmatrix} 0 & 0 & 0 \\ 1 & 0 & 0 \\ 0 & 1 & 1 \end{smallmatrix} \right), \{2,4,4\}, \left(\begin{smallmatrix} 0 & 0 & 0 \\ 0 & & \end{smallmatrix} \right) \right)$$

4   RTOS and Application Model

This section presents the modeling of the multi-core version of the Trampoline operating system and the application level. The complete model has been built with a systematic approach based on HCTPN translation rules Sect. 4.1 in ROMÉO, a tool for modeling and verifying timed systems using HCTPN. Trampoline is mainly written in the C language in over 20.000 lines long and includes 180 functions. The model is represented in the form of 115 Petri subnets which appear independent but form only one. In total, the model contains 600 transitions, 550 places, with 250 variables and 55 functions described under a C-like syntax file, included to ROMÉO. We developed a module in the Trampoline OIL compiler to extract the data structures from the OIL description of the application and automatically generate the C-like file. ROMÉO provides a variable *any* that gives the integer value of the color used for the transition firing, representing the core number.

4.1   Principles of Modeling

The modeling is built on the following bases:

- Each Petri subnet describes a function of the operating system and faithfully describes its control flow.
- The variables, actions, and conditions used in the model are those of the operating system control variables.
- The Petri net transitions include the same imperative expressions as those present in the source code.
- Pointers are translated to arrays in the model.
- The number of colors represents the number of cores in the model.
- All kernel transitions are fired in a time interval $[0,0]$, the time depends on a specific material target, and the hardware is abstracted.
- The application model is described by API function calls and captures all the possible API calls interleaving.

Atomicity. The code associated with a transition in a HCTPN is executed sequentially but is considered atomic. This code can be one or a sequence of instructions. In the modeling step, the association of an instruction sequence to a transition allows to reduce the state space. An update can read and/or write variables and when it is a variable of the modeled system, one must be careful to reproduce the competition situations of the real system. Therefore the modification of a shared variable must be cut in two: the reading on a transition, the writing on the following transition. We thus have the following property:

PROPERTY 5.1: Our model composed of the operating system program, and the application contains all the interleaving transitions that modify the shared variables. However, the complete model contains all the paths that might be traversed by the whole system during its execution modulo the atomicity. The formal model and the RTOS then have the same state space over the RTOS variables.

Function Call. When the Petri subnet models a called function, we represent a function call by a token deposit in its initial place. Then, we wait for the execution's end via a transition guard to receive the token. The arguments are passed, and the results are returned using arrays of global variables indexed by the number of the core on which the function call is made. When the function is written in ROMÉO language, we associate its call with the model's transitions. These functions are atomic and generally do not need an instruction-level check (e.g., functions used for result and error comparison).

4.2   RTOS Model

The RTOS model is composed of the API services and the kernel. Each modeled Trampoline source code function is described by a Petri subnet and, if needed, by a ROMÉO function described in a C-like syntax to reduce the state space.

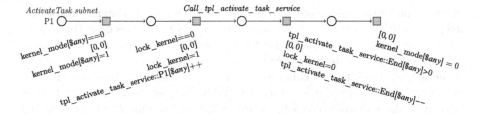

Fig. 3. Example of the `ActivateTask` service modeling

API Services Modeling. The API contains the various services available to the application. An application making a service call is shown in Fig. 4. Let us consider the API `ActivateTask` function model shown in Fig. 3. The transition guard associated with the first transition of the model ($kernel\_mode[\$any] == 0$) describes that an API function's call is always made in user mode to execute the requested service. The update of the $kernel\_mode$ variable to 1 means that the core switches to kernel mode when an API function is called. $lock\_kernel$ represents the *BigLock* and prevents simultaneous service calls by different cores. The first place of the Petri subnet represents the initial location of the function, and each transition describes the execution state of the function. Upon calling this Petri subnet, it calls the kernel function `tpl_activate_task_service`, itself modeled by a Petri subnet, to execute the requested service[1]. This function unlocks the kernel when it completes its execution, and another service can then be called. The final place of the called function is emptied to avoid token accumulation. All other services are similarly modeled.

Kernel Modeling. The Kernel contains all the low-level functions on which the Trampoline services are based. It ensures the start and shutdown of the OS and allows the activation of tasks, their scheduling, and their synchronization. The Trampoline kernel comprises three modules: the task manager, the counter manager and the scheduler; Each of these modules includes several functions.

4.3 Application Model

An application contains a concurrent set of tasks that interact with the operating system through system calls such as `ActivateTask()` or `TerminateTask()`. The attributes of the objects (tasks, resources, alarms, spinlocks, ...): Periods, priorities, core on which a task runs, ... constitute part of the model variables. Figure 4 shows a modeling example of an application using 3 tasks. The $IsReady(task_i)$ guards on Act_{task_i} means that the task model is ready for execution. The $IsRunning()$ guards on transitions returns 1 when the task $task_i$ is

---

[1] The two double dot (::) are equivalent to an arc in the model. This syntax proposed by ROMÉO allows a clear and better organization of the Petri subnet in different XML files, which form only one Petri net. Thus a function call is ensured by the following syntax: the XML file name of the Petri subnet:: the place name to which we want to send a token.

scheduled on the assigned core, and we are in the user mode (`kernel_mode==0`). $task_1$ is running on core 0 and activates $task_2$ on core 1. In this case, the *Biglock* is taken by core 0 when the `ActivateTask` service is called, and core 1 waits actively for its release to take over the interrupt and make the context switch. In the model, handling the concurrency of service calls in parallel on different cores is represented by the *lock_kernel* variable. It is set to 1 and reset to 0 at the end of the execution of each service call. Since the interrupts are masked and can not run concurrently, a *kernel_mode* table is used, allowing simultaneous access through the *any* variable. All transitions have a firing interval set in order to verify the behavior with and without the competition of execution of the services.

5   Formal Verification

Trampoline includes an OSEK/AUTOSAR test suite used to test the real implementation. This test suite has been run on several different hardware targets showing Trampoline RTOS compliance.

With a method similar to the approach represented in [3], we have modeled the AUTOSAR multi-core test suite with HCTPN allowing, by checking a simple temporal logic formula on the Trampoline formal model (given in Sect. 4), to verify Trampoline RTOS compliance.

Our goal is now to study rare situations with simultaneous service calls in parallel on several cores that are almost impossible to test on real implementation but that we will be able to obtain by our model checking approach.

We use the ROMÉO model checker that takes TCTL temporal logic formula as input and provides efficient on-the-fly algorithms over bounded HCTPN.

5.1   Case Studies

Case Study 1. Let us consider the system of the Fig. 4. Once the autostart $task_1$ is started on core 0 at system start-up time, it activates $task_2$ on core 1, and terminates afterwards. The purpose is to check that $task_2$ will run and terminate its execution on core 1, whatever the interleaving. $task_3$, which is an autostart task and has a lower priority than $task_2$, is assumed to be preempted by $task_2$.

Formal Analysis. We run a complete analysis of the application and the RTOS, using ROMÉO. We check that all the application's tasks complete their execution in a concurrent context. We verify that the places $TerminateTask_i[task_i.core\_id]$ are always marked by a token with the property: $AF(TerminateTask_1[0] > 0 \ and \ TerminateTask_2[1] > 0 \ and \ TerminateTask_3[1] > 0)$. ROMÉO replies that the property is not satisfied, and a counter-example execution trace is generated, proving the place $TerminateTask_2[1]$ is never reached in the given case:

1. StartOS: We start the operating system. It first makes some initializations, activates the autostart tasks and alarms, performs the scheduling, and executes the highest priority task. Thus, the autostart $task_1$ and $task_3$ are run in this startup phase;

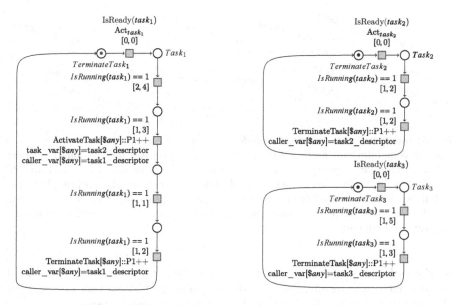

Fig. 4. Application model: activation of a higher priority task $Prio(task_1)$ < $Prio(task_3)$ < $Prio(task_2)$; $task_1$ runs on core 0 which is associated with the red color; $task_2$ and $task_3$ run on core 1 which is associated with the blue color. At start $task_1$ and $task_3$ are running on their respective core. Here we want to check that $task_2$ will run on core 1, whatever the interleaving.

2. ActivateTask: The service is called by $task_1$ running on core 0 in order to activate $task_2$ on core 1. The rescheduling for core 1 is performed on core 0, where the service call occurs. Core 0 sends an inter-core interrupt request to core 1 by setting the variable it_flag. Figure 5 presents the interrupt handler model. Core 1 actively waits for the local and global lock release;

3. TerminateTask: The service is called by $task_3$ running on core 1. $task_3$ ends its execution on core 1 and the context switch is performed to $idle$ task;

4. Handler: Core 1 enter the kernel to execute the inter-core interrupt and perform the context switch (Fig. 5). Since the need_switch flag of the tpl_kern structure is set to NO_NEED_SWITCH after the execution of the idle task on core 1, the context switch is not achieved. Thus, we return to the execution of the $idle$ task;

5. TerminateTask: The service is called by $task_1$ running on core 0; $task_1$ ends its execution and the context switch is performed to the $idle$ on this core.

The rescheduling performed by core 0 for core 1 in step 2, elects $task_2$ and extracts it from the ready_list. When the inter-core interrupt is executed, the context switch is performed to the task extracted from the ready_list if the need_switch flag is true. By calling the TerminateTask service in step 3 before executing the interruption, the first element of the ready_list is extracted, which is the $idle$ task. Thus the problem occurs, and the context switch is made

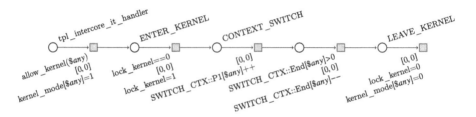

Fig. 5. Intercore interrupt handler model. To notify an interruption, a token with a color corresponding to the target core is put in the `tpl_intercore_it_handler` place. `allow_kernel($any)` is true if the corresponding core is in user mode and able to handle interrupts. Then interrupts are masked on the core (`kernel_mode[$any]=1`), the global lock is taken if possible (`lock_kernel=1`). Next, the context switch is performed. Finally, the global lock is released, and the core returns to user mode, unmasking interrupt consequently.

to *idle* task instead of $task_2$. In other words, the activation of $task_2$ on core 1 is lost because the termination of task $task_3$ on core 1 elects task *idle* without checking that the already elected task ($task_2$) has a lower priority.

Table 1 shows the computing time and the amount of memory used in this analysis. The second column gives the data for the application model shown in Fig. 4. The third column corresponds to an application running on three cores. It is obtained by duplicating $task_3$ and assigning it to the third core to evaluate the model-checking computation time when increasing state space.

Case Study 2. Let us consider a modification of the application presented in Fig. 4 and obtained by replacing the call to the `TerminateTask` service with a call to the `GetTaskID` service in $task_3$. `GetTaskID` writes in the `TaskID` variable the identifier of the task currently running. If no task is running, for example if `GetTaskID` was called from an ISR (Interrupt Service Routine), `INVALID_TASK` is returned. We want to verify if the *Biglock* is enough to protect the OS data structures access when we have concurrent calls to `ActivateTask` and `GetTaskID` services. Since `GetTaskID` is not a service that causes rescheduling, calling it should have no influence.

Formal Analysis. We conduct the same reachability verification with the ROMÉO model checker leading to the detection of the following problem: When the `GetTaskID` service call is made in concurrence with the execution of the inter-core interrupt on core 1, the `need_switch` and `need_save` flags are reset by the system call handler. The information is therefore lost for the inter-core interrupt handler. The trace provided by the model checker is as follows:

1. StartOS: We start the operating system and the autostart $task_1$, $task_3$ and $task_4$ are run;
2. ActivateTask: $task_1$ calls the service on core 0 to activate $task_2$ on core 1. Core 0 sends an inter-core interrupt request to core 1 after the rescheduling.

3. GetTaskID: The service is called by $task_3$ on core 1. The need_switch and need_save flags of the tpl_kern structure are reset (tpl_kern[1].need_switch=0).
4. Handler: The inter-core handler (Fig. 5) is called to execute the interrupt on core 1 and effect the context switch. The context switch is not performed since the tpl_kern structure flags, need_switch and need_save, are reset after the GetTaskID execution on core 1. Thus, $task_2$ is never executed on core 1.

The computation time and the amount of memory used in this analysis are given in Table 1. As in Case Study 1, the three-core system is obtained by duplicating $Task_3$ and assigning it to a third core.

Table 1. Computing time and memory used before correction.

	Case study 1		Case study 2	
	$AF(TerminateTask_i[task_i.core\_id] > 0)$		$AF(GetTaskID_2[task_2.core\_id] > 0)$	
Number of cores	2	3	2	3
Model checker result	False		False	
Memory used	96.0 MB	174.9 MB	56.6 MB	114.0 MB
Computing time	7.1 s	10.7 s	2.6 s	3.7 s

5.2   Correction of the Error

The errors found in Sect. 5.1 hold for any application, independently of the number of tasks on two or more cores, as the system call handler always resets the kernel data structure before calling the corresponding kernel function, resulting in a loss of information. In addition, while the executing OS call service leads to rescheduling, the ready list is modified. The problems have been reported to the developers, and solutions have been proposed to fix them formally in the model. Verification showed the property satisfaction. Table 2 represents the computing time after fixing the error in the model. The verification time is longer because all possible interleavings are considered, and property checking requires exploring the entire state space.

Case Study 1. We have to test before the extraction of the task at the front of the ready list that it has a higher priority than the elected one. If the elected task has a priority equal to or higher than the first task in the ready list, then the rescheduling is correct, and the extraction is useless. This modification guarantees a context switch to either the already elected task or the newly elected task with the highest priority.

Case Study 2. The solution we adopted is to move at the end of the sc_handler the reset of the need_switch and need_save flags. Instead of resetting them before the kernel function is called, they are reset when they are taken into account to perform the context switch. In this way, services that do not cause a context switch leave `need_switch` and `need_save` unchanged, and the information is not lost to the inter-core interrupt.

Table 2. Computing time and memory used after correction.

	Case study 1		Case study 2	
	$AF(TerminateTask_i[task_i.core\_id] > 0)$		$AF(GetTaskID_2[task_2.core\_id] > 0)$	
Number of cores	2	3	2	3
Model checker result	True		True	
Memory used	117.6 MB	127.8 MB	96.7 MB	150.1 MB
Computing time	51.1 s	2629.2 s	13.3 s	914.8 s

Scalability. The scalability of the approach is based on the number of cores, the number of tasks and their time interval, and the number of system calls that can be simultaneous. All these factors can increase the computation time during verification. Additional verifications with four cores, more than what is currently found in automotive embedded systems, each executing a task making concurrent system calls, run in 1124.8 s with 1141.3 MB of memory used and show that the approach scales to realistic automotive systems.

6   Conclusion

In this paper, we presented the model of the Trampoline RTOS, a compliant RTOS with the OSEK/VDX and AUTOSAR standards, and the application using High-level Colored Time Petri Nets formalism. AUTOSAR test cases do not test the kernel in concurrency situations and are therefore unsuitable as a basis for verifying the correctness of the kernel's mutual exclusion and communication mechanisms. Therefore, we applied our verification approach to check the rescheduling performed by the cores and the inter-core interrupt, considering case studies with simultaneous service calls on the cores. We found that the rescheduling and the context switching in concurrent situations are not functional. The model checker provided counter-example traces. A complete research door is opened to find implementation errors with several multi-core concurrent examples based on the verification approach.

In the next step, we aim to allow the simultaneous execution of the kernel on different cores by replacing the *BigLock* with several locks protecting shared data within the kernel. Furthermore, we want to avoid manual construction of the model by developing a Domain-Specific Language (DSL) from which the RTOS source code and its Petri net model would be generated automatically.

References

1. AUTOSAR GbR: Specification of operating system (2009)
2. Béchennec, J.L., Briday, M., Faucou, S., Trinquet, Y.: Trampoline an open source implementation of the OSEK/VDX RTOS specification. In: IEEE Conference on Emerging Technologies and Factory Automation, ETFA 2006, pp. 62–69 (2006)
3. Béchennec, J.L., Roux, O.H., Tigori, T.: Formal model-based conformance verification of an OSEK/VDX compliant RTOS. In: International Conference on Control, Decision and Information Technologies (CODIT 2018). IEEE (2018)
4. Boyer, M., Diaz, M.: Multiple enabledness of transitions in petri nets with time. In: 9th International Workshop on Petri Nets and Performance Models, PNPM 2001, pp. 219–228. IEEE Computer Society (2001)
5. Choi, Y.: Safety analysis of trampoline OS using model checking: an experience report. In: 2011 IEEE 22nd International Symposium on Software Reliability Engineering, pp. 200–209 (2011)
6. Espinosa, T., Leon, G.: Formal verification of a real-time operating system. Master thesis, University of Saskatchewan (2012)
7. Gadelha, M.R., Monteiro, F.R., Morse, J., Cordeiro, L.C., Fischer, B., Nicole, D.A.: ESBMC 5.0: an industrial-strength C model checker, pp. 888–891. Association for Computing Machinery, New York (2018)
8. Gu, R., et al.: Building certified concurrent OS kernels. Commun. ACM **62**(10), 89–99 (2019)
9. Haur, I., Béchennec, J.L., Roux, O.H.: High-level colored time petri nets for true concurrency modeling in real-time software. In: International Conference on Control, Decision and Information Technologies (CODIT 2022). IEEE (2022)
10. Haur, I., Béchennec, J.L., Roux, O.H.: Formal schedulability analysis based on multi-core RTOS model. In: 29th International Conference on Real-Time Networks and Systems, RTNS 2021, pp. 216–225 (2021)
11. Hillah, L., Kordon, F., Petrucci, L., Trèves, N.: PN standardisation: a survey. In: Najm, E., Pradat-Peyre, J.-F., Donzeau-Gouge, V.V. (eds.) FORTE 2006. LNCS, vol. 4229, pp. 307–322. Springer, Heidelberg (2006). https://doi.org/10. 1007/11888116_23
12. ISO: ISO 26262:2018 road vehicles – functional safety. Technical report, ISO (2018)
13. Klein, G., et al.: Sel4: formal verification of an OS kernel. In: Proceedings of the ACM SIGOPS 22nd Symposium on Operating Systems Principles, SOSP 2009, New York, NY, USA, pp. 207–220 (2009)
14. Lamport, L.: Proving the correctness of multiprocess programs. IEEE Trans. Softw. Eng. **SE–3**(2), 125–143 (1977)
15. Lime, D., Roux, O.H., Seidner, C., Traonouez, L.-M.: Romeo: a parametric model-checker for petri nets with stopwatches. In: Kowalewski, S., Philippou, A. (eds.) TACAS 2009. LNCS, vol. 5505, pp. 54–57. Springer, Heidelberg (2009). https:// doi.org/10.1007/978-3-642-00768-2_6
16. OSEK Group: OSEK/VDX OS test plan version 2.0 (1999)
17. Tigori, K.T.G., Béchennec, J.L., Faucou, S., Roux, O.H.: Formal model-based synthesis of application-specific static RTOS. ACM Trans. Embed. Comput. Syst. (TECS) **16**(4), 1–25 (2017)

SMT-Based Model Checking of Industrial Simulink Models

Daisuke Ishii[1]([⊠]), Takashi Tomita[1], Toshiaki Aoki[1], The Quyen Ngo[2], Thi Bich Ngoc Do[3], and Hideaki Takai[4]

[1] Japan Advanced Institute of Science and Technology, Ishikawa, Japan
{dsksh,tomita,toshiaki}@jaist.ac.jp
[2] VNU University of Science, Hanoi, Vietnam
ngoquyenbg@hus.edu.vn
[3] Posts and Telecommunications Institute of Technology, Hanoi, Vietnam
ngocdtb@ptit.edu.vn
[4] GAIO Technology Co., Tokyo, Japan
takai.h@gaio.co.jp

Abstract. The development of embedded systems requires formal analysis of models such as those described with MATLAB/Simulink. However, the increasing complexity of industrial models makes analysis difficult. This paper proposes a model checking method for Simulink models using SMT solvers. The proposed method aims at (1) automated, efficient and comprehensible verification of complex models, (2) numerically accurate analysis of models, and (3) demonstrating the analysis of Simulink models using an SMT solver (we use Z3). It first encodes a target model into a predicate logic formula in the domain of mathematical arithmetic and bit vectors. We explore how to encode various Simulink blocks exactly. Then, the method verifies a given invariance property using the k-induction-based algorithm that extracts a subsystem involving the target block and unrolls the execution paths incrementally. In the experiment, we applied the proposed method and other tools to a set of models and properties. Our method successfully verified most of the properties including those unverified with other tools.

Keywords: SMT solvers · Model checking · MATLAB/Simulink

1 Introduction

Complex embedded systems are developed using a model-based approach, in which a *model* of a system is developed virtually before the actual implementation [18]; typical development targets are vehicles and robots. *MATLAB/Simulink* (Sect. 2) is a tool for developing cyber-physical system (CPS) models. It provides a graphical language and a numerical simulation engine.

As ISO 26262 recommends, formal analysis of models is important to assure the quality of products in the model-based development. A MATLAB toolbox

---

This work was supported by JSPS KAKENHI Grant Numbers 18K11240, 18H03220.

A. Riesco and M. Zhang (Eds.): ICFEM 2022, LNCS 13478, pp. 156–172, 2022.
https://doi.org/10.1007/978-3-031-17244-1_10

Simulink Design Verifier (SLDV) (Sect. 6) provides a set of blocks to represent properties and dedicated model checking functions. Notably, checking invariance properties plays a crucial role in test generation. However, as industrial models become complex, several issues arise in the formal analysis:

- *Scalability issue* due to the increase in the time taken by checking properties.
- *Reliability issue* due to the approximation applied during model checking by the tools such as SLDV.
- *Explainability issue*. The detail of the model checking process and the underlying "formal methods" of the tool are unknown.

SMT solvers [17] are a core technology of formal methods [3]. They handle decision problem instances in various domains e.g. reals, integers, and bit vectors. Recently, it has become possible to verify properties on floating-point (FP) numbers [7]. In terms of application, they have been applied to analysis of Simulink models (e.g. [5,12,22]). Yet state-of-the-art solvers are efficient, their scalability is limited in principle; in our preliminary experiments, the execution time blew up when analyzing industrial Simulink models directly.

The objective of this paper is to realize an invariance model checking method that is efficient, formal and comprehensible. We also aim at a feasibility study of analyzing industrial Simulink models using SMT solvers. The contributions of this paper are summarized as follows:

- *SMT-based model checking method*. We consider invariance properties and verify them with SMT-based model checking (Sect. 3). The method consists of an encoder from Simulink models to logic formulas (in SMT-LIB format) and a model checker. We present two encoding methods (Sect. 4): *Approximate encoding* based on mathematical numerals and *exact encoding* based on bit vectors. For model checking, we propose an algorithm that iteratively applies k-induction while expanding the paths unrolled and the local subsystem scope (Sect. 5).
- *Experimental results with artificial and industrial Simulink models*. Sect. 6 reports the results of the verification of nine models; we experimented using the proposed method, SLDV and CoCoSim for comparison. We explain that our method processed the models correctly and effectively; the advantages over the other tools and the validity of using our method in industrial settings are discussed.

2   Simulink

Simulink[1] is a MATLAB toolbox for modeling synchronous and hybrid systems based on a graphical language. The targets are described as timed models, either with a continuous timeline or with a timeline discretized with a fixed sample time; in this work, we assume the latter. Simulink models are diagrams representing hierarchical directed graphs with edges, called *lines*, and nodes, called *blocks*, of various kinds.

---

[1] https://www.mathworks.com/products/simulink.html.

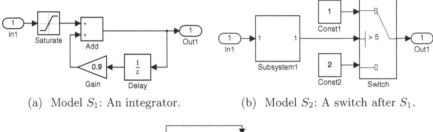

(a) Model S_1: An integrator.   (b) Model S_2: A switch after S_1.

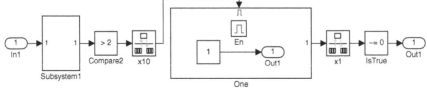

(c) Model S_3: An example with multiple rates and an enabled subsystem.

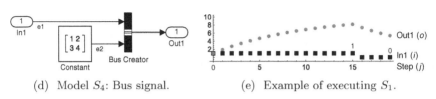

(d) Model S_4: Bus signal.   (e) Example of executing S_1.

Fig. 1. Example Simulink models.

Example Simulink models are shown in Fig. 1. Model S_1 describes an integration with a feedback loop, in which the input value is added with the output value of the previous step with gain 0.9; here, blocks of type **Add**, **Constant**, **Gain** and **Unit Delay** are utilized; also, block **Saturate** is used to limit the input range to $[-1, 1]$. Each block is configured with its *parameters* such as gain factor, saturation threshold, and data type of the signal to be processed. Model S_2 embeds S_1 as a *subsystem* to model in a hierarchical way. S_2 describes a branch using a **Switch** block that outputs a constant signal with a value of 1 or 2, depending on whether the input is greater than 5 or not. Model S_3 is a more complex example with rate transition and a subsystem with an **Enable** port. Initially, the subsystem **One** is deactivated (outputs 0); it will be activated when **Compare2** outputs true, but the activation occurs at a 10-fold period. Model S_4 exemplifies matrix and bus signals. It outputs a signal that combines two named elements, a scalar signal **e1** and a matrix signal **e2**.

The primary function of Simulink is numerical simulation, i.e. to obtain output signals of models. In this paper, we regard a *signal* as a bounded sequence of output values; j-th value is output at time $j \times st$ ($j \geq 0$ and st is a configured sample time). Example input and output signals are shown in Fig. 1e.

Simulink models have a tree structure consisting of subsystems as shown in Fig. 1. Accordingly, each block in models can be located by a path i.e. a sequence of subsystem names ending with a block name; e.g., "S_2/**Subsystem1/Saturate**" locates `Saturate` in S_2. Our proposed subsystem-wise method uses this hierarchical structure of subsystems. The method in Sect. 5 refers to the length of a path by d.

Formalization of Simulink Models. A discrete-time Simulink model can be regarded as a transition system.

Definition 1. *Assume sets V_i, V_o and V_s of input, output, and state variables. For a set of variables $V = \{v_1, \ldots, v_n\}$, we denote their domain $D_1 \times \cdots \times D_n$ by $D(V)$. A transition system $(\mathcal{I}, \mathcal{T})$ consists of an initial condition $\mathcal{I} \subseteq D(V_s)$ and a transition relation $\mathcal{T} \subseteq D(V_s) \times D(V_s) \times D(V_i) \times D(V_o)$.*

The model S_1 is interpreted as $(\mathcal{I}_1, \mathcal{T}_1)$, where:

$$\mathcal{I}_1(s) :\Leftrightarrow s = 0, \quad \mathcal{T}_1(s, s', i, o) :\Leftrightarrow o = \max\{-1, \min\{i, 1\}\} + 0.9\,s \wedge s' = o.$$

Input/output variable i/o represents the value of an input/output signal at a step. The state variable s/s' is necessary for `Delay` to represent signal values before/after the transition. In the same way, S_2 is interpreted as $(\mathcal{I}_2, \mathcal{T}_2)$:

$$
\begin{aligned}
\mathcal{I}_2(s) &:\Leftrightarrow \mathcal{I}_1(s), \\
\mathcal{T}_2(s, s', i, o) &:\Leftrightarrow \exists i', \exists o', \ \mathcal{T}_1(s, s', i', o') \ \wedge \ i = i' \ \wedge \ o = \begin{cases} 1 & \text{if } o' > 5, \\ 2 & \text{else.} \end{cases}
\end{aligned}
$$

Predicates are defined based on $(\mathcal{I}_1, \mathcal{T}_1)$. Note how variables are handled when subsystemizing; state variables of S_1 are inherited to S_2; placeholders for the input and output of S_1 are prepared locally in the rhs.

We assume that variables are typed as an instance of Ty_C, defined inductively as follows:

$$
\begin{aligned}
Ty_C &::= Ty_N \mid d\,Ty_N \mid (d_1 \times \cdots \times d_m)\,Ty_N \mid Bus \\
Ty_N &::= \texttt{boolean} \mid \texttt{uint}n \mid \texttt{int}n \mid \texttt{double} \mid \texttt{single} \mid \texttt{half}
\end{aligned}
$$

where $d_\square \in \mathbb{N}$, $m \geq 2$, and $n \in \{8, 16, 32, 64\}$. Each term of Ty_C represents scalars, d-ary vectors, (possibly higher-dimension) matrices, and buses. Buses are concatenated values that combine named members of certain types; see Sect. 4.2 for how buses are analyzed. Ty_N consists of Boolean type, unsigned/signed integer types and three types for FP numbers. Basically, Simulink models are statically typed based on their descriptions and dialog settings. For instance, the variables i, o and s of S_1 can be typed as scalar numerical type t, e.g. `uint8` and `double`. Also, they can be typed as dt, where $d \in \mathbb{N}$, by configuring each block for element-wise processing of vector values.

Signals obtained by numerical simulation are formalized by execution paths.

Definition 2. *Given $(\mathcal{I}, \mathcal{T})$, execution paths (or executions) of length k are*

$$s_{-1} \xrightarrow{i_0/o_0} s_0 \xrightarrow{i_1/o_1} s_1 \cdots s_{k-2} \xrightarrow{i_{k-1}/o_{k-1}} s_{k-1},$$

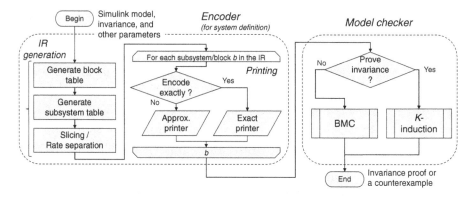

Fig. 2. The process of SMT-based model checking.

where $s_\square \in D(\mathcal{V}_s)$, $i_\square \in D(\mathcal{V}_i)$, $o_\square \in D(\mathcal{V}_o)$, $\mathcal{I}(s_{-1})$, *and* $\mathcal{T}(s_{j-1}, s_j, i_j, o_j)$ *holds for* $j \in [0, k-1]$. Input, output *and* state signals *are the traces* $i_0 \cdots i_{k-1}$, $o_0 \cdots o_{k-1}$, *and* $s_{-1} \cdots s_{k-1}$ *of an execution path.*

The input and output signal values at the initial time are represented by i_0 and o_0. Signals can be depicted as in Fig. 1e.

The formalization in this paper may not be applicable to some discrete-time Simulink models, e.g. signal delays for variable lengths. In addition to the above signal data types, there are types for fixed-point numbers, strings, enumeration values, and user-defined `ValueType` objects. Support for general models and types is a future work.

3   SMT-Based Model Checking

SMT (satisfiability modulo theories) solvers are automated provers for the satisfiability of logic formulas that involve predicates in various theories e.g. integer, real and FP arithmetic. In this paper, we apply a representative implementation $Z3^2$ to the analysis of Simulink models.

We assume an invariance property of a Simulink model and verify that it holds for the model or violated in an execution. Typically, such properties can represent a test objective; a counterexample corresponds to a test case and a valid invariance indicates a dead logic.

Definition 3. *Given a model* $(\mathcal{I}, \mathcal{T})$, *an invariance is described by a formula* $\square\phi$, *where* $\phi \subseteq D(\mathcal{V}_i) \times D(\mathcal{V}_s)$ *is a predicate on the input and state variables. Assume an execution path involving input signal* $i_0 \cdots i_{k-1}$ *and state signals* $s_{-1} \cdots s_{k-1}$. *Then, it is a* counterexample *if* $\neg\phi(i_j, s_{j-1})$ *holds for a* $j \in [0, k-1]$. *Invariance* $\square\phi$ *holds for a model iff there is no counterexample of any length.*

---

² https://github.com/Z3Prover/z3.

For example, control condition of the `Switch` block in S_2 is described by an invariance $\Box(o' > 5)$, where o' represents $\max\{-1, \min\{i, 1\}\} + 0.9s$. S_2 does not satisfy $\Box(o' > 5)$ as shown in Fig. 1e. The objectives in Simulink coverage testing are regarded as invariance properties defined for some block types.[3]

In this paper, we propose a process illustrated in Fig. 2 for checking an invariance $\Box\phi$ of a Simulink model $(\mathcal{I}, \mathcal{T})$. It mainly consists of two parts:

1. Encode a target Simulink model and a property into the input format of SMT solvers (Sect. 4). It generates a definition of the transition system $(\mathcal{I}, \mathcal{T})$ represented by the model. The predicate ϕ is instrumented in the definition. The process consists of generation of intermediate representation (IR) of the model and printing of the IR. The process involves several steps to handle industrial models. Notably, there are a printing step that can generates exact machine representation of numerals (Sect. 4.1), and steps for slicing and separation of different rate portions of a model (Sect. 4.2).
2. Model checking of the invariance $\Box\phi$ (Sect. 5). Verification is basically done by encoding a bounded execution path of the model and by feeding it to an SMT solver. We use two methods: A bounded model checking (BMC) method for falsification and a k-induction method to prove the invariance. We propose an iterative process regarding the parameter k (Algorithm 1) and a strategy to efficiently expand the target subsystem.

The basic techniques employed by the proposed method are known ones; the results of encoding are similar to those obtained by a combination of the CoCoSim [5] and Kind2 [10] tools; BMC and k-induction are basic SMT-based methods. In this work, we extend the techniques; for example, we support the encoding of industrial models and we examine a subsystem-wise model checking for efficiency; see also discussions in Sect. 7.

Subsystem-Wise Model Checking. If a property $\Box\phi$ holds in a subsystem S' of a Simulink model S, then a model checking process that verifies locally for S' will be more efficient than one that verifies for S. Therefore, our subsystem-wise method starts from a local verification and gradually attempts the verification for the parent systems until the invariance is proved. In a subsystem verification, the system description to be analyzed is simplified because the externals of the subsystem are abstracted by the input and output variables.

Suppose ϕ is described with variables in $\mathcal{V}_i' \cup \mathcal{V}_s'$ of a subsystem S'. To verify $\Box\phi$ for a parent system S, we consider the translation $\phi {\uparrow} S$ of the property with variables in $\mathcal{V}_i \cup \mathcal{V}_s$ of S, which is straightforward since $\mathcal{V}_s' \subseteq \mathcal{V}_s$ and the model S should describe a relation in $D(\mathcal{V}_i) \times D(\mathcal{V}_s) \times D(\mathcal{V}_i')$ (note that $\phi \subseteq D(\mathcal{V}_i') \times D(\mathcal{V}_s')$). For instance, a predicate $\phi \Leftrightarrow i < 1$ describing a condition of the `Saturate` block of S_1 is translated as $\phi {\uparrow} S_2 \Leftrightarrow i' < 1$ where i' belongs to $\mathcal{V}_i$ of S_2. There is the following relationship between the two:

---

[3] https://www.mathworks.com/help/slcoverage/ug/model-objects-that-receive-coverage.html.

```
1   ;; Variable representing the current step.
2   (declare-const curr_step Int)
3   ;; Whether to verify the induction step.
4   (declare-const flag_kind Bool)
5
6   ;; Specification of subsystem S1.
7   (define-fun init1 ((s@0 Real)) Bool (= s@0 0))
8   (define-fun trans1
9     ((c Int) (s@0 Real) (s@1 Real) (i Real) (o Real)) Bool
10    (let ((lv (saturate 1 (- 1) i)))
11      (and (= o (+ lv (* 0.9 s@0))) (= s@1 o)) ))
12
13  ;; Specification of the parent system S2.
14  (define-fun init2 ((s@0 Real)) Bool (init1 s@0))
15  (define-fun trans2
16    ((c Int) (s@0 Real) (s@1 Real) (i Real) (o Int)) Bool
17    (exists ((i_ Real) (o_ Real))
18      (and (trans1 c s@0 s@1 i_ o_) (= i_ i) (= o (ite (> o_ 5) 1 2))
19
20        ;; Objective instrumentation.
21        (=> (= c curr_step) (not (> o_ 5)))
22        ;; Assumption for the induction step.
23        (=> flag_kind (=> (< c curr_step) (> o_ 5))) )))
24
25  ;; Encoding of the execution path.
26  (declare-const s@i Real) (assert (init2 s@i))
27
28  (declare-const s@0 Real) (declare-const i@0 Real)
29  (declare-const o@0 Int) (assert (trans2 0 s@i s@0 i@0 o@0))
30
31  (declare-const s@1 Real) (declare-const i@1 Real)
32  (declare-const o@1 Int) (assert (trans2 1 s@0 s@1 i@1 o@1))
33
34  ;; Check the reachability at step 1.
35  (check-sat-assuming (and (= curr_step 1) (not flag_kind)))
```

Fig. 3. Simulink models S_1 and S_2 encoded in SMT-LIB.

Proposition 1. *If $\Box\phi$ holds for S', $\Box(\phi \uparrow S)$ holds for S.*

Proof. The contraposition obviously holds because a counterexample of $\Box\phi$ can be extracted from that of $\Box(\phi \uparrow S)$.

4   SMT-LIB Encoding of Simulink Models

SMT-LIB [2] is an input format for SMT solvers, which has a LISP-like prefix grammar. Here, we describe the encoding method with an example. Figure 3 lists an encoded SMT-LIB description of the model S_2 (and S_1 as a subsystem). At **Lines 6–11**, predicates $\mathcal{I}_1$ and $\mathcal{T}_1$ of S_1 are defined as Bool-valued functions init1 and trans1. **Lines 13–18** define $(\mathcal{I}_2, \mathcal{T}_2)$ in the same way. The encoding process is either *approximate* or *exact* (Sect. 4.1); the example is an approximate encoding. Assuming that variables s, s', i and o of S_1 are typed as FP numbers, they are encoded with variables s@0, s@1, i and o of sort Real, which represents mathematical rational numbers. In the same way, variable o of S_2 is sorted as unbounded integers. **Lines 20–23** instrument the invariance $\square(\text{o\_} > 5)$. Two global variables curr_step and flag_kind and the argument c of transition predicates are introduced for the verification (Sect. 5). **Lines 25–32** describe a length-2 execution path where values at each step are parameterized by fresh variables. The predicate init2 is asserted for the initial step -1 and trans2 is asserted for the later steps. State variables are shared between two steps. Finally, at **Line 35**, command (check-sat-assuming c) will invoke a solving process; it will assume the argument constraint c temporarily. With setting a step number to curr_step and disabling flag_kind, the violation of the invariance at step 1, i.e. reachability to the state such that $\neg(\text{o\_} > 5)$, should be checked. This example will result in unsat; unrolling the execution path up to step 6 will result in sat.

4.1   Exact Encoding of Machine-Representable Numbers

For reliable analysis, we propose to encode FP numbers and integers using the vocabulary provided by the SMT-LIB theories FloatingPoint and BitVector. This encoding method exactly describes rounded values, overflow cases, etc. Solving exact formulas tends to be expensive; thus, we use this method along with the approximate method. FloatingPoint provides the sorts (e.g. Float64 for double-precision FP numbers), arithmetic operators (e.g. fp.add for addition), and utility functions (e.g. (_ fp.to_sbv n) that converts an FP number to a signed bit vectors of length n). For machine integers, we prepare necessary vocabularies based on BitVector as in [1]; we use the sort (_ BitVec n) to represent n-bit integers and define the functions for arithmetic operations, e.g. int64.add (they are defined in the beginning of the encoder outputs).

For example, the first equation in Line 11 of Fig. 3 is encoded as:

```
(= o (fp.add RNE lv (fp.mul RNE (fp #b0 #b01111111110
  #b1100110011001100110011001100110011001100110011001101 ) s@0 )))
```

Variables o, lv and s@0 are of sort Float64. RNE represents a rounding mode.

4.2   Encoding of Complex Simulink Models

This section describes techniques for more complex models.

A subsystem $(\mathcal{I}, \mathcal{T})$ can be executed conditionally by adding an activation port, e.g. EnablePort in Fig. 1c. When deactivated, the subsystem outputs the initial value or the previous value. We encode such subsystems by introducing wrappers for $\mathcal{I}$ and $\mathcal{T}$. For example, $\mathcal{T}$ of the subsystem One in Fig. 1c is encoded into the following wrapper predicate:

```
(define-fun trans ( (ien Bool) (so@0
  (ite ien
    ;; Activate the body transition predicate.
    (and (trans_body o) (= so@1 o) )
    ;; Else, output the prev value and keep the state unchanged.
    (and (= o so@0) (= so@1 so@0)) ))
```

It assumes that the body content (to output constant 1) `trans_body` is pre-defined. Output variable o of sort t is inherited from `trans_body`. Variables `ien`, `so@0` and `so@1` are introduced to represent a signal input to the `EnablePort` and state variables to keep track of a previous output value when deactivated. $\mathcal{I}$ is also wrapped and the initial output value is configured.

Activation using `TriggerPort` is encoded with a wrapper and a behavioral description of the trigger signal such as `Rising` (we pre-define pattern functions as in [24]). We also use wrapper predicates to encode multi-rate models (e.g. S_3 in Fig. 1c). For a subsystem configured to be executed with a slower rate, we encode with a wrapper equipped with a local counter variable, which computes the activation period and activates the body predicate accordingly. Multiple rates may be present in a subsystem; in such a case, we run a preprocess to divide the subsystem into separate *dummy* subsystems for each rate (Sect. 4.3).

Encoding of vector signals is simply done by preparing scalar variables for each element of vector values. For bus signals, we utilize their schema externally specified by a *bus object data type*.[4] Based on the specification, we introduce an SMT-LIB sort that represents bus signal values. For the model S_4 in Fig. 1d, the sort and accessors for the elements are declared as follows:

```
(declare-sort BO 0)
(declare-fun BO_e1 (BO) Int) ;; Accessor for member e1.
(declare-fun BO_e2_1_1 (BO) Real) ;;Accessor for member e2.
;; BO_e2_1_2, BO_e2_2_1, and BO_e2_2_2 are also declared.
```

Given a value bo of sort BO, `(BO_e2_1_1 bo)` represents the element at $(1,1)$ of the matrix-typed member e2. Using the sort BO, $\mathcal{T}_4$ is defined as follows:

```
(define-fun trans ((c Int) (i Int) (o BO)) Bool
  (and (= (BO_e1 o) i) (= (BO_e2_1_1 o) 1) (= (BO_e2_1_2 o) 2)
                       (= (BO_e2_2_1 o) 3) (= (BO_e2_2_2 o) 4) ))
```

4.3   Implementation of the Encoder

We have implemented the encoder as a MATLAB script (about 9000 LOCs). The script implements the IR generation process and printers as shown in Fig. 2.

In IR generation, we first prepare a *block table* (BT), an array of `struct` (record) data where each element represents a block (or a subsystem). Most content of a Simulink model can be accessed via command `get` (or `get_param`) in a script. So, BT collects necessary information, e.g. block-line graph structure and type signature of each inport/outport. Second, we generate another `struct`

---

[4] We consider only *nonvirtual* buses.

array, *subsystem table* (ST), that represents the tree structure of subsystems. Each element corresponds to a transition system and contains lists of variables and a list of child subsystems. Third, we modify BT and ST to support multi-rate models and to slice the target portion of the content. Slicing is done by a backward reachability analysis on BT, starting from the objective block of the invariance property. For each multi-rate ST element, we classify the blocks rate-wise, and then introduce dummy subsystems with dummy inports and outports.

Approximate and exact printers basically translate the content of a ST into an SMT-LIB description. Each ST element is printed as definitions of corresponding $\mathcal{I}$ and $\mathcal{T}$. The body of each definition mainly contains assignments to the variables and their rhs are printed by traversing BT.

Our implementation supports encoding of 37 block types (but not all parameter settings). Unsupported block instances are stubbed with local unconstrained variables in a predicate definition. These local variables do not affect the soundness of the invariance proof, but undermine the soundness of the falsification (may lead to false counterexamples).

5   Model Checking Methods

As described in Sect. 3, we consider two methods for verifying an invariance $\Box\phi$ of a Simulink model $(\mathcal{I}, \mathcal{T})$, i.e. BMC and k-induction. In the following, we abbreviate $\langle$check-sat-assuming $c\rangle$ to CSA(c), curr_step in Fig. 3 to c and flag_kind to f, respectively.

Given $k \geq 1$, the BMC method searches for a counterexample of length-k or less. It performs the following steps for each $j \in [0, k-1]$. (0) Assume that $(\mathcal{I}, \mathcal{T})$ instrumented with ϕ has been encoded. (1) Encode the length-$(j+1)$ execution paths. (2) Feed the encoded result to an SMT solver and then solve the command CSA($c = j \wedge f = \bot$). The process is done efficiently by incrementing from $j = 1$, encoding only $\mathcal{T}$ for the j-th step in (1).

The k-induction method [23] consists of the proofs of the following facts:

- *Base case*: "ϕ is invariant for execution paths of length $k-1$ or less."
- *Induction step*: "Assume execution paths of length k that are not initialized. Let $j \in [0, k-2]$, and if ϕ holds for every j-th step of a path, then ϕ holds at the last $(k-1)$-th step of the path."

Algorithm 1 is an incremental procedure for proving the two facts. We assume an SMT solver process running in the background. The algorithm generates SMT-LIB expressions in several stages and feeds them to the solver at each stage. The definition of the model is generated at **Line 1** and predicate $\mathcal{T}$ reaching step j is generated at **Line 3**. Then, it verifies the base case (**Line 5**) and induction step (**Line 4**; checked one iteration after). Based on the locality (Proposition 1), $(\mathcal{I}, \mathcal{T})$ can be a subsystem, but it is needed to be the top-level system to falsify the invariance (**Line 6**).

Algorithm 1: A k-induction procedure.

Input   : Simulink model $(\mathcal{I}, \mathcal{T})$, Invariance $\Box\phi$, $k \in \mathbb{N}_{\geq 2}$, Encode exactly? b
Output: true, false or maybe

1 EncodeSystemAndAssert$_b(\mathcal{I}, \mathcal{T}, \phi)$;
2 **for** $j \in [0, k-1]$ **do**
3 | EncodeTransAndAssert$_b(\mathcal{T}, j)$;
4 | **if** $j > 0 \wedge \mathsf{CSA}(\mathsf{c}{=}j \wedge \mathsf{f}{=}\top) =$ unsat **then return** true; **end**
5 | **if** $\mathsf{CSA}(\mathsf{EncodeInit}_b(\mathcal{I}) \wedge \mathsf{c}{=}j \wedge \mathsf{f}{=}\bot) =$ sat **then**
6 | | **If** $(\mathcal{I}, \mathcal{T})$ is top-level **then return** false; **else return** maybe; **end**
7 | **end**
8 **end**
9 **return** maybe;

Implementation. BMC and k-induction methods have been implemented as MATLAB scripts (about 2500 LOCs). In addition to the encoding process, they generate SMT-LIB expressions for execution paths during a verification process. For SMT solving, they communicate with an external server that wraps Z3 via a TCP socket.

The k-induction script conducts verification subsystem-wise, starting from the objective subsystem of the invariance property. The script repeatedly invoke Algorithm 1, controlling the following two factors (initially $d := 1$ and $k := 1$):

1. *Number d of subsystem hierarchies.* We start applying Algorithm 1 on the subsystem ($d = 1$) that is targeted by the property. When the result is inconclusive, we increase the value of d, i.e. to invoke Algorithm 1 in the upper hierarchy.
2. *Bound k on the path lengths.* Once the whole hierarchy has been analyzed, we increase the value k exponentially (and repeat for each subsystem again). Algorithm 1 is modified to skip the verification for an initial range of $[1, k-1]$ that has been processed in the previous round.

6   Experimental Evaluation

This section describes an empirical evaluation of the proposed method (abbreviated as "PM" in the following). We have verified artificial and industrial Simulink models using our implementation and exiting tools (SLDV and CoCoSim). Here, the purpose was to answer: **RQ1**: Does PM correctly handle the collected Simulink models? **RQ2**: How is the scalability of PM? **RQ3**: Is the performance of PM better than other tools?

Experiments were conducted on 64-bit Ubuntu 20.04 virtual machines (with 4 cores and 8 GB RAM), running on a 2.2 GHz Intel Xeon E5-2650v4 processor (12 cores) with 128 GB RAM. We used MATLAB R2022a. Execution time was limited to 1 h.

Evaluated Tools. We used the following three tools.

(i) *PM* implemented (cf. Sect. 4.3 and 5) as an add-on to a proprietary tool PROMPT.[5] In the experiment, we applied the BMC method to obtain counterexamples of false properties, and the k-induction method to prove true properties. BMC was performed against the entire system, while k-induction (Algorithm 1) was performed subsystem-wise. Each verification was performed in two ways using either approximate or exact encoder; we respectively refer to them by "PM/A" and "PM/E."

(ii) *SLDV*,[6] a tool for analyzing Simulink models based on formal methods. Also, it seems to apply approximations in the analysis. Among various functions of SLDV, we used the *"property proving (PP)"* function in this experiment. If a `Proof Objective` block representing an invariance property is added to a Simulink model, it performs verification of whether it holds or be falsified by a counterexample. We enabled the option "FindViolation" for false properties and "Prove" for true properties.

(iii) *CoCoSim* (version 1.2), a front-end tool for applying formal tools to Simulink. Its "prove properties" function allows invariance verification using Kind2 (version 1.2), a model checker for Lustre programs. Process of the function consists of translation from Simulink to Lustre and invocation of Kind2.

Target Simulink Models. We have prepared 5 artificial and 4 industrial examples to ensure that the different types of models could be handled correctly and effectively. We refer to the models as **(1)**–**(9)**; also, we refer to a model with a parameter p as $(i)_p$. Model $(1)_{th}$ represents S_2 in Sect. 2 with switching threshold th. Models $(2)_{th}$ and $(3)_{th}$ describe second and fourth-order digital filters with threshold th on the output signals. Model $(4)_{th}$ describes 32 nested counters that are reset at threshold th.[7] Model **(5)** is the multi-rate model S_3 with additional logic blocks. Models **(6)**–**(8)** are taken from the Lockheed Martin challenge [11,19]. We used the first, fourth and sixth problems. Model **(9)** describes a realistic controller using various types of blocks and externally-controlled subsystems. The size of each model is shown in Table 1.

6.1   Results

For each model, we considered 2 or 4 invariance properties such that half of them are false and the rest are true; false and true instances are denoted by $(i)_{Pj}$ and $(i)_{Qj}$, respectively ($j \in \{1, 2\}$). The properties prepared can be regarded as test objectives for a block or subsystem, such as conditions on input/output signals and activation conditions. We verified them using the tools. The execution time

---

[5] https://www.en.gaio.co.jp/products/prompt-2/.

[6] https://www.mathworks.com/products/simulink-design-verifier.html.

[7] https://github.com/dsksh/sl-examples.

of PM and SLDV is shown in Fig. 4. The right side of Table 1 shows the parameters of PM used for each property; the number of sliced blocks that belong to the analyzed subsystems, the maximum bound k used in the model checking, and the number d of analyzed subsystem hierarchies (cf. Sect. 5 "Implementation"). Results of the SMT-LIB encoding of the models (other than **(9)**) are available at https://doi.org/10.5281/zenodo.6781295.

Table 1. Statistics on the models and the solving process. The abbreviations "s's" and "b's" represent "subsystems" and "sliced blocks," respectively. Parameters k and d of the model checker are also shown. Third to sixth sections correspond to false and true properties.

Model	# blocks	# s's	P1 # b's	k	P2 # b's	k	Q1 # b's	k	d	Q2 # b's	k	d
(1)$_{th}$	12	1	11	7	—		11	1	1	—		
(2)$_{th}$	16	1	14	2	14	7	14	10	2	14	29	2
(3)$_{th}$	24	1	22	15	—		22	≥ 34	2	—		
(4)$_{th}$	290	32	289	12	—		289	1	1	—		
(5)	33	8	26	21	—		25	1	1	—		
(6)	479	39	321	2	327	1	259	1	1	321	1	2
(7)	291	18	116	1	103	1	58	1	2	9	1	3
(8)	712	188	27	1	327	1	27	1	3	327	1	3
(9)	574	30	19	1	407	≥ 1	12	1	1	407	1	3

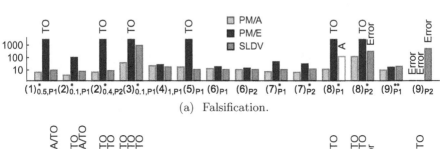

(a) Falsification.

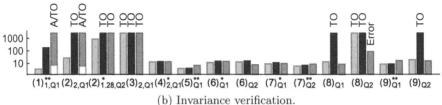

(b) Invariance verification.

Fig. 4. Execution time in seconds. Results marked with "TO" are timeouts. "A" means "solved under approximation (white portion shows time required)." Superscript * (resp. **) indicates that PM/A (resp. PM/A and PM/E) outperforms SLDV.

6.2 Discussions

RQ1 (correctness). All the conclusive results of PM were confirmed correct. For false properties, we manually simulated the obtained counterexamples using Simulink and confirmed that they were indeed so. For true properties, we confirmed that the results of PM were the same as SLDV. Errors on $(9)_{P2}$ occurred due to unsupported blocks by the encoder. Some block types, e.g. lookup tables and nonlinear arithmetic functions, are difficult to encode and/or to analyze. Our tool either causes an error when falsifying, or abstract them with stub variables in the encoding for an invariance proof.

RQ2 (scalability). Using a parameterized model, we can observe the nearly exponential growth of execution time. Right figure shows the time needed to falsify the instances $(1)_{th,P1}$ with several th's. The scalability of PM/A was better than SLDV on more than half of the instances and thus we believe it is enough to handle most of the prepared models. PM/E scaled orders of magnitude worse, limiting the number of instances it could handle. As shown in Table 1 and Fig. 4, for

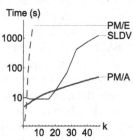

the same model, the execution time increases basically with the number of analyzed blocks, "#b's" $\times\ k$.[8] For example, this is the case for (2), $(7)_{Qj}$, (8) and $(9)_{Qj}$. To improve the applicability, slicing and subsystem-wise process of PM is significant. Table 1 shows that the numbers of encoded blocks were reduced from those contained in the models, contributing to the number of instances verified in time.

RQ3 (tool comparison). PM/A outperformed the other tools for 17 out of 28 instances. PM/E was able to handle 15 instances including industrial ones, although its performance was worse than PM/A (it ran out of time for the others). Notably, we verified 3 instances that could not be handled by other tools ($(8)_{P2}$, exact verification of $(1)_{1,Q1}$ and approximate verification of $(2)_{1.28,Q2}$). Regarding the encoding method, PM/E should be used to prove a property reliably. When falsifying properties, counterexamples obtained by PM/A can be certified by a simulation using Simulink.

SLDV resulted in timeouts for 4 true instances. On $(1)_{1,Q1}$ and $(2)_{2,Q1}$, it first indicated "valid under approximation" and then ran out of time to prove the validity accurately. It is not clear whether the "approximation" method is similar to PM. Errors on $(8)_{P2/Q2}$ and $(9)_{P2}$ were "due to nonlinearities."

CoCoSim handled only model $(1)_{th}$. 5 models were resulted in errors during conversion to Lustre (due to unsupported blocks). Verification of 3 models failed in the model checking process of Kind2.

---

[8] It is likely to depend on other factors, e.g. the form of encoded formulas and the number of solutions; a detailed analysis is omitted from this paper.

7   Related Work

Model checking techniques using SAT/SMT solvers have been applied to various domains [3]. Bourbouh et al. [5] have developed the CoCoSim tool for Simulink models using an SMT-based model checker, Kind2 [10]. The basic process in this paper is similar but we provide an exact encoding method and more support for industrial models. Filipovikj et al. [12] have proposed a bounded model checking method for Simulink models, although the target is a subset. A related technology is model checking for the synchronous language Lustre [8,14]. Versions of the Kind tool [10,13,16] and Zustre [15] have been developed. They have implemented techniques such as IC3 [6], parallel solving, and Horn clause encoding; they can be implemented in our method in the future. Kind2 supports accurate encoding with machine integers; our method handles FP numbers in addition.

SMT-based methods require formalization of the target Simulink models. Some of the existing work has formalized via translation to Lustre [5,8,24]. The basic concepts of Simulink are naturally mapped to the Lustre counterparts. A node definition describes the relation between input and output values of a Simulink subsystem at each step, and the method in this paper encodes in basically the same way. Additionally, translation methods for multi-rate (or multi-periodic) models and conditionally executed subsystems have examined [5,24]. Our method handles multi-rates in the same way but differs in that we directly encode to SMT-LIB descriptions, whereas the above methods use the when construct of Lustre. Zhou et al. [25] have proposed a translation method into input-output finite automata. They also formalized conditioning on subsystems and multi-rate models. The result of the transformation is a flat automaton with no subsystem structure. Bouissou et al. [4] have formalized the simulator for continuous-time models implemented in Simulink, which involves numerical integration and zero crossing detection.

There are SMT-based test generation methods that translate Simulink models to constraints and perform a symbolic analysis [9,22], which is performed to obtain a test case as a solution that satisfies constraints. They do not consider to verify invariance properties explicitly. The SmartTestGen tool [20,21] combines four approaches of test generation; one of them considers invariance checking to guide the coverage strategy. From their evaluation, the effectiveness of the tool for our example models is not clear.

8   Conclusions

We have presented an SMT-based model checking method for the invariance verification of Simulink models. Experimental result shows that it is useful in industrial setting; we had compared the results with the state-of-the-art tool, SLDV; our tool handled models that could not be properly analyzed by other tools. The verification process is comprehensible by the intermediate encoded representation and the parameters such as k and d. The resulting invariance proofs are reliable based on exact encoding with bit vectors.

There are several future issues such as improvement of the model checking algorithm and the SMT-LIB encoding method for faster verification, and experiments on the analysis of larger and more complex models.

References

1. Baranowski, M., He, S., Lechner, M., Nguyen, T.S., Rakamarić, Z.: An SMT theory of fixed-point arithmetic. In: Peltier, N., Sofronie-Stokkermans, V. (eds.) IJCAR 2020. LNCS (LNAI), vol. 12166, pp. 13–31. Springer, Cham (2020). https://doi.org/10.1007/978-3-030-51074-9_2

2. Barrett, C., Fontaine, P., Tinelli, C.: The SMT-LIB Standard (Version 2.6) (2021). https://smtlib.cs.uiowa.edu/

3. Biere, A., Kröning, D.: SAT-based model checking. In: Clarke, E., Henzinger, T., Veith, H., Bloem, R. (eds.) Handbook of Model Checking, pp. 277–303. Springer, Cham (2018). https://doi.org/10.1007/978-3-319-10575-8_10

4. Bouissou, O., Chapoutot, A.: An operational semantics for Simulink's simulation engine. ACM SIGPLAN Notices **47**(5), 129–138 (2012). https://doi.org/10.1145/2345141.2248437

5. Bourbouh, H., Garoche, P.l., Loquen, T., Noulard, E., Pagetti, C.: CoCoSim, a code generation framework for control/command applications. In: ERTS, pp. 1–11 (2020)

6. Bradley, A.R.: SAT-based model checking without unrolling. In: Jhala, R., Schmidt, D. (eds.) VMCAI 2011. LNCS, vol. 6538, pp. 70–87. Springer, Heidelberg (2011). https://doi.org/10.1007/978-3-642-18275-4_7

7. Brain, M., Schanda, F., Sun, Y.: Building better bit-blasting for floating-point problems. In: Vojnar, T., Zhang, L. (eds.) TACAS 2019. LNCS, vol. 11427, pp. 79–98. Springer, Cham (2019). https://doi.org/10.1007/978-3-030-17462-0_5

8. Caspi, P., Curic, A., Maignan, A., Sofronis, C., Tripakis, S., Niebert, P.: From simulink to SCADE/Lustre to TTA: a layered approach for distributed embedded applications. ACM SIGPLAN Notices **38**(7), 153–162 (2003). https://doi.org/10.1145/780731.780754

9. Chakrabarti, S., Ramesh, S.: SymTest: a framework for symbolic testing of embedded software. In: ISEC, pp. 48–58 (2016). https://doi.org/10.1145/2856636.2856642

10. Champion, A., Mebsout, A., Sticksel, C., Tinelli, C.: The KIND 2 model checker. In: Chaudhuri, S., Farzan, A. (eds.) CAV 2016. LNCS, vol. 9780, pp. 510–517. Springer, Cham (2016). https://doi.org/10.1007/978-3-319-41540-6_29

11. Elliott, C.: Cyber-physical V&V challenges for the evaluation of state of the art model checkers. In: Safe and Secure Systems and Software Symposium (S5) (2016)

12. Filipovikj, P., Rodriguez-Navas, G., Seceleanu, C.: Bounded invariance checking of simulink models. In: SAC, pp. 2168–2177 (2019). https://doi.org/10.1145/3297280.3297493

13. Hagen, G., Tinelli, C.: Scaling up the formal verification of Lustre programs with SMT-based techniques. In: FMCAD, pp. 1–9. IEEE (2008). https://doi.org/10.1109/FMCAD.2008.ECP.19

14. Halbwachs, N., Lagnier, F., Raymond, P.: Synchronous observers and the verification of reactive systems. In: Algebraic Methodology and Software Technology (AMAST), pp. 83–96 (1993)

15. Kahsai, T., Gurfinkel, A.: Zustre (2018). https://github.com/coco-team/zustre

16. Kahsai, T., Tinelli, C.: PKind: a parallel k-induction based model checker. In: International Workshop on Parallel and Distributed Methods in verification (PDMC), vol. 72, pp. 55–62 (2011). https://doi.org/10.4204/eptcs.72.6

17. Kroening, D., Strichman, O.: Decision Procedures, 2nd edn. Springer, Heidelberg (2016). https://doi.org/10.1007/978-3-662-50497-0

18. Lee, E.A., Seshia, S.A.: Introduction to Embedded Systems. A Cyber-Physical Systems Approach, 2nd edn. MIT Press, Cambridge (2017). http://leeseshia.org

19. Mavridou, A., et al.: The ten lockheed martin cyber-physical challenges: formalized, analyzed, and explained. In: IEEE International Conference on Requirements Engineering, pp. 300–310 (2020). https://doi.org/10.1109/RE48521.2020.00040

20. Peranandam, P., Raviram, S., Satpathy, M., Yeolekar, A., Gadkari, A., Ramesh, S.: An integrated test generation tool for enhanced coverage of Simulink/Stateflow models. In: DATE, pp. 308–311. IEEE (2012). https://doi.org/10.1109/date.2012.6176485

21. Raviram, S., Peranandam, P., Satpathy, M., Ramesh, S.: A test suite booster for enhanced structural coverage. In: Roychoudhury, A., D'Souza, M. (eds.) ICTAC 2012. LNCS, vol. 7521, pp. 164–167. Springer, Heidelberg (2012). https://doi.org/10.1007/978-3-642-32943-2_13

22. Ren, H., Bhatt, D., Hvozdovic, J.: Improving an industrial test generation tool using SMT solver. In: Rayadurgam, S., Tkachuk, O. (eds.) NFM 2016. LNCS, vol. 9690, pp. 100–106. Springer, Cham (2016). https://doi.org/10.1007/978-3-319-40648-0_8

23. Sheeran, M., Singh, S., Stålmarck, G.: Checking safety properties using induction and a SAT-solver. In: Hunt, W.A., Johnson, S.D. (eds.) FMCAD 2000. LNCS, vol. 1954, pp. 127–144. Springer, Heidelberg (2000). https://doi.org/10.1007/3-540-40922-X_8

24. Tripakis, S., Sofronis, C., Caspi, P., Curic, A.: Translating discrete-time simulink to Lustre. ACM Trans. Embed. Comput. Syst. 4(4), 779–818 (2005). https://doi.org/10.1145/1113830.1113834

25. Zhou, C., Kumar, R.: Semantic translation of simulink diagrams to input/output extended finite automata. Discrete Event Dyn. Syst. Theory Appl. 22(2), 223–247 (2012). https://doi.org/10.1007/s10626-010-0096-1

PFMC: A Parallel Symbolic Model Checker for Security Protocol Verification

Alex James, Alwen Tiu$^{(\boxtimes)}$, and Nisansala Yatapanage

School of Computing, The Australian National University, Canberra, Australia
alwen.tiu@anu.edu.au, yatapanage@acm.org

Abstract. We present an investigation into the design and implementation of a parallel model checker for security protocol verification that is based on a symbolic model of the adversary, where instantiations of concrete terms and messages are avoided until needed to resolve a particular assertion. We propose to build on this naturally lazy approach to parallelise this symbolic state exploration and evaluation. We utilise the concept of *strategies* in Haskell, which abstracts away from the low-level details of thread management and modularly adds parallel evaluation strategies (encapsulated as a monad in Haskell). We build on an existing symbolic model checker, OFMC, which is already implemented in Haskell. We show that there is a very significant speed up of around 3–5 times improvement when moving from the original single-threaded implementation of OFMC to our multi-threaded version, for both the Dolev-Yao attacker model and more general algebraic attacker models. We identify several issues in parallelising the model checker: among others, controlling growth of memory consumption, balancing lazy vs strict evaluation, and achieving an optimal granularity of parallelism.

1 Introduction

A security protocol describes a sequence of actions and message exchanges between communicating partners in a networked system, in order to achieve certain security goals, such as authentication and secrecy. The analysis of security protocols against a stated security property is a challenging problem, not just from a computational complexity perspective (e.g., the problem of establishing the secrecy property of a protocol is undecidable in general [13]), but also from a protocol designer perspective, since proofs of security properties are dependent on the adversary model, which can be challenging to precisely formalise.

A commonly used adversary model is the Dolev-Yao model [12]. The Dolev-Yao model assumes that the attacker controls the network, and hence will be able to intercept, modify and remove messages. However, the attacker is also assumed to be unable to break the basic cryptographic primitives used in the protocol. For example, an encrypted message can only be decrypted by the attacker if and only if the attacker possesses the decryption key. The Dolev-Yao model may be further extended by adding various abstract algebraic properties (e.g.,

© Springer Nature Switzerland AG 2022
A. Riesco and M. Zhang (Eds.): ICFEM 2022, LNCS 13478, pp. 173–189, 2022.
https://doi.org/10.1007/978-3-031-17244-1_11

theories for modelling exclusive-or, or Abelian groups in general). In the context of protocol analysis, the Dolev-Yao model and/or its algebraic extensions are sometimes referred to as the symbolic model.

In this paper, we are concerned with verifying protocols with a bounded number of sessions in the symbolic model, and we restrict to only proving reachability properties, i.e., those properties that can be expressed as a predicate on a single trace of a protocol run, such as secrecy and authentication. Bounded verification aims primarily at finding attacks, but even for a small number of sessions, the complexity of finding attacks is still very high, e.g., NP-complete for the standard Dolev-Yao model [20]. Another interesting use of bounded verification is to lift the result of such verification to the unbounded case, for a certain class of protocols [3]. A related work by Kanovich et al. [15] on a bounded-memory adversary (which implies bounded number of sessions) also points to the fact that many attacks on existing protocols can be explained under a bounded-memory adversary. These suggest that improving the performance of bounded protocol verifiers may be a worthwhile research direction despite the prevalence of protocol verifiers for unbounded sessions such as Proverif [7] and Tamarin [18].

A bounded-session protocol verifier works by state exploration (search), so naturally we would seek to improve its performance by parallelising the search. Given the ubiquity of multicore architecture in modern computing, it is quite surprising that very few protocol verifiers have attempted to benefit from the increase in computing cores to speed up their verification efforts. An important consideration in our attempt is avoiding excessive modification of the (implementation of) decision procedures underlying these verifiers, as they are typically complex and have been carefully designed and optimised. This motivates us to consider a language where parallelisation (of a deterministic algorithm) can be added as an effect – Haskell parallelisation monads (e.g., [17]) fit this requirement very well. In this work, we use OFMC, which is implemented in Haskell, as the basis of our study, looking at ways to introduce parallelisation without changing the underlying implementation of its decision procedures. This will hopefully provide us with a recipe for applying similar parallelisation techniques to other protocol verifiers written in Haskell, notably Tamarin.

We have implemented a parallel version of OFMC [19], which we call PFMC, in Haskell. We show that PFMC significantly improves the performance of OFMC, with a speed-up of around 3–5 times faster than OFMC, when run on 4–16 cores. This promising result allows us to push the boundary of bounded protocol verification. As part of the implementation of PFMC, we have designed what we believe are several novel parallel evaluation strategies for buffered (search) trees in the context of symbolic model checking for protocol verification, which allows us to achieve parallelism with a generally constant memory residency.

Related Work. Currently, there are not many major protocol verifiers that explicitly support parallelisation. The only ones that we are aware of are the DEEPSEC prover [10] and the Tamarin prover [18]. DEEPSEC uses a process-level parallelisation, i.e., each subtask in the search procedure is delegated to a child process and there is no support for a more fine-grained thread-level parallelisation. Tamarin is implemented in Haskell, which has a high-level modular way of turning a deterministic program into one which can be run in parallel, sometimes called semi-explicit parallelisation. This is the method that we will adopt, as it seems like the most straightforward way to gain performance with minimal effort. As far as we know, there has been no published work on systematically evaluating the performance of Tamarin parallelisation; see [14] for a preliminary investigation into its parallelisation performance. Some of the established protocol verifiers such as Proverif [7], DEEPSEC [10], SATEQUIV [11], SPEC [22] or APTE [9] are implemented in OCaml, and the support for multicore is not as mature as other languages. For an overview of protocol verification tools, see a recent survey article by Barbosa et al. [5].

Outline. The rest of the paper is organised as follows. Section 2 provides an overview of the state transition system arising from symbolic protocol analysis. Section 3 gives a brief overview of Haskell parallelisation features. Section 4 presents the parallelisation strategies implemented in PFMC and the evaluation of their performance on selected protocol verification problems. Section 5 concludes and discusses future directions. The full source code of PFMC is online.[1]

2   Protocol Specifications and Transition Systems

There are a variety of approaches for modelling protocols and their transition systems, such as using multiset rewriting [8], process calculus [1], strand spaces [21] or first-order Horn clauses [6]. OFMC supports the modelling language IF (Intermediate Format), but it also supports a more user-friendly format known as AnB (for *Alice and Bob*). The AnB syntax can be translated to the IF format, for which a formal semantics is given in [2]; we refer the interested reader to that paper for details.

The operational semantics of OFMC is defined in terms of strand spaces. One can think of a strand as a sequence of steps that an agent takes. The steps could be a sending action, a receiving action, checking for equality between messages and special events (that may be used to prove certain attack predicates). We use the notation $A_1 \| \ldots \| A_n$ to denote n parallel strands, $A_1, \ldots, A_n$, that may be associated with some agents. A *state* is a triple consisting of a set of strands of honest agents, a strand for the attacker, and a set of events which have occurred. The attacker strand consists of the messages the attacker receives by intercepting communication between honest agents, and the messages the attacker synthesises and sends to honest agents. OFMC represents these strands symbolically. For example, the messages the attacker synthesises are initially represented as variables and *concretised* as needed when agents check for equality between messages. The attacker strand is represented as a set of deducibility constraints, and the transition relation must preserve satisfiability of these constraints.

In OFMC, the state transition relation is defined from an adversary-centric view. This means in particular that what matters in the transition is the update to the attacker's knowledge, and the only way to update the attacker's knowledge

---

[1] https://gitlab.anu.edu.au/U4301469/pfmc-prover.

is through the output actions of the honest agents. Therefore, it makes sense to define a state transition as a combination of input action(s) that trigger an output action from an honest agent, rather than using each individual action to drive the state transition. Due to the presence of parallel composition protocol specifications, the (symbolic) state transitions can generate a large number of possible traces, due to the interleaving of parallel strands. The search procedure for OFMC is essentially an exploration of the search tree induced by this symbolic transition system.

3   Haskell Parallelisation Strategies

This section provides a very brief overview of Haskell parallelisation features and discusses some initial unsuccessful attempts (in the sense that we did not achieve meaningful improvements) to parallelise OFMC, to motivate our designs in Sect. 4. We use the semi-explicit parallelisation supported by Haskell. We assume the reader is familiar with the basics of Haskell programming, and will only briefly explain the parallelisation approach we use here.

In the semi-explicit parallelism approach in Haskell, the programmer specifies which parts of the code should be paralellised, using primitives such as `par`. The statement `x par y` is semantically identically to `y`. However, the former tells the Haskell runtime system (RTS) to create a worker to evaluate `x` and assigns it to an available thread to execute. In Haskell terminology, such a unit of work is called a *spark*. The programmer does not need to explicitly create and destroy threads, or schedule the sparks for execution. The RTS uses a *work-stealing* scheduling to execute sparks opportunistically. That is, each available core keeps a queue of sparks to execute and if its queue is empty, it looks for sparks in other cores' queues and 'steals' their sparks to execute. This should ensure all available cores are used during runtime. An appealing feature of this approach is that one does not need to be concerned with low-level details of thread management and scheduling, as they are all handled automatically by the Haskell runtime system.

Determining the Granularity of Parallelisation. There are three main subproblems in the search for attacks that we examined for potential parallelisation:

- checking the solvability of a constraint system,
- enumerating all possible next states from the current state and
- the overall construction of the search tree itself.

The search for the solutions for a constraint problem can itself be a complex problem, depending on the assumed attacker model. Thus it may seem like a good candidate to evaluate in parallel. However, it turns out that when verifying real-world protocols, most of the constraints generated are simple, and easily solvable sequentially. Attempting to parallelise this leads to worse performance than executing them sequentially, as it ends up creating too many lightweight sparks. It may be the case that as the number of sessions grows, the constraints generated become larger the deeper down the search tree, so at a deeper node in the search tree, such a parallelisation might be helpful. However, to reach that stage, there would likely be a lot of simple constraints that need to be solved for which the overhead of paralellisation outweighs its benefit.

Our next attempt was to parallelise the process for enumerating successor states, which involves solving the intruder constraint problem. This led to some improved performance, but was harder to scale up, as it still created too many sparks, many of which ended up being garbage collected, a sign that there were too many useless sparks. The final conclusion seems to be that focussing on parallelising the construction of the search tree, executing the constraint solving and the successor state enumeration sequentially, produces the most speed up.

Lazy Evaluation and Parallelism. Haskell by default uses a lazy evaluation strategy in evaluating program expressions. By default, functions in Haskell are evaluated to *weak head normal form* (WHNF). Haskell provides libraries to force a complete evaluation of a program expression, e.g. via the `force` function. This, however, needs to be used with extreme care as it can create unnecessary computation and a potential termination issue.

One advantage of lazy evaluation, when parallelising a search algorithm, is that it allows one to decouple the search algorithm and the parallelisation strategy. In our case, we can implement the search algorithm as if it is proceeding sequentially, constructing a potentially infinite tree of states, without considering termination, as each node will be evaluated lazily only when needed, i.e. when the attack predicate is evaluated against the states in the search tree. Thus, at a very high level, given a function `f` that constructs a search tree sequentially, and a strategy `s` for parallelisation, the sequential execution of `f` can be turned into a parallel execution using the composition:

```
1    (withStrategy s) o f
```

Applying this strategy to OFMC, we applied a custom parallelisation strategy (see Sect. 4.1) to the construction of the search tree. The search algorithm itself does not make any assumption about termination of the search. It does, however, allow the user to specify the depth of search, so any nodes beyond a given depth will not be explored further.

Profiling the runtime behaviour of the parallelisation strategy revealed that a significant amount of time is spent on garbage collection. When searching at a depth d, OFMC keeps the subtrees at depth $> d$, which end up being garbage collected, as they are not needed in the final evaluation of the attack predicate. A solution is to prune the search tree prior to evaluating the predicate on the nodes. This seems to significantly reduce the memory footprint of the program.

4   Parallel Strategies for Search Trees

We now present a number of parallelisation strategies implemented in PFMC. The actual implementation contains more experimental parallelisation strategies not covered here, as they did not seem to offer much improvements over the main strategies presented here. We note that it is possible to directly benefit from multicore support for the Haskell runtime by compiling the program with the `-threaded` option. However, doing so results in worse performance compared to the single-threaded version, at least in the case for OFMC.

A main difficulty in designing an efficient parallelisation strategy in the case of OFMC is that the branching factor of a given node in the search tree is generally unbounded. Based on our profiling of the search trees of some sample protocols, the branching factor is highly dependent on the number of sessions of the protocol, the assumed intruder model (e.g., constraint solving for some algebraic theories can yield a variable number of solutions), and the depth of the search tree. This makes it difficult to adapt general parallel strategies for bounded trees such as the ones discussed in [23].

The source code for each strategy discussed here can be found in the file `src/TreeStrategies.hs` in the PFMC distribution.

4.1   parTreeBuffer: A Buffered Parallel Strategy for Search Trees

A naive parallelisation strategy for OFMC is to simply spark the entire search tree, i.e., for each node in the search tree, we create a spark and evalute it eagerly in parallel. In our tests, it quickly exhausted the available memory in our test server for large benchmark problems, so it does not scale well. Haskell (through the `Control.Parallel.Strategies` library) provides two ways to avoid creating a large number of sparks simultaneously, via a *chunking* strategy (`parChunk`), and a *buffered* strategy (`parBuffer`). They are however restricted to lists. The chunking strategy, as the name suggests, attempts to partition the input list into chunks of a fixed size, and executes all chunks in parallel, but keeping the sequential execution within each chunk. The buffered strategy attempts to stall the creation of sparks, by first creating n sparks (for a given value n), and then *streaming* the sparks one at a time as needed.

It was not clear what would be an equivalent of `parChunk` applied to potentially unbounded search trees. In an initial attempt, we tried to flatten the search tree to a list, use the chunking strategy for lists, and 'parse' the list back to a tree. This did not produce the desired effect. We instead designed an approximation of a buffered strategy, but applied to search trees, by controlling the depth of sparking, which we call *par-depth*. For example, for a *par-depth* of 2, all nodes at depth less than or equal to 2 will be sparked, and anything beyond depth 2 will be suspended – by returning their WHNF immediately. The sparks created for nodes that have only been evaluated to WHNF will not attempt to create more sparks for the subtrees. When a suspended node is required by the main thread (e.g., when it needs to be evaluated against a security property), it will trigger another round of sparking (up to *par-depth*)). Figure 1 shows a situation where some of the left-most nodes (marked with the green color) have completed their tasks, and the main thread is starting to query the next suspended node (grey node). This triggers sparking of a subtree of depth 2. As can be seen, the strategy essentially sparks a chunk of seven nodes at a time, in a depth-first manner. The grey nodes represent those that have been only evaluated to WHNF. The yellow nodes represent nodes that may be either finished performing their task, or waiting for results from their child nodes.

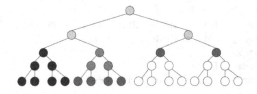

Fig. 1. A buffered search tree. (Color figure online)

This example shows a balanced binary tree. In reality, the search tree may not be balanced, and the branching factor can vary from one node to another. It may be theoretically possible to create a search tree that is infinitely branching, so our strategy cannot completely guarantee that the number of sparks at any given time would be bounded. Indeed, based on our profiling of search trees for a number of benchmarks in OFMC, the search trees can be quite unbalanced, and the branching factors vary greatly between different depths of the search tree. For three sessions of the Kerberos protocol, for example, the branching factors seem to congregate at two extremes: between 1–3 branches at the lower-end versus 40–50 branches at the higher end. In our experiments, we witnessed a relatively constant memory consumption throughout the execution of the benchmark problems up to three sessions. Going beyond four sessions, for large protocols such as Kerberos, the longer the benchmark is executed, the memory consumption may grow substantially, to the point that the entire system memory can be exhausted. Nevertheless, this buffered strategy is simple enough and serves as a good starting point in investigating various trade-offs between the number of cores, the degree of parallelisation and the memory consumption.

Our buffered strategy is implemented as shown in Fig. 2. The difference between sparking new nodes and stalling the sparking lies in the use of par-Buffer vs. parList: the former evaluates a node into WHNF and returns without creating a new spark, whereas the latter would spark the entire list.

To evaluate the performance of the `parBufferTree` strategy, we selected three benchmark problems: a flawed version of Google Single Sign-On (SSO) protocol [4], the TLS protocol and a basic version of the Kerberos protocol. All experiments were performed on a server with 96 Intel(R) Xeon(R) Gold 6252 physical cores at 2.10 GHz (192 logical cores), and 196 GB of RAM. We show some details here for the simplified versions of Google SSO and Kerberos protocols; see [14] further details. For each experiment, we specified the number of sessions and the depth of the search, and the *par-depth* for the clustering of parallel search. The protocols used for these experiments were all specified in the AnB format. These experiments were restricted to a *par-depth* of 3, which seems to strike a reasonable balance between performance and memory consumption. For a protocol with n steps per session, the length of the run of k concurrent sessions of the protocol is bounded by $n * k$, which corresponds to the depth of search. Therefore, to prove the security of a protocol with k steps for n sessions, the depth of the search must be at least $n * k$. Note that since the search procedure in OFMC (and therefore also in PFMC) aims to find attacks, the benefit

```
1    data Tree a = Node a [Tree a]
2    parTreeBuffer :: Int → Int → Strategy a → Strategy (Tree a)
3    parTreeBuffer _ _ strat (Node x []) = do
4      y ← strat x
5      return (Node y [])
6    parTreeBuffer 0 n strat (Node x l) = do
7      y ← strat x
8      l' ← parBuffer 50 (parTreeBuffer n n strat) l
9      return (Node y l')
10   parTreeBuffer !m n strat (Node x l) = do
11     y ← strat x
12     l' ← parList (parTreeBuffer (m-1) n strat) l
13     return (Node y l')
```

Fig. 2. A buffered parallel strategy for search trees

of parallelisation is in general clearer when verifying protocols for which there are no attacks (under the symbolic model).

To check whether our parallelisation strategy did indeed distribute the work to multiple cores, we perform a profiling of runtime workload distributions among different cores. For this test, we used the Google Single Sign-On (SSO) protocol formalisation which comes with the OFMC distribution. The runtime profiles (Fig. 3) were generated using the threadscope software [16]. Figure 3a shows the overall profile. The green 'bar' on the top is the overall workload of all cores combined, and the bars below (labelled HEC 0 - HEC 3) correspond to the activities for each core. The green bars represent the actual workload of the program being run. The orange bars denote time spent on garbage collection and the light orange bars represent idle time. As we can see in the figure, the work is distributed evenly across all cores, but there are gaps between activities. Figure 3b shows an individual activity in more detail. The workload component is only slightly longer than the combined GC and idle time. As we will see later, this ratio of workload vs overhead (GC + idle time) is consistently observed throughout our benchmarks.

For the Kerberos protocol, we witnessed a huge increase in the number of states to verify. For 3 sessions and a search depth of 10, using a naive (unbuffered) strategy (e.g. parTree), the verifier occasionally entered a state where it consumed a huge amount of memory (close to 190 GB) and the program was terminated by the operating system. The problem became worse when moving to 4 sessions (with a search depth of 12); the memory consumption rose to around 130 GB within 3 min of runtime. This is thus an example that shows the advantage of the buffered search tree strategy in PFMC.

For this case study, we performed two sets of experiments. The first experiment used 3 sessions of the protocol, with a search depth of 10, while the second one increased the search depth to 18 (hence it covered all possible interleavings of actions from the 3 sessions). The purpose of this was primarily to see how the verification effort scales up with the increase of search depth.

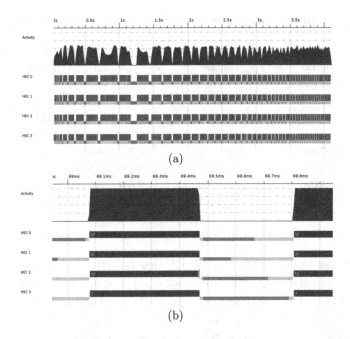

Fig. 3. Profiling workload distributions: (a) overall and (b) an individual activity. (Color figure online)

The results of the experiments are summarised in Tables 1 and 2 and Fig. 4. The *Total (elapsed)* column shows the total elapsed time (wall time). The *Total (CPU)* column shows the total CPU time spent by all cores. The *GC* column shows the (elapsed) time spent on garbage collection, and *MUT* shows the actual productive time spent on the workload. The last column shows the maximum memory residency, i.e., the largest amount of memory used at any time. The two experiments look remarkably similar. We see a steep improvement in elapsed time up to 10–12 cores, before the curves flatten out. The performance speed-ups in the best cases were 5.1 (for the first experiment, with 16 cores) and 3.8 (for the second experiment, with 14 cores). In the second experiment, the single-threaded OFMC took slightly over 24 hours, but the parallel version, in the best case, terminated after 6 hours or so.

The long tails of distributions of performance gain in the previous experiments do not necessarily mean that we have reached the limit of parallelisation. Rather, it seems to be an effect on the limit of the *par-depth* (and hence also the memory ceiling). Tweaking the *par-depth* parameter slightly may result in better or worse performance. For the Kerberos verification, for 3 sessions and a search depth of 18, increasing the *par-depth* to 4 from 3 gained us some improvement: the elapsed time was 21765.3 s (so about 1.12 speed up over the execution time using a *par-depth* of 3), GC time 14271.5 s and MUT time 7494.8 s. However, the resident memory rose to 20 GB (from 6.8 GB). Raising the memory ceiling also allows more cores to be used to gain further performance improvement. For

Table 1. Kerberos protocol verification for 3 sessions and search depth 10.

Core#	Total (elapsed) (s)	Total (CPU) (s)	GC (s)	MUT (s)	Mem. res. (MB)
1	7990.432	7989.687	4539.233	3451.164	255.4
2	4992.650	9967.061	3324.002	1668.644	3609.8
4	2891.620	11422.235	1989.502	902.115	3954.3
6	2123.020	12443.051	1483.549	639.460	4122.6
8	1753.690	13493.416	1232.658	521.021	3930.3
10	1627.630	15456.142	1162.774	464.846	3861.1
12	1679.090	18870.687	1219.576	459.509	3829.5
14	1634.090	21193.560	1197.041	437.042	4120.1
16	1563.200	22944.665	1147.829	415.366	4204.5

Table 2. Kerberos protocol verification for 3 sessions and search depth 18.

Core#	Elapse time (s)	CPU time (s)	GC time (s)	MUT (s)	Mem. res. (MB)
1	88804.862	88796.110	46791.364	42013.268	2195.3
2	56400.770	111668.513	34207.638	22193.131	6589.9
4	35479.590	133237.707	22194.304	13285.284	6766.1
6	29285.870	157276.399	18348.008	10937.858	6689.4
8	25753.490	177285.007	16184.376	9569.108	6742.4
10	24328.190	201795.566	15171.428	9156.752	6795.9
12	22916.410	221311.255	14186.897	8729.507	6823.9
14	23114.540	254643.338	14284.919	8829.614	6864.3
16	24443.140	304698.207	15330.385	9112.746	6868.6

example, for the same Kerberos benchmark, with a *par-depth* of 4, raising the number of cores to 20 resulted in a total elapsed time of 20789.7 s, with resident memory of 20.8 GB. Generally, increasing the *par-depth* results in higher memory consumption, but may allow all cores to be maximally used at all times. When tested with a *par-depth* of 6, the verification of Kerberos (3 sessions, search depth 18) exhausted the server's memory (196 GB) and was terminated by the operating system. These suggest that there are still performance improvements to be gained from `parTreeBuffer` if we can reduce the overall memory footprint of PFMC, allowing us to use a greater *par-depth*. However, generally, `parTreeBuffer` is rather unsatisfactory as the memory consumption can grow unpredictably and crash the verifier. In our next strategies, we attempt to address this issue.

Garbage collection currently seems to be the largest source of inefficiency in our experiments, taking up almost half of the execution time per core. This is, however, not due to the parallelisation, as it is also observed in the runtime for the single-core cases. Our conjecture is that this is an inherent issue with the search procedures underlying OFMC, which may involve creation of search nodes that end up not being evaluated and later discarded by the garbage collector.

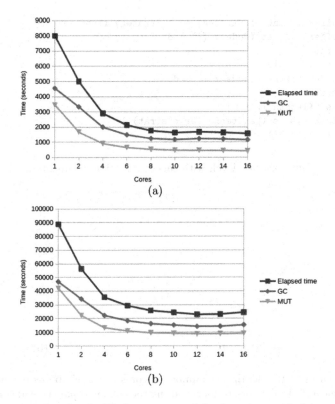

Fig. 4. Execution time for the Kerberos protocol for 3 sessions with (a) a search depth of 10 and (b) a search depth of 18.

4.2   Enhanced parTreeBuffer

This strategy was a modification to the original `parTreeBuffer` strategy which led to a dramatic improvement in both speed and memory consumption. The modification consists of two parts. First, the *par-depth* limitation is removed, and `parBuffer` is called at each node's children. This increases speed-up at the cost of memory overhead. However, this memory cost increase is offset by the second modification. The second change, which is the key modification, involves eagerly evaluating the *spine* of the list of children at each node, without evaluating each individual node in the list, prior to calling `parBuffer`, as shown in Fig. 5.

To understand why the second modification is significant, recall that due to the lazy evaluation of Haskell, when a function that returns a list is called, Haskell will stop evaluating the function as soon as the topmost constructor is evaluated, i.e., when the result is of the form `(x:l)`, where the head `x` and the tail `l` of the list are unevaluated expressions. In the case of PFMC, this list contains the successors of the underlying transition system encoding the protocol and the attacker moves. Deducing possible transitions may involve solving deducibility constraints, and as the number of sessions and the depth search grow, the

```
ı parTreeBuffer :: Int → Strategy a → Strategy (Tree a)
₂ parTreeBuffer _ strat (Node x []) = do
ı    y ← strat x
ı    return (Node y [])
ı parTreeBuffer c strat (Node x l) = do
ı    y ← strat x
ı    n ← rseq (length l)
ı    l' ← parBuffer c (parTreeBuffer c strat) l
ı    return (Node y l')
```

Fig. 5. parBuffer at each level, with eager evaluation of subchildren length.

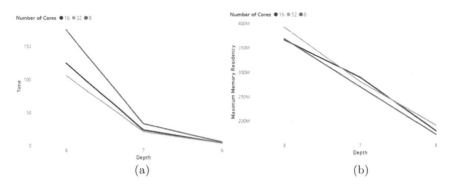

(a)   (b)

Fig. 6. The effect of the depth and number of cores of the Kerberos protocol on (a) execution time and (b) memory residency, using the enhanced **parTreeBuffer** strategy.

accumulated constraints can be significant; we conjecture that evaluating this eagerly allows some of the large lazy terms to be simplified in advance, at little computation cost, which reduces the memory footprint significantly. This small change decreases the memory consumption of the strategy tenfold in many cases. Figure 6 shows the effect of the depth and number of cores on execution time and memory residency, using the basic Kerberos protocol.

4.3   parTreeChunkSubtrees

This strategy aims at controlling exactly the overall number of sparks created. It uses a concept of *fuel* and fuel splitting, motivated by [23]. It starts at the root node of the search tree with a given number of sparks (i.e., the fuel) to be created. It then divides this number between each subtree, evaluating nodes sequentially. When the number of sparks reaches one, a spark is created to evaluate the remaining subtrees in parallel. This method is extremely memory efficient and performs well on smaller trees. However, as the number of sparks requested increases, the sequential portion towards the root of the tree becomes larger. Therefore, this method is not suitable for large problem sizes. Nevertheless, the

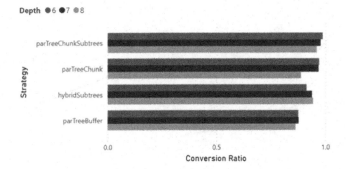

Fig. 7. Conversion Ratio using the `hybridSubtrees` strategy for the Kerberos protocol.

overall memory consumption of this strategy is extremely low, so it has potential applications where memory use is a priority, as well as for smaller problem sizes. An extension to this strategy which resolves this issue is `hybridSubtrees`.

4.4   hybridSubtrees

The `hybridSubtrees` strategy divides a certain number of sparks over the tree. However, instead of evaluating sequentially until it runs out of fuel, it recursively calls `parBuffer` at each level, and divides the remaining sparks between its children. When the strategy can no longer create a full buffer, it creates a spark for the remaining subtree. This strategy therefore has a strict upper bound on the degree of parallelism. It also affords better control over the trade-off between memory and performance in general. When given enough sparks, it behaves similarly to `parTreeBuffer`. Given fewer sparks, the average granularity increases, the performance slows, and the memory consumption decreases. A benefit of sparking subtrees may also be that nodes deeper in the tree are less likely to require evaluation, meaning less work for the relatively overloaded subtree sparks. This is evidenced by its conversion rate when compared to other strategies, which indicates fewer fizzled and garbage collected sparks, as shown in Fig. 7.

A limitation of this strategy is that the sparks are not evenly divided between subtrees, and the number of sparks created is usually significantly lower than the number requested. Overall, the strategy performed slightly better than `parTreeBuffer` at certain problem sizes. However when testing very large problem sizes (4 sessions or depths greater than 10), spark creation as a proportion of the spark cap provided decreased, and it became difficult to assign adequate sparks to offer comparable speeds to `parTreeBuffer` without thoroughly testing for a given depth to explore its sparking characteristics. Figure 8 shows the execution time and memory residency using this strategy on the Kerberos protocol.

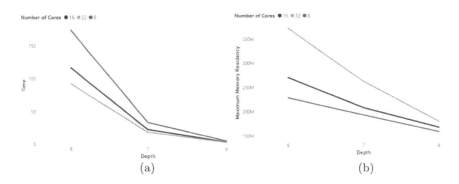

Fig. 8. The effect of the depth and number of cores of the Kerberos protocol on (a) execution time and (b) memory residency, using the `hybridSubtrees` strategy.

4.5 Strategies with Annotation

The above strategies make assumptions about the shape of the tree which could impact performance for particular problems. For example, sparks could be left unused by `hybridSubTrees` due to the unbalanced nature of the tree. Learning more about the search tree before applying a strategy could help to offset this. We experimented with several strategies using annotation methods inspired by [23], by annotating each node in the search tree with information about the number of subnodes, in order to achieve better sparking and load balancing characteristics. The core of these strategies was at each node developing a list of slightly different strategies to apply to each subtree, based on the annotation information. For example, in the case of fuel-splitting strategies such as `parTreeChunkSubtrees` or `hybridSubtrees`, annotation was used to ensure excess fuel was not passed to subtrees without sufficient nodes to make use of it.

However, in all cases these strategies did not justify their additional cost in performance and memory. This may be due to the fact that many nodes in the tree are not evaluated under normal conditions, but the annotation runs force a degree of evaluation in order to count nodes, and this overhead is not offset by any performance gains. It is also possible that the chosen method of annotation is inefficient, and better methods using, for example, a heuristic technique may perform better.

4.6 Comparison

The enhanced `parTreeBuffer` strategy offers reliably good results for most problem sizes, with improved speed-up and memory consumption in all cases over the `parTreeBuffer` strategy. For small trees, the simpler `parTreeChunkSubtrees` performs better in both measures than any alternatives, but at these problem sizes the difference is not significant. The `hybridSubTrees` strategy performs well if assigned adequate fuel, but this can become difficult for greater depths.

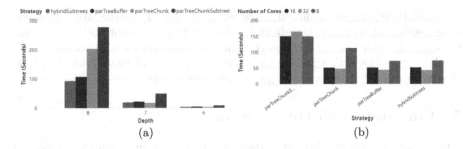

Fig. 9. (a) Best execution time vs depth and (b) average execution time for varying numbers of cores for each of the strategies.

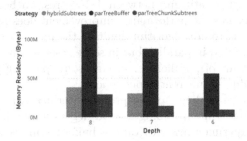

Fig. 10. Maximum memory residency vs depth for some of the strategies.

For very large problems, where `parTreeBuffer` may overflow memory due to excessive spark creation, `hybridSubtrees` can also be used to limit parallelism while still benefiting from parallel speed-up. It performed consistently better in terms of memory consumption compared to `parTreeBuffer` and offers more explicit control over the degree of parallelism. Figures 9 and 10 show the comparisons of execution time and memory for the different strategies.

These observations apply only to PFMC, and testing on a variety of other problems would be required for commenting on the more general performance characteristics of the strategies. Finer granularity of problem size at each node would make chunking strategies more applicable, whereas problems which require the evaluation of the entire tree at each execution would not benefit as much from the buffering approach and may be better served by fuel-splitting or some other strategy.

4.7 Enabling the Verification of Protocols with Algebraic Operators

OFMC also supports extensions of Dolev-Yao attacker models with algebraic operators. Some of these operators, such as XOR, are supported by default, but the user has the ability to add their own equational theory for custom operators. The custom theories, however, are supported only when the input is specified in the AVISPA Intermediate Format (IF) format [19], which is not very user-friendly. OFMC does provide a translator from AnB format to IF format, but currently there are some issues in recognising the custom theories. We have made some modifications to the translator to allow us to experiment with verification of protocols with algebraic properties. In terms of performance speed-up, the results are in line with what we have seen in the case of Dolev-Yao attackers. Further details of these experiments are available in [14].

5 Conclusion and Future Work

Our preliminary results show that there is a significant improvement in moving towards moderate parallelisation of security protocol verification based on symbolic constraint solving. We managed to achieve 3–5 times speed up compared to the sequential verifier, utilising between 4–16 cores, on benchmarks with 3 sessions. Beyond 16 cores the performance improvement does not seem substantial. This is partly due to our algorithm limiting the memory usage, preventing more tasks to be executed in parallel, but in some cases it could also be that the problem has hit a limit of parallelisation, e.g., some parts of the search could not be parallelised due to inherent dependencies.

One major issue in scaling up the protocol verification is controlling the memory consumption, while attaining a good degree of parallelisation. To this end we have been experimenting with various buffering and chunking strategies. The extended `parTreeBuffer` and the `hybridSubTree` strategies (Sect. 4) seem to so far provide a good balance of memory consumption and performance, with `parTreeBuffer` generally performing better, but with a worse memory footprint.

For future work, we plan to explore annotation methods to achieve better load balancing in sparking the search trees, perhaps by moving to a limited shared-memory concurrent setting. We also plan to apply our light-weight parallelisation approach to improve the performance of other protocol verifiers, e.g., Tamarin.

References

1. Abadi, M., Gordon, A.D.: A calculus for cryptographic protocols: the SPI calculus. Inf. Comput. **148**(1), 1–70 (1999)
2. Almousa, O., Mödersheim, S., Viganò, L.: Alice and bob: reconciling formal models and implementation. In: Bodei, C., Ferrari, G.-L., Priami, C. (eds.) Programming Languages with Applications to Biology and Security. LNCS, vol. 9465, pp. 66–85. Springer, Cham (2015). https://doi.org/10.1007/978-3-319-25527-9_7
3. Arapinis, M., Delaune, S., Kremer, S.: From one session to many: dynamic tags for security protocols. In: Cervesato, I., Veith, H., Voronkov, A. (eds.) LPAR 2008. LNCS, vol. 5330, pp. 128–142. Springer, Heidelberg (2008). https://doi.org/10.1007/978-3-540-89439-1_9
4. Armando, A., Carbone, R., Compagna, L., Cuéllar, J., Tobarra, L.: Formal analysis of SAML 2.0 web browser single sign-on: breaking the SAML-based single sign-on for google apps. In: Proceedings of the 6th ACM Workshop on Formal Methods in Security Engineering, FMSE 2008, pp. 1–10. ACM (2008)
5. Barbosa, M., Barthe, G., Bhargavan, K., Blanchet, B., Cremers, C., Liao, K., Parno, B.: SoK: computer-aided cryptography. IACR Cryptology ePrint Archive 2019/1393 (2019)

6. Blanchet, B.: Using horn clauses for analyzing security protocols. In: Formal Models and Techniques for Analyzing Security Protocols. Cryptology and Information Security Series, vol. 5, pp. 86–111. IOS Press (2011)
7. Blanchet, B.: Modeling and verifying security protocols with the applied Pi calculus and ProVerif. Found. Trends Priv. Secur. 1(1–2), 1–135 (2016)
8. Cervesato, I., Durgin, N.A., Lincoln, P., Mitchell, J.C., Scedrov, A.: A meta-notation for protocol analysis. In: Proceedings of the 12th IEEE Computer Security Foundations Workshop, CSFW 1999, pp. 55–69. IEEE Computer Society (1999)
9. Cheval, V.: APTE: an algorithm for proving trace equivalence. In: Ábrahám, E., Havelund, K. (eds.) TACAS 2014. LNCS, vol. 8413, pp. 587–592. Springer, Heidelberg (2014). https://doi.org/10.1007/978-3-642-54862-8_50
10. Cheval, V., Kremer, S., Rakotonirina, I.: DEEPSEC: deciding equivalence properties in security protocols theory and practice. In: Proceedings of 2018 IEEE Symposium on Security and Privacy, SP 2018, pp. 529–546. IEEE Computer Society (2018)
11. Cortier, V., Dallon, A., Delaune, S.: Efficiently deciding equivalence for standard primitives and phases. In: Lopez, J., Zhou, J., Soriano, M. (eds.) ESORICS 2018. LNCS, vol. 11098, pp. 491–511. Springer, Cham (2018). https://doi.org/10.1007/978-3-319-99073-6_24
12. Dolev, D., Yao, A.C.: On the security of public key protocols. IEEE Trans. Inf. Theory 29(2), 198–207 (1983)
13. Durgin, N.A., Lincoln, P., Mitchell, J.C., Scedrov, A.: Undecidability of bounded security protocols. In: Workshop on Formal Methods and Security Protocols (1999)
14. James, A., Tiu, A., Yatapanage, N.: PFMC: a parallel symbolic model checker for security protocol verification. CoRR, abs/2207.09895 (2022)
15. Kanovich, M.I., Kirigin, T.B., Nigam, V., Scedrov, A.: Bounded memory Dolev-Yao adversaries in collaborative systems. Inf. Comput. 238, 233–261 (2014)
16. Marlow, S., Jones, D., Singh, S.: ThreadScope (software package). https://wiki.haskell.org/ThreadScope
17. Marlow, S., Newton, R., Jones, S.L.P.: A monad for deterministic parallelism. In: Proceedings of the 4th ACM SIGPLAN Symposium on Haskell, Haskell 2011, Tokyo, Japan, 22 September 2011, pp. 71–82. ACM (2011)
18. Meier, S., Schmidt, B., Cremers, C., Basin, D.: The TAMARIN prover for the symbolic analysis of security protocols. In: Sharygina, N., Veith, H. (eds.) CAV 2013. LNCS, vol. 8044, pp. 696–701. Springer, Heidelberg (2013). https://doi.org/10.1007/978-3-642-39799-8_48
19. Mödersheim, S., Viganò, L.: The open-source fixed-point model checker for symbolic analysis of security protocols. In: Aldini, A., Barthe, G., Gorrieri, R. (eds.) FOSAD 2007-2009. LNCS, vol. 5705, pp. 166–194. Springer, Heidelberg (2009). https://doi.org/10.1007/978-3-642-03829-7_6
20. Rusinowitch, M., Turuani, M.: Protocol insecurity with finite number of sessions is NP-complete. In: 14th IEEE Computer Security Foundations Workshop (CSFW-14 2001), pp. 174–187. IEEE Computer Society (2001)
21. Thayer, F.J., Herzog, J.C., Guttman, J.D.: Strand spaces: proving security protocols correct. J. Comput. Secur. 7(1), 191–230 (1999)
22. Tiu, A., Nguyen, N., Horne, R.: SPEC: an equivalence checker for security protocols. In: Igarashi, A. (ed.) APLAS 2016. LNCS, vol. 10017, pp. 87–95. Springer, Cham (2016). https://doi.org/10.1007/978-3-319-47958-3_5
23. Totoo, P.: Parallel evaluation strategies for lazy data structures in Haskell. Ph.D. thesis, Heriot-Watt University (2016)

A Formal Methodology for Verifying Side-Channel Vulnerabilities in Cache Architectures

Ke Jiang[1(✉)], Tianwei Zhang[1(✉)], David Sanán[2], Yongwang Zhao[3,4], and Yang Liu[1]

[1] School of Computer Science and Engineering, Nanyang Technological University, Singapore, Singapore
ke006@e.ntu.edu.sg, tianwei.zhang@ntu.edu.sg
[2] Information and Communication Technologies, Singapore Institute of Technology, Singapore, Singapore
[3] ZJU-Hangzhou Global Scientific and Technological Innovation Center, Zhejiang University, Hangzhou, China
[4] School of Cyber Science and Technology, College of Computer Science and Technology, Zhejiang University, Hangzhou, China

Abstract. Security-aware CPU caches have been designed to mitigate side-channel attacks and prevent information leakage. How to validate the effectiveness of these designs remains an unsolved problem. Prior works assess the security of architectures empirically without a formal guarantee, making the evaluation results less convincing. In this paper, we propose a comprehensive methodology based on formal methods for security verification of cache architectures. Specifically, we design an entropy-based noninterference reasoning framework with two unwinding conditions to assess the information leakage of the cache designs. The reasoning framework quantifies the dependency relationships by the mutual information between the distributions of input and output of side channels. Given a cache design, we formalize its behavior specification along with the cache layouts into an abstract state machine, to instantiate the parameterized reasoning framework that discloses any potential vulnerabilities. We use our methodology to assess eight state-of-the-art cache architectures to demonstrate reliability as well as flexibility.

Keywords: Cache designs · Side-channel attacks · Security verification

1 Introduction

Micro-architectural side-channel attacks have incurred serious threats to computer security over the past decades [19]. These side-channel attacks mainly exploit the timing observations from hardware components (e.g., CPU cache [21,23], Translation Look-aside Buffer (TLB) [3,10]) to infer confidential information. The essence of these attacks is the interference [9] from the memory accesses between different programs or even inside one program. Such interference leaves regular footprints on certain hardware components, which can be

© Springer Nature Switzerland AG 2022
A. Riesco and M. Zhang (Eds.): ICFEM 2022, LNCS 13478, pp. 190–208, 2022.
https://doi.org/10.1007/978-3-031-17244-1_12

captured by an adversary to recover confidential information about the victim program. Past works have demonstrated successful attacks to steal cryptographic keys (symmetric ciphers [2], asymmetric ciphers [18,35,38], signature algorithms [1,25,34], post-quantum ciphers [11]), keystrokes [29], visited websites [26], and system configurations [14]. In this paper, we focus on cache-based side channels.

To mitigate cache side-channel attacks, a variety of defense solutions have been proposed. One promising direction is to design security-aware hardware components to reduce or prevent side-channel information leakage. These designs mainly follow two kinds of strategies. The partitioning-based solutions [31] physically partition the shared cache components into multiple zones for different domain applications to achieve strong isolation. The randomization-based solutions [24,31–33] obfuscate the adversary's observations by randomizing the cache states. These architectures exhibit great generalization and efficiency in protecting the programs running atop them. Although these architectures have been thoroughly considered and evaluated by researchers during the design phase, *it is still important to check whether there are any potential security vulnerabilities in these sophisticated cache systems before fabricating the actual chips.*

Over the past years, various methods have been proposed to evaluate cache side-channel vulnerabilities in hardware components. Unfortunately, they suffer from certain limitations, making it hard to apply them for practical and comprehensive verification. Specifically: **(1)** Some works [24,31–33] simulate the mechanisms of the newly designed caches against different types of side-channel attacks and empirically evaluated their effectiveness. Due to the lack of formal verification, they are not comprehensive, and can possibly miss some side-channel vulnerabilities. It also takes a lot of time to perform the cycle-accurate simulations in order to obtain convincing evaluation results. **(2)** A couple of approaches [7,8,30] abstractly describe the cache behaviors and define the execution paths that are treated as suspicious behaviors under a side-channel attack. Thereafter, they exhaustively search whether these suspicious behaviors are hidden in the cache behavior combinations. However, the modeling process is not formally guaranteed. Besides, the analysis is based on the exhaustive exploration of the execution traces, which can easily suffer from the combinatorial explosion issue. **(3)** Another challenge in verifying cache architectures is their probabilistic behaviors. To handle this issue, some works introduce methods based on statistics and entropy for security analysis. Zhang et al. [37] formally construct a cache state transition simulation through model checking techniques to get stable probability matrices within finite steps. To quantify information leakage, they calculate the mutual information between the input distribution and observable outputs. He et al. [13] establish a probabilistic information flow graph to model the interaction between the victim and attacker programs in the CPU cache. They define the concept of security-critical paths as the union of an attacker's observation and a victim's information flow. Equal probability of each node throughout the security-critical paths means the attacker cannot distinguish the victim's cache-accessed information. These methods face the balance issue between probability accuracy and state explosion. Besides, manual analysis and associating the probability to hardware behaviors can lead to incomprehensive conclusions. (4) New hardware description languages (HDL) were introduced to design secure hardware circuits [6,16,36] with formal proof. These solutions are not comprehensive for side-channel analysis: they can only be applied to the partitioning-based caches while failing to evaluate the randomization-based designs with stochastic behaviors. Besides, they are not user-friendly and need manual work for attaching security labels and defining security policies.

To overcome the limitations of assessing the security of cache designs, this paper introduces a novel methodology based on formal methods by theorem proving to comprehensively verify the security of cache architectures against side-channel attacks. First, we formalize the specifications of cache designs in an event-state machine way. We offer functional correctness proofs to guarantee the consistency between the specifications and designs, which is ignored in prior works. Second, we design a noninterference reasoning framework to verify the side-channel vulnerability resident in the cache specifications. It adopts the concept of entropy [4,5] as the theoretical basis to assess the information leakage. We propose two unwinding conditions to unify and evaluate different types of secure caches (e.g., partitioning-based, randomization-based), making our solution comprehensive. Third, we implement our framework in Isabelle/HOL [20], and adopt it to verify eight state-of-the-art cache designs. In summary, we make the following contributions:

- We implement a noninterference reasoning framework based on information entropy that unifies both the deterministic and non-deterministic event models. We define nonleakage as security property by mutual information and derive two general unwinding conditions. We design interfaces for this framework to offer verification services.
- We formally specify each cache design in an event-state machine way on top of general set-associative cache layouts, forming a complete cache specification. We prove the cache specification is an instantiation of the reasoning framework, hence can be efficiently verified security properties.
- We evaluate our entropy-based noninterference reasoning framework on eight state-of-the-art cache designs. The verification practice shows that our methodology possesses high theoretical reliability and flexibility.

We present the background about cache side-channel attacks and mutual information in Sect. 2. We give the threat model and briefly describe the methodology in Sect. 3. The design of reasoning framework is shown in Sect. 4. Section 5 presents a case-study, and Sect. 6 analyzes the verification results of eight state-of-the-art cache architectures. Section 7 concludes this paper.

2 Background

2.1 Cache Side-Channel Attacks

Cache Hierarchy. Most CPU caches are organized in a n-way set-associative way. A n-way set-associative cache can be treated as a two-dimensional data array. Each row is called a *cache set*, which is further divided into n *cache lines*. Each memory block is mapped to one cache set indexed by its memory address. This block can be stored in any cache lines in this set, determined by a replacement policy. When a CPU core wants to access a memory block, if it resides in the cache, the CPU can directly obtain it, resulting in a cache hit with a fast access speed. The CPU has to fetch the data from the main memory to the cache, otherwise. This results in a cache miss with a much slower access speed. Particularly, a cache with only one way in each set (i.e., $n = 1$) is a direct-mapped cache, while a cache with only one set is called fully-associative.

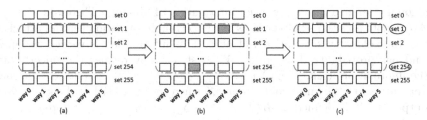

Fig. 1. Side-channel attack scheme. Sub-figure (a) represents the preparation phase, (b) the waiting phase, and (c) the observation phase.

Cache Attacks. The first cache attacks deduce cryptographic secrets by observing the whole execution time [2,15,22,27]. In recent days, cache side-channel attack techniques narrow down to a smaller granularity. The timing difference between a cache hit and a cache miss can reveal information about the program's access traces. A cache side-channel attack typically involves three steps (see Fig. 1). (1) Preparation: the adversary manipulates the states of certain cache lines with its own address space [28]. For instance, PRIME-PROBE attack [21] fills up the entire critical cache sets, while a FLUSH-RELOAD attack [35] and a FLUSH-FLUSH attack [12] evict certain cache lines through the *clflush* instruction. The area controlled by the adversary is shared with the victim. And, the adversary has the knowledge that the victim's access pattern in this area is related to its confidential information. (2) Waiting: the adversary does nothing until the victim finishes several execution circles. The victim may load its data blocks into the cache and replace the cache lines occupied by the adversary. (3) Observation: the adversary collects the footprints left by the victim program. For example, the PRIME-PROBE attack re-accesses the critical cache set to check if certain blocks were evicted by the victim. The FLUSH-RELOAD attack reloads the target cache lines to determine if it has been touched by the victim. The FLUSH-FLUSH attack re-flushes the target cache lines to check whether data is loaded into these lines by the victim. The victim's cache access pattern is thus leaked to the attacker.

2.2   Mutual Information

Intuitively, the concept of noninterference tells that one domain (denoted as victims) does not affect the observation of another domain (denoted as adversaries). The concept is consistent with the cache side-channel attack schemes because an adversary can deduce the victim's memory access patterns that are associated with secrets when its observation depends on the victim's behaviors. Furthermore, from the perspective of the probability distribution, information leakage of the side-channel is equivalent to the existence of a dependency relationship between the input (victim's behaviors) and output (adversary's observation). And, this kind of dependency relationship can be calculated by mutual information. This is the motivation of this work where we interpret the cache side-channel attack schemes by noninterference and measure the information flow of this noninterference through mutual information of Shannon Theory [4,5].

We denote a victim's behaviors as the uncertain information that an attacker wishes to explore by side-channel attacks. This information is viewed as input X and has probability distribution $\mathcal{X}$. First, entropy defines the uncertainty of the information itself, of $H(X) = -\sum_{x \in \mathcal{X}} p(x) log_2 p(x)$. Second, conditional entropy measures the uncertainty about X when the attacker has the knowledge of output Y. It is defined as $H(X|Y) = -\sum_{y \in \mathcal{Y}} p(y) \sum_{x \in \mathcal{X}} p(x|y) log_2 p(x|y)$. Lastly, mutual information between X and Y measures the information that an adversary can learn about X if he gains the knowledge through output Y, defined as $I(X;Y) = H(X) - H(X|Y)$. One property of mutual information is that it is symmetry: $I(X;Y) = I(Y;X)$. It can be calculated through a joint probability matrix, as shown in Eq. 1.

$$I(X;Y) = \sum_{x \in \mathcal{X}} \sum_{y \in \mathcal{Y}} p(x,y) log_2 \frac{p(x,y)}{p(x)p(y)} \tag{1}$$

$$= \sum_{x \in \mathcal{X}} \sum_{y \in \mathcal{Y}} p(x)p(y|x) log_2 \frac{p(y|x)}{p(y)} \tag{2}$$

2.3 Isabelle/HOL

Isabelle/HOL [20] is a higher-order logic theorem prover. It offers common types (e.g., naturals (nat), integers (int) and booleans ($bool$)). The keyword $datatype$ is used to define an inductive data type. Composed data types include tuple, record, list, and set. Projection functions fst and snd return elements t_1 and t_2 of a tuple $(t_1 \times t_2)$. Isabelle/HOL offers record type to include multiple elements of different data types. Assignment symbol $=$ is used to initialize the contents of a record, while $:=$ is used to update it. Lists are defined by an empty list denoted as [], and a concatenation constructor represented as #. The ith component of a list xs is accessed by $xs!i$. The cardinality of a set s (i.e., $|s|$) is denoted as $card\ s$, returning zero when set s is infinite. Isabelle/HOL provides $definition$ command to specify a non-recursive function, while $primrec$ command for primitive recursions.

Isabelle/HOL supports parametric theories with the keyword $locale$. A $locale$ includes a series of parameter declarations (with keyword $fixes$) and assumptions (with keyword $assumes$). Isabelle/HOL users can instantiate a locale through $interpretation$ command, where concrete data is assigned to parameters and declarations are added to the current context. We construct a parametric non-interference reasoning framework through $locale$ command and instantiate it in different cache architecture scenarios through $interpretation$ command.

3   Methodology Overview

3.1   Threat Model

We consider the cache architectures to be verified are involved in the following threat model. The victim and the attacker share the same cache environment and a cross-core/VM attack allows the attacker and the victim to execute in parallel on different cores/VMs. The attacker cannot directly observe the memory content from the CPU, probing cache states to check whether the victim's data is resident in the cache indirectly instead. This model captures most cache side-channel attacks in the literature. For example, EVICT-TIME attack [21] measures the latency of victim's program, PRIME-PROBE attack [18,21,23], FLUSH-RELOAD attack [35] and FLUSH-FLUSH attack [12] measure the latency of attacker's program.

We also mention that the attacker accurately monitors both cache set and cache line granularities. This is because modern OS adopts the page sharing technique that removes the duplication of shared libraries, enabling probing the shared libraries narrow to a cache line.

3.2   Architecture

The workflow of our proposed methodology is shown in Fig. 2. It includes two components. (1) A reasoning framework is designed to quantify the information leakage of the target system. The essence of the framework is to interpret the non-interference property through mutual information. (2) A complete cache specification includes the cache behavior formalization and the general cache layouts. The cache behavior is described as an event-state transition. Its formalization is first proved to meet the consistency with its design. The cache specification instantiates the interface layer offered by the reasoning framework. Therefore, for verifying whether a cache specification satisfies the security properties, we only need to verify whether it satisfies two unwinding conditions. Violations of both conditions indicate the cache design is vulnerable to side-channel attacks. In this work, we mainly focus on the fundamentals of information leakage, while skipping the analysis of adversarial strategies for extracting the secrets from the footprints of the victim program. As shown in Fig. 2, the reasoning framework contains the following components.

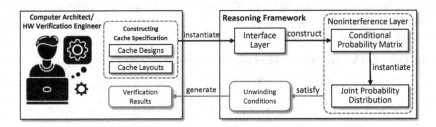

Fig. 2. Workflow of our proposed approach.

Interface Layer: this layer is used to connect the given cache specification to the noninterference layer. The interface layer offers an event-state transition function and output function to parse cache behaviors into probabilistic representations.

Noninterference Layer: this is the core of our reasoning framework. It introduces a parameterized joint probability distribution between the victim's information X and attacker's observation Y. We calculate the mutual information $I(X;Y)$ as information flow security property to quantify how much information the attacker can learn about X from Y. The joint probability distribution can be constructed by multiplying a series of probabilistic inputs and a conditional probability matrix. The conditional probability matrix models the relationships between the input and the output of cache designs.

Unwinding Conditions: this defines the conditions to satisfy information flow security property, meaning to make the mutual information zero according to Eq. 2. We deduce two unwinding conditions as shown in Eq. 3, when we stipulate that each input probability is greater than zero. The first condition $C1$ indicates that the attacker learns nothing when there is no observation. The second condition $C2$ shows the attacker's observation is constant and independent of the victim's behaviors.

$$C1 : \forall x \ y. \ p(y|x) = 0 \longrightarrow I(X;Y) = 0$$
$$C2 : \forall x \ y. \ p(y|x) = p(y) \longrightarrow I(X;Y) = 0$$

$$(3)$$

4   Design of Reasoning Framework

In this section, we provide more details about our reasoning framework.

4.1   Interface Layer—An Abstract State Machine

A cache specification implements a state machine through instantiating the interface layer. We construct the interface layer for the purpose of re-usability because verification of any cache architecture only requires instantiating the interface functions.

First, we model the input distribution space as $\mathbb{P}(\mathcal{I} \times \mathcal{P})$, which is the powerset of type $\mathcal{I} \times \mathcal{P}$. Label $\mathcal{I}$ describes the input content and $\mathcal{P}$ is of real type describing probabilities. We further stipulate any valid input distribution is neither empty nor infinite[1]. We omit input elements with zero-probability because they will not result in any outputs. We also guide that all inputs are different and the sum of the probabilities of all inputs equals one. We use the operator . to denote an attribute of a input, e.g., $x.i$ and $x.p$ represent the content and probability of input x, respectively.

Definition 1 (Valid Input Distribution Sets).

$$makeInput \triangleq \{\mathcal{X}. \ | \mathcal{X} | > 0 \wedge (\forall m \ n \in \mathcal{X}. \ m \neq n \longrightarrow m.i \neq n.i) \wedge$$
$$(\forall d \in \mathcal{X}. \ d.p > 0) \wedge \sum_{d \in \mathcal{X}} d.p = 1\}$$

---

[1] We follow the Isabelle/HOL definition where the cardinality of infinite sets is zero.

Next, we formalize the event-state transition function as ψ, which describes a non-deterministic event model. It is a single step execution triggered by the event label and the input, of type $\mathcal{E} \times \mathcal{X} \rightarrow \mathbb{P}(\mathcal{S} \times \mathcal{S})$. Label $\mathcal{S}$ represents the state space and $\mathcal{E}$ is the set of event labels. We use $\psi(e, x)/s$ to represent that all event-state transitions happen when we execute the event e on the state s with input x.

Definition 2 (Event-state Transition Function from State s).

$$\psi(e, x)/s \triangleq \{t. \; t \in \psi(e, x) \wedge (\exists s'. \; t = (s, s'))\}$$

Then, we define an abstract output function that extracts the output from each transition tuple (s, s'), of type $\varpi : (\mathcal{S} \times \mathcal{S}) \rightarrow \mathcal{O}$. Label $\mathcal{O}$ describes the output content. With these functions, we construct an abstract state machine in the interface layer.

Definition 3. *The interface layer implements an abstract state machine $\mathcal{M}$ as tuple $\langle \mathcal{S}, \mathcal{E}, \mathcal{X}, \mathcal{O}, \psi, \varpi \rangle$, where $\mathcal{S}$ is the state space, $\mathcal{E}$ is the set of event labels, $\mathcal{X}$ and $\mathcal{O}$ are the valid input distribution and output content respectively, ψ is the event-state transition function, and ϖ is the output function.*

4.2 Noninterference Layer

The concept of noninterference indicates that the behaviors of one domain do not affect the observation of another domain [9]. In our reasoning framework, these two domains correspond to the victim's input and the attacker's observation in the side channel. To describe such a side-channel mechanism, we construct a joint probability distribution through the functions from the interface layer step by step. We quantify the effect of the interaction between the victim and attacker by calculating mutual information from the joint probability distribution.

A joint probability can be written as $P(X)P(Y|X)$. Therefore, to instantiate a joint probability distribution is to construct the input distribution $P(X)$ and a conditional probability matrix $P(Y|X)$. The input distribution can be directly inherited from the interface layer. For example, it is any set that satisfies $\mathcal{X} \in makeInput$.

To construct a conditional probability matrix, we first introduce a conditional probability transition function Cpt. It first applies output function to each state transition tuple to get all possible outputs, shown as $\mathcal{O} = \{d. \; \exists t \in \psi(e, x)/s. \; d = \varpi(t)\}$. Then, for each output $o \in \mathcal{O}$, it counts all the transitions that produce the output o to get the probability, which is the proportion of these transitions in the total transitions. The definition of Cpt is as follows. The result of this function is the output distribution $\mathcal{Y}$, of type $\mathbb{P}(\mathcal{O} \times \mathcal{P})$.

Definition 4 (Conditional Probability Transition Function).

$$Cpt(e, x)/s \triangleq \{y. \exists o \in \mathcal{O}.$$

$$\mathcal{T}_{sub} = \{t. \ t \in \psi(e, x)/s \wedge \varpi(t) = o\} \wedge$$

$$y.o = o \wedge y.p = \frac{|\mathcal{T}_{sub}|}{|\psi(e, x)/s|}\}$$

$$where \ \mathcal{O} = \{d. \ \exists t \in \psi(e, x)/s. \ d = \varpi(t)\}$$

The function Cpt only takes one input while the valid input distribution $\mathcal{X}$ contains limited input contents. Therefore, the next step is to apply the function Cpt to each input in $\mathcal{X}$. The result of this process is a conditional probability matrix $\mathcal{W}$. Each row of the matrix $(w[y_1|x_i], \ w[y_2|x_i] \ \dots \ w[y_{|Y|}|x_i])$ can be viewed as the representation of the conditional probability distribution of output $y_1, \ y_2 \dots y_{|Y|}$ under the input x_i.

Now it is time to build the joint probability distribution. The following function $makeJoint$ matches each input x that belongs to the input distribution $\mathcal{X}$ with any conditional probability y that is part of $Cpt(e, x)/s$. Then the joint probability is the product of the corresponding probabilities of these two elements. Joint distribution $\mathcal{J}$ is defined as $\mathbb{P}((\mathcal{I} \times \mathcal{O}) \times \mathcal{P})$.

Definition 5 (Joint Probability Distribution).

$$makeJoint \triangleq \{j. \exists x \in \mathcal{X}. \ \exists y \in Cpt(e, x)/s.$$

$$j.i = x.i \wedge j.o = y.o \ \wedge j.p = x.p * y.p\}$$

The computation of mutual information from Eq. 1 requires two marginal probability distributions. We take the marginal probability of the input x as an example: we first collect the subset $\mathcal{J}_{sub} = \{j. \ j \in makeJoint. \ j.i = x.i\}$ that takes all elements whose input dimension is equal $x.i$ from the joint probability distribution. Then the marginal probability is the sum of the probabilities of all such elements. Its definition is shown below. We omit the definition of $margOutput$ due to the space limit.

Definition 6 (Input Marginal Probability Distribution).

$$margInput \triangleq \{mi. \exists x \in \mathcal{X}. \ \mathcal{J}_{sub} = \{j. \ j \in makeJoint. \ j.i = x.i\} \wedge$$

$$mi.i = x.i \wedge mi.p = \sum_{d \in \mathcal{J}_{sub}} d.p\}$$

Now we give the definition of mutual information based on Eq. 1. Function $mutualInfo$ takes each element $j \in makeJoint$ from the joint probability distribution, and then calculates the marginal probabilities of the input (mi) and output (mo) respectively. Afterwards, the value of the mutual information is the accumulation of $j.p * log_2 \frac{j.p}{mi.p*mo.p}$, when iterating the element j.

Definition 7 (Mutual Information).

$$mutualInfo \triangleq \sum_{j \in makeJoint} j.p * log_2 \frac{j.p}{mi.p * mo.p}$$

4.3   Unwinding Conditions

With mutual information calculated above, we assess the information leakage of noninterference by the following definition.

Definition 8 (Information Leakage).

$$nonleakage \triangleq \forall e\ \mathcal{X}\ s.\ mutualInfo = 0$$

According to Eq. 3, two unwinding conditions imply that the mutual information equals zero. We give the definitions of these two unwinding conditions and prove the implication relationships.

Theorem 1 (Condition 1: No Observation).

$$\forall e\ s.\ \forall x \in \mathcal{X}.\forall y \in Cpt(e,x)/s.$$
$$y.p = 0 \longrightarrow mutualInfo = 0$$

Proof. When the conditional probability $y \in Cpt(e,x)/s$ equals zero, the corresponding joint probability $j.p = x.p * y.p$ also equals zero. Then unfolding the definition of $mutualInfo$ and substituting $j.p$ as 0, the accumulated result $0 * log_2 \frac{0}{mi.p*mo.p}$ is zero. In the end, the mutual information is zero.

Theorem 1 gives the advice that if the attacker cannot observe anything from the footprints released by the victim, then the cache dose not leak any information. This condition can be used in some partitioning-based designs [31].

Theorem 2 (Condition 2: Constant Observation).

$$\forall e\ s.\ \forall x \in \mathcal{X}.\ \forall y \in Cpt(e,x)/s.$$
$$y.p = \sum_{d \in \mathcal{J}_{sub}} d.p \longrightarrow mutualInfo = 0$$
$$where\ \mathcal{J}_{sub} = \{j.\ j \in makeJoint.\ j.o = y.o\}$$

Proof. For any joint probability $j \in makeJoint$, its corresponding marginal probability of the input $mi.p$ equals its input probability $x.p$ because the sum of the probabilities of all elements in $Cpt(e,x)/s$ equals one. Also, the joint probability $j.p$ can be calculated by $x.p * y.p$. We have $y.p = \sum_{d \in \mathcal{J}_{sub}} d.p$, where $\mathcal{J}_{sub} = \{j.\ j \in makeJoint.\ j.o = y.o\}$ according to the condition 2 above. The accumulated result in the definition of $mutualInfo$, $j.p * log_2 \frac{j.p}{mi.p*mo.p}$ of Eq. 1, is then folded and substituted as $x.p * \sum_{d \in \mathcal{J}_{sub}} d.p * log_2 \frac{x.p*\sum_{d \in \mathcal{J}_{sub}} d.p}{x.p*\sum_{d \in \mathcal{J}_{sub}} d.p}$. Its value equals zero, leading the mutual information to be zero as well.

Theorem 2 describes a scenario where the conditional probability distribution is constant for any input. Therefore, the footprints caused by any input are the same. Note that Theorem 2 only requires the values of each column in the matrix $\mathcal{W}$ to be the same. When this condition is applied into cache designs, we can find that some randomization-based strategies further manipulate that the values of $w[y_1|x_i]$, $w[y_2|x_i] \ldots w[y_{|Y|}|x_i]$ are in the same probability, which is one special case of the above condition.

In the end, either of these two unwinding conditions can imply no information leakage, as shown in the following theorem.

Theorem 3 (Unwinding Conditions Reasoning).

$$(condition1 \vee condition2) \Longrightarrow nonleakage$$

5   Application of Our Methodology: A Case-study

In this section, we demonstrate how to verify an existing randomization-based cache design, i.e., Random Permutation (RP) cache [31] with our methodology.

5.1   The General Cache Layouts Specification

We start with the specification of the general cache layouts. A cache line is the smallest unit among cache layouts, which is defined as a **record** $ca\_line = ca\_set, ca\_way, ca\_tag, valid, lock, owned$. The first three fields directly represent the cache index, cache way and cache tag. The following fields denote whether the cache line is used, whether its content is protected, and which process is occupying it. We define the cache structure and the specification it needs to satisfy as follows: the parameterized cache layouts are constructed by a list whose length is **M**, where each element of the list represents a cache set with **W** cache lines (i.e., W-ways). In a cache set, the ca_set identifier of each cache line equals its cache set index, and all cache lines in one cache set have different ca_way.

Definition 9 (The Cache Structure).

$Cache :: \text{``}(ca\_line\ set)\ list\text{''}\ and\ it\ satisfies : |\ Cache\ | = M\ \wedge$
$(\forall l < M.\ |\ Cache\ !\ l\ | = W) \wedge (\forall l < M.\ \forall e \in (Cache\ !\ l).\ e.ca\_set = l)\ \wedge$
$(\forall l < M.\ \forall e_i\ e_j.\ e_i \in (Cache\ !\ l) \wedge e_j \in (Cache\ !\ l).$
$\qquad e_i \neq e_j \longrightarrow e_i.ca\_way \neq e_j.ca\_way)$

With the cache layouts definition, we formalize the memory request that acts as the input from the victim and is performed by the corresponding cache design on the cache layouts. A memory request is denoted as a **record** $mem\_req = tagbits, setbits, protected, process$. Label $tagbits$ is used to compare the tag field of a cache line, and $setbits$ is sent to the cache mapping to get the actual cache index. Label $protected$ denotes whether the memory data is protected by its owner, and $process$ represents the owner of this memory block in two values: **H** and **L** denote the confidential and non-confidential processes respectively. Last, we design the system state that includes the cache structure and the mapping structure from a memory request to the cache set index. The structure is formally defined as **record** $state = Cache, Mapping$.

5.2   The RP Cache Specification

For the RP cache, the workflow of handling memory requests is shown in Fig. 3. RP cache utilizes three strategies to randomize the observation of the adversary. (1) When there is an external cache miss (Column 1: the mapped cache line does not belong to the current process), RP cache randomly chooses a cache set and selects one cache line according to the replacement policy in this set to replace the request memory. (2) When there is an internal miss (Column 2: the mapped cache line belongs to the current process but has a different protection flag), RP cache randomly chooses a cache set and selects one cache line according to the replacement policy in this set to evict it without caching. These two strategies will result in non-deterministic cache state transitions. (3) For the external cache miss (Column 1), RP cache also dynamically changes the memory-to-cache mapping, so even if the attacker can deduce the mapping for one read operation, it would fail for the next time.

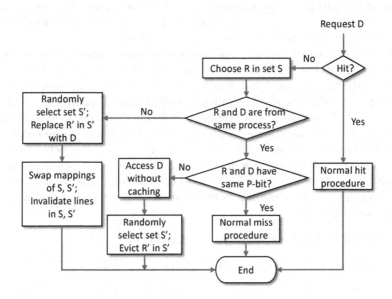

Fig. 3. Random permutation cache

The specification of RP cache is defined in a way of the event-state transition function and is omitted here. We give a lemma to prove the correctness of cache layout when a RP cache read is issued and a miss happens. It indicates that there will be multiple state transitions when a cache miss happens, showing non-deterministic execution. For each transition, there will be one cache line from a random cache set updated, while other cache sets remain the same. Here, l_{mr} refers to the original mapped cache set index.

Lemma 1 (Correctness of RP Cache Read).

$$[\![\forall e \in s.Cache \ ! \ l_{mr}. \ e.ca\_tag \neq mr.tagbits]\!] \Longrightarrow$$
$$[\![\forall s' \in rp\_read \ mr \ s. \ \exists!l. \ (\forall l' \neq l. \ s'.Cache \ ! \ l' = s.Cache \ ! \ l') \ \wedge$$
$$|\ (s'.Cache \ ! \ l) \cap (s.Cache \ ! \ l) \ | = | \ s.Cache \ ! \ l \ | -1]\!]$$

5.3 Security Verification of RP Cache

With the instantiation of the event-state transition function (i.e., the RP cache specification), we instantiate the remaining two functions to complete the instantiation of the interface layer of the reasoning framework.

Due to direct inheritance, the memory request distribution issued from the victim is regarded as $\mathcal{X}$, of concrete type $\mathbb{P}(mem\_req \times \mathcal{P})$. Next, we instantiate the observation function ϖ. According to the correctness proofs, only one cache set is updated inside those state transitions for each cache miss. Therefore, the attacker can regard the state transition with the same updated cache set as the same observation when re-accessing the cache. For convenience, we use the cache set index to represent the observable state transitions.

Now, we construct the attack-simulated cache layout specification that statically demonstrates how the attacker manipulates the cache layout with its data. It describes the circumstances of the preparation phase shown in the leftmost picture of Fig. 1. A cache line e can be differentiated through identifier $e.owned = \mathbf{H}$ and $e.owned = \mathbf{L}$, denoting e is occupied by a confidential or non-confidential process. An attacker use a series of memory accesses without cache collision to fill part of the cache. The specification of manipulated cache below indicates that the attacker's accesses to each memory address in the m_s will result in a cache hit. Thereafter, the victim's access to these manipulated cache areas will change their ownership, resulting in observation to the attacker if re-accessing this memory space.

Definition 10 (The Attack-simulated Cache Layout).

$$m\_s :: \ \text{``mem\_req set''} \ and \ it \ satisfies :$$
$$\forall m \in m\_s. \ (m.process = L) \wedge (\exists!e \in Cache \ ! \ (Mapping \rightharpoonup m.setbits).$$
$$e.ca\_tag = m.tagbits \wedge e.owned = L)$$

As for the replacement policy in a cache set, we follow the practice in [18] where they consider the age replacement (e.g., LRU replacement or FIFO replacement) and stipulate that the adversary re-accesses a cache set in a reversed order. In such a way, the victim evicts the oldest cache line at the adversary's waiting state, shown in the middle picture of Fig. 1. If the adversary probes the cache set in his original order, then the second-oldest (same for the followings) cache line is evicted, leading to a miss on every probe. In contrast, if the attacker probes the cache set in a reversed order, the cache line evicted by the victim can be precisely probed without causing a miss on every probe. We leave the random replacement policy as future work.

With all the preparations above, we turn to the security verification of RP cache read operation. It breaks the first unwinding condition but preserves the second one, which means it produces constant observations to the attacker regardless of the victim's input. We prove the theorem of RP cache read as follows.

Theorem 4 (RP Cache Read Produces Constant Observation).

$$\forall x \in \mathcal{X}.\, Cpt(rp\_read, x)/s = \{y.\, \exists o \in \{0\,..\,M-1\}.\, y = (o, \frac{1}{M})\} \wedge$$

$$(\forall y \in Cpt(rp\_read, x)/s.\, y.p = \sum_{d \in \mathcal{J}_{sub}} d.p)$$

$$where\ \mathcal{J}_{sub} = \{j.\, j \in makeJoint.\, j.o = y.o\}$$

Proof. With the attack specification, any input that causes an external or internal cache miss requires the RP cache to select one cache line according to replacement policy from each set for replacement or eviction. Therefore, the range of the observation is the whole cache set index under the extreme circumstance, where the attacker can control the whole cache. This is shown in the first line of the above theorem. Meanwhile, the probability of each cache set index equals $\frac{1}{M}$, where M is the length of the whole cache index. When applying this knowledge to the reasoning framework, we can prove that the RP cache read operation satisfies the second unwinding condition. The observation range narrows under the non-extreme circumstance, while all the observations have a uniform probability. Therefore, there is no information leakage through this process.

6   Security Verification Results and Analysis

We successfully verify eight state-of-the-art cache designs. We implement all the verification work in Isabelle/HOL[2]. Table 1 shows the verification results, as well as the implementation complexity (lines of codes) for each cache. We give the security analysis of eight state-of-the-art cache designs as follows.

Table 1. Verification results of cache designs.

Cache design	No-observation	Constant-observation	Leakage	LOC
Set-Associative Cache	×	×	yes	490+
Random Fill Cache	×	×	yes	930+
Partition Locked Cache	√	○	no	380+
Random Permutation Cache	×	√	no	1490+
NewCache	×	√	no	1260+
CEASE Cache	×	×	yes	510+
CEASER Cache	×	×	yes	580+
SCATTER Cache	×	×	yes	500+

---

[2] Interested readers can refer here for the reasoning framework and verification cases.

Set-Associative (SA) Cache. This conventional cache is well known to be vulnerable to side-channel attacks. Among the cache regions controlled by the attacker, any memory request from the victim can cause an observation with a conditional probability of 1 due to the deterministic execution. Therefore, the cache operation breaks the first condition. Also, a program owns multiple memory address mapped to different cache sets, resulting in different observations. Then, there exists a marginal output that is not equal to the conditional probability of 1, breaking the second condition. Hence, SA cache leaks side-channel information.

Random Fill (RF) Cache [17]. RF cache fills the cache line to be replaced with a random memory line from a neighborhood window of the request memory line. It can result in observations to the attacker, breaking the first condition. Although it randomly picks up a memory line among a stated window, it cannot promise to produce the same range of observations and of equal probability. In extreme cases, RF cache can degrade to a SA cache if the neighborhood window is small, making each memory line mapped to the same cache set. This property cannot imply the second condition. Therefore, there exists information leakage.

Partition Locked (PL) Cache [31]. PL cache with prefetching strategy adds a lock mechanism to the cache line. A replacement policy will work only when the cache line chosen to be replaced is unlocked or belongs to the same process. Therefore, an attacker has no chance to obtain any observations. This cache design is the only one that satisfies the first unwinding condition.

Random Permutation (RP) Cache [31]. Any memory request that causes an external or internal cache miss requires the RP cache to select one cache line from each set for replacement or eviction. Therefore, the range of the observation is the whole cache set index under the extreme circumstance, where the attacker can control the whole cache. Meanwhile, the probability of each cache set index equals $\frac{1}{M}$, where M is the length of the whole cache index. We can prove that the RP cache operation satisfies the second unwinding condition. The observation range narrows under the non-extreme circumstance, while all the observations have a uniform probability. Therefore, there is no information leakage through this progress.

NewCache [32]. For the protected memory requests, NewCache employs similar strategies as the RP cache. Therefore, it responses to an external or internal cache access by selecting one cache line from each cache set to replace the memory block or to cause an eviction deliberately. Applying similar verification proves the security of NewCache against side-channel attacks.

CEASE Cache [24]. The CEASE cache employs encryption over the physical address and uses the ciphertext to index the cache. However, the memory to cache-set mapping remains constant as long as the encryption key remains the same. Unfortunately, it degenerates to a set-associative cache, which means an adversary can observe a deterministic change for each cache miss. As a result, the CEASE cache may leak confidential information.

CEASER Cache [24]. CEASER cache is an advanced version of CEASE, which adopts dynamic remapping to periodically change the key and remap the lines based on the new key. In the phase when both the current and next keys exist, previous remapping and the victim's access can provide useful observations to the attacker. Therefore, it breaks the first unwinding condition. Although part of the observations is created by remapping of cache lines, the attacker can obtain a deterministic observation during each epoch, and thus there exists such a marginal output that is not equal to its corresponding conditional probability. Therefore, it can not satisfy the second unwinding condition, and information leakage exits.

SCATTER Cache [33]. The SCATTER cache employs the index derivation function that takes the secure domain identifier, the encryption key, and the memory request as inputs to form a nominal cache set (the cache line of each cache way comes from different cache sets). The mapping table is deterministic to a process as long as the encryption key is constant. Another characteristic is that the conditional probability of each output is uniform, while the ranges of these outputs are inconsistent. Therefore, it can not satisfy the second unwinding condition, leaving a trail of telltale information.

7   Conclusions and Future Work

In this paper, we propose a novel verification methodology to verify side-channel vulnerabilities resident in the cache designs. We construct an entropy-based non-interference reasoning framework with two unwinding conditions for the evaluation of side-channel threats. We use our methodology to successfully assess and evaluate the security of eight state-of-the-art cache solutions. The verification practice indicates that our verification framework offers strong accuracy and persuasion for the verification of cache side channels.

Although our methodology provides a strong guarantee for the security verification of cache designs from the perspective of formal methods, it still has drawbacks. Our reasoning framework asks a high-level requirement of professionalism of theory proving on users and cannot offer an automated derivation process. Therefore, in future work, we plan to automate the validation process and provide more refined cache models.

Acknowledgements. This work has been supported in part by Singapore National Research Foundation under its National Cybersecurity R&D Programme (NCR Award NRF2018 NCR-NCR009-0001), Singapore Ministry of Education (MOE) AcRF Tier 1 RS02/19, NTU Start-up grant, and the National Natural Science Foundation of China (NSFC) under the Grant No. 62132014 and by Key R&D Program of Zhejiang Province under the Grant No. 62132014.

References

1. Aranha, D.F., Novaes, F.R., Takahashi, A., Tibouchi, M., Yarom, Y.: LadderLeak: breaking ECDSA with less than one bit of nonce leakage. In: Proceedings of the 2020 ACM SIGSAC Conference on Computer and Communications Security, pp. 225–242 (2020)
2. Bernstein, D.J.: Cache-timing attacks on AES (2005)
3. Canella, C., et al.: Fallout: leaking data on meltdown-resistant CPUs. In: Proceedings of the 2019 ACM SIGSAC Conference on Computer and Communications Security, pp. 769–784 (2019)
4. Chatzikokolakis, K., Chothia, T., Guha, A.: Statistical measurement of information leakage. In: Esparza, J., Majumdar, R. (eds.) TACAS 2010. LNCS, vol. 6015, pp. 390–404. Springer, Heidelberg (2010). https://doi.org/10.1007/978-3-642-12002-2_33
5. Cover, T.M.: Elements of Information Theory. Wiley, Hoboken (1999)
6. Deng, S., et al.: SecChisel framework for security verification of secure processor architectures. In: Proceedings of the 8th International Workshop on Hardware and Architectural Support for Security and Privacy, pp. 1–8 (2019)
7. Deng, S., Xiong, W., Szefer, J.: Cache timing side-channel vulnerability checking with computation tree logic. In: Proceedings of the 7th International Workshop on Hardware and Architectural Support for Security and Privacy, pp. 1–8 (2018)
8. Deng, S., Xiong, W., Szefer, J.: Analysis of secure caches using a three-step model for timing-based attacks. J. Hardware Syst. Secur. 3(4), 397–425 (2019)
9. Goguen, J.A., Meseguer, J.: Security policies and security models. In: 1982 IEEE Symposium on Security and Privacy, pp. 11–11. IEEE (1982)
10. Gras, B., Razavi, K., Bos, H., Giuffrida, C.: Translation leak-aside buffer: defeating cache side-channel protections with TLB attacks. In: 27th USENIX Security Symposium (USENIX Security 2018), pp. 955–972 (2018)
11. Groot Bruinderink, L., Hülsing, A., Lange, T., Yarom, Y.: Flush, gauss, and reload – a cache attack on the BLISS lattice-based signature scheme. In: Gierlichs, B., Poschmann, A.Y. (eds.) CHES 2016. LNCS, vol. 9813, pp. 323–345. Springer, Heidelberg (2016). https://doi.org/10.1007/978-3-662-53140-2_16
12. Gruss, D., Maurice, C., Wagner, K., Mangard, S.: Flush+Flush: a fast and stealthy cache attack. In: Caballero, J., Zurutuza, U., Rodríguez, R.J. (eds.) DIMVA 2016. LNCS, vol. 9721, pp. 279–299. Springer, Cham (2016). https://doi.org/10.1007/978-3-319-40667-1_14
13. He, Z., Lee, R.B.: How secure is your cache against side-channel attacks? In: Proceedings of the 50th Annual IEEE/ACM International Symposium on Microarchitecture, pp. 341–353 (2017)
14. Hund, R., Willems, C., Holz, T.: Practical timing side channel attacks against kernel space ASLR. In: 2013 IEEE Symposium on Security and Privacy, pp. 191–205. IEEE (2013)
15. Kocher, P.C.: Timing attacks on implementations of Diffie-Hellman, RSA, DSS, and other systems. In: Koblitz, N. (ed.) CRYPTO 1996. LNCS, vol. 1109, pp. 104–113. Springer, Heidelberg (1996). https://doi.org/10.1007/3-540-68697-5_9
16. Li, X., et al.: Sapper: a language for hardware-level security policy enforcement. In: Proceedings of the 19th International Conference on Architectural Support for Programming Languages and Operating Systems, pp. 97–112 (2014)
17. Liu, F., Lee, R.B.: Random fill cache architecture. In: 2014 47th Annual IEEE/ACM International Symposium on Microarchitecture, pp. 203–215. IEEE (2014)

18. Liu, F., Yarom, Y., Ge, Q., Heiser, G., Lee, R.B.: Last-level cache side-channel attacks are practical. In: 2015 IEEE Symposium on Security and Privacy, pp. 605–622. IEEE (2015)

19. Lou, X., Zhang, T., Jiang, J., Zhang, Y.: A survey of microarchitectural side-channel vulnerabilities, attacks, and defenses in cryptography. ACM Comput. Surv. (CSUR) **54**(6), 1–37 (2021)

20. Nipkow, T., Paulson, L.C., Wenzel, M.: Isabelle/HOL: A Proof Assistant for Higher-Order Logic. Springer, Heidelberg (2002). https://doi.org/10.1007/3-540-45949-9

21. Osvik, D.A., Shamir, A., Tromer, E.: Cache attacks and countermeasures: the case of AES. In: Pointcheval, D. (ed.) CT-RSA 2006. LNCS, vol. 3860, pp. 1–20. Springer, Heidelberg (2006). https://doi.org/10.1007/11605805_1

22. Page, D.: Theoretical use of cache memory as a cryptanalytic side-channel. Cryptology ePrint Archive (2002)

23. Percival, C.: Cache missing for fun and profit (2005)

24. Qureshi, M.K.: CEASER: mitigating conflict-based cache attacks via encrypted-address and remapping. In: 2018 51st Annual IEEE/ACM International Symposium on Microarchitecture (MICRO), pp. 775–787. IEEE (2018)

25. Ryan, K.: Return of the hidden number problem. IACR Trans. Cryptogr. Hardware Embed. Syst. 146–168 (2019)

26. Shusterman, A., et al.: Robust website fingerprinting through the cache occupancy channel. In: 28th USENIX Security Symposium (USENIX Security 2019), pp. 639–656 (2019)

27. Tsunoo, Y., Saito, T., Suzaki, T., Shigeri, M., Miyauchi, H.: Cryptanalysis of DES implemented on computers with cache. In: Walter, C.D., Koç, Ç.K., Paar, C. (eds.) CHES 2003. LNCS, vol. 2779, pp. 62–76. Springer, Heidelberg (2003). https://doi.org/10.1007/978-3-540-45238-6_6

28. Vila, P., Köpf, B., Morales, J.F.: Theory and practice of finding eviction sets. In: 2019 IEEE Symposium on Security and Privacy (SP), pp. 39–54. IEEE (2019)

29. Wang, D., et al.: Unveiling your keystrokes: a cache-based side-channel attack on graphics libraries. In: NDSS (2019)

30. Wang, L., Zhu, Z., Wang, Z., Meng, D.: Analyzing the security of the cache side channel defences with attack graphs. In: 2020 25th Asia and South Pacific Design Automation Conference (ASP-DAC), pp. 50–55. IEEE (2020)

31. Wang, Z., Lee, R.B.: New cache designs for thwarting software cache-based side channel attacks. In: Proceedings of the 34th Annual International Symposium on Computer Architecture, pp. 494–505 (2007)

32. Wang, Z., Lee, R.B.: A novel cache architecture with enhanced performance and security. In: 2008 41st IEEE/ACM International Symposium on Microarchitecture, pp. 83–93. IEEE (2008)

33. Werner, M., Unterluggauer, T., Giner, L., Schwarz, M., Gruss, D., Mangard, S.: {ScatterCache}: thwarting cache attacks via cache set randomization. In: 28th USENIX Security Symposium (USENIX Security 2019), pp. 675–692 (2019)

34. Yarom, Y., Benger, N.: Recovering OpenSSL ECDSA Nonces using the FLUSH+RELOAD cache side-channel attack. Cryptology ePrint Archive (2014)

35. Yarom, Y., Falkner, K.: FLUSH+ RELOAD: a high resolution, low noise, L3 cache side-channel attack. In: 23rd {USENIX} Security Symposium ({USENIX} Security 2014), pp. 719–732 (2014)

36. Zhang, D., Wang, Y., Suh, G.E., Myers, A.C.: A hardware design language for timing-sensitive information-flow security. ACM SIGPLAN Notices **50**(4), 503–516 (2015)

37. Zhang, T., Lee, R.B.: New models of cache architectures characterizing information leakage from cache side channels. In: Proceedings of the 30th Annual Computer Security Applications Conference, pp. 96–105 (2014)
38. Zhang, Y., Juels, A., Reiter, M.K., Ristenpart, T.: Cross-VM side channels and their use to extract private keys. In: Proceedings of the 2012 ACM Conference on Computer and Communications Security, pp. 305–316 (2012)

Refined Modularization for Bounded Model Checking Through Precondition Generation

Marko Kleine Büning[(⊠)], Johannes Meuer, and Carsten Sinz

Karlsruhe Institute of Technology (KIT), Karlsruhe, Germany
johannes.meuer@student.kit.edu,
{marko.kleinebuening,carsten.sinz}@kit.edu

Abstract. Modularization is a widespread approach to tackle software complexity, not only in development but also in verification. Most approaches are either based on manual specifications, which are labor-intensive for large-scale projects, or on program abstractions that have the potential to create false positives. In this paper, we propose an approach for modular bounded model checking extended by refined modularization based on program abstractions and learning of preconditions. Modules, which consist of subsets of a program's functions, are extended by including increasingly larger calling contexts. Potentially under-approximated preconditions are generated by enumerating relevant information from bounded model checking generated counterexamples, including memory assignments. These preconditions are then extended through a tree-based learning approach that generalizes the generated data-points. Through substitution of function calls, preconditions are iteratively pushed through the program to eliminate potential false positives. We evaluate our approach on three real-world software projects demonstrating a significant increase in precision.

1 Introduction

The formal verification of real-world applications is an ongoing challenge and while Bounded Model Checking (BMC) is a powerful technique to verify software, it can not naively be applied to larger systems. Encoding a complete program often produces a formula that is too large to be solved or even read-in by current solvers. Even minimizing the problem by unrolling and inlining loops and functions only once does not counterbalance the mere size of current real-world programs. Thus, the complexity of bounded model checking necessitates modularization and approximations. Design by contract [17] systematically requires users to provide preconditions, postconditions, and (loop) invariants. Through these specifications, programs can be modularized and verified in a divide and conquer style. Often, the generation of precise specifications is the main challenge. Manual specifications, as for example used in [21], are not practical when verifying large projects. Fully automatic modularization as presented in [12] utilize structural abstractions of program behavior and through

© Springer Nature Switzerland AG 2022
A. Riesco and M. Zhang (Eds.): ICFEM 2022, LNCS 13478, pp. 209–226, 2022.
https://doi.org/10.1007/978-3-031-17244-1_13

over-approximations can divide the program with quite general module specifications. This leads to a fast and modular analysis but is prone to false positives (error messages where there are no errors).

In this paper, we present an approach that refines structural abstractions for C-programs. We incrementally increase the size of modules to exhaust the limits of bounded model checkers. Furthermore, we refine abstractions through automatically generated preconditions. Based on an enhanced output of the bounded model checking approach, we generate enumerative preconditions that represent erroneous input (including memory) for the entry function of a module. These possibly under-approximated preconditions are then generalized by a tree-based learning approach. By substitution of function calls with preconditions, the approach can refine the verification task and thus minimize false positives. The approaches are implemented and evaluated on real-world software projects, including SQLite with nearly half a million lines of code. The generated preconditions are human-readable and can thus be examined and adjusted.

2 Preliminaries

We consider programs in a procedural programming language, i.e. the program consists (mainly) of a set of functions, and functions may call each other. To automatically check for errors, we assume that program statements (instructions) may be annotated with correctness conditions, which we will also call assertions or *checks*. Thus, more formally, we can write $P = \{F_1, \ldots, F_n\}$ for a program P consisting of functions F_i. The set of checks C in a program P can be partitioned according to the functions F_i. We write $C(F)$ to denote the checks annotated to instructions in function F. Thus $C = \dot{\bigcup}_{F \in P} C(F)$.

In order to check the properties of a program modularly, we will, on one hand, partition the set of checks C. On the other hand, we try to prove checks not on the complete program P, but only on a fraction $M \subseteq P$ of it. By ensuring that the fractions correspond to over-approximations of the program behavior, we can guarantee that a "no error" answer on a fraction also holds wrt. the complete program. The converse does not hold, however, such that in case of an "error" answer a refinement step is needed. We will also say *modules* instead of program fractions and denote the functions and checks of a module M by $F(M)$ and $C(M)$, respectively. Typically, we use as checks C in a module M either (a) all checks occurring in M, i.e., $C = \dot{\bigcup}_{F \in M} C(F)$; (b) exactly those checks of one particular function $F^* \in M$, i.e. $C = C(F^*)$, or (c) exactly one check c, i.e. $C = \{c\}$. The functions of a module should not be arbitrarily selected, as that would make it hard to guarantee the over-approximation property. We, therefore, make use of the call graph to specify closure-properties of a module. Consider the function call relation $\to_P$ of a program P. (We might drop the index P if it is clear from the context.) $F \to G$ indicates that there is a call from function F to function G (in program P). By $\to^+$, $\to^*$ and $\leftrightarrow$ we denote the transitive, reflexive-transitive and symmetric closure of $\to$, respectively. For a module M, we now demand that (a) if $F_1, F_2 \in M, G \in P$ and $F_1 \to^* G \to^* F_2$ then $G \in M$;

and (b) that the vertex-induced subgraph of a module M is weakly connected, i.e. $F_1 \leftrightarrow^* F_2$ for all $F_1, F_2 \in M$. Moreover, we call a module M *callee-closed* if all call instructions in M invoke functions that are already part of M, i.e. if $F \in M$ and $F \to G$, then $G \in M$. We call a module *caller-closed* if all calling functions of a module's function are already included in the module, i.e., if $G \in M$ and $F \to G$, then $F \in M$. We assume that each module possesses a unique function F_e, the *entry point function*, which has no callers in the module. In this paper, we will mainly deal with callee-closed modules. These form over-approximations of the program behavior, as they are contiguous fractions of programs, where simply the calling context of the entry point function F_e is dropped.

Modular Bounded Model Checking. Bounded model checking (BMC) is a common technique for formal verification of software, with a number of different tools implementing and optimizing the BMC approach, e.g., CBMC [14], ESBMC [19], LLBMC [16], or SeaHorn [10]. Given a callee-closed module $M \subseteq P$ with an entry point function F_e and a set of properties $C \subseteq C(M)$ to be checked, bounded model checking unrolls loops and inlines function calls into F_e up to a bound b. The transformed program is, together with the negation of desired properties (checks), encoded into an SMT formula,

$$\text{BMC}(F_e, P, C, b) = \text{Encode}(F_e, P, b) \wedge \neg \bigwedge_{c \in C} \text{Encode}(c) , \tag{1}$$

and solved. If the solver returns UNSAT (or false) the properties hold and if the solver returns SAT (or true) at least one property is violated. Several tools like LLBMC and SeaHorn utilize the LLVM Framework [15] as an intermediate representation of source code to simplify compilation and encoding. Compared to approaches that (over-)approximate value ranges like abstract interpretation, bounded model checking has the capability to extract exact error traces.

Modularization. To handle the increasing size of the software to be verified and the scalability issue of the BMC approach, we apply a fully automatic modularization approach as introduced in [12]. Through abstractions of function environments and function calls, modules of arbitrary size can be created. In this work, we will concentrate on function environment abstractions that will be refined by preconditions (callee-closed modules), while we leave the abstraction of function calls out of scope of this paper. For a module M, we will consider as checks C for this module exactly those occurring in the module's entry function F_e, i.e. $C = C(F_e)$. A *modularization* $\mathcal{M}$ of a program P is a set of modules, such that all checks of the program are covered by a module. Of course, there are many ways how to achieve this. The method we chose works by constructing, for each function F in a program P, a callee-closed module with F_e as its entry point function and set of checks set to $C(F_e)$. An example of such a modularization is shown in Fig. 1. Here, P consists of four functions, say, F, G, H_1, H_2, from top to bottom. The four callee-closed modules are then: $M_1 = \{H_1\}, M_2 = \{H_2\}, M_3 = \{G, H_1, H_2\}$ and $M_4 = \{F, G, H_1, H_2\}$, and the modularization $\mathcal{M} = \{M_1, \ldots, M_4\}$.

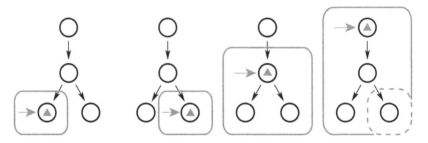

Fig. 1. Modularization into four independent modules (boxes) based on abstraction of call environment. The entry point(arrow) for every module is the function containing the checks (triangle). Through the abstraction of the call environment no prior functions have to be included into modules.

3   Bird's Eye View of the Method

```
void bot(int x, int y){          void mid1(int x, int y){
    if(y >= 0 && y < 100){           if(x > 0){
        // assert(x < 2147483646);       x = x - 1;
        x = x + 2;  }                    bot(x,y);}
}                                }


void mid2(int x, int y){         void top(int x, int y){
    if(y > 100){                     if(x > 0){
        bot(x,y);  }                     x = x - 1;
}                                        mid1(x,y);
                                         mid2(x,y);  }
                                 }
```

Fig. 2. Example for bird's eye view of the method.

We present an overview of the method on a simple example given in Fig. 2. Function top calls functions mid1 and mid2, which in turn call function bot. Modularization, as presented above, will produce four modules $M_1 = \{\text{bot}\}$, with checks $C(\text{bot})$, $M_2 = \{\text{mid1}, \text{bot}\}$, with $C(\text{mid1})$, $M_3 = \{\text{mid2}, \text{bot}\}$, with $C(\text{mid2})$ and $M_4 = \{\text{top}, \text{mid1}, \text{mid2}, \text{bot}\}$, with $C(\text{top})$. Our goal is to verify that the addition $x = x + 2$ in function bot does not overflow (assuming 32-bit integers). In our modular approach, we start by verifying M_1. The bounded model checker returns unsafe, because both x and y are unrestricted inputs assumed to take arbitrary values.

By **inclusion of callers**, we can refine these arbitrary values by taking the calling functions of bot into account. Our approach creates new modules $M_1^{mid1} = \{\text{mid1}, \text{bot}\}$ and $M_1^{mid2} = \{\text{mid2}, \text{bot}\}$, checking $C(\text{bot})$ with entry point functions mid1 and mid2, respectively. The bounded model checker recognizes that M_1^{mid2} is safe, because of the restriction on y, but M_1^{mid1} is still unsafe. Thus, a third new module is created $M_1^{top} = \{\text{top}, \text{mid1}, \text{mid2}, \text{bot}\}$, checking $C(\mathtt{bot})$ with entry function $\mathtt{top}$. Note that $\mathtt{mid1}$ has to be included, for M_1^{top} to be verifiable. The bounded model checker can prove the safety of the arithmetic operation in $\mathtt{bot}$ but had to include all functions of P in module M_1^{top}. It is more efficient and more scalable to not include functions but preconditions representing the input space for which the check is $\mathtt{unsafe}$ to the module.

Enumerative Preconditions are based on the counterexamples generated by the bounded model checker. For function $\mathtt{bot}$, the approach would generate data points like $(x = 2147483647 \wedge y = 1)$. In a refinement step, this input assignment is negated and added as an assumption to the SMT formulae that is rechecked through incremental SMT-solving. Such, the algorithm can enumerate all input assignments leading to an error. In our example, 200 (2 values for x times 100 values for y) data points would be generated, which combined represent the enumerative precondition. While enumerating 200 input assignments takes under a second for such a small example, it is often not feasible for larger modules with more parameters. Therefore, we enumerate a smaller amount of assignments producing a possibly under-approximated precondition.

Learned Preconditions generalize the under-approximated precondition. In addition to the enumerated error data points, we generate inputs that are guaranteed to be safe by negating all assumptions and assertions in the program to be checked by the bounded model checker. Then, through a featurizer and synthesizer based on the ID3-algorithm [24], we iteratively generalize the data points leading to a complete (or over-approximated) precondition. For our example, the learning process produces the complete precondition $((x \neq 2147483647 \wedge x \neq 2147483646) \vee y > 99 \vee y < 0)$.

Through **substitution** of function calls of $\mathtt{bot}$ with the generated precondition, we can refine the verification without enlarging the module size. The algorithm including callers is reused, but this time with function bodies substituted by preconditions. Therefore, $M_1^{mid1} = \{\mathtt{mid1}, pre(\mathtt{bot})\}$ and $M_1^{mid2} = \{\mathtt{mid2}, pre(\mathtt{bot})\}$, checking $C(\mathtt{bot})$ are not containing the function $\mathtt{bot}$ but the much smaller representation of erroneous inputs. While M_1^{mid2} would again be verified as safe, the approach would generate a new precondition for M_1^{mid1} because of the new restriction on x. This precondition is then substituted in function $\mathtt{top}$ leading to $M_1^{top} = \{\mathtt{top}, pre(\mathtt{mid1})\}$. For the final verification of $C(\mathtt{bot})$, the function call of $\mathtt{mid2}$ can be ignored, because it was already classified as $\mathtt{safe}$ and has no relevant return value or memory writes influencing the function call of $\mathtt{mid1}$. The overall process of our approach with its three refinement steps is depicted in Fig. 3.

4 Module Extension by Caller Inclusion

We define a verification task as a triple $vt = (f_e, m, r)$, f_e being the unique entry point function, m being the module containing the properties to be checked and r representing the verification result, with $r \in \{\mathtt{safe}, \mathtt{cond.safe}, \mathtt{cond.unsafe}, \mathtt{unsafe}, \mathtt{unknown}\}$. Potential false positives are summarized as $\mathtt{cond.unsafe}$,

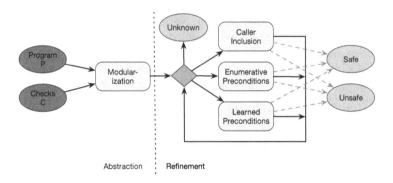

Fig. 3. Overall approach, starting with an abstracting modularization step, followed by several heuristically chosen refinement steps.

they are mostly generated by over-approximations of program behavior, e.g., by abstracting the call environment. Results that so far have been shown to be safe, but are potentially false negatives, are considered `cond.safe`; they are often produced by under-approximations like the loop-bound restriction of BMC.

For simplicity of exposition, we from now on assume that every module contains exactly one check to be analyzed. Conceptually, if there are several checks in one function, we can create copies of the module with separate checks. As the starting point of our verification, we assume a set of callee-closed modules and a modularization as shown in the example in Fig. 1. We generate a set of verification tasks, $VT = \{vt_1, ..., vt_m\}$, one for each module, where the result is set to `unknown`. We then run our BMC on each verification task, updating the results. Those tasks resulting in `safe` or `unsafe` are completed and need not be considered further. For the remaining tasks VT' (with results `unknown`, `cond.safe` and `cond.unsafe`) a refinement step is needed. In both cases we refine the abstraction introduced by modularization and add callers of the respective module's entry point function. Note that for `cond.safe` results we could also choose to increase the loop bound, but extending the call environment is also a viable alternative, as it often introduces additional constraints to derive smaller loop bounds. Thus, for such $vt_i = (f_e, m, \texttt{cond.unsafe})$, we include functions that are calling f_e, denoting the set by $Callers(f_e) = \{f_1, ..., f_n\}$. In order to maintain the single-entry-point property of a module, we then define a set of n new refined verification tasks, taking each caller of f_e in turn into account. To ensure that the module is $callee-closed$, all called functions of the caller f_i are added to the module. For these new verification tasks we have $m_i = \{m \cup \{f_i\} \cup callees(f_i)\}$, the entry point function is unchanged.

After verification of the n extended modules (for each vt_i) by the BMC, these n results, say r_j for $1 \leq j \leq n$, have to be summarized. If there is one $r_j = \texttt{unsafe}$, the property is violated and the overall check is `unsafe`. Otherwise, as long as there is a sub-result marked as abstracted (`cond.*`), we again search for all callers and reiterate the process until (1) there is a `unsafe` result, (2) all results are **safe** or (3) the limitations of the underlying BMC is reached and the verification runs into a time- or memory-out and returns **unknown**.

5 Refined Modularization Through Preconditions

Through preconditions, we are able to include callers of entry-point functions in our analysis without steadily increasing the size of modules. After creation of a precondition that represents the input space at f_e leading to an error, we can substitute function calls of f_e with such precondition. Encoding the precondition simplifies the problem, because it represents only constraints over input parameters in reference to a specific check, instead of the whole function. We present a novel approach that first creates enumerative (sometimes under-approximated) preconditions based on failed proof attempts (counterexamples). Afterward, we employ a tree-based learning approach to generalize the precondition to a complete (or over-approximated) precondition based on the enumerated data points.

5.1 Generation of Enumerative Preconditions Based on BMC

We introduce our approach of generating enumerative preconditions by example:

Example 1 (Example 1). The module contains a single function **example1**. The input space is defined as $I = \{x, y, *c, *g\}$.

```
char *g = nondet_ptr();
void example1(int x, char y, char *c) {
    if(c[1] == 'z' && *g == 'a')
        x = x + 2; } // possible arithmetic overflow
```

If the **if**-statement is **true**, the addition $x = x + 2$ leads to an undefined overflow for **INT_MAX** and **INT_MAX**-1. Verifying **example1** results in a task vt with $vt.r =$ **cond.unsafe**, so, for refinement, we generate counterexamples, in turn on the SMT, LLVM IR, and, finally, the C-code level. Both during encoding and solving of the formulae the underlying BMC-approaches optimize and eliminate variables. We have to track these optimizations but can also benefit from them. If an input parameter is not part of the formula or the SAT-model, it is not relevant to the erroneous execution and can thus be removed from the input space. In our example, variable y would be eliminated. We obtain a counterexample consisting of two functions $A : (Var \rightarrow Val)$ returning a value (either constant or pointer) for each program variable and $Mem : (Loc \rightarrow Val)$ returning the value saved at a given address location in memory.[1]

Special handling is needed for pointer values during refinement, as we want to exclude values stored in memory rather than particular addresses used for storing them. We thus refine only pointer goals (for primitive, non-pointer values), but not memory addresses.

---

[1] We assume memory accesses occur only to allocated memory.

Excluding Values. For refining the counterexample we gather relevant elements of the input space I_m of module m and its entry-point function f_e, which are: parameters of f_e, global variables and memory locations accessed in m. Excluding the complete counterexample would lead to a massive under-approximation. Finding a minimal conjunction of values to exclude could be computed by following def-use chains backwards from the check's variables, including memory-based dependencies (via LLVM IR's loads and stores), but this would be extremely expensive. We therefore over-approximate the use-def chain leading to under-approximated preconditions. Our approach distinguishes between non-pointer and pointer parameters. For non-pointer parameters, the approach excludes the value assigned by the counterexample, for all parameter but those which have been optimized out by the solver. For pointer parameters, we first list all loaded addresses in m. We minimize this set of loaded locations by including only locations that are loaded prior to the validation check, by excluding reoccurring load instructions and concentrating on the first occurrence of a memory location. For direct loads, like char or integer pointers, we are able to enquire first the address and then the value stored at that address from the module created by the SMT solver. For indirect loads to struct or array members, we check additional parameters like index and type of the pointer, such that we are able to exclude values for struct and array members instead of the address of the overall struct.

Given the set of relevant elements, we divide them into non-pointer (denoted by $e^n \in I_m^n$) and pointer (denoted by $e^p \in I_m^p$). Due to single error points given by the counterexample, we only use the $=$ or $\neq$ relations in our preconditions. Given functions A and Mem, we generate the following precondition:

$$pre(I_m) = \neg \left(\bigwedge_{e_n \in I_m^n} e^n = A(e^n) \wedge \bigwedge_{e_p \in I_m^p} e^p = A(Mem(e^p)) \right).$$

For our Example 1, the relevant input space is $I_m = \{x, c[1], *g\}$ removing y and handling the array access for $*c$. A preliminary precondition would then be:

$$pre(I_m) = \{\neg (x = 2147483647 \wedge *g = \text{'a'} \wedge c[1] = \text{'z'})\}.$$

Enumerative Preconditions. A single bounded model checking run creates a partial precondition (also called single error data point). By adding the partial precondition to the SMT-formula of the module, we can exclude this particular assignment and generate more counterexamples. The effort for re-checking can be minimized by utilizing incremental SAT/SMT-solving. As long as the BMC approach is able to generate more counterexamples, the precondition is not complete, thus we refine the under-approximation of the precondition iteratively until the precondition is complete or a given bound is met. In every iteration, we exclude single values that are guaranteed to generate an error and can thus never over-approximate the precondition.

Definition 1 (Enumerative Precondition). *Given a bound k for the number of iterations, the enumerative precondition is created by:*

$$pre(I_m) = \bigwedge_{i=1}^{k} pre_i(I_m).$$

For our Example 1, the approach generates the following complete precondition after two iterations:

$$pre(I_m) = \{\neg\,(x = 2147483647 \wedge {}^*g = \text{'a'} \wedge c[1] = \text{'z'}) \wedge$$
$$\neg\,(x = 2147483646 \wedge {}^*g = \text{'a'} \wedge c[1] = \text{'z'})\}.$$

Disregarding time and memory limitations, enumerative preconditions guarantee complete preconditions as long as the bound k is chosen big enough. In practice, choosing a large enough k might be prohibitive, especially if the number of variables in I_m is large. Thus the enumerative approach might not be sufficient to generate a complete precondition. Nevertheless, enumerative preconditions can be deployed to find bugs and can give a human user an idea of which inputs lead to an error.

5.2 Learning General Preconditions from Data Points

For some examples, the enumerative approach would need billions of iterations for a complete precondition. Therefore, we implemented a learning approach that can generalize from data points to the relevant input space that has to be excluded. The approach generalizes preconditions by learning from data points generated by both erroneous and error-free verification runs for the module. In our implementation, the preconditions are human-readable and are parsed directly into C-code.

Our technique is based on a white-box teacher black-box learner approach, as for example presented in [9], the main difference being that the teacher will be handled by our static-analysis tool LLBMC. Compared to dynamic testing approaches this brings three advantages: (1) Modules can be verified without needing to be executable. (2) A static-analysis technique like LLBMC typically finds more error points than testing. (3) LLBMC can serve as a data-set generator, reliably providing inputs for both successful and erroneous executions.

From this data set, a `featurizer` extracts features, classifying sets of data-points with characteristics. The `synthesizer` refines these features to a Boolean function, resulting in the minimal number of features that suffice to represent the data set. The result is the precondition that applies to the enumerated data points. This cycle continues, until the bounded model checker is not able to find any erroneous data points, implying completeness, as well as data points resulting in a successful execution, implying maximality.

Enumerating Data Points with BMC. Additionally to the presented approach to generate enumerative preconditions (called negative data points here), the learning approach needs positive data points representing the input space for error-free executions of the module. Otherwise it would over-approximate the precondition such that `assume(false)` would always be a valid option. To generate positive executions, we negate the disjunction of checks and the conjunction of assumptions and cover special cases, where the assertions are in branches. If there exists an assertion in one side of a branch, we have to generate a failed assertion in the other side of that branch. We thereby generate a program execution where the assertion can hold. This assertion is then added to the conjunction of negated assertions. Through this extension, LLBMC is able to generate both positive and negative data points for the learning approach.

Featurizer. The task of the featurizer is the extraction of characteristics from the data-set provided by LLBMC. All features combined should be able to represent the relevant properties for preconditions. The approach of feature extraction is based on the algorithm implemented in the tool PIE by Padhi et al. [22]. Initially the algorithm considers a set of random sample values that are classified as program failures or successes. Then a conflict group is defined as a set of differently classified data-points which can not be distinguished because they are represented by the same valuation of current features. As long as such a conflict group exists, the current features do not sufficiently describe the data-set and a new feature has to be determined and added. Such a feature is determined by iterating over existing features from a predefined *feature pool*. We enhance [22] by dynamically expanding the feature pool on demand. The feature pool is defined as a set containing Boolean combinations of relational formulae. Every atomic formula consists of variables, constants, comparison operands $\{<, >, \leq, \geq, =, \neq\}$ and arithmetic operations $\{+, -, *, \div\}$. The feature pool is initially considered empty. If no conflict resolving feature exists in the current feature pool, it is extended by more complex features, continuing until a conflict resolving feature has been found.

Example 2. We consider function `divide` from `stdlib.h`. Division by zero and division of `INT_MIN` by -1 lead to undefined behavior and are treated as errors.

```
#include <stdlib.h>
div_t divide(int numer,int denom) {
div_t result;
result.quot = numer / denom;
result.rem = numer % denom;
return result;
}
```

The approach generates the feature `denom = 0` in the first iteration. After running the synthesizer and realizing that the feature is not strong enough to generate a fitting precondition, it adds the feature `denom = -1` and then in the third iteration the feature `numer = -2147483648`.

In principle, such featurizers are able to generate preconditions when provided with a complete data set. However, the featurizer alone is much less scalable than an approach in which the precondition generation is extended by a

Boolean learning processes, the synthesizer. The featurizer is restricted by a given parameter limiting the size of regarded conflict groups.

Synthesizer. After resolving all conflicts from the data-set, the selected features suffice to separate the data-set into correct classes. But the feature set is not necessarily minimal. Imagine the featurizer learned the features $x < 5$ and the redundant $x < 6$. We use the synthesizer to create a decision tree on the features in order to represent their structure and relations. As many previous precondition learning techniques [1,25] did, we apply the ID3-classification algorithm [24] to learn decision trees. The ID3-algorithm is an entropy-based classifier. First, the entropy H of the complete data-set S is calculated. Then, the information gain of each feature regarding the data set is computed in order to determine the feature with the highest information gain. This feature is selected as the root node of the decision tree, and the algorithm is applied recursively, considering only the leftover features and dividing the data-set into two subsets: Subset 1 contains all data-points for which the feature with the highest information gain is true, and Subset 2 all data-points for which this feature is false. The recursion terminates, when the decision tree is able to classify every data-point from the data-set correctly. We can transform this decision tree into a precondition by traversing every path from the root to a leaf. For each path, we build a conjunction of the nodes' features where a feature is negated if its node is left by a *No* edge. The disjunction of all paths leading to a *success* leaf then represents the precondition guaranteeing a successful program execution.

For Example 2, our approach generates the decision tree and the precondition in three iterations as shown in Fig. 4.

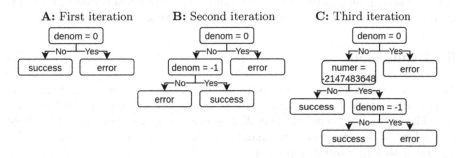

Fig. 4. Decision trees created by the ID3-classification algorithm

$$(\mathtt{denom} \neq 0 \wedge \mathtt{numer} \neq -2147483648) \vee$$
$$(\mathtt{denom} \neq 0 \wedge \mathtt{numer} = -2147483648 \wedge \mathtt{denom} \neq -1)$$

The precondition excludes all divisions by zero as well as integer overflows resulting from dividing INT_MIN with -1.

Such preconditions are inserted directly into C-code via `assume` statements that are placed at the beginning of the regarded function. The precondition can still be incomplete, if the sampling does not represent all relevant inputs. Thus, the precondition is strengthened by another run of the bounded model checker LLBMC generating more data points. Generally, the approach is able to iteratively refine the precondition with new data points until it's complete. If time-limitations are reached without concluding a complete precondition, the algorithm returns the latest over-approximated precondition.

5.3   Subsumption of Preconditions

The enumerative and the generalized preconditions can be applied to refine the modularization without massively increasing the size of verified modules. Similar to the caller inclusion, we extend the module. However, instead of including the original entry-point function f_e, we substitute the function call of f_e with a generated precondition, thereby omitting the encoding of f_e and all successively called functions. The precondition is inserted as an intrinsic function call (similar to inserted checks). The parameters of the function call are equivalently kept as input parameters for the new intrinsic call. If there are multiple function calls of f_e, each call is substituted. If f_e has a return value it is generally ignored and assumed to be an undefined value. This leads to an over-approximation in case the return value influences input parameters of later function calls of f_e and thereby the preconditions. This case only occurs if there are multiple calls of f_e or the function is called inside a loop. In the current implementation such cases are excluded and no precondition substitution takes place. While merging results of different callers, the algorithm tracks if the precondition is under-approximated (enumerative), thus regarding only result transitions to unsafe, over-approximated (over-generalized), regarding only safe checks or complete.

6   Evaluation

To evaluate our refinements, we implemented the caller inclusion and the generation and substitution of enumerative preconditions into the tool `QPR Verify` [13]. The learning approach to generalize preconditions was prototypically implemented in the separate tool `precondition-learner` and could thus not yet be evaluated on larger software projects.[2]

The aim of this evaluation is to demonstrate the advantage of our novel refinement steps compared to the pure modularization presented in Sect. 2 and previously published in [12]. The evaluation results presented in Subsect. 6.1 show a clear reduction of potential false positives compared to the pure modularization. Afterwards, we compare the refined modular bounded model checking approach with the abstract interpretation tool Polyspace [8], which is, together

---

[2] Instructions to replicate the bmi160 results and experiment with `QPR Verify` and the `precondition-learner` in a prepared VM can be found under https://baldur. iti.kit.edu/qpr/QPR_Verify-2021-info.txt.

with Astreé [2], the most applied static analysis tools for software written in
C/C++ for German industry companies. The evaluation results show that our
approach produces more precise verification results due to our abstraction refinement compared to Polyspace. The approaches are evaluated on three software
projects written in C-code. The open-source library BMI160-Driver [3] is a low
power control unit driver designed for mobile applications. It is implemented by
the Robert Bosch GmbH with around 2000 lines of code plus libraries.[3] MNAV
[18] is an open-source control software for fixed-wing aircrafts provided by [11]
and first verified by Gurfinkel et al. in [10], who concentrated on the verification
of buffer overflows and managed a 4% warning rate for 815 buffer overflow checks.
MNAV contains 2190 lines of original source code, including external header files
totaling in 160K LOC [10]. SQLite is a C-language library that implements one
of the most used SQL database engines in the world [26]. It contains around
400K LOC without included libraries.

6.1   Evaluation Results

Table 1 shows the results of running QPR Verify on the three benchmarks with
different solving strategies. The whole-program analysis is denoted as **Global**.
The modularization approach with call environment abstraction is denoted as
Modular. The refinement strategies presented in this paper are marked with the
prefix **Refined** and the addition of **CI(x)** for caller inclusion of depth x, **EP(x)**
for enumerative preconditions with x enumerations of errors. Note that our BMC
approach is able to recognizing if no loop-bound needed to be approximated
during encoding. It can therefore produce safe results for checks.

   In general, one can observe that the refinement strategies lead to longer
runtimes (most right column) but therefore to a reduced number of potential
false positives (cond. unsafe). Furthermore, they can refine loop-bound safe
results and categorize them as safe.

   The BMI160-Driver was verified with a loop-bound of 1. The modular approach takes 798 s and leads to 15% potential false positives. Enumerative preconditions with five data points, reduces the amount of cond. unsafe results
to 9% with a minimal time overhead of around 100 s. Due to the small size
of BMI160, including callers leads to module sizes verifiable by the underlying
bounded model checker. Therefore, the refined verification with including callers
to depth five results in only 1% cond. unsafe checks that would have to be
analyzed by a developer. However, the time usage increases significantly to more
than 4,5 h. Notably, our approach is able to find 40 locations, where functions
can crash due to wrong inputs for the top-level API functions.

   The MNAV benchmark has a main function and is of medium size. Thus a
global analysis is able to verify the program. The autopilot system is nested in
an infinite loop, leading to only loop-bound safe results as a best case. Different verification runs showed minimal differences between loop-bounds between

---

[3] We slightly adapted the source code to overcome current technical limits of our tool,
   e.g. by removing irrelevant function pointers in structs.

Table 1. Results of Global, Modular and Refined verification strategies.

	safe	loop-bound safe	cond. unsafe	unsafe	unknown	Time(sec)
BMI160						
Global	not applicable due to missing main function					
Modular	349 (61%)	140 (24%)	84 (15%)	0 (0%)	1 (0%)	798
Refined-EP(5)	386 (67%)	134 (23%)	49 (9%)	5 (1%)	0 (0%)	899
Refined-CA(5)	497 (87%)	32 (6%)	5 (1%)	40 (7%)	0 (0%)	16,485
MNAV						
Global	0 (0%)	324 (100%)	0 (0%)	0 (0%)	0 (0%)	375
Modular	0 (0%)	230 (71%)	76 (23%)	0 (0%)	28 (9%)	15,484
Refined-EP(5)	0 (0%)	301 (93%)	19 (6%)	0 (0%)	4 (1%)	8,973
Refined-CI(5)	0 (0%)	310 (96%)	14 (4%)	0 (0%)	0 (0%)	56,882
SQLite						
Global	0 (0%)	0 (0%)	0 (0%)	0 (0%)	8,371 (100%)	TO
Modular	698 (8%)	2,095 (25%)	3,138 (37%)	0 (0%)	2,426 (29%)	3,8'893
Refined-EP(5)	1,965 (23%)	791 (9%)	3,135 (37%)	54 (1%)	2,426 (29%)	4,45'147
Refined-CI(1)	698 (8%)	2,096 (25%)	2,769 (33%)	369 (4%)	2,439 (29%)	6,39'563

one and five and Table 1 depicts result for loop-bound one. For smaller programs with a main function, the global approach is best. However, we can utlize this benchmark to analyze the real number of false positives introduced by the modularization of [12] and the reduction through our novel refinement approaches. The modularization introduced 23% false positives, which can be reduced to 6% by enumerative preconditions and to 4% by caller inclusion.

SQLite was verified with a loop-bound of 1 and it is to large to be verifiable or even to encode into a single formulae. The modular approach leads to 37% potential false positives, which our preconditions can not reduce due to a large global memory state that our enumerative preconditions can not grasp without generalization. Applying the learning algorithm to such complex preconditions is part of future work. However, preconditions only describing loop bounds given as parameter lead to a reduction of **loop-bound safe** result from 25% to 9%. Caller inclusion can reduce the amount of false negatives by 4%, which is an improvement but still shows the limitations of increased module size and module splitting. Especially, the splitting of modules leads to an large overhead in verification time. However, we estimate that a parallel verification of the independent modules would significantly reduce run-time.

6.2   Comparison to Polyspace

We ran Polyspace version 2017b[4] with default configurations on BMI160, MNAV and SQLite. We chose a generic compiler with an i368 processor style and left the precision and verification level at default value 2 for BMI160 and MNAV and value 1 for SQLite. Polyspace first verifies the program by propagating sets

---

[4] Due to licensing, 2017b was the latest available version of Polyspace for evaluation.

represented as static integer domains and in level 2 applies a polyhedron model to refine the verification. The results of running Polyspace on the three benchmarks are displayed in Table 2.

Table 2. Results of verifying benchmarks with Polyspace.

Polyspace	Green	Orange	Red	Grey	Total	Time
BMI160	45 (19%)	142 (61%)	0 (0%)	46 (20%)	233	988 s
MNAV1.5	110 (87%)	12 (9%)	1 (1%)	4 (3%)	123	154 s
SQLite	unsuccessfully aborted after 24 h					

It is difficult to compare different static analysis tools on industrial software, because there is no distinct definition of properties that are verified. There are initiatives working towards exchangeable and comparable static analysis results but they are currently not established in research or most commercial static analysis tools. For our verification, we thus concentrate on percentages of solved properties and of potential false positives (orange checks for Polyspace and cond.unsafe for QPR Verify). Comparing Polyspace results for BMI160 and MNAV1.5, one can see that the percentage of false positives (orange and cond.unsafe checks) are significantly higher for Polyspace then for QPR Verify. Especially, due to our refinement strategies presented in this paper, we are able to reduce the amount of manual labor that comes with false positives. SQLite with around 400 k lines of code is too large to be verified by any standard bounded model checking tool and apparently also to large for Polyspace. We set precision levels to minimal values and started an analysis on the whole program without any user-given timeout. After 24 h Polyspace terminated the analysis, because it was not able to translate the program into its internal intermediate representation. If the translation of the given program into their IR fails, Polyspace assumes that no verification will be possible. Polyspace 2017b has the option to create a modularization of the program. For SQLite this modularization produced a single module containing the whole program. We assume that for a more meaningful partition an expert user would have to give partition specifications. Therefore, Polyspace is not able to produce any verification results for SQLite.

Summary. We verified three different real-world applications with sizes between 2000 and 400 k lines of code plus external libraries and showed the applicability and improvements of our refinement strategies implemented into QPR Verify. The two main improvements of our approach compared to the state-of-the-art are: (1) Reduction of false positives through caller inclusion and automatically generated preconditions and therefore fewer ''orange'' warnings compared to Polyspace. (2) Precondition generation and substitution produces precise results in relatively short time compared to no refinements with call environment abstraction or increased module sizes through caller inclusion.

Overall, our refined modularization advances the state-of-the-art of static analysis for large scale software projects compared both to standard bounded model checking and abstract interpretation approaches like Polyspace.

7   Related Work

Program verification through manual specifications [6,21] is not comparable to our approach due to the significant effort of writing specifications. The two approaches most closely related to our work are automatic precondition interference by Cousot et al. [7] introduced a framework for automatic inference of under-approximated (they call it necessary) preconditions based on abstract interpretation techniques. They argue that developers will object to over-approximated preconditions due to the occurrence of false positives. The tool BLITZ [5] is not openly available for comparison but implements a composition verification approach for a bounded model checking based verification. They create under-approximated preconditions through the extension of information gained by SAT-proofs leading to a property violation. While the bounded model checker can extract and exploit this information, they are not human-readable. Furthermore, they are only applied in the context of bug finding and not whole program verification. We contrary argue that the context of the verification tasks can necessitate stronger preconditions. When verifying safety critical software, it is the aim to guarantee and prove an error free execution. While finding errors is an important step, software is only accepted in safety critical environments when error-free execution is guaranteed.

Over-approximated (or sufficient) preconditions can be generated by different techniques. In [4], Hoare triples are established to produce preconditions for shape analysis. [20] presents modular assertion checking through a mixture of abstract interpretation and weakest precondition calculus and [23] produces over-approximated preconditions for heaps. Generally, such approaches do not substitute functions at their call-sites with generated preconditions and do not consider whole program verification of larger programs. This also applies to learning algorithms presented in tools like PIE [22] and others. Furthermore, such approaches rely on data generated by test-runs, which can never guarantee the completeness of preconditions.

8   Conclusion

We presented a refined modularization approach based on bounded model checking and precondition learning. Given a modularization that divides a program into smaller modules by fully abstracting the call environment of functions containing checks, we refined this abstraction by first extending the module size through caller inclusion before generating preconditions representing input space that leads to erroneous execution of the module. Based on counterexamples from the BMC approach, we generated (under-approximated) enumerative preconditions and then generalized these preconditions utilizing an ID3-based learning approach. The preconditions can be successively pushed through the program leading to a more precise verification. The preconditions are user-readable and can be examined and extended by the user. The evaluation shows the potential to verify large projects and to reduce both false positives and false negatives significantly through caller inclusion and preconditions.

Currently, the refinement leads to significant overhead in verification time which can be minimized through a parallel verification of modules and a database supporting effective handling of thousands of checks. Furthermore, we aim to investigate the impact of precondition simplifications and better integrate the precondition-learner, function-pointer handling and function call abstraction into QPR Verify and our evaluation.

References

1. Astorga, A., Madhusudan, P., Saha, S., Wang, S., Xie, T.: Learning stateful preconditions modulo a test generator. In: Proceedings of the 40th ACM SIGPLAN Conference on Programming Language Design and Implementation, pp. 775–787. ACM (2019)
2. Bertrane, J., et al.: Static analysis and verification of aerospace software by abstract interpretation. In: AIAA Infotech@ Aerospace 2010, p. 3385 (2010)
3. Bosch. Bosch Sensortec Sensor Driver (2020)
4. Calcagno, C., Distefano, D., O'Hearn, P.W., Yang, H.: Footprint analysis: a shape analysis that discovers preconditions. In: Nielson, H.R., Filé, G. (eds.) SAS 2007. LNCS, vol. 4634, pp. 402–418. Springer, Heidelberg (2007). https://doi.org/10.1007/978-3-540-74061-2_25
5. Cho, C. Y., D'Silva, V., Song, D.: Blitz: compositional bounded model checking for real-world programs. In: 2013 28th IEEE/ACM International Conference on Automated Software Engineering (ASE), pp. 136–146. IEEE (2013)
6. Cousot, P., Cousot, R.: Modular static program analysis. In: Horspool, R.N. (ed.) CC 2002. LNCS, vol. 2304, pp. 159–179. Springer, Heidelberg (2002). https://doi.org/10.1007/3-540-45937-5_13
7. Cousot, P., Cousot, R., Logozzo, F.: Contract precondition inference from intermittent assertions on collections. In: VMCAI, pp. 150–168 (2011)
8. Deutsch, A.: Static verification of dynamic properties. In: ACM SIGAda 2003 Conference (2003)
9. Garg, P., Löding, C., Madhusudan, P., Neider, D.: ICE: a robust framework for learning invariants. In: Biere, A., Bloem, R. (eds.) CAV 2014. LNCS, vol. 8559, pp. 69–87. Springer, Cham (2014). https://doi.org/10.1007/978-3-319-08867-9_5
10. Gurfinkel, A., Kahsai, T., Navas, J.A.: SeaHorn: a framework for verifying C programs (competition contribution). In: Baier, C., Tinelli, C. (eds.) TACAS 2015. LNCS, vol. 9035, pp. 447–450. Springer, Heidelberg (2015). https://doi.org/10.1007/978-3-662-46681-0_41
11. Jang, J.S., Liccardo, D.: Automation of small UAVs using a low cost mems sensor and embedded computing platform. In: 2006 IEEE/AIAA 25TH Digital Avionics Systems Conference, pp. 1–9. IEEE (2006)
12. Kleine Büning, M., Sinz, C.: Automatic modularization of large programs for bounded model checking. In: Ait-Ameur, Y., Qin, S. (eds.) ICFEM 2019. LNCS,

vol. 11852, pp. 186–202. Springer, Cham (2019). https://doi.org/10.1007/978-3-030-32409-4_12

13. Kleine Büning, M., Sinz, C., Faragó, D.: QPR verify: a static analysis tool for embedded software based on bounded model checking. In: Christakis, M., Polikarpova, N., Duggirala, P.S., Schrammel, P. (eds.) NSV/VSTTE -2020. LNCS, vol. 12549, pp. 21–32. Springer, Cham (2020). https://doi.org/10.1007/978-3-030-63618-0_2

14. Kroening, D., Tautschnig, M.: CBMC – c bounded model checker. In: Ábrahám, E., Havelund, K. (eds.) TACAS 2014. LNCS, vol. 8413, pp. 389–391. Springer, Heidelberg (2014). https://doi.org/10.1007/978-3-642-54862-8_26

15. Lattner, C., Adve, V.: LLVM: a compilation framework for lifelong program analysis & transformation. In: International Symposium on Code Generation and Optimization, 2004. CGO 2004, pp. 75–86. IEEE (2004)

16. Merz, F., Falke, S., Sinz, C.: Bounded model checking of C and C++ programs using a compiler IR. In: Joshi, R., Müller, P., Podelski, A. (eds.) VSTTE 2012. LNCS, vol. 7152, pp. 146–161. Springer, Heidelberg (2012). https://doi.org/10.1007/978-3-642-27705-4_12

17. Meyer, B.: Applying 'design by contract'. Computer **25**(10), 40–51 (1992)

18. Micro NAV autopilot software. http://sourceforge.net/projects/micronav/. Accessed 14-oct-2021

19. Morse, J., Ramalho, M., Cordeiro, L., Nicole, D., Fischer, B.: ESBMC 1.22. In: Ábrahám, E., Havelund, K. (eds.) TACAS 2014. LNCS, vol. 8413, pp. 405–407. Springer, Heidelberg (2014). https://doi.org/10.1007/978-3-642-54862-8_31

20. Moy, Y.: Sufficient preconditions for modular assertion checking. In: Logozzo, F., Peled, D.A., Zuck, L.D. (eds.) VMCAI 2008. LNCS, vol. 4905, pp. 188–202. Springer, Heidelberg (2008). https://doi.org/10.1007/978-3-540-78163-9_18

21. Müller, P. (ed.): : Modular specification and verification of frame properties. In: Modular Specification and Verification of Object-Oriented Programs. LNCS, vol. 2262, pp. 143–194. Springer, Heidelberg (2002). https://doi.org/10.1007/3-540-45651-1_5

22. Padhi, S., Sharma, R., Millstein, T.: Data-driven precondition inference with learned features. ACM SIGPLAN Notices **51**(6), 42–56 (2016)

23. Podelski, A., Rybalchenko, A., Wies, T.: Heap assumptions on demand. In: Gupta, A., Malik, S. (eds.) CAV 2008. LNCS, vol. 5123, pp. 314–327. Springer, Heidelberg (2008). https://doi.org/10.1007/978-3-540-70545-1_31

24. Quinlan, J.R.: Induction of decision trees. Mach. Learn. **1**(1), 81–106 (1986). https://doi.org/10.1007/BF00116251

25. Sankaranarayanan, S., Chaudhuri, S., Ivančić, F., Gupta, A.: Dynamic inference of likely data preconditions over predicates by tree learning. In: Proceedings of the 2008 International Symposium on Software Testing and Analysis, pp. 295–306. ACM (2008)

26. SQLite. http://sqlite.org. Accessed: 14 oct 2021

TTT/ik: Learning Accurate Mealy Automata Efficiently with an Imprecise Symbol Filter

Paul Kogel$^{(\boxtimes)}$, Verena Klös, and Sabine Glesner

Software and Embedded Systems Engineering, TU Berlin, Berlin, Germany
{p.kogel,verena.kloes,sabine.glesner}@tu-berlin.de

Abstract. Active automata learning algorithms like TTT infer accurate automata models of black-box applications and thereby help developers to understand the behavior of increasingly complex cyber-physical systems. However, learning systems with large input alphabets often takes very long or is not feasible at all. We present *TTT/ik*, an extension of TTT that exploits an *imprecise symbol filter* that uses imprecise prior knowledge of state local alphabets to learn accurate Mealy automata more efficiently. We show across seven realistic case studies that our method almost always dramatically reduces queries and symbols even with imprecise knowledge, while still being accurate, thus, greatly improving runtime in practice.

Keywords: Active automata learning · Symbol filter · Imprecise knowledge

1 Introduction

With the rapidly growing complexity of modern cyber-physical systems (CPS), developers increasingly struggle to understand the behavior of existing software components without accurate and up-to date behavioral models. Such models, however, are often unavailable, as legacy and black-box third-party components rarely provide these, and increasingly shortening release cycles leave developers little time to create and maintain them for new software. Active automata learning algorithms like the highly efficient TTT [7] could fill this gap by inferring an accurate automaton model of the target through input queries, but learning automata for systems with large input alphabets, like CPS, often takes very long or is not feasible at all. Here, *symbol filters* that ignore queries for symbols without effect typically improve learning performance greatly. This is because state local alphabets in CPS are usually significantly smaller than global alphabets. However, information about alphabets of black-box systems is almost always limited before learning, e.g., due to incomplete system traces, or approximate user knowledge. Using a symbol filter based on such imprecise information leads to inaccurate models, and thus, wrong assumptions about the target.

We address this problem by extending the TTT active automata learning algorithm for an *imprecise symbol filter* (ISF) that may falsely accept queries

A. Riesco and M. Zhang (Eds.): ICFEM 2022, LNCS 13478, pp. 227–243, 2022.
https://doi.org/10.1007/978-3-031-17244-1_14

for symbols that have no effect in a state, and falsely reject queries for symbols that do. Our resulting method *TTT/ik* provides the following key advantages. First, and most critically, it always learns accurate models. Second, it reduces queries and the total number of symbols contained in these even with imprecise knowledge, thus, greatly reducing runtime even in applications that were unable to use a symbol filter before. Finally, it is widely applicable, as it is domain independent and integrates ISF implementations that use knowledge from different sources easily, like models generated by AI or *passive* automata learning [13].

We target event-driven systems that can be modelled as deterministic Mealy machine and silently ignore illegal symbols. We use TTT as foundation because it is the state-of-the-art active learning algorithm [3]. We provide three novel extensions. First, we design and integrate a heuristic for *false accept handling* that identifies symbols that were potentially falsely accepted by the ISF to improve efficiency. Second, we create a method for *extended counterexample analysis* that identifies falsely rejected symbols efficiently to resolve model inaccuracies. Finally, we replace the *discriminator search* that TTT uses to optimize performance with our new *opportunistic discriminator search* method that maintains accuracy with falsely rejected symbols and improves performance with correctly rejected ones. We implement our method in *LearnLib* [8] and validate its accuracy and efficiency using seven realistic case studies from different domains.

The rest of this paper is structured as followed. First, we give an overview of related work (Sect. 2) and present our system model (3). In Sect. 4, we summarize background on active automata learning and the TTT algorithm that we extend. Then, we describe our method in detail (5). We follow with our practical evaluation (6), and a conclusion (7) that also looks at future work.

2   Related Work

Knowledge-based *query filters* like the ISF that we introduce and the closely related *mappers* have been used to improve efficiency in active automata learning for some time. The basic idea behind both is to reduce irrelevant queries with an intermediary component between learner and teacher. This component processes queries using expert knowledge so that fewer redundant requests reach the target. Margaria et al. [10] demonstrate an early application of different knowledge-based filters. Later, Aarts and Vaandrager [1] introduce a user-defined symbol filter called *learning purpose* to reduce complexity when learning I/O-automata. Another important example is the *StateLocalInputSUL* component included in the latest release of the automata learning framework *LearnLib* [8] that ignores inputs that are not available in the current target system state. While effective, all these methods lead to incomplete or incorrect models when using incorrect expert knowledge for filtering, unlike our method. Leucker et al. [9] introduce limited support for imprecise knowledge with a learner that supports an *inexperienced teacher*. This teacher may be unable to answer some queries. While their learner infers minimal deterministic automata, the authors assume that the imprecision is inherent to the membership oracle. Hence, their method cannot always infer all aspects of the target system behavior, different to our method.

Mappers [3] perform more complex operations on queries than filters. They translate *abstract* symbols in queries sent by the learner to *concrete* symbols before passing them to the target, and vice-versa. The idea is to define a mapping so that the learner can use a minimal abstract alphabet. Manually defining such mappings, though, is challenging and causes inaccurate models when the mapping is faulty. Howar et al. [5] overcome this challenge through automation. Their seminal *Automated Alphabet Abstraction Refinement* (AAR) method automatically maps concrete symbols with the same effect to a single abstract symbol. Users may provide an initial mapping that is then refined using counterexample analysis. AAR is a key technique for learning systems with large alphabets efficiently [3]. On the downside, defining an initial mapping in the format required by AAR is challenging when having only limited knowledge of the target. Providing a faulty mapping can cause inaccuracies. This is different to our method, where we can provide initial alphabets easily and always learn accurate models regardless of the initially accepted or rejected symbols. AAR has been adapted for state-local alphabets by Isberner et al. [6], but their approach has the same limitations for imprecise knowledge as AAR. Moreover, they use the L^* learning algorithm, which is less efficient than the TTT algorithm that we extend in our method.

3   System Model

Before presenting our method, we introduce our system model and define notation. We target systems that can be modelled as a deterministic state local input Mealy automaton $\mathcal{M} = \langle Q^{\mathcal{M}}, q_0^{\mathcal{M}}, \Sigma^{\mathcal{M}}, \Omega^{\mathcal{M}}, \delta^{\mathcal{M}}, \lambda^{\mathcal{M}} \rangle$ that is defined as follows. $Q^{\mathcal{M}}$ is the state set of $\mathcal{M}$, with $q_0^{\mathcal{M}} \in Q^{\mathcal{M}}$ as initial state. $\Sigma^{\mathcal{M}}$ is its *global alphabet* and $\Omega^{\mathcal{M}}$ contains its output symbols. Both sets are finite. $\delta^{\mathcal{M}} : Q^{\mathcal{M}} \times \Sigma^{\mathcal{M}} \to Q^{\mathcal{M}}$ is the transition function and $\lambda^{\mathcal{M}} : Q^{\mathcal{M}} \times \Sigma^{\mathcal{M}} \to \Omega^{\mathcal{M}}$ the output function. We also define the function $mq_{\mathcal{M}} : \Sigma^{\mathcal{M}^*} \to \Omega^{\mathcal{M}^*}$ that gives the concatenated output when successively inputting $w \in \Sigma^{\mathcal{M}^*}$, starting at $q_0^{\mathcal{M}}$. $mq'_{\mathcal{M}}$, in turn, gives the last symbol given by $mq_{\mathcal{M}}$. In these and the following expressions, we omit the automaton name when clear from context.

We extend this definition with state locality. We define a *state local alphabet* $\Sigma_q^{\mathcal{M}} \subseteq \Sigma^{\mathcal{M}}$ for each $q \in Q^{\mathcal{M}}$. We call symbols $s \in \Sigma^{\mathcal{M}}, \Sigma_q^{\mathcal{M}}$ *legal* in q and symbols only in $\Sigma^{\mathcal{M}}$ but not in $\Sigma_q^{\mathcal{M}}$ *illegal* in q. We extend this notion s.t. transitions using symbols that are legal in its source state are *legal transitions* and transitions using symbols that are illegal there are *illegal transitions*. Not all systems produce an error for illegal symbols. Thus, we model illegal transitions as silent self loops to make our method widely applicable. Like [1], we assume that we can observe silence, e.g., using timeouts. We represent silence by $void \in \Omega^{\mathcal{M}}$. We also allow silent legal transitions. We assume that the state local alphabets of $\mathcal{M}$ are significantly smaller than $\Sigma^{\mathcal{M}}$, to give the ISF sufficient savings potential.

As usual, we use ϵ as the empty word, $\cdot$ as concatenation, and $|w|$ as the length of $w \in \Sigma$. Finally, we define $w[a, b]$ with $1 \le a \le b \le |w|$ as the *subsequence* of w starting at index a and ending at b, both inclusively.

4   Background: Active Automata Learning and TTT

Having presented our system model, we discuss relevant background next. We summarize fundamentals of active automata learning and describe the TTT active automata learning algorithm that we extend to support imprecise symbol filters. We focus on the behavior for Mealy automata and use the automaton from Fig. 1 as running example.

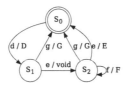

Fig. 1. Example SUL $\mathcal{M}$ (illegal transitions are omitted)

Active automata learning methods attempt to learn an accurate automaton model of a target system (*system under learning, SUL*) through direct interaction with it. Most active automata learning methods, including TTT and the traditional L^* algorithm, implement the *minimally adequate teacher* (MAT) framework to achieve this. There, a *learner* with no access to a SUL $\mathcal{M}$ asks a *teacher* multiple queries [3]. The learner uses the responses to gradually *refine* a *hypothesis automaton* $\mathcal{H}$ until $\mathcal{H} \equiv \mathcal{M}$. We describe this process for TTT below.

MAT-based learners use *access sequences* and *discriminators* to discover and identify states. Assume a Mealy automaton $\mathcal{M}$. An *access sequence* for a state $q \in Q^{\mathcal{M}}$ is an input $w \in \Sigma^*$ that leads from q_0 to q. We write $\mathcal{M}[w] = q$ and $\lfloor q \rfloor_{\mathcal{M}} = w$. In our example, $\lfloor s_1 \rfloor_{\mathcal{M}} = d$. In algorithms like TTT, each state has a unique access sequence. There, $\lfloor w \rfloor_{\mathcal{M}}$ returns this sequence, shortening potentially longer alternative ones. In our example, $\lfloor ddd \rfloor_{\mathcal{M}} = d$. A *discriminator* for two states $q, q' \in Q^{\mathcal{M}}$ is an input $v \in \Sigma^*$ that yields different output in these. In our example, f is a discriminator for s_1 and s_2. It has the output *void* in the former and F in the latter. We can use known access sequences and discriminators to identify transition targets. Assume we want to identify the target of e in s_1. This transition corresponds to the input $\lfloor s_1 \rfloor_{\mathcal{M}} \cdot e = d \cdot e$. We know that f discriminates s_2 from s_0 and s_1. Due to $mq_{\mathcal{M}}(d \cdot e \cdot f) = mq_{\mathcal{M}}(\lfloor s_2 \rfloor_{\mathcal{M}} \cdot f) = F$, our target must be s_2.

TTT is a MAT-based learning algorithm introduced by Isberner et al. in [7] that uses significantly fewer queries than other approaches like L^*. In the following, we describe its learning process. TTT subsequently performs the key steps *initialization, refinement*, and *finalization*[1]. During *initialization*, the TTT learner creates a hypothesis with a single initial state and adds outgoing transitions for each $s \in \Sigma$. To add transitions, TTT retrieves their output and identifies their respective target in $\mathcal{H}$ using known discriminators, similarly to the

---

[1] We omit the *stabilization* step that is irrelevant to our method.

process described above. During both, TTT uses *membership queries* $mq_\mathcal{M}(w)$ to retrieve the output for an input $w \in \Sigma^*$.

After initialization, the learner asks the teacher to check whether $\mathcal{H} \equiv \mathcal{M}$ (*equivalence query*). Since $\mathcal{M}$ is typically a blackbox, this check is usually approximated with conformance testing, e.g., comparing output for random words [3]. When $\mathcal{H} \equiv \mathcal{M}$, learning concludes. Otherwise, the teacher provides the learner a *counterexample* $c \in \Sigma^*$ that gives different output in $\mathcal{H}$ and $\mathcal{M}$.

With c, the learner enters *refinement*. Because we received c, $\mathcal{M}$ must contain at least one state that is distinct from all states in $\mathcal{H}$. Hence, we need to add at least one new state to our hypothesis. To identify this state, TTT first decomposes c into $c = u \cdot a \cdot v$ with $u, v \in \Sigma^*, a \in \Sigma$ s.t. $mq_\mathcal{M}(\lfloor u \rfloor_\mathcal{H} \cdot a \cdot v) \neq mq_\mathcal{M}(\lfloor u \cdot a \rfloor_\mathcal{H} \cdot v)$. We call this a *valid decomposition* of c. Hence, providing a to $\lfloor u \rfloor_\mathcal{H}$ yields a different state in $\mathcal{H}$ and $\mathcal{M}$. Thus, TTT *splits* the state $q := \mathcal{H}[u]$ at a. It adds a new state q' with $\lfloor q' \rfloor_\mathcal{H} := \lfloor q \rfloor_\mathcal{H} \cdot a$, and stores v as discriminator for q' and the previous target for a in q. Then, it adds outgoing transitions for each input in Σ to q' and identifies their respective successors in $\mathcal{H}$, as it did during initialization.

Long counterexamples give long discriminators, causing excessive input. TTT reduces this by treating new discriminators as *temporary* and replacing them with shorter *final* ones during *finalization*. It achieves this with a two-step search. Assume a set $Q^\mathcal{B}$ of at least two states. In the first search step, TTT tries to find a symbol $s \in \Sigma$ in which at least two states from $Q^\mathcal{B}$ have different output. Naturally, such a symbol then discriminates them. If there is no such symbol, TTT attempts to extend a known final discriminator in the second step. First, it identifies successors in $\mathcal{H}$ for each symbol. Then, it searches for a known final discriminator for these. Appending these discriminators to their corresponding symbol then yields a new discriminator. For instance, providing e to s_1 and s_2 returns s_2 and s_0, respectively. These have the known final discriminator d. Hence, $e \cdot d$ discriminates s_1 and s_2. For efficiency, TTT uses the shortest new discriminator found. Note that TTT may not find a known final discriminator. However, the process guarantees that all discriminators are finalized before the learner asks the next equivalence query.

TTT enters refinement again after finalization when c still has different output in $\mathcal{H}$ and $\mathcal{M}$. Otherwise, it submits a new equivalence query.

With the key steps of original TTT discussed, we describe next how we extend these to learn accurate Mealy automata with an ISF.

5   The TTT/ik Method

We now present our *TTT/ik* method that learns accurate Mealy automata efficiently by exploiting an imprecise symbol filter. We first give an overview of our method, and then describe our main contributions in detail.

Our method extends the *initialization, refinement,* and *finalization* steps of the TTT active learning algorithm with new algorithms to enable the support

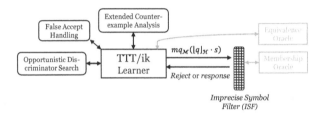

Fig. 2. Main components and interaction

of an ISF. Figure 2 shows the main components involved in learning. The *membership* and *equivalence oracles* are the components of the teacher that process membership and equivalence queries. They are outside our scope.

Let us now look at how our method achieves accuracy and efficiency with an ISF. Consider a SUL $\mathcal{M}$, a hypothesis $\mathcal{H}$, and a common input alphabet Σ. Further assume that the *ISF* has been initialized with imprecise knowledge about the state-local alphabets of $\mathcal{M}$, e.g., based on system traces or expert users. That is, it answers whether a symbol is legal in a state but this answer may be incorrect. Consider a state $q \in Q^{\mathcal{H}}$ that we just discovered. During initialization and refinement, original TTT creates outgoing transitions for each input $s \in \Sigma$. It queries their output $mq_{\mathcal{M}}(\lfloor q \rfloor_{\mathcal{H}} \cdot s)$ and determines their targets using known discriminators. Our *TTT/ik learner*, however, first sends $mq_{\mathcal{M}}(\lfloor q \rfloor_{\mathcal{H}} \cdot s)$ to the *ISF*, to save queries when $s \notin \Sigma_q^{\mathcal{M}}$. When the *ISF* assumes $s \in \Sigma_q^{\mathcal{M}}$, it passes the query to the *membership oracle* and returns the response. Then, we proceed like original TTT. When assuming $s \notin \Sigma_q^{\mathcal{M}}$, in contrast, the *ISF* rejects the query. Then, we mark s illegal in q and model it as silent self-loop, saving any further queries.

The *ISF* may falsely accept and reject queries. Falsely accepting illegal symbols causes redundant queries, reducing performance. We integrate *false accept handling* (FAH) to counter this effect. Falsely rejecting legal symbols is more severe, as it leads to inaccurate models. We only filter queries for the output of new transitions. Hence, equivalence queries are not filtered and inaccuracies from false rejects show in counterexamples. Thus, we can use counterexample analysis to improve our knowledge, like [6]. To do so, we design a new method for *extended counterexample analysis* that identifies false rejects and normal inaccuracies efficiently and integrate it with our *learner*. Assume that our analysis of a counterexample showed that the *ISF* falsely rejected s in q. Then, our *learner* legalizes s in q. It marks it legal, queries the output of the associated transition, and determines its target, as usual. Note that we only update the alphabets stored in the *learner*. This allows us to interact with diverse *ISF* implementations easily, regardless of whether these can adapt their stored knowledge as well. After counterexample analysis, TTT searches for short final discriminators during finalization. We replace the original search process with our new *opportunistic discriminator search* that ensures accuracy by also identifying false rejects and improves efficiency when handling illegal symbols.

We describe FAH, counterexample analysis, and discriminator search in detail in the following.

5.1 False Accept Handling

False accepts make our learner less efficient. Hence, we design a basic heuristic to reduce their impact on performance. We know that illegal transitions are always silent. Thus, when the initial membership query for a symbol s returns *void*, we mark s illegal. When it is not actually illegal, we rejected it incorrectly. Hence, s appears to our method as false reject and is discovered as usual during counterexample analysis or discriminator search. FAH is not limited to models with few silent legal transitions. As we show in our evaluation, it still improves total performance in models with many silent legal transitions, despite the additional false rejects.

5.2 Extended Counterexample Analysis

Different to false accepts, false rejects lead to model inaccuracies. These inaccuracies show in counterexamples. In the following, we motivate and describe how we extend the original TTT counterexample analysis to discover false rejects, and subsequently show that our method operates correctly.

TTT counterexample analysis decomposes a counterexample $c \in \Sigma^*$ to identify states that need to be split. Recent TTT implementations use binary search to discover such decompositions efficiently. To extend TTT counterexample analysis, we need to consider how false rejects show in counterexamples first. Assume a counterexample $c \in \Sigma^*$, a hypothesis $\mathcal{H}$, a SUL $\mathcal{M}$, and a silent transition t with input $s \in \Sigma$ that starts at $q \in Q^{\mathcal{H}}$. Let there also be $q' \in Q^{\mathcal{M}}$ s.t. $\mathcal{M}[\lfloor q \rfloor_{\mathcal{H}}] = q'$, and a transition t' starting at q' with the same input s. We reject s correctly when t' is also a silent self-loop. Otherwise, we differentiate the following cases of false reject:

I. t' is silent, but not a self-loop.
II. t' is neither silent, nor a self-loop.
III. t' is not silent, but a self-loop.

In case I, s triggers a silent state change in $\mathcal{M}$. Hence, if case I shows in c, there is a valid decomposition $c = u \cdot s \cdot v$ s.t. $mq_{\mathcal{M}}(\lfloor u \rfloor_{\mathcal{H}} \cdot s \cdot v) \neq mq_{\mathcal{M}}(\lfloor u \cdot s \rfloor_{\mathcal{H}} \cdot v)$, with $v \in \Sigma^*$ and $u = \lfloor q \rfloor_{\mathcal{H}}$. The symbol s also triggers a state change in case II, but this change is not silent. Thus, case II can show as valid decomposition of c like case I but may also do so as different output in the last symbol of c, without valid decomposition. This is because a valid decomposition requires a non-empty suffix, but a counterexample only needs to contain any output deviation. We call the former instance of case II *case IIa* and the latter *case IIb*. In IIb, $c = u \cdot s$ and $mq_{\mathcal{M}}(\lfloor u \rfloor_{\mathcal{H}} \cdot s) \neq mq_{\mathcal{M}}(\lfloor u \cdot s \rfloor_{\mathcal{H}})$, with $u = \lfloor q \rfloor_{\mathcal{H}}$. Case III behaves like case IIb.

Based on these observations, we choose the following basic approach for our extended counterexample analysis. We exploit the decomposition search already used by TTT to identify cases I, IIa, and normal inaccuracies. For cases IIb and III, we perform additional analysis of output deviations.

Method. We now describe our method in detail. As outlined above, we identify cases I, IIa, and normal inaccuracies using decomposition search. Cases IIb and III do not show as valid decompositions. Thus, we need to discover them by comparing the output $mq_{\mathcal{M}}(c)$ and $mq_{\mathcal{H}}(c)$ for a counterexample $c \in \Sigma^*$. This is challenging. Finding an output deviation at a specific index x of c does not necessitate that the symbol $c[x]$ was falsely rejected in cases IIb or III. Instead, the deviation may also be caused by any yet undetected state change that occurred before x. Thus, $mq_{\mathcal{M}}(u \cdot s) = mq_{\mathcal{M}}(\lfloor u \rfloor_{\mathcal{H}} \cdot s)$, with $s = c[x]$ and $u = c[1, x-1]$, not always holds. For it to hold, we must ensure that the subsequence $c[1, x-1]$ shows no yet undetected state changes. To do so, we search for any valid decomposition in $c[1, x]$ and fix the corresponding false rejects or normal inaccuracies until there is no further valid decomposition. This approach causes redundant queries when applying decomposition search without finding a valid decomposition. To reduce these queries, we use the following heuristic. If $c[x]$ belongs to case IIb or III, $c[x] \in \Sigma^{\mathcal{H}}_{\mathcal{H}[u]}$ and $mq'_{\mathcal{M}}(u \cdot c[x]) \neq void$, with $u = [c[1, x-1]]$. Thus, when these conditions hold, we check $mq'_{\mathcal{M}}(\lfloor \mathcal{H}[u] \rfloor_{\mathcal{H}} \cdot c[x]) \neq void$ to validate that we found an actual false reject. If true, we can skip decomposition search, saving the corresponding queries. If false, there are still undetected state changes in $c[1, x]$, and we need to apply decomposition search as usual.

This gives the following algorithm, taking a counterexample c, a hypothesis $\mathcal{H}$, and a SUL $\mathcal{M}$:

1. Cut c after the first output deviation between $\mathcal{H}$ and $\mathcal{M}$ and only keep the first part.
2. When $a \notin \Sigma^{\mathcal{H}}_q$ and $mq'_{\mathcal{M}}(u \cdot a) \neq void$ with $c = u \cdot a$ and $q \leftarrow \mathcal{H}[u]$, validate that the last symbol a of c was falsely rejected: iff $mq'_{\mathcal{M}}(\lfloor q \rfloor_{\mathcal{H}} \cdot a) \neq void$, falsely rejected a (cases IIb, III). Terminate and add a to $\Sigma^{\mathcal{H}}_q$.
3. Find any valid decomposition $c = u \cdot a \cdot v$. Then, set $q \leftarrow \mathcal{H}[u]$.
   – If $a \notin \Sigma^{\mathcal{H}}_q$, falsely rejected a (cases I, IIa). Terminate and add a to $\Sigma^{\mathcal{H}}_q$.
   – If $a \in \Sigma^{\mathcal{H}}_q$, we found a normal inaccuracy. Terminate and refine $\mathcal{H}$.

The reference implementation of TTT in *LearnLib* already applies the first step by default. Like it, we use binary decomposition search to find valid decompositions efficiently. We also analyze the same counterexample again after refinement when it still shows differences between hypothesis and SUL. We show the correctness of our method in the following.

Correctness. Our counterexample analysis operates correctly iff it identifies false rejects and normal inaccuracies and does not incorrectly legalize a correctly rejected symbol. We show in our evaluation that our method always learns accurate models, thus, it identifies false rejects and inaccuracies correctly. We show that we also do not incorrectly legalize symbols in the following. Consider a hypothesis $\mathcal{H}$ and a SUL $\mathcal{M}$. Let $q' \in Q^{\mathcal{M}}$ be a state in $\mathcal{M}$ where a symbol $s \in \Sigma$ is illegal, and $q \in Q^{\mathcal{H}}$ with $q' \equiv q$ be its corresponding state in $\mathcal{H}$. Due to $q' \equiv q$, $\mathcal{M}[\lfloor q \rfloor_{\mathcal{H}}] = q'$. This also applies over multiple iterations of $\mathcal{H}$ because access sequences of discovered states are immutable in TTT. Now assume any counterexample $c = u \cdot s \cdot v$ with $\mathcal{H}[u] = q$ and $u, v \in \Sigma^*$. Note that $c = u \cdot s \cdot v$ is not necessarily a valid decomposition of c.

We first look at cases IIb and III where $v = \epsilon$. We incorrectly legalize s in q iff $mq'_{\mathcal{M}}(u \cdot s) \neq void$ and $mq'_{\mathcal{M}}(\lfloor q \rfloor_{\mathcal{H}} \cdot s) \neq void$. Using $q' \equiv q$ gives us $mq'_{\mathcal{M}}(\lfloor q \rfloor_{\mathcal{H}} \cdot s) = mq'_{\mathcal{M}}(\lfloor q' \rfloor_{\mathcal{M}} \cdot s)$. From $s \notin \Sigma^{\mathcal{M}}_{q'}$ follows $mq'_{\mathcal{M}}(\lfloor q' \rfloor_{\mathcal{M}} \cdot s) = void$. Thus, $mq'_{\mathcal{M}}(\lfloor q \rfloor_{\mathcal{H}} \cdot s) = void$ and thereby our initial condition never holds. Hence, our method never incorrectly legalizes s $\square$

We apply a similar argument in cases I and IIa. We incorrectly legalize s in q iff $c = u \cdot s \cdot v$ is a valid decomposition of c. Due to $q \equiv q'$, we can set $mq_{\mathcal{M}}(\lfloor u \rfloor_{\mathcal{H}} \cdot s \cdot v)$ to $mq_{\mathcal{M}}(\lfloor q' \rfloor_{\mathcal{M}} \cdot s \cdot v)$ and $mq_{\mathcal{M}}(\lfloor u \cdot s \rfloor_{\mathcal{H}} \cdot v)$ to $mq_{\mathcal{M}}(\lfloor \lfloor q' \rfloor_{\mathcal{M}} \cdot s \rfloor_{\mathcal{M}} \cdot v)$. From $s \notin \Sigma^{\mathcal{M}}_{q'}$ follows $mq_{\mathcal{M}}(\lfloor q' \rfloor_{\mathcal{M}} \cdot s \cdot v) = mq_{\mathcal{M}}(\lfloor \lfloor q' \rfloor_{\mathcal{M}} \cdot s \rfloor_{\mathcal{M}} \cdot v)$. Hence, $c = u \cdot s \cdot v$ never is a valid decomposition, and therefore, our method does not incorrectly legalize s $\square$

5.3 Opportunistic Discriminator Search

TTT uses discriminator search to finalize long temporary discriminators. With false rejects, however, the implemented search may give incorrect results. In the following, we motivate the need for an alternative approach, and present our opportunistic discriminator search design that supports false rejects. We use the hypothesis automaton in Fig. 3 for the SUL from Fig. 1 as running example.

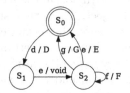

Fig. 3. Example hypothesis $\mathcal{H}$ (illegal transitions are omitted)

Assume we want to find a discriminator for the states $Q^{\mathcal{B}} = \{s_1, s_2\}$ from $\mathcal{H}$. As shown in the example, we falsely rejected g in s_1. With the original discriminator search, our learner would thus falsely assume that g has silent output in s_1, and thus, discriminates s_1 and s_2. Moreover, it would assume that providing g to s_1 leads to s_1 instead of s_0. As g in s_2 would still lead to s_0, it would then use any known final discriminator for s_0 and s_1, like d. Hence, giving the incorrect discriminator $g \cdot d$ for s_1 and s_2. Continuing learning with such an incorrect discriminator results in an inaccurate hypothesis that we cannot correct through our extended counterexample analysis. Consequently, we need a new approach for discriminator search.

A naive solution to ensure correct discriminators would be to query the output of illegal transitions and identify their targets using known discriminators, as we do when creating legal transitions. However, this would lead to redundant queries in all states in $Q^{\mathcal{B}}$ where an analyzed symbol is actually illegal. Thus, eliminating savings from not asking queries for these correctly rejected symbols. Therefore, we design a new and more efficient approach that analyzes symbols opportunistically.

We observe that we need different numbers of queries to check if a symbol yields a discriminator directly or by extending a known final one. This query count depends on the number of states where they are legal, and the output they have there. Therefore, to reduce queries, we classify all symbols in Σ based on their expected query count in analysis and analyze them subsequently from fewest to most. We terminate when finding a valid discriminator or a false reject. Thus, we rarely analyze all symbols, unlike the original TTT discriminator search. Therefore, we may not always return the shortest discriminator. Still, our opportunistic method dramatically outperforms the naive approach in practice, as we show in our evaluation.

We separate symbols in a set $Q^{\mathcal{B}}$ of at least two states into the following classes:

1. Symbols that are marked legal by our learner in all states of $Q^{\mathcal{B}}$.
2. Symbols that are marked legal in at least one state $q \in Q^{\mathcal{B}}$, marked illegal in at least one state $q' \in Q^{\mathcal{B}}$, and are not silent in q.
3. Symbols that appear to have silent output in all states of $Q^{\mathcal{B}}$.

In our example, the first class only contains e, as we falsely rejected g. We analyze these symbols directly with original TTT discriminator search, needing no additional queries to the SUL. Symbols in the second class are discriminators if there is at least one correct reject. Then, they show an output deviation in at least two states of $Q^{\mathcal{B}}$. In our case, the second class contains $\{f, g\}$. As the ISF uses imprecise knowledge, we cannot be certain that f and g are actually illegal in s_1. Hence, we pick any symbol s from this class and a state from $q' \in Q^{\mathcal{B}}$ where we marked it illegal, and ask a single query $mq'_{\mathcal{M}}(\lfloor q' \rfloor_{\mathcal{H}} \cdot s)$. If as for f in s_1 the output is silent, our picked symbol is a discriminator and we terminate. Otherwise, as for g, we discovered a false reject. In this case, we terminate and legalize the symbol, to use a more accurate hypothesis during the next discriminator search. Note that we still identify g as false reject when picking f, either through our extended counterexample analysis or in another run of our opportunistic discriminator search.

Symbols in the third class may yield a discriminator but analyzing them could require many membership queries. In our example, the third class only contains d. To use d as part of a valid discriminator, we must ensure that it actually forms silent self-loops in s_1 and s_2. Identifying the target of a correctly rejected transition, however, introduces redundant queries. To avoid these, we design a two-step approach. In the first step, we check for obvious false rejects. We validate that our analyzed symbol s from the third class has silent output in each state in $Q^{\mathcal{B}}$ where we marked it illegal. To do this, we use a single membership query in each of these states. If we encounter any non-silent output, we found a false reject. We then terminate and legalize s.

For the second step, we combine the transition-based discriminator search of TTT with its method for identifying transition targets. TTT stores known discriminators in a tree, where inner nodes are discriminators and leaves are states. When identifying a transition target, TTT traverses this tree from root to leaves until reaching a state or a temporary discriminator. When identifying a known discriminator for two states, it moves from the corresponding leaves upwards, taking their first common ancestor.

We adapt this downwards traversal and apply it collectively to all transitions from Q^B where our analyzed symbol is marked illegal. Like TTT, our *light sifting* approach stops traversal when encountering a leaf or temporary node but we stop even earlier when possible to save redundant queries. First, we stop when at least two supposedly illegal transitions have different output at a discriminator, as this discriminator clearly differentiates their targets. Thus, we can append it to our analyzed symbol to retrieve a valid discriminator. Second, we stop when discovering a false reject. When, as in our example, d has been correctly rejected in s_1, it must form a self-loop there. Thus, we must reach s_1 or one of its ancestors eventually. Hence, we would terminate and legalize d in s_1 when we encountered a node that is not an ancestor of s_1. Third, assuming we know states $Q' \subseteq Q^B$ where s is legal, we stop when reaching the discriminator of their targets for s or a discriminator that is not ancestor of it. We return the corresponding node, as we cannot find a lower common discriminator. To further improve performance, we sort symbols in class 3 by the number of associated transitions that are marked illegal and start our two-step process where these are lowest.

6   Evaluation

We have validated our *TTT/ik* method in practice. We discuss the results of our evaluation in the following. All models are available online[2].

Table 1. Case studies

Model	States	$|\Sigma|$	Legal transitions	Local alphabet sizes relative to $|\Sigma|$ [%]		
				Minimum	Maximum	Average
CAS	8	7	18	29	43	32
Edentifier2	8	8	46	38	100	72
TcpLinux	15	10	90	40	70	60
Heater	9	15	36	13	40	27
LaneDetection	16	13	79	8	62	38
Smartfarm	20	51	732	67	78	72
WindowControl	85	20	674	10	55	40

We have selected seven realistic case studies of different structure across different domains to validate the wide applicability of our method. We have focused on larger systems with large global and small state-local alphabets, as

---

[2] https://git.tu-berlin.de/pkogel/ttt-ik-supp.

these promise the most savings potential with our method. We have simulated these systems using models to simplify our evaluation setup without limiting validity. Table 1 lists all systems with their key structural properties. From the Radboud University automata benchmark collection[3], we have taken the *Edentifier2* and *TcpLinux* models. The former specifies the behavior of a smart card reader used for Internet banking, while the latter corresponds to a TCP client implementation on Linux. We have removed redundant self-loops in both models so that they do not accept every symbol in each state. We have not chosen other models from this collection, because they are either too small or have very large local alphabets that we cannot reduce without additional domain knowledge. In addition, we have selected models of a heating controller from [11] and a car alarm system (*CAS*) from [2] that is frequently used in automata learning. We have also added several models from our own collection. *LaneDetection* models the lane detection approach used by an autonomous robot in a student project, while *Smartfarm* specifies an automated crop care system that controls irrigation, fertilization, and plant protection. *WindowControl*, finally, models a controller for power windows. All except the benchmark systems have been modelled as statechart. Hence, we have transformed them to Mealy automata to use them with our method.

Table 2. Tested settings for the Mock ISF

	pf	ar1	ar2	ar3	ar4	ar5	ar7	no
False accept ratio [%]	0	10	20	30	40	50	70	100
False reject ratio [%]	0	10	20	30	40	50	70	100

We have implemented our method in the latest release of the automata learning framework *LearnLib* [8], as it is widely used and contains the TTT reference implementation. We have added a query cache to improve performance and created a *Mock ISF* to test different ISF behavior easily. The *Mock ISF* allows us to specify how many illegal transitions it falsely accepts, and how many legal transitions it falsely rejects. It chooses the corresponding transitions randomly. Testing all potential Mock ISF settings is not feasible. Therefore, we have used a selection of settings, shown in Table 2. *pf* corresponds to perfect knowledge of all state local alphabets, and *no* to completely incorrect information.

6.1   Accuracy

First, we have validated that we learn accurate models. We have applied our method across all case studies and ISF settings and compared the learned automata to the original models. We have chosen a reliable equivalence oracle that always delivers counterexamples until hypothesis and SUL match. Like all MAT-based methods, including TTT, we fundamentally require such an oracle to learn accurate models. In all cases, our method has always learned an accurate model of its target.

---

[3] https://automata.cs.ru.nl/Overview.

6.2 Efficiency

The main goal of our method is to improve learning performance when only imprecise knowledge is available. In the following, we describe how we have evaluated the efficiency of our approach and discuss results.

We have measured performance in total queries sent to the SUL, and the total number of symbols contained in these, as these metrics typically determine runtime in practice [7]. We have used original TTT with a standard query cache as baseline and focused on the best-case performance of both TTT and TTT/ik. This focus has allowed us to analyze the maximum potential of our method. Finally, we have not considered knowledge-based filters or mappers due to their shortcomings described in Sect. 2.

We have chosen a *Wp-method* equivalence oracle [4] that approximates equivalence queries by testing the output of semi-random words to measure the queries and symbols used for counterexample search in practice. We have limited the number of generated words to reduce redundant queries. As a result, the oracle has sometimes failed to provide a counterexample for inaccurate hypotheses, both with original TTT and our method. We have reattempted these runs with different random seeds, to still retrieve significant results. We have observed that TTT and TTT/ik perform best at different counterexample generator settings. Hence, we have chosen the most efficient configuration among several word lengths and counts for the generator. The optimal configuration for TTT/ik has often varied per Mock ISF setting. We usually do not know the precision of the ISF in practice. Therefore, we have chosen the configuration with the best average performance.

Table 3. Results per case study. *Format = queries/symbols*

Model	Baseline		Relative overhead [%]						
		pf	ar1	ar2	ar3	ar4	ar5	ar7	no
CAS	235.7/	**-49.2/**	**-48.7/**	**-47.8/**	**-45.0/**	**-44.8/**	**-43.4/**	**-41.2/**	**-46.0/**
	1327.3	**-32.6**	**-32.4**	**-29.4**	**-26.7**	**-24.4**	**-23.8**	**-18.7**	**-29.1**
Edentifier2	198.3/	**-3.7/**	**-3.2/**	0.7/	11.8/	6.6/	11.6/	7.7/	3.7/
	959.7	4.3	2.1	18.0	34.6	33.8	50.6	39.8	28.9
TcpLinux	616.3/	**-37.5/**	**-33.1/**	**-29.7/**	**-24.4/**	**-29.4/**	**-25.2/**	**-18.7/**	**-17.1/**
	3643.0	**-39.4**	**-32.0**	**-28.2**	**-17.3**	**-19.1**	**-10.5**	**-2.4**	5.4
Heater	655.0/	**-67.9/**	**-68.3/**	**-65.3/**	**-63.8/**	**-63.2/**	**-61.2/**	**-57.8/**	**-51.0/**
	2884.0	**-54.9**	**-55.9**	**-52.9**	**-49.8**	**-50.2**	**-47.9**	**-43.5**	**-34.6**
LaneDetection	1130.0/	**-44.5/**	**-43.0/**	**-43.9/**	**-45.2/**	**-42.5/**	**-44.9/**	**-43.9/**	**-41.1/**
	4864.0	**-10.4**	**-3.0**	**-5.8**	**-7.6**	0.4	**-6.8**	**-8.2**	**-5.2**
Smartfarm	2032.7/	**-28.3/**	**-21.5/**	**-18.1/**	**-16.7/**	**-14.5/**	**-13.1/**	**-9.3/**	**-4.5/**
	7653.0	**-24.1**	29.0	45.4	48.6	65.5	88.9	107.2	105.5
WindowControl	7377.7/	**-59.0/**	**-52.2/**	**-48.0/**	**-43.8/**	**-40.0/**	**-36.3/**	**-34.0/**	**-28.7/**
	68462.0	**-50.6**	**-33.4**	**-26.0**	**-14.8**	**-5.6**	**-4.1**	6.1	21.9

We have measured the relative overhead per ISF setting and case study to the baseline. We have averaged all results over three successful runs to account for the randomness of the equivalence oracle and our Mock ISF. Table 3 shows the results for all tested ISF settings for queries and symbols and the corresponding baselines. In this and the subsequent tables, negative overhead is an improvement and printed bold. The results clearly demonstrate the efficiency of our method. Across all case studies, our method has reduced queries for at least one ISF setting with imprecise knowledge. In all systems except *Edentifier2* this also applies to symbols. More precise knowledge generally pays off. Almost all systems have performed best with perfect knowledge, while reducing false accepts and rejects has almost always improved performance. Only *Edentifier2* and *Heater* have performed best at *ar1* instead of *pf*. This is likely due to the structure of the randomly generated counterexamples at these settings. Even quite imprecise knowledge has almost always improved performance. In all systems but *Smartfarm* and *Edentifier2*, we have reduced both queries and symbols at *ar5* (50% false rejects, 50% false accepts). Even in the complex *WindowControl* system, we have reduced queries by 36.3% and symbols by 4.1% at *ar5*, while *ar2* has yielded 48% less queries and 26% fewer symbols. In less complex systems, knowledge may even be less precise. For instance, for *Heater*, we have saved 57.8% queries and 43.5% symbols even with *ar7*. For *TcpLinux*, *ar7* has given us 18.7% fewer queries and 2.4% fewer symbols. These results underline the great benefit of having a learner that can exploit imprecise knowledge.

Table 4. Equivalence query overhead per case study.

Model	Baseline	Relative overhead [%]							
		pf	ar1	ar2	ar3	ar4	ar5	ar7	no
CAS	5.0	66.6	66.6	66.6	73.4	73.4	73.4	106.6	120.0
Edentifier2	4.7	7.1	28.5	71.3	107.1	142.6	178.4	235.6	185.4
TcpLinux	9.0	0.0	40.8	92.6	163.0	207.4	211.1	311.1	451.9
Heater	7.3	36.4	22.8	22.8	54.6	36.4	72.9	91.0	131.9
LaneDetection	9.3	267.9	289.4	243.0	271.6	278.7	253.7	253.7	296.6
Smartfarm	2.0	0.0	2233.5	3416.5	4266.5	4566.5	4833.5	5383.5	6483.5
WindowControl	14.3	293.1	539.7	802.5	1053.7	1195.7	1358.5	1637.6	2130.8

We have identified counterexample generation as the primary influence on the performance of our method. Ideally, we could discover multiple inaccuracies per counterexample. As shown in Table 4, though, our method often has asked dramatically more equivalence queries than TTT. For instance, *WindowControl* has already required about 540% more equivalence queries at *ar1* than TTT. This is because generating effective examples with a semi-random oracle like W_p becomes difficult with an increasing false reject count and system size. A large global alphabet like in *Smartfarm* and many states reduce the chance of choosing transitions that show inaccuracies. Hence, the oracle must test more words until finding a counterexample, and a single counterexample is likely to show fewer inaccuracies, adding queries and inputs. More counterexamples also necessitate more rounds of our extended counterexample analysis, adding further queries. Their impact, however, is comparatively low, as we use efficient binary search. This ineffective generation affects the potential savings of our method particularly in systems with large local alphabets. For instance, in *Edentifier2*, we have quickly outweighed the benefits of ignoring its few illegal transitions. In *WindowControl*, in contrast, we have still achieved significant savings despite its high number of states. We expect to improve savings across even more systems with more effective counterexample generation, like chaining different equivalence oracles as in [13].

Table 5. Relative performance overhead [%] for opportunistic and naive discriminator search with selected settings. *Format = queries/symbols*

	pf		ar1	
Model	Opportunistic	Naive	Opportunistic	Naive
CAS	**−49.2/−32.6**	**−5.9/−4.7**	**−48.7/−32.4**	**−5.7/−4.7**
Edentifier2	**−3.7/4.3**	**−8.6/−5.5**	**−3.2/2.1**	**−7.9/−5.2**
TcpLinux	**−37.5/−39.4**	1.1/−9.2	**−33.1/−32.0**	0.8/−11.0
Heater	**−67.9/−54.9**	**−0.7/−0.1**	**−68.3/−55.9**	**−0.7/−0.1**
LaneDetection	**−44.5/−10.4**	**−0.1/0.0**	**−43.0/−3.0**	0.0/0.0
Smartfarm	**−28.3/−24.1**	**−25.1/−22.4**	**−21.5/29.0**	**−18.4/27.6**
WindowControl	**−59.0/−50.6**	**−12.4/8.5**	**−52.2/−33.4**	**−9.0/−0.3**

FAH and our opportunistic discriminator search have clearly improved the efficiency of our method. We have found that FAH had improved the average performance per ISF setting in all case studies, although it introduces false rejects for legal transitions that are silent. This includes even systems like *LaneDetection*, where 52% of all legal transitions are silent. In Sect. 5.3, we assume that our opportunistic discriminator search is more efficient than a naive approach that legalizes all illegal transitions in a set of states Q^B. We have rerun our method with the naive approach to validate this assumption. Table 5 shows the resulting overhead of both approaches for the *pf* and *ar1* settings, where the naive approach has performed best. As shown, the naive approach has only performed better for *Edentifier2*. Here, the additional legalizations during discriminator search have eliminated the need for additional equivalence queries. These limit performance for this model, as discussed above. In all other cases, our opportunistic search shows its clear advantage by leading to dramatically fewer queries and symbols.

Hence, we have shown that our method effectively reduces queries and symbols across a wide range of applications.

7   Conclusion and Future Work

We have presented *TTT/ik*, a method for learning accurate Mealy automata efficiently with an imprecise symbol filter. Our method provides three novel extensions to the TTT active learning algorithm. Our *extended counterexample analysis* and *opportunistic discriminator search* methods replace TTT counterexample analysis and discriminator search and efficiently assure accurate models when falsely rejecting symbols, while our *false accept handling* improves performance when encountering falsely accepted ones. We have described our extensions in detail and shown across seven realistic case studies of varying complexity that our method learns accurate models, while also nearly always reducing queries and symbols drastically over TTT with a query cache only, even when falsely accepting and rejecting symbols. Hence, our method reduces runtime in practice and critically also does so in systems that were unable to use a symbol filter before.

We see several exciting possibilities for future work. First, we intend to explore methods to create counterexamples more tailored towards our method. We have seen that increasing false rejects also increase equivalence queries, hence, reducing these would make our method even more effective. With a more efficient counterexample generator in place, we also intend to analyze the scalability of our method systematically. Second, we plan to integrate our method with *alphabet abstraction* [6]. This would make it more efficient with large CPS, where different symbols often have the same effect. Finally, we would like to test our method with different ISF implementations and explore its applicability to more expressive models. Our method fundamentally assumes automata where inputs directly trigger outputs and it can distinguish illegal transitions from legal self-loops. Hence, it is also applicable to other models based on Mealy automata, like Mealy Machines with timers [12].

References

1. Aarts, F., Vaandrager, F.: Learning I/O automata. In: Gastin, P., Laroussinie, F. (eds.) CONCUR 2010. LNCS, vol. 6269, pp. 71–85. Springer, Heidelberg (2010). https://doi.org/10.1007/978-3-642-15375-4_6
2. Aichernig, B.K., Brandl, H., Jöbstl, E., Krenn, W.: UML in action. ACM SIGSOFT Softw. Eng. Notes **36**(1), 1–8 (2011). https://doi.org/10.1145/1921532.1921559
3. Ali, S., Sun, H., Zhao, Y.: Model learning: a survey of foundations, tools and applications. Front. Comput. Sci. **15**(5), 1–22 (2021). https://doi.org/10.1007/s11704-019-9212-z
4. Fujiwara, S., Bochmann, G.V., Khendek, F., Amalou, M., Ghedamsi, A.: Test selection based on finite state models. IEEE Trans. Softw. Eng. **17**(6), 591–603 (1991). https://doi.org/10.1109/32.87284
5. Howar, F., Steffen, B., Merten, M.: Automata learning with automated alphabet abstraction refinement. In: Jhala, R., Schmidt, D. (eds.) VMCAI 2011. LNCS, vol. 6538, pp. 263–277. Springer, Heidelberg (2011). https://doi.org/10.1007/978-3-642-18275-4_19

6. Isberner, M., Howar, F., Steffen, B.: Inferring automata with state-local alphabet abstractions. In: Brat, G., Rungta, N., Venet, A. (eds.) NFM 2013. LNCS, vol. 7871, pp. 124–138. Springer, Heidelberg (2013). https://doi.org/10.1007/978-3-642-38088-4_9

7. Isberner, M., Howar, F., Steffen, B.: The TTT algorithm: a redundancy-free approach to active automata learning. In: Bonakdarpour, B., Smolka, S.A. (eds.) RV 2014. LNCS, vol. 8734, pp. 307–322. Springer, Cham (2014). https://doi.org/10.1007/978-3-319-11164-3_26

8. Isberner, M., Howar, F., Steffen, B.: The open-source LearnLib. In: Kroening, D., Pǎsǎreanu, C.S. (eds.) CAV 2015. LNCS, vol. 9206, pp. 487–495. Springer, Cham (2015). https://doi.org/10.1007/978-3-319-21690-4_32

9. Leucker, M., Neider, D.: Learning minimal deterministic automata from inexperienced teachers. In: Margaria, T., Steffen, B. (eds.) ISoLA 2012. LNCS, vol. 7609, pp. 524–538. Springer, Heidelberg (2012). https://doi.org/10.1007/978-3-642-34026-0_39

10. Margaria, T., Raffelt, H., Steffen, B.: Knowledge-based relevance filtering for efficient system-level test-based model generation. Innovations Syst. Softw. Eng. 1(2), 147–156 (2005). https://doi.org/10.1007/s11334-005-0016-y

11. Taylor, J.T., Taylor, W.T.: Patterns in the Machine. Apress, Newyork (2021). https://doi.org/10.1007/978-1-4842-6440-9

12. Vaandrager, F., Bloem, R., Ebrahimi, M.: Learning mealy machines with one timer. In: Leporati, A., Martín-Vide, C., Shapira, D., Zandron, C. (eds.) LATA 2021. LNCS, vol. 12638, pp. 157–170. Springer, Cham (2021). https://doi.org/10.1007/978-3-030-68195-1_13

13. Yang, N., et al.: Improving model inference in industry by combining active and passive learning. In: 2019 IEEE 26th International Conference on Software Analysis, Evolution and Reengineering (SANER). IEEE (2019). https://doi.org/10.1109/saner.2019.8668007

A Proof System for Cyber-Physical Systems with Shared-Variable Concurrency

Ran Li[1], Huibiao Zhu[1(✉)], and Richard Banach[2]

[1] Shanghai Key Laboratory of Trustworthy Computing,
East China Normal University, Shanghai, China
hbzhu@sei.ecnu.edu.cn

[2] Department of Computer Science, University of Manchester, Oxford Road,
Manchester M13 9PL, UK

Abstract. Cyber-physical system (CPS) is about the interplay of discrete behaviors and continuous behaviors. The combination of the physical and the cyber may cause hardship for the modeling and verification of CPS. Hence, a language based on shared variables was proposed to realize the interaction in CPS. In this paper, we formulate a proof system for this language. To handle the parallel composition with shared variables, we extend classical Hoare triples and bring the trace model into our proof system. The introduction of the trace may complicate our specification slightly, but it can realize a compositional proof when the program is executing. Meanwhile, this introduction can set up a bridge between our proof system and denotational semantics. Throughout this paper, we also present some examples to illustrate the usage of our proof system intuitively.

Keywords: Cyber-physical System (CPS) · Shared variables · Trace model · Hoare logic

1 Introduction

Cyber-physical system (CPS) [6,7] is an integration of discrete computer control behaviors and continuous physical behaviors. In CPS, computer programs can influence physical behaviors, and vice versa. It has covered a wide range of application areas, including healthcare equipment, intelligent traffic control and environmental monitoring, etc.

The interaction between the cyber and the physical brings convenience for many applications, while it may also complicate the design and the modeling of systems. Thus, some specification languages are proposed to describe and model CPS. Henzinger described hybrid systems with hybrid automata [3]. Zhou et al. developed a language called Hybrid CSP [12] which supports parallel composition via the communication mechanism, and Liu et al. proposed a calculus for it [9]. He et al. presented a hybrid relational modeling language (HRML) [2]. Different from them, we proposed a language whose parallel mechanism is based on shared

© Springer Nature Switzerland AG 2022
A. Riesco and M. Zhang (Eds.): ICFEM 2022, LNCS 13478, pp. 244–262, 2022.
https://doi.org/10.1007/978-3-031-17244-1_15

variables in our previous work [1]. Further, we elaborated this language and proposed its denotational and algebraic semantics [8].

In this paper, we give a proof system for this language based on our previous work [1,8]. The major challenge of formulating our proof system is how to cope with the parallel programs that contain shared variables. For parallel programs supported by shared variables, there are two main classical verification methods. In the well-known Owicki & Gries system [11], they defined interference-free to realize parallel composition. However, it may require proving numerous assertions when we check the property of interference-free. Therefore, a compositional method called rely-guarantee was proposed [5]. This approach adds a rely condition and a guarantee condition in its specification, so that compositionality is achieved. In [10], Lunel et al. employed this approach to present a component-based verification technique for Computer Controlled System (CCS) in differential dynamic logic. Nevertheless, it takes some effort to determine the corresponding rely condition and guarantee condition.

Slightly different from the two ways, we introduce the trace model into our proof system. For the feature of shared variables in the parallel mechanism, we define a *Merge* function to solve it. Thanks to the trace model, programs can perceive environment's actions and they can be composed during their executions consequently. However, the trace model is not a panacea. We add the corresponding preconditions and postconditions (similar to those in Hoare Logic [4]) to record the state of continuous variables, in that the trace only tracks values of discrete variables. Further, we attach the global clock variable now to our proof system. Therefore, it can capture the real-time feature of CPS. Altogether, we extend the traditional triple in Hoare Logic [4] $\{p\}$ S $\{q\}$ to $[tr \bullet p_c]$ S $[tr' \bullet q_c]$. tr and tr' are responsible for recording values of discrete variables. p_c and q_c contain the pre/postcondition of continuous variables and the starting/termination time of S. Because the focus of the proof is the initial and terminal data state of the program, we present a transformation rule to build the bridge between our proof system and traditional Hoare Logic.

Although the introduction of the trace model complicates the expression form slightly, it realizes compositional proof during the programs' executions which cannot be done in Owicki & Gries system. What's more, since the trace model records all data states, it can provide more precise conditions of the environment compared with the rely-guarantee approach. Moreover, our approach can link our proof system with denotational semantics, since the trace model is used in the description of our denotational semantics [8]. Overall, we give several rules for basic commands and compound constructs in this paper. Besides, to aid the understanding of our proof system, we also apply it to an example of a battery management system.

The remainder of this paper is organized as follows. In Sect. 2, we recall the syntax of this language and introduce the trace model briefly. Based on the feature of this language and trace model, the specification of our proof system is given. In Sect. 3, we list a set of rules used to specify and prove the correctness of CPS. To showcase the application of our proof system, Sect. 4 is dedicated to the example of a battery management system. We conclude our work and discuss some future work in Sect. 5.

2   Semantic Model

In this section, we first recall the syntax of the language to describe CPS. Then, we introduce the trace model to support our proof system in the next section. On this basis, the specification of our proof system is given as well.

2.1   Syntax of CPS with Shared-Variable Concurrency

As shown in Table 1, we follow the syntax proposed and elaborated in [1,8]. Here, x is a discrete variable and v is a continuous variable. b stands for a Boolean expression and e represents a discrete or continuous expression. The process in our language contains discrete behaviors Db, continuous behaviors Cb and various compositions of Db and Cb.

Table 1. Syntax of CPS

Process	$P, Q ::= Db$	(Discrete behavior)
	$\mid Cb$	(Continuous behavior)
	$\mid P; Q$	(Sequential composition)
	$\mid$ **if** b **then** P **else** Q	(Conditional construct)
	$\mid$ **while** b **do** P	(Iteration construct)
	$\mid P \parallel Q$	(Parallel composition)
Discrete behavior	$Db ::= x := e \mid @gd$	
Continuous behavior	$Cb ::= R(v, \dot{v})$ **until** g	
Guard condition	$g ::= gd \mid gc \mid gd \vee gc \mid gd \wedge gc$	
Discrete guard	$gd ::= true \mid x = e \mid x < e \mid x > e \mid\ gd \vee gd \mid gd \wedge gd \mid \neg gd$	
Continuous guard	$gc ::= true \mid v = e \mid v < e \mid v > e \mid\ gc \vee gc \mid gc \wedge gc \mid \neg gc$	

- **Db:** There are two discrete actions in our language.
  - $x := e$ is a discrete assignment and it is an atomic action. Through this assignment, the expression e is evaluated and the value gained is assigned to the discrete variable x.
  - $@gd$ is a discrete event guard. It is triggered if gd is satisfied. Otherwise, the process waits for the environment to trigger gd. Note that the environment stands for the other program given by the parallel composition. For example, if the whole system is $P \parallel Q$ and we now analyze the program P, then Q is P's environment.
- **Cb:** To define the continuous behaviors in CPS, we introduce differential relation in our language.
  - $R(v, \dot{v})$ **until** g is the syntax of describing continuous behavior. $R(v, \dot{v})$ is a differential relation which defines the dynamics of the continuous variable v. The evolution of v will follow the differential relation until the guard condition g is triggered. Four kinds of guard condition g are allowed in our language, including the discrete guard gd, continuous guard gc, mixed guards $gd \wedge gc$ and $gd \vee gc$.

– **Composition:** Also, a process can be comprised of the above commands. Our language supports sequential composition, iteration construct and parallel composition.
  - $P; Q$ is sequential composition. The process Q is executed after the process P's successful termination.
  - **if** b **then** P **else** Q is a conditional construct. If the Boolean condition b is true, then P is executed. Otherwise, Q is executed.
  - **while** b **do** P is an iteration construct. P keeps running repeatedly until the Boolean condition b does not hold.
  - $P \parallel Q$ is parallel composition. It indicates P executes in parallel with Q. The parallel mechanism is based on shared variables. In our language, shared writable variables only focus on discrete variables.

2.2 Trace Model

The parallel mechanism in our language is based on shared variables. We introduce a trace model to record the communication during their execution. Trace is defined to describe the behavior of a program, and it is composed of a series of snapshots. A snapshot specifies the behavior of an atomic action, and it is expressed as a triple (t, σ, μ).

– t: It records the time when the action occurs.
– σ: We use σ to record the states of data (i.e., discrete variables) contributed by the program itself or its environment (i.e., the other program given by the parallel composition) during the program's runtime.
– μ: We introduce it to indicate whether the action is done by the program itself or by the environment. If $\mu = 1$, it means that this action is performed by the program itself. If $\mu = 0$, it implies that this action is contributed by the environment. The introduction of μ can support the data exchange for the components of a parallel process with the help of the *Merge* function.

We list the following projection functions $\pi_i (i = 1, 2, 3)$ to get the ith element of a snapshot.

$$\pi_1((t, \sigma, \mu)) =_{df} t, \quad \pi_2((t, \sigma, \mu)) =_{df} \sigma, \quad \pi_3((t, \sigma, \mu)) =_{df} \mu$$

Further, we also define some operators of traces and snapshots.

– $last(tr)$ stands for the last snapshot of the trace tr.
– $tr_a \,^\frown tr_b$ denotes the concatenation of the trace tr_a and tr_b.
– Assume that tr contains at least one snapshot, the notation $tr - last(tr)$ indicates the rest of tr after deleting the last snapshot of tr.
– Assume that the snapshot sp is not the first one in its trace tr, $pre(sp, tr)$ denotes the previous snapshot of sp in tr.
– $tr = tr_a \lor tr_b$ is equivalent to $tr = tr_a \lor tr = tr_b$. It implies that there are two possible cases of tr. We introduce this notation to represent different execution orders under parallel composition.

2.3   Specification

Based on the trace model, we introduce the formalism to specify and verify CPS with shared-variable concurrency that is modeled by our language.

The classic Hoare triples [4] have the form of $\{p\}\ S\ \{q\}$. p, q and S denote precondition, postcondition and program respectively. It indicates that if the program S is executed under the precondition p, the final state of S satisfies the postcondition q when S terminates.

For parallelism with shared variables, slightly different from the two existing methods (i.e., interference-free checking [11] and rely-guarantee [5]), we can pave the way for parallel composition in the light of the above trace model. The trace model gives the process an insight into the behaviors of the environment. Whereas, since trace can only record the state of discrete variables in our model, we also need to utilize traditional precondition and postcondition to mark values of continuous variables. Besides, time is a crucial element in CPS, so we add a global clock variable called *now* in our assertions.

Altogether, the formula has the new form of $[tr \bullet p_c]\ S\ [tr' \bullet q_c]$. tr and tr' represent the initial trace and ending trace. p_c and q_c record the states of continuous variables and the starting/termination time of S.

3   Proof System

In this section, we present a proof system for our language to prove the correctness of CPS with shared-variable concurrency. We give auxiliary rules, rules for basic commands and rules for compound constructs in turn. Also, some programs are attached and act as examples to illustrate the usage of these rules.

3.1   Auxiliary Rules

We give two auxiliary rules in this subsection. **Rule 1** is defined to convert the formula of the trace form to the classic form in Hoare Logic. **Rule 2** is similar to the traditional consequence rule in Hoare Logic.

Rule 1. Transformation

$$\frac{[tr \bullet p_c]\ S\ [tr' \bullet q_c],\ (last(tr) \bullet p_c) \rightsquigarrow p,\ (last(tr') \bullet q_c) \rightsquigarrow q}{\{p\}\ S\ \{q\}}$$

Actually, when we prove the correctness of program, the real focus is data state. Thus, we link our proof system with traditional Hoare Logic through this rule. We introduce the notation of $\rightsquigarrow$ as below. It maps the elements of the snapshot sp to the corresponding data states, and it is different from the normal implication (i.e., $\rightarrow$). $PL(\sigma)$ translates the mapping relations in the data state into expressions of predicate logic. For example, if $\sigma =_{df} \{x \mapsto 0, y \mapsto 1\}$, then $PL(\sigma) = (x = 0 \land y = 1)$.

$$(sp \bullet p_c) \rightsquigarrow p =_{df} (PL(\pi_2(sp)) \land p_c) \rightarrow p$$

Rule 2. Consequence

$$\frac{[tr_1 \bullet p_{c1}] \; S \; [tr_1' \bullet q_{c1}], \; (tr \bullet p_c) \xrightarrow{c} (tr_1 \bullet p_{c1}), \; (tr_1' \bullet q_{c1}) \xrightarrow{c} (tr' \bullet q_c)}{[tr \bullet p_c] \; S \; [tr' \bullet q_c]}$$

We use this rule to strengthen the precondition and weaken the postcondition. The notation of $\xrightarrow{c}$ is used to define the implication relation of data states.

$$(tr \bullet p_c) \xrightarrow{c} (tr_1 \bullet p_{c1}) =_{df} ((tr - last(tr)) = (tr_1 - last(tr_1)))$$
$$\wedge ((PL(\pi_2(last(tr))) \wedge p_c) \to (PL(\pi_2(last(tr_1))) \wedge p_{c1}))$$

3.2   Proof Rules for Basic Commands

In this subsection, we give proof rules for basic commands, including $x := e$, $@(gd)$ and $R(v, \dot{v})$ **until** g.

3.2.1 Assignment

Rule 3. Assignment

$$\frac{tr \xrightarrow{env} (tr' - last(tr')), \; pre(last(tr'), tr') \rightsquigarrow PL(\pi_2(last(tr')))[e/x]}{[tr \bullet p_c] \; x := e \; [tr' \bullet p_c]}$$

Here, $PL(\sigma)[e/x]$ is the same as $PL(\sigma)$ except that all free instances of variable x are substituted for expression e. We define $\xrightarrow{env}$ to describe the relationship between tr and tr'. It implies that only environment steps are performed between the end of tr and the end of tr'. This is due to the fact that when "x" is a shared variable, it can be modified by the environment's action.

$$tr_1 \xrightarrow{env} tr_2 =_{df} \exists s \cdot (tr_2 = tr_1 \hat{\;} s \wedge \forall ttr \in s \cdot \pi_3(ttr) = 0)$$

An example of an application of this rule is:

$$[tr_0 \bullet v = 1.25 \wedge now = 0] \; x := x + 1 \; [tr_1 \bullet v = 1.25 \wedge now = 0].$$

Here, $tr_0 =_{df} \langle (0, \sigma_0, 1) \rangle$, $tr_1 =_{df} \langle (0, \sigma_0, 1), (0, \sigma_1, 1) \rangle$, $\sigma_0 =_{df} \{x \mapsto 0\}$ and $\sigma_1 =_{df} \{x \mapsto 1\}$. $v = 1.25 \wedge now = 0$ represents the initial state of continuous variables and the starting time, and it remains unchanged. This is because the discrete assignment does not change continuous values, and it is an atomic action which takes no time.

3.2.2 Discrete Event Guard

For the discrete event guard @gd, it can be triggered by the program itself or by the environment, so we divide it into two rules as follows.

(1) Rule 4-1 describes that gd is triggered due to the program's own action.
Rule 4-1. Guard_SelfTrig

$$\frac{last(tr) \rightsquigarrow gd}{[tr \bullet p_c]\ @gd\ [tr \bullet p_c]}$$

$last(tr) \rightsquigarrow gd$ means that the current trace can trigger gd, that is, the event guard gd is triggered by the program itself without waiting for the environment to trigger. Due to this immediate trigger action, nothing needs to change.

By utilizing this rule, we can prove the following formula. Here, $tr_1 =_{df} \langle (0, \sigma_0, 1), (0, \sigma_1, 1) \rangle$, $\sigma_0 =_{df} \{x \mapsto 0\}$ and $\sigma_1 =_{df} \{x \mapsto 1\}$.

$$[tr_1 \bullet v = 1.25 \land now = 0]\ @(x > 0)\ [tr_1 \bullet v = 1.25 \land now = 0].$$

(2) Rule 4-2 implies gd waits for the environment to trigger it.
Rule 4-2. Guard_EnvTrig

$$\frac{last(tr) \rightsquigarrow \neg gd,\ last(s) \rightsquigarrow gd,\ \forall ttr \in s \cdot \pi_3(ttr) = 0,\ \forall ttr \in (s - last(s)) \cdot ttr \rightsquigarrow \neg gd}{[tr \bullet p_c]\ @gd\ [tr^{\frown}s \bullet p_c[\pi_1(last(s))/now]]}$$

When the process cannot trigger the guard under the current state (i.e., $last(tr) \rightsquigarrow \neg gd$), the process will wait for environment's action to trigger gd. $\forall ttr \in s \cdot \pi_3(ttr) = 0$ implies that all the actions in the trace s are contributed by the environment. $\forall ttr \in (s - last(s)) \cdot ttr \rightsquigarrow \neg gd$ and $last(s) \rightsquigarrow gd$ emphasize that it is the last action of s triggers gd and none of the previous actions can trigger gd. The global clock now is updated to $\pi_1(last(s))$ because of the consumption of waiting.

With this rule, we can deduce:

$$[tr_1 \bullet v = 1.25 \land now = 0]\ @(y > 0)\ [tr_2 \bullet v = 1.25 \land now = 2].$$

Here, $tr_1 =_{df} \langle (0, \sigma_0, 1), (0, \sigma_1, 1) \rangle$, $tr_2 =_{df} tr_1^{\frown} \langle (1, \sigma', 0), (2, \sigma'', 0) \rangle$, $\sigma_0 =_{df} \{x \mapsto 0\}$, $\sigma_1 =_{df} \{x \mapsto 1\}$, $\sigma' =_{df} \{x \mapsto 1, y \mapsto 0\}$ and $\sigma'' =_{df} \{x \mapsto 1, y \mapsto 1\}$.

3.2.3 Continuous Behavior

For the continuous behavior $R(v, \dot{v})$ **until** g, we list the following four types of rules according to the types of guard g. More specifically, we further detail each type of rules on the basis of the time when g is triggered (i.e., triggered at the beginning or not).

(1) Rule 5-1-1 and **Rule 5-1-2** describe the situation where the guard condition is merely determined by continuous variables (i.e., $g \equiv gc$). Hence, we can omit trace in this rule and focus on the states of continuous variables in them.

Rule 5-1-1. Cb_ContGuard_1

$$\frac{gc(v_{now})}{[tr \bullet p_c] \; R(v, \dot{v}) \; \textbf{until} \; gc \; [tr \bullet p_c]}$$

Rule 5-1-2. Cb_ContGuard_2

$$\frac{p_c[t_0/now] \wedge \exists t' \in (t_0, \infty) \cdot \boxed{(gc(v_{t'}) \wedge \forall t \in [t_0, t') \cdot \neg gc(v_t) \wedge now = t')} \\ \wedge R(v, \dot{v}) \; \textbf{during} \; [t_0, now) \to q_c}{[tr \bullet p_c] \; R(v, \dot{v}) \; \textbf{until} \; gc \; [tr \bullet q_c]}$$

As shown in **Rule 5-1-1**, if gc is satisfied at the beginning of the program (i.e., $gc(v_{now})$), then the state will not change. Here, $gc(v_t)$ means that the value of continuous variables v at the time t makes gc true.

Rule 5-1-2 describes the situation where gc is not triggered at the beginning. Here, t_0 is a fresh variable representing the initial time. The program waits for gc to be triggered (highlighted in **Rule 5-1-2**). now is updated to t' and the continuous variable v is evolving as $R(v, \dot{v})$ during this period, expressed by $R(v, \dot{v})$ **during** $[t_0, now)$.

By applying this rule, we can get the following proof. Here, $tr_0 =_{df} \langle (0, \sigma_0, 1) \rangle$ and $\sigma_0 =_{df} \{x \mapsto 0\}$.

$$[tr_0 \bullet v = 1.25 \wedge now = 0] \; \dot{v} = 1 \; \textbf{until} \; v \geqslant 2.5 \; [tr_0 \bullet v = 2.5 \wedge now = 1.25].$$

(2) Rule 5-2-1 and **Rule 5-2-2** contain rules that the guard concerns purely discrete variables (i.e., $g \equiv gd$). Different from the above rules, we need to track the traces. This is because the states of discrete variables are recorded in traces.

Rule 5-2-1. Cb_DiscGuard_1

$$\frac{last(tr) \rightsquigarrow gd}{[tr \bullet p_c] \; R(v, \dot{v}) \; \textbf{until} \; gd \; [tr \bullet p_c]}$$

Rule 5-2-2. Cb_DiscGuard_2

$$\frac{p_c[t_0/now] \wedge EnvTrig2(gd) \wedge now = \pi_1(last(s)) \wedge R(v, \dot{v}) \; \textbf{during} \; [t_0, now) \to q_c}{[tr \bullet p_c] \; R(v, \dot{v}) \; \textbf{until} \; gd \; [tr\widehat{}s \bullet q_c]}$$

The process is evolving as $R(v, \dot{v})$ until the guard gd is triggered. Similarly, as shown in **Rule 5-2-1**, if gd is triggered when the program starts, then nothing needs to change.

Otherwise, as presented in **Rule 5-2-2**, gd waits to be triggered by the environment, defined by $EnvTrig2(gd)$. The definition of $EnvTrig2(gd)$ below is similar to **Rule 4-2**.

$$EnvTrig2(gd) =_{df} last(tr) \rightsquigarrow \neg gd \wedge last(s) \rightsquigarrow gd \wedge \forall ttr \in s \cdot \pi_3(ttr) = 0$$
$$\wedge \forall ttr \in (s - last(s)) \cdot ttr \rightsquigarrow \neg gd$$

This rule leads to:

$$[tr_1 \bullet v = 1.25 \wedge now = 0] \; \dot{v} = 1 \textbf{ until } y > 0 \; [tr_2 \bullet v = 3.25 \wedge now = 2].$$

Here, $tr_1 =_{df} \langle (0, \sigma_0, 1), (0, \sigma_1, 1) \rangle$, $tr_2 =_{df} tr_1 {}^\frown \langle (1, \sigma', 0), (2, \sigma'', 0) \rangle$, $\sigma_0 =_{df} \{x \mapsto 0\}$, $\sigma_1 =_{df} \{x \mapsto 1\}$, $\sigma' =_{df} \{x \mapsto 1, y \mapsto 0\}$ and $\sigma'' =_{df} \{x \mapsto 1, y \mapsto 1\}$.

(3) Rule 5-3-1 and **Rule 5-3-2** denote the condition where the guard is a hybrid one with the form of $gd \wedge gc$.

Rule 5-3-1. Cb_HybridGuard1_1

$$\frac{gc(v_{now}) \wedge (last(tr) \rightsquigarrow gd)}{[tr \bullet p_c] \; R(v, \dot{v}) \textbf{ until } gd \wedge gc \; [tr \bullet p_c]}$$

Rule 5-3-2. Cb_HybridGuard1_2

$$\frac{p_c[t_0/now] \wedge (last(tr {}^\frown s) \rightsquigarrow gd) \wedge Await(gd \wedge gc)}{\wedge \exists t' \geqslant \pi_1(last(tr {}^\frown s)) \cdot (gc(v_{t'}) \wedge now = t') \wedge R(v, \dot{v}) \textbf{ during } [t_0, now) \rightarrow q_c}{[tr \bullet p_c] \; R(v, \dot{v}) \textbf{ until } gd \wedge gc \; [tr {}^\frown s \bullet q_c]}$$

For the hybrid guard $gd \wedge gc$, only when gd and gc are both triggered, the relevant continuous evolution terminates. **Rule 5-3-1** depicts that $gd \wedge gc$ is satisfied at the beginning.

We apply **Rule 5-3-2** to present the condition where $gd \wedge gc$ is not triggered at the beginning. We can first wait for gd to become true. Once gd holds, we wait for gc. $Await(gd \wedge gc)$ defined below states that both guards do not hold in the intervening period, and the highlighted part formalizes gd is not satisfied at t. Since gd can only be changed at discrete time points, it keeps unchanged until the next discrete action happens. As illustrated in Fig. 1, we define $LClosest(tr {}^\frown s, t)$ (i.e., the closest discrete action's time point to t) to imply gd's state at t. Here, π_1^* is lifted from a single snapshot to a sequence of snapshots. The demonstration of this rule is presented in Fig. 2(a).

$$Await(gd \wedge gc) =_{df} \forall t < \pi_1(last(tr {}^\frown s)) \cdot$$
$$\left(\begin{array}{c} \neg gc(v_t) \vee \\ \left(\exists ttr \in (tr {}^\frown s - pre(last(tr))) \cdot (\pi_1(ttr) = LClosest(tr {}^\frown s, t) \wedge ttr \rightsquigarrow \neg gd) \right) \end{array} \right),$$

$$LClosest(tr {}^\frown s, t) = t_c,$$

$$\textbf{if } t_c \in \pi_1^*(tr {}^\frown s) \cdot \left(t_c \leqslant t \wedge (\forall time \in \pi_1^*(tr {}^\frown s) \cdot (time \leqslant t \rightarrow t_c \geqslant time)) \right)$$

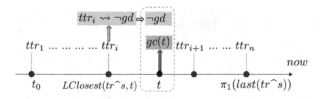

Fig. 1. Demonstration of *Await*

Also, we give an example to show this rule. Here, $tr_1 =_{df} \langle (0, \sigma_0, 1), (0, \sigma_1, 1) \rangle$, $tr_2 =_{df} tr_1{}^\frown \langle (1, \sigma', 0), (2, \sigma'', 0) \rangle$, $\sigma_0 =_{df} \{x \mapsto 0\}$, $\sigma_1 =_{df} \{x \mapsto 1\}$, $\sigma' =_{df} \{x \mapsto 1, y \mapsto 0\}$ and $\sigma'' =_{df} \{x \mapsto 1, y \mapsto 1\}$.

$$[tr_1 \bullet v = 1.25 \wedge now = 0] \; \dot{v} = 1 \textbf{ until } y > 0 \wedge v \geqslant 2.5 \; [tr_2 \bullet v = 3.25 \wedge now = 2]$$

(4) Rule 5-4-1 and **Rule 5-4-2** include rules that the guard is a hybrid guard with the form of $gd \vee gc$.

Rule 5-4-1. Cb_HybridGuard2_1

$$\frac{gc(now) \vee (last(tr) \leadsto gd)}{[tr \bullet p_c] \; R(v, \dot{v}) \textbf{ until } gd \vee gc \; [tr \bullet p_c]}$$

Rule 5-4-2. Cb_HybridGuard2_2

$$\frac{p_c[t_0/now] \wedge AwaitTrig(gd \vee gc) \wedge R(v, \dot{v}) \textbf{ during } [t_0, now) \to q_c}{[tr \bullet p_c] \; R(v, \dot{v}) \textbf{ until } gd \vee gc \; [tr{}^\frown s \bullet q_c]}$$

For the hybrid guard $gd \vee gc$, the continuous variable v evolves until the guard gd or gc is satisfied. **Rule 5-4-1** portrays that at least one guard condition is satisfied at the beginning.

If the current data state cannot meet gd and gc, the program will wait to be triggered. As given in **Rule 5-4-2**, we define $AwaitTrig(gd \vee gc)$ to describe the waiting and the eventual triggering process. The first two lines in the bracket indicate that gc and gd are both unsatisfied before the terminal time t'. The third line informs that it meets gc or gd at the time t'. The demonstrative figure is shown in Fig. 2(b).

$$AwaitTrig(gd \vee gc) =_{df} \exists t' \in (t_0, \infty) \cdot$$

$$\begin{pmatrix} (\forall t < t' \cdot \neg gc(v_t)) \\ \wedge (\forall ttr \in (tr{}^\frown s - pre(last(tr))) \cdot (\pi_1(ttr) < t') \to (ttr \leadsto \neg gd)) \\ \wedge (gc(v_{t'}) \vee (\pi_1(last(tr{}^\frown s)) = t' \wedge last(tr{}^\frown s) \leadsto gd)) \wedge now = t' \end{pmatrix}$$

According to this rule, we can get:

$$[tr_1 \bullet v = 1.25 \wedge now = 0] \; \dot{v} = 1 \textbf{ until } y > 0 \vee v \geqslant 2.5 \; [tr_1' \bullet v = 2.5 \wedge now = 1.25].$$

Here, $tr_1 =_{df} \langle (0, \sigma_0, 1), (0, \sigma_1, 1) \rangle$, $tr_1' =_{df} tr_1{}^\frown \langle (1, \sigma', 1) \rangle$, $\sigma_0 =_{df} \{x \mapsto 0\}$, $\sigma_1 =_{df} \{x \mapsto 1\}$ and $\sigma' =_{df} \{x \mapsto 1, y \mapsto 0\}$.

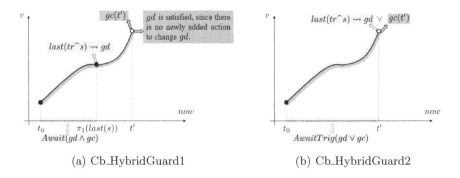

(a) Cb_HybridGuard1   (b) Cb_HybridGuard2

Fig. 2. Cb_HybridGuard

3.3   Proof Rules for Compound Constructs

In this subsection, rules for compound constructs (Sequential Composition, Iteration Construct and Parallel Composition) are enumerated.

Rule 6. Sequential Composition

$$\frac{[tr \bullet p_c] \; P \; [tr_m \bullet p_m], \; [tr_m \bullet p_m] \; Q \; [tr' \bullet q_c]}{[tr \bullet p_c] \; P; Q \; [tr' \bullet q_c]}$$

It requires that the trace and the continuous variables' values in P's post-condition are consistent with those in Q's precondition.

As an example, we assume that $tr_0 =_{df} \langle (0, \sigma_0, 1) \rangle$, $tr_1 =_{df} \langle (0, \sigma_0, 1), (0, \sigma_1, 1) \rangle$, $\sigma_0 =_{df} \{x \mapsto 0\}$ and $\sigma_1 =_{df} \{x \mapsto 1\}$. From

$$[tr_0 \bullet v = 1.25 \wedge now = 0] \; x := x + 1 \; [tr_1 \bullet v = 1.25 \wedge now = 0]$$
$$[tr_1 \bullet v = 1.25 \wedge now = 0] \; \dot{v} = 1 \; \textbf{until} \; v \geqslant 2.5 \; [tr_1 \bullet v = 2.5 \wedge now = 1.25],$$

through **Rule 6**, we have:

$$[tr_0 \bullet v = 1.25 \wedge now = 0] \; x := x + 1; \dot{v} = 1 \; \textbf{until} \; v \geqslant 2.5 \; [tr_1 \bullet v = 2.5 \wedge now = 1.25].$$

Rule 7. Conditional Choice

$$\frac{[b \& \; (tr \bullet p_c)] \; P \; [tr' \bullet q_c]}{[\neg b \& \; (tr \bullet p_c)] \; Q \; [tr' \bullet q_c]}{[tr \bullet p_c] \; \textbf{if} \; b \; \textbf{then} \; P \; \textbf{else} \; Q \; [tr' \bullet q_c]}$$

The first line of this rule implies that we need to prove $[tr \bullet p_c] \; P \; [tr' \bullet q_c]$, if the Boolean condition b is satisfied in the data state of $last(tr) \bullet p_c$ (i.e., $last(tr) \bullet p_c \rightsquigarrow b$). On the contrary, the second line means that if the data state cannot meet b, then we need to prove $[tr \bullet p_c] \; Q \; [tr' \bullet q_c]$.

We define that $tr_0 =_{df} \langle (0, \sigma_0, 1) \rangle$, $tr_1 =_{df} \langle (0, \sigma_0, 1), (0, \sigma_1, 1) \rangle$, $\sigma_0 =_{df} \{x \mapsto 0\}$ and $\sigma_1 =_{df} \{x \mapsto 1\}$. From this rule, we can prove:

$[tr_0 \bullet v = 1.25 \wedge now = 0]\textbf{if} \; x \geqslant 0 \; \textbf{then} \; x := x + 1 \; \textbf{else} \; x := x - 1[tr_1 \bullet v = 1.25 \wedge now = 0].$

Rule 8. Iteration Construct

$$\frac{(last(tr) \bullet p_c) \rightsquigarrow I, \ \{I \wedge b\} \ P \ \{I\}, \ (last(tr') \bullet q_c) \rightsquigarrow (I \wedge \neg b)}{[tr \bullet p_c] \ \textbf{while} \ b \ \textbf{do} \ P \ [tr' \bullet q_c]}$$

For the iteration construct, we follow the classic definition in Hoare logic and employ loop invariant [4] to prove it. Here, I is the invariant of this iteration and it can be inferred from the precondition. We only need to focus on the last element of tr, since the trace can be generated by the previous programs. The assertion of $\{I \wedge b\} \ P \ \{I\}$ stays the same as that in traditional Hoare Logic. When the program terminates, the data state should satisfy $I \wedge \neg b$ (i.e., $(last(tr') \bullet q_c) \rightsquigarrow (I \wedge \neg b)$).

We take the program below as an example to explain this rule.

$$[tr_0 \bullet v = 1.25 \wedge now = 0] \ \textbf{while} \ x \leqslant 2 \ \textbf{do} \ x := x + 1 \ [tr_3 \bullet v = 1.25 \wedge now = 0]$$

Here, $tr_0 =_{df} \langle (0, \sigma_0, 1) \rangle$, $tr_3 =_{df} \langle (0, \sigma_0, 1), (0, \sigma_1, 1), (0, \sigma_2, 1), (0, \sigma_3, 1) \rangle$ and $\sigma_i =_{df} \{x \mapsto i\}(i = 0, 1, 2, 3)$. In order to prove this formula, we need to prove the following three premises. We define $x \leqslant 3$ as the invariant I.

- $(last(tr) \bullet p_c) \rightsquigarrow I$ and $(last(tr') \bullet q_c) \rightsquigarrow (I \wedge \neg b)$: They can be deduced with predicate logic directly.
- $\{I \wedge b\} \ P \ \{I\}$: To prove this, we transform it to the form of trace, i.e.,

$$[tr_{Ib}] \ x := x + 1 \ [tr_{I'}]$$

Here, tr_{Ib} stands for the trace whose data state satisfies $I \wedge b$ and $tr_{I'}$ is the terminal trace after executing $x := x + 1$. We define $tr_{Ib} =_{df} \langle (0, \sigma_{Ib}, 1) \rangle$, $PL(\sigma_{Ib}) \rightarrow x \leqslant 2$, $tr_{I'} =_{df} tr_{Ib} \smallfrown \langle (0, \sigma_{I'}, 1) \rangle$ and $\sigma_{I'} = \sigma_{Ib}[x + 1/x]$. With **Rule 3**, $[tr_{Ib}] \ x := x + 1 \ [tr_{I'}]$ is proved. Next, **Rule 1** leads to $\{I \wedge b\} \ P \ \{I\}$.

Rule 9. Parallel Composition

$$\frac{\begin{array}{l} [tr \bullet p_c] \ P \ [tr_1 \bullet (q_{c1} \wedge now = t_1)], \\ [tr \bullet p_c] \ Q \ [tr_2 \bullet (q_{c2} \wedge now = t_2)], \\ q_c = q_{c1} \wedge q_{c2}, \ tr_{add} \in Merge(tr_1 - tr, tr_2 - tr), \ tr' = tr \smallfrown tr_{add} \end{array}}{[tr \bullet p_c] \ P \ || \ Q \ [tr' \bullet q_c[max\{t_1, t_2\}/now]]}$$

In our approach, we employ the trace model to reflect the interaction between the parallel components, so that we can focus on the individual components first and then combine them.

We assume that continuous variables cannot be shared writable in our language. It makes sense, since a continuous variable only has a determined value at one time in the real-world. Therefore, q_{c1} and q_{c2} have no shared writable variables. Thus, we can simply combine q_{c1} and q_{c2} as $q_{c1} \wedge q_{c2}$. Besides, the maximal terminal time of P and Q is the terminal time of $P \parallel Q$. As for the final trace of $P \parallel Q$, we propose a *Merge* function to define the terminal trace of parallel composition. We define $Merge(trace_1, trace_2)$ as below. Here, $trace_1$, $trace_2$ and $trace_3$ stand for the newly added traces of P, Q and $P \parallel Q$ respectively.

$$Merge(trace_1, trace_2) =_{df}$$

$$\left\{ \begin{array}{c} (\pi_1^*(trace_3) = \pi_1^*(trace_1) = \pi_1^*(trace_2)) \wedge \\ trace_3 | (\pi_2^*(trace_3) = \pi_2^*(trace_1) = \pi_2^*(trace_2)) \wedge \\ (\pi_3^*(trace_3) = \pi_3^*(trace_1) + \pi_3^*(trace_2)) \wedge (2 \notin \pi_3^*(trace_3)) \end{array} \right\}$$

Here, π_i^* is lifted from a single snapshot to a sequence of snapshots. As defined in Sect. 3, a snapshot in the trace is a tuple (t, σ, μ). The first two conditions imply that the time and data stored in the trace of the parallel composition (i.e., $trace_3$) should be the same as those in both parallel components (i.e., $trace_1$ and $trace_2$). The third one indicates that the actions of parallel components P and Q are also the actions of their parallel composition. The last condition restricts that every snapshot can only be contributed by one parallel component. In the trace model, although the two parallel components can do actions at the same time, snapshots of them need to be added to the trace one by one.

Considering the following parallel program, we illustrate this rule. As an example, from

$$[tr_0 \bullet v = 0 \wedge now = 0] \; x := x + 1; \dot{v} = 1 \text{ until } v \geqslant 1 \; [tr_1' \bullet v = 1 \wedge now = 1],$$
$$[tr_0 \bullet u = 0 \wedge now = 0] \; x := 2; \dot{u} = 2 \text{ until } u \geqslant 4 \; [tr_2' \bullet u = 4 \wedge now = 2],$$

through **Rule 9**, we have:

$$[tr_0 \bullet v = 0 \wedge u = 0 \wedge now = 0]$$
$$(x := x + 1; \dot{v} = 1 \text{ until } v \geqslant 1) \parallel (x := 2; \dot{u} = 2 \text{ until } u \geqslant 4)$$
$$[tr' \bullet v = 1 \wedge u = 4 \wedge now = 2]$$

where,

$$\sigma_i =_{df} \{x \mapsto i\} (i = 0, 1, 2, 3), \; tr_0 =_{df} \langle (0, \sigma_0, 1) \rangle,$$
$$tr_1' =_{df} \langle (0, \sigma_0, 1), (0, \sigma_2, 0), (0, \sigma_3, 1) \rangle \vee \langle (0, \sigma_0, 1), (0, \sigma_1, 1), (0, \sigma_2, 0) \rangle,$$
$$tr_2' =_{df} \langle (0, \sigma_0, 1), (0, \sigma_2, 1), (0, \sigma_3, 0) \rangle \vee \langle (0, \sigma_0, 1), (0, \sigma_1, 0), (0, \sigma_2, 1) \rangle,$$
$$tr' =_{df} \langle (0, \sigma_0, 1), (0, \sigma_2, 1), (0, \sigma_3, 1) \rangle \vee \langle (0, \sigma_0, 1), (0, \sigma_1, 1), (0, \sigma_2, 1) \rangle.$$

Here, as introduced before, $tr = tr_a \vee tr_b$ denotes that there are two possible cases of tr, i.e., tr can be equal to tr_a or tr_b. In the above sample parallel program, tr_1' and tr_2' both have two possible traces because they represent two different execution orders of $x := x + 1$ and $x := 2$. As a consequence, the final trace of their parallel composition tr' has two cases through *Merge* function.

4   Case Study

In this section, we present an example of a Battery Management System (BMS) to illustrate the usage of our proof system. We first give the BMS program to demonstrate the syntax of our language. Then, we prove some related properties using our proof system.

4.1   Description of BMS

We employ the process of heat management in BMS as an example to illustrate our language. For simplicity, we assume that the battery works properly if its temperature is between $T_{safemin}$ and $T_{safemax}$. When the vehicle is moving and the temperature does not exceed the threshold value T_{MAX}, the temperature increases linearly. BMS will cool down the battery if the temperature is equal to or greater than $T_{safemax}$. Also, the temperature decreases linearly when BMS is cooling and the temperature does not reach the threshold value T_{MIN}. If the temperature is equal to or less than $T_{safemin}$, BMS will stop cooling.

$$BMS =_{df} Ctrl \parallel Temp;$$

$$Ctrl =_{df} \textbf{while } DT < 60 \textbf{ do}$$

$$\left\{ \begin{array}{l} @(caron = 1); \ \dot{t} = 1 \textbf{ until } t \geqslant DT + 1; \\ \textbf{if}(\theta \geqslant T_{safemax})\textbf{then } coolon := 1; \ \textbf{else } coolon := coolon; \\ \textbf{if}(\theta \leqslant T_{safemin})\textbf{then } coolon := 0; \ \textbf{else } coolon := coolon; \\ DT := t; \end{array} \right\}$$

$$Temp =_{df} \textbf{while } DT < 60 \textbf{ do}$$

$$\left\{ \begin{array}{l} \textbf{if}(coolon == 0)\textbf{then } \dot{\theta} = 1 \textbf{ until}(\theta \geqslant T_{MAX} \vee coolon = 1); \\ \qquad\qquad \textbf{else } \dot{\theta} = -2 \textbf{ until}(\theta \leqslant T_{MIN} \vee coolon = 0); \end{array} \right\}$$

Here, DT is an auxiliary variable to realize the delay operation. t and θ represent the time and the temperature, and we assume $\theta = 10$ and $t = 0$ at the beginning. $caron = 1$ means that the car is moving. $coolon$ stands for the switch of cooling, BMS starts to cool down the battery if $coolon = 1$. We set $T_{MIN} = 0$, $T_{MAX} = 100$, $T_{safemin} = 10$ and $T_{safemax} = 40$.

4.2   Proof for BMS

We first give an overview of the proof, and then present the proof outline of $Ctrl$ and $Temp$. Finally, we prove the whole program with **Rule 9**.

4.2.1. Overview

The program of BMS should meet that the battery must begin to cool down once the temperature is equal to or greater than $T_{safemax}$, and it stops cooling when the temperature is equal to or lower than $T_{safemin}$. Further, the temperature of the battery is guaranteed to be controlled between $T_{safemin}$ and $T_{safemax}$. Altogether, the program BMS should satisfy the following correctness formula.

$$\{Init\}\ BMS\ \{DI \wedge CI\}$$

where,

$$Init =_{df} caron = 1 \wedge DT = 0 \wedge coolon = 0 \wedge \theta = 10 \wedge t = 0,$$
$$DI =_{df} (\theta \geqslant T_{safemax} \rightarrow coolon = 1) \wedge (\theta \leqslant T_{safemin} \rightarrow coolon = 0)$$
$$\wedge DT \leqslant 60 \wedge caron = 1,$$
$$CI =_{df} T_{safemin} \leqslant \theta \leqslant T_{safemax}.$$

We first convert this correctness formula to the form of trace model.

$$[tr \bullet p_c \wedge now = 0]\ BMS\ [tr' \bullet q_c \wedge now = 60]$$

Here, since we are only concerned with the last snapshot of tr', we abstract the intermediate snapshots done by the loop body as a sequence of three dots $(...)$. $PL(\sigma') \rightarrow (DI \wedge DT = 60)$ indicates that the terminal data state σ' meets $DI \wedge DT = 60$.

$$p_c =_{df} \theta = 10 \wedge t = 0,\ q_c =_{df} 10 \leqslant \theta \leqslant 40 \wedge t = 60,$$
$$tr =_{df} \langle(0, \sigma, 1)\rangle,\ tr' =_{df} \langle(0, \sigma, 1), ..., (60, \sigma', 1)\rangle,$$
$$\sigma =_{df} \{caron \mapsto 1, DT \mapsto 0, coolon \mapsto 0\},\ PL(\sigma') \rightarrow (DI \wedge DT = 60).$$

4.2.2. Proof for Ctrl

In this part, we focus on the process of $Ctrl$ and we want to prove $[tr \bullet p_c \wedge now = 0]\ Ctrl\ [tr_1 \bullet q_{c1} \wedge now = 60]$. The proof outline of $Ctrl$ is given below.

$[tr \bullet p_c \wedge now = 0]$

while $DT < 60$ **do**

$$
\begin{cases}
\quad [tr_{Ib} \bullet p_{dt} \wedge now = DT]...[1] \\
\quad @(caron = 1); \\
\quad [tr_{Ib} \bullet p_{dt} \wedge now = DT]...[2] \\
\quad t = 1 \text{ \textbf{until} } t \geqslant DT + 1; \\
\quad [tr_{Ib} \bullet p_{dt+1} \wedge now = DT + 1]...[3] \\
\quad \textbf{if}(\theta \geqslant T_{safemax})\textbf{then} \\
\qquad \begin{cases} [(\theta \geqslant 40)\&(tr_{Ib} \bullet p_{dt+1} \wedge now = DT + 1)]...[3.1] \\ \quad coolon := 1; \\ [tr_{Ib}{}^\frown\langle(now, \sigma_{c1}, 1)\rangle \bullet p_{dt+1} \wedge now = DT + 1]...[3.2] \end{cases} \\
\quad \textbf{else} \\
\qquad \begin{cases} [\neg(\theta \geqslant 40)\&(tr_{Ib} \bullet p_{dt+1} \wedge now = DT + 1)]...[3.3] \\ \quad coolon := coolon; \\ [tr_{Ib}{}^\frown\langle(now, \sigma_{Ib}, 1)\rangle \bullet p_{dt+1} \wedge now = DT + 1]...[3.4] \end{cases} \\
\quad [tr_{Ib}{}^\frown\langle(now, \sigma_{Ib}, 1)\rangle \bullet p_{dt+1} \wedge now = DT + 1]...[4] \\
\quad \textbf{if}(\theta \leqslant T_{safemin})\textbf{then} \\
\qquad \begin{cases} [(\theta \leqslant 10)\&(tr_{Ib1} \bullet p_{dt+1} \wedge now = DT + 1)]...[4.1] \\ \quad coolon := 0; \\ [tr_{Ib1}{}^\frown\langle(now, \sigma_{c2}, 1)\rangle \bullet p_{dt+1} \wedge now = DT + 1]...[4.2] \end{cases} \\
\quad \textbf{else} \\
\qquad \begin{cases} [\neg(\theta \leqslant 10)\&(tr_{Ib1} \bullet p_{dt+1} \wedge now = DT + 1)]...[4.3] \\ \quad coolon := coolon; \\ [tr_{Ib1}{}^\frown\langle(now, \sigma_{Ib}, 1)\rangle \bullet p_{dt+1} \wedge now = DT + 1]...[4.4] \end{cases} \\
\quad [tr_{Ib1}{}^\frown\langle(now, \sigma_{Ib}, 1)\rangle \bullet p_{dt+1} \wedge now = DT + 1]...[5] \\
\quad DT := t; \\
\quad [tr_{Ib2}{}^\frown\langle(now, \sigma_t, 1)\rangle \bullet p_{dt+1} \wedge now = DT + 1]...[6] \\
\quad [tr_{I'} \bullet p_{dt+1} \wedge now = DT + 1]...[7]
\end{cases}
$$

$[tr_1 \bullet q_{c1} \wedge now = 60]$

Also, some notations are defined as below. Among them, $\sigma_{Ib}[1/coolon]$ is the same as σ_{Ib} except that the value of *coolon* is now assigned to 1.

$$p_{dt} =_{df} t = DT, \; p_{dt+1} =_{df} t = DT + 1, \; q_{c1} =_{df} true,$$

$$tr_1 =_{df} tr', \; tr_{Ib} =_{df} \langle(now, \sigma_{Ib}, 1)\rangle, \; tr_{Ib1} =_{df} tr_{Ib}{}^\frown\langle(now, \sigma_{Ib}, 1)\rangle,$$

$$tr_{Ib2} =_{df} tr_{Ib1}{}^\frown\langle(now, \sigma_{Ib}, 1)\rangle, \; tr_{I'} =_{df} tr_{Ib2}{}^\frown\langle(now, \sigma_I, 1)\rangle,$$

$$PL(\sigma_I) \rightarrow DI, \; PL(\sigma_{Ib}) \rightarrow (DI \wedge DT < 60),$$

$$\sigma_{c1} =_{df} \sigma_{Ib}[1/coolon], \; \sigma_{c2} =_{df} \sigma_{Ib}[0/coolon], \; \sigma_t =_{df} \sigma_{Ib}[t/DT].$$

4.2.3. Proof for Temp

In this part, we want to prove $[tr \bullet p_c \wedge now = 0] \; Temp \; [tr_2 \bullet q_{c2} \wedge now = 60]$. For gaining it, we present the proof outline of $Temp$ as below.

$$[tr \bullet p_c \wedge now = 0]$$

while $DT < 60$ **do**

$\left\{ \begin{array}{l} [tr_{Ib'} \bullet \theta = \theta_i \wedge now = t_i]...[1] \\ \mathbf{if}(coolon == 0)\mathbf{then} \\ \quad [(coolon == 0)\&(tr_{Ib'} \bullet \theta = \theta_i \wedge now = t_i)]...[1.1] \\ \qquad \dot\theta = 1 \; \mathbf{until}(\theta \geqslant T_{MAX} \vee coolon = 1); \\ \quad [tr_{Ib'}\widehat{} \langle (now, \sigma_{c1}, 0) \rangle \bullet \theta = 40 \wedge now = t_i + 40 - \theta_I]...[1.2] \\ \mathbf{else} \\ \quad [\neg(coolon == 0)\&(tr_{Ib'} \bullet \theta = \theta_i \wedge now = t_i)]...[1.3] \\ \qquad \dot\theta = -2 \; \mathbf{until}(\theta \leqslant T_{MIN} \vee coolon = 0); \\ \quad [tr_{Ib'}\widehat{} \langle (now, \sigma_{c2}, 0) \rangle \bullet \theta = 10 \wedge now = t_i + \theta_i - 10]...[1.4] \\ \quad [tr_{I''} \bullet \theta_I \wedge now = (t_i + 40 - \theta_i) \vee (t_i + \theta_i - 10)]...[2] \end{array} \right.$

$$[tr_2 \bullet q_{c2} \wedge now = 60]$$

where,

$$10 \leqslant \theta_i \leqslant 40, \; q_{c2} =_{df} CI, \; \theta_I =_{df} CI, \; tr_{Ib'} =_{df} \langle (now, \sigma_{Ib}, 0) \rangle,$$
$$tr_{I''} =_{df} tr_{Ib'}\widehat{} \langle (now, \sigma_I, 0) \rangle, \; tr_2 =_{df} \langle (0, \sigma, 1), ..., (60, \sigma', 0) \rangle.$$

4.2.4. Parallel Composition of Ctrl and Temp

Based on the above proof, we now prove the parallel composition of $Ctrl$ and $Temp$. By means of **Rule 9**, we get:

$$[tr \bullet p_c \wedge now = 0] \; Ctrl \; [tr_1 \bullet q_{c1} \wedge now = 60],$$
$$[tr \bullet p_c \wedge now = 0] \; Temp \; [tr_2 \bullet q_{c2} \wedge now = 60],$$
$$\frac{q_c = q_{c1} \wedge q_{c2}, \; tr_{add} \in Merge(tr_1 - tr, tr_2 - tr), \; tr' = tr\widehat{}tr_{add}}{[tr \bullet p_c \wedge now = 0] \; Ctrl \parallel Temp \; [tr' \bullet q_c \wedge now = 60]}$$

In $Ctrl \parallel Temp$, we note that the actions of $Temp$ are all continuous. As a result, the actions recorded in tr' are exactly the same as those in tr_1 that were done by $Ctrl$. Thus, snapshots in $tr_1 - tr$ and $tr_2 - tr$ are structurally similar and vary only in their values of μ. μ is equal to 1 in $tr_1 - tr$ and 0 in $tr_2 - tr$. Then, the satisfaction of $tr_{add} \in Merge(tr_1 - tr, tr_2 - tr)$ is obvious. We employ **Rule 1**, and obtain the final desirable result, i.e., $\{Init\} \; BMS \; \{DI \wedge CI\}$.

5   Conclusion and Future Work

In this paper, we have presented a proof system for the language which is proposed to model cyber-physical systems based on our previous work [1,8].

The proof system is comprised of auxiliary rules, rules for basic commands and rules for compound constructs. We extended the triple in classical Hoare Logic $\{p\}\ S\ \{q\}$ to $[tr \bullet p_c]\ S\ [tr' \bullet q_c]$. In this specification, tr and tr' are introduced to pave the way for the proof of parallel programs with shared variables. Considering that trace can only record the values of discrete variables, we also appended a precondition p_c and a postcondition q_c to indicate the states of continuous variables. now, the global clock variable, is added to catch the feature of real-time in CPS as well. Our proof system is mainly supported by the trace model, it can not only realize compositional proof, but also link the proof system with denotational semantics [8]. For an intuitive demonstration of this proof system's usage, we also provided the example of a battery management system in this paper.

In the future, considering that the traditional approach of building the link between the proof system and semantics is mainly based on operational semantics, we will investigate the link between our proof system and our denotational semantics [8] in detail.

Acknowledgements. This work was partly supported by the National Key Research and Development Program of China (Grant No. 2018YFB2101300), the National Natural Science Foundation of China (Grant Nos. 61872145, 62032024), Shanghai Trusted Industry Internet Software Collaborative Innovation Center, and the Dean's Fund of Shanghai Key Laboratory of Trustworthy Computing (East China Normal University).

References

1. Banach, R., Zhu, H.: Language evolution and healthiness for critical cyber-physical systems. J. Softw. Evol. Process. **33**(9), e2301 (2021)
2. Jifeng, H., Qin, L.: A hybrid relational modelling language. In: Gibson-Robinson, T., Hopcroft, P., Lazić, R. (eds.) Concurrency, Security, and Puzzles. LNCS, vol. 10160, pp. 124–143. Springer, Cham (2017). https://doi.org/10.1007/978-3-319-51046-0_7
3. Henzinger, T.A.: The theory of hybrid automata. In: LICS, pp. 278–292. IEEE Computer Society (1996)
4. Hoare, C.A.R.: An axiomatic basis for computer programming. Commun. ACM **12**(10), 576–580 (1969)
5. Jones, C.B.: Accommodating interference in the formal design of concurrent object-based programs. Formal Meth. Syst. Des. **8**(2), 105–122 (1996). https://doi.org/10.1007/BF00122417
6. Lanotte, R., Merro, M., Tini, S.: A probabilistic calculus of cyber-physical systems. Inf. Comput. **279**, 104618 (2021)
7. Lee, E.A.: Cyber physical systems: design challenges. In: ISORC, pp. 363–369. IEEE Computer Society (2008)
8. Li, R., Zhu, H., Banach, R.: Denotational and algebraic semantics for cyber-physical systems. In: ICECCS, pp. 123–132. IEEE (2022)
9. Liu, J., et al.: A calculus for hybrid CSP. In: Ueda, K. (ed.) APLAS 2010. LNCS, vol. 6461, pp. 1–15. Springer, Heidelberg (2010). https://doi.org/10.1007/978-3-642-17164-2_1

10. Lunel, S., Mitsch, S., Boyer, B., Talpin, J.-P.: Parallel composition and modular verification of computer controlled systems in differential dynamic logic. In: ter Beek, M.H., McIver, A., Oliveira, J.N. (eds.) FM 2019. LNCS, vol. 11800, pp. 354–370. Springer, Cham (2019). https://doi.org/10.1007/978-3-030-30942-8_22
11. Owicki, S.S., Gries, D.: An axiomatic proof technique for parallel programs I. Acta Informatica **6**, 319–340 (1976). https://doi.org/10.1007/BF00268134
12. Chaochen, Z., Ji, W., Ravn, A.P.: A formal description of hybrid systems. In: Alur, R., Henzinger, T.A., Sontag, E.D. (eds.) HS 1995. LNCS, vol. 1066, pp. 511–530. Springer, Heidelberg (1996). https://doi.org/10.1007/BFb0020972

Theorem Proving for Maude Specifications Using Lean

Rubén Rubio[✉] and Adrián Riesco

Facultad de Informática, Universidad Complutense de Madrid, Madrid, Spain
{rubenrub,ariesco}@ucm.es

Abstract. Maude is a specification language based on rewriting logic whose programs can be executed, model checked, and analyzed with other techniques, but not easily theorem proved. On the other hand, Lean is a modern proof assistant based on the calculus of inductive constructions with a wide library of reusable proofs and definitions. This paper presents a translation from the first formalism to the second, and a tool that derives a Lean program from a Maude module in a predictable way. Hence, theorems can be proved in Lean about Maude specifications.

1 Introduction

Formal methods comprise a wide spectrum of specification formalisms and verification techniques for describing and checking the behavior of systems against their expected properties. These formalisms are usually influenced by the intended applications and verification approach, with varying automation and user intervention degrees. For instance, model checking has been widely used in industry because of the unattended nature and smooth learning curve, but it can only work for concrete size-bounded instances of a system unless non-trivial abstractions are used. On the contrary, interactive theorem proving demands more effort, knowledge and training from the user, but it can handle more general properties by induction [20]. Having the possibility of applying different techniques on the same specification and interoperate with different formalisms and tools is convenient for effective verification in an affordable way.

Maude [3,4] is a specification language based on rewriting logic [14,15], which extends membership equational logic [2] with non-deterministic rewrite rules that naturally represent concurrent computation. For modeling a system under this formalism, states are described as terms in an order-sorted signature modulo equations, while transitions are represented by rewrite rules acting on these terms. Specifications in Maude are organized in modules and can be executed with the multiple commands available in the interpreter. This combination of a simple but expressive syntax, powerful semantics, and efficient implementation makes Maude an appropriate tool for specifying a large number of systems. Moreover, a builtin LTL model checker [11] and other verification tools make Maude a convenient tool for formal verification. Regarding inductive theorem proving, the Maude ITP tool was presented in 2006 [5], but its features are not

© Springer Nature Switzerland AG 2022
A. Riesco and M. Zhang (Eds.): ICFEM 2022, LNCS 13478, pp. 263–280, 2022.
https://doi.org/10.1007/978-3-031-17244-1_16

comparable to those of widespread proof assistants, its reasoning capabilities are limited to the equational part of rewriting logic and induction on the relations is not supported, and it is currently incompatible with the latest Maude releases.

Lean [19] is a proof assistant based on the proposition-as-types paradigm of the calculus of inductive constructions, borrowed from Coq [1]. Notable features of Lean are powerful resolution with Haskell-like type classes, a metaprogramming framework, support for proof automation, a multithreaded type checker, and an intuitive interactive interface. The tool counts with a significant community-driven library of reusable definitions and proofs called *mathlib* [7], used to formalize non-trivial mathematical theories from undergraduate to novel research topics. The presentation in the current paper targets Lean 3, but the approach can be easily applied to the new ongoing version Lean 4 [18].

This paper presents a translation from rewriting logic to the calculus of constructions with inductive types used by the Lean language. The translation is implemented in a tool that automatically derives a Lean specification from a Maude module. It can be used to reason inductively and prove theorems about Maude-specified models, their terms, and their equational and rewriting relations. The transformed specification is constructive, predictable, and configurable and some lemmas are provided to facilitate building proofs on it. Indeed, the Lean simplifier can handle sorts and reduction to canonical form in most cases.

The structure of the paper is as follows: Sect. 2 briefly describes the formalisms and tools involved in this work, Sect. 3 presents the proposed translation, and Sect. 4 outlines the associated tool with an example. A more suggesting application is summarized in Sect. 5, Sect. 6 discusses on related work, and finally Sect. 7 concludes with ideas for future extension. The tool is available at github.com/fadoss/maude2lean.

2   Preliminaries

In this section we describe Maude and Lean, focusing on their underlying logics.

2.1   Rewriting Logic and Maude

Maude [4] is a high-performance logical framework and specification language based on rewriting logic [14]. This logic is parameterized by an equational logic, which in the case of Maude is membership equational logic [2], a logic that, in addition to *sorts* and *equations*, allows users to state *membership axioms* characterizing the elements of a sort. Rewriting logic extends membership equational logic with *rewrite rules*, which stand for transitions in concurrent systems.

In equational logic, a *many-sorted signature* $\Sigma = (S, \Sigma)$ is usually defined as a set of sorts S and an $(S^* \times S)$-indexed family $\Sigma = \{\Sigma_{s_1 \cdots s_n, s} : s_1 \cdots s_n \in S^*, s \in S\}$ of symbols. We say that a symbol $f \in \Sigma_{s_1 \cdots s_n, s}$ has range sort s and arity n, and receives that many arguments of sorts $s_1, \ldots, s_n$. Given a S-indexed family of variables $X = \{X_s\}$, the sets $T_{\Sigma, s}(X)$ of terms of sort s in

Σ are inductively defined as the variables $x \in X_s$ and the syntactic elements $f(t_1, \ldots, t_n)$ for any $f \in \Sigma_{s_1 \cdots s_n, s}$ and any $t_k \in T_{\Sigma, s_k}(X)$ for $1 \leq k \leq n$. An *order-sorted* signature is a many-sorted signature with a partial order $\leq_S$ defined on S representing a subsort relation. In this case, the definition of terms is updated so that $T_{\Sigma, s}(X) \subseteq T_{\Sigma, s'}(X)$ if $s \leq_S s'$. Terms without variables $T_{\Sigma, s}(\emptyset)$ are called *ground terms*. Membership equational logic is constructed on top of a *many-kinded signature* (K, Σ), i.e., a many-sorted signature where we have renamed *sort* to *kind* and S to K. The word *sort* is used for a K-indexed family $S = \{S_k\}$ of sorts.

Theories in membership equational logic are defined with by two classes of atomic sentences, *equations* $t = t'$ and sort *membership axioms* $t : s$, which respectively identify terms and assign them a sort. They can be combined to yield conditional Horn clauses of the form

$$t = t' \qquad \text{if} \bigwedge_i u_i = u_i' \wedge \bigwedge_j v_j : s_j \qquad\qquad t : s \qquad \text{if} \bigwedge_i u_i = u_i' \wedge \bigwedge_j v_j : s_j$$

Membership equational theories (Σ, E) are the combination of a signature and a set of such axioms. We usually partition the set of equations into *structural axioms* and normal equations, where the first is a fixed set of common identities like associativity and commutativity that cannot be applied in practice without losing executability.

Similarly, rewriting logic theories can contain the sentences above and rewrites rules, of the form:

$$l \Rightarrow r \qquad \text{if} \bigwedge_i u_i = u_i' \wedge \bigwedge_j v_j : s_j \wedge \bigwedge_k w_k \Rightarrow w_k'$$

Notice that rules can also be conditioned by rewriting clauses, which hold whenever the term w_k can be rewritten to a term that matches the pattern w_k'.

In Maude, membership equational logic specifications are defined in functional modules, with syntax fmod NAME is SENS endfm, where NAME is the module name and SENS is a set of sentences. We will illustrate Maude syntax by describing how to implement natural numbers[1] with addition and distinguishing even numbers. First, the PEANO module is stated, defining the sorts Nat (for natural numbers), Even (for even numbers), and NzNat (for non-zero natural numbers) by using the sorts keyword:

```
fmod PEANO is
   sorts Nat Even NzNat .
```

Because both even and non-zero numbers are particular cases of natural numbers, we can use a subsort declaration to state it:

```
subsorts NzNat Even < Nat .
```

We define how terms of these sorts are built by using operators:

---

[1] Although Maude provides a predefined module for natural numbers, functions are not defined by means of Maude equations but at the C++ level.

```
op  0 :  -> Even [ctor] .
op  s_ : Nat -> NzNat [ctor] .
```

Note that operators are defined with the keyword op followed by the operator name (where underscores stand for placeholders), a colon, the arity (which is empty in the case of constants), the keyword ->, the coarity, and a set of attributes enclosed in square brackets. In this case only the ctor attribute, stating that the operators are *constructors* of the corresponding sorts, is used. Finally, note that the constant 0 has sort Even, while the successor (s_) receives any natural number and returns a non-zero natural number. Similarly, the addition operator would be defined as:

```
op  _+_ : Nat Nat -> Nat .
```

where we have not used some standard attributes such as assoc, stating that the function is *associative*, because we will prove in the next sections that our definition, by means of its equations, fulfills this property. Next, we define some variables of sort Nat that will be used later in membership axioms and equations:

```
vars N M : Nat .
```

We can now use membership axioms, with syntax mb (cmb for *conditional* membership axioms) to distinguish those terms that cannot be identified only by their constructors. In our case, even numbers are recursively identified as:

```
cmb s s N : Even if N : Even .
```

It is important to note that subsorts (which can be understood as membership axioms) and membership axioms determine the kinds of the signature, that we identify with the connected components of each sort S under the subsort relation. The kind of the sort s is written [s] and Maude introduces an additional sort with the same name as the kind for its error terms, that is, those that cannot be assigned a proper sort. In our case, the sorts Nat, NzNat, and Even have the same kind because they are related by a subsort. We identify this kind by [Nat] because Nat is the top sort in the relation.

It is important to note that, from the Maude point of view, operator declarations are internally transformed to both a kind-level declaration of the symbol and a membership axiom stating that the result sort is the given one if the arguments have the correct sorts. For example, the addition operator above would be transformed into:

```
op  _+_ : [Nat] [Nat] -> [Nat] .
mb  N + M : Nat .
```

where the variable definition of N and M implicitly requires that these variables have the appropriate sort.

Equations are introduced with syntax eq (ceq for conditional equations). The equations for the addition can be defined as follows by distinguishing constructors in the second argument:

```
eq N + 0 = N .
eq N + s M = s (N + M) .
endfm
```

where the `endfm` keyword indicates the module has been closed.

Rewrite theories are specified in *system modules*, with syntax mod `NAME` is `SENS` endm, where `NAME` is the module name and `SENS` is a set of sentences including any of the ones described for functional modules plus rewrite rules. The module `PEANO-WITH-RULE` below imports the `PEANO` module and introduces a rule, with label `cancel`, for transforming an odd number into the previous one:

```
mod PEANO-WITH-RULE is
  protecting PEANO .
  var N : Nat .
  crl [cancel] : s N => N if N : Even .
endm
```

2.2 Dependent Type Theory and Lean

Interactive theorem provers are tools that assist humans in writing formal specifications and proving theorems about them. Usually, they do not only check the proof steps specified by the human, but also provide automation features to simplify routine work. Well-know examples are Isabelle/HOL [21], Agda [22], Coq [1], and Lean [19]. The logical foundations of the last three are extensions of Martin-Löf dependent type theory with inductive types, where propositions are seen as types whose elements are their proofs.

Given a universe of types $\mathcal{U}$, for any type A and for any A-indexed collection $B : A \to \mathcal{U}$ of them, two dependent type constructors $\Pi_{x:A}B(x)$ and $\Sigma_{x:A}B(x)$ are considered. Intuitively, elements of $\Pi_{x:A}B(x)$ are functions that given an $a : A$ produces a result $b : B(a)$, where the type of the result may depend on the argument and not only its value. If there is no such a dependency, we obtain a standard functional type $A \to B$. On the other hand, elements of $\Sigma_{x:A}B(x)$ are seen as pairs (a, b) for some $a : A$ and $b : B(a)$, whose independent case is the Cartesian product $A \times B$. Inductive dependent types $B(a_1, \ldots, a_n)$ are given by a finite collection of constructors $C_k : \Pi_{a_1:A_1} \cdots \Pi_{a_n:A_n(a_1,\ldots,a_{n-1})}B(a_1, \ldots, a_n)$ with arguments from other types and from the type itself.

From a logical point of view, as expressed in the Curry-Howard correspondence, types are seen as propositions, an element of type A is a proof that A holds, a function/implication $A \to B$ gives a proof of B for a proof of A, and so on. Elements of $\Pi_{x:A}B(x)$ give a proof of $B(a)$ for every a, so the type can be seen as a universally quantified formula and we also write $\forall x : A, B(x)$. Elements of $\Sigma_{x:A}B(x)$ give an element a and a proof of $B(a)$, so this type can be understood as an existentially quantified formula and written $\exists x : A, B(x)$. Equality can be defined as an inductive dependent type `eq` A B with a single constructor `refl` of type `eq` A A, so that equality only holds for identical terms. Other relations are defined similarly.

Lean [19] is a modern interactive theorem prover founded on a dependent type formalism called the calculus of inductive constructions, borrowed from Coq [1]. Developed by Microsoft Research, it counts with a unified and extensive library of mathematics *mathlib* [7] maintained by its community, used to formalize quite complex mathematical theories. The term language of Lean is a dependent λ-calculus with variables, constants, function application, λ-abstraction, function spaces, metavariables, and macros. There is a special type `Prop` for propositions, a hierarchy of types `Type` u parameterized by universes[2], and equality is defined as mentioned in the previous paragraphs. Inductive types, families, and definitions can be declared with the `inductive` and `def` keywords, axioms can be established with `axiom`, and results can be provided with `lemma` or `theorem`. In order to prove them, a collection of tactics are available, like `exact` to provide an element for the target type, `rw` to rewrite with an identity, `simp` to apply the Lean simplifier, `apply` to apply a hypothesis, `cases` to consider each case of an inductive type or obtain the witness of an existential claim, and `induction` to proceed by induction.

3   The Translation

Given a rewrite theory $\mathcal{R} = (\Sigma, A \cup E, R)$ where $\Sigma = (K, \Sigma, S)$ is a K-kinded signature with a K-indexed family S of sorts, A is a set of equations specifying builtin structural axioms like commutativity, E is a set of normal equations and membership axioms, and R is a set of rewrite rules, everything given by a Maude module M, we define the following specification in Lean.

In a nutshell, terms in the Maude signature are represented as elements of some inductive types, one for each kind $k \in K$, and the sort membership, equational, and rewriting relations are inductively defined on them. More precisely, we declare an inductive type `MSort` of constants enumerating the sorts S in the module, and for each kind $k \in K$

1. an inductive type k with a constructor for every operator $f \in \bigcup_{d \in K^*} \Sigma_{d,k}$ to represent the terms $T_{\Sigma,k}(X)$ of kind k. Specifically, the inductive type is named **k**s where s is the most general sort of the kind k (if there are many, the first one to be declared).
2. a binary relation k.`has_sort` of type $k \rightarrow$ `MSort` $\rightarrow$ `Prop` where k.`has_sort` t s means $t \in T_{\Sigma,s}(X)$. In Lean and in this paper, we use the overloaded infix notation $t \triangleright s$.
3. two binary relations k.`eqa` and k.`eqe` of type $k \rightarrow k \rightarrow$ `Prop` for the equivalence relation of terms modulo structural axioms and modulo equations, respectively. Again, we use the overloaded infix notation `=A` and `=E` for them.
4. k.`rw_one` and k.`rw_star` of type $k \rightarrow k \rightarrow$ `Prop` for the one-step sequential rule-rewrite relation and for its reflective and transitive closure. In infix form, we write `=>1` and `=>*`.

We detail the concrete definition of these elements in the rest of the section. Because these relations always have cross dependencies between them and with their counterparts for other kinds, their definitions should be mutually inductive.

---

[2] Type universes form a countable non-cumulative hierarchy $\mathcal{U}_0, \mathcal{U}_1, \mathcal{U}_2, \ldots$ to avoid Russell-like paradoxes.

Regarding the representation of terms, symbols $f \in \Sigma_{d_1 \cdots d_n, k}$ in $\mathcal{R}$ are mapped one-to-one to their homonym constructors $f : d_1 \to \cdots \to d_n \to k$ of the inductive type k, so there is an isomorphism of Σ-algebras between $T_{\Sigma, k}(\emptyset)$ and the elements of the type k. The translation does not distinguish by default between constructor and defined operators, since marking operators with the `ctor` attribute is not common practice, and deciding whether they are completely defined is non-trivial [12]. Unlike other works [13,16] that represent each Maude sort as a type with coercions to pass from the subsort to the supersort, our translation works with types at the kind level and handles sort membership with the explicit `has_sort` relation, as explained in the next paragraphs.

Statements in Maude (explicit membership axioms, equations, and rewrite rules) are translated under the same general principles. Every statement takes the form "φ if $\varphi_1 \wedge \cdots \wedge \varphi_n$" where $\varphi, \varphi_1, \ldots, \varphi_n$ are atomic sentences that may contain some variables $a_1, \ldots, a_m$ of sorts $s_1, \ldots, s_m$. The sort-membership sentence $l : s$ in Maude is translated to $l \rhd s$ in Lean, the equality sentences $l = r$ and $l := r$ to $l =E \ r$[3], and the rewriting sentence $l => r$ to $l =>* \ r$ in the condition and to $l =>1 \ r$ in the main sentence φ. Thus, we translate the above statement to the chain of implications or the dependent functional type

$$\forall a_1 : k_1, \ldots, a_m : k_m, \ a_1 \rhd s_1 \to \cdots \to a_m \rhd s_m \to \qquad\qquad$$
$$T(\varphi_1) \to \cdots \to T(\varphi_n) \to T(\varphi) \qquad (\star)$$

where $T(\psi)$ is the translation of the atomic sentence ψ. This chain is logically equivalent to $(\bigwedge_{i=1}^{m} a_i \rhd s_i \wedge \bigwedge_{j=1}^{n} T(\varphi_j)) \to T(\varphi)$. In addition to its own condition, statements also include sort-membership obligations for the variables, since their type in Lean is only associated to a kind.

The schema in the previous paragraphs is used to specify the sort membership, equational, and rewriting relations enumerated in (2–4). Each relation is declared as an *inductive family* in Lean, in other words, as a dependent parameterized type defined by an inductive enumeration of cases. The only self-contained relation is equivalence modulo structural axioms =A, which is given by the following constructors

- `refl` (reflexivity) of type $\forall \ a : k, \ a =A \ a$.
- `symm` (symmetry) of type $\forall \ a, b : k, \ a =A \ b \to b =A \ a$.
- `trans` (transitivity) of type $\forall \ a, b, c : k, \ a =A \ b \to b =A \ c \to a =A \ c$.
- f_`assoc` of type $\forall \ a, b, c : k, \ f \ a \ (f \ b \ c) =A \ f \ (f \ a \ b) \ c$ for every associative operator f in k.
- f_`comm` of type $\forall \ a, b : k, \ f \ a \ b =A \ f \ b \ a$ for every commutative operator f.
- Similar constructors f _`left_id`, f_`right_id`, and f_`idem` for operators with left and right identity elements, and for idempotent operators.
- `eqa`_f (congruence) of type $\forall_{i=1}^{n} a_i : k_i, \ a_1 =A \ b_1 \to \cdots \to a_n =A \ b_n \to f \ a_1 \cdots a_n =A \ f \ b_1 \cdots b_n$ for every operator f of arity n in the kind. Notice that =A may be the counterpart relation k_i.`eqa` of other kind.

---

[3] The atomic sentence $l := r$ is equivalent to $l=r$ but allowing free variables in the left-hand side to be instantiated by matching, which does not make a difference here.

Although we have written the types of the constructors as first order formulas for readability, they represent dependent types where universal quantification $\forall a : k$ can be replaced by $\Pi_{a:k}$. For example, `refl` has type $\Pi_{a:k}$ `k.eqa` a a. Intuitively, the constructors of the inductive relation are the closed set of axioms defining it. A statement l `=A` r is true iff it can be derived from these axioms, and we can reason by induction whether a statement holds or not. Technically, terms of type l `=A` r built with these constructors are proofs that the relation holds for l and r, and inhabited types are exactly the true propositions. For example, if `f` is an associative and commutative symbol, a proof of `f` a `(f` b c`)` `=A` `f` `(f` b a`)` c is

trans f_assoc (eqa_f f_comm refl)

where we have omitted the universally quantified variables in the constructor applications (indeed, they are defined as implicit arguments in Lean, which are inferred by the tool from the context) and their namespaces for readability.

The sort-membership relation k.`has_sort`, written $\triangleright$ in infix form, consists of the following constructors

- `subsort` of type $\forall t : k,\ r, s :$ `MSort`,   `subsort` r s $\rightarrow$ $t \triangleright r$ $\rightarrow$ $t \triangleright s$ where `subsort` : `MSort` $\rightarrow$ `MSort` $\rightarrow$ `Prop` is the generator of the subsorting relation specified with `subsort` declarations in Maude.
- f`_decl` of type $\forall_{i=1}^n t_i : k,\ t_1 \triangleright s_1 \rightarrow \cdots \rightarrow t_n \triangleright s_n \rightarrow (f\ t_1 \cdots t_n) \triangleright s$ for each operator declaration $f : s_1 \cdots s_n \rightarrow s$ as its implicit membership axiom.
- For each `mb` or `cmb` statement in Maude, a constructor whose type is derived as in $(\star)$.

Equivalence modulo equations and structural axioms `=E`, also k.`eqe`, is given by the constructors

- `from_eqa` of type $\forall\ a, b : k,\ a$ `=A` $b \rightarrow a$ `=E` b stating that `=A` is finer than `=E`.
- Both `symm` and `trans` as defined for `=A`. However, `refl` follows from the constructors of `=A` and `from_eqa`, so it is not introduced as a constructor.
- For each symbol f in the kind, a congruence constructor `eqe_`f with the same definition as `eqa_`f where `=A` has been replaced by `=E`.
- For each `eq` and `ceq` statement in Maude, a constructor whose type is derived as in $(\star)$.

Standard axioms like reflexivity and transitivity are marked with builtin attributes in the Lean specification to facilitate their use within the system and by its automation infrastructure.

Rewriting relations are specified in a very similar way. We first define the one-step rule relation k.`rw_one` (or `=>1` in infix form) and then make k.`rw_star` (`=>*`) its reflective and transitive closure. However, since conditional rules with reachability premises are allowed, the definitions of `=>1` and `=>*` should be simultaneous and mutually recursive. The one-step relation is given by the following constructors

- `eqe_left` to apply a rewrite modulo equations on the left, of type $\forall\ a, b, c : k,\ a$ `=E` $b \rightarrow b$ `=>1` $c \rightarrow a$ `=>1` c.

- **eqe_right** to apply a rewrite modulo equations on the right, of type $\forall\, a, b, c : k,\ a \mathrel{=>1} b \to b \mathrel{=E} c \to a \mathrel{=>1} c$.
- For each operator f of arity n and each $0 \leq i < n$, a constructor **sub_f_i** to apply a rule inside the ith argument of f, whose type is $\forall_{j=0}^{n} t_j, t_i'$: $k,\ t_i \mathrel{=>1} t_i' \to (f\, t_1 \cdots t_i \cdots t_n) \mathrel{=>1} (f\, t_1 \cdots t_i' \cdots t_n)$.
- For each **rl** and **crl** statement in Maude, a constructor whose type is derived as in $(\star)$.

On the other hand, $\mathrel{=>*}$ is defined with three constructors

- **refl** (reflexivity) with type $\forall\, a, b : k,\ a \mathrel{=E} b \to a \mathrel{=>*} b$,
- **step** of type $\forall\, a, b : k,\ a \mathrel{=>1} b \to a \mathrel{=>*} b$, and
- **trans** for transitivity, whose type coincides *mutatis mutandis* with the equivalent constructors for previous relations.

Some basic and useful properties when elaborating proofs are a consequence of the previous axioms, like the extension of the **sub_f_i** axioms for the $\mathrel{=>*}$ relation. In order to facilitate proofs, these and other properties are generated and proven as lemmas by our translation. The following proposition establishes the soundness of the translated specification for proving theorems about rewriting logic specifications in Lean.

Proposition 1. *Given a rewrite theory $\mathcal{R}$, two terms $t, t' \in T_{\Sigma,k}(X)$ for some kind k, and a sort $s \in S_k$, and with $\vdash A$ meaning that the type A is inhabited:*

1. *There is an isomorphism T of Σ-algebras between the Maude and the Lean specifications.*
2. $t \in T_{\Sigma,s}(X)$ *iff* $\vdash T(t) \triangleright T(s)$.
3. $t =_A t'$ *iff* $\vdash T(t) \mathrel{=A} T(t')$
4. $t =_E t'$ *iff* $\vdash T(t) \mathrel{=E} T(t')$
5. $t \to_R^1 t'$ *iff* $\vdash T(t) \mathrel{=>1} T(t')$
6. $t \to_R^* t'$ *iff* $\vdash T(t) \mathrel{=>*} T(t')$

Proof. See Appendix A.

4   The Translation Tool

The translation explained in the previous section is implemented in a Python script using the **maude** Python library [27]. Given a Maude source file and selected a module, obtaining its translation to Lean is simply invoking the command

$$\texttt{./maude2lean}\ \langle \textit{Maude source} \rangle\ [\langle \textit{module} \rangle]\ [\texttt{-o}\langle \textit{output file} \rangle]$$

Instead of a Maude file, the user can also provide a JSON or YAML specification of the translation, allowing some customization of the Lean output. For instance, a custom renaming can be specified for operator names, optimizations can be activated like the removal of membership conditions for most general sorts in error-free kinds, the notation used for relations can be selected, and so on. All these parameters are documented in the repository of the tool.

In order to build proofs using the axioms of the translated specification, it is important to know their names. The tool uses the predictable and systematic nomenclature of Sect. 3, although the generated Lean code is organized and includes comments to easily locate the desired elements. Statements are named after their labels prefixed by `mb_`, `eq_`, or `rl_` to avoid ambiguities. In the absence of a label, the name of the top symbol in the left-hand side is used. In case multiple statements are assigned the same name with the just described procedure, a number is appended according to the position of the statements in the file. All symbols and axioms are declared inside the namespace of its corresponding kind.

For example, let us show the result of the translation for the system module `PEANO-WITH-RULE` in Sect. 2. The generated Lean code starts with the inductive type `MSort` enumerating the sorts in the module. This list includes the sort `Bool` because the predefined `BOOL` module is implicitly imported by default into any Maude module. Moreover, the generator of their subsort relation is introduced as an inductively-defined relation

```
inductive MSort              def subsort : MSort → MSort → Prop
  | Bool                       | MSort.NzNat MSort.Nat := true
  | Nat                        | MSort.Even  MSort.Nat := true
  | Even                       | _           _          := false
  | NzNat
```

The definition of the kinds and their operators follows. In the `PEANO-WITH-RULE` module there is only two kinds, `[Nat]` and `[Bool]`, written here as `kNat` and `kBool`. Here is the definition of `kNat`.

```
inductive kNat
  | zero
  | s      : kNat → kNat
  | sum    : kNat → kNat → kNat
```

Some optional definitions can also be generated like `kind` to map sorts to kinds and `ctor_only` to recognize terms all whose symbols are declared as constructors in Maude.

```
def kind : MSort → Type
  | MSort.Bool   := kBool
  | MSort.Nat    := kNat
  | MSort.Even   := kNat
  | MSort.NzNat  := kNat
```

We then find the specification of the equational relations, with k.`eqa` and the potentially mutually related k.`has_sort` and k.`eqe`.

```
mutual inductive kBool.has_sort, kNat.has_sort, kBool.eqe, kNat.eqe
```

The following is an excerpt of the sort-membership relation for `kNat` with some implicit axioms derived from the operator declarations and with the constructor `mb_s` for the explicit membership axiom `cmb s s N : Even if N : Even .`

```
with kNat.has_sort : kNat → MSort → Prop
  | subsort {t a b} : subsort a b → kNat.has_sort t a
                                  → kNat.has_sort t b
  | zero_decl : kNat.has_sort kNat.zero MSort.Even
  | s_decl {a : kNat} : kNat.has_sort a MSort.Nat →
                        kNat.has_sort (kNat.s a) MSort.NzNat
  ...
  | mb_s {n} : kNat.has_sort n MSort.Even →
                        kNat.has_sort (kNat.s (kNat.s n)) MSort.Even
```

Equality modulo equations is given by the following constructors, among others, where eqe_s is the congruence axiom for the successor symbol and the last one corresponds to the first equation for the sum.

```
with kNat.eqe : kNat → kNat → Prop
  | from_eqa {a b} : kNat.eqa a b → kNat.eqe a b
  ...
  | eqe_s {a b : kNat} : kNat.eqe a b → kNat.eqe (kNat.s a) (kNat.s b)
  ...
  | eq_sum₀ {n} : kNat.has_sort n MSort.Nat →
                  kNat.eqe (kNat.sum n kNat.zero) n
```

Finally, k.rw_one and k.rw_star are defined in a similar way, with a constructor rl_s for the only rule crl [cancel] : s N => N if N : Even .

```
mutual inductive kBool.rw_one, kNat.rw_one, kBool.rw_star, kNat.rw_star
  ...
with kNat.rw_one : kNat → kNat → Prop
  ...
  | sub_sum₀ {a₁ a b} : kNat.rw_one a b →
                        kNat.rw_one (kNat.sum a a₁) (kNat.sum b a₁)
  ...
  | rl_cancel {n} : kNat.has_sort n MSort.NzNat →
                    kNat.rw_one (kNat.s n) n
```

In addition to these definitions, some lemmas are also generated for various properties of the relations. For instance, we have

```
@[refl] lemma eqe_refl (a : kBool) : a =E a := eqe.from_eqa eqa.refl
```

for the reflexivity of =E that follows from the similar property of =A. The lemma is prepended by the attribute refl that tells Lean to use this lemma with refl, simp, and other builtin tactics. In general, constructors and lemmas for standard properties like reflexivity, symmetry, transitivity, and congruence are marked with predefined Lean attributes that announce them to the automation and interactive tactics of the theorem prover. For instance, the Lean simplifier simp is able to automatically reduce Maude terms with equations and prove sort membership claims. We also derive lemmas like

```
lemma rw_star_sub_s (a b : kNat) : a =>* b → s a =>* s b
  := by infer_sub_star ''(rw_one.sub_s) ''(eqe.eqe_s)
```

claiming that a derivation with =>* in an argument yields a derivation in the whole term. This follows by induction on the definitions of =>1 and =>*, where infer_sub_star is a tactic we have programmed to share this proof among their multiples instances.

4.1 Proving the Associativity of the Sum

Using all these ingredients, we can prove properties of the PEANO module, like the associativity of the sum. Instead of directly proving the statement, we start with a first lemma, sum_assoc_aux, with an additional premise o.ctor_only telling that the operand o consists only of zero and successor symbols (since these have been marked with the ctor attribute in Sect. 2).

```
lemma sum_assoc_aux (n m o : kNat) (oh : o.ctor_only) :
      n.sum (m.sum o) =E (n.sum m).sum o :=
begin
  induction o,
  case kNat.zero {                      -- goal: n + (m + 0) =E (n + m) + 0
    simp,                -- applies the equations and the reflexivity of =E
  },
  case kNat.s : o ih {                  -- goal: n + (m + o.s) =E (n + m) + o.s
    simp,                  -- reduces to (n + (m + o)).s =E ((n + m) + o).s
    apply kNat.eqe_s,             -- congruence axiom for s under =E
    rw kNat.ctor_only at oh,      -- oh from o.s.ctor_only to o.ctor_only
    exact ih oh,                          -- induction hypothesis
  },
  case kNat.sum : l r hl hr {
    rw kNat.ctor_only at oh,   -- (l.sum .r).ctor_only evaluates to false
    contradiction,                      -- this case is not possible
  },
end
```

This lemma can be easily extended to arbitrary terms after the following sufficient-completeness result, whose proof is available in the repository.

```
lemma sc_nat (n : kNat) : ∃ w, n =E w ∧ w.ctor_only
```

Indeed, an arbitrary term o can be replaced by its equivalent constructor term w provided by sc_nat, and then sum_assoc_aux can be invoked to conclude.

```
theorem sum_assoc (n m o : kNat) : n.sum (m.sum o) =E (n.sum m).sum o
:= begin
  cases (sc_nat o) with w h,            -- yields h : o =E w ∧ w.ctor_only
  simp [h.left],                        -- simplify with o =E w
  exact sum_assoc_aux n m w h.right,
end
```

Similarly, other properties like commutativity are also proven in the repository.

5   Example: The Dining Philosophers

For illustrating more practical applications of the translation, we summarily describe in this section the proof in Lean by induction of a simple property of a Maude specification of the classical concurrency problem of the dining philosophers. It has been specified in Maude several times [10, 24] and multiples properties have been proven or refuted by model checking [28]. However, model checking can only handle instances of the problem for a fixed number of philosophers, so it is impossible to prove that a deadlock state is always reachable regardless of the number of messmates. Inductive reasoning can solve this problem easily, so we can provide an inductive proof in Lean for the property in the same specification we have already model checked.

The full specification of the problem is available and thoroughly explained in [28], so we only give an overview of the proof at a high level. In the initial configuration of the problem, generated by a Maude function initial(n), there are n philosophers with empty hands and n forks between them in the circular table. Our first goal is proving that from the initial term we can always reach a configuration where every philosopher has taken its right fork, as expressed below.

$$< (\text{o} \mid 0 \mid \text{o}) \; \psi \; \cdots \; \psi \; (\text{o} \mid n-1 \mid \text{o}) \; \psi >$$
$$\rightarrow^* < (\text{o} \mid 0 \mid \psi) \quad \cdots \quad (\text{o} \mid n-1 \mid \psi) >$$

In Lean, we realize this as the has_deadlock theorem that can be proven by a standard induction on n

```
theorem has_deadlock (n : N) : ∃ t,
  (initial (nat_l2m n)) =>* t ∧ t.every_phil_has_right_fork
```

where nat_l2m and every_phil_has_right_fork are Lean definitions to convert natural numbers from Lean to Maude and to recognize the desired final state. However, we still need to prove that such a final state is actually deadlocked, i.e. that no rule rewrite can take place on it. This is proven in the following theorem in Lean

```
theorem ephrf_deadlock (a b : kTable)
  (h : every_phil_has_right_fork a) : ¬ (a =>1 b)
```

Its proof essentially relies on the constructive definitions of the relations, since we derive this negative property by induction on the type a =>1 b. Therefore, this theorem cannot be proven in any of the related tools mentioned in Sect. 6. The complete commented proofs are available in the tool's repository.

6   Related Work

In this section we briefly discuss related proposals to theorem proving. First, the Heterogeneous Tool Set (Hets) [17] integrates different logics by defining them as institutions and translations between them as comorphisms. In this way, systems can be defined in the most convenient logic and then translated in order to prove their properties in other formalisms supporting different types of theorem proving. Maude has been integrated into Hets [6], so some automatic theorem provers for first-order logic and more powerful tools such as Isabelle/HOL [25] could be used. However, the translation generated some proof obligations when importations were required that made the approach difficult to use. Moreover, this integration has not been adapted to newer versions of Maude and Hets, so it does not support some features and theorem provers. Note that in our case the translation is not as general as the one in Hets because we do not intend to build a general framework where several formalisms are combined, but a particular translation between two systems. This allows us to use a simpler approach and focus on strategies to simplify the translation and the proofs. Furthermore, the translation from order-sorted specifications to many-sorted algebras for theorem proving has been explored in [13,16]. However, these translations follow a different approach by replicating the order-sorted structure in the types of the target specification, and they do not cover the rule rewriting relations.

Different theorem provers have been implemented in Maude. The ITP [5] is an inductive theorem prover for Maude specifications that has been used to verify some properties of Maude systems. However, it only implements basic strategies, does not include decision procedures or simplification strategies, and does not take advantage of Maude features like unification and narrowing [3], making it useful for basic systems only. The theorem prover in [26], although originally developed for CafeOBJ specifications [8], supports Maude specifications and provides automatic mechanisms for inferring proofs. However, these mechanisms rely on a reduced set of basic commands and heuristics focusing on observational transitions systems [23], so it cannot be straightforwardly applied to any specification. In both cases, our translation provides three important advantages: (i) it supports reasoning about rewrite rules, not just equations; (ii) relations are specified constructively, letting users prove negative properties; and (iii) it integrates into a widespread proof assistant with a broad library of definitions and proofs.

Finally, Maude is integrated with different SMT solvers [3], which allows users to discharge proof obligations generated from Maude specifications. Moreover, *reachability logic* [29] and its associated tools can also be used to deductively reason about Maude programs. Although these automated proof methodologies are useful in practice they cannot deal with several properties that require more powerful techniques, hence it complements but does not replace the approach presented here.

7   Conclusions and Future Work

In this paper, we have described a translation from rewriting logic to the calculus of inductive constructions, implemented in a tool that produces programs for the Lean theorem prover from Maude specifications. Consequently, Lean can be used to reason and prove properties about Maude models, as we have shown with two small examples. The sort membership, equational, and rewriting relations have been specified inductively to allow proving negative properties that would not follow from a purely axiomatic specification. Finally, lemmas and integration with tactics are provided to facilitate reasoning and automation. The contributions of this work are (i) support for reasoning about rule rewriting in addition to equations, (ii) a constructive specification of the relations that allows proving useful negative properties of the models like deadlock, and (iii) a practical translation to a well-known and community-active proof assistant with a wide library of reusable definitions and proofs. This translation can be easily adapted to other tools based on the same or a similar formalism, like Coq [1].

There are some paths for future extension of this work. For instance, our translation operates on the flattened version of a module, without leveraging on the modular nature of Maude specifications to reason compositionally in Lean. This means reusing the results about imported modules and instanciating the propositions obtained for parameterized ones. The translation can also be extended with more resources and lemmas to simplify the user task, including proofs of relevant properties of the data types in the standard prelude, and with support for other aspects of rewriting logic like parallel rewriting or rewriting strategies [9].

Acknowledgments. Work partially supported by the Spanish AEI project ProCode (PID2019-108528RB-C22/AEI/10.13039/501100011033) and CAM project BLOQUES-CM (S2018/TCS-4339) co-funded by EIE Funds of the European Union.

A   Proof of Proposition 1

Proposition 1. *Given a rewrite theory* $\mathcal{R}$, *two terms* $t, t' \in T_{\Sigma,k}(X)$ *for some kind* k, *and a sort* $s \in S_k$, *and with* $\vdash A$ *meaning that the type* A *is inhabited:*

1. *There is an isomorphism* T *of* Σ-*algebras between the Maude and the Lean specifications.*
2. $t \in T_{\Sigma,s}(X)$ *iff* $\vdash T(t) \triangleright T(s)$.
3. $t =_A t'$ *iff* $\vdash T(t)$ =A $T(t')$
4. $t =_E t'$ *iff* $\vdash T(t)$ =E $T(t')$
5. $t \rightarrow^1_R t'$ *iff* $\vdash T(t)$ =>1 $T(t')$
6. $t \rightarrow^*_R t'$ *iff* $\vdash T(t)$ =>* $T(t')$

Proof. (1) For each kind k of the Maude signature, an inductive type kk is defined in Lean with a constructor $f : kk_1 \rightarrow \cdots \rightarrow kk_n \rightarrow kk$ for each operator $f : k_1 \cdots k_n \rightarrow k$ in Maude. Terms are inductively defined in the same way for both formalisms, so the homomorphism of Σ-algebras that maps $T(k) = kk$ and $T(f(x_1, \cdots, x_n)) = f\, T(x_1) \cdots T(x_n)$ is an isomorphism.

(2–4) These claims follow from the fact that proof terms of membership equational logic [2] for $t =_A t'$, $t =_E t'$, and $t : s$ are in a one-to-one correspondence with the elements of $T(t)$ =A $T(t')$, $T(t)$ =E $T(t')$, and $T(t) \triangleright s$. Indeed, the inductive constructors of these types and the deduction rules of membership equational logic are very closely related. We omit the inductive proof for brevity and since it is much similar to the one below for the rewriting relations.

(5–6) The rule rewriting relations $\rightarrow^1$ and $\rightarrow^*$ are defined in [15, §3.1] by the finite application of the following five deduction rules with some restrictions.

1. *Reflexivity.* For each $t \in T_\Sigma(X)$, $\vdash t \to t$.
2. *Equality.* $u \to v, u =_E u', v =_E v' \vdash u' \to v'$.
3. *Congruence.* For each $f : k_1 \cdots k_n \to k$ in Σ, and $t_1, t_1', \ldots, t_n, t_n' \in T_\Sigma(X)$,

$$\frac{t_1 \to t_1' \quad \cdots \quad t_n \to t_n'}{f(t_1, \ldots, t_n) \to f(t_1', \ldots, t_n')}$$

4. *Replacement.* For each rule $r : t \to t'$ if $\bigwedge_i u_i = u_i' \wedge \bigwedge_j v_j : s_j \wedge \bigwedge_k w_k \to w_k'$ with variables $\{x_1, \ldots, x_n\}$ and each substitution such that $\sigma(x_i) = p_i$:

$$\frac{p_1 \to p_1' \quad \cdots \quad p_n \to p_n' \qquad \cdots \quad \sigma(u_i) =_E \sigma(u_i') \quad \cdots}{\cdots \quad \sigma(w_k) \to \sigma(w_k') \quad \cdots \qquad \cdots \quad \sigma(v_j) \in T_{\Sigma, s_j} \quad \cdots}$$
$$\sigma(t) \to \sigma[x_1 / p_1', \ldots, x_n / p_n'](t)$$

5. *Transitivity.* $t_1 \to t_2, t_2 \to t_3 \vdash t_1 \to t_3$.

One-step rewrites are those derivable from rules (1–4) with at least one application of rule (4), but allowing all rules (1–5) in the derivation of sequents. Sequential rewrites are those that can be derived from (1–5) where the premises $p_i \to p_i'$ of (3) are not derived with (3) and at most one premise of (4) is derived with (3). Both relations, $\to^1$ and $\to^*$, are sequential and $\to^1$ is also one-step. We will prove by structural induction that, for any two terms $t, t' \in T_{\Sigma, k}(X)$, there is a one-to-one correspondence between the proof trees of $t \to^1 t'$ (respectively, $t \to^* t'$) and the terms of type k.rw_one $T(t)$ $T(t')$ (respectively, k.rw_star $T(t)$ $T(t')$). First, given a proof tree, we show the corresponding proof term.

1. The tree $\vdash t \to t$ produced by rule (1) can only prove the statement $t \to^* t$, since there is no application of rule (3). An element of type $T(t) \texttt{=>*} T(t)$ is k.rw_star.refl (k.eqe.from_eqa k.eqa.refl).
2. For the *equality* rule, we have a term α of sort $T(u) \texttt{=>1} T(v)$ (the same with $\texttt{=>*}$) by induction hypothesis. Since $u =_E u'$ and $v =_E v'$, we have terms β_u of type $T(u) \texttt{=E} T(u')$ and β_v of type $T(v) \texttt{=E} T(v')$. An element of type $T(u') \texttt{=>1} T(v')$ is k.rw_one.eqe_left β_u (k.rw_one.eqe_right α β_v). An element of type $T(u') \texttt{=>*} T(v')$ is k.rw_star.trans (k.rw_star.refl β_u) (k.rw_star.trans α (k.rw_star.refl β_v)).
3. For the *congruence* rule, suppose $f(t_1, \ldots, t_n) \to^1 f(t_1', \ldots, t_n')$, so exactly one of the derivations $t_i \to t_i'$ uses (3), say the jth one. This implies $t_i =_E t_i'$ for $i \neq j$ and $t_j \to^1 t_j'$. By induction hypothesis, there is a term α_j of type $T(t_j) \texttt{=>1} T(t_j')$ and terms α_i of type $T(t_i) \texttt{=E} T(t_i')$. The element k.rw_one.eqe_right (k.rw_one.sub_f_j α_j) (k.eqe.eqe_f $\alpha_1 \cdots$ (k_j.eqe.from_eqa k_j.eqa.refl) $\cdots$ α_n) has type $f(T(t_1), \ldots, T(t_n)) \texttt{=>1}$ $f(T(t_1'), \ldots, T(t_n'))$. The $\to^*$ case can be proven similarly using the fact that $t_j \texttt{=>*} t_j' \to f(\ldots, t_j, \ldots) \texttt{=>*} f(\ldots, t_j', \ldots)$, which is proven as a lemma sub_star in the `infer_sub_star.lean` file of the repository.
4. For the *replacement* rule, given a rewrite rule $r : t \to t'$ (where the sort membership of variables can be assumed to be given by explicit conditions) and a substitution σ, if $\sigma(t) \to^1 \sigma[p_i/p_i'](t')$, by induction hypothesis, there

are elements α_i of type $T(\sigma(u_i))$ =E $T(\sigma(u_i'))$, β_j of type $T(\sigma(v_j)) \triangleright s_j$, γ_k of type $T(\sigma(w_k))$ =>* $T(\sigma(w_k'))$, and δ_l of type $T(p_l)$ =E $T(p_l')$, since (3) cannot be applied in $p_l \to p_l'$. The constructor rl_r, whose type is derived from r by (⋆), yields a term ξ of type $T(\sigma(t))$ =>1 $T(\sigma(t'))$ when applied the premises α_i, β_j, and γ_k in the appropriate order. Finally, we apply eqe_right to ξ and an appropriate term of type $T(\sigma(t'))$ =E $T(\sigma[p_i/p_i'](t'))$ built with eqe_f constructors and δ_l terms. The $\to^*$ case follows by applying rw_star.step to ξ, and then the lemma sub_star with the δ_l proof terms of type p_l =>* p_l'.

5. For the *transitivity* rule, which can only be applied to derive $t_1 \to^* t_3$, there are proof terms α of type $T(t_1)$ =>* $T(t_2)$ and β of type $T(t_2)$ =>* $T(t_3)$ by induction hypothesis. k.rw_star.trans α β has type $T(t_1)$ =>* $T(t_3)$.

Conversely, proof terms in rewriting logic can be built for any term of type t =>1 t' or t =>* t' in Lean. In fact, rw_one.eqe_left and rw_star.eqe_right follow from rule (2), the congruences sub_f_i from (1) and (3), and the concrete rule constructors follow from rule (4). For the $\to^*$ relation, rw_star.refl follows from rules (1) and (2), step from the less restrictive constraints on the application of the deduction rules, and trans from rule (5).

References

1. Bertot, Y., Castéran, P.: Interactive Theorem Proving and Program Development - Coq'Art: The Calculus of Inductive Constructions. Texts in Theoretical Computer Science. Springer, Heidelberg (2004). https://doi.org/10.1007/978-3-662-07964-5
2. Bouhoula, A., Jouannaud, J., Meseguer, J.: Specification and proof in membership equational logic. Theor. Comput. Sci. **236**(1–2), 35–132 (2000). https://doi.org/10.1016/S0304-3975(99)00206-6
3. Clavel, M., et al.: Maude Manual v3.2.1 (2022)
4. Clavel, M., et al.: All About Maude - A High-Performance Logical Framework. LNCS, vol. 4350. Springer, Heidelberg (2007). https://doi.org/10.1007/978-3-540-71999-1
5. Clavel, M., Palomino, M., Riesco, A.: Introducing the ITP tool: a tutorial. J. Univers. Comput. Sci. **12**(11), 1618–1650 (2006). https://doi.org/10.3217/jucs-012-11-1618
6. Codescu, M., Mossakowski, T., Riesco, A., Maeder, C.: Integrating maude into hets. In: Johnson, M., Pavlovic, D. (eds.) AMAST 2010. LNCS, vol. 6486, pp. 60–75. Springer, Heidelberg (2011). https://doi.org/10.1007/978-3-642-17796-5_4
7. mathlib community, T.: The Lean mathematical library. In: CPP 2020, pp. 367–381. ACM (2020). https://doi.org/10.1145/3372885.3373824
8. Diaconescu, R., Futatsugi, K.: Logical foundations of CafeOBJ. Theor. Comput. Scie. **285**(2), 289–318 (2002). https://doi.org/10.1016/S0304-3975(01)00361-9
9. Durán, F., et al.: Programming and symbolic computation in Maude. J. Log. Algebraic Methods Program. **110**, 100497 (2020). https://doi.org/10.1016/j.jlamp.2019.100497
10. Durán, F., Roldán, M., Vallecillo, A.: Invariant-driven strategies for Maude. ENTCS **124**(2), 17–28 (2005). https://doi.org/10.1016/j.entcs.2004.11.018
11. Eker, S., Meseguer, J., Sridharanarayanan, A.: The Maude LTL model checker. In: Gadducci, F., Montanari, U. (eds.) WRLA 2002. ENTCS, vol. 71, pp. 162–187. Elsevier (2004). https://doi.org/10.1016/S1571-0661(05)82534-4

12. Hendrix, J., Meseguer, J., Ohsaki, H.: A sufficient completeness checker for linear order-sorted specifications modulo axioms. In: Furbach, U., Shankar, N. (eds.) IJCAR 2006. LNCS (LNAI), vol. 4130, pp. 151–155. Springer, Heidelberg (2006). https://doi.org/10.1007/11814771_14

13. Li, L., Gunter, E.L.: A method to translate order-sorted algebras to many-sorted algebras. In: Cirstea, H., Sabel, D. (eds.) WPTE 2017. EPTCS, vol. 265, pp. 20–34 (2017). https://doi.org/10.4204/EPTCS.265.3

14. Meseguer, J.: Conditional rewriting logic as a unified model of concurrency. Theor. Comput. Sci. **96**(1), 73–155 (1992). https://doi.org/10.1016/0304-3975(92)90182-F

15. Meseguer, J.: Twenty years of rewriting logic. J. Log. Algebr. Program. **81**(7–8), 721–781 (2012). https://doi.org/10.1016/j.jlap.2012.06.003

16. Meseguer, J., Skeirik, S.: Equational formulas and pattern operations in initial order-sorted algebras. Formal Aspects Comput. **29**(3), 423–452 (2017). https://doi.org/10.1007/s00165-017-0415-5

17. Mossakowski, T., Maeder, C., Lüttich, K.: The heterogeneous tool set, HETS. In: Grumberg, O., Huth, M. (eds.) TACAS 2007. LNCS, vol. 4424, pp. 519–522. Springer, Heidelberg (2007). https://doi.org/10.1007/978-3-540-71209-1_40

18. Moura, L., Ullrich, S.: The lean 4 theorem prover and programming language. In: Platzer, A., Sutcliffe, G. (eds.) CADE 2021. LNCS (LNAI), vol. 12699, pp. 625–635. Springer, Cham (2021). https://doi.org/10.1007/978-3-030-79876-5_37

19. de Moura, L., Kong, S., Avigad, J., van Doorn, F., von Raumer, J.: The lean theorem prover (system description). In: Felty, A.P., Middeldorp, A. (eds.) CADE 2015. LNCS (LNAI), vol. 9195, pp. 378–388. Springer, Cham (2015). https://doi.org/10.1007/978-3-319-21401-6_26

20. Newcombe, C.: Why amazon chose TLA$^+$. In: Ait Ameur, Y., Schewe, K.D. (eds.) Abstract State Machines, Alloy B TLA VDM and Z. Lecture Notes in Computer Science, vol. 8477, pp. 25–39. Springer, Berlin, Heidelberg (2014). https://doi.org/10.1007/978-3-662-43652-3_3

21. Nipkow, T., Wenzel, M., Paulson, L.C. (eds.): Isabelle/HOL. LNCS, vol. 2283. Springer, Heidelberg (2002). https://doi.org/10.1007/3-540-45949-9

22. Norell, U.: Dependently typed programming in Agda. In: Kennedy, A., Ahmed, A. (eds.) TLDI 2009, pp. 1–2. ACM (2009). https://doi.org/10.1145/1481861.1481862

23. Ogata, K., Futatsugi, K.: Proof scores in the OTS/CafeOBJ method. In: Najm, E., Nestmann, U., Stevens, P. (eds.) FMOODS 2003. LNCS, vol. 2884, pp. 170–184. Springer, Heidelberg (2003). https://doi.org/10.1007/978-3-540-39958-2_12

24. Ölveczky, P.C.: Teaching formal methods based on rewriting logic and Maude. In: Gibbons, J., Oliveira, J.N. (eds.) TFM 2009. LNCS, vol. 5846, pp. 20–38. Springer, Heidelberg (2009). https://doi.org/10.1007/978-3-642-04912-5_3

25. Paulson, L.C. (ed.): Isabelle. LNCS, vol. 828. Springer, Heidelberg (1994). https://doi.org/10.1007/BFb0030541

26. Riesco, A., Ogata, K.: An integrated tool set for verifying CafeOBJ specifications. J. Syst. Softw. **189**, 111302 (2022). https://doi.org/10.1016/j.jss.2022.111302

27. Rubio, R.: Maude as a library: an efficient all-purpose programming interface. In: Bae, K. (ed.) Rewriting Logic and Its Applications. Lecture Notes in Computer Science, vol. 13252, pp. 274–294. Springer, Cham (2022). https://doi.org/10.1007/978-3-031-12440-2_14

28. Rubio, R., Martí-Oliet, N., Pita, I., Verdejo, A.: Model checking strategy-controlled systems in rewriting logic. Autom. Softw. Eng. **29**(1), 1–62 (2021). https://doi.org/10.1007/s10515-021-00307-9

29. Skeirik, S., Stefanescu, A., Meseguer, J.: A constructor-based reachability logic for rewrite theories. Fundam. Informaticae **173**(4), 315–382 (2020). https://doi.org/10.3233/FI-2020-1926

On How to Not Prove Faulty Controllers Safe in Differential Dynamic Logic

Yuvaraj Selvaraj[1,3]([⊠]) [iD], Jonas Krook[1,3] [iD], Wolfgang Ahrendt[2] [iD],
and Martin Fabian[1] [iD]

[1] Department of Electrical Engineering, Chalmers University of Technology, Göteborg, Sweden
{yuvaraj,krookj,fabian}@chalmers.se
[2] Department of Computer Science and Engineering, Chalmers University of Technology,
Göteborg, Sweden
ahrendt@chalmers.se
[3] Zenseact, Göteborg, Sweden
{yuvaraj.selvaraj,jonas.krook}@zenseact.com

Abstract. Cyber-physical systems are often safety-critical and their correctness is crucial, as in the case of automated driving. Using formal mathematical methods is one way to guarantee correctness. Though these methods have shown their usefulness, care must be taken as modeling errors might result in proving a faulty controller safe, which is potentially catastrophic in practice. This paper deals with two such modeling errors in *differential dynamic logic*. Differential dynamic logic is a formal specification and verification language for *hybrid systems*, which are mathematical models of cyber-physical systems. The main contribution is to prove conditions that when fulfilled, these two modeling errors cannot cause a faulty controller to be proven safe. The problems are illustrated with a real world example of a safety controller for automated driving, and it is shown that the formulated conditions have the intended effect both for a faulty and a correct controller. It is also shown how the formulated conditions aid in finding a *loop invariant* candidate to prove properties of hybrid systems with feedback loops. The results are proven using the interactive theorem prover KeYmaera X.

Keywords: Hybrid systems · Automated driving · Formal verification · Loop invariant · Theorem proving

1 Introduction

Cyber-physical systems (CPS) typically consist of a digital *controller* that interacts with a physical dynamic system and are often employed to solve safety-critical tasks. For example, an automated driving system (ADS) has to control an autonomous vehicle (AV) to safely stop for stop signs, avoid collisions, etc. It is thus paramount that CPS

This work was supported by FFI, VINNOVA under grant number 2017–05519, *Automatically Assessing Correctness of Autonomous Vehicles – Auto-CAV*, and by the Wallenberg AI, Autonomous Systems and Software Program (WASP) funded by the Knut and Alice Wallenberg Foundation.

The original version of this chapter was revised: This chapter contains errors in many tables and equations mistakes and has been submitted by mistake. The complete paper was corrected. The correction to this chapter is available at
https://doi.org/10.1007/978-3-031-17244-1_26

A. Riesco and M. Zhang (Eds.): ICFEM 2022, LNCS 13478, pp. 281–297, 2022.
https://doi.org/10.1007/978-3-031-17244-1_17

work correctly with respect to their requirements. One way to ensure correctness of CPS is to use formal verification, which requires a formal model of the CPS. An increasingly popular family of models of CPS are *hybrid* systems, which are mathematical models that combine discrete and continuous dynamics.

To reason about the correctness of a CPS, hybrid systems can model different components of the CPS and their interactions, thus capturing the overall *closed-loop* behavior. In general, hybrid systems that model real world CPS may involve three main components: a *plant* model that describes the physical characteristics of the system, a controller model that describes the control software, and an *environment* model that captures the behaviors of the surrounding world in which the controller operates, thereby defining the *operational domain*. The goal for the controller is to choose control actions such that the requirements are fulfilled for *all* possible behaviors of the hybrid system.

Typically, the environment is modeled using nondeterminism to capture all possible behaviors. However, assumptions on the environment behavior are necessary to limit the operational domain and remove behaviors that are too hostile for any controller to act in a safe manner. For example, if obstacles are assumed to appear directly in front of an AV when driving, no controller can guarantee safety. While the assumptions in the formal models are necessary to make the verification tractable, there are subtle ways in which formal verification can provide less assurance than what is assumed [4]. In other words, as a result of the verification, the designer may conclude the controller to be safe in the entire assumed operational domain, whereas in reality some critical behaviors where the controller is actually at fault might be excluded from the verification. One possible cause for such a disparity between what is verified and what is assumed to be verified is the presence of modeling errors. In such cases, if a controller is verified to be safe, it leads to unsafe conclusions which might be catastrophic in practice. This paper deals with two such modeling errors by making them subject to interactive verification. In the first erroneous case, the environment assumptions and the controller actions interact in such a way that the environment behaves in a friendly way to adapt to the actions of a controller that exploits its friendliness. Then, it is possible that a faulty controller can be proven safe since the environment reacts to accommodate the bad control actions. An example of this is a faulty ADS controller that never brakes, together with an environment that reacts by always moving obstacles to allow the controller not to brake.

In the second erroneous case, the assumptions about the environment and/or other CPS components remove all behaviors in which any action by the controller is needed. In this case, the assumptions over-constrain the allowed behaviors. For example, if the assumptions restrict the behavior of the AV to an extent that only braking is possible, then a faulty ADS controller can be proven safe because nothing is proven about the properties of the controller. In the worst-case, the assumptions remove all *possible* behaviors, thereby making the requirement vacuously true.

In both cases, a faulty controller can be proven safe with respect to the requirements for the wrong reasons, i.e., unintended modeling errors, thus resulting in potentially catastrophic operation of the CPS in practice. Modeling errors are in general hard to address because every model is an abstraction and there exists no ubiquitous notion of what a *correct model* means. Therefore, a systematic way to identify and avoid modeling errors is highly desirable as it reduces the risk of unsound conclusions when a model is formally proven safe with respect to the requirements. Typically, the requirements specify (un)desired behavior of the closed-loop system within the operational domain and are expressed in some logical formalism to apply formal verification. *Differential dynamic logic* (dL) [8,9] is a specification and verification language that can be used to formally describe and verify hybrid systems. The interactive theorem prover KeYmaera X [2] implements a sound proof calculus [8,9] for dL and can thus mathematically prove that the models fulfill their specified requirements.

The main contributions of this paper, Theorem 1 and Theorem 2, formulate and prove conditions that when fulfilled, ensure the model cannot be proven safe if it is susceptible to the above modeling errors. Essentially, a loop invariant is used not only to reason about the model inductively but also to ensure that the interaction between the controller and the other components in the model is as intended; the two theorems provide conditions on the relation between the assumptions and the loop invariant. Furthermore, these conditions give hints as to when a suggested loop invariant for the model is sufficiently strong to avoid modeling errors. The problems are illustrated with a running example of an automated driving controller that shows that they can appear in real models. It is then proven that the formulated conditions have the intended effect. Finally, it is shown by example that the method captures the problematic cases and also increases confidence in a correct model free from the considered modeling errors.

2   Preliminaries

The logic dL uses *hybrid programs* (HP) to model hybrid systems. An HP α is defined by the following grammar, where α, β are HPs, x is a variable, e is a term[1], and P and Q are formulas of first-order logic of real arithmetic (FOL)[2]:

$$\alpha ::= x := e \mid x := * \mid ?P \mid x' = f(x) \,\&\, Q \mid \alpha \cup \beta \mid \alpha; \beta \mid \alpha^*$$

Each HP α is semantically interpreted as a reachability relation $[\![\alpha]\!] \subseteq \mathcal{S} \times \mathcal{S}$, where $\mathcal{S}$ is the set of all states. If $\mathcal{V}$ is the set of all variables, a state $\omega \in \mathcal{S}$ is defined as a mapping from $\mathcal{V}$ to $\mathbb{R}$, i.e., $\omega \colon \mathcal{V} \to \mathbb{R}$. The notation $(\omega, \nu) \in [\![\alpha]\!]$ denotes that final state ν is reachable from initial state ω by executing the HP α. $\omega[\![e]\!]$ denotes the value of term e in state ω, and for $x \in \mathcal{V}$, $\omega(x) \in \mathbb{R}$ denotes the real value that variable x holds in state ω. Given a state ω_1, a state ω_2 can be obtained by assigning the terms $\{e_1, \ldots, e_n\}$ to the variables $y = \{y_1, \ldots, y_n\} \subseteq \mathcal{V}$ and letting the remaining variables in $\mathcal{V}$ be as in ω_1, that is, $\omega_2(y_i) = \omega_1[\![e_i]\!]$ for $1 \leq n$ and $\omega_2(\nu) = \omega_1(\nu)$ for all $\nu \in \mathcal{V} \setminus y$. Let $\omega_2 = \omega_1(y_1 := e_1, \ldots, y_n := e_n)$ be a shorthand for this assignment. For a FOL formula P, let $(\!|P|\!) \subseteq \mathcal{S}$ be the set of all states where P is true, thus $\omega \in (\!|P|\!)$ denotes that P is true in state ω. If P is parameterized by $y_1, \ldots, y_n$, then $\omega \in (\!|P|\!)$ means that $\omega \in (\!|P(\omega(y_1), \ldots, \omega(y_n))|\!)$. A summary of the program statements in HP and their transition semantics [9] is given in Table 1.

---

[1] Terms are polynomials with rational coefficients defined by $e, \tilde{e} ::= x \mid c \in \mathbb{Q} \mid e + \tilde{e} \mid e \cdot \tilde{e}$.
[2] First-order logic formulas of real arithmetic are defined by $P, Q ::= e \geq \tilde{e} \mid e = \tilde{e} \mid \neg P \mid P \wedge Q \mid P \vee Q \mid P \to Q \mid P \leftrightarrow Q \mid \forall x P \mid \exists x P$.

Table 1. Semantics of HPs [9]. P, Q are first-order formulas, α, β are HPs.

Statement	Semantics
$[\![x := e]\!]$	$= \left\{ (\omega, \nu) : \nu = \omega(x := e) \right\}$
$[\![x := *]\!]$	$= \left\{ (\omega, \nu) : c \in \mathbb{R} \text{ and } \nu = \omega(x := c) \right\}$
$[\![?P]\!]$	$= \left\{ (\omega, \omega) : \omega \in (\![P]\!) \right\}$
$[\![x' = f(x) \& Q]\!]$	$= \left\{ (\omega, \nu) : \phi(0) = \omega(x' := f(x)) \text{ and } \phi(r) = \nu \text{ for a solution } \phi : [0, r] \to \mathcal{S} \right.$
	$\left. \text{of any duration } r \text{ satisfying } \phi \models x' = f(x) \wedge Q \right\}$
$[\![\alpha \cup \beta]\!]$	$= [\![\alpha]\!] \cup [\![\beta]\!]$
$[\![\alpha; \beta]\!]$	$= [\![\alpha]\!] \circ [\![\beta]\!] = \left\{ (\omega, \nu) : (\omega, \mu) \in [\![\alpha]\!], (\mu, \nu) \in [\![\beta]\!] \right\}$
$[\![\alpha^*]\!]$	$= [\![\alpha]\!]^* = \bigcup\limits_{n \in \mathbb{N}_0} [\![\alpha^n]\!] \text{ with } \alpha^0 \equiv ?true \text{ and } \alpha^{n+1} \equiv \alpha^n; \alpha.$

The sequential composition $\alpha; \beta$ expresses that β starts executing after α has finished. The *nondeterministic choice* operation expresses that the HP $\alpha \cup \beta$ can nondeterministically choose to follow either α or β. The *test* action $?P$ has no effect in a state where P is true, i.e., the final state ω is same as initial state ω. If however P is false when $?P$ is executed, then the current execution of the HP *aborts*, meaning that no transition is possible and the entire current execution is removed from the set of possible behaviors of the HP. The *nondeterministic repetition* α^* expresses that α repeats n times for any $n \in \mathbb{N}_0$. Furthermore, test actions can be combined with sequential composition and the choice operation to define *if-statements* as:

$$\text{if } (P) \text{ then } \alpha \text{ fi} \equiv (?P; \alpha) \cup (?\neg P) \tag{1}$$

HPs model continuous dynamics as $x' = f(x) \& Q$, which describes the *continuous evolution* of x along the differential equation system $x' = f(x)$ for an arbitrary duration (including zero) within the *evolution domain constraint* Q. The evolution domain constraint applies bounds on the continuous dynamics and are first-order formulas that restrict the continuous evolution within that bound. x' denotes the time derivative of x, where x is a vector of variables and $f(x)$ is a vector of terms of the same dimension.

The formulas of dL include formulas of first-order logic of real arithmetic and the modal operators $[\alpha]$ and $\langle \alpha \rangle$ for any HP α [8,9]. A formula θ of dL is defined by the following grammar (ϕ, ψ are dL formulas, $e, \tilde{e}$ are terms, x is a variable, α is an HP):

$$\theta ::= e = \tilde{e} \mid e \geq \tilde{e} \mid \neg \phi \mid \phi \wedge \psi \mid \forall x \phi \mid [\alpha] \phi \tag{2}$$

The dL formula $[\alpha] \phi$ expresses that *all* non-aborting executions of HP α (i.e., the executions where all test actions are successful) end in a state in which the dL formula ϕ is true. The formal semantics are defined by $(\![[\alpha] \phi]\!) = \{\omega \in \mathcal{S} : \forall \nu \in \mathcal{S}. (\omega, \nu) \in [\![\alpha]\!] \to \nu \in (\![\phi]\!)\}$. The dL formula $\langle \alpha \rangle \phi$ means that there exists *some* non-aborting execution leading to a state where ϕ is true. $\langle \alpha \rangle \phi$ is the dual to $[\alpha] \phi$, defined as $\langle \alpha \rangle \phi \equiv \neg [\alpha] \neg \phi$. Similarly, $>, \leq, <, \vee, \to, \leftrightarrow, \exists x$ are defined using combinations of the operators in (2). A dL formula θ is *valid*, denoted $\models \theta$ if $(\![\theta]\!) = \mathcal{S}$.

The logic dL and the interactive theorem prover KeYmaera X support the specification and verification of hybrid systems. The dL formula $(init) \to [\alpha] (guarantee)$ can

---

Model 1: The general model considered

$$(init) \rightarrow [(env;\ aux;\ ctrl;\ plant)^*]\,(guarantee) \tag{3}$$

$$env \triangleq e := *;\ ? P(s, e, a) \tag{4}$$

$$aux \triangleq a := *;\ ? Q(s, e, a) \tag{5}$$

$$ctrl \triangleq \text{if } \neg ok(s, e, a) \text{ then } a := *;\ ? C(s, e, a)\, \text{fi} \tag{6}$$

$$plant \triangleq \tau := 0;\ s' = f(s),\ \tau' = 1\ \&\ F(s, e, a, \tau) \wedge \tau \leq T \tag{7}$$

---

be used to specify the correctness of an HP α with respect to the requirement *guarantee*. It expresses that, if the initial conditions described by the formula *init* are true, then all (non-aborting) executions of α only lead to states where formula *guarantee* is true. KeYmaera X takes such a dL formula as input and successively decomposes it into several sub-goals according to the sound proof rules of dL to prove the formula [8,9].

Often, modeling CPS as HPs involves execution of a controller together with a plant in a loop described by the nondeterministic repetition α^*. To prove properties of loops, like the property $(init) \rightarrow [\alpha^*]\,(guarantee)$, KeYmaera X uses *loop invariants*, provided by the user, to inductively reason about all (non-aborting) executions. Given a loop invariant (candidate) ζ, applying the loop invariant rule to the above formula would make the proof branch into the following three cases:

loop(i): $(init) \rightarrow \zeta$, i.e., the initial state satisfies the invariant,

loop(ii): $\zeta \rightarrow [\alpha]\,\zeta$, i.e., invariant remains true after one iteration of α from any state where the invariant was true,

loop(iii): $\zeta \rightarrow (guarantee)$, i.e., the invariant implies the requirement.

3   Problem Scope

The scope of CPS considered in this paper are hybrid systems with closed-loop feedback control as described by Model 1. The dL formula (3) models the CPS as a HP that repeatedly executes in a loop and expresses the requirement on the CPS by the formula *guarantee*. The HP in (3) is composed of four different components, each of which is an HP and assigns four variables: the dynamic state s which evolves continuously, the control actions a, the environment actions e, and the time progress τ. Though the variables in Model 1 are scalars, they can in general be vectors of any dimension.

The environment (*env*) in (4) describes the environment behavior using a nondeterministic assignment followed by a test. The environment action e is nondeterministically assigned a real value which is then checked by the subsequent test for adherence to the environment assumptions P, which define the operational domain. The auxiliary system (*aux*) describes the internal digital system that the controller interacts with, in addition to the environment. Similarly to *env*, *aux* (5) nondeterministically assigns a real value to the control action a followed by a subsequent test which checks whether the internal assumptions Q hold. These internal assumptions typically describe conditions that stem from the design of the CPS such as physical limits on the system actuators.

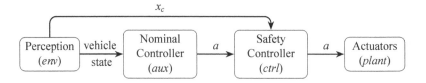

Fig. 1. Architecture of the automated driving feature.

The controller's (*ctrl*) task is to ensure that the requirement *guarantee* is fulfilled and is modeled as an if-statement as seen in (6). First, the control action *a* set by *aux* is tested with *ok*. If the test is not *ok*, then *ctrl* overrides the control action *a* by the control law *C*, and finally it passes on the control action to the *plant* (7), which models the physical part of the system. It is described as an ordinary differential equation. However, the sampling time of *ctrl* is bounded, so the evolution of *plant* must stop before the sampling time T [11].

In the most abstract setting, the parameterized FOL formulas in Model 1 are treated as uninterpreted predicates, which could be replaced by any concrete hybrid model with specific formulas and HPs, as long as the assignment of values to variables follows the flow of Model 1. Hence, the conclusions drawn from Model 1 can be applied and used for a wide variety of hybrid systems.

Running Example: Automated Driving Controller

To illustrate the problems and solutions, this paper considers an example of an in-lane automated driving feature for an AV, the *ego-vehicle*. Figure 1 shows a simplified architecture of the automated driving feature, which can be modeled as a HP of the general form in Model 1. The safety requirement is for the ego-vehicle to safely stop for stationary obstacles that have entered its path.

The *perception* senses the world around the ego-vehicle and corresponds to the *env* in Model 1. The *env* models the perception algorithms that communicate the obstacle position x_c to the controller and thus the *env* assumptions describe the dynamics of the obstacles appearing in the ego-vehicle's path. The *nominal controller*, described by *aux*, represents any algorithm solving the nominal driving task subjected to different constraints (e.g. comfort) and requests a nominal acceleration. Thus, *aux* of the form in (5) allows to keep the model parametric to arbitrary nominal controller implementations while being regarded as a black box. The *aux* assumptions therefore capture design conditions on the nominal controller such as always requesting an acceleration within certain bounds.

The *safety controller* described by *ctrl* ensures that only safe control actions, i.e., acceleration commands *a*, are communicated to the actuators. It evaluates the nominal acceleration and overrides it with a safe acceleration if needed, thereby satisfying the safety requirement. Thus, the verification of the safety requirement can be limited to verifying the decision logic in one component, the safety controller.

The *plant* is a dynamic model of the ego-vehicle. It is modeled as a double integrator with position x and velocity v of the ego-vehicle as the dynamic states and the accel-

---

Model 2: Example hybrid system

$$init \triangleq v = 0 \land x \le x_c \land a_s^{min} > 0 \land a_n^{max} > 0$$
$$\land a_n^{min} > 0 \land a_s^{min} > a_n^{min} \land T > 0 \tag{8}$$

$$guarantee \triangleq (x \le x_c) \tag{9}$$

$$plant \triangleq \tau := 0;\ x' = v, v' = a, \tau' = 1\ \&\ v \ge 0 \land \tau \le T \tag{10}$$

---

eration a as control input, as seen in (10) of Model 2. The ego-vehicle is not allowed to drive backwards, so v must be non-negative through the entire evolution. In other words, the evolution would stop before v gets negative.

In the next section, the general dL formula in (3) is refined with concrete descriptions of env, aux, and $ctrl$ to illustrate the modeling errors where a faulty controller can be proven safe. However, $init$, $plant$, and $guarantee$ remain unchanged in the subsequent models and are shown in Model 2. The initial condition $init$ (8) specifies that the ego-vehicle starts stationary ($v = 0$) at an arbitrary position x before the position x_c of an obstacle. It also sets up assumptions on the *constant* parameters such as the minimum safety and nominal acceleration a_s^{min} and a_n^{min}, and maximum nominal acceleration, a_n^{max}, and that the sampling time T is positive. These constant parameters do not change value during the execution of the HP [$(env;\ aux;\ ctrl;\ plant)^*$], and therefore the assumptions on the constant parameters remain true in all contexts. The requirement that the ego-vehicle must stop before stationary obstacles is expressed by the post condition $guarantee$ (9), which says that the obstacle's position may not be exceeded.

4   Discover Modeling Errors

This section presents two erroneous models to illustrate how a faulty $ctrl$ can be proven safe with respect to $guarantee$. In the first case, shown in Model 3, improper interaction between env and $ctrl$ results in env adapting to faulty $ctrl$ actions. Such an erroneous model can be proven safe since the loop invariant ζ is not strong enough to prevent improper interactions. Theorem 1 gives conditions to strengthen ζ to avoid such issues. In the second erroneous case, Model 4, the error arises due to over-constrained env and aux assumptions that discard executions where $ctrl$ is at fault. Theorem 2 presents conditions to identify and avoid errors due to such over-constrained assumptions.

4.1   Exploiting Controller

Consider Model 3 where the assumptions on env and aux are given by (11) and (12) respectively. env assigns x_c such that it is possible to brake and stop before the position of the obstacle. This is necessary since if an obstacle appears immediately in front of the moving ego-vehicle it is physically impossible for any controller to safely stop the vehicle. aux is a black box, but it is known that the nominal acceleration request a is bounded. The $ctrl$ test ok (14) checks whether maximal acceleration for a time period of T leads to a violation of the requirement, and if it does, the controller action C (15)

Model 3: *ctrl* is exploiting

$$env \triangleq x_c := *; \ ? \left(x_c - x \geq \frac{v^2}{2a_n^{min}} \right) \tag{11}$$

$$aux \triangleq a := *; \ ?(-a_n^{min} \leq a \leq a_n^{max}) \tag{12}$$

$$ctrl \triangleq \text{if } \neg ok(x, v, x_c, a) \text{ then } a := *; \ ? \, C(x, v, x_c, a) \, \text{fi} \tag{13}$$

$$ok(x, v, x_c, a) \triangleq \left(x_c - x \geq vT + \frac{a_n^{max} T^2}{2} \right) \tag{14}$$

$$C(x, v, x_c, a) \triangleq a = -a_s^{min} \tag{15}$$

---

sets the deceleration to its maximum. This maximum deceleration is a symbolic value, parameterized over the other model variables.

Denote by θ the dL formula (3) together with the definitions of Model 2 and Model 3. θ is proved [12] with the loop invariant $\zeta_1 \equiv x \leq x_c$. Though the goal is to find a proof that θ is valid, and thereby establish that *ctrl* is safe with respect to *guarantee*, it is in this case incorrect to draw that conclusion from the proof, as will now be shown.

The *env* assumption (11) discards executions where the distance between the obstacle position x_c and the ego-vehicle position x is less than the minimum possible braking distance of the ego-vehicle. This assumption is reasonable as it only discards situations where it is physically impossible for *ctrl* to safely stop the vehicle. Still, infinitely many *env* behaviors are possible since x_c is nondeterministically assigned any value that fulfills the assumption. Among other behaviors, this allows x_c to remain constant, as would be the case for stationary obstacles. However, due to improper interaction between *env* and a faulty *ctrl*, *env* can be forced by *ctrl* to not have x_c constant.

Consider a state $\omega_0 \in (\!\lvert \zeta_1 \rvert\!)$, illustrated in Fig. 2a, such that

$$\omega_0(x) = 0 \qquad \omega_0(x_c) = 1 \qquad \omega_0(T) = 1$$
$$\omega_0(v) = 0 \qquad \omega_0(a) = 1.8 \qquad \omega_0(a_n^{max}) = 2 \qquad \omega_0(a_n^{min}) = 3 \ .$$

The ego-vehicle is currently at $(x, v) = (0, 0)$ as shown by the black circle. The hatched area represents all the points in the xv-plane from which it is possible to stop before the obstacle position, x_c, at the dashed vertical line. It holds that $(\omega_0, \omega_0) \in [\![env]\!]$ since $x_c - x = 1 \geq 0^2/(2 \times 3) = v^2/(2a_n^{min})$, so the assumptions on *env* allow $x_c = 1$. This can also be seen in the figure since the black circle is within the hatched area. The arrow labeled a in Fig. 2a represents the acceleration request by *aux*, and if *plant* evolves for 1 s with a as input, the ego-vehicle ends up at the white circle. As a is within the bounds of *aux*, it holds that $(\omega_0, \omega_0) \in [\![aux]\!]$. The controller *ctrl* is *ok* with this choice since x_c is not passed if maximum acceleration a_n^{max} is input to *plant*, as illustrated by the gray circle in the figure. Formally, $x_c - x = 1 \geq 0 \times 1 + 2 \times 1^2/2 = vT + a_n^{max}T^2/2$ and therefore it holds by (14) that $\omega_0 \in (\!\lvert ok(x, v, a_n, a) \rvert\!)$. Thus, $(\omega_0, \omega_0) \in [\![ctrl]\!]$. Let $\omega_1 = \omega_0(x := 0.9, v := 1.8)$. Now it holds that $(\omega_0, \omega_1) \in [\![plant]\!]$, i.e., starting at $x = 0$ and $v = 0$, with $a = 1.8$ as input, *plant* evolves to $x = 0.9$ and $v = 1.8$ in 1 s.

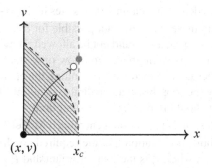

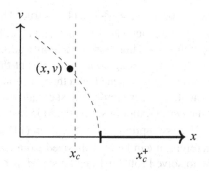

(a) Graphical representation of the state ω_0. The hatched area contains all points in the xv-plane from which it is possible to stop before the obstacle x_c. The invariant ζ_1 evaluates to true in the shaded area.

(b) Graphical representation of the state ω_1. A friendly *env* discards all obstacle positions in the interval between x_c and the start of the thick black line, and places the obstacle along the interval indicated by x_c^+.

Fig. 2. The controller chooses an action such that the *plant* evolves to a state where $x \leq x_c$. In the next loop iteration, *env* moves x_c to adapt to the controller's action.

After *plant* has evolved and the system has transited to ω_1, the ego-vehicle is now at the black circle in Fig. 2b. It is clear that $\omega_1 \in (\!| \zeta_1 |\!)$ as $x \leq x_c$. The intersection of the dashed curve with the x-axis in Fig. 2b represents the lower bound for x_c to satisfy (11) in the state ω_1. Therefore, in the next iteration, x_c can only be positioned somewhere along the interval indicated by the thick black line in Fig. 2b and all other values are discarded by (11). Semantically, as $x_c - x = 0.1 < 2^2/(2 \times 3) = v^2/(2a_n^{min})$, it follows that $(\omega_1, \omega_1) \notin [\![env]\!]$ so x_c cannot be kept constant between iterations.

To summarize, it holds that $\omega_0 \in (\!| \zeta_1 |\!)$, $(\omega_0, \omega_1) \in [\![env; aux; ctrl; plant]\!]$, and $\omega_1 \in (\!| \zeta_1 |\!)$. The acceleration requested by *aux* is *ok*'d by *ctrl* in ω_0 because the worst-case acceleration a_n^{max} in ω_0 leads to a state that fulfills ζ_1, and therefore also fulfills *guarantee*. Since there exists no control action allowed by the system dynamics in the assumed operational domain that can fulfill *guarantee* from ω_1, the decision made by *ctrl* is unsafe in this case. However, since $(\omega_1, \omega_1) \notin [\![env]\!]$, Model 3 can be proven to fulfill *guarantee* with this faulty *ctrl*.

So, the model is proven to fulfill *guarantee* only because *env* is not allowed to keep the obstacle stationary. Thus, *ctrl* exploits the behavior of *env* to move the obstacle so *ctrl* can keep accelerating rather than stopping safely. Though *env* is assumed to discard only those behaviors where it is physically impossible for *ctrl* to fulfill *guarantee*, the interaction between *env* and *ctrl* causes *env* to behave in a friendly way to adapt to faulty *ctrl* actions, thereby discarding *env* behaviors in which x_c remains constant.

Problem 1. How can the dL formula (3) be guaranteed not to be valid with a controller that exploits the environment?

Observe from Fig. 2b that for the state ω_0, the shaded area describes the region where the loop invariant ζ_1 holds. The hatched area describes the states from where it is possible for *ctrl* to stop before the obstacle x_c, i.e., all the xv-points for which the *env* assumption $x_c - x \geq \frac{v^2}{2a_n^{min}}$ in (11) is true. The shaded area contains some states in the xv-plane that are outside of the hatched area. From these states it is not possible for *ctrl* to stop before x_c. Thus, control actions leading to such states should not be allowed. However, ζ_1 is not strong enough to prevent this. If ζ_1 is strengthened to allow only states contained in the hatched area then the controller is prevented from exploiting the environment. In other words, any state allowed by the loop invariant shall also be allowed by the *env* assumptions, i.e., the loop invariant should imply the *env* assumptions.

The assumption $x_c - x \geq \frac{v^2}{2a_n^{min}}$ in (11) corresponds to P in the generalized Model 1. Therefore, it can be hypothesized from the above observation that the required condition to solve Problem 1 can be stated as $\zeta \rightarrow P$, where ζ is the loop invariant and P is the *env* assumptions. Indeed, the condition $\zeta \rightarrow P$ solves Problem 1 for Model 3. However, Problem 1 is not specific to Model 3 and it remains unestablished whether $\zeta \rightarrow P$ solves Problem 1 for models of the general form considered in Model 1. For example, in Model 3, the controller exploits the friendliness of *env* to not keep the obstacle position x_c constant between iterations, i.e., $x_c \neq x_c^+$ for two *env* actions (x_c, x_c^+). Admittedly, such a behavior does not characterize friendly behavior in all models. In general, the relation between two *env* actions (e_0, e_1) can be any relation $R \subseteq \mathbb{R} \times \mathbb{R}$ such that $(e_0, e_1) \in R$. Note that R only defines certain behaviors in the assumed operational domain. In Model 3, the exploiting controller could be proven safe because the environment behaves *friendly* by discarding some behaviors characterized by R. This is illustrated in Fig. 2b where x_c cannot be kept constant as $(\omega_1, \omega_1) \notin [\![env]\!]$.

Definition 1. *If there exists two states ω_0 and ω_1 that differ only in the assignment of the env variable e, i.e., $\omega_0(e) = e_0$ and $\omega_1 = \omega_0(e := e_1)$, and such that $(e_0, e_1) \in R$ and $(\omega_0, \omega_1) \notin [\![env]\!]$, then the environment env is* friendly *w.r.t the relation R. Thus, env is* unfriendly *if $(e_0, e_1) \in R \rightarrow (\omega_0, \omega_1) \in [\![env]\!]$ is true in all states ω_0 and ω_1 that differ only in the assignment of the env variable e.*

The hypothesis $\zeta \rightarrow P$ can now be generalized to include the relation R to describe the existence of an unfriendly *env* as:

$$\rho \equiv \forall s. \forall e. \forall e_1. \big(\zeta(s, e) \wedge R(e, e_1) \rightarrow \langle env \rangle (e = e_1)\big), \tag{16}$$

where ζ is parameterized to make it explicitly depend on the variables of the HP. The meaning of ρ is that, if a state fulfills the invariant, then for every next *env* action e_1 characterized by R there is at least one execution of *env* in which the action e_1 is chosen.

The loop invariant $\zeta_1 \equiv x \leq x_c$ is used to prove the dL formula (3) with the definitions of Model 2 and Model 3. Thus, it follows that $\models \zeta_1 \rightarrow [env; aux; ctrl; plant]\zeta_1$ holds by loop (ii). But, ζ_1 is not strong enough to prevent control actions that exploit friendly *env* behaviors. For instance, as illustrated in Fig. 2, the control action that leads to ω_1 from ω_0 should not be allowed since *env* must discard some behaviors from ω_1 to preserve ζ_1. These discarded behaviors include all executions where $(aux; ctrl; plant)$ do not preserve ζ_1. Thus *ctrl exploits env* to act friendly such that ζ_1 is preserved.

Definition 2. *A controller ctrl* exploits *a friendly environment env w.r.t the relation R if the loop invariant ζ is preserved by the loop body, i.e. $\models \gamma$, where*

$$\gamma \equiv \forall s. \forall e. \big(\zeta(s, e) \rightarrow [env; aux; ctrl; plant]\zeta(s, e)\big), \tag{17}$$

but

$$\exists s.\ \exists e.\ \exists e_0.\ \big(\zeta(s, e_0) \wedge R(e_0, e) \wedge \langle aux;\ ctrl;\ plant\rangle \neg \zeta(s, e)\big).\tag{18}$$

Thus, *ctrl* exploits *env* if it makes it necessary for *env* to behave friendly. In the following theorem it is shown that an exploiting controller can be prevented if the loop invariant is strong enough to ensure the existence of an unfriendly environment.

Theorem 1. *Let s and e be variables used in plant and env respectively as defined in Model 1. Let $\zeta(s, e)$ be a loop invariant candidate, and let R be a relation over the domain of e. Let γ (17) be the* dL *formula from the inductive step* loop *(ii) of the loop invariant proof rule, and let ρ be as defined by (16). If $\gamma \wedge \rho$ is valid, then the loop invariant candidate $\zeta(s, e)$ is sufficiently strong to prevent an exploiting controller.*

Proof. The following dL formula is proved [12] in KeYmaera X:

$$\gamma \wedge \rho \rightarrow \forall s.\ \forall e_0.\ \forall e.\ \big(\zeta(s, e_0) \wedge R(e_0, e) \rightarrow [aux;\ ctrl;\ plant]\,\zeta(s, e)\big).\tag{19}$$

This asserts that the loop invariant is strong enough to prevent *ctrl* from exploiting *env*'s friendly behavior because the clause implied by $\gamma \wedge \rho$ in (19) is the negation of (18). □

In addition to solving Problem 1, Theorem 1 gives hints on how the loop invariant must be constructed. In some cases, as in Fig. 2 where $x_c \leq x_c^+$, it suggests that $\zeta \equiv P$ might be a loop invariant candidate. In summary, Theorem 1 is useful in two ways: (i) By adding ρ to a dL formula, it is known that a proof of validity is not because *env* is friendly to *ctrl*, (ii) ρ can also be a useful tool to aid in the search for a loop invariant.

For the specific model instance considered in this section, and probably others, changes to the model can ensure that the environment is not too friendly. However, as this paper deals with modeling errors and ascertaining that models cannot be proven valid for wrong reasons, such changes do not solve the general problem, but might nonetheless be good as best practices to avoid modeling pitfalls.

4.2 Unchallenged Controller

The previous section dealt with modeling problems where *ctrl* causes *env* to exhibit friendly behaviors despite correct *env* assumptions. This section discusses modeling problems due to over-constrained assumptions, whereby *ctrl* is never challenged.

Consider Model 4, identical to Model 3, except for *aux* ((20) and (21)). As before, *aux* is a black box. However, in addition to the acceleration bounds, *aux* also fulfills a design requirement *req* given by (21). *req* describes that the nominal controller only requests an acceleration *a* such that the ego-vehicle does not travel more than the braking distance (with a_n^{min}) from any given state in one execution of *T* duration. Similar to Model 3, the requested acceleration is passed to the *plant* if the *ctrl* test *ok* (14) is true; if not, the controller action *C* (15) sets the maximal possible deceleration.

To verify that *ctrl* fulfills *guarantee* (9), the dL formula (3) together with the definitions in Model 2 and Model 4 must be proven valid. Though the validity can indeed be proven in KeYmaera X using the loop invariant $\zeta_1 \equiv x \leq x_c$, *ctrl* is faulty. Strong *env* and *aux* assumptions might result in the invariant ζ being true in all HP executions

---

Model 4: *ctrl* is unchallenged

$$aux \triangleq a := *; \ ?\left(-a_n^{min} \leq a \leq a_n^{max} \wedge req\right) \tag{20}$$

$$req \triangleq (v + aT \geq 0) \rightarrow vT + \frac{aT^2}{2} \leq \frac{v^2}{2a_n^{min}} \tag{21}$$

$$\wedge \ (v + aT < 0) \rightarrow a \leq -a_n^{min}$$

---

irrespective of *ctrl*'s actions, and hence *ctrl* is never verified. This manifests itself in Model 4; *env* assigns x_c such that it is possible to brake to stop before the position of the obstacle, and *aux* assumes that the ego-vehicle does not travel more than the braking distance in T time. Therefore, *guarantee* is true for all executions of [*env*; *aux*; *plant*], i.e., the model fulfills *guarantee* no matter which branch of *ctrl* is executed. Thus, this problem with strong *env* and *aux* assumptions, i.e., an over-constrained model such that *ctrl* is not challenged in any HP execution, may allow a faulty controller be proven safe.

Problem 2. How can the dL formula (3) be guaranteed not to be valid with an un-challenged controller?

In general, if *aux* and/or *env* assumptions are too strong, many relevant executions may be discarded when the respective tests fail. A worst-case situation is when a contradiction is present in the assumption, thereby discarding all possible executions of the HP. In that case, the dL formula (3) is vacuously true, irrespective of the correctness of *ctrl*. In situations where all possible executions are discarded due to failed tests, a potential work-around is to check for such issues by proving the validity of *init* $\rightarrow$ ⟨*env*; *aux*; *ctrl*; *plant*⟩ (*guarantee*) to verify that there exists at least one execution of the hybrid program that fulfills *guarantee*. However, that work-around is not helpful to discover models susceptible to Problem 2 because it is possible to prove that there is at least one execution of ⟨*env*; *aux*; *ctrl*; *plant*⟩ for which *guarantee* is true even in over-constrained systems as seen in the HP with definitions of Model 2 and Model 4.

Observe that if *ctrl* is removed from the dL formula (3) and the formula is still valid, then *ctrl* is not verified. Equivalently, if the invariant is preserved when *ctrl* is removed from the dL formula, i.e., $\chi \equiv \forall s.\forall e.\forall a.\zeta \rightarrow$ [*env*; *aux*; *plant*] ζ is valid, then *ctrl* is not verified. So the negation, i.e.,

$$\neg\chi \equiv \exists s. \exists e. \exists a. \zeta \wedge ⟨env; aux; plant⟩\neg\zeta . \tag{22}$$

can be proved to ascertain the absence of Problem 2 in the proof of (3).

Definition 3. *For hybrid systems described by Model 1 where the loop body is defined by (env; aux; ctrl; plant), ctrl is challenged w.r.t. env, aux, plant, and the loop invariant* ζ *if* $\zeta \wedge ⟨env; aux; plant⟩ \neg\zeta$ *is true in some state.*

However, proving $\neg\chi$ (22) might not be beneficial in practice. While failed attempts to prove $\neg\chi$ might illuminate modeling errors, the presence of *env*, *aux*, *plant*, and their interaction might complicate both the proof attempts and the identification of problematic fragments of the HP, especially for large and complicated models.

Note that if there exists one execution of (*env*; *aux*) that does not preserve the invariant ζ, then *ctrl* must choose a safe control action such that the hybrid system can be controlled to remain within the invariant states, i.e., $(\lvert \zeta \rvert)$. However, this is not sufficient to conclude that the controller is verified to be safe since it could be the case that for all such invariant violating executions, the *plant* forces the hybrid system back into the invariant states. Therefore, it is necessary that not all executions of the uncontrolled *plant* reestablish the invariant. So, if (*env*; *aux*) does not preserve the invariant, *plant* does not reestablish the invariant, then *ctrl* is indeed verified to be safe as shown in Theorem 2.

Theorem 2. *Let s, e, and a be variables used in plant, env, and ctrl respectively as defined in Model 1, and let the loop invariant candidate $\zeta(s, e, a_1)$ be a specific instantiation of the* dL *formula* $\zeta(s, e, a)$. *Let*

$$\psi \equiv \exists s. \exists e. \exists a_1. \left(\zeta(s, e, a_1) \wedge \langle env; \, aux \rangle \left(\neg \zeta(s, e, a) \wedge \langle plant \rangle \neg \zeta(s, e, a_1) \right) \right). \qquad (23)$$

Then, if ψ is valid, ctrl is challenged in some executions of [*env*; *aux*; *ctrl*; *plant*].

Proof. The following dL formula is proved [12] in KeYmaera X:

$$\psi \rightarrow \exists s. \exists e. \exists a_1. \zeta(s, e, a_1) \wedge \langle env; \, aux; \, plant \rangle \neg \zeta(s, e, a_1). \qquad (24)$$

The dL formula ψ (23) states that there exists at least one execution of (*env*; *aux*) where the invariant is not preserved, and *plant* does not always reestablish the invariant. The implied clause (24) asserts that *ctrl* is challenged by Definition 3.   □

By the conjunction of ψ (23) to a dL formula of the form (3), Theorem 2 can be used to identify Problem 2 and also the problematic fragments in all models of the form of Model 1. Furthermore, in HPs of the form (*env*; *ctrl*; *plant*)*, with no distinction between *env* and *aux*, Theorem 2 can still be used to determine whether the *env* assumption is over-constrained. In addition, ψ provides insights to aid in the search of a loop invariant and its dependency on the HP variables.

5   Results

This section shows how Theorem 1 and Theorem 2 are used to (i) identify that Model 3 and Model 4 are deceptive for the verification of *ctrl*, (ii) aid in the identification of a candidate loop invariant, and (iii) increase confidence in the fidelity of Model 5 where the errors are corrected. The HPs and the KeYmaera X proofs are available from [12].

The dL formula (3) with the definitions in Model 2 and Model 3, denoted as θ, is proved in KeYmaera X with the loop invariant $\zeta_1 \equiv x \le x_c$. Therefore it follows from loop (ii) that $\models \gamma$, where $\gamma \equiv \zeta_1 \rightarrow [env; \, aux; \, ctrl; \, plant] \zeta_1$. By Theorem 1, ρ must hold for Model 3 to conclude the absence of Problem 1. The formula

$$\neg \rho_1 \equiv \exists x. \exists v. \exists x_c. \exists x_c^+. \neg \left(x \le x_c \wedge x_c \le x_c^+ \rightarrow \right.$$
$$\left. \langle x_c := *; \, ? (v^2 \le 2a_n^{min}(x_c - x)) \rangle (x_c = x_c^+) \right), \qquad (25)$$

expressed from (16) for Model 3 with $\zeta(x, v, x_c) \equiv \zeta_1$ and $R(x_c, x_c^+) \equiv x_c \le x_c^+$ is proven valid in KeYmaera X, thereby confirming that Model 3 is susceptible to Problem 1.

Table 2. Summary of validity results for incorrect and correct models

Model	Loop invariant	Conjuncts	Valid	Reason
3	ζ_1	-	Yes	Exploiting controller
3	ζ_1	ρ_1	No	Invariant not strong enough
3	ζ_2	ρ_2	No	Controller does not fulfill requirement
4	ζ_1	-	Yes	Unchallenged controller
4	ζ_1	$\neg\chi_1$	No	Invariant preserved without controller
5	ζ_1	-	Yes	
5	ζ_1	$\rho_1 \wedge \neg\chi_1$	No	Invariant not strong enough
5	ζ_2	$\rho_2 \wedge \neg\chi_2$	Yes	

As $\models \neg\rho_1$, it follows that a stronger loop invariant is needed to not verify an exploiting *ctrl*. A possible candidate is the *env* assumptions themselves, so let $\zeta_2 \equiv v^2 \leq 2a_n^{min}(x_c - x)$. For this choice of loop invariant, ρ_2 is valid with $\zeta(x, v, x_c) \equiv \zeta_2$ and $R(x_c, x_c^+) \equiv x_c \leq x_c^+$. However, γ cannot be proven with ζ_2 since the *ctrl* actions do not maintain ζ_2, as already illustrated in Fig. 2. Hence, the exploiting *ctrl* cannot be proven to fulfill *guarantee*. These results are summarized in the first three rows of Table 2.

The next two rows of Table 2 summarize the results of the dL formula (3) with the definitions in Model 2 and Model 4 which is proved using the loop invariant ζ_1. Therefore it follows from `loop` (ii) that $\models \gamma$. By Theorem 2, $\models \neg\chi$ (22) must hold to ensure that *ctrl* is indeed verified safe. However the dL formula χ_1 (26) with ζ_1 and *env*, *aux*, *plant* defined by (11), (20), and (10), respectively, is proven in KeYmaera X and thus, it follows that Model 4 is vulnerable to Problem 2.

$$\chi_1 \equiv (x \leq x_c) \rightarrow [env;\ aux;\ plant]\,(x \leq x_c) \tag{26}$$

Model 5: Correct *env*, *aux*, and *ctrl*

$$env \triangleq x_c := *;\ ?\left(x_c - x \geq \frac{v^2}{2a_n^{min}}\right) \tag{27}$$

$$aux \triangleq a_n := *;\ ?\left(-a_n^{min} \leq a \leq a_n^{max}\right) \tag{28}$$

$$ctrl \triangleq \text{if } \neg ok(x, v, x_c, a) \text{ then } a := *;\ ?\,C(x, v, x_c, a)\,\text{fi} \tag{29}$$

$$ok \triangleq x_c - x \geq vT + \frac{a_n^{max}\,T^2}{2} + \frac{(v + a_n^{max}\,T)^2}{2a_n^{min}} \tag{30}$$

$$C(x, v, x_c, a) \triangleq a = -a_s^{min} \tag{31}$$

The last three rows of Table 2 summarize the results of the dL formula (3) with the definitions in Model 2 and Model 5, where all three parts conjuncted together is denoted by κ. Based on the insights about Model 3 and Model 4 from Table 2, Model 5 rectifies Problem 1 and Problem 2. Similar to the previous models, the *env* assumption (27) assigns x_c such that it is possible to brake to stop before the obstacle and *aux* (28) is a black box. Unlike the previous models, the *ctrl* test *ok* in (30) not only checks whether the worst-case acceleration is safe in the current execution but also checks whether, in doing so *guarantee* is fulfilled in the next loop execution.

The dL formula κ is proved in KeYmaera X using the loop invariant $\zeta_1 \equiv x \leq x_c$. Since $R(x_c, x_c^+) \equiv x_c \leq x_c^+$ is also applicable for Model 5, it follows from $\models \neg\rho_1$ (25) that ζ_1 is not sufficiently strong to solve Problem 1. The stronger invariant candidate $\zeta_2 \equiv v^2 \leq 2a_n^{min}(x_c - x)$ is used to prove κ and since $\models \rho_2$, it is concluded that ζ_2 is sufficiently strong to solve Problem 1 for Model 5.

Finally, to confirm that Model 5 is not susceptible to Problem 2, ψ from Theorem 2 must hold. The dL formula ψ_2 (32) is proven in KeYmaera X:

$$\psi_2 \equiv \exists x. \exists v. \exists x_c. \Big(\zeta(x, v, x_c, a_n^{min}) \wedge$$
$$\langle env;\ aux \rangle \big(\neg\zeta(x, v, x_c, a) \wedge \langle plant \rangle \neg\zeta(x, v, x_c, a_n^{min})\big)\Big), \tag{32}$$

where *env*, *aux* and *plant* are as defined in (27), (28) and (10) respectively, and the loop invariant $\zeta_2 \equiv \zeta(x, v, x_c, a_n^{min})$ is a specific instantiation of the dL formula $\zeta(x, v, x_c, a)$ given by:

$$\zeta(x, v, x_c, a) \equiv (v + aT \geq 0) \rightarrow (v + aT)^2 \leq 2a_n^{min}\left(x_c - x - vT - \frac{aT^2}{2}\right) \wedge$$
$$(v + aT < 0) \rightarrow v^2 \leq 2a_n^{min}(x_c - x).$$

With this result, it holds that $\models \psi_2$, and therefore it follows from Theorem 2 that $\models \neg\chi_2$ for the choice of ζ_2. Thus, it entails that Model 5 is bereft of Problem 1 and Problem 2, as summarized in the last row of Table 2.

6 Related Work

The models considered in this paper are similar to the models used to verify the European Train Controller System (ETCS) [10]. Though not explicitly stated, the modeling pitfalls are avoided for the ETCS models by the use of an *iterative refinement process* that determines a loop invariant based on a controllability constraint. The process is used to design a correct controller rather than to verify one.

An alternative to guarantee CPS correctness is *runtime validation* [6], where runtime monitors are added to the physical implementation, monitoring whether the system deviates from its model. If it does, correctness is no longer guaranteed, and safe fallbacks are activated. However, for Model 3, the safe fallback would be activated too late since *ctrl* had already taken an unsafe action when the violation of the *env* assumptions are detected. Furthermore, the safe fallbacks might cause spurious braking for Model 4.

The issue in Model 3 is not unique to dL; the issue manifests itself similarly in reactive synthesis [1,5]. The cause of the issue, in both paradigms, stems from the logical implication from the *env* assumptions to the *ctrl* actions and requirements. Instead of taking actions to fulfill the consequent, an exploiting *ctrl* can invalidate the premise to fulfill the implication. However, Bloem et al. [1] conclude that none of the existing approaches completely solve the problem and emphasize the need for further research.

Theorems 1 and 2 put conditions on individual components, but these conditions, in the form of the loop invariant, stem from the same global requirement. Müller et al. [7] take the other approach and start with separate requirements for each of the components to support the global requirement. The goal of the decomposition is to ease the modeling and verification effort, and not directly to validate the model. However, these methods would likely be beneficial in tandem.

The contributions of this paper give additional constraints, apart from the three implications of the loop rule, that can aid the construction of invariants. This might be useful in automatic invariant inference, which is a field of active research where loop invariants are synthesized. Furia and Meyer [3] note that the automatic synthesis of invariants based on the implementation (or the model) might be self-fulfilling, and go on to argue that the postconditions and the global requirements must be considered in the invariant synthesis. This paper, however, suggests that, for certain models, it might not be sufficient to consider only the postconditions in the invariant synthesis.

7 Conclusion

Modeling errors present a risk of unsound conclusions from provably safe erroneous models, if used in the safety argument of safety-critical systems. This paper formulates and proves conditions in Theorem 1 and Theorem 2 that, when fulfilled, help identify and avoid two kinds of modeling errors that may result in a faulty controller being proven safe. Furthermore, the formulated conditions aid in finding a loop invariant which is typically necessary to verify the safety of hybrid systems.

Using a running example of an automated driving controller, the problematic cases are shown to exist in practical CPS designs. The formulated conditions are then applied to the erroneous models to show that the errors are captured. Finally, the errors are rectified to obtain a correct model, which is then proved using a loop invariant that satisfies the formulated conditions, thus ensuring absence of the two modeling errors discussed in this paper.

A natural extension of this work will be to investigate also other kinds of modeling errors that might arise in the verification of complex CPS designs. Moreover, it would also be beneficial to investigate the connection between loop invariants and differential invariants, which are used to prove properties about hybrid systems with differential equations without their closed-form solutions.

References

1. Bloem, R., Ehlers, R., Jacobs, S., Könighofer, R.: How to handle assumptions in synthesis. In: Chatterjee, K., Ehlers, R., Jha, S. (eds.) Proceedings 3rd Workshop on Synthesis, SYNT. EPTCS, vol. 157 (2014). https://doi.org/10.4204/EPTCS.157.7
2. Fulton, N., Mitsch, S., Quesel, J.-D., Völp, M., Platzer, A.: KeYmaera X: an axiomatic tactical theorem prover for hybrid systems. In: Felty, A.P., Middeldorp, A. (eds.) CADE 2015. LNCS (LNAI), vol. 9195, pp. 527–538. Springer, Cham (2015). https://doi.org/10.1007/978-3-319-21401-6_36
3. Furia, C.A., Meyer, B.: Inferring loop invariants using postconditions. In: Blass, A., Dershowitz, N., Reisig, W. (eds.) Fields of Logic and Computation. LNCS, vol. 6300, pp. 277–300. Springer, Heidelberg (2010). https://doi.org/10.1007/978-3-642-15025-8_15
4. Koopman, P., Kane, A., Black, J.: Credible autonomy safety argumentation. In: 27th Safety-Critical Systems Symposium (2019)
5. Majumdar, R., Piterman, N., Schmuck, A.-K.: Environmentally-friendly GR(1) synthesis. In: Vojnar, T., Zhang, L. (eds.) TACAS 2019. LNCS, vol. 11428, pp. 229–246. Springer, Cham (2019). https://doi.org/10.1007/978-3-030-17465-1_13
6. Mitsch, S., Platzer, A.: ModelPlex: verified runtime validation of verified cyber-physical system models. Formal Methods Syst. Des. 49(1), 33–74 (2016). https://doi.org/10.1007/s10703-016-0241-z
7. Müller, A., Mitsch, S., Retschitzegger, W., Schwinger, W., Platzer, A.: Tactical contract composition for hybrid system component verification. Int. J. Softw. Tools Technol. Transf. 20(6), 615–643 (2018). https://doi.org/10.1007/s10009-018-0502-9
8. Platzer, A.: Logics of dynamical systems. In: 27th Annual IEEE Symposium on Logic in Computer Science, pp. 13–24. IEEE (2012). https://doi.org/10.1109/LICS.2012.13
9. Platzer, A.: Logical Foundations of Cyber-physical Systems, vol. 662. Springer, Cham (2018). https://doi.org/10.1007/978-3-319-63588-0
10. Platzer, A., Quesel, J.-D.: European train control system: a case study in formal verification. In: Breitman, K., Cavalcanti, A. (eds.) ICFEM 2009. LNCS, vol. 5885, pp. 246–265. Springer, Heidelberg (2009). https://doi.org/10.1007/978-3-642-10373-5_13
11. Selvaraj, Y., Ahrendt, W., Fabian, M.: Formal development of safe automated driving using differential dynamic logic. arXiv:2204.06873 (2022)
12. Selvaraj, Y., Krook, J.: model-pitfalls-dl (2022). https://doi.org/10.5281/zenodo.6821673

Declassification Predicates for Controlled Information Release

Graeme Smith[(✉)] [iD]

School of Information Technology and Electrical Engineering,
The University of Queensland, Brisbane, Australia
`smith@itee.uq.edu.au`

Abstract. Declassification refers to the controlled release of sensitive information by a program. It is well recognised that security analyses, formal or otherwise, need to take declassification into account to be practically usable. This paper introduces the concept of *declassification predicates* which enable a programmer to define precisely *what* can be declassified in a given program, and *where* in the program it can be released. We show how declassification predicates can be added to an existing information flow logic, and how the extended logic can be implemented within the Dafny program verifier.

1 Introduction

Information flow analyses track the flow of data through a program, and can hence detect when sensitive data flows to program locations which are considered to be accessible by an attacker. Such analyses range from simple security type systems [12,15] to more advanced logics which use predicates to represent the program state and the potentially dynamic security classifications of program variables [11,16]. These analysis techniques typically equate security with the notion of *non-interference* [5]. Non-interference holds when sensitive data does not influence the data held in program locations considered to be accessible to an attacker.

While non-interference provides a highly intuitive notion of information flow security, it is too strict to be used with many programs in practice. Consider, for example, a simple password checking program. In such a program, a user's password would be regarded as sensitive data. But this sensitive data influences what an attacker sees (success or failure) when they enter a guess for the password. Other examples include a program in which employees' salaries are sensitive, but their average may be released for statistical purposes, or a program which determines (and hence releases) whether a financial transaction can proceed although the balance of the account from which the money is being transferred is sensitive. In all cases, the information which is released, and hence accessible to an attacker, is influenced by the sensitive data.

This realisation has led to a range of proposals for weakening non-interference to allow *controlled* declassification of sensitive information. Sabelfeld and Sands [14] identify four dimensions of declassification related to how the release of

A. Riesco and M. Zhang (Eds.): ICFEM 2022, LNCS 13478, pp. 298–315, 2022.
https://doi.org/10.1007/978-3-031-17244-1_18

information is controlled: *what* information can be released; *where* in the program the information can be released; *who* can release the information; and *when* the information can be released. While approaches considering the who and when dimensions have been developed, e.g., Zdancewic and Myers consider the who dimension with their notion of *robust declassification* [17], there has been a significant focus on the what and where dimensions.

To capture the what dimension of declassification, Sabelfeld and Myers [13] introduce the concept of *delimited release*. It requires the programmer to specify a number of expressions in a program, referred to as *escape hatches*, whose values can be released. An escape hatch is specified in the program via a declassify annotation. When such an escape hatch is specified, other occurrences of the expression, either before or after the annotated expression, are also declassified. Hence, the notion is concerned solely with *what* information can be released and not *where* in the program it can be released.

In contrast, Mantel and Sands define a notion of security based on *intransitive non-interference* [8] which considers solely the where dimension. Declassification is allowed at any annotated program step, but only at annotated program steps. A similar approach is provided by Mantel and Reinhard [7] along with two notions of security to capture the what dimension of declassification.

To capture both the what and where dimensions in a single definition of security, Askarov and Sabelfeld introduce *localized delimited release* [3]. As with delimited release, the programmer specifies the expressions which can be released via a declassify annotation. However, only the annotated occurrence of a particular expression, and those following it, are declassified. The annotation therefore marks the point in the program from which the expression becomes declassified.

In this paper we present a new notion of security, *qualified release*, which combines the what and where dimensions, and demonstrate that it is more general, i.e., applicable to more programs, than localized delimited release. The key to our definition is a concept we call *declassification predicates*. These are predicates that must be true at the point in the program where declassification occurs. They can be used to describe a range of values that an escape-hatch expression can take at the point where its value is released. We begin in Sect. 2 with an overview of the earlier work described above. Then, in Sect. 3, we demonstrate how declassification predicates can overcome the shortcomings of existing approaches and define the notion of qualified release. In Sect. 4, we show how qualified release can be enforced by encoding declassification predicates in an existing information flow logic from Winter et al. [16]. In Sect. 5, we present an implementation of the logic with declassification predicates in the Dafny program verification tool [6]. We conclude in Sect. 6.

2 Exisiting Approaches

2.1 Non-interference

In information flow analyses in which declassification is not considered, the standard definition of security is *non-interference* [5]. Given a lattice of security classifications, non-interference states that data classified at a level lower than or equal to a given level ℓ cannot be influenced by data at levels higher than ℓ. When ℓ is the highest level of data accessible to an attacker, this means the attacker cannot deduce anything about the data classified higher than level ℓ. We refer to data classified at a security level higher than ℓ as *high data* and all other data as *low data*. Similarly, a variable that is able to hold high or low data is referred to as a *high variable*, and a variable that is only able to hold low data as a *low variable*.

Non-interference can be formally defined in terms of comparing two runs of the program under consideration. For concurrent programs, if the runs start with the same low data then at each point in the program the low data should remain the same [9].[1] Let a program configuration $\langle c, m \rangle$ denote a program c and memory, i.e., mapping of variables to values, m, and let $\langle c, m \rangle \longrightarrow \langle c', m' \rangle$ and $\langle c, m \rangle \longrightarrow^n \langle c', m' \rangle$ denote that $\langle c, m \rangle$ reaches configuration $\langle c', m' \rangle$ in one or $n \geq 1$ program steps, respectively. Let $m_1 =_\ell m_2$ denote that memories m_1 and m_2 are indistinguishable at security levels ℓ and below. This relation between memories is referred to as *low equivalence*.

Definition 1. Non-interference for program c
Program c is secure if the following holds.

$$\forall m_1, m_2, n, c', m_1' \cdot$$
$$m_1 =_\ell m_2 \land \langle c, m_1 \rangle \longrightarrow^n \langle c', m_1' \rangle \Rightarrow$$
$$\exists m_2', c'' \cdot \langle c, m_2 \rangle \longrightarrow^n \langle c'', m_2' \rangle \land m_1' =_\ell m_2'$$

This can equally be defined in terms of a bisimulation over configurations. Here we use an intuitive definition based on that for sequential programs. The premise of the implication in the above definition does not require the high data to be the same in m_1 and m_2. Hence, if high data which differs between m_1 and m_2 is declassified in c and then assigned to a low variable, the condition fails. Non-interference is, therefore, too strong to use in the presence of declassification.

2.2   Delimited Release

Delimited release [13] is a weakening of non-interference that allows identified expressions, referred to as *escape hatches*, to be declassified in a program. Escape hatches are identified as annotated expressions of the form declassify(e, d) where e is the expression to be declassified, i.e., e is the escape hatch, and d the level to which it is to be declassified. It is a requirement that d is not higher than ℓ, the security level accessible by an attacker.

Under delimited release, the condition $m_1' =_\ell m_2'$ in the consequent of Definition 1 need only hold when all escape hatches have the same value in the initial memories m_1 and m_2. Let $m_1 \, I(E) \, m_2$ denote that all expressions in set E are indistinguishable on memories m_1 and m_2.

---

[1] When concurrency is not a consideration, this definition (as well as the others in this section) can be weakened to only consider the point where the program terminates.

Definition 2. Delimited release of escape hatches E on program c
Program c is secure if the following holds.

$$\forall m_1, m_2, n, c', m_1' \cdot$$
$$m_1 =_\ell m_2 \wedge \langle c, m_1 \rangle \longrightarrow^n \langle c', m_1' \rangle \Rightarrow$$
$$\exists m_2', c'' \cdot \langle c, m_2 \rangle \longrightarrow^n \langle c'', m_2' \rangle \wedge (m_1 \, I(E) \, m_2 \Rightarrow m_1' =_\ell m_2')$$

This definition obviously equates to non-interference when there are no declassified expressions in a program, i.e., when $E = \varnothing$. To illustrate how it captures the *what* dimension of declassification, consider the following examples adapted from [13].

Example 1. Average salary
   A program uses high variables $h_1, \ldots, h_n$ to store the salaries of employees in an organisation. While these salaries are sensitive and have a security level higher than ℓ (the level accessible by a potential attacker), the average can be released for statistical purposes. The average is stored in a low variable avg.

$$avg := \mathsf{declassify}((h_1 + \ldots + h_n)/n, \ell)$$

Given that the annotation of the expression does not change its value, this program does not satisfy non-interference since the final value of avg is influenced directly via the values of $h_1, \ldots, h_n$. However, it does satisfy delimited release which only requires avg to be the same after two runs of the program if those runs start from memories in which the average of the salaries is the same.
   Consider, however, extending the program as follows.

$$h_2 := h_1; \ldots h_n := h_1; avg := \mathsf{declassify}((h_1 + \ldots + h_n)/n, \ell)$$

In this case, the program releases not the average of the initial salaries, but the initial value of h_1. This program does not satisfy delimited release. For example, if one run starts with $h_1 = v$ and $h_2 = u$ and the other with $h_1 = u$ and $h_2 = v$, for some values u and v, then the runs will start from memories in which the average of the salaries are the same. Yet the values of avg won't agree after the runs; it will be v for the first run and u for the second.
   It is in this way that delimited release controls *what* is released; in this case the average of the initial salaries. ◊

Example 2. Electronic wallet
   An electronic wallet indicates whether a transaction of amount k can proceed despite the balance h being sensitive and having a security level higher than ℓ (the level accessible by a potential attacker). The amount of a successful transaction is removed from h and added to a low variable amt.

$$\text{if } \mathsf{declassify}(h \geq k, \ell) \text{ then } h := h - k; amt := amt + k \text{ else } skip$$

Again this program does not satisfy non-interference (since amt is influenced by h), but does satisfy delimited release (since amt will have the same final value for two runs of a program in which it has the same initial value and same value for the released expression $h \geq k$ in the initial state). When extended as follows, however, the program does not satisfy delimited release.

$n := 0;$
while$(n < N)$
        if declassify$(h \geq k, \ell)$ then $h := h - k; amt := amt + k$ else $skip$
        $n := n + 1$

Rather than releasing the expression $h \geq k$ (as specified), this program releases how many transactions of amount k between 0 and an arbitrary value N can occur. It does not satisfy delimited release since the expression $h \geq k$ will be the same for an initial memory with $h = 2 * k$ and another with $h = 4 * k$, but the value released through amt will be different when $N \geq 2$.   ◇

2.3   Localized Delimited Release

Consider the following program where out_1 and out_2 have security level ℓ, and h has a security level higher than ℓ.

$$out_1 := h; out_2 := \mathsf{declassify}(h, \ell)$$

This satisfies delimited release even though it seems it is releasing the value of h early. Definition 2 only requires two runs to agree on out_1 when they agree on the value of h (identified as an escape hatch expression in the second instruction). That is, the definition is concerned with *what* can be released, not *where*.

To weaken non-interference for the where dimension of declassification, Mantel and Sands [8] modify the bisimulation underlying non-interference. Instructions which declassify an expression only need to maintain low equivalence of memories when the expression is equivalent in both memories. All other instructions need to always maintain low equivalence. Hence, the above program would be regarded as insecure since the first instruction does not maintain low equivalence for memories with different values of h. However, the extended versions of Examples 1 and 2 would be regarded as secure (since only the where, and not the what, dimension is considered by this definition). This is also true of other approaches which focus on the where dimension, including those which represent the knowledge of the attacker [2,4].

Localized delimited release [3] combines the idea of escape hatches from delimited release with a similar modification of the bisimulation underlying non-interference. Let $\langle c, m, E \rangle$ denote a program configuration with an additional element E denoting the set of escape hatches encountered so far in the program.

Definition 3. Localized delimited release on program c
Program c is secure if for all initial states i_1 and i_2 such that $i_1 =_\ell i_2$, there exists a bisimulation R_{i_1,i_2} such that $\langle c, i_1, \varnothing \rangle R_{i_1,i_2} \langle c, i_2, \varnothing \rangle$ and for all programs c_1 and c_2, and memories m_1 and m_2, the following holds.

$$\langle c_1, m_1, E_1 \rangle\, R_{i_1, i_2}\, \langle c_2, m_2, E_2 \rangle \Rightarrow$$

1. $(i_1\, I(E_1)\, i_2 \Leftrightarrow i_1\, I(E_2)\, i_2) \land$
2. $(i_1\, I(E_1)\, i_2 \Rightarrow$
   (i) $m_1 =_\ell m_2 \land$
   (ii) $\forall c_1', m_1', E_1' \cdot$

$$((\langle c_1, m_1, E_1 \rangle \longrightarrow \langle c_1', m_1', E_1' \rangle \Rightarrow$$
$$\exists c_2', m_2', E_2' \cdot$$
$$\langle c_2, m_2, E_2 \rangle \longrightarrow \langle c_2', m_2', E_2' \rangle \land$$
$$\langle c_1', m_1', E_1' \rangle\, R_{i_1, i_2}\, \langle c_2', m_2', E_2' \rangle)))$$

The configurations related by R_{i_1, i_2} correspond to those reached by two runs of the program c which start from any low-equivalent states. Note that the escape hatches encountered during two runs of a program may differ due to branching on high data. (Any branch taken based on low data will be the same for two runs whose states are low-equivalent.) The definition of R_{i_1, i_2} requires that the escape hatches of the first run are indistinguishable in the initial states of the runs, i_1 and i_2, precisely when the escape hatches of the second run are indistinguishable in i_1 and i_2 (requirement 1). Furthermore, when they are indistinguishable in the initial states, the current program states are low-equivalent (requirement 2(i)), and any step of the first run can be matched by a step of the second run to reach configurations again related by R_{i_1, i_2} (requirement 2(ii)).

Localized delimited release agrees with delimited release for the programs in Examples 1 and 2. However, the program $out_1 := h; out_2 := \mathsf{declassify}(h, \ell)$ is insecure under localized delimited release.

3   Declassification Predicates

Sabelfeld and Sands [13] define a security type system for ensuring delimited release. As well as tracking information flow, the type system keeps track of which variables have been updated and which have been declassified. The key constraint placed on secure programs is that escape-hatch variables must not be updated before they are declassified. The same type system is shown to also enforce localized delimited release by Askarov and Sabelfeld [3].

It is easy to see that this type system will find the extended programs in Examples 1 and 2 insecure (as required). Both extended programs change high variables before declassifying them. Relying on such a simple check, however, limits how declassification can be used. For example, consider the following program in which employees are awarded an annual bonus (which is between 0 and 10% of their salary) before the average of their salaries are released. $b_1, \ldots, b_n$ are the bonuses provided as inputs to the program.

$$h_1 := h_1 + b_1; \ldots h_n := h_n + b_n; avg := \mathsf{declassify}((h_1 + \ldots + h_n)/n, \ell)$$

This program illustrates a reasonable release of information, but would be regarded as insecure by the type system.

Similarly, consider an electronic wallet which can indicate whether two transactions of amount k can proceed.

$n := 0;$
$\mathsf{while}(n < 2)$
    $\mathsf{if}\ \mathsf{declassify}(h \geq k, \ell)\ \mathsf{then}\ h := h - k; amt := amt + k\ \mathsf{else}\ skip$
    $n := n + 1$

Again this is a reasonable release of information, but cannot be shown to be secure using the type system.

In both examples above, we want to declassify the identified expression in the current state of the program. The type system, however, requires the current values of escape-hatch variables to be equal to their initial state values. As the examples of Sect. 2 show, this is key to capturing *what* is declassified. Modifying Definitions 2 and 3 to refer to the current states in place of the initial states of the runs would result in them capturing the where dimension of declassification, and no longer the what dimension. As a consequence, the extensions of both Example 1 and 2 would be regarded as secure.

To allow such a modification and not lose the what dimension, we propose introducing constraints at the points of declassification. These constraints, which we call *declassification predicates*, provide a specification of precisely what can be released with respect to the initial state of the program. For the salaries example above, we want to release a value between the average of the initial values (corresponding to the case where all employees get a minimal bonus of 0) and the average of the values obtained by adding 10% to each of the initial values (corresponding to the case where all employees get the maximal bonus). The declassification predicate is written as a function $P_i(e)$ where e is the expression being declassified and i is the initial state of the run in which the predicate is being evaluated. Let $[\![v]\!]^i$ denote the value of variable v in state i. The declassification predicate for the salaries program is

$$P_i(e) \hat{=}$$
$$([\![h_1]\!]^i + \ldots + [\![h_n]\!]^i)/n \leq e \leq ([\![h_1]\!]^i + [\![h_1]\!]^i/10 + \ldots + [\![h_n]\!]^i + [\![h_n]\!]^i/10)/n$$

Provided the inputs $b_1, \ldots, b_n$ are between 0 and 10% of the salaries $h_1, \ldots, h_n$ respectively, this predicate will hold at the point of declassification. Hence, the above program will be regarded as secure. However, the predicate will not hold at the point of declassification of the extended program of Example 1, making that program insecure (as desired).

For the electronic wallet example, we want to release the information about whether $[\![h]\!]^i \geq k$ and then, after a successful transaction, whether $[\![h]\!]^i - k \geq k$. A suitable declassification predicate is

$$P_i(e) \hat{=} ([\![h]\!]^i \geq k \Leftrightarrow e) \vee ([\![h]\!]^i - k \geq k \Leftrightarrow e)$$

In general, there may be more than one declassification predicate associated with a program, and each declassified expression must be annotated with the predicate which needs to hold. When a declassification predicate does not hold, the expression is interpreted with its usual, i.e., non-declassified, security classification.

To support declassification predicates, we define a notion of security which we call *qualified release*. Qualified release differs from localized delimited release since it assumes that an escape-hatch expression is only released at the instruction where it is annotated as being declassified (similarly, to the approach of Mantel and Sands [8]). In contrast, with localized delimited release once an escape-hatch expression is released, it remains released for the rest of the program. For example, the program $out_1 := \mathsf{declassify}(h, \ell); out_2 := h$ is secure under localized delimited release when h is a high variable, and out_1 and out_2 are low.

Hence, we modify requirement 1 and the premise of requirement 2 of Definition 3 so that the escape-hatch expressions are compared in the current states of the runs, m_1 and m_2, rather than the initial states, i_1 and i_2. That is, the conditions on low-equivalence of current and future states (requirements 2(i) and 2(ii)) need only hold when all escape hatches have the same value in the state at which they are released. Furthermore, an annotated expression is only considered to be an escape hatch when the associated declassification predicate holds.

Qualified release is defined below where we let $\varepsilon_i(c, m)$ denote the set of expressions e where

- the first instruction in c has an expression $\mathsf{declassify}(e, d)$ such that d is not higher than ℓ, the security level accessible by an attacker (the requirement from Sect. 2), and
- m satisfies the associated declassification predicate $P_i(e)$ where i is the initial state of the run that led to the configuration $\langle c, m \rangle$.

Definition 4. Qualified release on program c
Program c is secure if for all initial states i_1 and i_2 such that $i_1 =_\ell i_2$, there exists a bisimulation R_{i_1, i_2} such that $\langle c, i_1 \rangle \, R_{i_1, i_2} \, \langle c, i_2 \rangle$ and for all programs c_1 and c_2, and memories m_1 and m_2, the following holds.

$$\langle c_1, m_1 \rangle \, R_{i_1, i_2} \, \langle c_2, m_2 \rangle \Rightarrow$$

1. $(m_1 \, I(\varepsilon_{i_1}(c_1, m_1)) \, m_2 \Leftrightarrow m_1 \, I(\varepsilon_{i_2}(c_2, m_2)) \, m_2) \, \wedge$
2. $(m_1 \, I(\varepsilon_{i_1}(c_1, m_1)) \, m_2 \Rightarrow$
   - (i) $m_1 =_\ell m_2 \, \wedge$
   - (ii) $\forall c_1', m_1' \cdot$
     $$(\langle c_1, m_1 \rangle \longrightarrow \langle c_1', m_1' \rangle \Rightarrow$$
     $$\exists c_2', m_2' \cdot \langle c_2, m_2 \rangle \longrightarrow \langle c_2', m_2' \rangle \wedge \langle c_1', m_1' \rangle \, R_{i_1, i_2} \, \langle c_2', m_2' \rangle))$$

For requirement 1 and the premise of requirement 2, the escape-hatch expressions are compared in the current states of the runs, m_1 and m_2, rather than the initial states, i_1 and i_2, as in Definition 3. This allows the variables in the escape-hatch expressions to be modified before declassification.

Like localized delimited release, when there is no declassification in a program qualified release is equivalent to non-interference. It requires that the states reached by a pair of runs, after any given number of steps from low-equivalent states, are low-equivalent.

In programs with declassification, the where dimension of declassification is captured by only enforcing low-equivalence when the escape-hatch expressions in the *current* states of the runs are indistinguishable. Note that when the two runs have identical values for their high variables initially, all escape-hatch expressions will be indistinguishable allowing the bisimulation to traverse the entire program.

The *what* dimension of declassification is enforced by the declassification predicates which must hold for each associated expression to be in $\varepsilon_{i_1}(c_1, m_1)$, and hence be declassified.

4   Enforcing Qualified Release

Due to the need to be able to evaluate arbitrary predicates $P_i(e)$ for qualified release, it cannot be enforced by a simple security type system (such as that designed for delimited release in [13]). A program logic which keeps track of the current state is required. In this section, we show how it can be enforced in the program logic developed by Winter et al. [16]. For presentation purposes, we focus on a subset of this logic supporting static security classifications of variables in single-threaded programs. Our approach, however, is equally applicable to the full logic for dynamic security classifications that change as the program executes (often referred to as *value-dependent* security classifications [11]) and multi-threaded programs.

In this subset of the logic, the function $\mathcal{L}$ maps each program variable to its (static) security classification. In a secure program, each program variable x is only allowed to hold data whose security level is lower than or equal to $\mathcal{L}(x)$. The security level of the data held in variable x, when it can be determined from the program, is captured in an auxiliary variable Γ_x. The security level of an expression e in a program which is so far judged to be secure is calculated from the security level of each variable x in e as follows.

$$\Gamma_E(e) \mathrel{\widehat{=}} \bigsqcup_{x \in vars(e)} (\Gamma_x \sqcap \mathcal{L}(x))$$

Note that $\sqcup$ denotes the join operator (or least upper bound) of the security lattice and $\sqcap$ denotes the meet operator (or greatest lower bound). Hence, if the security level of x can be determined, since it will be less than or equal to $\mathcal{L}(x)$, the expression $\Gamma_x \sqcap \mathcal{L}(x)$ equates to Γ_x. If it cannot be determined, the expression equates to $\mathcal{L}(x)$, accounting for all possible values of Γ_x. The security level of expression e is the highest of the values for each of its variables.

The logic is then expressed in terms of a weakest precondition predicate transformer *wpif* over a simple language comprising skips, assignments, conditionals (if-then-else) and loops (while).[2] Starting from the last line of code and

---

[2] For capturing concurrent algorithms, the simple language also supports atomic compare-and-swap (CAS) instructions which are not considered in this paper.

the postcondition *true*, the predicate transformer introduces proof obligations associated with information flow which are then transformed successively over the rest of the code to a predicate which must hold in the code's initial state. That is, a program c starting in an initial state satisfying S_0 is secure when $S_0 \Rightarrow wpif(c, true)$.

A skip instruction has no effect.

$$wpif(\text{skip}, Q) \mathrel{\widehat{=}} Q$$

For an assignment instruction, the predicate transformer is defined as follows where $def(e)$ is true when e is defined, i.e., won't throw an exception.

$$wpif(x := e, Q) \mathrel{\widehat{=}} \Gamma_E(e) \sqsubseteq \mathcal{L}(x) \wedge def(e) \wedge Q[x \leftarrow e, \Gamma_x \leftarrow \Gamma_E(e)]$$

The first conjunct is a check that the expression e's security level is lower than or equal to that which x is allowed to hold. The second conjunct ensures e is defined. This is needed since throwing of exceptions can reveal information about sensitive data. For example, a divide-by-zero exception can reveal that a sensitive variable holds value 0. The final conjunct updates the values of x and Γ_x in the postcondition Q as in the standard weakest precondition transformer for a pair of assignments.

For a conditional instruction, we require that the branching condition is defined and has a security level lower than or equal to ℓ, the highest security level of data which a potential attacker can access. This is not common to all information flow logics, but is used in Winter et al. [16] to prohibit information being leaked when an attacker can observe the timing of the chosen branch (and hence deduce the value of the branching condition [1,10]).

$$wpif(\text{if } b \text{ then } c_1 \text{ else } c_2, Q) \mathrel{\widehat{=}}$$
$$\Gamma_E(b) \sqsubseteq \ell \wedge def(b) \wedge (b \Rightarrow wpif(c_1, Q)) \wedge (\neg b \Rightarrow wpif(c_2, Q))$$

The final two conjuncts are the standard weakest precondition transformer for conditionals (with $wpif$ replacing wp).

For while loops, the security level of the guard similarly needs to be defined and low for each iteration of the loop, i.e., whenever the loop's invariant is true. For a program with variables $x_1, \ldots, x_n$ we have

$$wpif(\text{while}(b)\, c, Q) \mathrel{\widehat{=}}$$
$$(\forall x_1, \ldots, x_n \cdot Inv \Rightarrow def(b) \wedge \Gamma_E(b) \sqsubseteq \ell) \wedge$$
$$Inv \wedge (\forall x_1, \ldots, x_n \cdot (Inv \wedge b \Rightarrow wpif(c, Inv)) \wedge (Inv \wedge \neg b \Rightarrow Q))$$

where the final two conjuncts are the standard weakest precondition transformer for partial correctness of loops (with $wpif$ replacing wp). Note that since guards do not contain sensitive data (as ensured by the first conjunct), whether or not a loop terminates does not leak information.

To add declassification predicates to the logic, we introduce program annotations of the form declassify$_P(\ldots)$ where P is the associated declassification predicate with initial values of variables replaced by auxiliary variables, $v_1^0, \ldots, v_n^0$, i.e., additional variables which do not affect the program execution. These auxiliary variables are initialised to the corresponding program variables to determine if a program c is secure. That is, we check $S_0 \Rightarrow wpif(c', true)$ where c' is $v_1^0 := v_1; \ldots; v_n^0 := v_n; c$.

We assume that when an expression is declassified, the declassification is applied to the entire expression. That is, the syntax added to include annotations is $x := \mathsf{declassify}_P(e, \ell)$ for assignments, and $\mathsf{if}\ \mathsf{declassify}_P(b, \ell)\ \mathsf{then}\ c_1\ \mathsf{else}\ c_2$ and $\mathsf{while}(\mathsf{declassify}_P(b, \ell))\ c$ for conditionals and loops.

The logic is then extended with the following rules, where d is the level to which information is being declassified and ℓ is the level of access of an attacker.

$$wpif(x := \mathsf{declassify}_P(e, d), Q) \,\hat{=}\,$$
$$d \sqsubseteq \mathcal{L}(x) \wedge P(e) \wedge def(e) \wedge Q[x \leftarrow e, \Gamma_x \leftarrow d]$$
$$wpif(\mathsf{if}\ \mathsf{declassify}_P(b, d)\ \mathsf{then}\ c_1\ \mathsf{else}\ c_2, Q) \,\hat{=}\,$$
$$d \sqsubseteq \ell \wedge P(b) \wedge def(b) \wedge (b \Rightarrow wpif(c_1, Q)) \wedge (\neg b \Rightarrow wpif(c_2, Q))$$
$$wpif(\mathsf{while}(\mathsf{declassify}_P(b, d))\ c, Q) \,\hat{=}\,$$
$$(\forall x_1, \ldots, x_n \cdot Inv \Rightarrow def(b) \wedge P(b)) \wedge d \sqsubseteq \ell \wedge$$
$$Inv \wedge (\forall x_1, \ldots, x_n \cdot (Inv \wedge b \Rightarrow wpif(c, Inv)) \wedge (Inv \wedge \neg b \Rightarrow Q))$$

Each of the rules checks that the declassification predicate holds at the point of declassification. Hence, they will judge a program which does not satisfy a declassification predicate as insecure. This is stricter than necessary since an expression can be used with its usual classification when the predicate does not hold. However, the rules provide a simple extension to the logic which suffices in most situations. A proof of soundness of the extended logic with respect to Definition 4 is provided in Appendix A. To provide an intuitive understanding of the new rules, we revisit the suggested extensions to Examples 1 and 2 of Sect. 3.

Example 3. Average salary with bonuses

Let $b_1, \ldots, b_n$ be between 0 and 10% of the salaries $h_1, \ldots, h_n$ respectively. Let $P(e) \,\hat{=}\, (h_1^0 + \ldots + h_n^0)/n \le e \le (h_1^0 + h_1^0/10 + \ldots + h_n^0 + h_n^0/10)/n$ and c be the following program (where $n > 0$ and avg has security level ℓ).

$$h_1 := h_1 + b_1; \ldots h_n := h_n + b_n; avg := \mathsf{declassify}_P((h_1 + \ldots + h_n)/n, \ell)$$

The program is secure since the proof obligation $P((h_1 + \ldots + h_n)/n)$ introduced by $wpif$ over the final instruction, is transformed to

$$(h_1^0 + \ldots + h_n^0)/n \le (h_1 + b_1 + \ldots + h_n + b_n)/n)$$
$$\le (h_1^0 + h_1^0/10 + \ldots + h_n^0 + h_n^0/10)/n$$

by the preceding instructions. It is further transformed to

$$(h_1 + \ldots + h_n)/n \le (h_1 + b_1 + \ldots + h_n + b_n)/n)$$
$$\le (h_1 + h_1/10 + \ldots + h_n + h_n/10)/n$$

by the initialisation of the auxiliary variables $h_1^0 := h_1; \ldots; h_n^0 := h_n$, which then evaluates to true given the constraints on $b_1, \ldots, b_n$.   ◇

Example 4. Electronic wallet, two withdrawals

Let $P(e) \triangleq (h^0 \geq k \Leftrightarrow e) \vee (h^0 - k \geq k \Leftrightarrow e)$ and c be the following program (where $k \geq 0$ and amt has security level ℓ).

$n := 0;$

while$(n < 2)$

      if declassify$_P(h \geq k, \ell)$ then $h := h - k; amt := amt + k$ else *skip*

      $n := n + 1$

Since the final instruction of this program is a loop, we need a loop invariant to apply the logic. It is easy to see from the loop body, that when $n = 0$, $h = h^0$ and when $n = 1$, either $h = h^0$ when the if condition evaluated to false on the first loop iteration, or $h = h^0 - k$ when the if condition evaluated to true. Hence we choose the following as the invariant.

$$(n = 0 \Rightarrow h = h^0) \wedge$$
$$(n = 1 \Rightarrow (h^0 \geq k \Rightarrow h = h^0 - k) \wedge (h^0 < k \Rightarrow h = h^0))$$

The while loop introduces this invariant and the proof obligation $P(h \geq k)$ which is $(h^0 \geq k \Leftrightarrow h \geq k) \vee (h^0 - k \geq k \Leftrightarrow h \geq k)$. The former is transformed to $h = h^0$ by the first instruction (since n is replaced by 0) while the latter (which does not refer to n) is not changed. They are then both transformed to true by the initialisation of the auxiliary variable $h^0 := h$.   ◇

5   Dafny Encoding

Being based on weakest precondition calculations, the *wpif*-based information flow logic is readily encoded in a program verification tool such as Dafny [6]. The lattice of security levels can be encoded as an enumerated type along with functions defining when two levels are ordered, and for returning the meet and join of any two levels. For example, a standard diamond lattice where level A is higher than levels B and C which are in turn higher than level D (but B and C are not ordered) can be encoded in Dafny as follows.

```
datatype SL = A | B | C | D

function order(l1:SL, l2:SL):bool {
    l1 == A || l1 == l2 || l2 == D
}

function join(l1:SL, l2:SL):SL {
    if order(l1,l2) then l1 else if order(l2,l1) then l2 else A
}

function meet(l1:SL, l2:SL):SL {
    if order(l1,l2) then l2 else if order(l2,l1) then l1 else D
}
```

Note that $order(l_1, l_2)$ is true precisely when $l_2 \sqsubseteq l_1$. To check the encoding is indeed a lattice, the following lemmas, which can be proved automatically by Dafny, are added.

```
lemma partialorder(l1:SL, l2:SL, l3:SL)
    ensures order(l1,l1)
    ensures order(l1,l2) && order(l2,l1) ==> l1 == l2
    ensures order(l1,l2) && order(l2,l3) ==> order(l1,l3)

lemma joinLemma(l1:SL,l2:SL,l3:SL)
    ensures order(join(l1,l2),l1) && order(join(l1,l2),l2)
    ensures order(l3,l1) && order(l3,l2) ==> order(l3,join(l1,l2))

lemma meetLemma(l1:SL,l2:SL,l3:SL)
    ensures order(l1,meet(l1,l2)) && order(l2,meet(l1,l2))
    ensures order(l1,l3) && order(l2,l3) ==> order(meet(l1,l2),l3)
```

Then for each program variable x, *ghost* variables (which are used for specification purposes and are not part of the compiled program) can be added for $\mathcal{L}(x)$, Γ_x and the initial value of x. These allow the security checks (including declassification predicates) added by the *wpif* rules to be encoded as program assertions. For example, consider Example 3 with salaries $h1$, $h2$ and $h3$ and their associated bonuses at security level C, and an attacker able to access data at security level D. This can be encoded within a Dafny class as follows (for readability the full encoding for $h2$ and $h3$ is elided, but follows that for $h1$).

```
var h1:int, h2:int, h3:int, avg: int;   // salaries
ghost var h01:int, h02:int, h03:int, avg0:int;   // initial values
ghost const L_h1 := C; ...; const L_avg := D;
ghost var Gamma_h1: SL, ..., Gamma_avg: SL;

predicate P(e:int)
    reads this   // allows read access to the variables declared above
{
    (h01+h02+h03)/3 <= e <= (h01+h01/10+h02+h02/10+h03+h03/10)/3
}

method average(b1:int, b2:int, b3:int)
    requires 0 <= b1 <= h1/10 && ...
    modifies this   // allows changes to the variables declared above
{
    h01 := h1; h02 := h2; h03 := h3;   // set initial values
    assert order(L_h1,join(meet(Gamma_h1,L_h1),C)) && ...
    h1 := h1 + b1; Gamma_h1 := join(meet(Gamma_h1,L_h1),C); ...;
    assert order(L_avg,D) && P((h1+h2+h3)/3);
    avg := (h1+h2+h3)/3; Gamma_avg := D;   // declassify to level D
}
```

The program of Example 3 is captured by the method *average*. The requires clause of the method ensures the bonuses are within 10% of the associated salaries. The assertions capture the checks required by the *wpif* rules for the instructions which follow them (note that Dafny automatically checks for definedness of expressions).

For example, consider the final line of code which represents the assignment $avg := \mathsf{declass}_P((h1+h2+h3)/3)$. Applying the *wpif* rule for assignments involving declassification, we would get $D \sqsubseteq \mathcal{L}(avg) \wedge P((h1+h2+h3)/3) \wedge \mathit{def}((h1+h2+h3)/3) \wedge Q[avg \leftarrow (h1+h2+h3)/3, \Gamma_{avg} \leftarrow D]$. The final two conjuncts are routinely checked by Dafny (given that we have explicitly included the update to Γ_{avg}). The other conjuncts are included in the assertion and are hence also checked. Dafny can prove each assertion in this example automatically, proving that the program is secure. Similarly, other examples in this paper can be automatically proven to be secure or insecure as required. Importantly, the insertion of the assertions into the code, as well as the declaration and updates of ghost variables (apart from the values of $\mathcal{L}$ which must be provided) can be readily automated to reduce the programmer's burden.

6   Conclusion

In this paper, we have introduced declassification predicates and an associated notion of security called qualified release. Declassification predicates enable program developers to precisely specify *what* sensitive information can be released by a program, and *where* in the program it can be released. We have shown how they can be incorporated into an information flow logic for checking program security, and checked using the Dafny program verifier. Future research includes investigating the application of declassification predicates to a wide range of scenarios where information release is required, and their use in larger, real-world programs.

Acknowledgements. Thanks to Kirsten Winter for her feedback on this paper.

A   Soundness

Theorem 1. *Given a program c with variables $v_1, \ldots, v_n$ and set of initial states S_0, if $S_0 \Rightarrow wpif(v_1^0 := v_1; \ldots; v_n^0 := v_n; c, true)$, where $v_1^0, \ldots, v_n^0$ are fresh, then qualified release (Definition 4) holds for all initial states $i_1, i_2 \in S_0$.*

Proof
Let m_1 and m_2 be two program states such that $m_1 =_\ell m_2$. Following Definition 4, we need to prove that there exists a relation R_{m_1,m_2} such that $\langle c, m_1 \rangle R_{m_1,m_2} \langle c, m_2 \rangle$ for each program c considered secure under *wpif*. The proof is by induction over the instructions of the simple programming language whose operational semantics with respect to an initial state i is given below.

Let stop denote the program with no instructions, and $\varepsilon_i(\text{stop}, m) = \varnothing$.

$\langle \text{skip}, m \rangle \longrightarrow \langle \text{stop}, m \rangle$ $\varepsilon_i(\text{skip}, m) = \varnothing$

$\langle x := e, m \rangle \longrightarrow \langle \text{stop}, m[x \mapsto e'] \rangle$ when $e = \text{declassify}_P(e', d)$

$\langle x := e, m \rangle \longrightarrow \langle \text{stop}, m[x \mapsto e] \rangle$ otherwise

$\varepsilon_i(x := e, m) = \{e'\}$ when $e = \text{declassify}_P(e', d)$ and $d \sqsubseteq \ell$ and
$\qquad\qquad\qquad\qquad m$ satisfies $P(e')$

$\varepsilon_i(x := e, m) = \varnothing$ otherwise

$\langle c_1; c2, m \rangle \longrightarrow \langle c_1'; c2, m' \rangle$ when $\langle c_1, m \rangle \longrightarrow \langle c_1', m' \rangle$

$\langle c_1; c2, m \rangle \longrightarrow \langle c2, m' \rangle$ when $\langle c_1, m \rangle \longrightarrow \langle \text{stop}, m' \rangle$

$\langle \text{if } b \text{ then } c_1 \text{ else } c_2, m \rangle \longrightarrow \langle c_1, m \rangle$ when b is true

$\langle \text{if } b \text{ then } c_1 \text{ else } c_2, m \rangle \longrightarrow \langle c_2, m \rangle$ when b is false

$\varepsilon_i(\text{if } b \text{ then } c_1 \text{ else } c_2, m) = \{b'\}$ when $b = \text{declassify}_P(b', d)$ and $d \sqsubseteq \ell$ and
$\qquad\qquad\qquad\qquad m$ satisfies $P(b')$

$\varepsilon_i(\text{if } b \text{ then } c_1 \text{ else } c_2, m) = \varnothing$ otherwise

$\langle \text{while}(b)\, c, m \rangle \longrightarrow \langle c; \text{while}(b)\, c, m \rangle$ when b is true

$\langle \text{while}(b)\, c, m \rangle \longrightarrow \langle \text{stop}, m \rangle$ when b is false

$\varepsilon_i(\text{while}(b)\, c, m) = \{b'\}$ when $b = \text{declassify}_P(b', d)$ and $d \sqsubseteq \ell$ and
$\qquad\qquad\qquad\qquad m$ satisfies $P(b')$

$\varepsilon_i(\text{while}(b)\, c, m) = \varnothing$ otherwise

skip According to the operational semantics, the skip instruction changes neither the state m nor introduces escape-hatch expressions, and results in the program stop. Therefore, choosing $R_{m_1, m_2} = \{(\langle \text{skip}, m_1 \rangle, \langle \text{skip}, m_2 \rangle), (\langle \text{stop}, m_1 \rangle, \langle \text{stop}, m_2 \rangle)\}$ will satisfy Definition 4. For both configuration pairs, requirement 1 of Definition 4 holds trivially and requirement 2(i) holds due to $m_1 =_\ell m_2$ holding in the starting state. Requirement 2(ii) holds for the second pair due to there being no further program steps and, since it holds for the second pair, also holds for the first pair.

$x := e$ An assignment updates the state m and results in the program stop. If the assignment has a declassification annotation then (according to the *wpif* rule) the program will only be secure when the associated predicate is true in any state that may hold immediately before the assignment. Assume this is the case, and hence the declassification predicate is true in m_1 and m_2. Given this, any escape hatches introduced only depend on e and the level of declassification d (see the operational semantics). Hence, requirement 1 of Definition 4 trivially holds. Consider the relation $R_{m_1, m_2} = \{(\langle x := e, m_1 \rangle, \langle x := e, m_2 \rangle), (\langle \text{stop}, m_1' \rangle, \langle \text{stop}, m_2' \rangle)\}$, where m_1' and m_2' are derived from m_1 and m_2, respectively, by updating the value of x.

For the first configuration pair, if the released expressions are distinguishable on m_1 and m_2 then there is nothing further to prove. If they are indistinguishable then, since the assignments will replace x by an expression which is in the released expressions and at a level $d \sqsubseteq \ell$ (as required by the *wpif* rule), requirement 2(i) (which holds for the first pair) is preserved. Requirement 2(ii) also holds for the second pair (as argued for skip) and hence holds for the first pair.

If the assignment does not have a declassification annotation then no escape hatches will be introduced and requirement 1 trivially holds. The value of x will be replaced by e for both initial states. The *wpif* rule for assignment only holds when $\Gamma_E(e) \sqsubseteq \mathcal{L}(x)$. Hence, if x is low so is e, and low equivalence of states (requirement 2(i)) is preserved. Requirement 2(ii) is also satisfied by the first pair due to the second pair satisfying all requirements.

$c_1; c_2$ By the induction hypothesis, there exists a relation $R^1_{m_1,m_2}$ such that $\langle c_1, m_1 \rangle R^1_{m_1,m_2} \langle c_1, m_2 \rangle$ and $R^1_{m_1,m_2}$ satisfies Definition 4. Let $\langle c_1, m_1 \rangle \rightarrow^n \langle c'_1, m'_1 \rangle$ and $\langle c_1, m_2 \rangle \rightarrow^n \langle c'_1, m'_2 \rangle$, for some n. Note that both ending configurations have the same program, c'_1, since the logic does not allow branching on high data.

If $\neg(m'_1 \, I(\varepsilon_i(c'_1, m'_1)) \, m'_2)$ then there are no further requirements to prove and the following relation satisfies Definition 4 for $c_1; c_2$.

$$R_{m_1,m_2} = \{(\langle c^1_1; c_2, m'_1 \rangle, \langle c^2_1; c_2, m'_2 \rangle)|$$
$$\exists n \cdot \langle c_1, m_1 \rangle \longrightarrow^n \langle c^1_1, m'_1 \rangle \wedge \langle c_1, m_2 \rangle \longrightarrow^n \langle c^2_1, m'_2 \rangle \wedge$$
$$\langle c^1_1, m'_1 \rangle R^1_{m_1,m_2} \langle c^2_1, m'_2 \rangle\}$$

If $m'_1 \, I(\varepsilon_i(c'_1, m'_1)) \, m'_2$ and $\langle c'_1, m'_1 \rangle \rightarrow \langle \text{stop}, m''_1 \rangle$ and $\langle c'_1, m'_2 \rangle \rightarrow \langle \text{stop}, m''_2 \rangle$, i.e., c'_1 terminates after its next instruction, then $m''_1 =_\ell m''_2$ by Definition 4. By the induction hypothesis, there exists a relation $R^2_{m''_1,m''_2}$ satisfying Definition 4 where $\langle c_2, m''_1 \rangle R^2_{m''_1,m''_2} \langle c_2, m''_2 \rangle$. Consider then the following relation.

$$R_{m_1,m_2} = \{(\langle c^1_1; c_2, m'_1 \rangle, \langle c^2_1; c_2, m'_2 \rangle)|$$
$$\exists n \cdot \langle c_1, m_1 \rangle \longrightarrow^n \langle c^1_1, m'_1 \rangle \wedge \langle c_1, m_2 \rangle \longrightarrow^n \langle c^2_1, m'_2 \rangle \wedge$$
$$\langle c^1_1, m'_1 \rangle R^1_{m_1,m_2} \langle c^2_1, m'_2 \rangle\}$$
$$\cup \{(\langle c^1_2, m'''_1 \rangle, \langle c^2_2, m'''_2 \rangle)|$$
$$\exists n \cdot \langle c_2, m''_1 \rangle \longrightarrow^n \langle c^1_2, m'''_1 \rangle \wedge \langle c_2, m''_2 \rangle \longrightarrow^n \langle c^2_2, m'''_2 \rangle \wedge$$
$$\langle c^1_2, m'''_1 \rangle R^2_{m''_1,m''_2} \langle c^2_2, m'''_2 \rangle\}$$

This clearly relates $\langle c_1; c_2, m_1 \rangle$ and $\langle c_1; c_2, m_2 \rangle$. We now show that it also satisfies Definition 4 by considering two cases: a sequence of steps in program c_1, and a sequence of steps in program c_2.

First case: $\langle c_1, m_1 \rangle \longrightarrow^n \langle c^1_1, m'_1 \rangle$ and $\langle c_1, m_2 \rangle \longrightarrow^n \langle c^2_1, m'_2 \rangle$ such that $\langle c^1_1, m'_1 \rangle R^1_{m_1,m_2} \langle c^2_1, m'_2 \rangle$. The latter implies requirements 1 and 2(i) for R_{m_1,m_2}. If c^1_1 has not terminated then requirement 2(ii) follows from requirement 2(ii) of $R^1_{m_1,m_2}$. If c^1_1 has terminated, i.e., $m'_1 = m''_1$ and $m'_2 = m''_2$ (since the absence of branching on high data means the runs will terminate together), then from the operational semantics for sequential composition we know that $\langle c_1; c_2, m_1 \rangle \longrightarrow^n \langle c_2, m''_1 \rangle$ and $\langle c_1; c_2, m_2 \rangle \longrightarrow^n \langle c_2, m''_2 \rangle$. And since $\langle c_2, m''_1 \rangle$ and $\langle c_2, m''_2 \rangle$ are related by $R^2_{m''_1,m''_2}$, they are also related by R_{m_1,m_2} and we have requirement 2(ii).

Second case: $\langle c_2, m_1'' \rangle \longrightarrow^n \langle c_2^1, m_1''' \rangle$ and $\langle c_2, m_2'' \rangle \longrightarrow^n \langle c_2^2, m_2''' \rangle$ such that $\langle c_2^1, m_1''' \rangle R_{m_1,m_2}^2 \langle c_2^2, m_2''' \rangle$. As before, the latter implies requirements 1 and 2(i) for R_{m_1,m_2}. In this case, requirement 2(ii) of R_{m_1,m_2} also follows from requirement 2(ii) of $R_{m_1'',m_2''}^2$.

if b then c_1 else c_2 By the induction hypothesis, there exists relations R_{m_1,m_2}^1 and R_{m_1,m_2}^2 satisfying Definition 4 such that $\langle c_1, m_1 \rangle R_{m_1,m_2}^1 \langle c_1, m_2 \rangle$, and $\langle c_2, m_1 \rangle R_{m_1,m_2}^2 \langle c_2, m_2 \rangle$. Consider the first configuration pair of the following relation.

$$R_{m_1,m_2} = \{ (\langle \text{if } b \text{ then } c_1 \text{ else } c_2, m_1 \rangle, \langle \text{if } b \text{ then } c_1 \text{ else } c_2, m_2 \rangle) \}$$
$$\cup\ R_{m_1,m_2}^1 \cup R_{m_1,m_2}^2$$

If the guard has a declassification annotation then, following the proof for assignment, requirements 1 and 2(i) trivially hold, and requirement 2(ii) follows from the requirements holding for subsequent configurations. These hold due to the fact that the *wpif* rule for conditionals requires $\Gamma_E(b) \sqsubseteq \ell$ or, when b is declassified to security level d, $d \sqsubseteq \ell$. Hence, when any released expressions are indistinguishable on m_1 and m_2, the choice of branch c_1 or c_2 will be the same for the low-equivalent states m_1 and m_2 (according to the operational semantics). Therefore, all resulting configurations will be related by either R_{m_1,m_2}^1 or $R_{m1,m2}^2$.

while$(b)\,c$ The *wpif* rule for loops requires a loop invariant which holds in both m_1 and m_2 to be provided. Let M be the set of all memories satisfying the loop invariant and consider the following relation. By the induction hypothesis, for each $m_1', m_2' \in M$ such that $m_1' =_\ell m_2'$ there exists a relation R_{m_1,m_2}^1 such that $\langle c, m_1' \rangle R_{m_1',m_2'}^1 \langle c, m_2' \rangle$ and $R_{m_1',m_2'}^1$ satisfies Definition 4.

$$R_{m_1,m_2} = \bigcup\nolimits_{m_1',m_2' \in M} \{ (\langle \text{while}(b)\,c, m_1' \rangle, \langle \text{while}(b)\,c, m_2' \rangle), \langle \text{stop}, m_1' \rangle, \langle \text{stop}, m_2' \rangle \}$$
$$\cup\ R_{m_1',m_2'}^1$$

Given $m_1, m_2 \in M$, the proof follows the proof for conditionals with the following changes based on the operational semantics: (i) when b is false, the subsequent program is stop and the state is unchanged, and (ii) when b is true, the subsequent program is c; while$(b)\,c$. Note that in the latter case, since the loop invariant will be true after c terminates, requirement 2(ii) will hold due to the distributed union over all states satisfying the invariant in the definition of R_{m_1,m_2}. $\square$

References

1. Almeida, J.B., Barbosa, M., Barthe, G., Dupressoir, F., Emmi, M.: Verifying constant-time implementations. In: Holz, T., Savage, S. (eds.) 25th USENIX Security Symposium, USENIX Security 2016, pp. 53–70. USENIX Association (2016)
2. Askarov, A., Sabelfeld, A.: Gradual release: unifying declassification, encryption and key release policies. In: 2007 IEEE Symposium on Security and Privacy (S&P 2007), pp. 207–221. IEEE Computer Society (2007). https://doi.org/10.1109/SP. 2007.22

3. Askarov, A., Sabelfeld, A.: Localized delimited release: combining the what and where dimensions of information release. In: Hicks, M.W. (ed.) Proceedings of the 2007 Workshop on Programming Languages and Analysis for Security, PLAS 2007, pp. 53–60. ACM (2007). https://doi.org/10.1145/1255329.1255339

4. Chudnov, A., Naumann, D.A.: Assuming you know: epistemic semantics of relational annotations for expressive flow policies. In: 31st IEEE Computer Security Foundations Symposium, CSF 2018, pp. 189–203. IEEE Computer Society (2018). https://doi.org/10.1109/CSF.2018.00021

5. Goguen, J.A., Meseguer, J.: Security policies and security models. In: 1982 IEEE Symposium on Security and Privacy, pp. 11–20. IEEE Computer Society (1982). https://doi.org/10.1109/SP.1982.10014

6. Leino, K.R.M.: Dafny: an automatic program verifier for functional correctness. In: Clarke, E.M., Voronkov, A. (eds.) LPAR 2010. LNCS (LNAI), vol. 6355, pp. 348–370. Springer, Heidelberg (2010). https://doi.org/10.1007/978-3-642-17511-4_20

7. Mantel, H., Reinhard, A.: Controlling the what and where of declassification in language-based security. In: De Nicola, R. (ed.) ESOP 2007. LNCS, vol. 4421, pp. 141–156. Springer, Heidelberg (2007). https://doi.org/10.1007/978-3-540-71316-6_11

8. Mantel, H., Sands, D.: Controlled declassification based on intransitive noninterference. In: Chin, W.-N. (ed.) APLAS 2004. LNCS, vol. 3302, pp. 129–145. Springer, Heidelberg (2004). https://doi.org/10.1007/978-3-540-30477-7_9

9. Mantel, H., Sands, D., Sudbrock, H.: Assumptions and guarantees for compositional noninterference. In: Proceedings of the 24th IEEE Computer Security Foundations Symposium, CSF 2011, pp. 218–232. IEEE Computer Society (2011). https://doi.org/10.1109/CSF.2011.22

10. Molnar, D., Piotrowski, M., Schultz, D., Wagner, D.: The program counter security model: automatic detection and removal of control-flow side channel attacks. In: Won, D.H., Kim, S. (eds.) ICISC 2005. LNCS, vol. 3935, pp. 156–168. Springer, Heidelberg (2006). https://doi.org/10.1007/11734727_14

11. Murray, T.C., Sison, R., Engelhardt, K.: COVERN: a logic for compositional verification of information flow control. In: 2018 IEEE European Symposium on Security and Privacy, EuroS&P 2018, pp. 16–30. IEEE (2018). https://doi.org/10.1109/EuroSP.2018.00010

12. Sabelfeld, A., Myers, A.C.: Language-based information-flow security. IEEE J. Sel. Areas Commun. 21(1), 5–19 (2003). https://doi.org/10.1109/JSAC.2002.806121

13. Sabelfeld, A., Myers, A.C.: A model for delimited information release. In: Futatsugi, K., Mizoguchi, F., Yonezaki, N. (eds.) ISSS 2003. LNCS, vol. 3233, pp. 174–191. Springer, Heidelberg (2004). https://doi.org/10.1007/978-3-540-37621-7_9

14. Sabelfeld, A., Sands, D.: Declassification: dimensions and principles. J. Comput. Secur. 17(5), 517–548 (2009). https://doi.org/10.3233/JCS-2009-0352

15. Volpano, D.M., Irvine, C.E., Smith, G.: A sound type system for secure flow analysis. J. Comput. Secur. 4(2/3), 167–188 (1996). https://doi.org/10.3233/JCS-1996-42-304

16. Winter, K., Coughlin, N., Smith, G.: Backwards-directed information flow analysis for concurrent programs. In: 34th IEEE Computer Security Foundations Symposium, CSF 2021, pp. 1–16. IEEE (2021). https://doi.org/10.1109/CSF51468.2021.00017

17. Zdancewic, S., Myers, A.C.: Robust declassification. In: 14th IEEE Computer Security Foundations Workshop (CSFW-14 2001), 11–13 June 2001, pp. 15–23. IEEE Computer Society (2001). https://doi.org/10.1109/CSFW.2001.930133

Trace Refinement in B and Event-B

Sebastian Stock[1](✉) ⓘ, Atif Mashkoor[1](✉) ⓘ, Michael Leuschel[2]ⓘ,
and Alexander Egyed[1](✉) ⓘ

[1] Johannes Kepler University, Linz, Austria
{sebastian.stock,atif.mashkoor,alexander.egyed}@jku.at
[2] Heinrich Heine University, Düsseldorf, Germany
leuschel@hhu.de

Abstract. Traces are used to show whether a model complies with the intended behavior. A modeler can use trace checking to ensure the preservation of the model behavior during the refinement process. In this paper, we present a trace refinement technique and tool called *BERT* that allows designers to ensure the behavioral integrity of high-level traces at the concrete level. The proposed technique is evaluated within the context of the B and Event-B methods on industrial-strength case studies from the automotive domain.

Keywords: B method · Event-B · Animation · Traces · Refinement

1 Introduction

In a correct-by-construction model development process, refinement takes center stage. The idea is to incrementally enrich a model in detail (horizontal or vertical refinement) while preserving the correctness of already introduced functionalities and properties. This correctness assurance process requires both verification and validation. While proof obligations (POs) [1] can ensure that the model is verifiable, validation obligations (VOs) [26] can be used to assess the validity of the model.

A trace can ascertain two conditions: 1) a specific end-state is reachable after executing steps in a specific order, and 2) a specific order of transitions is feasible. When creating a trace for a model, the designer may be interested in keeping the specific trace throughout the refinement chain as evidence that particular behavior is preserved. However, the time invested in creating the trace may be lost during the refinement process. Furthermore, the trace may no longer be replayable due to a change in the operations or the addition of new operations. One could argue that the designer could postpone validation until the model is concrete or recreate the trace on the refined machine. However, the first approach

This research presented in this paper has been conducted within the IVOIRE project, which is funded by "Deutsche Forschungsgemeinschaft" (DFG) and the Austrian Science Fund (FWF) grant # I 4744-N. The work of Austrian authors has been partly funded by the LIT Secure and Correct Systems Lab sponsored by the province of Upper Austria.

A. Riesco and M. Zhang (Eds.): ICFEM 2022, LNCS 13478, pp. 316–333, 2022.
https://doi.org/10.1007/978-3-031-17244-1_19

is against the spirit of early validation in the modeling process, while the latter case entails additional work and complexity.

In this paper, we present a technique and tool called *BERT* (<u>B</u> and <u>E</u>vent-B Trace <u>R</u>efinement <u>T</u>echnique) showing how traces on abstract models can be refined automatically to replay on later stages of the refinement chain. With this technique and tool, we aim to make traces transferable between an abstract and refining machine in the context of B [1], and Event-B [2]. The ability to transfer traces increases the worth of traces in multiple aspects. For one, we can assure ourselves of the presence of abstract behavior in the refinement, which helps us validate the specification. Additionally, we encourage tracing and the exploration of the model via animation in general. With BERT, designers can automatically transfer the findings of their experiments to the next stage of development, i.e., the next refinement step. This is an aspect of early validation, which is desirable when writing formal models. However, we aim not to establish a refinement relationship but to transform a trace from an abstract machine M_A to a concrete machine M_C. So trace refinement in our context means not *establishing a refinement relationship via traces* but *refinement of a trace*. Trace refinement enables *comfortable* early validation of models via trace checking. We choose B and Event-B as candidate formal methods in this endeavor. The proposed technique is implemented as an add-on for the animator and model checker ProB [19]. The proposed technique is validated using industrial-strength case studies from the automotive domain.

The rest of the paper is structured as follows. Section 2 introduces formal methods B and Event-B and the tool-set ProB. Section 3 discusses the relationship between refinement checking and trace refinement and formalizes the technique of this paper. Section 4 introduces the techniques used for trace refinement. In Sect. 5 BERT is evaluated on two mid-size Event-B case studies. In Sect. 6 the observations regarding algorithm and case studies are presented. Section 7 compares the presented technique with the related work. Finally, Sect. 8 concludes the paper.

2   Formal Methods B and Event-B

The B modeling language, and its successor Event-B, shown in Fig. 1a, are formal methods based on set theory and first-order predicate logic. Although the methods differ in various ways, as explained by Leuschel [17] and Mashkoor et al. [25], both promote the correct-by-construction development paradigm. Designers can describe a machine that behaves like a state automaton with both languages. In B, so-called `operations` are used to make transitions between states, while in Event-B, the transitions are made via `events`. Both events and operations manipulate the state of the machine[1]. The events have guards consisting of predicates checked against the machine's state. Depending on whether a guard is met, the transition is enabled. With the events, we can manipulate variables written in the `variables` section of the machine. For a machine, we can also

---

[1] In the following, events and operations will be used as interchangeable words.

define `invariants` that constrain the state space and are also used to define variables.

2.1 Refinement

In B and Event-B, refinement is a way to enrich the model by adding new variables or events or by replacing existing variables with more complex constructs. The key to refinement is that the concrete model preserves abstract behavior. Refinement enhances the abilities of a model without violating its properties.

In classical B, refinement of operations happens in a strict 1:1 relation. Practically this means that every operation from the abstract machine is refined in the concrete one only once, and no new operations are introduced. Furthermore, the name of the operation and the number and name of its parameters cannot change in the concrete machine M_C once defined in the abstract machine M_A.

In Event-B, refinement is more liberal. For example, it is allowed to rename events, and it is allowed to introduce new events in M_C that refine the invisible `skip` event from M_A. Furthermore, unlike B, in Event-B, multiple events in M_C can refine one abstract event from M_A, and the parameters can also be changed. To check for the consistency of an Event-B refinement, one can use proofs showing a refinement does not violate the abstract model. These proofs are supported by, for example, the Rodin platform [3].

Figure 1a shows an abstract model of a traffic light taken from the Rodin handbook [10]. We see two variables, one for pedestrians and one for cars, stating whether they can pass. We can manipulate these variables with events. Additionally, the invariant @*inv3* ensures that cars and people cannot pass at the same time.

Figure 1b shows the refinement of Fig. 1a. Here, two main features are implemented. First, we replace the Boolean variables with actual colors introduced in Fig. 1c and couple the abstract and concrete states with @inv7 and @inv8, thus ensuring that the safety invariant established in Fig. 1a is also present in Fig. 1b. Furthermore, we have two colors for pedestrians and four for a car traffic light. The fact that these four phases[2] have a specific order is accounted for in `set_cars_colors` where we have four consecutive phases for the lights. namely: `green → yellow → red → red,yellow → green`. Second, we introduce a new behavior in the form of the `activateSystem` event that refines `skip`. This event symbolizes the start of the system and is fired once.

In Event-B, stuttering events are allowed. Stuttering describes the phenomenon when one abstract transition/state is replaced with multiple concrete ones. From the perspective of the abstract model, the concrete one has the same behavior. From the concrete model perspective, one may have to do multiple steps in the concrete state-space to mirror one abstract step. The abstract handling of the traffic light contains two consecutive phases for cars `TRUE → FALSE` and the concrete version contains four consecutive color phases, as mentioned earlier. Abstract and concrete states are coupled via the witness `@new_value`,

---

[2] We model them in the way how German traffic lights operate.

such that the light is **green** whenever the Boolean variable would be TRUE and vice versa, thus mapping one abstract state to multiple concrete ones.

2.2   ProB

ProB [6] is a model checker and animator for formal methods, including B and Event-B. ProB allows for sophisticated manipulation and reasoning about models of different formal languages with its extensions and libraries, making it a suitable tool for trace refinement. BERT is implemented as an add-on to ProB and utilizes its infrastructure, e.g., Java APIs of the kernel, to execute the necessary tasks.

3   Trace Refinement Concept

Back and Wright [5] showed how to establish a refinement relationship by showing that the behavior of the concrete machine simulates the abstract machine. We are not establishing a refinement relationship here but transforming a trace from M_A to M_C. The target of trace refinement is to find a trace in M_C that contains the behavior of the trace from M_A. This is achieved step-wise by transforming the abstract trace's transitions and adapting them for the concrete machine. However, as Back and Wright's approach works well for transforming a concrete trace back to an abstract one, one cannot simply conclude the other way around. This is because not every abstract trace has a concrete counterpart. Similarly, only because an abstract trace can be refined for a concrete machine, those machines are not necessarily in a correct refinement relationship. However, the concrete machine mimics the behavior of the abstract machine encoded in the form of a trace.

3.1   Trace Refinement in B

For B, the concept of trace refinement is implemented in the form of refinement checking to ensure that an abstract machine contains all concrete traces [7,9,18]. We define a trace T as an ordered list of transitions $t_1, \ldots, t_n$, which describe the operation's name, the parameters used, and the state reached. For a B machine, it is refined to T' iff every transition t, consisting of a state and an operation, from the abstract trace has 1) a distinguishable counterpart in the corresponding concrete trace, 2) transitions and states have the same order, and 3) the length of the abstract trace and the concrete trace is equal. These attributes are directly derived from the notion of refinement of B refinement and the findings of Leuschel and Butler [18] regarding refinement checking via traces.

3.2   Trace Refinement in Event-B

Trace refinement in Event-B is commonly established via proofs. In terms of our trace refinement algorithm, it is more challenging than the B version. Let us

```
machine mac

variables
cars_go peds_go

invariants
@inv1 peds_go ∈ BOOL
@inv2 cars_go ∈ BOOL
@inv3 ¬(cars_go=TRUE∧peds_go=TRUE)

events
  event INITIALISATION
  then
  @act1 peds_go = FALSE
  @act2 cars_go = FALSE
  end

  event set_peds_go
  when
  @grd1 cars_go = FALSE
  then
  @act1 peds_go = TRUE
  end

  event set_peds_stop
  then
  @act1 peds_go = FALSE
  end

  event set_cars
  any new_value
  where
  @grd1 new_value ∈ BOOL
  @grd2 new_value = TRUE → peds_go=FALSE
  then
  @act1 cars_go=new_value
  end
end
```

(a) Abstract machine with binary light status

```
machine mac1 refines mac sees Colours

variables cars_color peds_color activated

invariants
@inv4 peds_color ∈ {red, green}
@inv5 cars_color ⊆ colours
@inv7 (peds_go = TRUE) → (peds_color = green)
@inv8 (cars_go = TRUE) → (green ∈ cars_color)
@inv9 activated ∈ BOOL

events
  event INITIALISATION
  then
  @act3 cars_color = {red}
  @act4 peds_color = red
  @act5 activated = FALSE
  end

  event activateSystem
  where
  @grd1 activated = FALSE
  then
  @act2 activated = TRUE
  end

  event set_peds_green refines set_peds_go
  where
  @grd2 green ∉ cars_color
  @grd3 activated = TRUE
  then
  @act2 peds_color = green
  end

  event set_peds_red refines set_peds_stop
  where
  @grd3 activated = TRUE
  then
  @act2 peds_color = red
  end

  event set_cars_colors refines set_cars
  any new_value_color
  where
  @grd1 new_value_color ⊆ colours
  @grd2 green ∈ new_value_color → peds_color = red
  @grd3 cars_color = {yellow} → new_value_color = {red}
  @grd4 cars_color = {red} → new_value_color = {red, yellow}
  @grd5 cars_color = {red, yellow} → new_value_color = {green}
  @grd6 cars_color = {green} → new_value_color = {yellow}
  @grd7 activated = TRUE
  with
  @new_value (new_value = TRUE) → (green ∈ new_value_color)
  then
  @act1 cars_color = new_value_color
  end
end
```

(b) Refined machine with colors

```
context Colours

sets
colours

constants
red yellow green

axioms
@axm1 partition(colours, {red}, {yellow}, {green})
end
```

(c) Context for colors

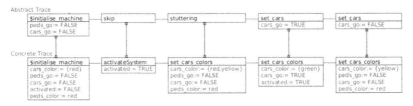

(d) Example of trace refinement result visualization outputted by BERT

Fig. 1. Traffic light refinement example

consider a small example trace for Fig. 1a. INITIALISATION → set_cars(TRUE) → set_cars(FALSE) represents the abstract model allowing the cars to go and stops them afterwards. Now we want to refine the trace and adapt it to Fig. 1b. Consider Fig. 1d as a reference to a successful refinement[3]. Figure 1d shows two traces, both to be read horizontally. Each rectangle represents a trace transition, with the upper part being the operation and the body representing the changed values. The different transitions are connected via the red lines. The connection between the abstract and concrete transitions is marked with strokes with a square head on both ends, e.g., the concrete initialization contains a more sophisticated set of variables than the abstract one. Two placeholders skip and stuttering were inserted in the places where the concrete trace diverges from the abstract - those two transitions were not part of the abstract trace. The event activateSystem that refines skip has become a necessity in order to progress further in the trace. Same goes for set_cars_colors, which is a stuttering action. Note the values of the machine here. While it was possible to directly switch from TRUE to FALSE in the abstract version, a stuttering action is needed as FALSE is mapped to red and red,yellow in the concrete version.

For a successful trace refinement, we borrow some of the attributes from Sect. 3.1: 1) pairs of abstract and concrete states are distinguishable, and 2) order persevering. However, with 3), the trace might get lengthier as new observable behaviors might become necessary to mirror the abstract behavior in the concrete model. Though acceptable, being unavoidable, the addition of new behaviors is not preferable.

A significant challenge for the trace refinement algorithm is stuttering, skip refinements, and their ability to introduce divergence [8]. Divergence means that the model neither runs in a deadlock nor terminates but evolves in a way not observable from an abstract standpoint. For refinement in Event-B, this can be the case as skip and refines keywords add behaviors not observable from an abstract viewpoint. We cannot be sure whether these behaviors terminate or deadlock at some point. Event-B offers a solution for this by annotating events as convergent associated with a proof that the event will occur only finite times often. Further challenges are that multiple events can refine a single one, thus forcing us to investigate all concrete events, and that renaming can occur.

To sum up: Trace refinement in Event-B, like in B, ensures that the abstract behavior is preserved in the concrete trace in the same order. However, there can be additional, new behaviors only observable in the concrete machine at any point in the concrete trace. If the related events are not annotated as convergent at some point, these concrete events can occur infinitely often. If the convergence is unproven, we can run into a situation where we often discover new concrete states that do not present in the abstract model, thus running into an endless loop without any abort condition.

---

[3] The graphical output shown in Fig. 1d is the result of BERT's automatic visualization. As ProBs internal representation is used, some names, for example *initalize_machine*, are held in the ProB style.

4   BERT

BERT[4] is a technique and tool for trace refinement. It needs M_A, M_C, and the trace to be refined. BERT uses the ProB libraries to prepare the machines on the implementation level. The actual refinement process is done with the help of the ProB animator. The solution can be stored in the trace format used by the animator[5]. It can be replayed on the concrete machine without additional measures. If there is no solution, an error message is displayed, and the last attempt is given as a trace. The visual representation provided by BERT is shown in Fig. 1d.

4.1   Trace Refinement for B

The existence of data refinement makes it necessary to observe abstract and concrete state space simultaneously when doing trace refinement as a designer can replace abstract variables with concrete ones. The consequence is that the abstract variables are no longer visible in the concrete machine. This could leave us unsure which transition to take when doing trace refinement, as each transition in the trace is formulated as a predicate over state variables and enabled operations. Missing information could lead to ambiguity. The problem is that machines are independent components. Therefore, we combine the state spaces of M_A and M_C to eliminate the data refinement problem. One way to achieve this is by merging abstract syntax trees (ASTs) and creating an intermediate machine. After a successful combination of state spaces, we can proceed with trace refinement.

Let $M(R, V, I, Op)$ be a simplified machine. Each of the four elements represents one of the ASTs node types.

- R is the set of references to other machines, represented as an identifier list
- V is the set of variables, represented as an identifier list
- I is the invariant, a conjunction of predicates
- Op is the set of operations. An operation has the form $op(N, In, Ou, B)$
    - N represents the name of the operation
    - In represents input variables of the operation
    - Ou represents output variables of the operation
    - B represents the body of the operation

Let $M_A(R_A, V_A, I_A, Op_A)$ be the abstract and $M_C(R_C, V_C, I_C, Op_C)$ be the concrete machine. An interleaved machine $M_I = M_A \| M_C$ has the form $M_I(R_A \cup R_C, I_A \wedge I_C, V_A \cup V_C, Op_A \| Op_B)$ and the operations are interleaved by $Op_A \| Op_B = \{op(N, In, Ou, B_1 \| B_2) | op(N, In, Ou, B_1) \in Op_A \wedge op(N, In, Ou, B_2) \in Op_C\}$. In the case of the operation bodies, $\|$ is the parallel substitution. As parameters cannot be changed, they stay untouched. In

---

[4] BERT is available as part of ProB2, see https://www3.hhu.de/stups/downloads/prob2/snapshot/.

[5] A demo is provided at https://doi.org/10.6084/m9.figshare.16909006.v2.

B machines with multiple, overlapping references, merging R_A and R_C can be challenging. This is because of the possibility that R_A and R_C could contain conflicting statements which would need to be resolved by renaming large parts of the AST to avoid conflicts. Currently, these cases are not treated in this work and should be considered as out of scope.

Algorithm 1 shows the process of the actual trace refinement. For reasoning, we borrow the $start \xrightarrow[M_C]{op} s$ notation from the work of Leuschel et al. [18] to describe the process of creating a transition. This notation expresses multiple things. First, a transition goes from a state $start$ to a state s. Furthermore, the transition uses the operation op. Finally, the transition is executed on the machine M_C. Internally, the transition is written as a predicate consisting of abstract variables, operation parameters, and the operation name. If an operation with the name exists that fulfills the predicates, the operation is seen as a valid transition.

Algorithm 1 aims to implement the condition for successful trace refinement we set up in Sect. 3.1: an order-preserving and length preserving image from an abstract transition to the concrete counterpart. In Algorithm 1, we show how B traces are refined. We take a transition, find its counterpart, and append the found concrete transition to our solution in each step. This happens in line 12 of Algorithm 1. As multiple solutions per transition are possible, we have to carry all those solutions with us, which result in the fact that we store all concrete traces that are candidates for being a solution in `currentTraces`. Due to the way we copy `resultTraces` into `currentTraces`, we dismiss those traces from further calculations that are no more qualified candidates. The way we use the coupled state spaces, the $start \xrightarrow[M_C]{op} s$ relation and reduce the trace in each step, we ensure that Algorithm 1 produces the correct result.

4.2 Trace Refinement for Event-B

Merging state spaces for Event-B is analogous to B, as shown in Sect. 4.1, with minor changes in how parameters and 1:n relations between concrete events are handled.

The trace refinement algorithm for Event-B is shown in Algorithm 2. Besides static information about alternatives and skip refinement, it includes a list of **trace** data structures, which itself is a triple and consists of the current concrete trace, the abstract transitions left, and the already visited nodes of the state space. We loop until we either have no further state to traverse and return unsuccessful or find a trace that refines all abstract steps and has found a solution. Inside the loop, we consider each **trace** structure, which is currently maintained as a possible solution for all valid successors. In line 13 of Algorithm 2, one can recognize the formulation already used in Algorithm 1 where a direct equivalent to an abstract transition exists. In this case, the abstract trace is reduced in size in line 16 of Algorithm 2, and the solution for this step is added to the set of solutions. In line 18 of Algorithm 2, we create all solutions for this step, erasing all stored states as we made progress in reducing the task size. New is

---

Algorithm 1. Algorithm of BERT for B

Require: M_C that has access to M_A, Trace T made out of a list of transitions $t_1, \ldots, t_n$
    with t = (op,s)
1: $resultTraces \leftarrow$ FINDPATH($\langle\langle(\_, root)\rangle\rangle$, T, M_C)
2: **if** resultTraces = $\langle\rangle$ **then**
3:     println(*"Trace could not be translated"*)
4: **else**
5:     selectAnySolution(resultTraces)   ▷ Hand selection of the result
6: **end if**
7: **function** FINDPATH(currentTraces, T, M_C)
8:     **for** (op, s) $\in$ T **do**
9:         resultTraces $\leftarrow \langle\rangle$
10:       **for** trace $\in$ currentTraces **do**
11:           (_, currentState) $\leftarrow$ last(trace)
12:           trans $\leftarrow \{(op, s') | currentState \xrightarrow[M_C]{op} s' \wedge s \sqsubseteq s'\}$ ▷ Next reachable states
13:           **for** tran $\in$ trans **do**   ▷ Collect all solutions
14:              resultTraces $\leftarrow$ append(resultTraces, append(trace, tran))
15:           **end for**
16:       **end for**
17:       currentTraces $\leftarrow resultTraces$
18:     **end for**
19:     **return** currentTraces
20: **end function**

---

the calculation for `skip` and stuttering in line 20. We remove every transition we have already seen from the found solutions to avoid being livelocked as we made no progress in reducing the task size. In line 23, we then construct the set of solution candidates. All solution candidates are then sent to the next iteration. As Algorithm 2 terminates when it reaches the first set of solutions, we can be sure that we find a minimal solution without added behavior if there is any.

4.3 Practical Limitations and Optimizations

Practically the state space explosion problem can hinder both algorithms from finding a solution if the machine running the algorithm runs out of memory. In the case of Event-B, introduced divergence can result in an endless loop. However, it is up to the designer to show the convergence of the events.

The designer may limit the search depth or the number of investigated branches to mitigate the state space problem. In our implementation and the resulting testing, we had good experiences with this. A further modification to the proposed algorithms was a mixed breadth/depth-first search resulting in quicker results in our test cases for the price that, in rare cases, not the shortest solution was found. Further optimization was comparing candidate sub-traces for their equality, resulting in pruning traces that occurred multiple times.

Algorithm 2. Algorithm of BERT for Event-B

Require: M_C that has access to M_A, Trace T made out of a list of transitions $t_1, \ldots, t_n$ with t = (op,s), a map *alt* mapping abstract to concrete operations, the list of transitions refining **skip**

1: $resultTrace \leftarrow$ FINDPATH($\langle trace(\langle (\_, root) \rangle), T, seenTrans) \rangle, M_C, alt, skip)$
2: **if** resultTraces = $\langle \rangle$ **then**
3:     println(*"Trace could not be translated"*)
4: **else**
5:     return selectAnySolution(resultTraces)
6: **end if**
7: **function** FINDPATH(currentTraces, M_C, alt, skip)
8:     **while** $|currentTraces| \neq 0 \land \nexists trace \in currentTraces \,.\, |trace(1)| = 0$ **do**
9:        resultTraces $\leftarrow \langle \rangle$
10:      **for** entry $\in$ currentTraces **do**
11:        (op, s) $\leftarrow$ first(entry(1))
12:        (_, cS) $\leftarrow$ last(entry(0))
13:        $t \leftarrow \{(op', s') | op' \in alt(op) \land cS \xrightarrow[M_C]{op'} s' \land s \sqsubseteq s'\}$
14:        **for** tran $\in$ t **do**
15:           T $\leftarrow$ entry(1)
16:           newT $\leftarrow$ drop(T,0)   ▷ Reduce the task size
17:           newTrace $\leftarrow$ append(entry(0), tran)
18:           resultTraces $\leftarrow$ append(resultTraces, trace(newTrace, newT, $\langle \rangle$))
19:        **end for**
20:        $t \leftarrow \{(op', s') | (op' \in skip \lor op' \in alt(tOp)) \land cS \xrightarrow[M_C]{op} s' \land s' \sqsubseteq cS\}$
21:        $t \leftarrow t \cap$ entry(2)   ▷ Remove all solutions leading into livelock
22:        **for** tran $\in$ t **do**
23:           seenTrans $\leftarrow$ tran $\cup$ entry(2)   ▷ Add seen transitions
24:           newTrace $\leftarrow$ append(entry(0), tran)
25:           mewEntry $\leftarrow$ trace(newTrace, entry(1), seenTrans)
26:           resultTraces $\leftarrow$ append(resultTraces, newEntry)
27:        **end for**
28:      **end for**
29:      currentTraces $\leftarrow$ resultTraces
30:     **end while**
31:     **return** $\{trace | trace \in currentTraces \land |trace(1)| = 0\}$
32: **end function**

---

5   Case Studies

In this section, we experiment to validate the proposed technique on two industrial-strength case studies, both implementing models of an automotive system [16]. For brevity, we demonstrate only the Event-B implementation as shown in Algorithm 2 on case studies as Event-B refinements pose a more significant challenge than B as far as trace refinement is concerned. In the first case study, we work out the quality aspect of trace refinement. In the second case study, we address the performance aspect.

5.1   Pitman Arm Controller

Case Study Description. The first case study is the pitman arm controller model
[20]. The authors modeled a pitman arm that controls car lights and the user's
interaction with it. The model consists of three machines forming a refinement
chain of:

$$BlinkLamps \rightarrow PitmanController \rightarrow PitmanControllerTime$$

BlinkLights models the light environment of a car and its behavior. It allows controlling lights. Furthermore, one can set a blinking timer emulating the actual
number of blinks of the lights. In the model itself, the amount is set via parameters of the SET_REMAININGBlinks and its refinements. -1 means forever, 3 means
three-time, and so on. The third feature is the tip blinking or comfort blinking
of modern cars, which is also modeled. The *PitmanController* extends the *BlinkLights* and adds an actual car environment building on top of the lamps. The
position of the Pitman arm and car's key state is modeled. In *PitmanController-
Time* the abstract time counting is replaced with a concrete one. Normally the
tip blinking of a car has a specified time interval, usually three to five times.
PitmanControllerTime models this behavior. For the experiment we will create
a trace on *BlinkLamps* and refine it step-wise to *PitmanControllerTime*. We will
present all three traces and evaluate what the refinement did to the trace and
which knowledge one can extract from this.

Results. In Fig. 2 one can see the abstract trace and its refinements. The abstract
trace in Fig. 2a captures the idea of first using the tip blinker, but the user then
decides to make the blinking permanent after one blink. Again, after one blink,
the user turns off the blinker entirely.

In Fig. 2b one can see the adaptation. The most important change is that it
is now necessary to turn on the engine, for the lamps to blink. A new transition at position 4 is introduced for this. Renaming introduced with the refinement is considered, and the events have been changed accordingly, for example,
SET_REMAININGBlinks is now called TIME_Tip_Blinking, SET_RightBlinkersOn
is now called ENV_Pitman_TipBlinkingRight_Blink, and SET_AllBlinkersOff
is now called ENV_Pitman_Reset_to_Neutral_Noblink.

For the third refinement, the introduction of time had a minor effect on the
existing behavior. This is mirrored in the resulting trace adaptation. In Fig. 2c we
see no change compared to Fig. 2b besides additional parameters for the events,
for example, on position 3.

We gathered multiple insights into the effectiveness of trace refinement from
our experiments. 1) The engine needs to be turned on for the lights to blink,
which can be checked against the specification to learn if it is intentional behavior. 2) The newly introduced event in *PitmanControllerTime* does not interfere
with existing behavior. Once again, one can check if this is intentional. 3) From
the perspective of animation, there is an event SET_RemainingBlinks that can
have parameters 1,2,3 as input. We observed that 2 always leads to a failing
adaptation process. When checking for the reason, it was found that the state in

which the remaining blinks are equal to 2 is no longer reachable. Therefore, all behaviors relying on this are no longer possible. Designers might want to check whether this is an intentional behavior with the stakeholders.

Position▲	Transition
0	---root---
1	SETUP_CONSTANTS
2	INITIALISATION
3	TIME_Nothing(newOnCycle=TRUE)
4	SET_RightBlinkersOn(rem=3)
5	TIME_BlinkerOff
6	TIME_BlinkerOn
7	SET_RemainingBlinks(rem=-1)
8	TIME_BlinkerOff
9	TIME_BlinkerOn
10	**SET_AllBlinkersOff**

(a) Original trace on BlinkLamps

Position▲	Transition
0	---root---
1	SETUP_CONSTANTS
2	INITIALISATION
3	TIME_Nothing(newOnCycle=TRUE)
4	ENV_Turn_EngineOn_Noblink
5	ENV_Pitman_TipBlinkingRight_Blink(rem=3)
6	TIME_BlinkerOff
7	TIME_BlinkerOn
8	TIME_Tip_blinking_Timeout(rem=-1)
9	TIME_BlinkerOff
10	TIME_BlinkerOn
11	**ENV_Pitman_Reset_to_Neutral_Noblink**

(b) Refined trace on PitmanController

Position▲	Transition
0	---root---
1	SETUP_CONSTANTS
2	INITIALISATION
3	TIME_Nothing(newOnCycle=TRUE, delta=500)
4	ENV_Turn_EngineOn_Noblink
5	ENV_Pitman_TipBlinkingRight_Blink(rem=3)
6	TIME_BlinkerOff(delta=500)
7	TIME_BlinkerOn(delta=500)
8	TIME_Tip_blinking_Timeout(rem=-1)
9	TIME_BlinkerOff(delta=500)
10	TIME_BlinkerOn(delta=500)
11	**ENV_Pitman_Reset_to_Neutral_Noblink**

(c) Refined trace on PitmanControllerTime

Fig. 2. Trace before and after the first and second step of trace refinement.

5.2 Automotive Adaptive Exterior Light System

Case Study Description. The second case study is more complex than the first one and is about the specification of the adaptive exterior light system of an automobile [22]. The case study focuses on the lights, their behavior, reaction to the user, and environmental changes. As a result, the refinement chain is more prolonged, reaching from *M0* as the most abstract machine to *M5* as the most concrete machine.

- *M0* introduces a simple event with the name *headLightSet* with the ability to set a specific light of the car to a specific level.
- *M1* introduces the interfaces allowing the user to interact with the car.
- *M2* introduces details to the direction indicators, the hazard lights, and the emergency brake light.
- *M3* introduces details for the low beam lights.
- *M4* introduces details for the cornering lights.
- *M5* introduces details for the high beam lights.

The introduction order of the features in *M2* up to *M5* was arbitrary. This is related to the problem of expressing topological orders in the strict Event-B refinement hierarchy even tho there are attempts, such as by Mashkoor et al. [24]. We provide an overview of the exact metrics of all refinement steps in table 1. Like the previous case study, the first refinement step sees a massive increase of events as several new features are introduced to model the user interface. The table shows that we have a continuous, stark growth of variables in each step, on average twelve, which heavily increased the state space in each step. The fact of the possible inputs further blows up the state-space for each event. As events had large sets of parameters, each step had a large set of possible parameter values. The resulting increase of the state space caused problems as generating all possible inputs for an event became very memory intensive. Thus, there was a need for cutting away solutions to not run out of memory. For this, the internal standard of ProB was used that provides the first five correct solutions to a predicate if not further modified. For the experiment, we create a longer trace (30 steps) and find an adaptation for each machine. As mentioned earlier, this quantitative experiment shows how well BERT deals with larger state spaces.

Table 1. Refinement chain statistics

Machine	M0	M1	M2	M3	M4	M5
Introduced Variables	1	15	9	12	12	12
Overall Variables	1	16	25	37	49	61
Introduced Events (via `skip`)	1	1	0	0	0	3
Refined Events	N/A	10	3	5	0	0
Extended Events	N/A	1	11	14	20	20
Overall Events	1	12	14	19	20	23

Results. With the introduced restrictions, a trace could be successfully adapted. The results are shown in Table 2. For our experiment, we measure four categories: 1) the input trace to the algorithm, 2) the time needed for adaptation, 3) the number of transitions that need to be added for a successful adaptation, and 4) the amount of solutions found for the input trace.

The trace was not refined for M1 as it was created on this machine, thus N/A. We can see that the number of transitions stays constant while the calculation time increases up to M4. The reason here seems to be the number of possible solutions and the increasing number of variables later leading to state space explosion. The decline in time for M5 can be explained because there were not many solutions to be explored. No transitions were added, which was expected as the refinement steps focused on adding new behaviors, so the abstract behavior was preserved.

Overall we conclude the experiment a success. We anticipated problems with larger state spaces when designing the algorithm back in Sect. 4.3. Nevertheless, we managed to refine a trace even under more challenging conditions.

Table 2. Trace refinement statistics for the trace refined with BERT

Machine	M1	M2	M3	M4	M5
Trace Input Size	N/A	96	96	96	96
Adaptation Time (ms)	N/A	1663	2289	8268	1938
Added Transitions	96	0	0	0	0
Individual solutions	N/A	3	4	10	2

5.3 Threat to Validity

The application of Algorithm 2 to case studies poses an internal threat. We used the readily available implementations. While the first case study was created to be animated, the second was not, meaning that creating traces was far more difficult for the second case study. We created meaningful traces for the first case study, and the results had meanings we could reason. The second case study was not created with animation in mind. Hence the traces created to test were not always meaningful. In the first case study, we observed quality features of the behavior of trace refinement, while in the second one, we could only observe quantitative behaviors.

6 Lessons Learned

- Trace early. Following this long-standing advice can indeed save from making poor design choices. Trace refinement can then help to design elegant refinement steps.
- Keep the refinement step simple and small, i.e., introduce one feature per refinement as also suggested by Mashkoor et al. [23]. This will simplify the refinement process and help understand the reasons for a failing trace refinement.
- Do not create unnecessary choice points. Checking choice points created by newly introduced events and non-deterministic choices can increase calculation time significantly. This was discovered when searching for a valid configuration that holds throughout the refinement chain. Whenever there was no first best choice but many second-best choices, the path branched heavily, leading to long-running times. This case can be handled by keeping the number of choice points introduced in each refinement step small.

Overall, BERT helped clarify whether a specific behavior in M_A is still valid in M_C. This seems particularly interesting from the designer's perspective as it can validate the assumption that refinement ruled out a particular behavior. In addition, the high level of details that a trace provides can help a designer understand why a specific behavior is not feasible in the refinement, thus identifying modeling flaws.

Especially interesting when using trace refinement is what can be learned from a failing adaptation. There are two reasons for a failing adaptation. Either there is no adaptation or the adaptation is not achievable within the set memory limits. If we expect a successful adaptation, a manual inspection of the resulting trace of the failed adaptation can uncover design flaws. It can hint at questionable design from the animation perspective, as shown in the second case study, where technical limitations made it hard to find solutions. One might want to rethink the model to keep it easily animatable and traceable. Also, with manual inspection of failing results, cases were encountered where events were not sound and forgot to reset a specific variable leading to a failing adaptation.

7   Related Work

We compare our technique to the related work's existing trace and scenario refinement techniques. We want to stress the difference between traces and scenarios. Even though the term 'scenarios' is heavily overused, we can extract a baseline of scenarios being high-level representations of intended behavior. With high-level, we mean only selected pre-selected variables and transitions of interest are observed. Traces, on the other hand, are more low level. As traces need to be precise, they contain all available information about states and transitions.

Trace Refinement. One important inspiration for this paper is how refinement is defined and established in state-of-the-art CSP [15] algorithms [12]. In CSP, one specification can refine another in multiple ways, i.e., trace- and failure refinement. The refinement relationship is established by showing that both specifications are equivalent regarding the traces they share or do not share. The notion of 'hiding' transitions was especially interesting for our technique. In Event-B, we encountered a similar situation when stuttering refinement occurred. Whenever a transition or variables only occur in the concrete specification, we 'hide' them to treat the situation like a case of B-trace refinement to check whether the trace is still valid in the concrete refinement.

Scenario Refinement. Arcaini and Riccobene [4] describe how to refine ASM scenarios, which are used as acceptance tests. Using their proposed tool, scenarios are translated into an LTL formula. Then M_C is loaded into the tool-related model checker, the LTL formula is negated, and the model checker will try to find a counter-example. This counter-example can be re-translated into a scenario. The authors define two mapping procedures from scenario to LTL formulas, one that is strict and will produce 1:1 traces and one that can produce 1:n traces. The latter will add new behaviors. Besides the obvious difference that the proposed technique deals with ASMs, the authors seem not to encounter divergences as part of the concrete model. The ASM technique completely rely on its existing framework using an existing scenario language and the LTL model checker. In contrast, in our technqiue, we can perform calculations only based on a state-space representation, and we have chosen the one provided by ProB. Therefore, we provide a common technique for trace refinement and a tool. The advantage of our technique is that whenever low level properties are of interest we are able to refine them.

Scenarios for Event-B were introduced, e.g., by Fischer and Dghyam [11] where Cucumber [29] is used as a description language. However, compared to our work, the refinement abilities described in the paper are minimal. The created tests are not further refined but statically generated for each model version. Another technique to Event-B scenarios, which catered for refinement, was proposed by Malik et al. [21] where for Event-B models, scenarios were encoded in CSP and then refined. However, this technique suffers from the need to encode scenarios in CSP, which loses exact information about states as CSP only supports reasoning about transitions. Furthermore, the problems tackled by our work are only partially tackled in this work. The idea of scenario refinement was then advanced by Snook et al. [27] where it is investigated how scenarios can be refined or applied to more abstract machines. The authors also suggested a tool [28] for scenario generation for Rodin that is currently not able to refine those scenarios.

Dual Animation. Our technique focuses on going from an abstract to a concrete level while the technique of Hallerstede et al. [13,14] proposes the opposite. In their technique, a concrete machine is linked to its predecessor, thus giving insight into how the abstraction behaves when the concrete model does something. This helps to explore the actual behavior of an abstract and concrete machine and the changes due to refinement. However, checking the preservation of behavior is a cumbersome, manual task and not a real option as too many details need to be considered. With our technique, this task is automatically done by the provided tool.

8   Conclusion and Future Work

This paper introduces BERT – a technique and a tool to refine traces that are explicit paths through state space. With this tool, it is possible to refine traces of abstract B and Event-B machines for their respective refinement. This transfer helps designers to ensure the presence of an abstract behavior in the concrete specification. We successfully conducted experiments on two case studies to showcase the validity of the proposed technique. While BERT produced the expected results, the case studies helped find its role as a support tool for designers. With its help, one can comprehend if and why a specific behavior is still allowed in a refined model. The benefit for the designer is the fine-grained details a trace provides that allow exact reproduction of the defined behavior.

We are currently tackling refinements for Event-B and using the usage of the REFINES keyword for B. In the future, we want to tackle B's alternative ways of enriching a machine's behavior, for example, INCLUDES or EXTENDS. This will leverage the burden of animating and refining B machines, making trace refinement through animation more convenient.

References

1. Abrial, J.R.: The B-book: Assigning Programs to Meanings. Cambridge University Press, Cambridge (2005)

2. Abrial, J.R.: Modeling in Event-B: System and Software Engineering. Cambridge University Press, Cambridge (2010)

3. Abrial, J.R., Butler, M., Hallerstede, S., Hoang, T.S., Mehta, F., Voisin, L.: Rodin: an open toolset for modelling and reasoning in Event-B. Int. J. Softw. Tools Technol. Transfer **12**(6), 447–466 (2010). https://doi.org/10.1007/s10009-010-0145-y

4. Arcaini, P., Riccobene, E.: Automatic refinement of ASM abstract test cases. In: 2019 IEEE International Conference on Software Testing, Verification and Validation Workshops (ICSTW), pp. 1–10 (2019)

5. Back, R.J.R., von Wright, J.: Trace refinement of action systems. In: Jonsson, B., Parrow, J. (eds.) CONCUR 1994. LNCS, vol. 836, pp. 367–384. Springer, Heidelberg (1994). https://doi.org/10.1007/978-3-540-48654-1_28

6. Bendisposto, J., et al.: PROB2-UI: a Java-based user interface for ProB. In: Lluch Lafuente, A., Mavridou, A. (eds.) FMICS 2021. LNCS, vol. 12863, pp. 193–201. Springer, Cham (2021). https://doi.org/10.1007/978-3-030-85248-1_12

7. Butler, M.: An approach to the design of distributed systems with B AMN. In: Bowen, J.P., Hinchey, M.G., Till, D. (eds.) ZUM 1997. LNCS, vol. 1212, pp. 221–241. Springer, Heidelberg (1997). https://doi.org/10.1007/BFb0027291

8. Derrick, J., Boiten, E.: Refinement: Semantics, Languages and Applications. Springer, Heidelberg (2018). https://doi.org/10.1007/978-3-319-92711-4

9. Dunne, S., Conroy, S.: Process refinement in B. In: Treharne, H., King, S., Henson, M., Schneider, S. (eds.) ZB 2005. LNCS, vol. 3455, pp. 45–64. Springer, Heidelberg (2005). https://doi.org/10.1007/11415787_4

10. Rodin User's Handbook. https://www3.hhu.de/stups/handbook/rodin/current/html/. Accessed 12 Sep 2022

11. Fischer, T., Dghyam, D.: Formal model validation through acceptance tests. In: Collart-Dutilleul, S., Lecomte, T., Romanovsky, A. (eds.) RSSRail 2019. LNCS, vol. 11495, pp. 159–169. Springer, Cham (2019). https://doi.org/10.1007/978-3-030-18744-6_10

12. Gibson-Robinson, T., Armstrong, P., Boulgakov, A., Roscoe, A.W.: FDR3 — a modern refinement checker for CSP. In: Ábrahám, E., Havelund, K. (eds.) TACAS 2014. LNCS, vol. 8413, pp. 187–201. Springer, Heidelberg (2014). https://doi.org/10.1007/978-3-642-54862-8_13

13. Hallerstede, S., Leuschel, M., Plagge, D.: Refinement-animation for Event-B — towards a method of validation. In: Frappier, M., Glässer, U., Khurshid, S., Laleau, R., Reeves, S. (eds.) ABZ 2010. LNCS, vol. 5977, pp. 287–301. Springer, Heidelberg (2010). https://doi.org/10.1007/978-3-642-11811-1_22

14. Hallerstede, S., Leuschel, M., Plagge, D.: Validation of formal models by refinement animation. Sci. Comput. Program. **78**(3), 272–292 (2013)

15. Hoare, C.A.R.: Communicating sequential processes. Commun. ACM **21**(8), 666–677 (1978)

16. Houdek, F., Raschke, A.: Adaptive exterior light and speed control system. In: Raschke, A., Méry, D., Houdek, F. (eds.) ABZ 2020. LNCS, vol. 12071, pp. 281–301. Springer, Cham (2020). https://doi.org/10.1007/978-3-030-48077-6_24

17. Leuschel, M.: Spot the difference: a detailed comparison between B and Event-B. In: Raschke, A., Riccobene, E., Schewe, K.-D. (eds.) Logic, Computation and Rigorous Methods. LNCS, vol. 12750, pp. 147–172. Springer, Cham (2021). https://doi.org/10.1007/978-3-030-76020-5_9

18. Leuschel, M., Butler, M.: Automatic refinement checking for B. In: Lau, K.-K., Banach, R. (eds.) ICFEM 2005. LNCS, vol. 3785, pp. 345–359. Springer, Heidelberg (2005). https://doi.org/10.1007/11576280_24

19. Leuschel, M., Butler, M.: ProB: an automated analysis toolset for the B method. Int. J. Softw. Tools Technol. Transfer **10**(2), 185–203 (2008)

20. Leuschel, M., Mutz, M., Werth, M.: Modelling and validating an automotive system in classical B and Event-B. In: Raschke, A., Méry, D., Houdek, F. (eds.) ABZ 2020. LNCS, vol. 12071, pp. 335–350. Springer, Cham (2020). https://doi.org/10.1007/978-3-030-48077-6_27

21. Malik, Q.A., Lilius, J., Laibinis, L.: Model-based testing using scenarios and Event-B refinements. In: Butler, M., Jones, C., Romanovsky, A., Troubitsyna, E. (eds.) Methods, Models and Tools for Fault Tolerance. LNCS, vol. 5454, pp. 177–195. Springer, Heidelberg (2009). https://doi.org/10.1007/978-3-642-00867-2_9

22. Mammar, A., Frappier, M., Laleau, R.: An Event-B model of an automotive adaptive exterior light system. In: Raschke, A., Méry, D., Houdek, F. (eds.) ABZ 2020. LNCS, vol. 12071, pp. 351–366. Springer, Cham (2020). https://doi.org/10.1007/978-3-030-48077-6_28

23. Mashkoor, A., Jacquot, J.P.: Guidelines for formal domain modeling in Event-B. In: 2011 IEEE 13th International Symposium on High-Assurance Systems Engineering, pp. 138–145 (2011)

24. Mashkoor, A., Jacquot, J.: Utilizing Event-B for domain engineering: a critical analysis. Requir. Eng. **16**(3), 191–207 (2011)

25. Mashkoor, A., Kossak, F., Egyed, A.: Evaluating the suitability of state-based formal methods for industrial deployment. Softw. Pract. Exp. **48**(12), 2350–2379 (2018)

26. Mashkoor, A., Leuschel, M., Egyed, A.: Validation obligations: a novel approach to check compliance between requirements and their formal specification. In: 2021 IEEE/ACM 43rd International Conference on Software Engineering: New Ideas and Emerging Results (ICSE-NIER), pp. 1–5 (2021)

27. Snook, C., Hoang, T.S., Dghaym, D., Fathabadi, A.S., Butler, M.: Domain-specific scenarios for refinement-based methods. J. Syst. Architect. **112**, 101833 (2021)

28. Snook, C., Hoang, T.S., Fathabadi, A.S., Dghaym, D., Butler, M.: Scenario checker: an Event-B tool forvalidating abstract models. In: Rodin Workshop (2021)

29. Wynne, M., Hellesoy, A., Tooke, S.: The Cucumber Book: Behaviour-driven Development for Testers and Developers. Pragmatic Bookshelf (2017)

Model Checking B Models via High-Level Code Generation

Fabian Vu$^{(\boxtimes)}$ ⓘ, Dominik Brandt, and Michael Leuschel ⓘ

Institut für Informatik, Universität Düsseldorf,
Universitätsstr. 1, 40225 Düsseldorf, Germany
{fabian.vu,dominik.brandt,leuschel}@uni-duesseldorf.de

Abstract. We present a new approach to improve the model checking performance for B models. We build on the high-level code generator B2PROGRAM, which unlike B's original code generators can already be applied at an early stage to high-level B models. We extend B2PROGRAM to generate efficient model checkers in Java and C++. The generated model checkers are customized and compiled for specific B models and include features like parallelization and caching. We evaluate the approach on a wide range of B models, comparing the performance to existing B model checkers. The results show that for some models we can obtain significant performance improvements, while for others PROB remains the tool of choice. For lower-level models, our new approach improves upon the existing TLC backend. In summary, the B2PROGRAM model checker is a very useful new tool addition for the B method.

Keywords: Code generation · B method · Model checking

1 Introduction and Motivation

When using formal methods, software is often modeled step-by-step until all desired features are encoded. During each development step, the model is verified, e.g., by model checkers such as PROB [24] or by provers such as ATELIERB [9]. In the B method [1], the model is refined until reaching an implementable subset of the language, called B0, before code generation is feasible. Thus, code generation is applied at the end of the development cycle to generate executable code. ATELIERB [9] contains several code generators, which translate B0 code to C and Ada. In an earlier work [31], we presented the code generator B2PROGRAM[1] which generates code from high-level B specifications to Java and C++. In contrast to ATELIERB, B2PROGRAM is capable of code generation

---

[1] Available at: https://github.com/favu100/b2program.

The works of Fabian Vu and Michael Leuschel are part of the IVOIRE project, which is funded by "Deutsche Forschungsgemeinschaft" (DFG) and the Austrian Science Fund (FWF) grant # I 4744-N.

A. Riesco and M. Zhang (Eds.): ICFEM 2022, LNCS 13478, pp. 334–351, 2022.
https://doi.org/10.1007/978-3-031-17244-1_20

```
MACHINE TrafficLight
SETS colors = {red, redyellow, yellow, green}
VARIABLES tl_cars, tl_peds
INVARIANT tl_cars : colors & tl_peds : {red, green} &
          (tl_peds = red or tl_cars = red)
INITIALISATION   tl_cars := red || tl_peds := red
OPERATIONS
cars_ry = SELECT tl_cars = red & tl_peds = red THEN tl_cars := redyellow END;
cars_y = SELECT tl_cars = green & tl_peds = red THEN tl_cars := yellow END;
cars_g = SELECT tl_cars = redyellow & tl_peds = red THEN tl_cars := green END;
cars_r = SELECT tl_cars = yellow & tl_peds = red THEN tl_cars := red END;
peds_r = SELECT tl_peds = green & tl_cars = red THEN tl_peds := red END;
peds_g = SELECT tl_peds = red & tl_cars = red THEN tl_peds := green END
END
```

Listing 1. Example of a Traffic Light Controller in B

from models using high-level data structures such as sets and relations. However, B2PROGRAM is not meant for generating code for safety-critical embedded systems, as it uses dynamic heap allocation. Nevertheless, the main advantage is that code generation, e.g., for efficient simulation, is feasible at an early stage without refining to B0.

The idea of this paper is to use B2PROGRAM for efficient explicit-state model checking. Indeed, existing model checkers like PROB or TLC [34] *interpret* the model, and using *compiled generated* code could lead to significantly improved performance. In this article, we extend B2PROGRAM to generate customized model checkers for high-level B models. A difficulty is that a model checker has to compute *all* enabled transitions of a model (and not just one), and has to be able to switch from one arbitrary state to another (and not just from one state to a successor state). Our main motivation is to achieve high performance, but the new model checker can also be used as a second toolchain with PROB to safe-guard against bugs in the tools (discussed in [31] and [15]).

Section 2 explains how B2PROGRAM is extended for model checking. Section 3 discusses the limitations of B2PROGRAM. Section 4 evaluates the performance compared to PROB and TLC (translation to TLA+ by TLC4B [15]). Finally, we compare this work with existing code generators and model checkers in Sect. 5, and conclude in Sect. 6.

2   Code Generation for Model Checking

This section presents how we extended B2PROGRAM for model checking. In the previous work [31], we generated code from a verified model for execution, while here we generate code for verification (or model checking to be precise).

A B specification is composed of B machines, each with its constants and variables. The state of a B machine consists of the values of the constants and variables; the latter can be modified by operations. Operations contain guards or preconditions which are used to define whether the operation is enabled. An important feature of B are the invariants, which often encode important safety properties. A running example (of a traffic light controlling cars and pedestrians) is shown in Listing 1.

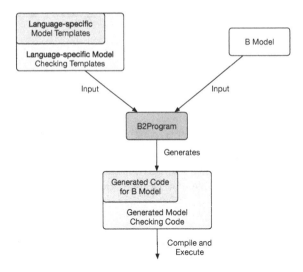

Fig. 1. Workflow of model checking

2.1   Extension of Generated Code

B2PROGRAM uses the STRINGTEMPLATE [28] engine which makes it possible to generate code for multiple languages. In this article, we focus on Java and C++, but other target languages (like TypeScript/JavaScript [32], Rust, and Python) are being added to B2PROGRAM. The earlier work [31] provided templates for B's operators and constructs; by instantiating and assembling these templates one obtains the target code for the given model. In the previous work, code was generated from the model's operations, while the execution had to be controlled by a manually implemented main function. Thus, there was no computation of enabled operations (all parameters were provided by the main function). Furthermore, it was assumed that the model was already verified, i.e., code generation was not applied for constructs that are relevant for verification such as the invariant or preconditions.

In this article, we have added language-specific model checking templates which are weaved into the target code (see Fig. 1).These templates contain the model checking algorithm, the computation of all enabled operations, and the evaluation of the invariant.A user can then verify invariants and deadlock-freedom in the model by compiling and executing the generated target code.When finding a violation, a counter-example is displayed showing a trace with states and executed events between them.By writing templates for model checking, it is possible to keep model checking code generation generic, i.e., to generate code for any B model (in B2PROGRAM's supported subset of B; discussed in Sect. 3) and for several languages with a single code generator.This avoids implementing a model checker for each B model.For Java and C++, we implemented the model checkers with placeholders for the model's constructs.

In the following, we will first describe the evaluation of the invariant, and the computation of enabled operations. Afterward, we will explain the features that are implemented in the model checking algorithm.

Checking Invariant. The invariant predicate is decomposed into its conjuncts, each translated to a Boolean function. By splitting the invariant, it is possible to implement invariant caching (discussed later in this section). The generated Java code for checking the invariant of Listing 1 is shown in Listing 2.

```
public boolean _check_inv_1() {
  return new BBoolean(_colors.elementOf(tl_cars).booleanValue()).booleanValue();
}
public boolean _check_inv_2() {
  return new BBoolean(new BSet<colors>(colors.red, colors.green)
          .elementOf(tl_peds).booleanValue())
          .booleanValue();
}
public boolean _check_inv_3() {
  return new BBoolean(tl_peds.equal(colors.red).booleanValue() ||
              tl_cars.equal(colors.red).booleanValue()).booleanValue();
}
```

Listing 2. Generated Java Code from INVARIANT of Listing 1

Computing Enabled Operations. Relevant B constructs for computing enabled transitions are PRE, SELECT, ANY, CHOICE substitutions, non-deterministic assignments, and high-level PROPERTIES constraining the possible values for the model's constants. In the previous work [31], we could treat any non-deterministic constructs in a simplified manner, such that only one possible execution path was chosen. In the context of model checking, it is necessary to cover *all* possible execution branches. It is, however, difficult to treat non-deterministic constructs deep within a B statement in Java or C++ code. A failed guard deep within a B statement could in principle be translated to an exception, but supporting all non-deterministic constructs is more difficult. Hence, we currently only allow non-determinism in top-level PRE and SELECT constructs; so the B model has to be rewritten to move non-determinism and guards to the top level.[2]

For operations without parameters, the guard or precondition is translated to a Boolean function evaluating whether the operation is enabled. Such a translation for cars_ry in Listing 1 to Java is shown in Listing 3.

```
public boolean _tr_cars_ry() {
  return new BBoolean(tl_cars.equal(colors.red).booleanValue() &&
              tl_peds.equal(colors.red).booleanValue()).booleanValue();
}
```

Listing 3. Generated Java Code to Compute Enabledness of cars_ry in Listing 1

---

[2] In the absence of the WHILE loop, such a rewriting is always possible (cf. the normal form for substitutions in Chap. 6 of [1]).

In contrast, the computation of enabled transitions for operations with parameters is more difficult. Here, B2PROGRAM calculates the set of parameters for which the operation is enabled. Let $p_1, \ldots, p_n$ be the operation's parameters constrained by the precondition or guard P. It is then translated similarly as the set comprehension $\{p_1, \ldots, p_n \mid P\}$.[3] The rules after which quantified constructs are translated can be found in Sect. 3.5 of [31] and ensure that B2PROGRAM can create code to enumerate all quantified values.

As an example, the function for computing all parameter values to make the operation SetCruiseSpeed(vcks, csam) = PRE vcks : BOOL & csam : BOOL & CruiseAllowed = TRUE THEN ... END enabled is generated as shown in Listing 4.

```
public BSet<BTuple<BBoolean, BBoolean>> _tr_SetCruiseSpeed() {
  BSet<BTuple<BBoolean, BBoolean>> _ic_set_1 =
    new BSet<BTuple<BBoolean,BBoolean>>();
  for(BBoolean _ic_vcks_1 : BUtils.BOOL) {
    for(BBoolean _ic_csam_1 : BUtils.BOOL) {
      if((CruiseAllowed.equal(new BBoolean(true))).booleanValue()) {
        _ic_set_1 = _ic_set_1.union(new BSet<BTuple<BBoolean, BBoolean>>
                              (new BTuple<>(_ic_vcks_1, _ic_csam_1)));
      }
    }
  }
  return _ic_set_1;
}
```

Listing 4. Generated Java Code to Compute Transitions for SetCruiseSpeed

Copy Machine. From any given state there can be multiple enabled operations. When executing a single transition, the machine's current state is modified. It is then necessary to restore the previous state to execute another transition. To achieve this, we copy the machine's state before executing a transition during model checking.

```
public TrafficLight_MC(colors tl_cars, colors tl_peds) {
  this.tl_cars = tl_cars;
  this.tl_peds = tl_peds;
}
public TrafficLight_MC _copy() {return new TrafficLight_MC(tl_cars, tl_peds);}
```

Listing 5. Generated Java Code to Copy Machine from Listing 1

On the technical side, a copy constructor and a copy function are generated returning a new instance of the machine. Here, only references and not the data itself are copied. Note that B2PROGRAM is designed such that operations on data structures are applied immutably. An example of a copy constructor and a copy function for Listing 1 is shown in Listing 5.

2.2 Model Checking Features

The core of the algorithm is standard and follows [3]. So far, B2PROGRAM implements explicit-state model checking, verifying invariants and deadlock-freedom.

---

[3] Note that top-level preconditions are treated as similar to guards, and we only allow top-level guards and preconditions as non-determinism.

LTL and symbolic model checking are not supported. When a violation is found, a counter-example is displayed showing a trace with states and executed events between them. Additionally, we implemented parallelization as well as invariant and guard caching to improve the performance.

Invariant and Guard Caching. The techniques implemented here are inspired by the work of Bendisposto and Leuschel [6], and Dobrikov and Leuschel [12], but for our purposes, we only use lightweight caching techniques without using proof information or performing semantic analyses.

Taking a look at Listing 1: If an operation does not modify the variable `tl_peds` (e.g. `cars_y`), the model checker does not have to check the invariant `tl_peds` : {red, green} after applying the operation (provided no invariant violation has been found thus far). Similarly, if a guard of an operation is not affected by an executed operation, the model checker does not have to check this guard in the following state. Before applying model checking, B2PROGRAM extracts some static information from the model:

- For each operation, it extracts which variables are written.
- For each guard, it extracts which variables are read.
- For each invariant conjunct, it extracts which variables are read.

From this, we derive a table about which event can affect which guard and invariant: a guard or invariant p depends on operation op if there exists a variable that is read by p and written by op.

As B2PROGRAM stops as soon as an invariant violation is encountered, we do not have to cache each invariant's status; they must be true. The model checker only needs to know how a state is reached. When reaching a state s_2 from a state s_1 via an operation op, only invariants modified by op are checked. As for guards, the algorithm caches each guard's status for each visited state. Furthermore, the model checker copies the values of guards from s_1 which do not depend on op.

Parallelization. B2PROGRAM is also capable of multi-threaded model checking. Here, the model checker consists of a user-specified number of worker threads with one additional thread acting as a coordinator. Figure 2 shows the corresponding workflow, which is as follows: The coordinator takes the next state to be processed (depending on the search strategy), and assigns it to a worker thread. The worker checks the provided state for deadlocks and invariant violations, and computes the enabled operations. Successor states that have not been visited are then added to the list of queued states. The coordinator continues assigning tasks as long as there are unvisited states in the queue. Otherwise, the coordinator waits for a worker's notification. For this, a worker notifies the coordinator upon completion of a task when either (1) the global queue contains states for processing, or (2) the worker is the only one running at the moment. In case (2), the coordinator can finish model checking, in case (1) it can (again) assign tasks to workers.

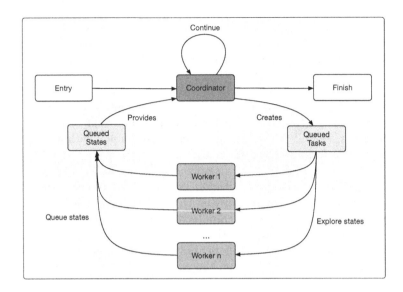

Fig. 2. Workflow: multi-threaded model checking

3   Limitations of High-Level Code Generation

Below, we discuss the limitations of model checking with B2PROGRAM. Compared to existing B0 code generators, B2PROGRAM supports high-level constructs such as sets, relations, and quantified constructs like set comprehensions, quantified predicates, or lambda expressions. While B2PROGRAM is high-level compared to B0 code generators, it still has restrictions compared to PROB.

Currently, the required format for quantified constructs is quite restrictive. Indeed, quantified variables $v_1, \ldots, v_n$ must be constrained by a predicate P where the i-th conjunct of P must be constraining v_i (as described in previous work [31] to enable finite enumeration of v_i's possible values). E.g., assuming that z is a machine's state variable, $\{x, y \mid x \in 1..10 \land x \neq z \land y \in x..10\}$ must be rewritten to $\{x, y \mid x \in 1..10 \land y \in x..10 \land x \neq z\}$. This restriction will disappear in the future. TLC4B can cater for interleaved pruning predicates like $x \neq z$ while PROB has no restriction on the order of the conjuncts at all.

Comparing code generation for model checking with simulation, we have already discussed limitations regarding inner guards and non-deterministic constructs in Sect. 2.1. Here, the user has to re-write the model to move guards and non-determinism to the top level of an operation. For now, constants must also be constrained to have a single possible value. (PROB does allow an arbitrary number of valuations for the constants.) DEFINITIONS must currently be inlined in the code by hand as well.

B2PROGRAM supports simple predicates using infinite sets on the right-hand side of $\in$, e.g., x ∈ NATURAL. Internally, the generated code checks whether x is greater than or equal to 0. Slightly more complicated constructs such as x ∈ NATURAL → NATURAL are supported as well. Here, the generated code performs the same check on each element in the domain and the range. Additionally, it checks whether x is a total function. Note that the expression on the left-hand side of the operation is finite. Currently, B2PROGRAM also allows (partial and total) function operators including injection, surjection, and bijection together with ∈. Nevertheless, we have disallowed constructs where it might be necessary to evaluate infinite sets or function operations explicitly. For example, we have disallowed the assignment of a variable to an infinite set like x := NATURAL. Furthermore, nested uses of infinite sets such as x ∈ NATURAL → (NATURAL → NATURAL) are not supported. Similarly, this work does not support assignment to function operations, e.g., x := 1 . . . m → 1 . . . n. The latter could be supported in the future, but the cardinality of those sets can grow very large.

On the technical side, there are also language-specific restrictions, e.g., the sum of B variables and constants must be less than 255 for generated Java code. To overcome this Java restriction, one would need to adapt the code generation technique to avoid creating large classes with too many parameters.[4]

However, as the next section shows, we can apply B2PROGRAM to a large number of examples. We also hope that many of the above restrictions will disappear in the future.

4   Empirical Evaluation of the Performance

This section evaluates the model checking performance compared to PROB, and TLC (via TLC4B). The generated Java model checking code is executed on *OpenJDK*. [5] The generated C++ code is compiled using *clang*[6] with -O1. For Java and C++, we benchmarked both *with* and *without* invariant and guard caching (cf. Sect. 2.2). We execute PROB in *1.12.0-nightly*,[7] and TLC4B in 2.06. Regarding PROB, we benchmark *with* and *without* operation re-use (a new technique described in [22]). Furthermore, we benchmark multi-threaded model checking (with six threads) for Java and C++ and compare the results with TLC. We have also measured the startup overhead time including parsing, translation, and compilation. The experiments in Table 2 (see Appendix A), Table 3 (see Appendix A), and Table 1 show the respective results for single-threaded, multi-threaded model checking, and the overhead. For single-threaded model checking, we show the bar chart relative to PROB (see Fig. 3). For multi-threaded model checking, we show the bar charts relative to TLC (see Fig. 4) and relative to the single-threaded speedups (see Fig. 5). A more detailed overview and more benchmarks (including C++ with -O2 optimization) are available in B2PROGRAM's repository. They are run on a MacBook Air with 8 GB of RAM

---

[4] Note that TLC also has problems when the number of variables of a model increases, in terms of stack consumption and runtime degradation.

[5] 64-Bit Server VM (build 15+36-1562, mixed mode, sharing).

[6] Apple clang version 13.0.0 (clang-1300.0.29.30).

[7] Revision b6d1b600dbf06b7984dd2a1dd7403206cfd9d394.

and a 1.6 GHz Intel i5 processor with two cores. Each model checking benchmark is run ten times with a timeout of one hour, and afterward, the median runtime and the median memory consumption (maximum resident set size) are measured. Regarding the overhead, we measure the median runtime. We omit the C++ -O2 benchmarks in this paper because the *clang++* compiler cannot optimize further for model checking.

The benchmarked models vary both in their complexity and in the focus of how they are modeled: Counter is a modified version of Lift from [31], consisting of operations to increment and decrement the counter between 0 and 1000000. It serves as a baseline benchmark for simple models with large state spaces.

The Volvo Cruise Controller uses mainly Boolean variables with many logical operations and assignments. The Landing Gear model (originally from Event-B [21]) also contains many logical operations and assignments, in addition to a large number of set operations.

Train and CAN Bus use set and relational operations. To keep the runtimes reasonable we benchmark a modified version [23] of the Train interlocking (with ten routes) from [2], where partial order reduction is applied manually. While PROB and TLC can be used directly, it is necessary to rewrite some constructs for B2PROGRAM. As PROB and TLC handle the original versions better, we benchmarked those for PROB and TLC.

We also benchmarked Nokia's NoTa (network on terminal architecture) model [27] which has many set operations. Here, it was necessary to rewrite the model to apply B2PROGRAM. The rewritten version leads to a reduced number of transitions, but does not affect the performance of PROB and TLC negatively. Compared to the other models, there are more power sets and quantified constructs. Also, its invariant contains more involved function type checks.

sort_1000 is a B model (originally from Event-B [29]) of an insertion sorting algorithm with 1000 elements.

As an opposite to the Counter model, we benchmark a B model of the N-Queens problem with $N = 4$. The model contains a B operation to solve the N-Queens puzzle and the state space will consist of all solutions to the puzzle (i.e., 2 for $N = 4$). While PROB and TLC apply to the original model, it is necessary to rewrite the model for B2PROGRAM. Similar to Train, we thus benchmarked the original model for PROB and TLC, and the rewritten model for B2PROGRAM.

In the previous work [31], code generation to Java and C++ for simulation was up to one or two magnitudes faster than PROB.Now, one can see in Fig. 3 that this is still the case for several models when model checking compared to PROB *without* the new operation caching feature.For the Cruise Controller, the runtimes are similar and N-Queens is the only model where PROB outperforms B2PROGRAM in all configurations.This is obviously due to PROB's constraint solving capabilities.With the operation caching feature [22], the situation changes somewhat.PROB is now faster than generated C++ model checkers for NoTa and faster than the Java model checkers for Train. The speedups obtained by the generated model checkers are still significant, but less than a factor of two for a few models.

Counter is the only model where the generated code strongly outperforms PROB (up to two magnitudes). One can also see that for some models, it is necessary to choose the right setting to outperform PROB with operation reuse. For example, model checking Train with B2PROGRAM only leads to a better runtime, when C++ with caching is chosen.

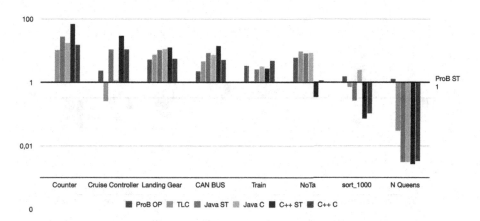

Fig. 3. Single-threaded Speedups relative to ProB ST as Bar Charts; ST = Standard, OP = Operation Reuse, C = Caching

Regarding model checking with TLC, there are models where PROB performs better and vice versa. Code generation to Java and C++ makes it possible to outperform TLC for most benchmarks (also for multi-threaded model checking as shown in Fig. 4). For NoTa, the generated Java model checkers have a similar performance to TLC, while C++ is much slower.

TLC can find all solutions for N-Queens faster than the generated model checkers, but slower than PROB. Similar to B2PROGRAM, TLC also lacks constraint solving features. The reason why TLC possibly performs better could be the restrictions of constraining predicates as discussed in Sect. 3. For both PROB and TLC, the generated code only performs better for sort_1000 if Java is chosen together with caching. In particular, the translation of the invariant generates large sets which could be avoided by caching successfully.

As shown in Fig. 5, parallelization makes it possible to improve the performance further for most benchmarks. For sort_1000 and Train, the additional speedup is around two. In some cases, e.g. Counter, CAN BUS or NoTa, the overhead results in a slowdown. Regarding the first two machines, this overhead can also be seen in TLC.

The implemented caching features in B2PROGRAM lead to overhead for most benchmarks. Nevertheless, a speedup could also be achieved for some models, e.g., Train. The reason could be the complex invariants and guards in both models. For sort_1000, caching only improves Java's runtime. One can also see (in

Table 2 and Table 3 in Appendix A) that our caching implementation increases
memory usage significantly. In contrast, PROB manages to keep memory consumption low when using operation reuse together with state compression [22].
A significantly increased memory consumption only occurs for Train. Overall,
the operation reuse feature in PROB is not only more complex, but is also much
more efficient than the caching technique implemented in this work.

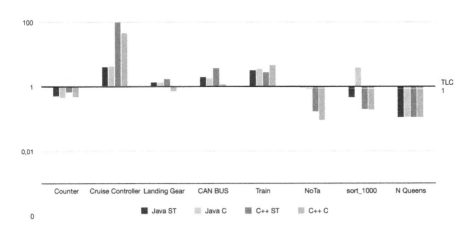

Fig. 4. Multi-threaded (6 Threads) speedups relative to TLC as bar charts; ST =
Standard, C = Caching

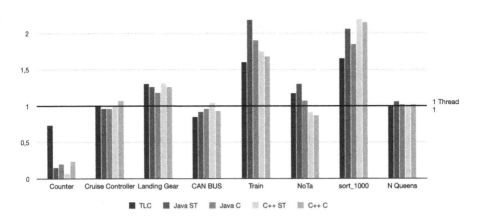

Fig. 5. Multi-threaded speedups relative to single-threaded speedups as bar charts; ST
= Standard, C = Caching

Table 1. Startup overhead in seconds (including parsing, translation and compilation) of ProB, TLC, and generated code in Java, and C++

Counter	ProB	TLC	Java	C++ -O1	C++ -O2
Parsing/Translation	2.52	2.95	1.32	1.35	1.35
Compiling	-	-	2.15	6.22	7.31
Cruise Controller (Volvo)	ProB	TLC	Java	C++ -O1	C++ -O2
Parsing/Translation	3.05	3.97	2.34	2.52	2.52
Compiling	-	-	3.33	20.84	37.48
Landing Gear [21]	ProB	TLC	Java	C++ -O1	C++ -O2
Parsing/Translation	3.04	3.91	2.53	2.74	2.74
Compiling	-	-	3.61	26.01	42.3
CAN BUS (J. Colley)	ProB	TLC	Java	C++ -O1	C++ -O2
Parsing/Translation	2.85	3.45	1.87	2.05	2.05
Compiling	-	-	3.05	16.17	23.45
Train (ten routes) [2,23]	ProB	TLC	Java	C++ -O1	C++ -O2
Parsing/Translation	2.9	3.59	2.07	2.21	2.21
Compiling	-	-	2.84	15.52	20.05
NoTa [27]	ProB	TLC	Java	C++ -O1	C++ -O2
Parsing/Translation	2.94	3.65	2.14	2.32	2.32
Compiling	-	-	3.03	29.23	39.76
sort_1000 [29]	ProB	TLC	Java	C++ -O1	C++ -O2
Parsing/Translation	2.61	3.1	1.53	1.58	1.58
Compiling	-	-	2.26	8.51	10.37
N-Queens with N=4	ProB	TLC	Java	C++ -O1	C++ -O2
Parsing/Translation	2.61	3.07	1.45	1.5	1.5
Compiling	-	-	2.2	9.11	11.33

Table 1 shows a small startup overhead for ProB, TLC, and B2PROGRAM with Java. Note that the ProB and Java times also contain the startup time of the ProB CLI, and the JVM (twice: generating code with B2PROGRAM, and compiling) respectively. The JVM's startup time is not included in the TLC overhead times.

The C++ startup time, however, can be considerable. In some cases, the compilation time is greater than the model checking time. Thus, in a setting where one wants to repeatedly modify and re-verify a model, the C++ overhead would be prohibitive. B2PROGRAM with C++ is thus only effective for long-running model checking such as Train. In the future, one could pre-compile some libraries to reduce the C++ compilation times.

5   More Related Work

The present work enabled us to make use of some of ProB's validation tests, namely the tests where counter-examples to over 500 mathematical laws are sought after using model checking [5]. This indeed uncovered several issues in B2PROGRAM, and helped us improve the stability of the core of B2PROGRAM.

Code Generators. There are several code generators for various formalisms such as Event-B [8,13,14,26,29], ASM [7], or VDM [17]. As far as we know, none of these code generators supports model checking (yet).

Model Checkers. We have already compared B2PROGRAM with the explicit-state model checkers PROB [24], and TLC [34] via TLC4B [15].

In the following, we add a few more points. In general, there are some limitations compared to PROB, as discussed in Sect. 3. Furthermore, B2PROGRAM only supports B, while PROB also supports Event-B, Z, TLA + CSP, or CSP || B. In the context of explicit-state model checking PROB supports various features such as state compression, efficient state hashing, use of proof information, partial order reduction, partial guard evaluation, invariant and operation caching. Still, B2PROGRAM leads to a faster runtime for most benchmarks thanks to custom model checkers without interpretation overhead. But especially, the operation reuse feature [22] makes it possible for PROB to keep up with TLC's and B2PROGRAM's performance. PROB has the advantage that model checking counter-examples are represented as traces and can be loaded into the animator for inspection. Furthermore, PROB also supports other techniques such as LTL model checking which are not available to B2PROGRAM yet. Again, PROB is also capable of visualization features, e.g., visualizing the state space.

As discussed in Sect. 3, parameters or quantified variables must be enumerated for B2PROGRAM in the exact order they are defined first, before additional predicates can be checked. In contrast, TLC allows interleaving of pruning predicates. Unlike TLC, B2PROGRAM supports code generation for sequential substitutions. The parallel model checking approach in TLC is implemented similar to B2PROGRAM. Within TLC, a worker always takes a state before processing it. A main feature of TLC is the efficient storage of the state space on disk. As result, TLC can handle very large state spaces, while the generated Java model checking code with B2PROGRAM depends on the JVM's memory. Nevertheless, there are also state collisions in TLC, which can lead to erroneous results, although they occur rarely. Unlike TLC, collisions between states are handled. When analyzing the performance (for both single-threaded and multi-threaded model checking), we have encountered that model checking with B2PROGRAM leads to a speedup compared to TLC.

Another toolset is LTSMIN [18] which supports explicit-state model checking and LTL model checking, as well as symbolic model checking. LTSMIN also supports parallelization and partial order reduction. As presented by Körner et al. [19] and Bendisposto et al. [4], LTSMIN was integrated into PROB, leading to a significant speedup. It, however, also has some drawbacks (see [22]) and the predicates and operations themselves are still computed by the PROB interpreter.

PYB is a second tool-chain of PROB, which can also model check B models. Similar to TLC and this work, PYB lacks constraint solving. Set operations in PYB were relatively slow, while integer operations can be applied efficiently [33].

The idea of generating code for model checking has already been implemented in SPIN [16]. Here, a problem-specific model checker in C is generated from a

Promela model. SPIN supports features such as state compression, bitstate hashing, partial order reduction, and LTL model checking. SPIN is a very efficient explicit-state model checker, but operates on a much lower-level language.

JavaPathfinder [25] is a model checker which runs executable Java bytecode on the JVM to check a program for race conditions and deadlocks. To cover all possible execution paths of a Java program, JavaPathfinder is implemented with backtracking features. B2PROGRAM currently only supports non-determinism for top-level guards and preconditions.

There are also bounded model checkers for C and Java, named CBMC [20] and JBMC [10] respectively. Both model checkers are capable of verifying memory safety, checking for exceptions, checking for various variants of undefined behavior, and checking user-specified assertions. In contrast to CBMC and JBMC, the main purpose of our work is to generate Java and C++ code for verification, not verifying Java and C++ programs themselves.

6   Conclusion and Future Work

In this work, we extended the high-level B code generator B2PROGRAM to generate specialized model checkers. One goal was to provide a baseline for model checking benchmarks, using tailored model checkers, compiled for each B model. The hope was to achieve fast model checking, exceeding TLC's (interpreter-based) performance and overcoming some of the limitations.

One major challenge was to adapt B2PROGRAM so that it produced *all* enabled operations (and not just one). This was achieved for top-level guards, parameters and preconditions but not yet for nested guards or preconditions and some nested non-deterministic constructs. In general, we have discovered some limitations of B2PROGRAM compared to PROB. In particular, some B constructs are too high-level for code generation to Java and C++. Furthermore, PROB also supports more formalisms than B2PROGRAM, which only supports B. The TLC4B approach shares some limitations of B2PROGRAM, e.g., the need for explicit enumeration predicates. There are, however, limitations of TLC which can be handled by B2PROGRAM and vice versa.

Our empirical evaluation has provided some interesting insights. We found out that code generation to Java and C++ leads to a speedup up to one magnitude wrt. PROB for certain interesting benchmarks. However, there are also models where PROB performs better, either due to its constraint solving capabilities or due to the recent operation caching technique [22]. In contrast, the invariant and guard caching in B2PROGRAM only improve performance in some cases (for very complex invariants or guards) and its overhead is not worthwhile in general. Parallelization improves the generated code's performance for most experiments. Code generation to Java and C++ outperforms TLC for most benchmarks. The fact that TLC performs better for some models could be caused by the restrictions of B2PROGRAM. Indeed, these restrictions also mean that PROB will quite often perform significantly better than B2PROGRAM for (original) models which have not been adapted for B2PROGRAM.

In future, we would like to remove the above-mentioned restrictions of B2PROGRAM. We will also improve the feedback, e.g., show which parts of the invariant are violated, or more information about the coverage. Furthermore, it would also be possible to improve the performance, e.g., by improving the state space's storage, or caching features (such as presented by Leuschel [22]). One could also generate code for existing model checkers, such as LTSmin, SPIN, SpinJA [11] (integrated into LTSmin [30]), JBMC [10], or JavaPathfinder [25]. This would enable features, such as LTL or symbolic model checking, without re-implementing them. Another main issue for the future is model checking non-deterministic parts deep in the specifications. To address non-determinism, B2PROGRAM could also be extended to target Prolog.

Acknowledgements. We would like to thank Florian Mager and Klaus Sausen. They have been working on a student's model checking project from which some ideas have emerged for this work. We would also like to thank Lucas Döring, who is currently improving B2PROGRAM's model checking performance. We would also like to thank Sebastian Stock for proofreading this paper and anonymous referees for their feedback.

A   Benchmarks

Table 2. Single-threaded runtimes of PROB, TLC, and generated code in Java, and C++ (Compiled with -O1) in seconds with state space size, speed-up relative to PROB, memory usage in KB, OP = Operation Reuse, ST = Standard, C = Caching

Counter		ProB OP	ProB ST	TLC	Java ST	Java C	C++ ST	C++ C
(1000001 states,	Runtime	90.06	87.98	8.52	3.24	5.16	1.29	5.88
2000001 transitions)	Speed-up	1	1.02	10.67	27.84	17.47	70.08	15.33
	Memory	1151604	1151556	325420	421034	654880	217920	878754
Cruise Controller		ProB OP	ProB ST	TLC	Java ST	Java C	C++ ST	C++ C
(Volvo,	Runtime	0.75	1.74	6.89	1.6	1.53	0.06	0.16
1360 states,	Speed-up	1	0.11	0.15	0.47	0.49	12.5	4.69
26149 transitions)	Memory	174954	174247	172016	121832	113110	2722	10912
Landing		ProB OP	ProB ST	TLC	Java ST	Java C	C++ ST	C++ C
Gear [21]	Runtime	36.85	188.87	25.68	18.23	17.22	15.1	34.38
(131328 states,	Speed-up	1	0.2	1.51	2.12	2.44	2.56	1.12
884369 transitions)	Memory	476783	469995	681308	751508	985684	186736	1053604
CAN BUS		ProB OP	ProB ST	TLC	Java ST	Java C	C++ ST	C++ C
(J. Colley,	Runtime	23.13	52.11	11.42	6.23	7.21	3.77	10.29
132599 states,	Speed-up	1	0.44	2.03	3.71	3.2	6.14	2.25
340266 transitions)	Memory	353338	352125	461096	450596	562440	196762	677544
Train [2,23]		ProB OP	ProB ST	TLC	Java ST	Java C	C++ ST	C++ C
(with ten routes,	Runtime	776.81	2564.03	2373.16	1004.45	799.37	940.32	533.78
672174 states,	Speed-up	1	0.3	0.33	0.77	0.97	0.83	1.46
2244486 transitions)	Memory	2995244	1278929	896422	1267960	2317640	1228082	2995064
NoTa [27]		ProB OP	ProB ST	TLC	Java ST	Java C	C++ ST	C++ C
(80718 states	Runtime	29.89	178.82	18.78	21.89	20.9	88.51	157.8
1797353 transitions)	Speed-up	1	0.17	1.59	1.37	1.43	0.34	0.19
	Memory	947413	946857	883470	974294	1063392	189306	993818
sort_1000 [29]		ProB OP	ProB ST	TLC	Java ST	Java C	C++ ST	C++ C
(500501 states,	Runtime	234.97	359.23	505.1	1365.79	146.72	3288.73	3468.77
500502 transitions)	Speed-up	1	0.65	0.47	0.17	1.6	0.07	0.07
	Memory	833697	602163	374906	521224	1314720	303293	947840
N-Queens		ProB OP	ProB ST	TLC	Java ST	Java C	C++ ST	C++ C
with N=4	Runtime	0.15	0.19	6.46	61.97	61.19	57.05	57.02
(4 states	Speed-up	1	0.79	0.02	0.002	0.002	0.003	0.003
6 transitions)	Memory	166608	166574	170972	351168	349608	48892	48886

Table 3. Multi-threaded (6 Threads) runtimes of TLC, and generated code in Java, and C++ (Compiled with -O1) in seconds with state space size, speed-up relative to TLC and relative to single-threaded, memory usage in KB, TH = Thread, ST = Standard, C = Caching

Counter		TLC	Java ST	Java C	C++ ST	C++ C
1000001 states,	Speed-up to TLC	1	0.51	0.45	0.67	0.48
2000001 transitions)	Speed-up to 1 TH	0.73	0.15	0.2	0.07	0.24
	Memory	294664	398248	728514	218086	878910
Cruise Controller		TLC	Java ST	Java C	C++ ST	C++ C
(Volvo,	Speed-up to TLC	1	4.1	4.3	114.33	45.73
1360 states,	Speed-up to 1 TH	1	0.96	0.96	1	1.07
26149 transitions)	Memory	172032	147498	142246	3048	10994
Landing		TLC	Java ST	Java C	C++ ST	C++ C
Gear [21]	Speed-up to TLC	1	1.36	1.36	1.71	0.72
(131328 states,	Speed-up to 1 TH	1.3	1.26	1.18	1.31	1.26
884369 transitions)	Memory	808976	954956	1179980	195566	1056952
CAN BUS		TLC	Java ST	Java C	C++ ST	C++ C
(J. Colley,	Speed-up to TLC	1	1.98	1.78	3.72	1.21
132599 states,	Speed-up to 1 TH	0.85	0.92	0.96	1.04	0.93
340266 transitions)	Memory	337404	498644	574292	204528	687058
Train [2, 23]		TLC	Java ST	Java C	C++ ST	C++ C
(with ten routes,	Speed-up to TLC	1	3.22	3.51	2.76	4.65
672174 states,	Speed-up to 1 TH	1.6	2.18	1.9	1.75	1.68
2244486 transitions)	Memory	1077022	1456166	2340918	1261254	3164336
NoTa [27]		TLC	Java ST	Java C	C++ ST	C++ C
(80718 states	Speed-up to TLC	1	0.95	0.82	0.17	0.09
1797353 transitions)	Speed-up to 1 TH	1.17	1.3	1.07	0.91	0.87
	Memory	898580	1100700	1138802	220648	1035806
sort_1000 [29]		TLC	Java ST	Java C	C++ ST	C++ C
(500501 states,	Speed-up to TLC	1	0.46	3.84	0.2	0.19
500502 transitions)	Speed-up to 1 TH	1.65	2.06	1.85	2.19	2.15
	Memory	503360	520850	1894494	304048	948392
N-Queens		TLC	Java ST	Java C	C++ ST	C++ C
with N=4	Speed-up to TLC	1	0.11	0.11	0.11	0.11
(4 states	Speed-up to 1 TH	1.0	1.06	1.02	1.01	1.02
6 transitions)	Memory	170934	360534	350706	49026	48920

References

1. Abrial, J., Hoare, A.: The B-Book: Assigning Programs to Meanings. Cambridge University Press, Cambridge (2005)

2. Abrial, J.-R.: Modeling in Event-B: System and Software Engineering. Cambridge University Press, Cambridge (2010)

3. Baier, C., Katoen, J.-P.: Principles of Model Checking. MIT Press, Cambridge (2008)

4. Bendisposto, J., et al: Symbolic Reachability Analysis of B Through ProB and LTSmin. ArXiv, abs/1603.04401 (2016)

5. Bendisposto, J., Krings, S., Leuschel, M.: Who watches the watchers: validating the prob validation tool. In: Proceedings F-IDE, EPTCS 149. Electronic Proceedings in Theoretical Computer Science (2014)

6. Bendisposto, J., Leuschel, M.: Proof assisted model checking for B. In: Breitman, K., Cavalcanti, A. (eds.) ICFEM 2009. LNCS, vol. 5885, pp. 504–520. Springer, Heidelberg (2009). https://doi.org/10.1007/978-3-642-10373-5_26

7. Bonfanti, S., Carissoni, M., Gargantini, A., Mashkoor, A.: Asm2C++: a tool for code generation from abstract state machines to Arduino. In: Barrett, C., Davies, M., Kahsai, T. (eds.) NFM 2017. LNCS, vol. 10227, pp. 295–301. Springer, Cham (2017). https://doi.org/10.1007/978-3-319-57288-8_21

8. Cataño, N., Rivera, V.: EventB2Java: a code generator for event-B. In: Rayadurgam, S., Tkachuk, O. (eds.) NFM 2016. LNCS, vol. 9690, pp. 166–171. Springer, Cham (2016). https://doi.org/10.1007/978-3-319-40648-0_13

9. ClearSy. Atelier B, User and Reference Manuals. Aix-en-Provence, France (2016). http://www.atelierb.eu/

10. Cordeiro, L., Kesseli, P., Kroening, D., Schrammel, P., Trtik, M.: JBMC: a bounded model checking tool for verifying java bytecode. In: Chockler, H., Weissenbacher, G. (eds.) CAV 2018. LNCS, vol. 10981, pp. 183–190. Springer, Cham (2018). https://doi.org/10.1007/978-3-319-96145-3_10

11. de Jonge, M., Ruys, T.C.: The SPINJA model checker. In: van de Pol, J., Weber, M. (eds.) SPIN 2010. LNCS, vol. 6349, pp. 124–128. Springer, Heidelberg (2010). https://doi.org/10.1007/978-3-642-16164-3_9

12. Dobrikov, I., Leuschel, M.: Enabling analysis for event-B. In: Proceedings ABZ, pp. 102–118 (2016)

13. Edmunds, A.: Templates for event-B code generation. In : Ait Ameur, Y., Schewe, K.D. (eds) Abstract State Machines, Alloy, B, TLA, VDM, and Z. ABZ 2014. Lecture Notes in Computer Science, vol. 8477, pp. 284–289. Springer, Heidelberg (2014). https://doi.org/10.1007/978-3-662-43652-3_25

14. Fürst, A., Hoang, T.S., Basin, D., Desai, K., Sato, N., Miyazaki, K.: Code generation for event-B. In: Albert, E., Sekerinski, E. (eds.) IFM 2014. LNCS, vol. 8739, pp. 323–338. Springer, Cham (2014). https://doi.org/10.1007/978-3-319-10181-1_20

15. Hansen, D., Leuschel, M.: Translating B to TLA + for Validation with TLC. In: Ait Ameur, Y., Schewe, K.D. (eds.) Proceedings ABZ, LNCS, vol. 8477, pp. 40–55. Springer, Heidelberg (2014)

16. Holzmann, G.: The SPIN Model Checker: Primer and Reference Manual, 1st edn. Addison-Wesley Professional, Boston (2011)

17. Jørgensen, P.W.V., Larsen, M., Couto, L.D.: A code generation platform for VDM. In: Proceedings of the 12th Overture Workshop. School of Computing Science, Newcastle University, UK, Technical Report CS-TR-1446 (2015)

18. Kant, G., Laarman, A., Meijer, J., van de Pol, J., Blom, S., van Dijk, T.: LTSmin: high-performance language-independent model checking. In: Baier, C., Tinelli, C. (eds.) TACAS 2015. LNCS, vol. 9035, pp. 692–707. Springer, Heidelberg (2015). https://doi.org/10.1007/978-3-662-46681-0_61

19. Körner, P., Leuschel, M., Meijer, J.: State-of-the-art model checking for B and event-B using PROB and LTSMIN. In: Furia, C.A., Winter, K. (eds.) IFM 2018. LNCS, vol. 11023, pp. 275–295. Springer, Cham (2018). https://doi.org/10.1007/978-3-319-98938-9_16

20. Kroening, D., Tautschnig, M.: CBMC – C bounded model checker. In: Ábrahám, E., Havelund, K. (eds.) TACAS 2014. LNCS, vol. 8413, pp. 389–391. Springer, Heidelberg (2014). https://doi.org/10.1007/978-3-642-54862-8_26

21. Ladenberger, L., Hansen, D., Wiegard, H., Bendisposto, J., Leuschel, M.: Validation of the ABZ landing gear system using ProB. Int. J. Softw. Tools Technol. Transf. **19**(2), 187–203 (2015). https://doi.org/10.1007/s10009-015-0395-9

22. Leuschel, M.: Operation Caching and State Compression for Model Checking of High-Level Models - How to have your cake and eat it. In: Proceedings iFM. LNCS, vol. 13274, pp. 129–145. Springer, Cham (2022). https://doi.org/10.1007/978-3-031-07727-2_8

23. Leuschel, M., Bendisposto, J., Hansen, D.: Unlocking the mysteries of a formal model of an interlocking system. In: Proceedings Rodin Workshop (2014)

24. Leuschel, M., Butler, M.: ProB: A model checker for B. In: Araki, K., Gnesi, S., Mandrioli, D. (eds.) FME 2003. LNCS, vol. 2805, pp. 855–874. Springer, Heidelberg (2003). https://doi.org/10.1007/978-3-540-45236-2_46

25. Mehlitz, P., Rungta, N., Visser, W.: A hands-on Java Pathfinder tutorial. In: Proceedings ICSE, pp. 1493–1495 (2013)

26. Méry, D., Singh, N.K.: Automatic code generation from event-B models. In: Proceedings SoICT, pp. 179–188. ACM ICPS (2011)

27. Oliver, I.: Experiences in using B and UML in industrial development. In: Julliand, J., Kouchnarenko, O. (eds.) B 2007. LNCS, vol. 4355, pp. 248–251. Springer, Heidelberg (2006). https://doi.org/10.1007/11955757_20

28. Parr, T.: StringTemplate Website. http://www.stringtemplate.org/ (2013). Accessed 23 Sep 2021

29. Rivera, V., Cataño, N., Wahls, T., Rueda, C.: Code generation for event-B. STTT **19**(1), 31–52 (2017)

30. van der Berg, F.I., Laarman, A.: SpinS: extending LTSmin with Promela through SpinJa. Electron. Notes Theor. Comput. Sci. **296**, 95–105 (2013)

31. Vu, F., Hansen, D., Körner, P., Leuschel, M.: A multi-target code generator for high-level B. In: Ahrendt, W., Tapia Tarifa, S.L. (eds.) IFM 2019. LNCS, vol. 11918, pp. 456–473. Springer, Cham (2019). https://doi.org/10.1007/978-3-030-34968-4_25

32. Vu, F., Happe, C., Leuschel, M.: Generating domain-specific interactive validation documents. In: Proceedings FMICS, pp. 32–49 (2022). To appear in LNCS 13487

33. Witulski, J.: A Python B Implementation - PyB A Second Tool-Chain. PhD thesis, Universitäts-und Landesbibliothek der Heinrich-Heine-Universität Düsseldorf (2018)

34. Yu, Y., Manolios, P., Lamport, L.: Model checking TLA$^+$ specifications. In: Pierre, L., Kropf, T. (eds.) CHARME 1999. LNCS, vol. 1703, pp. 54–66. Springer, Heidelberg (1999). https://doi.org/10.1007/3-540-48153-2_6

On Probabilistic Extension
of the Interaction Theory

Hongmeng Wang, Huan Long$^{(\boxtimes)}$ ⓘ, Hao Wu, and Qizhe Yang

BASICS, Shanghai Jiao Tong University, Shanghai, China
{whm2020,longhuan,wuhao_seiee,guili94}@sjtu.edu.cn

Abstract. In this paper, we propose a uniform interaction theory that covers both classical and randomized models. Under this framework, two basic relations, the equality relation within a model and the expressiveness relation between different models, are restudied. We also give an interesting comparison between the world of classical models and the world of randomized models.

1 Introduction

Motivation and Related Work. Process calculi study theoretical aspects of concurrency. Since the early 80s, lots of research has been done in this field. Two key topics are building formalisms for abstract specification of concurrent systems and studying their semantics, including structured operational semantics, congruence, bisimilarity etc. On one hand, so far an enormous number of process calculi have been proposed for theoretical or practical reasons. Representative process models include calculus of communicating systems (CCS), value-passing calculus (VPC) [19], π calculus [20], higher-order calculi [22] etc. based on basic models, and one of the most popular extension is the randomized models, i.e., probabilistic process calculi [1,6,14,15], which is the focus of this work. On the other hand, a powerful tool to characterize whether two concurrent systems behave in the same way is bisimulation [19]. Many variants of bisimulation have been proposed over the years [7,11]. There have also been a lot of work on different combinations of concurrent models and bisimulation relations.

The large number of calculi and equivalence relations calls for unification and classification. One way to achieve that is to reveal their relative expressiveness. Some representative work includes [5,8,12,13,17,22]. However, as people use different expressiveness criteria, this actually brings more variety into the pool. One would expect a uniform way to investigate different models. To non-probabilistic models, one work of special interest is given in [3], where the so-called *theory of interaction* is established. It gives model independent formulations for two fundamental relations in process calculi. The first one is the equality relation between objects of a single process calculus. The second is the relative expressiveness relation between two process calculi. The main results in [3] can be summed up as *the world of models* given in Fig. 3(a). However when it comes to probabilistic models, much less is known. In this work, we would hope to extend the work in [3] to randomized models and keep model independence.

© Springer Nature Switzerland AG 2022
A. Riesco and M. Zhang (Eds.): ICFEM 2022, LNCS 13478, pp. 352–369, 2022.
https://doi.org/10.1007/978-3-031-17244-1_21

We will take the convention *classical* model to specify a traditional, non-probabilistic model. To reach the above goal, we first need a uniform way to introduce probabilistic factors into classical models. In previous work, there used to be two kinds of channel randomness which are incomparable to each other. One is generative models [6] which bind probabilistic choice to external actions, and the other is reactive models [1,18] which interleave the non-deterministic choice with probabilistic distributions. As being explained in detail in [4], most of the weak and branching bisimilaries in earlier work fail to be a full scale congruence relation. The chance to extend uniform interaction theory to probabilistic models comes with [4], where a model independent approach for studying syntax, semantics and bisimulation of probabilistic models has been introduced. For example, to randomized CCS, it is shown that the corresponding bisimilarity is a congruence. Also an efficient equivalence checking algorithm and a complete axiomatization system for finite state randomized systems have been proposed [24]. Note that all these work can be generalized to other randomized process calculi, such as randomized high order calculi. However, to randomized process calculi, a uniform expressiveness theory is still missing. Besides, simple as it might seem to be, it would be natural to ask for a rigorous comparison between any classical model and its probabilistic extension.

Contribution. In this work, we give a thorough study on the interaction theory of classical and randomized models, especially on expressiveness theory. Our key contributions are two-fold:

1. We extend the theory of interaction to cover both classical and randomized models. More specifically, we formalize the subbisimilairty relation between models where some of them could have randomized operators. This is a non-trivial extension of [3] and is still model independent. It can be utilized to compare any models under the same framework.
2. We give two meta theories for expressiveness. Firstly we show that any classical interactive model is strictly less expressive than its probabilistic extension. Secondly we show that encodings between two classical models can be extended to their respectively probabilistic extensions, as long as the original encoding is deterministic.

In addition, for a better illustration of our work, we introduce two probabilistic calculi, randomized VPC and randomized C, as case studies. These two models are of independent interest. C has been proposed in [3], which meets the minimal properties of process calculus. Moreover, in C structural congruence coincides with absolute equality, which makes one believe C can serve as the least model. Any model M we will discuss should meet those properties and at least as expressive as C.

The rest of the paper is organized as follows. Section 2 introduces the randomized VPC and randomized C. Section 3 extends the model independent equality theory to randomized models; Sect. 4 recasts the expressiveness theory in a randomized framework; Sect. 5 ends this paper with some future work.

2   Randomized Calculi and the Bisimulation

In this section we give probabilistic extensions of classical value-passing calculus and C calculus. We call it randomized value-passing calculus (randomized C calculus resp.) for brevity and denote it by RVPC (RC resp.). The way to include probabilistic operators into classical models is model independent [4]. Thus RVPC (RC resp.) extends VPC (C resp.) in basically the same way as RCCS does to CCS in [4]. We only give necessary key or new conceptions.

2.1   Randomized Value-Passing Calculus

As one of the most classic concurrent models, VPC is especially suitable for modelling concurrency and data communication [2,19]. Following the notations in [2], we assume that the calculus is defined on top of a decidable first order theory Th of type Σ, where Σ is a countable vocabulary. The set of closed Σ-terms is denoted by T_Σ^0. To get the randomized extension from any model M to its randomized version RM, we simply include the model independent probabilistic choice operator in [4]:

$$\bigoplus_{i \in I} p_i \tau . T_i \xrightarrow{p_i \tau} T_i, \tag{1}$$

where $p_i \in (0,1)$ and $\sum_{i \in I} p_i = 1$. Following the notations in [4], we will also use $\bigoplus_{i \in I} p_i \tau . T_i \xrightarrow{\coprod_{i \in I} p_i \tau} \coprod_{i \in I} T_i$ to represent a *collective silent transition*, which indicates a collection of silent transitions.

The set of channel names $\mathcal{N}$ will be ranged over by lowercase letters such as a, b, c, d. The set of conames is defined as $\overline{\mathcal{N}} = \{\overline{a} \mid a \in \mathcal{N}\}$. The set of variables will be ranged over by x, y, z. As usual, if $n = \overline{a}$, then $\overline{n} = a$. The set of randomized value-passing *terms*, denoted by $\mathbb{T}_{\mathsf{RVPC}}$, is defined as follows and will be ranged over by capital letters R, S, T:

$$T := \mathbf{0} \mid \sum_{i \in I} \varphi_i a(x).T_i \mid \sum_{i \in I} \varphi_i \overline{a}(t_i).T_i \mid \bigoplus_{i \in I} p_i \tau . T_i \mid T|T' \mid (c)T \mid \varphi T \mid !a(x).T \mid !\overline{a}(t).T.$$

$$\tag{2}$$

where $\mathbf{0}$ is the nil process; φ is a boolean Σ-expression and I is a finite index set. The RVPC-term $\sum_{i \in I} \varphi_i \alpha_i . T_i$, which stands for either $\sum_{i \in I} \varphi_i a(x).T_i$ or $\sum_{i \in I} \varphi_i \overline{a}(t_i).T_i$, is called *conditional guarded choice*. When $|I| = 1$, φT is called *single condition*, and is interpreted as 'if φ then T'. Sometimes we use $[x = t].T$ as an abbreviation. Similarly we will use $[x \neq t].T$ as an abbreviation for 'if $x \neq t$ then T'. The prefix $a(x)$ is an input primitive which binds the Σ-variable x. The prefix $\overline{a}(t)$ is an output primitive which will output a closed Σ-term. As usual, for a term T, variables bound by input prefix are called *bound variables*, denoted by $bv(T)$, otherwise called *free*. The set of free variables in T is denoted by $fv(T)$. For some $S \in \mathbb{T}_{\mathsf{RVPC}}$ with $fv(S) = \{x_1, x_2, \ldots, x_n\}$, and some $T_1, T_2, \ldots, T_n \in \mathbb{T}_{\mathsf{RVPC}}$, the term $S\{T_1/x_1, T_2/x_2, \ldots T_n/x_n\}$ results from S by replacing each x_i with T_i. A RVPC-term without free variables is also called RVPC-*process*, denoted by $\mathbb{P}_{\mathsf{RVPC}}$. We use capital letters such as S, T to range over them. The probabilistic choice operator $\bigoplus_{i \in I} p_i \tau.T_i$ following (1), shows that T can do τ action with probability p_i and evolve into T_i for $i \in I$. The meanings of *structural equivalence* (notational $\equiv$), *composition*, *localization* and *guarded replication* are standard. The concrete semantics of RVPC is given by the labelled transition system (Fig. 1). Meanings of each rule are straightforward [2].

Action

$$\frac{}{\sum_{i \in I} \varphi_i a(x).T_i \xrightarrow{a(t)} T_i\{t/x\}} \; t \in T^0_\Sigma, \mathrm{Th} \vdash \varphi_i \qquad \frac{}{\sum_{i \in I} \varphi_i \bar{a}(t_i).T_i \xrightarrow{\bar{a}(t_i)} T_i} \; t \in T^0_\Sigma, \mathrm{Th} \vdash \varphi_i$$

Probabilistic choice

$$\frac{}{\bigoplus_{i \in I} p_i \tau.T_i \xrightarrow{p_i \tau} T_i} \; \forall i \in I, \; p_i \in (0,1), \; \sum_{i \in I} p_i = 1$$

Interaction

$$\frac{S \xrightarrow{a(t)} S' \quad T \xrightarrow{\bar{a}(t)} T'}{S \mid T \xrightarrow{\tau} S' \mid T'}$$

Structural

$$\frac{S \xrightarrow{\lambda} S'}{S \mid T \xrightarrow{\lambda} S' \mid T} \qquad \frac{T \xrightarrow{\lambda} T'}{S \mid T \xrightarrow{\lambda} S \mid T'} \qquad \frac{T \xrightarrow{\lambda} T'}{(c)T \xrightarrow{\lambda} (c)T'} \; c \text{ is not in } \lambda$$

Condition

$$\frac{T \xrightarrow{\lambda} T'}{\varphi T \xrightarrow{\lambda} T'} \; \mathrm{Th} \vdash \varphi$$

Replication

$$\frac{}{!a(x).T \xrightarrow{a(t)} T\{t/x\} \mid !a(x).T} \; t \in T^0_\Sigma \qquad \frac{}{!\bar{a}(t).T \xrightarrow{\bar{a}(t)} T \mid !\bar{a}(t).T} \; t \in T^0_\Sigma$$

Fig. 1. LTS for RVPC

A numeric system for RVPC is defined as $\langle \{\hat{0}, \hat{1}, \cdots, \hat{n}, \cdots\}, S_d(x) \rangle$ [2]. It contains a countable subset $\{\hat{0}, \hat{1}, \cdots, \hat{n}, \cdots\}$ of T^0_Σ, and $S_d(x) \in \mathbb{T}_{\mathsf{RVPC}}$, which is, intuitively, the successor function. It has been proved that all recursive functions are definable in VPC equipped with numeric system [2], which means if VPC has a numeric system, it can simulate all recursive functions. Finally we define the action sets. The external action set contains the input and output actions, which is denoted by $\mathrm{Act}^e = \{a(t) \mid t \in T^0_\Sigma \text{ and } a \in \mathcal{N} \cup \overline{\mathcal{N}}\}$ and ranged over by α, β. The silent action set Act^s contains τ, and the probabilistic action $p\tau$ (where $p \in (0,1)$). For simplicity we will interpret τ as 1τ. Then $\mathrm{Act}^s = \{p\tau \mid p \in (0,1]\}$. The action set $\mathrm{Act} = \mathrm{Act}^e \cup \mathrm{Act}^s$ will be ranged over by ℓ, λ.

2.2 Randomized C

C is a basic interactive model which any interactively complete model should be able to explain [3]. C is a minimal extension of computable function which supports interaction. To the randomized extension, the probabilistic operator also comes from (1). The set of RC terms, denoted by $\mathbb{T}_{RC}$, is given below:

$$P := \mathbf{0} \mid \Omega \mid F_a^b(f(x)) \mid \bar{a}(\underline{i}) \mid P|P \mid \bigoplus_{i \in I} q_i \tau.P_i \qquad (3)$$

where $f(x)$ is a unary recursive function and $\underline{i}$ represents a numeral. Figure 2 gives the operational semantics.

Function

$$\frac{}{F_a^b(f(x)) \xrightarrow{a(\underline{m})} \bar{b}(\underline{n})} \text{ if } f(m) = n \qquad \frac{}{F_a^b(f(x)) \xrightarrow{a(\underline{m})} \Omega} \text{ if } f(m) \text{ is undefined}$$

Value and divergence

$$\frac{}{\bar{a}(\underline{n}) \xrightarrow{\bar{a}(\underline{n})} \mathbf{0}} \qquad \frac{}{\Omega \xrightarrow{\tau} \Omega}$$

Probabilistic choice

$$\frac{}{\bigoplus_{i \in I} p_i \tau.T_i \xrightarrow{p_i \tau} T_i} \quad \forall i \in I \; p_i \in (0,1), \; \sum_{i \in I} p_i = 1$$

Interaction

$$\frac{P \xrightarrow{a(\underline{n})} P' \quad Q \xrightarrow{\bar{a}(\underline{n})} Q'}{P \mid Q \xrightarrow{\tau} P' \mid Q'}$$

Structural

$$\frac{P \xrightarrow{\lambda} P'}{P \mid Q \xrightarrow{\lambda} P' \mid Q} \qquad \frac{Q \xrightarrow{\lambda} Q'}{P \mid Q \xrightarrow{\lambda} P \mid Q'}$$

Fig. 2. LTS for RC

The function component $F_a^b(f(x))$ can input, say $\underline{m}$, at channel a, compute the function $f(m)$ and become $\bar{b}(\underline{n})$ if $f(m) = n$ or Ω if $f(m)$ is undefined. We will use Act_C^e (Act_{RC}^e resp.) and Act_C^s (Act_{RC}^s resp.) to stand for the set of external or silent actions for C (RC resp.).

2.3   Branching Bisimulation Congruence

Branching bisimulation [7] preserves the branching structure of processes, in the sense that it preserves computations together with the potentials in all intermediate states that are passed through. In this section, we introduce branching bisimulation for randomized models [4]. We will only introduce conceptions which are necessary for our discussion. As conception in this part is basically model independent, we use RVPC as an example. Corresponding conceptions for RC can be obtained similarly.

For an equivalence relation $\mathcal{R}$ over $\mathbb{P}_{\mathsf{RVPC}}$, we write $A\mathcal{R}B$ if $(A, B) \in \mathcal{R}$. $\mathbb{P}_{\mathsf{RVPC}}/\mathcal{R}$ stands for the set of equivalence classes with respect to $\mathcal{R}$. The equivalence class A belongs to is denoted by $[A]_{\mathcal{R}}$. The transition $A \xrightarrow{\ell} \mathcal{C}$, where $\mathcal{C} \in \mathbb{P}_{\mathsf{RVPC}}/\mathcal{R}$, is interpreted as $A \xrightarrow{\ell} A' \in \mathcal{C}$ for some A'. A silent action $A \xrightarrow{\tau} A'$ is called *state-preserving* if $A\mathcal{R}A'$, and otherwise *state-changing*. We write $A \xrightarrow{\tau}_{\mathcal{R}} A'$, if $A \xrightarrow{\tau} A'\mathcal{R}A$ for some A', which indicates the silent action is state-preserving. As usual, $\Longrightarrow_{\mathcal{R}}$ is the reflexive and transitive closure of $\xrightarrow{\tau}_{\mathcal{R}}$. A process A is $\mathcal{R}$-*divergent* if there is an infinite sequence $A \xrightarrow{\tau}_{\mathcal{R}} A_1 \xrightarrow{\tau}_{\mathcal{R}} \cdots A_k \xrightarrow{\tau}_{\mathcal{R}}$ $\cdots$. To achieve the random version of $\Longrightarrow_{\mathcal{R}}$, ϵ-tree [4] is introduced.

Definition 1 (ϵ-tree). *Let $\mathcal{R}$ be an equivalence relation on $\mathbb{P}_{\mathsf{RVPC}}$ and $A \in$ $\mathbb{P}_{\mathsf{RVPC}}$. An ϵ-tree $t_{\mathcal{R}}^A$ of A with regard to $\mathcal{R}$ is a labelled tree which validates the following conditions:*

1. *The root is labelled by A. All the nodes of $t_{\mathcal{R}}^A$ are in the class $[A]_{\mathcal{R}}$;*
2. *Every edge is labelled by a real number in $(0, 1]$;*
3. *If $A \xrightarrow{q} A'$ is an edge in $t_{\mathcal{R}}^A$ ($q \in (0,1)$), there must be a collective silent transition $A \xrightarrow{\coprod_{i \in I} p_i \tau} \coprod_{i \in I} A_i$, and A_i ($i \in I$) are the only children of A;*
4. *If $A \xrightarrow{1} A'$ is an edge in $t_{\mathcal{R}}^A$, then A' is the only child of A with $A \xrightarrow{\tau} A'$.*

In [4], divergence in randomized models has been formalized through ϵ-tree. For ϵ-tree t, we use $\mathsf{P}(\pi)$ to stand for the probability of executing a path π in t. The probability of finite branches of t is defined as $\mathsf{P}^f(t) = \lim_{k \to \infty} \mathsf{P}^k(t)$, where $\mathsf{P}^k(t) = \sum\{\mathsf{P}(\pi) \mid \pi \text{ is a finite branch of} t \text{ such that} |\pi| \leq k\}$. A ϵ-tree $t_{\mathcal{R}}^A$ is called *regular* if $\mathsf{P}^f(t_{\mathcal{R}}^A) = 1$; or *divergent* if $\mathsf{P}^f(t_{\mathcal{R}}^A) = 0$.

Given $A \in \mathbb{P}_{\mathsf{RVPC}}$, A may evolve into class $\mathcal{B} \in \mathbb{P}_{\mathsf{RVPC}}/\mathcal{R}$ in two ways:

- Via an action $\ell \in \mathsf{Act}^e$, or $\ell = \tau \wedge [A]_{\mathcal{R}} \neq \mathcal{B}$. An ℓ-transition from A to $\mathcal{B}$ consists of a regular ϵ-tree $t_{\mathcal{R}}^A$ with regard to $\mathcal{R}$ and a transition $L \xrightarrow{\ell} L' \in \mathcal{B}$ for every leaf L of $t_{\mathcal{R}}^A$. An ℓ-transition will be denoted as $A \rightsquigarrow_{\mathcal{R}} \xrightarrow{\ell} \mathcal{B}$.
- Via probabilistic actions. Suppose L is a leaf of $t_{\mathcal{R}}^A$ and $L \xrightarrow{\coprod_{i \in I} p_i \tau}$ $\coprod_{i \in I} L_i$ such that $L_i \in \mathcal{B}$ for some $i \in I$. Define $\mathsf{P}\left(L \xrightarrow{\coprod_{i \in I} p_i \tau} \mathcal{B}\right) =$ $\sum_{i \in I}\left\{p_i \mid L \xrightarrow{p_i \tau} L_i \in \mathcal{B}\right\}$. The *normalized probability* [4] with respect to an equivalence $\mathcal{R}$ is defined as $\mathsf{P}_{\mathcal{R}}\left(L \xrightarrow{\coprod_{i \in I} p_i \tau} \mathcal{B}\right) = \dfrac{\mathsf{P}\left(L \xrightarrow{\coprod_{i \in I} p_i \tau} \mathcal{B}\right)}{\left(1 - \mathsf{P}\left(L \xrightarrow{\coprod_{i \in I} p_i \tau} [A]_{\mathcal{R}}\right)\right)}$.

Thus the normalized probability is just given L's leaving states in $[A]_{\mathcal{R}}$, L's chance of reaching some state in $\mathcal{B}$. To process A, we could define q-transition. It consists of a *regular* ϵ-tree $t_{\mathcal{R}}^A$ and a collective silent transition $L \xrightarrow{\coprod_{i \in I} p_i \tau} \coprod_{i \in I} L_i$ for every leaf L in $t_{\mathcal{R}}^A$, such that $\mathsf{P}_{\mathcal{R}}\left(L \xrightarrow{\coprod_{i \in I} p_i \tau} \mathcal{B}\right) = q$.

A q-transition is denoted by $A \rightsquigarrow_{\mathcal{R}} \xrightarrow{q} \mathcal{B}$.

Then we can define branching bisimulation for RVPC.

Definition 2. *An equivalence $\mathcal{R}$ on $\mathbb{P}_{\mathsf{RVPC}}$ is a branching bisimulation if the following statements are satisfied:*

1. *If $B\mathcal{R}A \leadsto_{\mathcal{R}} \xrightarrow{\ell} \mathcal{C} \in \mathcal{P}/\mathcal{R}$, where $(\ell \in Act^e) \vee (\ell = \tau \wedge \mathcal{C} \neq [A]_{\mathcal{R}})$,*
   then $B \leadsto_{\mathcal{R}} \xrightarrow{\ell} \mathcal{C}$;
2. *If $B\mathcal{R}A \leadsto_{\mathcal{R}} \xrightarrow{q} \mathcal{C} \in \mathcal{P}/\mathcal{R}$ such that $\mathcal{C} \neq [A]_{\mathcal{R}}$, then $B \leadsto_{\mathcal{R}} \xrightarrow{q} \mathcal{C}$.*

Note that Definition 2 is stated in [23] in a different but equivalent way, except the normalized part, in terms of a lifting relation between probabilistic spaces. It has been proved in [4] that the branching bisimulation for randomized CCS is a congruence. The same proof works for RVPC and is omitted for conciseness.

3   Generalized Equality Theory

As mentioned earlier, there are two fundamental relations in process calculi. The first one is the equality relation between objects of one model. In this section we give the randomized extension of the model independent equality theory.

3.1   Absolute Equality for Randomized Process Models

Absolute equality is a model independent equivalence relation which takes into account of the time, space, computation and interaction invariance [3]. To extend it to probabilistic circumstances, the only probabilistic operator we will allow is the model independent probabilistic choice operator (1). We will use superscript [R] to highlight the fact that we are dealing with the more general randomized calculi. We start by giving corresponding conceptions for randomized models. Some notations in Sect. 2 are overloaded for brevity. We will simply replace RVPC with a randomized interactive model M. Meanings of the resulting notations will still be clear. For example, $\mathbb{P}_{\mathsf{M}}$ stands for the set of processes of model M. All conceptions in this section are model independent, in the sense that they can be initialized as any concrete models. Note that some relations are defined as equivalence for brevity.

Definition 3 (Time invariance[R]). *An equivalence relation $\mathcal{R} \subseteq \mathbb{P}_{\mathsf{M}} \times \mathbb{P}_{\mathsf{M}}$ is* bisimilar *if the following statements are valid:*

1. *If $Q\mathcal{R}^{-1}P \leadsto_{\mathcal{R}} \xrightarrow{\tau} \mathcal{P}' \in \mathcal{P}/\mathcal{R}$ and $\mathcal{P}' \neq [P]_{\mathcal{R}}$, then $Q \leadsto_{\mathcal{R}} \xrightarrow{\tau} \mathcal{P}'$;*
2. *If $Q\mathcal{R}^{-1}P \leadsto_{\mathcal{R}} \xrightarrow{q} \mathcal{P}' \in \mathcal{P}/\mathcal{R}$ and $\mathcal{P}' \neq [P]_{\mathcal{R}}$, then $Q \leadsto_{\mathcal{R}} \xrightarrow{q} \mathcal{P}'$.*

Definition 4 (Space invariance[R]). *A binary relation $\mathcal{R} \subseteq \mathbb{P}_{\mathsf{M}} \times \mathbb{P}_{\mathsf{M}}$ is* extensional *if it satisfies:*

1. *If $P\mathcal{R}Q$ and $M\mathcal{R}N$, then $P|M \ \mathcal{R} \ Q|N$;*
2. *If $P\mathcal{R}Q$, then $(a)P \ \mathcal{R} \ (a)Q$ for all $a \in \mathcal{N}$.*

Definition 5 (Computation invariance^R). *An equivalence relation $\mathcal{R} \subseteq \mathbb{P}_M \times \mathbb{P}_M$ is divergence-sensitive if it validates the following statements whenever $P\mathcal{R}Q$:*

- *If P has a divergent ϵ-tree $t_{\mathcal{R}}^P$, then Q has a divergent ϵ-tree $t_{\mathcal{R}}^Q$.*

As in [3], a process P is called observable, notational $P \Downarrow$, if there exists some external action $\lambda \in \text{Act}^e$ and process P', such that $P \leadsto_{\mathcal{R}} \xrightarrow{\lambda} P'$. The classical version of Definition 5 and variants are stated in [9] in detail.

Definition 6 (Interaction invariance^R). *A binary relation $\mathcal{R} \subseteq \mathbb{P}_M \times \mathbb{P}_M$ is equipollent if $P \Downarrow$ implies $Q \Downarrow$ whenever $P\mathcal{R}Q$.*

Finally we can propose the generalized absolute equality for randomized models.

Definition 7 (Absolute equality^R). *The absolute equality $=_M$ of model M is the largest equivalence relation on $\mathbb{P}_M$ which is equipollent, extensional, divergence-sensitive, and bisimilar.*

We also give a natural extension of the famous bisimulation lemma for randomized process models [3,21].

Lemma 1 *If P has a regular ϵ-tree $t_{=_M}^P$, and for every leaf P' in ϵ-tree $t_{=_M}^P$, $P' =_M Q$, at the same time Q has a regular ϵ-tree $t_{=_M}^Q$ and for every leaf Q' in ϵ-tree $t_{=_M}^Q$, $Q' =_M P$, then $P =_M Q$.*

3.2 External Characterization for $=_{RVPC}$

On one hand, $=_M$ enjoys the model independence and thus can be applied to any interactive model. On the other hand, the label-based semantics, i.e., the model dependent semantics, is the basis for the traditional observation theory. For a model M, if we can find a label-based equivalence which however coincides with $=_M$, i.e., an *external characterization* of $=_M$, then we can simplify the proof in many cases. Especially when it comes to some delicate problems (for example, expressiveness), the external characterization tends to be more convenient. We build the external characterization of $=_{RVPC}$ as Theorem 1.

Definition 8. *A divergence-sensitive, branching bisimulation $\mathcal{R}$ on $\mathbb{P}_{RVPC}$ is called a RVPC-bisimulation.*

Definition 8 is a probabilistic extension of branching bisimilarity in [9], which coincides with the orignal one in terms of colored traces in [10]. Following the same strategy in [4], we can prove the following fact:

Lemma 2. *If $\{\mathcal{R}_i\}_{i \in I}$ is a collection of divergence-sensitive, branching bisimulation on $\mathbb{P}_{RVPC}$, so is $(\bigcup_{i \in I} \mathcal{R}_i)^*$.*

This lemma allows us to define RVPC-bisimilarity, notational $\simeq_{\mathsf{RVPC}}$, to be the largest RVPC-bisimulation. Obviously $\simeq_{\mathsf{RVPC}}$ is reflexive, equipollent, divergence-sensitive, and bisimilar. We show that it is also extensional.

Lemma 3. *On* $\mathbb{P}_{\mathsf{RVPC}}$, $\simeq_{\mathsf{RVPC}}$ *is extensional.*

Proof. The proof is carried out by constructing relation $\mathcal{R}$ from $\simeq_{\mathsf{RVPC}}$ which is closed under composition and localization. Then following the same case study strategy in [4], we can show that $\mathcal{R}^\circ \overset{\text{def}}{=} (\mathcal{R} \cup \simeq_{\mathsf{RVPC}})^*$ is a branching bisimulation. Details are omitted here for its similarity to the proof for RCCS in [4].

Now we can show that $\simeq_{\mathsf{RVPC}}$ is the external characterization of $=_{\mathsf{RVPC}}$.

Theorem 1. *To* $\mathbb{P}_{\mathsf{RVPC}}$, *the* RVPC-*bisimilarity* $\simeq_{\mathsf{RVPC}}$ *coincides with the absolute equality* $=_{\mathsf{RVPC}}$.

Proof. $\simeq_{\mathsf{RVPC}} \subseteq =_{\mathsf{RVPC}}$ is immediate from Lemma 3 and earlier discussion. We then show the validity of $=_{\mathsf{RVPC}} \subseteq \simeq_{\mathsf{RVPC}}$. The proof resembles its non-randomized counterpart and is given in Appendix A.1 for space limitation.

According to Theorem 1, we can switch between $=_{\mathsf{RVPC}}$ and $\simeq_{\mathsf{RVPC}}$ freely.

3.3 External Characterization for $=_{\mathsf{RC}}$

First we have one more observation about the probabilistic operator: note that all internal actions in a C process are state-changing unless it is a silent action from some Ω component (i.e., from $\Omega \overset{\tau}{\to} \Omega$). However this is not the case for RC. In the process $\frac{1}{2}\tau.F_a^b(x) \bigoplus \frac{1}{2}\tau.F_a^b(x)$, both probabilistic actions are state-preserving. This shows that randomized model is more intricate compared with the classical version. To the external characterization of C, denoted by $\simeq_{\mathsf{C}}$, its coincidence with $=_{\mathsf{C}}$ can be found in [3]. We can define $\simeq_{\mathsf{RC}}$ for RC similar to Definition 8 by simply replacing $\mathbb{P}_{\mathsf{RVPC}}$ with $\mathbb{P}_{\mathsf{RC}}$ and then take the largest relation. Next we show it coincides with $=_{\mathsf{RC}}$. Note we cannot reuse the proof in [3]. In C, the branching bisimulation coincides with the structural congruence, which is not the case for RC. For example, obviously $p\tau.F_a^b(x) \bigoplus (1-p)\tau.F_a^b(x) =_{\mathsf{RC}} F_a^b(x)$ for any $p \in (0,1]$, while they are not structurally congruent to each other. One possible way to solve this is to introduce a set of rewritten rules (axioms) for RC and show that such rules are sound and complete, as we have done for RCCS [24]. Instead, here we present another Proposition which is simpler yet enough for building the external characterization.

Proposition 1. *For* $P, Q \in \mathbb{P}_{\mathsf{RC}}$, *if* $P =_{\mathsf{RC}} Q$ *then* P *and* P's *derivations have the same set of observable actions as* Q *and* Q's *derivations.*

Proof. Suppose there exists a name e such that some branch of derivation sequence starts with P can finally expose e on its leaves, while any derivation from Q cannot. We use P' to stand for the last time such case happens. Surely $P' =_{\mathsf{RC}} Q'$ for some Q'.

The key observation is that, for every RC process S, we can design a so-called *contra-process* S_c such that $S|S_c$ can evolve into an unobservable process. S_c is given inductively and its termination is obvious:

- $S = F_a^b(f(x))$
  - If $f(\underline{0}) = \underline{k}$ for some numeral $\underline{k}$, then $S_c = \bar{a}(\underline{0})|F_b^{b'}(\uparrow)$, where $\uparrow$ is an abbreviation for the empty function.
  - If $f(\underline{0})$ is undefined then $S_c = \bar{a}(\underline{0})$.
- $S = \bar{a}(\underline{n})$ then $S_c = F_a^{a'}(\uparrow_{\underline{n}})$, where $\uparrow_{\underline{n}}$ is a function which diverge on input $\underline{n}$ and otherwise be the identity function.
- $S = \Omega$ then $S_c = \mathbf{0}$.
- $S = S^1|S^2$ then $S_c = S_c^1|S_c^2$.
- $S = \bigoplus_{i\in I} p_i \tau.T_i$ then $S_c = \bigoplus_{i\in I} p_i \tau.(T_i)_c$.

Thus to Q' we can also give its contra-process Q'_c. According to the above construction, e will not appear in Q'_c (for e will not appear in Q's derivations). As P' is selected as the *last* time the mentioned scenario happen. Considering the number of interactions over e starting from P' there are two possible cases:

1. zero: then P' can do either an input or output, but not both, action at e. All derivations of $P'|Q'_c$ are observable (on e) and thus cannot simulate $Q'|Q'_c$.
2. one: then P' must be of the form $F_e^b(f(x))|\bar{e}(\underline{n})|P''$ with $b \neq e$ or $f(\underline{n})$ undefined, and e does not appear in an active position of P''. This case considers the process $T \stackrel{\text{def}}{=} F_e^r(x+1)$ where r is a fresh name to P, Q. It should be true that $P'|T =_{\mathsf{RC}} Q'|T$. However, $P'|T \stackrel{\tau}{\to} P''' = F_e^b(f(x))|\bar{r}(\underline{n}+1)|P''$ while no derivations of $Q'|T$ can expose r. That is, we can repeat the previous argument on $P'|T$ and $Q'|T$ for name r, and it will reduce to the zero case and thus find the contradiction.

A quick corollary of the above proposition is that once $P =_{\mathsf{RC}} Q$, then P and Q must have the same multiset of executable output components in the composition level. For example, the process $\left(\frac{1}{3}\tau.\bar{a}(\underline{0}) + \frac{2}{3}\tau.(\bar{a}(\underline{1})|\bar{a}(\underline{1}))\right)|\bar{b}(\underline{2})$ has the executable output actions $\{\{\bar{a}(\underline{0}), \bar{b}(\underline{2})\}, \{\bar{a}(\underline{1}), \bar{a}(\underline{1}), \bar{b}(\underline{2})\}\}$, and the process $\left(\frac{1}{3}\tau.\bar{a}(\underline{0}) + \frac{2}{3}\tau.\bar{a}(\underline{0})\right)|\bar{b}(\underline{2}) =_{\mathsf{RC}} \bar{a}(\underline{0})|\bar{b}(\underline{2})$ has executable output actions $\{\{\bar{a}(\underline{0}), \bar{b}(\underline{2})\}\}$. Otherwise the same contra-process will not work for both of P and Q. Based on this we can give the coincidence theorem for RC model.

Theorem 2. *To* $\mathbb{P}_{\mathsf{RC}}$, $\simeq_{\mathsf{RC}}$ *coincides with* $=_{\mathsf{RC}}$.

Proof. As we have mentioned earlier, the proof of this theorem is different from its non-randomized counterpart, as the branching bisimulation does not coincides with structural congruence in RC. We put the detail in Appendix A.2.

Next we use $\simeq_{\mathsf{M}}$ to denote the external characterization of $=_{\mathsf{M}}$ for model M.

4   Generalized Expressiveness Theory

Relative expressiveness among process models is another fundamental relation in process calculi. As aforementioned, several types of criteria have been proposed [3,8,12,13]. Here we extend the model independent framework in [3] to randomized models. We start by exploring expressiveness between VPC and RVPC, and then generalize it to any model M and its randomized extension RM. Furthermore, we also answer the question that, given two classical models M and N where N is at least as expressive as M (i.e., $M \sqsubseteq N$), then in what condition can we conclude that $RM \sqsubseteq RN$ holds. Main results in this part are:

1. $M \sqsubset RM$ (Theorem 3).
2. If $M \sqsubseteq N$ and the encoding from M into N is deterministic, then $RM \sqsubseteq RN$ (Theorem 4).

We first extend the expressiveness criteria in [3] into randomized process models.

4.1   Subbisimilarity for Randomized Process Models

To models M_1 and M_2, an *encoding* from M_1 into M_2 is an effective function from $\mathbb{P}_{M_1}$ to $\mathbb{P}_{M_2}$, where certain criteria are satisfied. An *interpretation* from M_1 into M_2 is total relation from $\mathbb{P}_{M_1}$ to $\mathbb{P}_{M_2}$, which interprets a process of M_1 into a set of processes of M_2. Composing an encoding with an equality in the target model, e.g., $=_{M_2}$, will give an interpretation $\mathcal{T}$ from model M_1 to model M_2 [3]. The existence of $\mathcal{T}$ shows that M_2 is at least as expressive as M_1. For some process $P \in \mathbb{P}_{M_1}$, we use $\mathcal{T}(P)_{M_2}$ to specify the equivalence *class* of its interpretation in M_2.

We take the encoding criteria developed in [3] for their model independence. Still, we need to extend them to randomized process models. First a few preparations are needed. Definitions 9,10,11 are standard:

Definition 9. *An interpretation $\mathcal{T}$ is* complete *if for any $P, Q \in \mathbb{P}_{M_1}$, $P =_{M_1} Q$ implies $\mathcal{T}(P)_{M_2} = \mathcal{T}(Q)_{M_2}$.*

Definition 10. *An interpretation $\mathcal{T}$ is* sound *if $\mathcal{T}(P)_{M_2} = \mathcal{T}(Q)_{M_2}$ implies $P =_{M_1} Q$.*

Definition 11. *An interpretation $\mathcal{T}$ from M_1 to M_2 is* fully abstract *if it is both sound and complete.*

We call a relation $\mathcal{R} \subseteq \mathbb{P}_{M1} \times \mathbb{P}_{M2}$ to be bisimilar (extensional, divergence-sensitive, equipollent resp.) with natural changes to Definition 3 (4, 5, 6 resp.). Finally, the generalized expressiveness criteria are given as Definition 12.

Definition 12 (Subbisimilarity^R). *A relation $\mathcal{R}$ from M_1 to M_2 is a subbisimilarity, if the following requirements are satisfied:*

1. *The relation is total and sound;*
2. *The relation is equipollent, extensional, divergence-sensitive and bisimilar.*

We say M_1 is *subbisimilar* to M_2, denoted by $M_1 \sqsubseteq M_2$, if there is a subbisimilarity from M_1 to M_2. We write $M_1 \sqsubset M_2$ if $M_1 \sqsubseteq M_2$ while $M_2 \not\sqsubseteq M_1$. If $M_1 \not\sqsubseteq M_2$ and $M_2 \not\sqsubseteq M_1$, then we say M_1, M_2 are independent to each other. Similar to [3], we can prove that $\sqsubseteq$ is transitive.

4.2 Expressiveness of the Probabilistic Operator

We first explore the expressiveness of probabilistic operators of type (1). This is non-trivial, for even if $\mathbb{P}_{M_1}$ is a subset of $\mathbb{P}_{M_2}$, they can still be expressively independent [3,16]. However, we show that the probabilistic operator can strictly increase the expressiveness. We study the interpretation from VPC to its randomized extension, i.e., RVPC. Then we generalize VPC to any model M.

Proposition 2. VPC $\sqsubset$ RVPC.

Proof. We take the interpretation to be the identity function with respect to absolute equality. In another word, the interpretation of any VPC processes P into RVPC is simply $[P]_{=\mathsf{RVPC}}$. It is obvious that this interpretation is total, equipollent, extensional, codivergent and bisimilar. To the soundness property, i.e., for any $P_1, P_2 \in \mathbb{P}_{\mathsf{VPC}}$, $P_1 =_{\mathsf{VPC}} P_2$ implies $P_1 =_{\mathsf{RVPC}} P_2$. Similar to Theorem 1, in [2] it has been shown that $=_{\mathsf{VPC}}$ coincides with $\simeq_{\mathsf{VPC}}$. However, as neither P_1 nor P_2 has any probabilistic operator, the label-based bisimulation also holds in $\mathbb{P}_{\mathsf{RVPC}}$, i.e., $P_1 \simeq_{\mathsf{RVPC}} P_2$. Now by Theorem 1, we conclude that $P_1 =_{\mathsf{RVPC}} P_2$. Finally, to show RVPC $\not\sqsubseteq$ VPC, simply consider the RVPC process $S \overset{\text{def}}{=} \frac{1}{2}\tau.\bar{a}(\hat{0}) \bigoplus \frac{1}{2}\tau.\bar{b}(\hat{0})$. One cannot find any VPC process which can explain S and respect the time invariance criterion, as there is no q-transition in VPC at all.

The above argument for showing non-existence of interpretation works for comparing any two models, whenever exactly one of them is randomized.

Corollary 1. *For any probabilistic interactive model* RN *and classical interactive model* M, RN $\not\sqsubseteq$ M.

The proof of Proposition 2 can be extended to expressiveness study between any model M and its randomized version RM. The technical essentials are the coincidence of the external characterization with the absolute equality, and the Definition 3 of bisimilar. Actually such coincidence has been built for all interactive models mentioned in [3]. Since absolute equality is model independent, it is fair to require that the external characterization can be built for any interactive model. Thus we have the following theorem.

Theorem 3. *For any interactive model* M *and its randomized extension* RM, M $\sqsubset$ RM.

Instances of Theorem 3 and the external characterizations in [3] include, CCS $\sqsubset$ RCCS, C $\sqsubset$ RC , IM $\sqsubset$ RIM, $\pi \sqsubset$ Rπ etc. (IM is the interactive Turing machine). One can refer to [3] for more details. An interesting observation of this part is that, even though probabilistic Turing machine is computationally equivalent to Turing machine by Church-Turing thesis, the probabilistic operator does bring more distinguishing power when it comes to interaction theory.

4.3   Expressiveness Between Randomized Models

For two classical models M, N, if we know M $\sqsubseteq$ N, what is the relative expressiveness between their respectively randomized extensions, i.e., RM and RN? We start by exploring the relation between RC and RVPC. It is known that C $\sqsubseteq$ VPC [3]. The proof is relatively easy as in C absolute equality coincides with structural equivalence. However as this is not the case for RC, we will have to use the external characterization of RC instead.

Proposition 3. RC $\sqsubseteq$ RVPC.

Proof. The proof is carried out by building the encoding and then showing it is not only subbisimilar (Definition 12) but also *deterministic*. The key for proving C $\sqsubseteq$ VPC is an encoding $\mathcal{E}$ from recursive functions into $\mathbb{P}_{\text{VPC}}$ [2,3], where every function is explained as a VPC process which can get their parameters via input channels. This encoding relys on the fact that only guarded choices are allowed. Then if the function is defined on this input, the resulting value will be outputted. If the function is undefined, the corresponding VPC process diverges. The only possible external actions for realizing recursive functions in $\mathcal{E}$ are input and output (if the computation ends). In $\mathcal{E}$ all internal actions are state-preserving, i.e., encoding $\mathcal{E}$ satisfies:

1. If $f(\underline{m}) = \underline{n}$ then $\mathcal{E}(F_a^b(f(x))) \xrightarrow{a(\hat{m})} \Longrightarrow_{=\text{VPC}} \bar{b}(\hat{n})$.
2. If $f(\underline{m})$ is undefined, then $\mathcal{E}(F_a^b(f(x))) \xrightarrow{a(\hat{m})} \Longrightarrow_{=\text{VPC}} (c)(!c(x)|!\bar{c}(\hat{0}))$.

Based on this we give the extended encoding $\mathcal{E}'$ from RC into RVPC :

$$\mathcal{E}'(0) \overset{\text{def}}{=} 0 \qquad\qquad \mathcal{E}'(\bar{a}(\underline{i})) \overset{\text{def}}{=} \bar{a}(\hat{i})$$

$$\mathcal{E}'(\Omega) \overset{\text{def}}{=} (c)(!c(x) \mid !\bar{c}(\hat{0})) \qquad \mathcal{E}'(F_a^b(f(x))) \overset{\text{def}}{=} \mathcal{E}(F_a^b(f(x)))$$

$$\mathcal{E}'(P \mid Q) \overset{\text{def}}{=} \mathcal{E}'(P) \mid \mathcal{E}'(Q) \qquad \mathcal{E}'(\bigoplus_{i \in I} q_i \tau.P_i) \overset{\text{def}}{=} \bigoplus_{i \in I} q_i \tau.\mathcal{E}'(P_i).$$

For clarity we introduce some symbolic sugar. We extend $\mathcal{E}'$ to specify action labels (marked by subscript l): first we use τ_Ω to specify a divergent silent action, i.e. silent actions in $\Omega \xrightarrow{\tau} \Omega$. Then we introduce $\mathcal{E}'_l(\bar{a}(\underline{i})) \overset{\text{def}}{=} \bar{a}(\hat{i})$, $\mathcal{E}'_l(a(\underline{i})) \overset{\text{def}}{=} a(\hat{i})$, $\mathcal{E}'_l(\tau_\Omega) \overset{\text{def}}{=} \tau_\Omega$ and $\mathcal{E}'_l(q_i\tau) \overset{\text{def}}{=} q_i\tau$. Obviously $\mathcal{E}'_l$ is reversible. Intuitively, we will use T_l to represent the set of actions in the encoding which have an syntactical pre-image in RC. That is, if a label does not belong to T_l, then it is a *new* action introduced by encoding. Surely all such new actions are internal actions introduced by $\mathcal{E}$ to realize computation.

Next, we show $\mathcal{E}'$ provides a subbisimilarity from RC to RVPC. We start by verifying the following easy yet useful claim.

Claim. The structural encoding is *deterministic* in the sense that:

1. All external actions in the target process must come from processes of the form $\mathcal{E}'(\bar{a}(\hat{i}) \mid P)$ or $\mathcal{E}'(F_a^b(f(x)) \mid P)$. In another word, there is a one-to-one correspondence between external actions in the source and target calculi.

2. If $P \xrightarrow{\lambda} P'$, then $\mathcal{E}'(P) \xrightarrow{\mathcal{E}'_l(\lambda)} \Longrightarrow_{\text{RVPC}} \mathcal{E}'(P')$.

3. If $\mathcal{E}'(P) \xrightarrow{\ell_1} \ldots \xrightarrow{\ell_{i-1}} \xrightarrow{\ell_i}$ with $\ell_1, \ldots, \ell_{i-1} \in T_l$ while $\ell_i \notin T_l$, then $\ell_i = \tau$ and there exists $P' \in \text{RC}$ such that: $\mathcal{E}'(P) \xrightarrow{\ell_1} \ldots \xrightarrow{\ell_{i-1}} \xrightarrow{\ell_i} \Longrightarrow_{\text{RVPC}} \Longrightarrow_{\text{RVPC}} \equiv \mathcal{E}'(P')$ and $P \xrightarrow{\mathcal{E}'^{-1}_l(\ell_1)} \ldots \xrightarrow{\mathcal{E}'^{-1}_{l-1}(\ell_{i-1})} P'$.

4. Any ϵ-tree rooted with P in RC will have an isomorphic ϵ-tree rooted with $\mathcal{E}'(P)$ in RVPC.

The conditions of determinisitic encoding are carefully checked and detailed proof are given in Appendix. B.1.

The conception of *deterministic encoding* can be generalized to encodings between any two models. A careful look into the proof of Proposition 3 shows that, the key property we have used, the encoding between two models, is not just a subbisimilarity but also deterministic. We can generalize the result into the following theorem.

Theorem 4. *If* $M \sqsubseteq N$ *and there exists deterministic encoding from* M *into* N, *then* $RM \sqsubseteq RN$.

Remark 1. As the current description for *deterministic* do rely on models, especially the correspondence between external actions, Theorem 4 seems less elegant compared to Theorem 3. Yet as a matter of fact, all encoding schemes in [3] for establishing subbisimilarity are deterministic. However, finding a model independent way to characterize deterministic encoding is an interesting problem.

We end this section with Fig. 3. It gives a pictorial comparison of the work in [3] and this paper. An arrow from one model to another stands for the subbisimilarity relation from the former to the latter. Models are independent otherwise. All models in Fig. 3 are interactively complete. Again, one can refer to [3] for more explanations about each classical model.

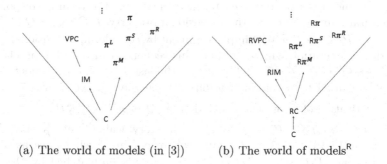

(a) The world of models (in [3])   (b) The world of models^R

Fig. 3. Comparison of the (non-)probabilistic theory of interaction

5 Concluding Remarks

In this paper we give the interaction theory for randomized models, including equality theory within one model and expressiveness theory for model comparison. We extend both absolute equality and subbisimilarity relation to randomized models, where all extensions are model independent. Some general expressiveness results are given, including that any interactive model is strictly less expressive than its randomized version, and subbisimilarity between two classical models can be lifted to their randomized versions as long as one can find an encoding satisfying some nice properties. We believe our work contributes in developing a more comprehensive understanding of process calculi. In the future, we would like to explore several topics on randomized process models, such as how to integrate testing semantics into this framework. Besides, we believe the existence of deterministic encoding is sufficient yet not necessary for the proof of Theorem 4. It would be interesting to dig deeper into this topic.

Acknowledgement. We are grateful to Prof. Yuxi Fu for valuable discussions and suggestions. We also thank the anonymous referees for their detailed comments. The support from the National Science Foundation of China (62072299) is acknowledged.

Appendix

A Proofs for Generalized Equality Theory

A.1 Proof of Theorem 1

Let $\mathcal{R} \overset{\text{def}}{=} \{(P, Q) \mid P =_{\mathsf{RVPC}} Q\}$. It will be enough to show that $\mathcal{R}$ is a RVPC-bisimulation. According to Definitions 2, 3, 8, we only need to discuss the cases when transitions are caused by observable actions $\beta \in \mathsf{Act}^e$.

1. $\beta = a(t)$. Suppose $P \leadsto_{\mathcal{R}} \xrightarrow{a(t)} P''$ with every leaf P'' of $t_{\mathcal{R}}^P$. Let $C = \bar{a}(t') + \bar{a}(t).\bar{b}(\hat{0})$ with $\mathsf{Th} \vdash t' \neq t$, where b is a fresh name which does not occur in P or Q, and $\hat{0}$ is just any fixed term, for instance, the term corresponding to natural number zero. By the extensional property, $P|C =_{\mathsf{RVPC}} Q|C$. Thus $P|C \leadsto_{\mathcal{R}} P''|C \xrightarrow{\tau} P'|\bar{b}(\hat{0})$. Simple argument by considering extensional under restriction operation will show that, this sequence can only be matched by $Q|C \leadsto_{\mathcal{R}} Q''|C \xrightarrow{\tau} Q'|\bar{b}(\hat{0}) \mathcal{R} P'|\bar{b}(\hat{0})$. As the last state-changing silent action must be caused by a communication between the context C (via $\bar{a}(t)$) and some derivation of Q, we can conclude that $Q \leadsto_{\mathcal{R}} \xrightarrow{a(t)} Q'\mathcal{R}P'$.

2. $\beta = \bar{a}(t)$. Suppose $P \leadsto_{\mathcal{R}} \xrightarrow{\bar{a}(t)} P'$ with every leaf P'' of $t_{\mathcal{R}}^P$. Let $D = a(x).[x = t]\bar{c}(\hat{0}) + a(x).[x \neq t]\bar{d}(\hat{0})$, where c, d are fresh names as above. The sequence $P|D \leadsto_{\mathcal{R}} P''|D \xrightarrow{\tau} P'|\bar{c}(\hat{0})$ can only be matched by $Q|D \leadsto_{\mathcal{R}} Q''|D \xrightarrow{\tau} Q'|\bar{c}(\hat{0}) \mathcal{R} P'|\bar{c}(\hat{0})$. Similar to the above argument, we can have that $Q \leadsto_{\mathcal{R}} \xrightarrow{\bar{a}(t)} Q'\mathcal{R}P'$ as desired.

Thus $=_{\mathsf{RVPC}} \subseteq \simeq_{\mathsf{RVPC}}$ holds. The two equivalence relations coincides.

A.2   Proof of Theorem 2

$\simeq_{\text{RC}}$ is bisimilar and divergence-sensitive by its definition. It is also equipollent for if only one of the two RC processes is observable, then the observable one can do an external action while the other cannot, which betrays bisimilar property. To show it is also extensional, again we consider the relation $\mathcal{R}^\circ \overset{\text{def}}{=} (\mathcal{R} \cup \simeq_{\text{RC}})^*$ as in [4], it is relatively easier because we only need to verify the composition case. Thus $\simeq_{\text{RC}} \subseteq =_{\text{RC}}$.

For the other direction, let $\mathcal{R} \overset{\text{def}}{=} \{(P, Q) \mid P =_{\text{RC}} Q\}$. It will be enough to show that $\mathcal{R}$ is a RC-bisimulation. Again the correspondence for silent moves (including probabilistic choices) has been satisfied by definition. We only need to discuss the cases when transitions are caused by some external actions $\beta \in \text{Act}_{\mathbb{C}}^e$.

1. $\beta = a(\underline{m})$. Suppose $P \rightsquigarrow_\mathcal{R} P'' \xrightarrow{a(\underline{m})} P'$ with every leaf P'' of $t_\mathcal{R}^P$. Surely $P'' \equiv F_a^b(f)|\tilde{P}$ for some function $f(\underline{m}) = \underline{n}$ and process $\tilde{P}$. The transitions can only be matched by $Q \rightsquigarrow_\mathcal{R} Q'' =_{\text{RC}} P''$. By extensional property we have $P''|\bar{a}(\underline{m}) =_{\text{RC}} Q''|\bar{a}(\underline{m})$. Next $P''|\bar{a}(\underline{m}) \xrightarrow{\tau} P'$ is a state-changing communication between P'' and $\bar{a}(\underline{m})$. $Q''|\bar{a}(\underline{m})$ will simulate this by reaching some state $Q''' =_{\text{RC}} P'$. Thus $Q''|\bar{a}(\underline{m})$ should do a pair of input-output communication where the input action $x(y)$ can only come from Q''. To verify that $x(y)$ is of the form $a(\underline{m})$, we take the previous analysis that $P''|\bar{a}(\underline{m})$ and $Q''|\bar{a}(\underline{m})$ should have the same multiset of executable output components, so does P' and Q'''. Therefore exactly one copy of $\bar{a}(\underline{m})$ will be consumed to get Q'''. Finally we can conclude $Q \rightsquigarrow_\mathcal{R} Q'' \xrightarrow{a(\underline{m})} Q' \equiv Q'''\mathcal{R}P'$

2. $\beta = \bar{a}(\underline{n})$. Suppose $P \rightsquigarrow_\mathcal{R} \xrightarrow{\bar{a}(\underline{n})} P'$ with every leaf P'' of $t_\mathcal{R}^P$. The proof is similar to the last case by composing with the process $F_a^e(h(x))$ where e is a fresh name, $h(\underline{x}) = \underline{0}$ if $x = \underline{n}$ and undefined otherwise. We can have that $Q \rightsquigarrow_\mathcal{R} \xrightarrow{\bar{a}(\underline{n})} Q'\mathcal{R}P'$ as desired.

Thus we also have $=_{\text{RC}} \subseteq \simeq_{\text{RC}}$. This finishes the proof.

B   Proofs for Generalized Expressiveness Theory

B.1   Proof of Proposition 3

Here we check the conditions of deterministic encoding. Correctness of items 1, 2, 3 is clear from the definition of $\mathcal{E}'$. To verify the 4th item, just note that $\mathcal{E}'$ does not introduce any new probabilistic silent action. Actually the first three items together is (a stronger version of) the so-called *operation correspondence* [12]. To the last item about ϵ-tree, it should be clear that $\mathcal{E}'\left(\bigoplus_{i \in I} q_i \tau.P_i\right) \overset{\text{def}}{=} \bigoplus_{i \in I} q_i \tau.\mathcal{E}'(P_i)$ is a natural encoding strategy for any randomized models whose randomness comes from the operator given in (1).

For the soundness, we consider the following relation:

$$\mathcal{R}^\bullet = \left\{ (\mathcal{E}'(P), \mathcal{E}'(Q)) \mid P, Q \in \mathbb{P}_{\text{RC}} \wedge P \simeq_{\text{RC}} Q \right\}.$$

We show that $\mathcal{R} \overset{\text{def}}{=} (\simeq_{\text{RVPC}}; \mathcal{R}^\bullet; \simeq_{\text{RVPC}} \cup \simeq_{\text{RVPC}})^*$ is a branching bisimulation. It is easy to show that $\mathcal{R}$ is an equivalence relation. For two $M, N \in \mathbb{P}_{\text{RVPC}}$, if $M\mathcal{R}N$, w.l.o.g, assume $M \simeq_{\text{RVPC}} \mathcal{E}'(P_1) \; \mathcal{R}^\bullet \; \mathcal{E}'(P_2) \simeq_{\text{RVPC}} N$ for some $P_1 \simeq_{\text{RC}} P_2$. Then we show M and N can simulate each other and their derivations keep in $\mathcal{R}$. We only give details for the output case as the others are similar.

- If $M \rightsquigarrow_{\simeq_{\text{RVPC}}} \overset{\bar{a}(\hat{i})}{\longrightarrow} [M']_{\simeq_{\text{RVPC}}}$, then as we have discussed earlier, all new internal actions introduced by $\mathcal{E}'$ are deterministic and the external actions are just one-to-one between RC and RVPC processes. Thus from $M \simeq_{\text{RVPC}} \mathcal{E}'(P_1)$,

    we have that $\mathcal{E}'(P_1) \rightsquigarrow_{\simeq_{\text{RVPC}}} \overset{\bar{a}(\hat{i})}{\longrightarrow} [\mathcal{E}'(P_1')]_{\simeq_{\text{RVPC}}} = [M']_{\simeq_{\text{RVPC}}}$ for some $P_1' \in$ $\mathbb{P}_{\text{RC}}$, and $P_1 \rightsquigarrow_{\simeq_{\text{RC}}} \overset{\bar{a}(\hat{i})}{\longrightarrow} [P_1']_{\simeq_{\text{RC}}}$. The trick is that, for the silent moves in $M \rightsquigarrow_{\simeq_{\text{RVPC}}} \overset{\bar{a}(\hat{i})}{\longrightarrow} [M']_{\simeq_{\text{RVPC}}}$ and $\mathcal{E}'(P_1) \rightsquigarrow_{\simeq_{\text{RVPC}}} \overset{\bar{a}(\hat{i})}{\longrightarrow} [\mathcal{E}'(P_1')]_{\simeq_{\text{RVPC}}} = [M']_{\simeq_{\text{RVPC}}}$, all $\simeq_{\text{RVPC}}$ equivalence classes can be replaced by $\mathcal{R}$-equivalence safely, for it is clear that $\simeq_{\text{RVPC}} \subseteq \mathcal{R}$. Then by the condition that $P_1 \simeq_{\text{RC}} P_2$, we have $P_2 \rightsquigarrow_{\simeq_{\text{RC}}} \overset{\bar{a}(\hat{i})}{\longrightarrow} [P_2']_{\simeq_{\text{RC}}} = [P_1']_{\simeq_{\text{RC}}}$ for some $P_2' \in \mathbb{P}_{\text{RC}}$. From the action correspondence, $\mathcal{E}'(P_2)$ can simulate the ϵ-tree rooted with $\mathcal{E}'(P_1)$, and then each leaf can do the $\bar{a}(\hat{i})$ action and reach some process equivalent to $\mathcal{E}'(P_2')$.

    Finally as $\mathcal{E}'(P_2) \simeq_{\text{RVPC}} N$, we have $N \rightsquigarrow_{\simeq_{\text{RVPC}}} \overset{\bar{a}(\hat{i})}{\longrightarrow} [N']_{\simeq_{\text{RVPC}}} = [\mathcal{E}'(P_2')]_{\simeq_{\text{RVPC}}}$. Similarly we can replace $\simeq_{\text{RVPC}}$ by $\mathcal{R}$-equivalence as well. Besides, as every leaf is equivalent to M' (in the ϵ-tree rooted with M), we have found the sequence $M' \simeq_{\text{RVPC}} \mathcal{E}'(P_1')\mathcal{R}^\bullet\mathcal{E}'(P_2') \simeq_{\text{RVPC}} N'$, it follows that $M' \; \mathcal{R} \; N'$. Thus $[M']_{\mathcal{R}} = [N']_{\mathcal{R}}$.

    Combing the above analysis, for any $M \rightsquigarrow_{\mathcal{R}} \overset{\bar{a}(\hat{i})}{\longrightarrow} [M']_{\mathcal{R}}$, we have $N \rightsquigarrow_{\mathcal{R}} \overset{\bar{a}(\hat{i})}{\longrightarrow}$ $[N']_{\mathcal{R}} = [M']_{\mathcal{R}}$. This shows that $\mathcal{R} \subseteq \simeq_{\text{RVPC}}$.

Now it is easy to prove that $\mathcal{E}'; =_{\text{RVPC}}$ is bisimilar, equipollent and divergence-sensitive. The extensional property is direct by definition. Thus, $\mathcal{E}'; =_{\text{RVPC}}$ is a subbisimilarity from RC to RVPC. It follows that RC $\sqsubseteq$ RVPC.

References

1. Deng, Y.: Semantics of Probabilistic Processes: An Operational Approach. Springer, Heidelberg (2014). https://doi.org/10.1007/978-3-662-45198-4
2. Fu, Y.: The value-passing calculus. In: Liu, Z., Woodcock, J., Zhu, H. (eds.) Theories of Programming and Formal Methods. LNCS, vol. 8051, pp. 166–195. Springer, Heidelberg (2013). https://doi.org/10.1007/978-3-642-39698-4_11
3. Fu, Y.: Theory of interaction. Theor. Comput. Sci. **611**, 1–49 (2016)
4. Fu, Y.: Model independent approach to probabilistic models. Theor. Comput. Sci. **869**, 181–194 (2021)
5. Fu, Y., Lu, H.: On the expressiveness of interaction. Theoret. Comput. Sci. **411**, 1387–1451 (2010)
6. Giacalone, A., Jou, C.C., Smolka, S.A.: Algebraic reasoning for probabilistic concurrent systems. In: Proceeding IFIP TC2 Working Conference on Programming Concepts and Methods. Citeseer (1990)

7. van Glabbeek, R.: Linear time-branching time spectrum i. In: Handbook of Process Algebra, pp. 3–99. North-Holland (2001)
8. van Glabbeek, R.: A theory of encodings and expressiveness (extended abstract). In: Foundations of Software Science and Computation Structures - 21st International Conference, FOSSACS 2018, pp. 183–202 (2018)
9. van Glabbeek, R., Luttik, B., Trčka, N.: Branching bisimilarity with explicit divergence. Fundam. Inf. **93**(4), 371–392 (2009)
10. van Glabbeek, R.J., Weijland, W.P.: Branching time and abstraction in bisimulation semantics. J. ACM **43**(3), 555–600 (1996)
11. Glabbeek, R.J.: The linear time — branching time spectrum II. In: Best, E. (ed.) CONCUR 1993. LNCS, vol. 715, pp. 66–81. Springer, Heidelberg (1993). https://doi.org/10.1007/3-540-57208-2_6
12. Gorla, D.: Towards a unified approach to encodability and separation results for process calculi. In: van Breugel, F., Chechik, M. (eds.) CONCUR 2008. LNCS, vol. 5201, pp. 492–507. Springer, Heidelberg (2008). https://doi.org/10.1007/978-3-540-85361-9_38
13. Gorla, D., Nestman, U.: Full abstraction for expressiveness: history, myths and facts. Math. Struct. Comput. Sci. **26**(4), 639–654 (2016)
14. Hansson, H., Jonsson, B.: A calculus for communicating systems with time and probabilities. In: 1990 Proceedings 11th Real-Time Systems Symposium, pp. 278–287. IEEE (1990)
15. Herescu, O.M., Palamidessi, C.: Probabilistic asynchronous π Calculus. In: Tiuryn, J. (ed.) FoSSaCS 2000. LNCS, vol. 1784, pp. 146–160. Springer, Heidelberg (2000). https://doi.org/10.1007/3-540-46432-8_10
16. Xue, J., Long, H., Fu, Y.: Remark on some π variants. In: Larsen, K.G., Sokolsky, O., Wang, J. (eds.) SETTA 2017. LNCS, vol. 10606, pp. 183–199. Springer, Cham (2017). https://doi.org/10.1007/978-3-319-69483-2_11
17. Lanese, I., Pérez, J.A., Sangiorgi, D., Schmitt, A.: On the expressiveness and decidability of higher-order process calculi. Inf. Comput. **209**(2), 198–226 (2011)
18. Larsen, K.G., Skou, A.: Bisimulation through probabilistic testing. Inf. Comput. **94**(1), 1–28 (1991)
19. Milner, R. (ed.): A Calculus of Communicating Systems. LNCS, vol. 92. Springer, Heidelberg (1980). https://doi.org/10.1007/3-540-10235-3
20. Milner, R., Parrow, J., Walker, D.: A calculus of mobile processes (parts i and ii). Inf. Comput. **100**(1), 1–77 (1992)
21. De Nicola, R., Montanari, U., Vaandrager, F.: Back and forth bisimulations. In: Baeten, J.C.M., Klop, J.W. (eds.) CONCUR 1990. LNCS, vol. 458, pp. 152–165. Springer, Heidelberg (1990). https://doi.org/10.1007/BFb0039058
22. Sangiorgi, D.: Expressing Mobility in Process Algebras: First-Order and Higher-Order Paradigms. Ph.D. thesis, University of Edinburgh (1992)
23. Segala, R., Lynch, N.: Probabilistic simulations for probabilistic processes. Nordic J. Comput. **2**(2), 250–273 (1995)
24. Zhang, W., Long, H., Xu, X.: Uniform random process model revisited. In: Proceedings of the 17th Asian Symposium on Programming Languages and Systems (APLAS 2019), pp. 388–404 (2019). https://doi.org/10.1007/978-3-030-34175-6_20

Extracting Weighted Finite Automata from Recurrent Neural Networks for Natural Languages

Zeming Wei, Xiyue Zhang, and Meng Sun$^{(\boxtimes)}$

Peking University, Beijing 100871, China
weizeming@stu.pku.edu.cn, {zhangxiyue,sunm}@pku.edu.cn

Abstract. Recurrent Neural Networks (RNNs) have achieved tremendous success in sequential data processing. However, it is quite challenging to interpret and verify RNNs' behaviors directly. To this end, many efforts have been made to extract finite automata from RNNs. Existing approaches such as exact learning are effective in extracting finite-state models to characterize the state dynamics of RNNs for formal languages, but are limited in the scalability to process natural languages. Compositional approaches that are scablable to natural languages fall short in extraction precision. In this paper, we identify the transition sparsity problem that heavily impacts the extraction precision. To address this problem, we propose a transition rule extraction approach, which is scalable to natural language processing models and effective in improving extraction precision. Specifically, we propose an empirical method to complement the missing rules in the transition diagram. In addition, we further adjust the transition matrices to enhance the context-aware ability of the extracted weighted finite automaton (WFA). Finally, we propose two data augmentation tactics to track more dynamic behaviors of the target RNN. Experiments on two popular natural language datasets show that our method can extract WFA from RNN for natural language processing with better precision than existing approaches. Our code is available at https://github.com/weizeming/Extract_WFA_from_RNN_for_NL.

Keywords: Abstraction · Weighted finite automata · Natural language models

1 Introduction

In the last decade, deep learning (DL) has been widely deployed in a range of applications, such as image processing [12], speech recognition [1] and natural language processing [11]. In particular, recurrent neural networks (RNNs) achieve great success in sequential data processing, e.g., time series forecasting [5], text classification [24] and language translation [6]. However, the complex internal design and gate control of RNNs make the interpretation and verification of their behaviors rather challenging. To this end, much progress has been

© Springer Nature Switzerland AG 2022
A. Riesco and M. Zhang (Eds.): ICFEM 2022, LNCS 13478, pp. 370–385, 2022.
https://doi.org/10.1007/978-3-031-17244-1_22

made to abstract RNN as a finite automaton, which is a finite state model with explicit states and transition matrix to characterize the behaviours of RNN in processing sequential data. The extracted automaton also provides a practical foundation for analyzing and verifying RNN behaviors, based on which existing mature techniques, such as logical formalism [10] and model checking [3], can be leveraged for RNN analysis.

Up to the present, a series of extraction approaches leverage explicit learning algorithms (e.g., L^* algorithm [2]) to extract a surrogate model of RNN. Such exact learning procedure has achieved great success in capturing the state dynamics of RNNs for processing formal languages [17,25,26]. However, the computational complexity of the exact learning algorithm limits its scalability to construct abstract models from RNNs for natural language tasks.

Another technical line of automata extraction from RNNs is the compositional approach, which uses unsupervised learning algorithms to obtain discrete partitions of RNNs' state vectors and construct the transition diagram based on the discrete clusters and concrete state dynamics of RNNs. This approach demonstrates better scalability and has been applied to robustness analysis and repairment of RNNs on large-scale tasks [7–9,22,23,27].

As a trade-off to the computational complexity, the compositional approach is faced with the problem of extraction consistency. Moreover, the alphabet size of natural language datasets is far larger than formal languages, but the extraction procedure is based on finite (sequential) data. As a result, the transition dynamics are usually scarce when processing low-frequency tokens (words).

However, the transition sparsity of the extracted automata for natural language tasks is yet to be addressed. In addition, state-of-the-art RNNs such as long short-term memory networks [13] show their great advantages on tracking long term context dependency for natural language processing, but the abstraction procedure inevitably leads to context information loss. This motivates us to propose a heuristic method for transition rule adjustment to enhance the context-aware ability of the extracted model.

In this paper, we propose an approach to extracting transition rules of weighted finite automata from RNNs for natural languages with a focus on the transition sparsity problem and the loss of context dependency. Empirical investigation in Sect. 5 shows that the sparsity problem of transition diagram severely impacts the behavior consistency between RNN and the extracted model. To deal with the transition sparsity problem that no transition rules are learned at a certain state for a certain word, which we refer to as *missing rows* in transition matrices, we propose a novel method to fill in the transition rules for the missing rows based on the semantics of abstract states. Further, in order to enhance the context awareness ability of WFA, we adjust the transition matrices to preserve part of the context information from the previous state, especially in the case of transition sparsity when the current transition rules cannot be relied on completely. Finally, we propose two tactics to augment the training samples to learn more transition behaviors of RNNs, which also alleviate the transition sparsity problem. Overall, our approach for transition rule extraction leads to better extraction consistency and can be applied to natural language tasks.

To summarize, our main contributions are:

(a) A novel approach to extracting transition rules of WFA from RNNs to address the transition sparsity problem;
(b) An heuristic method of adjusting transition rules to enhance the context-aware ability of WFA;
(c) A data augmentation method on training samples to track more transition behaviors of RNNs.

The organization of this paper is as follows. In Sect. 2, we show preliminaries about recurrent neural networks, weighted finite automata, and related notations and concepts. In Sect. 3, we present our transition rule extraction approach, including a generic outline on the automata extraction procedure, the transition rule complement approach for transition sparsity, the transition rule adjustment method for context-aware ability enhancement. We then present the data augmentation tactics in Sect. 4 to reinforce the learning of dynamic behaviors from RNNs, along with the computational complexity analysis of the overall extraction approach. In Sect. 5, we present the experimental evaluation towards the extraction consistency of our approach on two natural language tasks. Finally, we discuss related works in Sect. 6 and conclude our work in Sect. 7.

2   Preliminaries

In this section, we present the notations and definitions that will be used throughout the paper.

Given a finite alphabet Σ, we use Σ^* to denote the set of sequences over Σ and ε to denote the empty sequence. For $w \in \Sigma^*$, we use $|w|$ to denote its length, its i-th word as w_i and its prefix with length i as $w[:i]$. For $x \in \Sigma$, $w \cdot x$ represents the concatenation of w and x.

Definition 1 (RNN). *A Recurrent Neural Network (RNN) for natural language processing is a tuple $\mathcal{R} = (\mathcal{X}, \mathcal{S}, \mathcal{O}, f, p)$, where $\mathcal{X}$ is the input space; $\mathcal{S}$ is the internal state space; $\mathcal{O}$ is the probabilistic output space; $f : \mathcal{S} \times \mathcal{X} \rightarrow \mathcal{S}$ is the transition function; $p : \mathcal{S} \rightarrow \mathcal{O}$ is the prediction function.*

RNN Configuration. In this paper, we consider RNN as a black-box model and focus on its stepwise probabilistic output for each input sequence. The following definition of configuration characterizes the probabilistic outputs in response to a sequential input fed to RNN. Given an alphabet Σ, let $\xi : \Sigma \rightarrow \mathcal{X}$ be the function that maps each word in Σ to its embedding vector in $\mathcal{X}$. We define $f^* : \mathcal{S} \times \Sigma^* \rightarrow \mathcal{S}$ recursively as $f^*(s_0, \xi(w \cdot x)) = f(f^*(s_0, \xi(w)), \xi(x))$ and $f^*(s_0, \varepsilon) = s_0$, where s_0 is the initial state of $\mathcal{R}$. The RNN configuration $\delta : \Sigma^* \rightarrow \mathcal{O}$ is defined as $\delta(w) = p(f^*(s_0, w))$.

Output Trace. To record the stepwise behavior of RNN when processing an input sequence w, we define the *Output Trace* of w, i.e., the probabilistic output sequence, as $T(w) = \{\delta(w[:i])\}_{i=1}^{|w|}$. The i-th item of $T(w)$ indicates the probabilistic output given by $\mathcal{R}$ after taking the prefix of w with length i as input.

Definition 2 (WFA). *Given a finite alphabet Σ, a Weighted Finite Automaton (WFA) over Σ is a tuple $\mathcal{A} = (\hat{S}, \Sigma, E, \hat{s}_0, I, F)$, where $\hat{S}$ is the finite set of abstract states; $E = \{E_\sigma | \sigma \in \Sigma\}$ is the set of transition matrix E_σ with size $|\hat{S}| \times |\hat{S}|$ for each token $\sigma \in \Sigma$; $\hat{s}_0 \in \hat{S}$ is the initial state; I is the initial vector, a row vector with size $|\hat{S}|$; F is the final vector, a column vector with size $|\hat{S}|$.*

Abstract States. Given a RNN $\mathcal{R}$ and a dataset $\mathcal{D}$, let $\hat{O}$ denote all stepwise probabilistic outputs given by executing $\mathcal{R}$ on $\mathcal{D}$, i.e. $\hat{O} = \bigcup_{w \in \mathcal{D}} T(w)$. The abstraction function $\lambda : \hat{O} \to \hat{S}$ maps each probabilistic output to an abstract state $\hat{s} \in \hat{S}$. As a result, the output set is divided into a number of abstract states by λ. For each $\hat{s} \in \hat{S}$, the state $\hat{s}$ has explicit semantics that the probabilistic outputs corresponding to $\hat{s}$ has similar distribution. In this paper, we leverage the *k-means* algorithm to construct the abstraction function. We cluster all probabilistic outputs in $\hat{O}$ into some abstract states. In this way, we construct the set of abstract states $\hat{S}$ with these discrete clusters and an initial state $\hat{s}_0$.

For a state $\hat{s} \in \hat{S}$, we define the *center* of $\hat{s}$ as the average value of the probabilistic outputs $\hat{o} \in \hat{O}$ which are mapped to $\hat{s}$. More formally, the center of $\hat{s}$ is defined as follows:

$$\rho(\hat{s}) = \underset{\lambda(\hat{o})=\hat{s}}{\mathrm{Avg}} \{\hat{o}\}.$$

The center $\rho(\hat{s})$ represents an approximation for the distribution tendency of probabilistic outputs $\hat{o}$ in $\hat{s}$. For each state $\hat{s} \in \hat{S}$, we use the center $\rho(\hat{s})$ as its weight, as the center captures an approximation of the distribution tendency of this state. Therefore, the final vector F is $(\rho(\hat{s}_0), \rho(\hat{s}_1), \cdots, \rho(\hat{s}_{|\hat{S}|-1}))^t$.

Abstract Transitions. In order to capture the dynamic behavior of RNN $\mathcal{R}$, we define the abstract transition as a triple $(\hat{s}, \sigma, \hat{s}')$ where the original state $\hat{s}$ is the abstract state corresponding to a specific output y, i.e. $\hat{s} = \lambda(y)$; σ is the next word of the input sequence to consume; $\hat{s}'$ is the destination state $\lambda(y')$ after $\mathcal{R}$ reads σ and outputs y'. We use T to denote the set of all abstract transitions tracked from the execution of $\mathcal{R}$ on training samples.

Abstract Transition Count Matrices. For each word $\sigma \in \Sigma$, the abstract transition count matrix of σ is a matrix $\hat{T}_\sigma$ with size $|\hat{S}| \times |\hat{S}|$. The count matrices records the number of times that each abstract transition triggered. Given the set of abstract transitions T, the count matrix of σ can be calculated as

$$\hat{T}_\sigma[i,j] = T.count((\hat{s}_i, \sigma, \hat{s}_j)), \quad 1 \leq i,j \leq |\hat{S}|.$$

As for the remaining components, the alphabet Σ is consistent with the alphabet of training set $\mathcal{D}$. The initial vector I is formulated according to the initial state $\hat{s}_0$.

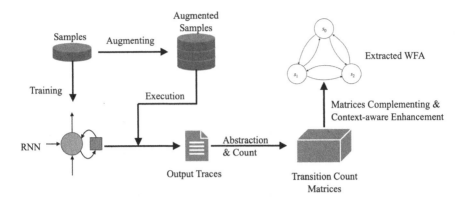

Fig. 1. An illustration of our approach to extracting WFA from RNN.

For an input sequence $w = w_1 w_2 \cdots w_n \in \Sigma^*$, the WFA will calculate its weight following

$$I \cdot E_{w_1} \cdot E_{w_2} \cdots E_{w_n} \cdot P.$$

3   Weighted Automata Extraction Scheme

3.1   Outline

We present the workflow of our extraction procedure in Fig. 1. As the first step, we generate augmented sample set $\mathcal{D}$ from the original training set $\mathcal{D}_0$ to enrich the transition dynamics of RNN behaviors and alleviate the transition sparsity. Then, we execute RNN $\mathcal{R}$ on the augmented sample set $\mathcal{D}$, and record the probabilistic output trace $T(w)$ of each input sentence $w \in \mathcal{D}$. With the output set $\hat{O} = \bigcup_{w \in \mathcal{D}} T(w)$, we cluster the probabilistic outputs into abstract states $\hat{S}$, and generate abstract transitions $\mathcal{T}$ from the output traces $\{T(w)|w \in \mathcal{D}\}$. All transitions constitute the abstract transition count matrices $\hat{T}_\sigma$ for all $\sigma \in \Sigma$.

Next, we construct the transition matrices $E = \{E_\sigma | \sigma \in \Sigma\}$. Based on the abstract states $\hat{S}$ and count matrices $\hat{T}$, we construct the transition matrix E_σ for each word $\sigma \in \Sigma$. Specifically, we use frequencies to calculate the transition probabilities. Suppose that there are n abstract states in $\hat{S}$. The i-th row of E_σ, which indicates the probabilistic transition distribution over states when $\mathcal{R}$ is in state $\hat{s}_i$ and consumes σ, is calculated as

$$E_\sigma[i, j] = \frac{\hat{T}_\sigma[i, j]}{\sum_{k=1}^{n} \hat{T}_\sigma[i, k]}. \tag{1}$$

This empirical rule faces the problem that the denominator of (1) could be zero, which means that the word σ never appears when the RNN $\mathcal{R}$ is in abstract state

$\hat{s}_i$. In this case, one should decide how to fill in the transition rule of the *missing rows* in E_σ. In Sect. 3.2, we present a novel approach for transition rule complement. Further, to preserve more contextual information in the case of transition sparsity, we propose an approach to enhancing the context-aware ability of WFA by adjusting the transition matrices, which is discussed in Sect. 3.3. Note that our approach is generic and could be applied to other RNNs besides the domain of natural language processing.

3.2   Missing Rows Complementing

Existing approaches for transition rule extraction usually face the problem of transition sparsity, i.e., *missing rows* in the transition diagram. In the context of formal languages, the probability of occurrence of missing rows is quite limited, since the size of the alphabet is small and each token in the alphabet can appear sufficient number of times. However, in the context of natural language processing, the occurrence of missing rows is quite frequent. The following proposition gives an approximation of the occurrence frequency of missing rows.

Proposition 1. *Assume an alphabet Σ with $m = |\Sigma|$ words, a natural language dataset $\mathcal{D}$ over Σ which has N words in total, a RNN $\mathcal{R}$ trained on $\mathcal{D}$, the extracted abstract states $\hat{S}$ and transitions $\mathcal{T}$. Let σ_i denote the i-th most frequent word occurred in $\mathcal{D}$ and $t_i = \mathcal{T}.count((*, \sigma_i, *))$ indicates the occurrence times of σ_i in $\mathcal{D}$. The median of $\{t_i | 1 \leq i \leq m\}$ can be estimated as*

$$t_{\lceil \frac{m}{2} \rceil} = \frac{2N}{m \cdot \ln m}.$$

Proof. The Zipf's law [21] shows that

$$\frac{t_i}{N} \approx \frac{i^{-1}}{\sum\limits_{k=1}^{m} k^{-1}}.$$

Note that $\sum\limits_{k=1}^{m} k^{-1} \approx \ln m$ and take i to be $\frac{m}{2}$, we complete our proof.

Example 1. In the QC news dataset [16], which has $m = 20317$ words in its alphabet and $N = 205927$ words in total, the median of $\{t_i\}$ is approximated to $\frac{2N}{m \cdot \ln m} \approx 2$. This indicates that about half of E_σ are constructed with no more than 2 transitions. In practice, the number of abstract states is usually far more than the transition numbers for these words, making most of rows of their transition matrices *missing rows*.

Filling the missing row with **0** is a simple solution, since no information were provided from the transitions. However, as estimated above, this solution will lead to the problem of transition sparsity, i.e., the transition matrices for uncommon words are nearly null. Consequently, if the input sequence includes some uncommon words, the weights over states tend to vanish. We refer to this solution as *null filling*.

Another simple idea is to use the uniform distribution over states for fairness. In [26], the uniform distribution is used as the transition distribution for unseen tokens in the context of formal language tasks. However, for natural language processing, this solution still loses information of the current word, despite that it avoids the weight vanishment over states. We refer to this solution as *uniform filling*. [29] uses the *synonym* transition distribution for an unseen token at a certain state. However, it increases the computation overhead when performing inference on test data, since it requires to calculate and sort the distance between the available tokens at a certain state and the unseen token.

To this end, we propose a novel approach to constructing the transition matrices based on two empirical observations. First, each abstract state $\hat{s} \in \hat{S}$ has explicit semantics, i.e. the probabilistic distribution over labels, and similar abstract states tend to share more similar transition behaviours. The similarity of abstract states is defined by their semantic distance as follows.

Definition 3 (State Distance). *For two abstract states $\hat{s}_1$ and $\hat{s}_2$, the distance between $\hat{s}_1$ and $\hat{s}_2$ is defined by the Euclidean distance between their center:*

$$dist(\hat{s}_1, \hat{s}_2) = \|\rho(\hat{s}_1) - \rho(\hat{s}_2)\|_2.$$

We calculate the distance between each pair of abstract states, which forms a *distance matrix* M where each element $M[i,j] = dist(\hat{s}_i, \hat{s}_j)$ for $1 \leq i, j \leq |\hat{S}|$. For a missing row in E_σ, following the heuristics that similar abstract states are more likely to have similar behaviors, we observe the transition behaviors from other abstract states, and simulate the missing transition behaviors weighted by distance between states. Particularly, in order to avoid numerical underflow, we leverage *softmin* on distance to bias the weight to states that share more similarity. Formally, for a missing row $E_\sigma[i]$, the weight of information set for another row $E_\sigma[j]$ is defined by $e^{-M[i,j]}$.

Second, it is also observed that sometimes the RNN just remains in the current state after reading a certain word. Intuitively, this is because part of words in the sentence do not deliver significant information in the task. Therefore, we consider simulating behaviors from other states whilst remaining in the current state with a certain probability.

In order to balance the trade-off between referring to behaviors from other states and remaining still, we introduce a hyper-parameter β named *reference rate*, such that when WFA is faced with a missing row, it has a probability of β to refer to the transition behaviors from other states, and in the meanwhile has a probability of $1 - \beta$ to keep still. We select the parameter β according to the proportion of self-transitions, i.e., transitions $(\hat{s}, \sigma, \hat{s}')$ in $\mathcal{T}$ where $\hat{s} = \hat{s}'$.

To sum up, the complete transition rule for the missing row is

$$E_\sigma[i,j] = \beta \cdot \frac{\sum_{k=1}^{n} e^{-M[i,k]} \cdot \hat{T}_\sigma[k,j]}{\sum_{l=1}^{n} \sum_{k=1}^{n} e^{-M[i,k]} \cdot \hat{T}_\sigma[k,l]} + (1-\beta) \cdot \delta_{i,j}. \tag{2}$$

Here $\delta_{i,j}$ is the Kronecker symbol:

$$\delta_{i,j} = \begin{cases} 1, & j = i \\ 0, & j \neq i \end{cases}.$$

In practice, we can calculate $\sum_{k=1}^{n} e^{-M[i,k]} \cdot \hat{T}_\sigma[k,j]$ for each j and then make division on their summation once and for all, which can reduce the computation overhead on transition rule extraction.

3.3 Context-Aware Enhancement

For NLP tasks, the memorization of long-term context information is crucial. One of the advantages of RNN and its advanced design LSTM networks is the ability to capture long-term dependency. We expect the extracted WFA to simulate the step-wise behaviors of RNNs whilst keeping track of context information along with the state transition. To this end, we propose an approach to adjusting the transition matrix such that the WFA can remain in the current state with a certain probability.

Specifically, we select a hyper-parameter $\alpha \in [0,1]$ as the *static probability*. For each word $\sigma \in \Sigma$ and its transition matrix E_σ, we replace the matrix with the *context-aware enhanced matrix* $\hat{E}_\sigma$ as follows:

$$\hat{E}_\sigma = \alpha \cdot I_n + (1 - \alpha) \cdot E_\sigma \tag{3}$$

where I_n is the identity matrix.

The context-aware enhanced matrix has explicit semantics. When the WFA is in state $\hat{s}_i$ and ready to process a new word σ, it has a probability of α (the *static probability*) to remain in $\hat{s}_i$, or follows the original transition distribution $E_\sigma[i,j]$ with a probability $1 - \alpha$.

Here we present an illustration of how context-aware enhanced matrices deliver long-term context information. Suppose that a context-aware enhanced WFA $\mathcal{A}$ is processing a sentence $w \in \Sigma^*$ with length $|w|$. We denote d_i as the distribution over all abstract states after $\mathcal{A}$ reads the prefix $w[:i]$, and particularly $d_0 = I$ is the initial vector of $\mathcal{A}$. We use Z_i to denote the decision made by $\mathcal{A}$ based on d_{i-1} and the original transition matrix E_{w_i}. Formally, $d_i = d_{i-1} \cdot \hat{E}_{w_i}$ and $Z_i = d_{i-1} \cdot E_{w_i}$.

The d_i can be regarded as the information obtained from the prefix $w[:i]$ by $\mathcal{A}$ before it consumes w_{i+1}, and Z_i can be considered as the decision made by $\mathcal{A}$ after it reads w_i.

Proposition 2. *The i-th step-wise information d_i which delivered by processing $w[:i]$ contains the decision information Z_j of prefix $w[:j]$ with a proportion of $(1-\alpha) \cdot \alpha^{i-j}$, $1 \leq j \leq i$.*

Proof. Since $\hat{E}_{w_i} = \alpha \cdot I_n + (1-\alpha) \cdot E_{w_i}$, we can calculate that

$$d_i = d_{i-1} \cdot \hat{E}_{w_i} = d_{i-1} \cdot [\alpha \cdot I_n + (1-\alpha) \cdot E_{w_i}] = \alpha \cdot d_{i-1} + (1-\alpha) \cdot Z_i. \tag{4}$$

Using (4) recursively, we have

$$d_i = (1 - \alpha) \sum_{k=1}^{i} \alpha^{i-k} \cdot Z_k + \alpha^i \cdot I.$$

This shows the information delivered by $w[: i]$ refers to the decision made by $\mathcal{A}$ on each prefix included in $w[: i]$, and the portion vanishes exponentially. The effectiveness of the context-aware transition matrix adjustment method will be discussed in Sect. 5.

The following example presents the complete approach for transition rule extraction, i.e., to generate the transition matrix $\hat{E}_\sigma$ with the missing row filled in and context enhanced, from the count matrix $\hat{T}_\sigma$ for a word $\sigma \in \Sigma$.

Example 2. Assume that there are three abstract states in $\hat{S} = \{\hat{s}_1, \hat{s}_2, \hat{s}_3\}$. Suppose the count matrix for σ is $\hat{T}_\sigma$.

$$\hat{T}_\sigma = \begin{bmatrix} 1 & 3 & 0 \\ 1 & 1 & 0 \\ 0 & 0 & 0 \end{bmatrix}, E_\sigma = \begin{bmatrix} 0.25 & 0.75 & 0 \\ 0.5 & 0.5 & 0 \\ 0.15 & 0.35 & 0.5 \end{bmatrix}, \hat{E}_\sigma = \begin{bmatrix} 0.4 & 0.6 & 0 \\ 0.4 & 0.6 & 0 \\ 0.12 & 0.28 & 0.6 \end{bmatrix}.$$

For the first two rows (states), there exist transitions for σ, thus we can calculate the transition distribution of these two rows in E_σ in the usual way. However, the third row is a *missing row*. We set the *reference rate* as $\beta = 0.5$, and suppose that the distance between states satisfies $e^{-M[1,3]} = 2e^{-M[2,3]}$, generally indicating the distance between $\hat{s}_1$ and $\hat{s}_3$ is nearer than $\hat{s}_2$ and $\hat{s}_3$. With the transitions from $\hat{s}_1$ and $\hat{s}_2$, we can complement the transition rule of the third row in E_σ through (2). The result shows that the behavior from $\hat{s}_3$ is more similar to $\hat{s}_1$ than $\hat{s}_2$, due to the nearer distance. Finally, we construct $\hat{E}_\sigma$ with E_σ. Here we take the *static probability* $\alpha = 0.2$, thus $\hat{E}_\sigma = 0.2 \cdot I_3 + 0.8 \cdot E_\sigma$. The result shows that the WFA with $\hat{E}_\sigma$ has higher probability to remain in the current state after consuming σ, which can preserve more information from the prefix before σ.

4   Data Augmentation

Our proposed approach for transition rule extraction provides a solution to the transition sparsity problem. Still, we hope to learn more dynamic transition behaviors from the target RNN, especially for the words with relatively low frequency to characterize their transition dynamics sufficiently based on the finite data samples. Different from formal languages, we can generate more natural language samples automatically, as long as the augmented sequential data are sensible with clear semantics and compatible with the original learning task. Based on the augmented samples, we are able to track more behaviors of the RNN and build the abstract model with higher precision. In this section, we introduce two data augmentation tactics for natural language processing tasks: *Synonym Replacement* and *Dropout*.

Synonym Replacement. Based on the distance quantization among the word embedding vectors, we can obtain a list of synonyms for each word in Σ. For a word $\sigma \in \Sigma$, the *synonyms* of w are defined as the top k most similar words of σ in Σ, where k is a hyper-parameter. The similarity among the words is calculated based on the Euclidean distance between the word embedding vectors over Σ.

Given a dataset $\mathcal{D}_0$ over Σ, for each sentence $w \in \mathcal{D}_0$, we generate a new sentence w' by replacing some words in w with their synonyms. Note that we hope that the uncommon words in Σ should appear more times, so as to gather more dynamic behaviors of RNNs when processing such words. Therefore, we set the probability that a certain word $\sigma \in w$ gets replaced to be in a negative correlation to its frequency of occurrence, i.e. the i-th most frequent word is replaced with a probability $\frac{1}{i+1}$.

Dropout. Inspired by the regularization technique *dropout*, we also propose a similar tactic to generate new sentences from $\mathcal{D}_0$. Initially, we introduce a new word named *unknown word* and denote it as $\langle \textbf{unk} \rangle$. For the sentence in $w \in \mathcal{D}_0$ that has been processed by synonym replacing, we further replace the words that hasn't been replaced with $\langle \textbf{unk} \rangle$ with a certain probability. Finally, new sentences generated by both synonym replacement and dropout form the augmented dataset $\mathcal{D}$.

With the dropout tactic, we can observe the behaviors of RNNs when it processes an unknown word $\hat{\sigma} \notin \Sigma$ that hasn't appeared in $\mathcal{D}_0$. Therefore, the extracted WFA can also show better generalization ability. An example of generating a new sentence from $\mathcal{D}_0$ is shown as follows.

Example 3. Consider a sentence w from the original training set $\mathcal{D}_0$, $w =$["I", "really", "like", "this", "movie"]. First, the word "like" is chosen to be replaced by one of its synonym "appreciate". Next, the word "really" is dropped from the sentence, i.e. replaced by the unknown word $\langle \textbf{unk} \rangle$. Finally, we get a new sentence $w' =$["I", "$\langle \textbf{unk} \rangle$", "appreciate", "this", "movie"] and put it into the augmented dataset $\mathcal{D}$.

Since the word "appreciate" may be an uncommon word in Σ, we can capture a new transition information for it given by RNNs. Besides, we can also observe the behavior of RNN when it reads an unknown word after the prefix ["I"].

Computational Complexity. The time complexity of the whole workflow is analyzed as follows. Suppose that the set of training samples $\mathcal{D}_0$ has N words in total and its alphabet Σ contains n words, and is augmented as $\mathcal{D}$ with t epochs (i.e. each sentence in $\mathcal{D}_0$ is transformed to t new sentences in $\mathcal{D}$), hence $|\mathcal{D}| = (t+1)N$. Assume that a probabilistic output of RNNs is a m-dim vector, and the abstract states set $\hat{S}$ contains k states.

To start with, the augmentation of $\mathcal{D}_0$ and tracking of probabilistic outputs in $\mathcal{D}$ will be completed in $\mathcal{O}(|\mathcal{D}|) = \mathcal{O}(t \cdot N)$ time. Besides, the time complexity of k-means clustering algorithm is $\mathcal{O}(k \cdot |\mathcal{D}|) = \mathcal{O}(k \cdot t \cdot N)$. The count of abstract transitions will be done in $\mathcal{O}(n)$. As for the processing of transition matrices, we need to calculate the transition probability for each word σ with each source state $\hat{s}_i$ and destination state $\hat{s}_j$, which costs $\mathcal{O}(k^2 \cdot n)$ time. Finally, the context-aware enhancement on transition matrices takes $\mathcal{O}(k \cdot n)$ time.

Note that $\mathcal{O}(n) = \mathcal{O}(N)$, hence we can conclude that the time complexity of our whole workflow is $\mathcal{O}(k^2 \cdot t \cdot N)$. So the time complexity of our approaches only takes linear time w.r.t. the size of the dataset, which provides theoretical extraction overhead for large-scale data applications.

5   Experiments

In this section, we evaluate our extraction approach on two natural language datasets and demonstrate its performance in terms of precision and scalability.

Datasets and RNNs models. We select two popular datasets for NLP tasks and train the target RNNs on them.

1. The CogComp QC Dataset (abbrev. QC) [16] contains news titles which are labeled with different topics. The dataset is divided into a training set containing 20k samples and a test set containing 8k samples. Each sample is labeled with one of seven categories. We train an LSTM-based RNN model $\mathcal{R}$ on the training set, which achieves an accuracy of 81% on the test set.
2. The Jigsaw Toxic Comment Dataset (abbrev. Toxic) [15] contains comments from Wikipedia's talk page edits, with each comment labeled toxic or not. We select 25k non-toxic samples and toxic samples respectively, and divide them into the training set and test set in a ratio of four to one. We train another LSTM-based RNN model which achieves 90% accuracy.

Metrics. For the purpose of representing the behaviors of RNNs better, we use *Consistency Rate (CR)* as our evaluation metric. For a sentence in the test set $w \in \mathcal{D}_{test}$, we denote $\mathcal{R}(w)$ and $\mathcal{A}(w)$ as the prediction results of the RNNs and WFA, respectively. The *Consistency Rate* is defined formally as

$$CR = \frac{|\{w \in D_{test} : \mathcal{A}(w) = \mathcal{R}(w)\}|}{|\mathcal{D}_{test}|}.$$

Missing Rows Complementing. As discussed in Sect. 3.2, we take two approaches as baselines, the *null filling* and the *uniform filling*. The two WFA extracted with these two approaches are denoted as $\mathcal{A}_0$ and $\mathcal{A}_U$, respectively. The WFA extracted by our *empirical filling* approach is denoted as $\mathcal{A}_E$.

Table 1 shows the evaluation results of three rule filling approaches. We conduct the comparison experiments on QC and Toxic datasets and select the cluster number for state abstraction as 40 and 20 for the QC and Toxic datasets, respectively.

The three columns labeled with the type of WFA show the evaluation results of different approaches. For the $\mathcal{A}_0$ based on blank filling, the WFA returns the

Table 1. Evaluation results of different filling approaches on missing rows.

Dataset	$\mathcal{A}_0$		$\mathcal{A}_U$		$\mathcal{A}_E$	
	CR(%)	Time(s)	CR(%)	Time(s)	CR(%)	Time(s)
QC	26	47	60	56	**80**	70
Toxic	57	167	86	180	**91**	200

weight of most sentences in $\mathcal{D}$ with **0**, which fails to provide sufficient information for prediction. For the QC dataset, only a quarter of sentences in the test set are classified correctly. The second column shows that the performance of $\mathcal{A}_U$ is better than $\mathcal{A}_0$. The last column presents the evaluation result of $\mathcal{A}_E$, which fills the missing rows by our approach. In this experiment, the hyper-parameter *reference rate* is set as $\beta = 0.3$. We can see that our empirical approach achieves significantly better accuracy, which is 20% and 5% higher than uniform filling on the two datasets, respectively.

The columns labeled *Time* show the execution time of the whole extraction workflow, from tracking transitions to evaluation on test set, but not include the training time of RNNs. We can see that the extraction overhead of our approach ($\mathcal{A}_E$) is about the same as $\mathcal{A}_U$ and $\mathcal{A}_0$.

Context-Aware Enhancement. In this experiment, we leverage the context-aware enhanced matrices when constructing the WFA. We adopt the same configuration on cluster numbers n from the comparison experiments above, i.e. $n = 40$ and $n = 20$. The columns titled *Configuration* indicate if the extracted WFA leverage context-aware matrices. We also take the WFA with different filling approaches, the uniform filling and empirical filling, into comparison. Experiments on null filling is omitted due to limited precision.

Table 2. Evaluation results of with and without context-aware enhancement.

Dataset	Configuration	$\mathcal{A}_U$		$\mathcal{A}_E$	
		CR(%)	Time(s)	CR(%)	Time(s)
QC	None	60	56	80	70
	Context	71	64	**82**	78
Toxic	None	86	180	91	200
	Context	89	191	**92**	211

The experiment results are in Table 2. For the QC dataset, we set the *static probability* as $\alpha = 0.4$. The consistency rate of WFA $\mathcal{A}_U$ improves 11% with the context-aware enhancement, and $\mathcal{A}_E$ improves 2%. As for the Toxic dataset, we take $\alpha = 0.2$ and the consistency rate of the two WFA improves 3% and 1%

respectively. This shows that the WFA with context-aware enhancement remains more information from the prefixes of sentences, making it simulate RNNs better.

Still, the context-aware enhancement processing costs little time, since we only calculate the adjusting formula (3) for each E_σ in E. The additional extra time consumption is 8 s for the QC dataset and 11 s for the Toxic dataset.

Data Augmentation Finally, we evaluate the WFA extracted with transition behaviors from augmented data. Note that the two experiments above are based on the primitive training set $\mathcal{D}_0$. In this experiment, we leverage the data augmentation tactics to generate the augmented training set $\mathcal{D}$, and extract WFA with data samples from $\mathcal{D}$. In order to get best performance, we build WFA with contextual-aware enhanced matrices.

Table 3. Evaluation results of with and without data augmentation.

Dataset	Samples	$\mathcal{A}_U$		$\mathcal{A}_E$	
		CR(%)	Time(s)	CR(%)	Time(s)
QC	$\mathcal{D}_0$	71	64	82	68
	$\mathcal{D}$	76	81	**84**	85
Toxic	$\mathcal{D}_0$	89	191	92	211
	$\mathcal{D}$	91	295	**94**	315

Table 3 shows the results of consistency rate of WFA extracted with and without augmented data. The rows labeled $\mathcal{D}_0$ show the results of WFA that are extracted with the primitive training set, and the result from the augmented data is shown in rows labeled $\mathcal{D}$. With more transition behaviors tracked, the WFA extracted with $\mathcal{D}$ demonstrates better precision. Specifically, the WFA extracted with both empirical filling and context-aware enhancement achieves a further 2% increase in consistency rate on the two datasets.

To summarize, by using our transition rule extraction approach, the consistency rate of extracted WFA on the QC dataset and the Toxic dataset achieves 84% and 94%, respectively. Taking the primitive extraction algorithm with uniform filling as baseline, of which experimental results in terms of CR are 60% and 86%, our approach achieves an improvement of 22% and 8% in consistency rate. As for the time complexity, the time consumption of our approach increases from 56 s to 81 s on QC dataset, and from 180 s to 315 s on Toxic dataset, which indicates the efficiency and scalability of our rule extraction approach. There is no significant time cost of adopting our approach further for complicated natural language tasks. We can conclude that our transition rule extraction approach makes better approximation of RNNs, and is also efficient enough to be applied to practical applications for large-scale natural language tasks.

6   Related Work

Many research efforts have been made to abstract, verify and repair RNNs. As Jacobsson reviewed in [14], the rule extraction approach of RNNs can be divided into two categories: pedagogical approaches and compositional approaches.

Pedagogical Approaches. Much progress has been achieved by using pedagogical approaches to abstracting RNNs by leveraging explicit learning algorithms, such as the L^* algorithm [2]. The earlier work dates back to two decades ago, when Omlin et al. attempted to extract a finite model from Boolean-output RNNs [18–20]. Recently, Weiss et al. proposed to levergae the L^* algorithm to extract DFA from RNN-acceptors [25]. Later, they presented a weighted extension of L^* algorithm that extracted probabilistic determininstic finite automata (PDFA) from RNNs [26]. Besides, Okudono et al. proposed another weighted extension of L^* algorithm to extract WFA from real-value-output RNNs [17].

The pedagogical approaches have achieved great success in abstracting RNNs for small-scale languages, particularly formal languages. Such exact learning approaches have intrinsic limitation in the scalability of the language complexity, hence they are not suitable for automata extraction from natural language processing models.

Compositional Approach. Another technical line is the compositional approach, which generally leverages unsupervised algorithms (e.g. k-means, GMM) to cluster state vectors as abstract states [4,28]. Wang et al. studied the key factors that influence the reliability of extraction process, and proposed an empirical rule to extract DFA from RNNs [23]. Later, Zhang et al. followed the state encoding of compositional approach and proposed a WFA extraction approach from RNNs [29], which can be applied to both grammatical languages and natural languages. In this paper, our proposal of extracting WFA from RNNs also falls into the line of compositional approach, but aims at proposing transition rule extraction method to address the transition sparsity problem and enhance the context-aware ability.

Recently, many of the verification, analysis and repairment works also leverage similar approaches to abstract RNNs as a more explicit model, such as *Deep-Steller* [9], *Marble* [8] and *RNNsRepair* [27]. These works achieve great progress in analyzing and repairing RNNs, but have strict requirements of scalability to large-scale tasks, particularly natural language processing. The proposed approach, which demonstrates better precision and scalability, shows great potential for further applications such as RNN analysis and Network repairment. We consider applying our method to RNN analysis as future work.

7   Conclusion

This paper presents a novel approach to extracting transition rules of weighted finite automata from recurrent neural networks. We measure the distance between abstract states and complement the transition rules of *missing rows*. In addition, we present an heuristic method to enhance the context-aware ability of the extracted WFA. We further propose two augmentation tactics to track more transition behaviours of RNNs. Experiments on two natural language datasets show that the WFA extracted with our approach achieve better consistency with target RNNs. The theoretical estimation of computation complexity and experimental results demonstrate that our rule extraction approach can be applied to natural language datasets and complete the extraction procedure efficiently for large-scale tasks.

Acknowledgements. This research was sponsored by the National Natural Science Foundation of China under Grant No. 62172019, 61772038, and CCF-Huawei Formal Verification Innovation Research Plan.

References

1. Abdel-Hamid, O., Mohamed, A.R., Jiang, H., Deng, L., Penn, G., Yu, D.: Convolutional neural networks for speech recognition. IEEE/ACM Trans. Audio Speech Lang. Process. **22**(10), 1533–1545 (2014)
2. Angluin, D.: Learning regular sets from queries and counterexamples. Inf. Comput. **75**(2), 87–106 (1987)
3. Baier, C., Katoen, J.P.: Principles of Model Checking. MIT press (2008)
4. Cechin, A.L., Regina, D., Simon, P., Stertz, K.: State automata extraction from recurrent neural nets using k-means and fuzzy clustering. In: 23rd International Conference of the Chilean Computer Science Society, 2003. SCCC 2003. Proceedings, pp. 73–78. IEEE (2003)
5. Che, Z., Purushotham, S., Cho, K., Sontag, D., Liu, Y.: Recurrent neural networks for multivariate time series with missing values. Sci. Rep. **8**(1), 1–12 (2018)
6. Datta, D., David, P.E., Mittal, D., Jain, A.: Neural machine translation using recurrent neural network. Int. J. Eng. Adv. Technol. **9**(4), 1395–1400 (2020)
7. Dong, G., et al.: Towards interpreting recurrent neural networks through probabilistic abstraction. In: 2020 35th IEEE/ACM International Conference on Automated Software Engineering (ASE), pp. 499–510. IEEE (2020)
8. Du, X., Li, Y., Xie, X., Ma, L., Liu, Y., Zhao, J.: Marble: model-based robustness analysis of stateful deep learning systems. In: Proceedings of the 35th IEEE/ACM International Conference on Automated Software Engineering, pp. 423–435 (2020)
9. Du, X., Xie, X., Li, Y., Ma, L., Liu, Y., Zhao, J.: Deepstellar: model-based quantitative analysis of stateful deep learning systems. In: Proceedings of the 2019 27th ACM Joint Meeting on European Software Engineering Conference and Symposium on the Foundations of Software Engineering, pp. 477–487 (2019)
10. Gastin, P., Monmege, B.: A unifying survey on weighted logics and weighted automata. Soft. Comput. **22**(4), 1047–1065 (2015). https://doi.org/10.1007/s00500-015-1952-6
11. Goldberg, Y.: Neural network methods for natural language processing. Synth. Lect. Hum. Lang. Technol. **10**(1), 1–309 (2017)
12. He, K., Zhang, X., Ren, S., Sun, J.: Deep residual learning for image recognition. In: Proceedings of the IEEE Conference on Computer Vision and Pattern Recognition (CVPR) (2016)

13. Hochreiter, S., Schmidhuber, J.: Long short-term memory. Neural Comput. **9**(8), 1735–1780 (1997)
14. Jacobsson, H.: Rule extraction from recurrent neural networks: Ataxonomy and review. Neural Comput. **17**(6), 1223–1263 (2005)
15. Jigsaw: Toxic comment classification challenge. https://www.kaggle.com/c/jigsaw-toxic-comment-classification-challenge. Accessed 16 Apr 2022
16. Li, X., Roth, D.: Learning question classifiers. In: COLING 2002: The 19th International Conference on Computational Linguistics (2002)
17. Okudono, T., Waga, M., Sekiyama, T., Hasuo, I.: Weighted automata extraction from recurrent neural networks via regression on state spaces. In: Proceedings of the AAAI Conference on Artificial Intelligence, vol. 34, pp. 5306–5314 (2020)
18. Omlin, C.W., Giles, C.L.: Extraction of rules from discrete-time recurrent neural networks. Neural Netw. **9**(1), 41–52 (1996)
19. Omlin, C.W., Giles, C.L.: Rule revision with recurrent neural networks. IEEE Trans. Knowl. Data Eng. **8**(1), 183–188 (1996)
20. Omlin, C., Giles, C., Miller, C.: Heuristics for the extraction of rules from discrete-time recurrent neural networks. In: Proceedings 1992 IJCNN International Joint Conference on Neural Networks, vol. 1, pp. 33–38. IEEE (1992)
21. Powers, D.M.: Applications and explanations of zipf's law. In: New Methods in Language Processing and Computational Natural Language Learning (1998)
22. Wang, Q., Zhang, K., Liu, X., Giles, C.L.: Verification of recurrent neural networks through rule extraction. arXiv preprint arXiv:1811.06029 (2018)
23. Wang, Q., Zhang, K., Ororbia, A.G., II., Xing, X., Liu, X., Giles, C.L.: An empirical evaluation of rule extraction from recurrent neural networks. Neural Comput. **30**(9), 2568–2591 (2018)
24. Wang, R., Li, Z., Cao, J., Chen, T., Wang, L.: Convolutional recurrent neural networks for text classification. In: 2019 International Joint Conference on Neural Networks (IJCNN), pp. 1–6. IEEE (2019)
25. Weiss, G., Goldberg, Y., Yahav, E.: Extracting automata from recurrent neural networks using queries and counterexamples. In: International Conference on Machine Learning, pp. 5247–5256. PMLR (2018)
26. Weiss, G., Goldberg, Y., Yahav, E.: Learning deterministic weighted automata with queries and counterexamples. In: Wallach, H., Larochelle, H., Beygelzimer, A., d' Alché-Buc, F., Fox, E., Garnett, R. (eds.) Advances in Neural Information Processing Systems, vol. 32. Curran Associates, Inc. (2019). https://proceedings.neurips.cc/paper/2019/file/d3f93e7766e8e1b7ef66dfdd9a8be93b-Paper.pdf
27. Xie, X., et al.: Rnnrepair: automatic rnn repair via model-based analysis. In: International Conference on Machine Learning, pp. 11383–11392. PMLR (2021)
28. Zeng, Z., Goodman, R.M., Smyth, P.: Learning finite state machines with self-clustering recurrent networks. Neural Comput. **5**(6), 976–990 (1993)
29. Zhang, X., Du, X., Xie, X., Ma, L., Liu, Y., Sun, M.: Decision-guided weighted automata extraction from recurrent neural networks. In: Thirty-Fifth AAAI Conference on Artificial Intelligence (AAAI), pp. 11699–11707. AAAI Press (2021)

RoboCert: Property Specification in Robotics

Matt Windsor$^{(\boxtimes)}$ ⬤ and Ana Cavalcanti$^{(\boxtimes)}$ ⬤

Department of Computer Science, University of York,
Deramore Lane, Heslington, York YO10 5GH, UK
{matt.windsor,ana.cavalcanti}@york.ac.uk

Abstract. RoboStar is a toolkit for model-based development using a domain-specific notation, RoboChart, with enriched UML-like state machines and a custom component model. We present RoboCert: a novel notation, based on UML sequence diagrams, which facilitates the specification of properties over RoboChart components. With RoboCert, we can express properties of a robotic system in a user-friendly, idiomatic manner. RoboCert specifications can be existential or universal, include timing notions such as deadlines and budgets, and both safety and liveness properties. Our work is faithful to UML where it can be, but presents significant extensions to fit the robotics application needs. RoboCert comes with tooling support for modelling and verification by model checking, and formal semantics in *tock*-CSP, the discrete-time variant of CSP.

Keywords: RoboChart · Timed properties · CSP · Sequence diagrams

1 Introduction

Mobile and autonomous robots are becoming common among us. While such systems come in many shapes and sizes, from vacuum cleaners to unmanned aerial vehicles, each must be designed such that we can trust it to operate correctly. A faulty robot risks mission or safety failures, causing reputational damage, financial loss, or injury.

Software and hardware engineering for *trustworthy* robotic systems is, therefore, a key research topic. One approach, embodied by RoboChart [13] and its associated notations, combines model-driven development and formal methods. RoboChart provides practitioners with intuitive, graphical notations that have a well-defined meaning rooted in a formal semantics.

While RoboChart is well-established, with many successful case studies,[1] its support for property specification is incomplete. Its assertion language is a thin layer atop the formalisms targeted by the RoboChart semantics—the CSP process algebra and the PCTL probabilistic logic—; users must be experts in

---

[1] https://robostar.cs.york.ac.uk/case_studies/.

A. Riesco and M. Zhang (Eds.): ICFEM 2022, LNCS 13478, pp. 386–403, 2022.
https://doi.org/10.1007/978-3-031-17244-1_23

those formalisms. We seek high-level notations resembling those already used by practitioners, which they can use with minimal adaptation to their workflows.

We introduce RoboCert, a notation for property specification over RoboChart models. RoboCert exposes a variant of the sequence, or interaction, diagrams of the Unified Modelling Language (UML) [18]. We choose sequence diagrams as they are a well-known notation for reasoning about reactive systems, with a large body of related literature (as seen in the next section).

Our key contributions are a formal metamodel and semantics for RoboCert. These, along with the domain specificity of our notation, address some of the issues highlighted as impeding UML usage in the empirical study by Petre [14]. Novelty comes from our treatment of time properties, both as novel constructs in RoboCert diagrams, and in its semantics, based on the *tock*-CSP dialect of CSP [2,15]. Timing properties are important for robotic systems, and so any useful property language must elegantly capture notions of delay and deadlock.

Section 2 outlines related work. Section 3 is a brief overview of RoboChart. Section 4 introduces RoboCert through examples. Section 5 explores the well-formedness conditions and formal semantics of RoboCert in *tock*-CSP. Section 6 presents tool support currently available. Finally, Sect. 7 gives conclusions.

2   Related Work

Before outlining RoboCert, we discuss existing work in the relevant fields.

Lindoso et al. [11] have adapted UML activity diagrams as a property notation for RoboChart. Their work has both a semantics in CSP and graphical tooling. That work, however, focus on internal, as opposed to visible like in Robo-Cert, behaviour of state machines, and does not yet consider time. Sequence and activity diagrams complement each other, and so our work is complementary. Since they are concerned with refinement checking, unsurprisingly, some of their constructs (any and until) have analogues in RoboCert.

The mainstream work on sequence diagrams is that of UML, which overlaps with work on the *Message Sequence Charts* standard [17]. Offshoots from these works pursue specific goals. *Live Sequence Charts* [4] (LSC) extend MSC to provide modalities for liveness analysis. *Property Sequence Charts* [1] (PSC) recast parts of UML and MSC alongside novel constructs for constraining message chaining. In RoboCert, like in LSC, we have facilities to define universal and existential properties. We have a notion similar to the constrained *intraMSGs* of PSC in RoboCert (our 'until' construct). Importantly, in terms of notation, what is novel in RoboCert are the explicit constructs to deal with time, and the specific combination of constructors to support refinement-based compositional reasoning about models of robotic systems.

STAIRS is a sequence-diagram refinement process [8] based on a trace-pair semantics of UML. In contrast, we use refinement to compare a RoboCert diagram to a RoboChart design, not different sequence diagrams. This is, of course, a possibility, given the nature of refinement reasoning. The notion of refinement in STAIRS, however, is different: it allows for addition of behaviours for incremental development of diagrams. RoboCert refinement captures safety, liveness,

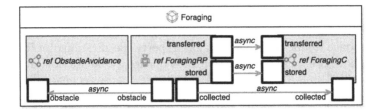

Fig. 1. The Foraging module.

reduction of nondeterminism, and timing preservation. Like STAIRS, RoboCert defines two forms of choice: internal and external. *Timed STAIRS* [7] extends STAIRS to consider UML timing constraints, which can specify budgets, like in RoboCert. In its semantics, events are time stamped.

Micskei and Waeselynck [12] surveyed the formal semantics for UML sequence diagrams available in 2011. They explored variants of the set of trace-pairs approach of UML, as well as other denotational and operational semantics. This comparison shows that different use cases and interpretations have given rise to different semantics. Two of them concern refinement: first, STAIRS; second, [6], where refinement is inclusion of languages defined by input-enabled automata for a collection of sequence diagrams. None of the works compared provides a reactive semantics for refinement based on a process algebra.

The treatments in [9,10] are closest to our work. They provide a process algebraic semantics to SysML and UML sequence diagrams, not including any time constructs. In contrast, RoboCert has constructs to define core properties of a timed system: time budgets, deadlines, and timeouts. RoboCert also adopts a component model (similar to that of RoboChart). There is a notion of robotic platform, system, and controller, as well as state machine. Messages correspond to events, operations, and variables that represent services of a robotic platform or other robotic components. A RoboCert sequence diagram is defined in the context of a specific component of a robotic system: the whole system, its sets of controllers, an individual controller, a set of timed state machines that define the behaviour of a controller, or, finally, a single machine.

3   RoboChart

RoboChart [13] is a notation for the design of robotic control software. It provides domain-specific constructs, such as the notion of service-based *robotic platforms* that abstract over the robotic hardware. Another key feature is its discrete-time constructs for specification of deadlines, delays, and time-outs.

A RoboChart model consists of several diagrams arranged in a hierarchy proceeding from the top-level *module* to individual *controllers*, each in turn containing state machines. Another diagram captures the robotic platform. Communications with the platform are asynchronous, reflecting their typical reification as sensors in the robot hardware. Communications between state machines are always synchronous; communications between controllers may be of either sort.

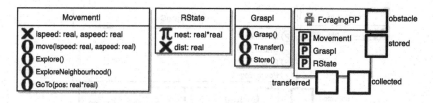

Fig. 2. The robotic platform and the interfaces it provides.

As a running example, we use the foraging robot of Buchanan et al. [3], which searches for items to store in a 'nest' location; it can transfer items to nearby robots and avoid obstacles. Figure 1 shows Foraging, the top-level module for our example. The platform block, ForagingRP, exposes four events to the software (depicted by white boxes and arrows). One (obstacle) signals to the ObstacleAvoidance controller that an obstacle is in the way. The others (collected, stored, and transferred) send item status to the ForagingC controller.

Figure 2 shows the robotic platform, ForagingRP. ForagingRP exposes the aforementioned events as well as three *provided interfaces* (**P**). Each (MovementI, GraspI, and RState) exposes operations (**O**), constants (π), and shared variables (**X**) for use by the software. For instance, the platform provides a move operation for setting linear and angular speed set-points. It then exposes the current speeds as variables lspeed and aspeed. A constant nest provides the fixed nest location. These elements abstract over actuators, sensors, and aspects of the environment.

Figure 3 depicts the controllers, and how they can both *require* (**R**) and locally define (**i**) interfaces. Both controllers contain state machines: ForagingC does so by reference to other diagrams, omitted here for space reasons, while ObstacleAvoidance directly contains Avoid. The complete example is available,[2] as well as many other case studies and RoboChart's reference manual and tutorial.

The behaviour of Avoid, after transitioning from the initial state i, is a cycle of Waiting for an event obstacle, then Turning, then stopping the turn once complete. Both behaviours are described by calls to move on the platform.

Avoid makes use of RoboChart time primitives. The marker #T on the obstacle transition resets a clock T. Subsequently, since(T) gets the number of discrete time units observed since the reset; this information forms part of a condition (in square brackets) which guards the transition back to Waiting. These primitives form a time-based check for the completion of the turn.

In RoboChart, state machines within a controller operate in parallel with one another, as do controllers within a module. This permits the modelling of multiple separate computational resources, threads, and other such constructs. Sequence diagrams, as a notation for capturing communications between parallel entities, capture these rich scenarios well. They are presented next.

---

[2] robostar.cs.york.ac.uk.

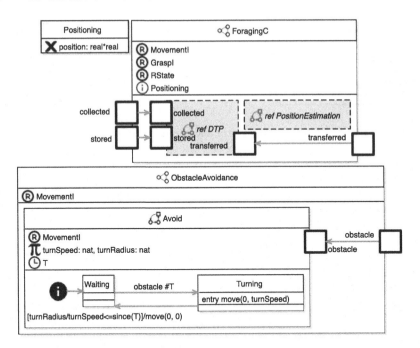

Fig. 3. The ForagingC and ObstacleAvoidance controllers.

4   RoboCert Sequence Diagrams

In this section, we present the main novel features of RoboCert sequence diagrams (or interactions, in UML terminology) via examples of properties of the foraging robot. A metamodel can be found in its reference manual [19], and formal semantics is discussed in Sect. 5. While it is not the focus of this paper, RoboCert includes the language presented in [13,16] for defining core properties (such as deadlock freedom and determinism) of RoboChart models.

A key characteristic of RoboCert compared to UML is that it adheres to the RoboChart component model. A RoboCert sequence diagram has a *target*: the RoboChart model element being constrained by the diagram. Each diagram also has a *world*: the environment of components residing above the target in the component hierarchy. Components are represented in diagrams by vertical *lifelines*, with downwards progression loosely representing the passage of time.

RoboCert sequence diagrams show traces of messages among components and the world, and associated time restrictions. Communications are represented by arrows between lifelines, with block-based control flow (parallelism, choice, and so on) depicted by boxes surrounding lifelines and relevant messages.

We can use RoboCert sequence diagrams to capture *existential* (stating *some* expected behaviours of the system) or *universal* (capturing *all* expected behaviours) properties [4]. We can check whether a target conforms to a sequence diagram according to two semantic models. In the 'traces' model, we only check

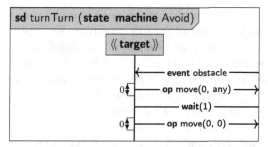

assertion A1: turnTurn **is not observed in the traces model**

Fig. 4. An existential property containing timing features.

trace-set inclusion, treating the passage of time as a trace event and ignoring liveness. In the 'timed' model, we require conformance in terms of liveness, and that timing properties in both specification and model are fully compliant.

In RoboCert, we decouple the method in which we use a diagram (existential versus universal, traces-model versus timed-model, and so on) from the diagram itself; the usage is instead part of the *assertions* over that diagram. While this differs from situations such as those in LSC (where existential diagrams are graphically distinct from universal diagrams), it allows the same diagram to be repurposed in different ways. Future work will enrich the assertion language to allow, for instance, parameterisation of diagrams at the assertion level.

Component Targets. There are two types of target: *component* and *collection* targets. Sequence diagrams for components capture black-box specifications of the behaviour of a component with respect to its world: they capture only the side of the communications visible to the target. Figure 4 shows a sequence diagram called turnTurn whose target is the **state machine** Avoid. Every diagram is given in a box; on its top left-hand corner, the label sd ('sequence diagram') gives the diagram name and, in parentheses, its target. In a component diagram, as in this example, there is a single lifeline, labelled ⟪ **target** ⟫. The world is represented by the box enclosing the diagram.

Diagrams with module targets show messages between the control software represented by the module and its robotic platform. Diagrams with controller targets depict controller interactions with the platform and other controllers. Finally, the world for state machine and operation diagrams includes other machines in the same controller, the other controllers, and the platform.

Below the diagram is a *sequence property* assertion, A1. Here, **not observed** denotes a negated existential property: we expect no traces to satisfy A1. To check universal properties, we use **does not hold** or **holds**. Also, **traces** states that we are checking A1 by traces refinement; for liveness proofs, we use **timed**. Properties are combinations of diagrams and assertions, with loose coupling between the two: a diagram can have zero, one, or many related assertions.

Time. As well as the UML constructs for loops, parallel composition, optionality, and alternative choice, RoboCert has constructs for capturing timing properties: deadlines, time budgets, and timeouts. The **deadline** fragment constrains the amount of time units that can pass on a lifeline. The **wait** occurrence pauses a lifeline for a given amount of time units, to define time budgets.

The diagram in Fig. 4 depicts traces that start with the event obstacle followed by an immediate (taking 0 time units) call to move(0, **any**), with arguments 0 and **any** other value, effecting a turn. Afterwards, we have a time budget (**wait**) of one time unit, and an immediate move call stopping the turn.

To specify a timeout, we use **wait** in conjunction with **until**, presented next.

Until. Another RoboCert extension to UML is **until** fragments, useful to define partial specifications, which characterise sets of traces, rather than single traces, of universal properties. These fragments permit the passage of time and exchange of *any* messages in a given set *until* some occurrence inside the body takes effect. (They are related to UML the concepts 'strict' and 'ignore'.)

Figure 5 shows a diagram targeting the Avoid state machine. Its first **until** fragment states that any messages can be exchanged (∗) **until** the event obstacle occurs. Afterwards, a series of messages can be exchanged immediately (with **deadline** 0) **until** a turn: a call to move(0, **any**). Other calls to move, in the set Move, whose definition we omit, are excluded in the **until** via ∗\Move. We define named sets such as Move outside of the diagrams, to allow reuse.

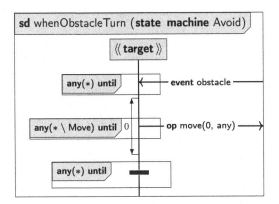

assertion A2: whenObstacleTurn **holds in the traces model**

Fig. 5. A universal property of the obstacle avoidance logic.

The last **until** fragment wraps a **deadlock** occurrence (━). This construct specifies that a lifeline has stopped making progress. Wrapping it in an **until** has the effect of allowing messages from the **until** set to occur indefinitely. This construct is useful for diagrams where we expect all traces to start with a certain pattern of behaviour, but, after that pattern has ended, we no longer constrain the behaviour; in other words, it captures universal diagrams over *partial* traces.

A third use of **until** is to wrap a **wait** occurrence to define a timeout. This permits messages in the set until the time specified by the **wait** has passed.

Temperature. We extend UML with a '**hot**/**cold**' modality for messages. This modality allows a form of liveness reasoning over message transmission, which is present in systems such as MSC [17] but not in UML. The presence of a **hot** message obliges a model to accept the message at any time, including immediately. By default, messages are **cold**; this weaker modality permits the model to refuse the messages for any length of time, including indefinitely.

For example, consider marking the obstacle message in Fig. 5 as **hot**. This changes the meaning of the first part of whenObstacleTurn: instead of 'Avoid can do anything, but *if* we see it accept obstacle, it must progress to the next part of the diagram', we now have the stronger obligation that Avoid must be ready to take an obstacle at any time during the **until**. This rules out implementations that, for instance, **wait** for some time before checking obstacle.

Mandatory Choice. As well as the UML **alt** fragment, RoboCert uses the **xalt** fragment. Informally, **alt** is a *provisional* choice where the model can decide which alternatives are available; **xalt** is a *mandatory* choice where the environment has full say and the model must accept all such choices.

The constructs **hot** and **xalt** add support to specify liveness aspects of a property. We can verify such a property by using the **timed** model.

Collections. Collection targets are defined by a component (module or controller), and reveal the internal representation of that component as a collection of subcomponents. In this case, the world remains the same as if the diagram had the corresponding component target, but each lifeline now maps to a distinct subcomponent; the target itself is not tangible here. We can observe both messages between the subcomponents and the world *as well as* messages from one subcomponent to another. Like in UML, the **component** lifelines produced by such subcomponents act in parallel except where connected by such messages.

Figure 6 gives an example over Foraging, describing traces that interleave activities of ObstacleAvoidance with those of ForagingC. First ForagingC calls the operation Explore() of the world (platform). Inputs are then provided to the controllers by the world via events obstacle and collected . The parallelism of the diagram means that Fig. 6 admits traces where collected occurs before obstacle. Finally, ObstacleAvoidance calls move with arguments 0 and **any**.

Other Features. Features not shown here for brevity and pragmatism include: a subset of the RoboChart expression language to define arguments and bounds; variables within interactions, with the possibility of capturing event and operation arguments to variables and using them within expressions; **loop**; and **par**.

5   Well-Formedness and Semantics

We now present a cross-section of the well-formedness conditions and semantics for RoboCert. A fuller treatment of both can be found in the manual [19].

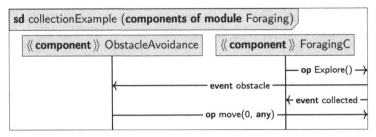

Fig. 6. Existential property of obstacle avoidance in parallel with the main logic.

5.1   Well-Formedness

To have a well-defined meaning, a sequence diagram must satisfy multiple well-formedness conditions. Diagrams must be well-typed and well-scoped; the typing and scoping rules are as one would expect for a language like RoboCert (such as 'variables referenced in a sequence must be defined in the sequence' and '**wait** durations must evaluate to natural numbers'), and so we leave them to its manual [19]. In addition, the referenced elements of RoboChart must comply with the well-formedness conditions of RoboChart.

Fragments are the main elements of sequence diagrams. They consist of *occurrences* (points on the vertical time axis, on which elements such as messages, deadlocks, and waits are located), and *combined fragments* (which implement control flow over other fragments), such as **deadline**, **until**, **opt**, for example.

Compound fragments contain one or more blocks of nested fragments; we call these their *operands*. Operands may have a guard, which must be true for the operand to be considered. By default, an operand's guard is **always**: a tautology. There are two other guard types: a Boolean expression, or **otherwise** (the negated disjunction of the guards of all operands in the fragment).

The following well-formedness conditions apply to fragments.

F1 *The operand of an* **opt** *or* **loop** *must not have an* **otherwise** *guard.* Since this guard is the negated disjunction of all other guards, and these fragments only have one operand, the **otherwise** guard would always be false.

F2 *At most one operand of* **alt**, **xalt**, *and* **par** *can have an* **otherwise** *guard.* Since this guard is the negated disjunction of all other guards, the two such guards would induce an ambiguous recursive definition.

F3 *An* **alt**, **xalt**, *or* **par** *must not have an operand with an* **always** *guard and one with* **otherwise**. The former would make the latter implicitly false.

F4 *A* **deadline**, **deadlock**, *or* **wait** *must not be* **on** *a* **world** *actor.* The **world** does not form a lifeline, so the fragment would not constrain anything.

F5 *An* **until** *must not contain another* **until**. Since the operand of an **until** defines the interrupting condition for the arbitrary occurrences of the allowed messages, it makes no sense for that condition to be an **until** itself.

Table 1. The *tock*-CSP operators used in our semantics (:: is borrowed from CSP_M)

Operator	Meaning	Operator	Meaning
tock	passage of one unit of time	*Skip*	termination
Stop	timed deadlock; refuses all events except *tock*	$TChaos(s)$	timed chaos; permits any event in s, *tock*, or deadlock
$Stop_U$	timelock; refuses all events including *tock*	$P \blacktriangleright n$	deadline; permit at most n *tocks* to pass within P
wait n	wait for n *tocks* to pass	$e \rightarrow P$	timed event prefixing
$g \,\&\, P$	guard (if g then P else *Stop*)	$\mu P \bullet f(P)$	recursive process definition
$P \bigtriangleup Q$	interrupt	$P \sqcap Q$	internal choice
$P \,\square\, Q$	external choice	$P \,\overset{\circ}{\circ}\, Q$	sequential composition
$P \mathbin{\vert\vert\vert} Q$	interleaving parallel	$P \mathbin{\lVert a \rVert} Q$	generalised parallel
$\mathbin{\vert\vert} x : a \bullet \alpha \circ P$	indexed alphabetised parallel	$P \sqsubseteq_m Q$	refined-by (under model m)
::	namespacing of identifiers		

Messages correspond to events, operation calls, and assignments to variables of the associated RoboChart model. In general terms, their use must be compatible with the RoboChart model. For example, the operation calls must have the right number of arguments of the right type. More interestingly, the source and target of an event message must be a component that defines that event, and there must be a connection between them associating these events. The specific conditions in this category are listed in the manual [19].

The semantics of diagrams defined next is for well-formed diagrams.

5.2 Semantics

The underlying verification strategy of RoboCert is refinement: that is, we map both the sequence diagram and the RoboChart model to objects capturing the sets of behaviours the diagram or model permits, and prove that the set from one object is a subset of ('refines') that from the other. As both sides of the refinement relation are the same type of object, we can check refinement in both directions; this is crucial for the ability of RoboCert to express both universal (model refines sequence diagram) and existential (sequence diagram refines model) properties.

Given the nature of robotic applications, namely concurrent reactive timed systems, we use *tock*-CSP [2], a discrete-time version of CSP to define the RoboCert formal semantics. Like in CSP, systems, their components, and properties are defined in *tock*-CSP as processes (the objects of the refinement relation). These define patterns of interaction via atomic and instantaneous events, with the special event *tock* used to mark the passage of time. Table 1 enumerates the operators we use, which behave as per Baxter et al. [2], where a denotational semantics for *tock*-CSP, and an encoding for model checking are provided.

Diagrams. The semantics of a diagram is a parallel composition of lifeline processes, as well as a process for handling **until** fragments. This reflects the UML semantics of weak sequencing on occurrences across lifelines; the separate **until** process lets us step out of this parallelism when inside an **until** fragment. Figure 7 presents the process $turn\,Turn$ defined by applying the semantics to Fig. 4.

$$turn\,Turn = \Big(\parallel a : \{t\} \bullet alpha(a) \circ lifeline(a) \Big) \setminus \{term\}$$

$$alpha(t) = ctl \ \cup \ \{Avoid :: obstacle.in\} \ \cup \ \{x \in \mathbb{R} \bullet Avoid :: moveCall.0.x\}$$

$$lifeline(t) = (\mu\, x \bullet (Avoid :: obstacle.in \rightarrow Skip) \sqcap tock \rightarrow x)$$

$$\mathbin{\overset{\circ}{\circ}} ((\mu\, x \bullet (Avoid :: moveCall.0?y \rightarrow Skip) \sqcap tock \rightarrow x) \blacktriangleright 0)$$

$$\mathbin{\overset{\circ}{\circ}} wait\ 1$$

$$\mathbin{\overset{\circ}{\circ}} ((\mu\, x \bullet (Avoid :: moveCall.0.0 \rightarrow Skip) \sqcap tock \rightarrow x) \blacktriangleright 0)$$

$$\mathbin{\overset{\circ}{\circ}} term \rightarrow Skip$$

Fig. 7. Semantics of turnTurn in $tock$-CSP – let t stand for $\langle\!\langle$ **target** $\rangle\!\rangle$

A diagram process, such as $turn\,Turn$, is defined by an iterated parallelism ($\parallel$) over its set of actors: just **target** in the example, abbreviated to t. It composes processes $lifeline(a)$, for each actor a, synchronising on the intersection of their sets of events $alpha(a)$. In our example, we have just one process $lifeline(t)$.

A $lifeline(a)$ process is defined as a sequence ($\mathbin{\overset{\circ}{\circ}}$) of processes representing the fragments of the lifeline, followed by a process $term \rightarrow Skip$, which uses the event $term$ to flag termination. This event is internal to RoboCert, and so we hide it at the top level using $\setminus \{term\}$. In turnTurn, the only lifeline has four fragments: an occurrence fragment including obstacle, a **deadline** fragment (with the call move(0,**any**)), another occurrence fragment with the **wait**, and a final **deadline** fragment. Accordingly, we have four fragment processes in $lifeline(t)$.

For fragments with a **cold** message, we have a process that makes repeated internal choices as to whether engage in the event representing the message or allow time to pass ($tock$). For example, the obstacle fragment is defined by a recursive process ($\mu\, x$) whose body makes an internal choice ($\sqcap$). The first option is to engage in the event $Avoid :: obstacle.in$ representing the input obstacle of the machine Avoid—the :: construct states that $obstacle$ is defined in a namespace $Avoid$, and is a CSP_M convention used within the RoboChart semantics—and terminate ($Skip$). The alternative choice engages in $tock$ and recurses (x). For a fragment with a **hot** message, the process engages in the event representing the message and terminates. There is no choice or recursion.

A **deadline** fragment has an operand: a list of fragments under a guard. Its semantics is a process defined by applying the $tock$-CSP deadline operator ($\blacktriangleright$) to the process for the operand, along with the number of $tock$s permitted to occur in said process. The semantics of an operand is a guarded process defined by a sequence of fragment processes. In the **deadline** fragments of our example, the operands are occurrence fragments. The semantics of a **wait** fragment is direct, since $wait$ is also a primitive of $tock$-CSP to model time budget.

$$whenObstacleTurn = \left(\left(\,\|\,a:\{t\}\bullet alpha(a)\circ lifeline(a)\right)[\![\,ctl\,]\!]\,until\right)\setminus ctl$$

$$lifeline(t) = (sync.0.in \rightarrow sync.0.out \rightarrow Skip)\,\fatsemi\,(sync.1.in \rightarrow sync.1.out \rightarrow Skip)\,\fatsemi$$

$$(sync.2.in \rightarrow sync.2.out \rightarrow Skip)\,\fatsemi\,term \rightarrow Skip$$

$$until = \mu\,x \bullet (term \rightarrow Skip)$$

$$\square\,(sync.0.in \rightarrow (TChaos(Events)\,\triangle\,Avoid::obstacle.in) \rightarrow sync.0.out \rightarrow x)$$

$$\square\,\dots$$

Fig. 8. Semantics of whenObstacleTurn in *tock*-CSP

For diagrams with **until** fragments, the lifelines must coordinate so that each is aware of when the fragments start and end. We consider a diagram with lifelines a, b, and c, a world w, a fragment **any** (m) **until**: $a \rightarrow b$: **event** e, and, below it, a fragment $c \rightarrow w$: **op** o(). While messages in m are being exchanged, c cannot progress past the **until** fragment to the **op** o() call. At the same time, that call becomes available as soon as **event** e occurs, even though c is not involved in that event. So, an **until** fragment affects all lifelines of a diagram.

To capture this semantics, we add a process to handle the bodies of **until** fragments, placing it in parallel with the lifeline processes. We synchronise lifelines with this process to effect the **until** fragments.

To illustrate, Fig. 8 sketches the *tock*-CSP translation of Fig. 5. The sequence process *whenObstacleTurn* composes the parallelism of the *lifeline* processes in parallel with a new process *until* synchronising on the events in the hidden channel set *ctl*. We define $ctl = \{term\} \cup sync$, where *sync* is a set of events representing synchronisation induced by **until**: there is a pair of events for each **until** fragment. Each event is of the form $sync.i.d$, where i is the index of an **until**, and d is an *in* or *out* direction with respect to the **until** block. For **any** (m) **until**: $a \rightarrow b$: **event** e in the example above, there is a pair $sync.i.in, sync.i.out$ where i is the index of the **until** fragment in the diagram. In Fig. 8, we have $sync.0.in$ and $sync.0.out$ capturing entering and exiting the fragment **any** (∗) **until**: $w \rightarrow t$: **event** obstacle, and similar pairs $(sync.1.in, sync.2.in)$ and $(sync.2.out, sync.2.out)$ for the next two fragments.

The *until* process is a recursion that offers either to acknowledge the termination of the lifeline processes and then terminates itself ($term \rightarrow Skip$) or to handle any of the three **until** fragments in Fig. 5 (we show one of the choices in Fig. 8). Each fragment choice is over an event on *sync* representing entering the fragment, followed by timed chaos (*TChaos*) on the events named in the fragment. (*TChaos*) captures the ability to perform any of the given events, consuming any amount of time or deadlocking. This can be interrupted ($\triangle$) by the trigger given in the fragment. Upon completion of a fragment, the process then engages in another *sync* event representing exiting the fragment, and recursing.

The *sync* communications synchronise with the *lifeline* processes. In our example, we only have **until** fragments; therefore, each fragment is modelled

Table 2. Selected semantic rules for RoboCert

Rule	Definition

$[\![-]\!]^{\mathsf{S}}$ For a diagram named s, with body $b = \langle b_1, \ldots, b_n \rangle$:

$$[\![\text{sequence } s \text{ actors } a_1, \ldots, a_n, b]\!]^{\mathsf{S}} \triangleq$$

$$\left(\left(\left\Vert a : \text{lines}(a_1, \ldots, a_n) \bullet \text{alpha}(a) \circ \text{lifeline}(a) \right) [\![\text{ctl}]\!] \text{ until} \right) \setminus \text{ctl}$$

$$\text{alpha}(a) = \alpha(a, b); \; \text{lifeline}(a) = [\![b_1]\!]^{\mathsf{F}}_{\{a\}} \; {}_9^\circ \ldots {}_9^\circ \; [\![b_n]\!]^{\mathsf{F}}_{\{a\}}; \; \text{until} = [\![\text{untils}(b)]\!]^{\mathsf{U}}$$

$[\![-]\!]^{\mathsf{U}}$ For a list $\langle f_1, \ldots f_n \rangle$ of **until** fragments:

$$[\![\langle f_1, \ldots f_n \rangle]\!]^{\mathsf{U}} \triangleq \mu x \bullet (\text{term} \rightarrow \text{Skip}) \; \square \; [\![f_1]\!]^{\mathsf{u}} \; \square \ldots \square \; [\![f_n]\!]^{\mathsf{u}}$$

$[\![-]\!]^{\mathsf{u}}$ For a single **until** fragment inside the *until* process:

$$[\![\text{any in } x \text{ until } p]\!]^{\mathsf{u}} \triangleq \text{sync.isync}(u).\text{in} \rightarrow (\text{TChaos}([\![r]\!]^{\mathsf{MS}}) \; \triangle \; [\![p]\!]^{\mathsf{P}}_{\mathsf{U}}) \rightarrow$$

$$\text{sync.isync}(u).\text{out} \rightarrow x$$

$[\![-]\!]^{\mathsf{F}}$ By case analysis on types of fragment:

$$[\![\text{alt } x_1 \text{ else } x_2 \text{ else } \ldots x_n \text{ end}]\!]^{\mathsf{F}}_a \triangleq [\![x_1]\!]^{\mathsf{P}} \sqcap [\![x_2]\!]^{\mathsf{P}} \sqcap \ldots \sqcap [\![x_n]\!]^{\mathsf{P}}$$

$$[\![\text{xalt } x_1 \text{ else } x_2 \text{ else } \ldots x_n \text{ end}]\!]^{\mathsf{F}}_a \triangleq [\![x_1]\!]^{\mathsf{P}} \; \square \; [\![x_2]\!]^{\mathsf{P}} \; \square \ldots \square \; [\![x_n]\!]^{\mathsf{P}}$$

$$[\![\text{opt } x \text{ end}]\!]^{\mathsf{F}}_a \triangleq [\![\text{alt } x \text{ else [always] nothing end}]\!]^{\mathsf{F}}_a$$

$$[\![\text{deadline } (d) \text{ on } o \; x \text{ end}]\!]^{\mathsf{F}}_a \triangleq \text{if } o \notin a \text{ then } ([\![x]\!]^{\mathsf{P}} \blacktriangleright [\![d]\!]^{\mathsf{E}}) \text{ else } [\![x]\!]^{\mathsf{P}}_a$$

$$[\![o]\!]^{\mathsf{F}}_a \triangleq \text{if } a \cap \Lambda(o) = \emptyset \text{ then } \text{Skip else } [\![o]\!]^{\mathsf{O}} \qquad (\text{occurrence fragments})$$

$$[\![u]\!]^{\mathsf{F}}_a \triangleq \text{sync.isync}(u).\text{in} \rightarrow \text{sync.isync}(u).\text{out} \rightarrow \text{Skip} \qquad (\text{until fragments})$$

$[\![-]\!]^{\mathsf{O}}$ By case analysis on types of occurrence:

$$[\![\text{deadlock on } a]\!]^{\mathsf{O}} \triangleq \text{Stop} \qquad [\![\text{wait}(x) \text{ on } a]\!]^{\mathsf{O}} \triangleq \text{wait} [\![x]\!]^{\mathsf{E}}$$

$$[\![m \text{ (hot)}]\!]^{\mathsf{O}} \triangleq [\![m]\!]^{\mathsf{M}} \qquad [\![m \text{ (cold)}]\!]^{\mathsf{O}} \triangleq \mu x \bullet [\![m]\!]^{\mathsf{M}} \sqcap \text{tock} \rightarrow x$$

by a process that engages in a pair of *sync* events corresponding to the appropriate fragment in *until*. These pairs effect the handing-over of control from lifelines to the **until** fragment, then the hand-back once it is finished. All *lifeline* processes synchronise on all *sync* events, so that they all handover control to *until*.

Table 2 presents selected rewrite rules, from RoboCert to *tock*-CSP, defining the semantics of diagrams as we have just illustrated. Grey font denotes metanotation; standard mathematical (italics) font denotes *tock*-CSP target notation.

Rule $[\![-]\!]^{\mathsf{S}}$ expands a diagram s with actors a_1 to a_n. With $\text{lines}(a_1, \ldots, a_n)$ we get the set of all actors except the world. The set $\alpha(a, b)$ is the *alphabet* of an actor a within the fragment list b. For Fig. 6, if o stands for ObstacleAvoidance, f for ForagingC, w for **world**, and b for the body of collectionExample, then

$$\alpha(o,b) = ctl \cup \{w \twoheadrightarrow o: \textbf{event } \mathsf{obstacle}\} \cup \{x \in \mathbb{R} \bullet o \twoheadrightarrow w: \textbf{op } \mathsf{move}(0,\ x)\}$$

The definition of $lifeline(a)$ expands, per actor, to the sequential composition of the fragment rule $[\![-]\!]^F$ for each fragment in b. That rule takes an actor set; some sequence elements only appear on the lifeline process if they relate to one of the actors in the set. Usually, the set contains only the actor of the lifeline being defined; the exception is when we expand fragments inside an **until**.

Let $untils(b)$ extract from fragment list b all **until**s nested in the list. For example, $untils$ over the body of the diagram in Fig. 5 yields:

$\langle$ **any in** $(*)$ **until**: $w \twoheadrightarrow t$: **event** obstacle,

　　any in $(* \setminus \mathsf{Moves})$ **until**: $t \twoheadrightarrow w$: **op** move(0, **any**),

　　any in $(*)$ **until**: **deadlock on** $t\rangle$

Rule $[\![-]\!]^U$ builds the process composing **until** fragment bodies, as extracted by $untils$. Inside a recursive process $\mu\,x$, we produce first the termination acknowledgement $term \rightarrow Skip$, then add, in parallel composition, one application of the sub-rule $[\![f]\!]^u_x$ for every fragment f in the list. This rule, in turn, produces the timed chaos over the message set of f, interrupted by the expansion of the trigger of f. This uses a rule $[\![-]\!]^P$ for fragment operands, which we omit for brevity. Each fragment expansion then ends in a recursive call to x.

Rule $[\![-]\!]^F$ gives the semantics of fragments. As mentioned, this rule takes as an extra argument the set of actors for which we are expanding the fragment semantics. For **alt**, we combine the semantics of the branches using internal choice. The semantics for **xalt** is identical, but uses external choice. As in UML, **opt** equates to an **alt** where one branch is the body and another branch is empty.

For **deadline** fragments, we lift the operand into the $tock$-CSP deadline operator if, and only if, its bound actor is one of the ones we are considering. Otherwise, we pass through the operand semantics unchanged.

For **until** fragments, we synchronise with the $until$ process. To do so, we find the correct $sync.i$ channel using $isync$, then emitting $sync.i.in$ followed by $sync.i.out$. While the fragment body is not used in this rule, it will execute sequentially on the $until$ process once all lifelines synchronise on $sync.i.in$.

We elide productions for **loop** and **par** in $[\![-]\!]^F$. The semantics for **loop** resembles the standard UML semantics; that is, no synchronisation between iterations. Furthermore, the semantics for **par** is similar to that of Lima et al. [10].

Occurrences at fragment position whose $relevant$ actors include any of the actors given to $[\![-]\!]^F$ map to their occurrence semantics. Otherwise, they become $Skip$. In the rule, $A(e)$ refers to the relevant actors for e: the actor bound in any **on** clause on e; the endpoints if e is a message; or U for any other e.

Finally, $[\![-]\!]^O$ is the semantic rule for occurrences. Both **deadlock** and **wait** map to their $tock$-CSP equivalents (respectively, $Stop$ and $wait$).[3] The message

---

[3] Nondeterministic waits, taking range expressions, are planned for future revisions.

productions wrap rule $[\![-]\!]^{\mathsf{M}}$ with the semantics of temperature modality, applying the previously mentioned recursive-process transformation on **cold** messages.

Since the full RoboCert semantics is available in [19], we elide some semantic rules for brevity, as well as the productions mentioned previously. We omit $[\![-]\!]^{\mathsf{E}}$ (expressions) as it is largely similar to its equivalent in the RoboChart semantics; the RoboChart semantics is fully defined in [13]. We also omit $[\![-]\!]^{\mathsf{MS}}$ (message sets), as it directly maps to set operations.

We omit the rule for messages $([\![-]\!]^{\mathsf{M}})$, as it follows that of the analogous RoboChart constructs. The semantics of **op** messages is that of RoboChart calls; for **event** messages, it is that of RoboChart communications. Instances of **any** become CSP inputs. For example, we translate the messages in Fig. 6 as:

$$[\![\,\mathsf{f} \,\twoheadrightarrow\, \mathsf{w}\colon \mathbf{op}\ \mathsf{Explore}()\,]\!]^{\mathsf{M}} \triangleq \mathit{ForagingC} :: \mathit{ExploreCall}$$

$$[\![\,\mathsf{w} \,\twoheadrightarrow\, \mathsf{o}\colon \mathbf{event}\ \mathsf{obstacle}\,]\!]^{\mathsf{M}} \triangleq \mathit{ObstacleAvoidance} :: \mathit{obstacle.in}$$

$$[\![\,\mathsf{w} \,\twoheadrightarrow\, \mathsf{f}\colon \mathbf{event}\ \mathsf{collected}\,]\!]^{\mathsf{M}} \triangleq \mathit{ForagingC} :: \mathit{collected.in}$$

$$[\![\,\mathsf{o} \,\twoheadrightarrow\, \mathsf{w}\colon \mathbf{op}\ \mathsf{move}(0, \mathbf{any})\,]\!]^{\mathsf{M}} \triangleq \mathit{ObstacleAvoidance} :: \mathit{moveCall.0?x}$$

6   Tool Support

RoboCert has tool support in the form of RoboTool Eclipse plug-ins.[4] It adopts a textual encoding of RoboCert diagrams loosely based on the *Mermaid*[5] markup language. The tool reifies the well-formedness rules and semantics in Sect. 5.

Listing 1.1 shows the encoding of the diagram in Fig. 4. In RoboTool, sequence diagrams are included in a *specification group* that has a name, and defines a target, possibly instantiating some of its constants. This is optional, but for successful verification by model checking, all constants need to have a value. In our example, the group is SAvoid. The **target** stanza sets the group's target as the **state machine** ObstacleAvoidance:,!:Avoid; other targets can be defined using **module, controller, operation**, or, for collection targets, **components of module** and **components of controller**. Each **set to** line fixes constants of the target.

A specification group also allows the definitions of (short)names for the **actors** such as **target**s, **world**s, and **component**s up-front for later use in the diagrams. In our example, we define names T and W for the target and the world.

In the sequence turnTurn, each occurrence inhabits its own line, with message occurrences denoting the source and target actors using the $\twoheadrightarrow$ syntax. Occurrences and fragments over particular actors have an 'on X' construct. A full syntax of RoboCert, while omitted here, is available in the report.

Below the group is a *sequence property* assertion, A1; this is the assertion seen in Fig. 4. Below A1 is a second assertion, over an example of a core property in the 'controlled English' language mentioned in Sect. 4. This assertion requires that

---

[4] https://github.com/UoY-RoboStar/robocert-evaluation.

[5] https://mermaid-js.github.io.

Listing 1.1. A RoboCert script textually encoding the sequence in Figure 4

```
specification  group SAvoid
  target  = state machine ObstacleAvoidance:\,\!:Avoid with
    turnRadius, turnSpeed  set to 2
  actors  = { target as T, world as W }
  sequence turnTurn
    actors T and W
    W→T: event obstacle
    deadline(0) on T: T→W: op move(0, any)
    wait(1) on T
    deadline(0) on T: T→W: op move(0, 0)

assertion A1  : SAvoid:\,\!:turnTurn is not observed in the traces model
assertion Ac  : target of SAvoid is deadlock−free
```

the target of SAvoid (that is, Avoid) is deadlock-free. The set of core properties is a broad subset of that of the existing RoboChart assertion language.

RoboTool compiles scripts such as those above using the semantic rules in Sect. 5. Before doing so, RoboTool performs syntax checking, scope analysis, and the verification of healthiness conditions. RoboTool outputs scripts in the CSP_M dialect of CSP understood by the FDR model checker [5]; we can then use FDR to model-check the CSP refinement and structural assertions corresponding to the sequence and core properties in the RoboCert script. By doing this, we validate the properties.

The RoboTool implementation validates our rules. Each rule is implemented separately, by its own method, and, apart from the fact that the rules are functional, and the implementation uses an imperative language, there is a one-to-one correspondence between the rule definitions and code.

The RoboCert plug-in uses the output of the existing RoboChart plugin to translate targets, either directly (for component targets) or with composition to reflect the top-level structure of the component (for collection targets). We can therefore use the RoboTool verification facilities to model check properties against the automatically generated semantics of the actual artefacts.

7   Conclusions

This paper has introduced a domain-specific property language for robotics based on UML sequence diagrams, but significantly enriched to deal with compositional reasoning and time properties. This language enriches the RoboStar model-based framework, and, in particular, supports the specification and verification by refinement of properties of design models written in RoboChart. We have shown that sequences capture flows of events and operations in RoboChart models in a natural way. We have also shown how the diagrams map onto *tock*-CSP.

RoboCert aims to be a unified toolbox for property specification of RoboStar models, and we plan to expand its notation set beyond core properties, sequence diagrams, CSP, and PCTL. As our work complements that of Lindoso et al. [11] on activity diagrams for RoboChart models, we will expand support in RoboTool to integrate such diagrams. Our goal is to discover and capture notations that are, or will be, useful among domain experts.

Our graphical notation is consistent and follows from the metamodel, but the diagrams here were manually created, and there is no mapping between graphical and textual notations except by translation of both to the metamodel. We aim to create *Mermaid*-style tooling for deriving graphical versions of textual scripts, but graphical creation of diagrams (as with RoboChart) would be very useful.

Evaluating RoboCert is an important next step. We intend to scale up from the small demonstrator seen in this paper to larger, real-world case studies; this will validate RoboCert and also help us to identify features and changes required to bring the language to maturity. Specific evaluation of usability among domain experts will also help to inform the evolution of the language.

Finally, the RoboStar notations allow for parallel modelling of both robotic software and hardware, with the goal of co-verification. Extending RoboCert to express hybrid properties over both (discrete, logical) software and (continuous, physical) hardware behaviour is in our plans.

Acknowledgements. This work has been funded by the UK EPSRC Grants EP/M025756/1, EP/R025479/1, and EP/V026801/2, and by the UK Royal Academy of Engineering Grant No CiET1718/45. We are also grateful to members of the RoboStar (www.cs.york.ac.uk/robostar/) group for several useful discussions; in particular, Pedro Ribeiro and Alvaro Miyazawa have given many insights as to how to best integrate RoboCert with the RoboStar ecosystem.

References

1. Autili, M., Inverardi, P., Pelliccione, P.: Graphical scenarios for specifying temporal properties: an automated approach. Autom. Softw. Eng. **14**, 293–340 (2007). https://doi.org/10.1007/s10515-007-0012-6
2. Baxter, J., Ribeiro, P., Cavalcanti, A.L.C.: Sound reasoning in tock-CSP. Acta Inform. (2021). https://doi.org/10.1007/s00236-020-00394-3, April 2021
3. Buchanan, E., Pomfret, A., Timmis, J.: Dynamic task partitioning for foraging robot swarms. In: Dorigo, M., et al. (eds.) ANTS 2016. LNCS, vol. 9882, pp. 113–124. Springer, Cham (2016). https://doi.org/10.1007/978-3-319-44427-7_10
4. Damm, W., Harel, D.: LSCs: breathing life into message sequence charts. Formal Methods Syst. Des. **19**(1), 45–80 (2001). https://doi.org/10.1023/A:1011227529550
5. Gibson-Robinson, T., Armstrong, P., Boulgakov, A., Roscoe, A.W.: FDR3 — a modern refinement checker for CSP. In: Ábrahám, E., Havelund, K. (eds.) TACAS 2014. LNCS, vol. 8413, pp. 187–201. Springer, Heidelberg (2014). https://doi.org/10.1007/978-3-642-54862-8_13
6. Grosu, R., Smolka, S.A.: Safety-liveness semantics for UML 2.0 sequence diagrams. In: 5th ACSD, pp. 6–14 (2005). https://doi.org/10.1109/ACSD.2005.31

7. Haugen, Ø., Husa, K.E., Runde, R.K., Stølen, K.: Why timed sequence diagrams require three-event semantics. In: Leue, S., Systä, T.J. (eds.) Scenarios: Models, Transformations and Tools. LNCS, vol. 3466, pp. 1–25. Springer, Heidelberg (2005). https://doi.org/10.1007/11495628_1

8. Haugen, Ø., Stølen, K.: STAIRS – steps to analyze interactions with refinement semantics. In: Stevens, P., Whittle, J., Booch, G. (eds.) UML 2003. LNCS, vol. 2863, pp. 388–402. Springer, Heidelberg (2003). https://doi.org/10.1007/978-3-540-45221-8_33

9. Jacobs, J., Simpson, A.: On a process algebraic representation of sequence diagrams. In: Canal, C., Idani, A. (eds.) SEFM 2014. LNCS, vol. 8938, pp. 71–85. Springer, Cham (2015). https://doi.org/10.1007/978-3-319-15201-1_5

10. Lima, L., Iyoda, J., Sampaio, A.: A formal semantics for sequence diagrams and a strategy for system analysis. In: MODELSWARD, pp. 317–324. SciTePress (2014). https://doi.org/10.5220/0004711603170324

11. Lindoso, W., Nogueira, S.C., Domingues, R., Lima, L.: Visual specification of properties for robotic designs. In: Campos, S., Minea, M. (eds.) SBMF 2021. LNCS, vol. 13130, pp. 34–52. Springer, Cham (2021). https://doi.org/10.1007/978-3-030-92137-8_3

12. Micskei, Z., Waeselynck, H.: The many meanings of UML 2 sequence diagrams: a survey. Softw. Syst. Model. **10**(4), 489–514 (2011). https://doi.org/10.1007/s10270-010-0157-9

13. Miyazawa, A., Ribeiro, P., Li, W., Cavalcanti, A., Timmis, J., Woodcock, J.: RoboChart: modelling and verification of the functional behaviour of robotic applications. Softw. Syst. Model. **18**(5), 3097–3149 (2019). https://doi.org/10.1007/s10270-018-00710-z

14. Petre, M.: UML in practice. In: ICSE, pp. 722–731. IEEE Press (2013). https://doi.org/10.1109/ICSE.2013.6606618

15. Roscoe, A.W.: Understanding Concurrent Systems. Texts in Computer Science, Springer, London (2011). https://doi.org/10.1007/978-1-84882-258-0

16. Ye, K., Cavalcanti, A., Foster, S., Miyazawa, A., Woodcock, J.: Probabilistic modelling and verification using RoboChart and PRISM. Softw. Syst. Model. **21**(2), 667–716 (2021). https://doi.org/10.1007/s10270-021-00916-8

17. Message Sequence Chart (MSC). Standard, ITU-T, February 2011. https://www.itu.int/rec/T-REC-Z.120-201102-I/en

18. OMG Unified Modeling Language. Standard, Object Management Group, December 2017. https://www.omg.org/spec/UML/2.5.1/PDF

19. RoboCert Reference Manual. Report, RoboStar, May 2022. https://robostar.cs.york.ac.uk/publications/reports/robocert.pdf

Formally Verified Animation
for RoboChart Using Interaction Trees

Kangfeng Ye[⊠], Simon Foster, and Jim Woodcock

University of York, York, UK
{kangfeng.ye,simon.foster,jim.woodcock}@york.ac.uk

Abstract. RoboChart is a core notation in the RoboStar framework. It is a timed and probabilistic domain-specific and state machine based language for robotics. RoboChart supports shared variables and communication across entities in its component model. It has a formal denotational semantics given in CSP. Interaction Trees (ITrees) is a semantic technique to represent behaviours of reactive and concurrent programs interacting with their environments. Recent mechanisations of ITrees along with ITree-based CSP semantics and a Z mathematical toolkit in Isabelle/HOL bring new applications of verification and animation for state-rich process languages, such as RoboChart. In this paper, we use ITrees to give RoboChart a novel operational semantics, implement it in Isabelle, and use Isabelle's code generator to generate verified and executable animations. We illustrate our approach using an autonomous chemical detector model. With animation, we show two concrete scenarios when the robot encounters different environmental inputs.

1 Introduction

The RoboStar[1] framework [1] brings modern modelling and verification technologies into software engineering for robotics. In this framework, models of the platform, environment, design, and simulations are given formal semantics in a unified semantic framework [2]. Correctness of simulation is guaranteed with respect to particular models using a variety of analysis technologies including model checking, theorem proving, and testing. Additionally, modelling, semantics generation, verification, simulation, and testing are automated and integrated in an Eclipse-based tool, RoboTool.[2] The core of RoboStar is RoboChart [3,4], a timed and probabilistic domain-specific language for robotics, which provides UML-like architectural and state machine modelling notations. RoboChart is distinctive in its formal semantics [3–5], which enables automated verification using model checking and theorem proving [6].

Previous work [3] gives RoboChart a denotational semantics based on the CSP process algebra [7,8]. This paper defines a direct operational semantics for RoboChart using Interaction Trees (ITrees) [9]. ITrees are coinductive structures

---

[1] https://robostar.cs.york.ac.uk.

[2] https://robostar.cs.york.ac.uk/robotool/.

© Springer Nature Switzerland AG 2022
A. Riesco and M. Zhang (Eds.): ICFEM 2022, LNCS 13478, pp. 404–420, 2022.
https://doi.org/10.1007/978-3-031-17244-1_24

that can model infinite behaviours of a reactive system interacting with its environment. ITrees have been mechanised in both Coq [9] and Isabelle/HOL [10]. ITrees are a powerful semantic technique for development of formal semantics that can unify trace-based failures-divergences semantics [8,11] for CSP and transition-based operational semantics, and so unifies verification and animation [10]. In previous work [10], we have proved a formal correspondence between the failures-divergences model and our ITree-based semantics.

The existing implementation of RoboChart's semantics in RoboTool is restricted to machine readable CSP (or CSP-M) for verification with FDR [12], and so only a subset of RoboChart's rich types and expressions can be supported and quantified predicates cannot be solved. Our contribution here is a richer ITree-based CSP semantics for RoboChart to address these restrictions. Our semantics also allows us to characterise systems with an infinite number of states symbolically, avoiding the need to generate an explicit transition system.

We mechanise the semantics in Isabelle/HOL and then utilise the code generator [13] to produce Haskell code for animation. Isabelle's code generator [13] is a translation from the source HOL logic to target functional languages (such as SML and Haskell) and the translation preserves semantics correctness using high-order rewrite systems [14]. As a result, the semantics of the source logic in Isabelle is preserved during code generation via translation to target functional languages. Our animation, therefore, is formally verified with respect to RoboChart's semantics in ITrees. Thanks to the equational logic, functional algorithms and data refinement are supported in code generation, and so less efficient algorithms and data structures, that are used for verification in Isabelle, can be replaced with more efficient ones for animation.

Our technical contributions are as follows: we (1) implement extra CSP operators (interrupt, exception, and renaming) to deal with the RoboChart semantics and a bounded sequence type for code generation; (2) define an ITree-based operational semantics for RoboChart; (3) implement the semantics of a RoboChart model for a case study; and (4) animate the model. With our mechanisation and the animation, we have detected a number of issues in this RoboChart model. All definitions and theorems in this paper are mechanised and accompanying icons (🐝) link to corresponding repository artifacts.

The remainder of this paper is organised as follows. In Sect. 2, we introduce RoboChart through an autonomous chemical detector example. Section 3 briefly describes the mechanisation of ITrees in Isabelle and presents the additional CSP operators in detail. Then we present the RoboChart semantics in ITrees in Sect. 4 and use the chemical detector as an example to illustrate animation in Sect. 5. We review related work in Sect. 6 and conclude in Sect. 7.

2   RoboChart

Modelling We describe features of RoboChart for modelling controllers of robots using as an example an autonomous chemical detector [3,15,16]. The robot is equipped with sensors to (1) analyse the air to detect dangerous gases; (2) detect obstacles; and (3) estimate change in position (using an odometer). The controller of the robot performs a random walk with obstacle avoidance. Upon

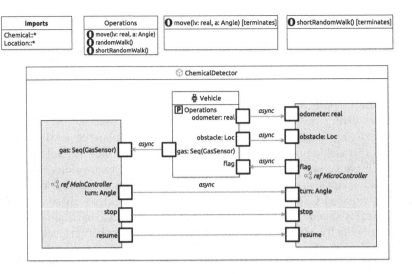

Fig. 1. The module of the autonomous chemical detector model.

detection of a chemical with its intensity above a threshold, the robot drops a flag and stops there. This model[3] [3] has been studied and analysed in RoboTool, using FDR4,[4] a CSP refinement checker.

The top level structure of a RoboChart model, a module, is shown in Fig. 1. The module ChemicalDetector contains a robotic platform Vehicle and two controller references MainController and MicroController. The physical robot is abstracted into the robotic platform through variables, events, and operations. The platform provides the controllers with services (1) to read its sensor data through three events: gas, obstacle, and odometer; (2) for movement through three operations: move, randomWalk, and shortRandomWalk as grouped in an interface Operations; and (3) to drop a flag through receiving a flag event.

A platform and controllers communicate using directional connections. For example, the platform is linked to MainController through an asynchronous connection on event gas of type seq(GasSensor), sequences of type GasSensor. Furthermore, the MainController and MicroController interact using the events turn, stop, and resume.

The types used in the module are defined in the two imported packages: Chemical and Location (whose diagrams are omitted here for simplicity). The two packages declare primitive types Chem and Intensity, enumerations Status, Angle, and Loc, a record GasSensor containing two fields (c of type Chem and i of type Intensity), and six functions, of which two are specified using preconditions and postconditions, and four are unspecified. An operation changeDireciton, with a parameter l of type Loc and a constant lv, is also defined using a state machine.

---

[3] https://robostar.cs.york.ac.uk/case_studies/autonomous-chemical-detector/autonomous-chemical-detector.html.

[4] https://cocotec.io/fdr/.

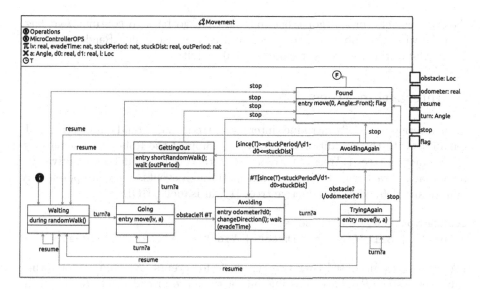

Fig. 2. Movement state machine of the autonomous chemical detector model.

MicroController is implemented using the Movement state machine shown in Fig. 2, and MainController using another state machine called GasAnalysis. The machine Movement declares various constants such as lv for linear velocity, four variables (a, d0, d1, and l) for preservation of values (angle, odometer readings, and location) carried on communication, and a clock T. The machine also contains a variety of nodes: one initial junction (●), seven normal states such as Waiting and Going, and a final state (Ⓕ). A state may have an entry action such as an operation call move(lv, a) of state Waiting, an exit action, or a during action such as an operation call randomWalk() of state Going.

In state machines, transitions connect states and junctions. Transitions have a label with the optional features: a trigger event, a clock reset, a guard condition, and an action. For example, the transition from TryingAgain to AvoidingAgain has an input trigger and an action odometer?d1 (an input communication). The transition from AvoidingAgain to Avoiding has a clock reset #T and a disjunctive guard in which since(T) counts elapsed time since the last reset of T.

This machine gives the behaviour of the robot's response to outcomes of the chemical analysis: (1) resume to state Waiting if no gas is detected (implemented in GasAnalysis); (2) stop to state Found and then terminate , if a gas above the threshold is detected; (3) turn to the direction, where a gas is detected but not above the threshold, with obstacle avoidance in state Going; (4) upon the first detection of an obstacle, reset T and start Avoiding with an initial odometer reading and the movement direction changed (software waits for evadeTime for the effect of that change); (5) if a gas is still detected after the changed direction, TryingAgain to turn and move to the gas direction; (6) if another obstacle is detected during avoidance, AvoidingAgain by reading the odometer to check the distance of two obstacles; (7) if the robot has moved far enough between the two obstacles or not got stuck long enough, go back to continue Avoiding; (8) otherwise, the robot has got stuck in a corner, use a shortRandomWalk for GettingOut of the area, then resume normal activities;

3   Interaction Trees

In this section we briefly introduce interaction trees, and extend our existing CSP semantics with three additional operators to support the RoboChart semantics.

Interaction trees (ITrees) [9] are a data structure for modelling reactive systems that interact with their environment through events. They are potentially infinite and defined as coinductive trees [17] in Isabelle/HOL.

```
codatatype ('e, 'r) itree =
  Ret 'r | Sil "('e, 'r) itree" | Vis "'e ⇸ ('e, 'r) itree"
```

ITrees are parameterised over two types: 'e for events (E), and 'r for return values or states (R). Three possible interactions are provided: (1) $Ret\,x$: termination $(\checkmark_x)$ with a value x of type R returned; (2) $Sil\,P$: an internal silent event $(\tau P$, for a successor ITree $P)$; or (3) $Vis\,F$: a choice among several visible events represented by a partial function F of type $E \nrightarrow (E, R)itree$. Partial functions are part of the Z toolkit[5] [18] which is also mechanised in Isabelle/HOL.

Deterministic CSP processes can be given an executable semantics using ITrees. Previously, the following CSP processes and operators are defined: (1) basic processes: *skip*, *stop*, and *div*; (2) input prefixing $c?x$; (3) output prefixing $c!v$; (4) *guard* b; (5) external choice $P \mathbin{\square} Q$; (6) parallel composition $P \parallel_E Q$; (7) hiding $P \setminus A$; (8) sequential composition $P \mathbin{;} Q$; (9) *loop* and *iterate*.

Here, we give an ITree semantics to three extra CSP operators to allow us to give an ITree-based semantics to RoboChart. The interrupt, exception, and renaming operators are used in the RoboChart's semantics to allow interruption of a during action, termination of a state machine, a controller, or a module, and alphabet transformation of processes. We restrict ourselves to deterministic operators as it makes animation of large models more efficient.

The first operator we introduce is interrupt [7,8], $P \mathbin{\triangle} Q$, which behaves like P except that if at any time Q performs one of its initial events then it takes over. We present partial functions as sets below. This operator, along with the other two, are defined corecursively, which allows them to operate on the infinite structure of an ITree. In corecursive definitions, every corecursive call on the right-hand side of each equation must be guarded by an ITree constructor.

Definition 3.1 (Interrupt).

$$(Sil\,P') \mathbin{\triangle} Q = Sil\,(P' \mathbin{\triangle} Q) \qquad P \mathbin{\triangle} (Sil\,Q') = Sil\,(P \mathbin{\triangle} Q')$$
$$(Ret\,x) \mathbin{\triangle} Q = Ret\,x \qquad\qquad P \mathbin{\triangle} (Ret\,x) = Ret\,x$$
$$(Vis\,F) \mathbin{\triangle} (Vis\,G) = Vis\left(\{e \mapsto (P' \mathbin{\triangle} Q) \mid (e \mapsto P') \in (dom(G) \mathbin{\lhd\!\!\!-} F)\} \oplus G\right)$$

---

[5] https://github.com/isabelle-utp/Z_Toolkit.

In the definition, $\lhd$ is called the domain anti-restriction, and $A \lhd R$ denotes the domain restriction of relation R to the complement of set A. The *Sil* cases allow τ events to happen independently with priority and without resolving $\triangle$. The *Ret* cases terminate with the value x returned from either left or right side of $\triangle$.

For the *Vis* cases, it is also *Vis* constructed from an overriding $\oplus$ of the further two sets, representing two partial functions. In the partial function, $(\text{dom}(G) \lhd F)$ restricts the domain of F to the complement of the domain of G. The first partial function denotes that an initial event e of P, that is not the initial event of Q, can occur independently (without resolving the interrupt) and its continuation is a corecursive call $P' \triangle Q$. The second function is just G, which denotes that the initial events of Q can happen no matter whether they are in F or not. This means if P and Q share events, Q has priority. This prevents nondeterminism.

Next, we present the exception operator, $P \llbracket A \rhd Q$, which behaves like P initially, but if P ever performs an event from the set A, then Q takes over.

Definition 3.2 (Exception).   🜂

$$(Ret\,x)\;\llbracket A \rhd Q = Ret\,x \qquad (Sil\,P')\;\llbracket A \rhd Q = Sil\,(P'\;\llbracket A \rhd Q)$$

$$(Vis\,F)\;\llbracket A \rhd Q = Vis\left(\begin{array}{l}\{e \mapsto (P'\;\llbracket A \rhd Q) \mid (e \mapsto P') \in (A \lhd F)\} \oplus \\ \{e \mapsto Q \mid e \in (A \cap \text{dom}(F))\}\end{array}\right)$$

The *Ret* case terminates immediately with the value x returned, and Q will not be performed. The *Sil* case allows the τ event to be consumed.

Similar to Definition 3.1, the *Vis* case is also represented by the overriding of two partial functions. The first partial function represents that an initial event e of P, that is not in A (that is, $e \in \text{dom}(A \lhd F)$), can occur independently and its continuation is a corecursive call $P'\;\llbracket A \rhd Q$. Following execution of an initial event e of P that is in A (that is, $e \in (A \cap \text{dom}(F))$, the exception behaves like Q, which is expressed by the second partial function.

The last operator we define for this work is renaming, $P\llbracket\rho\rrbracket$, which renames events of P according to the renaming relation $\rho : E_1 \leftrightarrow E_2$. We note this relation is possibly heterogeneous, and so E_1 and E_2 are different types of events. First, we define an auxiliary function for making a relation functional by removing any pairs that have duplicate distinct values. This is the case when the renaming relation, restricted to the initial events of P, is functional.

$$mk\_functional(R) = \{(x,y) \in R.\,\forall y'.(x,y') \in R \Rightarrow y = y'\}$$

This produces the minimal functional relation that is consistent with R. For example, $mk\_functional(\{e_1 \mapsto e_2, e_1 \mapsto e_3, e_2 \mapsto e_3\}) = \{e_2 \mapsto e_3\}$. This function is used to avoid nondeterminism introduced by renaming multiple events to a same event. We use this function to define the renaming operator.

Definition 3.3 (Renaming).   🜂

$$(Ret\,x)\,\llbracket\rho\rrbracket = Ret\,x \qquad (Sil\,P')\,\llbracket\rho\rrbracket = Sil\,(P'\llbracket\rho\rrbracket)$$

$$(Vis\,F)\,\llbracket\rho\rrbracket = \left(\begin{array}{l}\textbf{let}\;\; G = F \circ mk\_functional\left((\text{dom}(F) \lhd \rho)^{\sim}\right) \\ \bullet\; Vis\left(\{e_2 \mapsto (P'\llbracket\rho\rrbracket) \mid (e_2 \mapsto P') \in G\}\right)\end{array}\right)$$

The *Ret* case behaves like P and the renaming has no effect on it. The *Sil* case allows τ events to be consumed, since they are not subject to renaming.

In the *Vis* case, G is a partial function $(E_2 \nrightarrow (E_1, R)itree)$ that is the backward partial function composition $\circ$ of F and a partial function made using $mk\_functional$ from the inverse $\sim$ of the relation $(\mathrm{dom}(F) \lhd \rho)$ which is the domain restriction $\lhd$ of ρ to the domain $\mathrm{dom}(F)$ of F. Basically, the multiple events of E_1 that are mapped to a same event of E_2 in ρ and also are the initial events of P, or in $\mathrm{dom}(F)$, are removed in G. The renaming result is a partial function in which each event e_2 in the domain of G is mapped to a renamed process by a corecursive call $P'[\![\rho]\!]$ where $(e_2 \mapsto P') \in G$.

4   RoboChart Semantics in Interaction Trees

In this section, we describe how we give a semantics to RoboChart in terms of ITrees in Isabelle/HOL. These include types, instantiations, functions, state machines, controllers, and modules. In the implementation of RoboChart's semantics, we also take into account the practical details of the CSP semantics generation in RoboTool, such as naming and bounded primitive types.

Types. RoboChart has its type system based on that of the Z notation [19]. It supports basic types: PrimitiveType, Enumeration, records (or schema types), and other additional types from the mathematical toolkits of Z.

The core package of RoboTool provides five primitive types: boolean, naturals, integers, real numbers, and string. We map integers, naturals, and strings onto the corresponding types in Isabelle/HOL, but with support for code generation to target language types. This improve efficiency of evaluation and thus animation. RoboChart models can also have abstract primitive types with no explicit constructors, such as Chem and Intensity in the chemical detector model presented in Sect. 2. We map primitive types to finite enumerations for the purpose of code generation. We define a finite type `PrimType` parametrised over two types: `'t` for specialisation and a numeral type `'a` for the number of elements.

```
datatype ('t, 'a::finite) PrimType = PrimTypeC 'a          🦋
```

For example, Chem is implemented as a generic type (ChemT, 'a) PrimType (🦋). An example for a finite type `'a` is the numeral type in Isabelle, such as type 2 which contains two elements: zero (`0::2`) and one (`1::2`).

For enumerations and records, we use **datatype** and **record** in Isabelle. For finite sequences such as Seq(GasSensor), we also bound the length of each sequence in this type. We define bounded lists or sequences (`'a, 'n::finite`) `blist` (🦋) over two parametrised types: `'a` for the type of elements and a finite type `'n` for the maximum length of each list. For Seq(GasSensor), its bounded type in Isabelle is (`GasSensor, 2`) `blist` with length bounded to 2.

For other types, we have their counterparts in the Z toolkit.

```
    ƒ× intensity(gs: Seq(GasSensor)): Intensity
◄ size(gs)>0
▶ forall x: nat | 0<=x/\x<size(gs) @ goreq(result, gs[x].i)
▶ exists y: nat | 0<=y/\y<size(gs) @ result==gs[y].i
```

Fig. 3. The specification of function intensity.

Instantiations. The `instantiation.csp` file of the CSP semantics contains common definitions used by all models for verification using FDR. These include the definitions of bounded core types (named types in CSP) and arithmetic operators under which these bounded types are closed. We show below one example for type core_int and one for the plus operator, closed under a bounded type T.

```
nametype core_int = {-2 .. 2}
Plus(e1, e2, T) = if member(e1 + e2, T) then (e1 + e2) else e1
```

That is, if e1+e2 is within T then this is the result, otherwise it is e1. We use **locale** [20] in Isabelle to define these for reuse in all models. Locales allow us to characterise abstract parameters (such as `min_int` and `max_int`, to define bounded core type core_int) and assumptions in a local theory context.

Functions. Functions in RoboChart benefit from the rich expressions in Isabelle and the Z toolkit in Isabelle. The expressions that are not supported in CSP-M such as logical quantifications are naturally present in Isabelle. Using the code generator, the preconditions and postconditions of a function definition can be solved effectively, while this is not possible in CSP-M and FDR.

An example function is intensity, shown in Fig. 3, defined in the chemical detector model, whose two postconditions (▶) involve universal and existential quantifications where @ separates constraint and predicate parts, and goreq is a $\geq$ relation on intensities. The result of the function is the largest intensity in **gs**. The precondition (◄) is that the length (size) of the parameter **gs** is larger than 0. For verification with FDR in RoboTool, an explicit implementation of this function must be supplied. Our definition of this function in Isabelle, however, is directly from its specification and is shown below.

```
definition "pre_Chemical_intensity gs = (blength gs > 0)"
definition "Chemical_intensity gs = (THE result.
  (∀x::nat<blength gs. Chemical_goreq(result, gs_i (bnth gs x)))∧
  (∃x::nat<blength gs. result = gs_i (bnth gs x)))"
```

In the definitions, `blength gs` gives the length of a bounded sequence **gs**, `bnth gs n` gives the nth element in **gs**, and `gs_i` returns the field value in a record of type GasSensor. The two definitions are straightforward except that a definite description (`THE result`, denoting the unique result such that the predicate holds) is used to return the **result**. We have two definitions here corresponding to the definition of intensity: one for its precondition and one for its postconditions. This is due to the semantics of such a function f in RoboChart: a boolean guard (pre(f) & P) where pre(f) is the preconditions of f and f is called in process P, and so if the preconditions are not satisfied, the semantics deadlocks.

We note that there is an error in the definition of intensity in the original model where $\leq$ (instead of $<$) is used for comparison between x (and y) and size(gs). This is because sequences are zero-indexed. Our animation detects this error and so we have fixed it. Similarly, we also found another error in the postcondition of the function location: the postcondition is not strong enough to identify a unique result of the function.

State Machine Definitions. The RoboChart semantics of a state machine is a parallel composition of memory processes for its variables (MemoryVar) and transitions (MemoryTrans), and a process (STM) for its behaviour with internal events hidden and also catering for its termination using the exception operator.

STM is a parallel composition of the behaviour (STM_I) for its initial junction and the restricted behaviour (S_R) for each state S synchronising on state entering and exiting events. A state's behaviour S involves the entering of this state, the execution of its during action, and the execution of one of its transitions. The execution of a transition exits the state, executes the action of the transition, and enters the target state of the transition. Not all transitions are available for S, such as the transitions from sibling states of S and substates of S. These transitions are excluded in the restricted behaviour S_R.

The state machine semantics uses a general type InOut for the direction of an event in a connection, two data types for state and transition identifiers (SIDS and TIDS), and an event alphabet (E) for the process of this state machine. The event alphabet is represented by the parametrised type E of events which is declared through the **chantype** command. E is expressed by a finite set of channels declared in the command. We show below an example for the Movement machine in Fig. 2.

```
datatype InOut = din | dout
datatype SIDS_Movement = SID_Movement|SID_Movement_Waiting|...
datatype TIDS_Movement = TID_Movement_t1|TID_Movement_t2|...
chantype Chan_Movement = internal_Movement :: TIDS_Movement
  terminate_Movement::unit
  enter_Movement::"SIDS_Movement×SIDS_Movement" ...
  get_l_Movement::"Location_Loc"  set_l_Movement::"Location_Loc"
  obstacle__Movement::"TIDS_Movement×InOut×Location_Loc"
  obstacle_Movement::"InOut×Location_Loc" ...
  moveCall_Movement::"core_real×Chemical_Angle" ...
```

The channel type of Movement includes four kinds of channels. Firstly, flow control channels include (a) internal[6] for transitions without a trigger; (b) enter, entered, exit, and exited for the entering and exiting of a state; and

---

[6] In the Isabelle code, we include suffixes to ensure that names do not collide, but omit them here.

(c) **terminate** for the termination of the machine. Secondly, variable channels contain a **set** and a **get** channel for each variable with an additional **set_EXT** for each shared variable to accept an external update. Thirdly, event channels include two channels for each event of the machine, one such as **obstacle** for the event **obstacle** used in actions of RoboChart and another such as **obstacle_** (with an additional **TIDS** for its type) for the event **obstacle** used as triggers of transitions. The distinction of two event channels (**obstacle** and **obstacle_**) for each event (**obstacle**) is necessary because the guard of a transition is evaluated in **MemoryTrans**, and so only the trigger event (not action event) of the transition is subject to the guard evaluation, and, therefore, has a new channel (**obstacle_**) with a transition id. We note, however, that events **obstacle_.tid** of this new channel are eventually renamed to the event channel **obstacle** in the process for the machine. Fourthly, operation call channels include a channel such as **moveCall** for each call to the operation **move** provided by the platform.

The memory process **Memory_x** for a shared variable x is shown below.

$$loop\ (\lambda v.\ \texttt{get\_x!v} \rightarrow \checkmark_v\ \Box\ \texttt{set\_x?x} \rightarrow \checkmark_x\ \Box\ \texttt{set\_EXT\_x?x} \rightarrow \checkmark_x)$$

The process is an infinite loop. It provides three choices: output the value v on **get_x** without updating the variable and accept a local (or external) update of the variable through **set_x** (or **set_EXT_x**).

The memory process for transitions of the state machine Movement in Fig. 2 is partially (3 in 24 transitions) illustrated below.

$$loop\ (\lambda id.\ \texttt{internal!TID\_t1} \rightarrow \checkmark_{id}\ \Box\ \texttt{resume!(TID\_t0,din)} \rightarrow \checkmark_{id}\ \Box$$
$$(\texttt{get\_d1?d1} \rightarrow \texttt{get\_d0?d0} \rightarrow$$
$$(\texttt{d1-d0>stuckDist)\&(internal!TID\_t12} \rightarrow \checkmark_{id})\ \Box\ ...)$$

The state of this loop process is a constant **id** (used to identify a RoboChart module). Each choice corresponds to a transition: (1) the first choice for the default transition **t1** from the initial junction to state Waiting which has no trigger (hence **internal**); (2) the second for the self transition of state Waiting whose trigger is resume (an input so din); and (3) the third for the transition from AvoidingAgain to Avoiding whose guard is (d1-d0>stuckDist) (time semantics is ignored) and evaluated in this memory transition process.

The process S for the behaviour of a state S is sketched below.

$$S(id) = enter?sd : OSIDS \rightarrow S\_exec(id, fst\ sd)$$
$$S\_exec(id, s) = S\_entry \,\S\, entered!(s, SID\_S) \,\S\,$$
$$\left(\begin{array}{l} (S\_during \,\S\, stop) \, \triangle \\ \left(\begin{array}{l} \Box\, t : sTrans \bullet \left(\begin{array}{l} e\_t?(TID\_t, \_) \rightarrow exit!pSID\_S \rightarrow S\_exit \,\S\, \\ exited!pSID\_S \rightarrow enter!pSID\_S \rightarrow \\ S\_exec(id, SID\_S) \end{array} \right) \Box \\ \Box\, t : oTrans \bullet \left(\begin{array}{l} ... \,\S\, exited!pSID\_S \rightarrow enter!(SID\_S, SID\_td) \\ \rightarrow entered!(SID\_S, SID\_td) \rightarrow S(id) \end{array} \right) \Box \\ \Box\, e\_ : EvtChs \bullet \left(\begin{array}{l} e\_?(TID\_t, \_) \rightarrow exit?sd : OSIDS \rightarrow \\ (S\_exit \,\S\, exited?(fst\ sd, SID\_S) \rightarrow S(id)) \end{array} \right) \end{array} \right) \end{array} \right)$$

S and S_exec are defined by mutual recursion. Initially, S accepts *enter*ing from other nodes of the state machine containing S where *OSIDS* denotes a set of pairs $(oSID, SID\_S)$ ($oSID$ is SID for one of other nodes and SID_S is SID for S). Afterwards, the behaviour of S is given by S_exec with its second argument being the other node (the first element of sd).

S_exec, with a parameter s denoting the node entering S, executes the entry action of S first, if any, denoted by S_entry. Then S is *entered*. After that, the behaviour is given by an interrupt. The during action of S (S_during) can be executed if none of the initial events of the right side (external choices) of the interrupt is performed, that is, none of the self transitions $sTrans$ of S or other transitions $oTrans$ from S is taken, or none of trigger events $EvtChs$ of the state machine containing S is signalled. If, however, any of these transitions is taken or any of these trigger events is signalled, then the during action is interrupted. A *stop* process after S_during prevents the interrupt from being terminated and so interruption is always possible.

For each t of $sTrans$, it behaves as follows: (1) the corresponding event channel e_t for its trigger event, such as obstacle_, synchronises on t (identified by TID_t) only; (2) S starts to *exit* by itself where $pSID\_S$ denotes (SID_S, SID_S); (3) the exit action of S, denoted by S_exit, is executed; (4) S is *exited*; (5) t starts to *enter* S again because it is a self transition; and (6) finally S_exec is recursively called with the source state s being SID_S.

For each t of $oTrans$, the early behaviour is the same as above and so it is omitted (...). After S is *exited*, t starts to *enter* its target from S, identified by SID_td, and then the target is *entered*. Finally, S returns to its initial state ($S(id)$ is called) and accepts a further *enter* request.

For each trigger event e of the state machine containing S, there is a corresponding additional event channel e_ declared in the channel type of the machine. The set of these channels are denoted by $EvtChs$. If this event e of a transition t is signalled ($e?(TID\_t, \_)$), S accepts an *exit* from one of other nodes. Then its exit action, denoted by S_exit, is executed. Afterwards, S is *exited* from the node ($fst\ sd$). Finally, S returns to its initial state ($S(id)$ is called) and accepts a further *enter* request.

S and S_exec are implemented in ITrees through nested iterations: the outer iteration, corresponding to S, is an infinite *loop* and the inner, corresponding to S_exec, is a conditional iteration by the *iterate* constructor. The condition is true for self transitions and false otherwise. An example of the process for state Waiting in Movement can be found online (⚓).

Controllers. The event alphabet of the process for a controller contains termination, event and operation call channels. The event channels include not only the events of the controller, but also those in connections between its state machines.

Parallel composition of the heterogeneous state machine processes for a controller requires they all share a common event type E, and so we rename them. The events are renamed to the corresponding events in the controller alphabet, according to the connections between the controller and its state machines. For MicroController in Fig. 1, the terminate channel, the event channels, and the operation call channels of the process for Movement are mapped to the corresponding controller channels.

In particular, for a connection c from an event e of a state machine stm1 to an event e of another state machine stm2 of a controller, we declare a channel e_ctrl in the event alphabet of the controller. The channel in the process for stm1 is renamed to that of the controller with the same direction dout. Then the channel in the process for stm2 is renamed to that of the controller but with the opposite direction (din to dout). Finally, the processes (D_stm1 and D_stm2) for both stm1 and stm2 synchronise on the channels of the controller with direction dout, which is sketched below.

$$D\_\_stm1[\![\{(e\_stm1\ dout,\ e\_ctrl\ dout),\ldots\}]\!]$$
$$\|_{\{e\_ctrl\ dout,\ \ldots\}}$$
$$D\_\_stm2[\![\{(e\_stm2\ din,\ e\_ctrl\ dout),\ldots\}]\!]$$

Here $\|_E$ is parallel composition over event synchronisation set E. In this way, the output of e in stm1 synchronises with the input of e in stm2, which is the semantics of connection c.

Modules. Similar to the event alphabet of the process for a controller, that of the process for a module also contains a termination channel, event channels, and operation call channels. The event channels include not only the events of its platform, but also the events in connections between its controllers for the same reason. The process for a module is a parallel composition of the renamed processes for its controllers, memory processes, and buffer processes for asynchronous connections between its controllers such as the connection on event turn from MainController to MicroController in Fig. 1.

5   Code Generation, Animation, and Case Studies

As discussed previously in [10, Sect. 5], the animation of ITrees is achieved through code generation [13] in Isabelle. Infinite corecursive definitions over ITrees are implemented using lazy evaluation in Haskell. Associative lists are used as an implementation for partial functions in ITrees and a simple animator in Haskell is presented.

We illustrate two scenarios of the animation of the autonomous chemical detector in Figs. 4 and 5. Here, we instantiate Chem and Intensity to be a numeral type 2 and the sequence of GasSensor is bounded to 2, which is the same as the instantiations for the verification with FDR4. An animation scenario represents the interaction of the model with its environment: the lines starting with Events are produced by the model and represents all enabled events; and the lines starting with [Choose: 1-n] represents a user's choice of enabled events from number 1 to n. In Fig. 5, we omit the lines for enabled events and append the chosen event to the chosen number for simplicity.

Figure 4 illustrates the behaviour of the model when detecting a dangerous chemical: (1) initially the controller calls the platform to perform a random walk:

```
1   Starting ITree animation...
2   Events: (1) RandomWalkCall (); (2) Gas (Din, []); ...;
3   [Choose: 1-22]: 1
4   Events: (1) Gas []; (2) Gas [(0,0)]; (3) Gas [(0,1)]; (4) Gas [(1,0)];
5     (5) Gas [(1,1)]; (6) Gas [(0,0),(0,0)]; (7) Gas [(0,0),(0,1)]; (8) Gas
6     [(0,0),(1,0)]; (9) Gas [(0,0),(1,1)]; ...; (21) Gas [(1,1),(1,1)];
7   [Choose: 1-21]: 9
8   Events: (1) MoveCall (0,Chemical_Angle_Front);
9   [Choose: 1-1]: 1
10  Events: (1) Flag Dout;
11  [Choose: 1-1]: 1
12  Terminated: ()
```

Fig. 4. Animation of the example when dangerous chemical detected.

```
1   [Choose: 1-22]: 1 RandomWalkCall ()
2   [Choose: 1-21]: 4 Gas (Din,[(1, 0)])
3   [Choose: 1-22]: 1 MoveCall (1,Chemical_Angle_Front)
4   [Choose: 1-24]: 2 Obstacle (Din,Location_Loc_right)
5   [Choose: 1-23]: 1 Odometer (Din,0)
6   [Choose: 1-22]: 1 MoveCall (1,Chemical_Angle_Left)
7   [Choose: 1-21]: 8 Gas (Din,[(0, 0),(1, 0)])
8   [Choose: 1-22]: 1 MoveCall (1,Chemical_Angle_Front)
9   [Choose: 1-24]: 1 Obstacle (Din, Location_Loc_left)
10  [Choose: 1-23]: 2 Odometer (Din,1)
11  [Choose: 1-23]: 1 Odometer (Din,0)
12  [Choose: 1-22]: ...
```

Fig. 5. Animation of the example when chemical detected with low intensity.

the number 1 event is chosen on line #3, which corresponds to the call of the during action randomWalk() of state Waiting in Fig. 2; (2) then a sequence of gas sensor readings is received through the gas event, and we choose number 9 (among 21 enabled gas events shown on lines #4-6 where the first element Din of each event is omitted) on line #7: Gas [(0,0),(1,1)], representing a chemical being detected and its intensity is high in the second pair of the sequence; (3) the controllers call the move operation with speed 0 (on line #9), provided by the platform, to stop the robot; (4) the controllers indicate the platform to drop a flag (on line #11); and finally (5) the controllers terminate (on line #12).

In Fig. 5, we illustrate another scenario: a chemical is detected but its intensity is low for the two readings on lines #2 and #7. The model behaves as follows: (1) the initial behaviour is the same: calling the platform to request a random walk; (2) a sequence of gas sensor readings is received (on line #2); (3) the controllers call the move operation (the entry action of state Going in Fig. 2) to request the robot to move forward at speed 1 (on line #3); (4) an obstacle on its right is encountered (on line #4); (5) the odometer reading is 0 (on line #5);

(6) the controllers call move (the action of a transition in the defined operation changeDirection) to request the robot to move towards its opposite direction (left here) to the obstacle at speed 1 (on line #6); (7) another reading of the gas sensor shows there is still a chemical detected with low intensity (on line #7); (8) the controllers call move (the entry action of state TryingAgain in machine Movement) to request the robot to move towards its front at speed 1 (on line #8); (9) an obstacle on its left is encountered (on line #9); (10) the odometer reading (the action of the transition from state TryingAgain to state AvoidingAgain) is 1 (on line #10); (11) there is another odometer reading (0) on line #11, which corresponds to the entry action of state Avoiding (the entering of this state is resulted from the taken transition from state AvoidingAgain to state Avoiding due to its guard d1-d0>stuckDist is true where the values of d0 and d1 are the previous two odometer readings 0 and 1, and the value of stuckDist is set 0 in this animation); (12) we omit further interactions.

Based on the animation, we also observe that if no chemical is detected, the model returns to its initial state. If low intensity chemical is detected, even without progress of MicroController, the model can continuously read through the gas event without blocking. This is due to the connection between the controllers on event turn being asynchronous, and so MainController can continuously send a turn event without waiting for the synchronisation of MicroController.

6   Related Work

Animation is a lightweight formal method. Kazmierczak et al. [21] describe the advantages of using animation to verify models. It is highly automated and cheap to perform. It provides an insight into the specification and its implicit assumptions and is very suitable for demonstrating the system. It is a form of interactive testing of the model and its properties. It requires little expertise: less than model checking and much less than theorem proving. But its biggest drawback is that it cannot prove consistency, correctness, or completeness.

Animation can be tailored to specific application domains. For example, Boichut et al. [22] report on using animation to improve the formal specifications of security protocols. They animate these specifications to draw diagrams of typical executions of the protocols. They use this to visualise protocol termination and understand interleaved execution. They experiment with the animation to detect unwanted side effects. Finally, they use visualisation to simulate intruders to find attacks not detected by other protocol analysis tools.

We use ITrees to implement a framework for animation of formal specifications. The ProB animator and model checker provides a different framework [23]. ProB contains a model checker and a constraint-based checker, both of which can be used to detect various errors in B specifications. It implements a back-end in a framework for a variety of different specification languages, including the B language, Event-B, CSP-M, TLA+, and Z.

De Souza [24] provides another framework: Joker. This is a tool for producing animators for formal languages. The application is based on general labelled transition systems and provides graphical animation, supporting B, CSP, and Z.

Rosu et al. [25] develop K,[7] a rewriting-based executable semantic framework. Operational semantics of programming languages such as C [26] and Java [27] are proposed based on K. Our ITree-based approach is also an executable semantic framework enabling the definition of operational semantics, but for both abstract specification languages and concrete refinements. And so program development by refinement is supported in our framework. Higher-order logic and nondeterminism are some features of interaction trees, but not for K.

7   Conclusions

This work gives RoboChart an ITree-based operational semantics and enables animation of RoboChart using code generation in Isabelle/HOL. To provide animation support, we extend ITree-based CSP with three operators and present their definitions. We describe how the semantics of RoboChart is implemented in ITree-based CSP, and illustrate it with an autonomous chemical detector example. With the semantics of a RoboChart model in Isabelle, we generate Haskell code and animate it using a simple simulator. We show two concrete scenarios of the example using animation.

This work targets at deterministic RoboChart models and covers a large part of RoboChart features (but not all). Our immediate future work is to investigate support of nondeterminism and give a semantics to more features such as hierarchical state machines and timed semantics.

In this paper, we manually translate the RoboChart semantics to Isabelle. This process can be automated and our work brings insights on how RoboChart semantics in ITrees can be automatically generated. The simple animator will be improved to directly allow visualisation of RoboChart models in RoboTool.

With the RoboChart semantics in ITrees, we can also conduct verification in Isabelle/HOL, in addition to animation in this paper. We will investigate the use of temporal logics as a property language for verification of ITrees. We note that verification can also capitalise on the contributions of this work.

ITrees can also be extended to other semantic domains. Further work would be of great help in extending ITrees with probability and linking them to discrete-time Markov chains (DTMCs) [28,29], which will allow us give a ITree-based probabilistic semantics to RoboChart.

Our work has many potential applications in robotics. Further research could investigate the development of verified ROS nodes using code generation here for a concrete implementation of RoboChart controllers.

Acknowledgements. This work is funded by the EPSRC projects CyPhyAssure (https://www.cs.york.ac.uk/circus/CyPhyAssure/, Grant EP/S001190/1), RoboCalc (Grant EP/M025756/1), and RoboTest (Grant EP/R025479/1). The icons used in RoboChart have been made by Sarfraz Shoukat, Freepik, Google, Icomoon and Madebyoliver from www.flaticon.com, and are licensed under CC 3.0 BY.

---

[7] https://kframework.org/.

References

1. Cavalcanti, A., et al.: RoboStar technology: a roboticist's toolbox for combined proof, simulation, and testing. In: Cavalcanti, A., Dongol, B., Hierons, R., Timmis, J., Woodcock, J. (eds.) Software Engineering for Robotics, pp. 249–293. Springer, Cham (2021). https://doi.org/10.1007/978-3-030-66494-7_9
2. Hoare, C.A.R., He, J.: Unifying Theories of Programming. Prentice-Hall (1998)
3. Miyazawa, A., Ribeiro, P., Li, W., Cavalcanti, A., Timmis, J., Woodcock, J.: Robo-Chart: modelling and verification of the functional behaviour of robotic applications. Softw. Syst. Model. **18**(5), 3097–3149 (2019). https://doi.org/10.1007/s10270-018-00710-z
4. Ye, K., Cavalcanti, A., Foster, S., Miyazawa, A., Woodcock, J.: Probabilistic modelling and verification using RoboChart and PRISM. Softw. Syst. Model. **21**(2), 667–716 (2021). https://doi.org/10.1007/s10270-021-00916-8
5. Woodcock, J., Cavalcanti, A., Foster, S., Mota, A., Ye, K.: Probabilistic semantics for RoboChart. In: Ribeiro, P., Sampaio, A. (eds.) UTP 2019. LNCS, vol. 11885, pp. 80–105. Springer, Cham (2019). https://doi.org/10.1007/978-3-030-31038-7_5
6. Ye, K., Foster, S., Woodcock, J.: Automated reasoning for probabilistic sequential programs with theorem proving. In: Fahrenberg, U., Gehrke, M., Santocanale, L., Winter, M. (eds.) RAMiCS 2021. LNCS, vol. 13027, pp. 465–482. Springer, Cham (2021). https://doi.org/10.1007/978-3-030-88701-8_28
7. Hoare, C.A.R.: Communicating Sequential Processes. Prentice-Hall Int. (1985)
8. Roscoe, A.W.: Understanding Concurrent Systems. Texts in Computer Science, Springer, Heidelberg (2011)
9. Xia, L.Y., et al.: Interaction trees: representing recursive and impure programs in Coq. Proc. ACM Program. Lang. **4**(POPL) (2019)
10. Foster, S., Hur, C.K., Woodcock, J.: Formally verified simulations of state-rich processes using interaction trees in Isabelle/HOL. In: Haddad, S., Varacca, D. (eds.) 32nd International Conference on Concurrency Theory (CONCUR 2021). Leibniz International Proceedings in Informatics (LIPIcs), Dagstuhl, Germany, vol. 203, pp. 20:1–20:18. Schloss Dagstuhl - Leibniz-Zentrum für Informatik (2021)
11. Brookes, S.D., Hoare, C.A.R., Roscoe, A.W.: A theory of communicating sequential processes. J. ACM (JACM) **31**, 560–599 (1984)
12. Gibson-Robinson, T., Armstrong, P., Boulgakov, A., Roscoe, A.W.: FDR3—a modern refinement checker for CSP. In: Ábrahám, E., Havelund, K. (eds.) TACAS 2014. LNCS, vol. 8413, pp. 187–201. Springer, Heidelberg (2014). https://doi.org/10.1007/978-3-642-54862-8_13
13. Haftmann, F., Nipkow, T.: Code generation via higher-order rewrite systems. In: Blume, M., Kobayashi, N., Vidal, G. (eds.) FLOPS 2010. LNCS, vol. 6009, pp. 103–117. Springer, Heidelberg (2010). https://doi.org/10.1007/978-3-642-12251-4_9
14. Mayr, R., Nipkow, T.: Higher-order rewrite systems and their confluence. Theor. Comput. Sci. **192**(1), 3–29 (1998)
15. Hilder, J.A., et al.: Chemical detection using the receptor density algorithm. IEEE Trans. Syst. Man Cybern. Part C **42**(6), 1730–1741 (2012)
16. Miyazawa, A., et al.: RoboChart Reference Manual. Technical report, University of York (2020). https://www.cs.york.ac.uk/circus/publications/techreports/reports/robochart-reference.pdf
17. Blanchette, J.C., Hölzl, J., Lochbihler, A., Panny, L., Popescu, A., Traytel, D.: Truly modular (co)datatypes for Isabelle/HOL. In: Klein, G., Gamboa, R. (eds.)

ITP 2014. LNCS, vol. 8558, pp. 93–110. Springer, Cham (2014). https://doi.org/10.1007/978-3-319-08970-6_7

18. Spivey, J.M.: The Z Notation: A Reference Manual, 2nd edn. Prentice-Hall (1992)

19. Toyn, I. (ed.): Information Technology—Z Formal Specification Notation—Syntax, Type System and Semantics. ISO (2002). ISO/IEC 13568:2002(E)

20. Ballarin, C.: Locales and locale expressions in Isabelle/Isar. In: Berardi, S., Coppo, M., Damiani, F. (eds.) TYPES 2003. LNCS, vol. 3085, pp. 34–50. Springer, Heidelberg (2004). https://doi.org/10.1007/978-3-540-24849-1_3

21. Kazmierczak, E., Winikoff, M., Dart, P.W.: Verifying model oriented specifications through animation. In: 5th Asia-Pacific Software Engineering Conference (APSEC 1998), Taipei, Taiwan, ROC, 2–4 December 1998, pp. 254–261. IEEE Computer Society (1998)

22. Boichut, Y., Genet, T., Glouche, Y., Heen, O.: Using animation to improve formal specifications of security protocols. In: 2nd Conference on Security in Network Architectures and Information Systems, SARSSI 2007, pp. 169–182 (2007)

23. Leuschel, M., Butler, M.: ProB: a model checker for B. In: Araki, K., Gnesi, S., Mandrioli, D. (eds.) FME 2003. LNCS, vol. 2805, pp. 855–874. Springer, Heidelberg (2003). https://doi.org/10.1007/978-3-540-45236-2_46

24. de Souza, D.H.O.: Joker: an animator for formal languages. Ph.D. thesis, Departamento de Informática e Matemática Aplicada, Universidade Federal do Rio Grande do Norte (2011)

25. Rosu, G., Serbanuta, T.: An overview of the K semantic framework. J. Log. Algebraic Methods Program. **79**(6), 397–434 (2010)

26. Ellison, C., Rosu, G.: An executable formal semantics of C with applications. In: Field, J., Hicks, M. (eds.) Proceedings of the 39th ACM SIGPLAN-SIGACT Symposium on Principles of Programming Languages, POPL 2012, Philadelphia, Pennsylvania, USA, 22–28 January 2012, pp. 533–544. ACM (2012)

27. Bogdanas, D., Rosu, G.: K-Java: a complete semantics of Java. In: Rajamani, S.K., Walker, D. (eds.) Proceedings of the 42nd Annual ACM SIGPLAN-SIGACT Symposium on Principles of Programming Languages, POPL 2015, Mumbai, India, 15–17 January 2015, pp. 445–456. ACM (2015)

28. Kemeny, J.G., Snell, J.L., Knapp, A.W.: Denumerable Markov Chains (1976)

29. Kemeny, J.G., Snell, J.L.: Finite Markov Chains: With a New Appendix "Generalization of a Fundamental Matrix". Undergraduate Texts in Mathematics, Springer, Heidelberg (1983)

Machine-Checked Executable Semantics of Stateflow

Shicheng Yi[1,2], Shuling Wang[1(✉)], Bohua Zhan[1,2], and Naijun Zhan[1,2]

[1] State Key Laboratory of Computer Science, Institute of Software,
Chinese Academy of Sciences, Beijing, China
wangsl@ios.ac.cn
[2] University of Chinese Academy of Sciences, Beijing, China

Abstract. Simulink is a widely used model-based development environment for embedded systems. Stateflow is a component of Simulink for modeling event-driven control via hierarchical state machines and flow charts. However, Stateflow lacks an official formal semantics, making it difficult to formally prove properties of its models in safety-critical applications. In this paper, we define a formal semantics for a large subset of Stateflow, covering complex features such as hierarchical states and transitions, event broadcasts, early return, temporal operators, and so on. The semantics is formalized in Isabelle/HOL and proved to be deterministic. We implement a tactic for automatic execution of the semantics in Isabelle, as well as a translator in Python transforming Stateflow models to the syntax in Isabelle. Using these tools, we validate the semantics against a collection of examples illustrating the features we cover.

1 Introduction

Simulink [14] is an industrial model-based design environment for embedded systems. Its component Stateflow [15] extends it with event-driven control for modelling reactive systems based on the notions of hierarchical state machines and flow charts. Stateflow inherits Simulink's capabilities including graphical modelling, efficient simulation, and code generation to implementations of systems. However, due to the lack of formal semantics and incomplete coverage of simulation, design using Stateflow alone is insufficient for guaranteeing correctness of safety-critical systems, such as for applications in aerospace, medical services, and so on, where formal methods based rigorous semantics, analysis and verification may be required.

There have been prior works on formal semantics and verification of Stateflow, but they consider a limited set of Stateflow features, and many of these works also lack machine-checked implementation. There are also works translating Stateflow to other formal modelling languages, but the formal correctness of the translation is not guaranteed. To address the above issues, this paper defines formal semantics for a large subset of Stateflow which covers the most important features, and formalizes it in the proof assistant Isabelle/HOL. Furthermore, we implement an Isabelle tactic that automatically executes the semantics, as well as a tool translating Stateflow models to Isabelle syntax. This allows us to efficiently conduct testing on Stateflow examples and compare the results with simulation within Simulink.

© Springer Nature Switzerland AG 2022
A. Riesco and M. Zhang (Eds.): ICFEM 2022, LNCS 13478, pp. 421–438, 2022.
https://doi.org/10.1007/978-3-031-17244-1_25

Stateflow is a highly complex language whose official semantics is only described informally in its Users Guide [15] (the latest versions running over a thousand pages) and through simulation within Simulink. In this paper, we define an operational semantics for Stateflow, which characterizes the effect of executing different Stateflow constructs. The definitions are compositional, preserving the hierarchical structures of the charts. We formally define data types corresponding to Stateflow charts as well as information that are modified when running the chart. Based on these, we define operational semantics for execution of composition of states, transitions, actions, and so on. These are formalized in Isabelle/HOL, with proof that the semantics is deterministic. The semantics proposed in this paper covers all rules in Appendix A, and all but one of 35 examples in Appendix B of the Stateflow Users Guide [15].

In order to automate the execution of the semantics in Isabelle, we implement a tactic that automatically produces the result of executing the semantics for a given Stateflow model. We also implement a tool translating Stateflow graphical models in its XML format to its representation in Isabelle. This allows us to efficiently execute the semantics and compare execution results of Stateflow models against results of simulation within Simulink. We thoroughly validate the semantics we define using examples in the Stateflow Users Guide, as well as hand-crafted examples that are used to disambiguate some tricky behaviors in Stateflow. This gives us confidence in the correctness of the semantics we define.

This work also provides a semantic foundation for verification of Stateflow models against given properties, as well as for machine-checked proofs for correctness of translation from Stateflow to other formal languages and code generation to implementations of the system. On a larger scale, this work forms a part of a model-based development framework which aims to transform graphical models based on Simulink/Stateflow and AADL (Architecture Analysis & Design Language) to Hybrid CSP models [10,22] for formal analysis and verification [18], as well as code generation to SystemC implementations [19].

The remainder of this paper is organized as follows. We review related work in Sect. 1.1. Section 2 gives a brief introduction to Stateflow. Section 3 presents the formal syntax and the operational semantics of Stateflow as implemented in Isabelle/HOL. Section 4 describes the design of automatic execution of Stateflow models according to its semantics, as well as the translation from Stateflow models to Isabelle. We describe validation on Stateflow examples in Sect. 5, and conclude in Sect. 6.

1.1 Related Work

There have been plenty of works on semantics of Stateflow-like modeling languages. Statecharts, introduced by Harel [8], is a precursor of Stateflow for modelling reactive systems, and its semantics was extensively studied [4,9,16]. One version of the semantics in terms of hierarchical automata was formalized in Isabelle/HOL [11]. However, Stateflow is different from Statecharts in several aspects. In particular, the execution of Stateflow is deterministic, due to assignment of priorities to parallel states and transitions, whereas Statecharts is inherently non-deterministic. Hamon presented denotational semantics [6] and operational semantics [7] for a subset of Stateflow. These works provide a basis for later studies. However, they miss some important features of Stateflow such as temporal operators, early return caused by event broadcasts, and so on. Furthermore, the semantics was given as mathematical definitions without formalization in proof assistants. Bourbouh *et al.* adapted the denotational semantics to continuation-passing style, and used this to implement an interpreter and code generator for Stateflow [1]. Izerrouken *et al.* formalized a specification of sequencing of Simulink blocks in Coq, as part of the qualification process for the GENEAUTO code generator for Simulink [12]. It does not consider semantics for Stateflow.

Stateflow has also been translated to other modelling languages with formal semantics and verification support. Scaife *et al.* defined a safe subset of Stateflow and described the translation of the subset into Lustre for model checking [17]. Cavalcanti used Circus to specify Stateflow diagrams [2]. Chen *et al.* translated Stateflow to CSP# for formal analysis using the PAT model checker [3]. Jiang *et al.* proposed a translation from a subset of Stateflow to UPPAAL for verification [13]. The above work covers a larger subset of Stateflow and has been used on practical case studies. However, they lack a direct formalization of Stateflow semantics, and so the correctness of translation is difficult to guarantee. They also do not consider some of the more complex features in Stateflow, such as exact conditions for early return logic, graphical functions, and messages. This paper builds upon existing work of Zou *et al.* on translation of Stateflow to Hybrid CSP for verification using hybrid Hoare logic. The correctness of translation is proved using UTP theory [21,23], but without formalization in a theorem prover. Guo *et al.*. simplified this translation procedure as well as expanding the supported features [5].

Compared with the above works, we define an operational semantics that covers a wider range of important features in Stateflow, including exact conditions for early return logic, graphical functions, and messages. We also formalize the semantics in Isabelle/HOL, together with automatic execution of Stateflow models based on this semantics for validation and practical use.

2   A Brief Review of Stateflow

In this section, we first present an example of a Stateflow chart modeling a washing machine, to show how Stateflow may be used in practice. We then briefly describe the important features of Stateflow, illustrating the particularly tricky cases with examples.

2.1   An Example of Stateflow

Figure 1 shows a Stateflow model for a washing machine. The washing machine has two top-level states: *On* and *Off*. The *Off* state is divided into three substates: *Sleep*, *Ready*, and *Pending*. The *On* state is divided into two substates: *AddWater* and *Washing*. The model has three input events: *START*, *STOP*, and *SWITCH*.

The washing machine starts in state *Off* and its substate *Sleep*, as indicated by the default transitions. Variables *finish* and *time* are initialized to 0 in the entry action of *Sleep*. The entry and during actions of a given state are defined after the symbols *en* and *du* respectively. Event *START* triggers a transition from *Sleep* to *Ready*, then event *SWITCH* triggers a transition from *Ready* to substate *AddWater* of *On*. This *supertransition*, which crosses the state hierarchy, results in exit of both *Ready* and *Off*, then entry of both *On* and its substate *AddWater*.

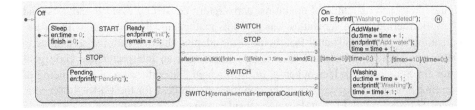

Fig. 1. A washing machine example

When in state *On*, the washing machine alternates between staying in *AddWater* for 5 ticks and staying in *Washing* for 10 ticks. This is controlled by the variable *time*, which is incremented every tick in both substates, and checked/reset in the transitions between the two substates. There are three transitions from *On* to *Off*, two controlled by events and the third by execution cycles. Transition 1 is triggered by *STOP* to stop the machine. Transition 2 is triggered by *SWITCH* to pause the machine, updating *remain* to the remaining working time (initially 45 ticks for the washing duration), and reaches *Pending*, which can return to state *On* as soon as *SWITCH* is received again. A history junction is defined in state *On* to record the previously active substate of *On* before pausing the machine, which will be reentered upon receiving *SWITCH*. Transition 3 is triggered when the washing duration is reached, as indicated by the temporal action after($remain$, tick), where tick is an implicit event in Stateflow representing the execution cycles of the active states. Then, the variable *finish* is set to 1 (to avoid infinite recursion of transition 3 due to event broadcast of E), *time* is reset to 0, and the local event E is broadcast, which triggers the on E action in state *On* to print the message Washing Completed!.

2.2   Stateflow Constructs

States, Junctions and Transitions. Each Stateflow chart consists of a number of *states* organized in a hierarchical way. Each state may specify entry, during, and exit actions, which execute when the state is activated, remains active during a step, and becomes inactive, respectively. There are two kinds of state compositions: And-composition for grouping parallel states and Or-composition for grouping exclusive states. When an And-composition becomes active, all its substates become active in a predefined order, while when an Or-composition becomes active, only one state (specified by default transition or history junction) becomes active. In the washing machine example, both *On* and *Off* are Or-compositions.

Transitions between states are specified in the form $E[c]\{a_c\}/\{a_t\}$, where E is the triggering event or message, c is the condition, a_c and a_t are the condition action and transition action respectively. When E occurs and c is true, the transition can be carried out, with a_c executed during the transition, and a_t accumulated onto a list, to be executed when a complete transition path reaching some target state is formed. Transitions originating from a state can be of two types: outer transitions and inner transitions, depending on whether the arrow leaves from the outer or inner boundary of the source state. Outer transitions are always attempted before inner transitions. Transitions crossing levels of the state hierarchy are called *supertransitions* (or inter-level transitions).

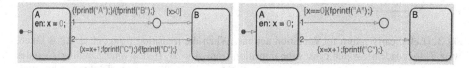

Fig. 2. (Left): Starting from state A, transition 1 is tried first, which prints A before failing the test $x > 0$. Then transition 2 is tried, which increments x and then prints C and D. The visible result is printing ACD and reaching state B. **(Right)**: Junctions with no outgoing transitions present a special case. Here transition 1 is tried first, which prints A and reaches a terminating junction. This stops the backtracking search, so transition 2 is not tried, and state B is not reached.

A *junction* forms an intermediate location for transitions. They connect different transitions to form a flow chart, which can be used to represent control flows such as conditionals and loops. A transition path between two states consists of a series of transitions with junctions as intermediate points. A *history junction* may be placed inside an Or-composition to remember the previously active substate. When the Or-composition becomes active again, the previously active substate is entered. Figure 2 shows two examples showing some of the subtleties concerning transition paths and junctions.

Events and Early Return Logic. Events trigger transitions or actions to occur. There are three types of events: input, output, and local events. In the washing machine example, there are three input events *START*, *STOP* and *SWITCH*, and one local event E. A local event is raised in actions and will cause immediate execution of its target: the entire Stateflow chart for *undirected* events, or some target state in the chart for *directed* events. As Stateflow charts execute in a sequential order, current activity will be interrupted to process events, and as soon as processing completes, execution continues the previous interrupted activity. Event broadcasts may cause *early return*: after the event broadcast, the context for performing the remaining actions may no longer be present, so they will be discarded. Figure 3 presents the two main cases for early return logic.

Other Functionality. Actions or transitions in a Stateflow chart may be guarded by events or temporal conditions. Some examples from the washing machine model are: the on E guard for printing Washing Completed, and the guard after($remain$, tick) on transition 3 from On to Off. Evaluating such guards necessitates keeping track of how many ticks (or seconds) the chart has stayed in any state.

Messages can hold data and are used to communicate between different states. After a message is sent, it is added onto a message queue according to its name. The message guard of a transition takes the top-most message from the corresponding queue, and the condition of a transition may test the content of the message (without taking new messages from the queue). Figure 4 gives an example of using messages.

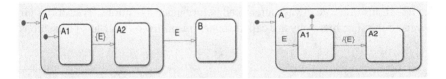

Fig. 3. (Left): early return for condition actions. When the transition from $A1$ to $A2$ is taken, event E is broadcast, which causes the transition from A to B. Hence, after handling E, states A and $A1$ are no longer active, and the transition to $A2$ is abandoned. **(Right):** early return for transition actions. The transition action of the transition from $A1$ to $A2$ is performed after exiting $A1$ and before entering $A2$. It broadcasts event E, which causes the re-entry of $A1$, so the transition to $A2$ is abandoned.

Fig. 4. In state A, a message with name M is sent with data 3. At the transition from A to B, the event guard M takes out this message, and the condition checks whether its data equals 3. The check passes so the chart transitions to B. At the transition from B to C, the check is performed on the same message and passes, so the chart transitions to C. At the transition from C to D, the event guard attempts to take out another message, but the queue for M is empty, so the transition to D will not be performed.

A Stateflow chart may also contain *Matlab functions* and *graphical functions*. A Matlab function is defined by a Matlab script, consisting of function name, a list of input variables, a list of output variables, and function body. A graphical function is similar to a Matlab function, except it is defined using a flow chart consisting of junctions. The evaluation of a graphical function largely follows that for junctions described above, except reaching a terminal junction means returning from the function.

2.3 Execution Cycle of a State

When a state becomes active, it is entered first, with the consequence of executing the entry action, then its substates (if any) are entered: all substates for And compositions and the default substate for Or compositions (if there is a history junction, the previously active substate is entered instead). As in the example, when *ON* is entered again due to switch, the previous substate recorded by the history function is entered.

During the execution of a state, first the outer transitions are checked according to the priority order. If there is one transition path that is able to reach a destination state, a state transition path occurs by exiting the source state, executing the transition actions, and the target state becomes active and is entered. If a terminal junction is reached during the execution, the execution of current state stops. If there is no enabled transition path away from current state, the during and on-event actions of the state executes. Then, the inner transitions of the state is checked in priority order. If still no one is enabled, the active substates inside the current state execute recursively.

When a state needs to be exited, first its substates are exited in the reverse order as they are entered. Then, the exit action of the state is performed.

As seen from the execution of Stateflow states explained above, entry, execution and exit of states are completely deterministic.

3   Syntax and Semantics of Stateflow

We define the syntax and semantics of Stateflow. All definitions given here have been formalized in Isabelle/HOL[1]. In this section, we write the syntax and semantics in usual mathematical notation.

3.1   Syntax of Stateflow Models

We formalize the syntax of Stateflow models as follows. In the syntax, e represents expressions, b Boolean variables, E events, f Matlab functions, and gf graphical functions.

$$
\begin{aligned}
TC &\ni tc := \mathsf{after}(n, E) \mid \mathsf{before}(n, E) \mid \mathsf{at}(n, E) \mid \mathsf{every}(n, E) \mid x = \mathsf{tempCount}(E) \\
Cond &\ni c := e_1 \ \mathbf{rel} \ e_2 \mid c_1 \wedge c_2 \mid c_1 \vee c_2 \mid \neg c \mid tc \quad \mathbf{rel} \in \{>, =, <\} \\
Act &\ni a := Skip \mid x ::= e \mid \mathsf{send}(E, b) \mid \mathsf{send}(E, b, p) \mid \mathsf{send}(M) \mid \mathsf{on} \ tc :: a \mid \mathsf{on} \ E :: a \\
&\qquad \mid \overline{x} ::= f\langle \overline{e} \rangle \mid \overline{x} ::= gf\langle\langle \overline{e} \rangle\rangle \mid \mathsf{print}(str) \mid a_1; a_2 \\
Trans &\ni t := (p_s, E, c, a_c, a_t, p_d) \qquad TranLs \ni tl := \varepsilon \mid t \# tl \\
States &\ni s \mid None \qquad Juncs \ni j \mid None \qquad Paths \ni p := \varepsilon \mid p.s \mid p.j \\
SDefs &\ni sd := (p, a_i, a_d, a_e, tl_i, tl_o, C) \qquad JDefs \ni J := \{j \mapsto tl, \cdots\} \\
Comp &\ni C := \mathsf{And}(L, sf) \mid \mathsf{Or}(tl, b, sf) \qquad SMaps \ni sf := \{s \mapsto sd, \cdots\} \\
fenv &\ni F := \{f_1 \mapsto (a_1, \overline{x}_1, \overline{y}_1), \cdots, f_m \mapsto (a_m, \overline{x}_m, \overline{y}_m)\} \\
genv &\ni G := \{g_1 \mapsto (t_1, \overline{z}_1, \overline{r}_1), \cdots, g_k \mapsto (t_k, \overline{z}_k, \overline{r}_k)\} \\
senv &\ni \Gamma := (root : Comp, F : fenv, G : genv, J : JDefs)
\end{aligned}
$$

A Stateflow chart Γ (called static environment later) consists of the following parts: the state composition *root* that is the root of all states in the chart; the collection of Matlab functions F; the collection of graphical functions G, and the collection of junctions J. Each Matlab function in *fenv* has the form $f \mapsto (a, \overline{x}, \overline{y})$, where action a is the body of the function, and $\overline{x}, \overline{y}$ are the lists of input and output variables. Each graphical function in *genv* has the form $g \mapsto (t, \overline{z}, \overline{r})$, where t is the initial transition, and $\overline{z}, \overline{r}$ are lists of input and output variables. Each junction in *JDefs* has the form $j \mapsto tl$, where tl is the list of outgoing transitions from the junction.

A state composition *Comp* is either an And-composition of the form $\mathsf{And}(L, sf)$, where L is the list of names of substates in priority order, and sf maps names to their definitions, or an Or-composition of the form $\mathsf{Or}(tl, b, sf)$, where tl is the list of default transitions, b denotes whether a history junction exists in the composition, and sf maps names of substates to their definitions.

---

[1] Implementation of the syntax and semantics, automatic tools, and examples can be found at https://gitee.com/bhzhan/mars/tree/master/Semantic_Stateflow.

A state definition sd is of the form $(p, a_i, a_d, a_e, tl_i, tl_o, C)$, where p is the path to this state, a_i, a_d, a_e are the entry, during and exit actions, tl_i and tl_o are the lists of inner and outer transitions in priority order, and C is the internal state composition. A path p is a sequence of state names, possibly ending in a junction name, indicating how to reach the state or junction starting from the root. E.g., the path to state *Sleep* in Fig. 1 is *root.Off.Sleep*. ε represents empty path (or empty transition list in the definition of tl). The path to a composition is defined as the path to its parent state.

A transition list tl is an ordered list of transitions. Each transition t has the form $(p_s, E, c, a_c, a_t, p_d)$, where p_s and p_d are the source and destination of t, E is the event or message guard of the transition, c is the condition, and a_c and a_t are the condition and transition actions.

We next describe the different actions in Stateflow. The undirected event broadcast $send(E, b)$ broadcasts event E to the whole chart, while the directed event $send(E, b, p)$ broadcasts E to state composition given by path p. Here parameter b indicates whether the sending event occurs in a transition action, to differentiate the two cases of early return in Fig. 3. Temporal action on $tc :: a$ means execution of action a is guarded by the temporal condition tc; while on $E :: a$ means a is guarded by the event E or message of name E. Calls to Matlab functions and graphical functions are denoted by $f\langle \overline{e} \rangle$ and $gf\langle\langle \overline{e} \rangle\rangle$ respectively. $print(str)$ prints a string str (in Matlab the function is fprintf). $a_1; a_2$ denotes sequential composition. Other control flow mechanisms, such as if-then-else and loops, are usually defined using flow charts in Stateflow.

Temporal conditions tc can be event-based or absolute time based, with respective intuitive meanings. E in tc is either an event or specified time units. Temporal expression $tempCount(E)$ counts the number of occurrences of an event, or the number of specified time units, since the activation of the associated state. The syntax for conditions c is as usual, with the addition of temporal conditions.

3.2 Configurations

The configuration of the operational semantics includes two parts: static and dynamic environments. The static environment is simply the Stateflow chart Γ. The dynamic environment α has the form (v, I), where v contains values of variables, event and timing information, and message lists, and I contains activation status and previously active substate remembered by history junctions.

$$vals \ni v \quad := (vv : var\_val, ev : event\_val, tv : time\_val, mv : message\_val)$$
$$info \ni i \quad := (is\_active : bool, active\_st : Paths, hj : Paths)$$
$$status \ni I := \{p_1 \mapsto i_1, \cdots, p_n \mapsto i_n\} \quad denv \ni \alpha := (v : vals, I : status)$$

The valuation v has the form (vv, ev, tv, mv). Here vv maps variables occurring in the chart to their values; ev maps path p and event e to the number of times that e has occurred since the activation of p; tv maps path p to the simulation time that has elapsed since the activation of p. Finally, mv maps message names to the corresponding message queues. The status I maps each path p (corresponding to a state composition) to its activation status. It consists of whether the given path is active (is_active), the currently active substate ($active\_st$) and previously active substate hj if there is a history junction. For And-compositions, all parallel states become active or inactive together, so the latter two components are not used (always with value ε).

3.3 Semantics

The semantics of expressions e is interpreted over valuations and states, represented by $[\![e]\!]_{v,p}$, which returns the value of e under valuation v and state p. Similarly, the semantics for conditions under a given valuation v and a state p is defined by $[\![c]\!]_{v,p}$. We leave their formal definitions to the report version [20].

The operational semantics consists of several kinds of arrows whose definitions mutually depend on each other. They range from performing a single action in the chart, to the top-level semantics for handling a sequence of events. We first explain the meaning of each of these arrows. The arrows have some common components: Γ in the context is the Stateflow chart, e on the top of the arrow indicates the current triggering event, and α_1, α_2 are the starting and ending dynamic environments, respectively. Several arrows take an additional path p in the context. For actions in a state, it is the path to that state; for actions in a transition, it is the path to the source state of the transition path.

- $\Gamma, p \vdash (a, \alpha_1) \xrightarrow{e}_a (\alpha_2, b)$ means performing action a transforms α_1 to α_2, and b is a flag for early return: $b = \bot$ indicates early return has occurred, so the remaining actions should be abandoned, while $b = \top$ indicates early return has not occurred.
- $\Gamma, p \vdash (t, \alpha_1) \xrightarrow{e}_t (\alpha_2, b, a_t, ts)$ means performing transition t transforms α_1 to α_2, b is the flag for early return, a_t the transition action to be accumulated, and ts is the target reached by the transition (either a state or a junction).
- $\Gamma, p \vdash (tl, \alpha_1) \xrightarrow{e}_{tl} (\alpha_2, vt, b, a_t s, ts, hp)$ means exploring a list of transitions tl transforms α_1 to α_2, vt indicates whether the transition has successfully reached a state, b is the flag for early return, $a_t s$ is the accumulated transition actions, ts is target state reached (if any), and hp is the lowest common ancestor of states and junctions along the transition path. There are three cases for vt: 1 means successfully reaching a state; 0 means failing to reach a state, and -1 means termination due to reaching a terminal junction.
- $\Gamma \vdash (p, \alpha_1) \xrightarrow{e}_{exS} (\alpha_2, b)$ means exiting from state p transforms α_1 to α_2, with b the flag for early return. $\Gamma \vdash (p, \alpha_1) \xrightarrow{e}_{exC} (\alpha_2, b)$ is the corresponding arrow for exiting from substates of p (the composition of p). The arrow exS consists of first performing exC, then calling the exit action of p and exiting from p itself.
- $\Gamma, h \vdash (p, \alpha_1) \xrightarrow{e}_{enS} (\alpha_2, b)$ means entering state p transforms α_1 to α_2, with b the flag for early return. Here h is a path (either ε or starting from p) specifying an eventual target for entry, which is needed to define behavior of supertransitions. $\Gamma, h \vdash (p, \alpha_1) \xrightarrow{e}_{enC} (\alpha_2, b)$ is the corresponding arrow for entering substate of p (the composition of p). The arrow enS consists of first entering p, calling the entry action of p, and then performing enC.
- $\Gamma, is \vdash (p, \alpha_1) \xrightarrow{e}_{runS} (\alpha_2, b)$ means running state p transforms α_1 to α_2, with b the flag for early return. Here is indicates whether the current execution is in the process of handling a local event. If yes (i.e. $is = \top$), the simulation time on states will not be incremented. $\Gamma, is \vdash (p, \alpha_1) \xrightarrow{e}_{runC} (\alpha_2, b)$ is the corresponding arrow for running substates of p (the composition of p).

– $\Gamma \vdash \alpha_1 \xrightarrow{[e_1,\cdots,e_n]}_{Ch} \alpha_2$ is the top-level arrow of the semantics, indicating that handling events e_1 through e_n by the entire chart carries α_1 to α_2.

Several additional functions are used in the definition of operational semantics below. $\mathsf{lca}(p_1,\ldots,p_n)$ is the least common ancestor of paths $p_1,\ldots,p_n$. $\mathsf{enb}(t,\alpha,e)$ indicates whether the transition t is enabled from dynamic environment α, when the current event is e. $\mathsf{state}(\Gamma,p)$ returns the state definition of p under Γ. $\mathsf{comp}(\Gamma,p)$ returns the composition of p under Γ. The definitions of these functions are straightforward and are omitted in this paper.

We now show rules for each of the arrows in the operational semantics. For reasons of space we can only show some of the representative rules. The full semantics is given in the report [20].

Semantics of Actions. The rules for performing event broadcasts, sequential composition of actions, and graphical functions are as follows.

$$\frac{\Gamma,\top \vdash (root,\alpha_1) \xrightarrow{e'}_{runC} ((v_2,I_2),b) \quad I_2(p) = (b_1,p_a,p_h)}{\Gamma,p \vdash (\mathsf{send}(e',0),\alpha_1) \xrightarrow{e}_a ((v_2,I_2),b_1)} \text{ SendF}$$

$$\frac{\Gamma,\top \vdash (root,\alpha_1) \xrightarrow{e'}_{runC} ((v_2,I_2),b) \quad I_2(\mathsf{parent}(p)) = (b_1,p_a,p_h)}{\Gamma,p \vdash (\mathsf{send}(e',1),\alpha_1) \xrightarrow{e}_a ((v_2,I_2),(b_1 \wedge p_a = \varepsilon))} \text{ SendT}$$

$$\frac{\Gamma,p \vdash (c_1,\alpha_1) \xrightarrow{e}_a (\alpha_2,\bot)}{\Gamma,p \vdash (c_1;c_2,\alpha_1) \xrightarrow{e}_a (\alpha_2,\bot)} \text{ SeqF}$$

$$\frac{\Gamma.G(gf) = (t,\overline{y},\overline{z}) \quad \Gamma,\varepsilon \vdash ([t],(v_1[\overline{y} \mapsto [\![\overline{w}]\!]_{v_1,p}],I_1)) \xrightarrow{e}_{tl} ((v_2,I_2),-1,\top,\_,\_,\_)}{\Gamma,p \vdash (\overline{x} ::= gf\langle\langle \overline{w} \rangle\rangle,(v_1,I_1)) \xrightarrow{e}_a ((v_2[\overline{x} \mapsto v_2(\overline{z})],I_2),\top)} \text{ GraF}$$

Rules (SendF) and (SendT) broadcast e' to the root of the chart, for the cases on whether or not event broadcast occurs in transition action. In consequence, the top composition $root$ executes under the context of handling local event e'. The resulting status I_2 is used for deciding early return logic: for (SendF), if p is still active, i.e. b_1 is true, then the remaining actions are continued; for (SendT), if the parent state of p, denoted by $\mathsf{parent}(p)$, is active, and all substates inside $\mathsf{parent}(p)$ are inactive, indicated by $p_a = \varepsilon$, then the remaining actions are continued.

For sequential composition, we list the case that if an early return occurs in c_1, then c_2 will be discarded and the early return will be propagated (rule SeqF).

Rule (GraF) defines the semantics for executing a graphical function. Suppose $\Gamma.G(gf)$ has the form $(t,\overline{y},\overline{z})$. The call to gf is equivalent to first assigning input variables $\overline{y}$ to their respective values, then executing the transition list $[t]$ (i.e. the flow chart of gf), and finally assigning values of output variables to $\overline{x}$. We use "_" to denote values in the tuple that are unused, or values that are unchanged in an assignment.

Example 1. The local event broadcast on transition 3 from *On* to *Off* in Fig. 1 is represented in our syntax by $\mathsf{send}(E,0)$, where 0 stands for condition action. The (rule

SendF) is applied, causing the execution of the entire chart using the arrow $runC$. The arrow outputs Washing Completed! but does not result in change of activation status of states, so state On is still active ($b_1 = \top$), and there is no early return.

Semantics of Transitions and Transition Lists. A transition $t = (p_s, E, c, a_c, a_t, p_d)$ is enabled under $\alpha_1 = (v_1, I_1)$ and event e, denoted $enb(t, \alpha_1, e)$, if $[\![c]\!]_{v_1, p_s}$ holds, and $E = e \vee E = \varepsilon \vee v_1.mv(E) \neq [\,]$ holds. If E is a message, it is necessary to pop a message from the message queue and record the message data. This is contained in the arrow $v_1 \rightarrow_E v_2$. Then the condition action a_c executes, and a_t accumulates to the transition action and p_d is recorded.

$$\frac{t = (p_s, E, c, a_c, a_t, p_d) \quad enb(t, \alpha_1, e) \quad v_1 \rightarrow_E v_2 \quad \Gamma, p \vdash (a_c, (v_2, I_1)) \xrightarrow{e}_a (\alpha_3, \top)}{\Gamma, p \vdash (t, (v_1, I_1)) \xrightarrow{e}_t (\alpha_3, \top, a_t, p_d)} \text{TrT}$$

We next list some rules for execution of a transition list. Suppose the transition list is in the form $t\#tl$. If t is enabled and reaches state d, then the execution of the transition list completes, with $vt = 1$, hp the lowest common ancestor of source p and target d, i.e. $\mathsf{lca}(p, d)$ (rule ToS). If t is enabled but reaches a junction d, then the process repeats on the outgoing transition list of d, i.e. $\Gamma.J(d)$. If the outgoing transitions of d finally reaches a state (returned vt is 1), a complete transition path is found (rule ToJ1); If the outgoing transitions of d fail to reach a state (returned vt is 0), then backtrack to the previous transition list tl to execute (rule ToJ2). But if tl is empty, the whole execution terminates and fails to reach a state (rule ToJ3); If the outgoing transitions of d reaches a terminal junction (returned vt is -1), the whole execution is recorded as reaching a terminal junction (rule ToJ4).

$$\frac{\Gamma, p \vdash (t, \alpha_1) \xrightarrow{e}_t (\alpha_2, \top, a, d) \quad d \in States}{\Gamma, p \vdash (t\#tl, \alpha_1) \xrightarrow{e}_{tl} (\alpha_2, 1, \top, a, d, \mathsf{lca}(p, d))} \text{ToS}$$

$$\frac{\Gamma, p \vdash (t, \alpha_1) \xrightarrow{e}_t (\alpha_2, \top, a_1, d) \quad d \in Juncs \quad \Gamma, p \vdash (\Gamma.J(d), \alpha_2) \xrightarrow{e}_{tl} (\alpha_3, 1, \top, a_2, d_2, p_2)}{\Gamma, p \vdash (t\#tl, \alpha_1) \xrightarrow{e}_{tl} (\alpha_3, 1, \top, (a_1; a_2), d_2, \mathsf{lca}(p, d, p_2))} \text{ToJ1}$$

$$\frac{tl \neq \varepsilon \quad \Gamma, p \vdash (t, \alpha_1) \xrightarrow{e}_t (\alpha_2, \top, a_1, d) \quad d \in Juncs \quad \Gamma, p \vdash (\Gamma.J(d), \alpha_2) \xrightarrow{e}_{tl} (\alpha_3, 0, \top, \varepsilon, None, \varepsilon) \quad \Gamma, p \vdash (tl, \alpha_3) \xrightarrow{e}_{tl} \gamma}{\Gamma, p \vdash (t\#tl, \alpha_1) \xrightarrow{e}_{tl} \gamma} \text{ToJ2}$$

$$\frac{\Gamma, p \vdash (t, \alpha_1) \xrightarrow{e}_t (\alpha_2, \top, a_1, d) \quad d \in Juncs \quad \Gamma, p \vdash (\Gamma.J(d), \alpha_2) \xrightarrow{e}_{tl} (\alpha_3, 0, \top, \varepsilon, None, \varepsilon)}{\Gamma, p \vdash ([t], \alpha_1) \xrightarrow{e}_{tl} (\alpha_3, 0, \top, \varepsilon, None, \varepsilon)} \text{ToJ3}$$

$$\frac{\Gamma, p \vdash (t, \alpha_1) \xrightarrow{e}_t (\alpha_2, \top, a_1, d) \quad d \in Juncs \quad \Gamma, p \vdash (\Gamma.J(d), \alpha_2) \xrightarrow{e}_{tl} (\alpha_3, -1, \top, \varepsilon, None, \varepsilon)}{\Gamma, p \vdash (t\#tl, \alpha_1) \xrightarrow{e}_{tl} (\alpha_3, -1, \top, \varepsilon, None, \varepsilon)} \text{ToJ4}$$

Example 2. Figure 2 (left) shows an example of backtracking. Starting from state A, transition 1 is tried first and reaches a junction. Since the transition following the junction cannot execute, it returns $vt = 0$. This causes backtracking, and transition 2 is tried, which reaches state B and returns $vt = 1$ (rule ToS), so executing the whole transition list reaches B and returns $vt = 1$ by (rule ToJ2).

Figure 2 (right) shows an example of stopping due to reaching a terminal junction. Starting from state A, transition 1 is tried first and reaches the junction, but there is no outgoing transitions from the junction, so it returns $vt = -1$. This causes execution of the whole transition list to return $vt = -1$ according to (rule ToJ4).

Semantics of State Entry and Exit. After a transition completes successfully, the source state exits and the target state is entered. Whenever a state is entered or exited, the activation status of the state, its substates, some of its superstates, as well as their sibling states will be changed (the latter two in the case of supertransitions).

Rule exS defines how to exit from state p: first exit from its internal composition, then execute the exit action a_e of p, and finally updates the status of p to be inactive.

Rule exO defines how to exit from an Or-composition: first exit from the active substate of C, i.e. p_a, then update the active substate of C to be empty, and if the flag b in the composition is true, indicating presence of history junction, record the previously active substate p_a.

$$\frac{\mathsf{state}(\Gamma,p)=(p,a_i,a_d,a_e,tl_i,tl_o,C) \quad \Gamma,p\vdash(a_e,\alpha_2)\xrightarrow{e}_a((v_3,I_3),\top)}{\Gamma\vdash(p,\alpha_1)\xrightarrow{e}_{exS}((v_3,I_3[p\mapsto(\bot,\_,\_)]),\top)}\text{ exS}$$

$$\frac{\mathsf{comp}(\Gamma,p)=\mathsf{Or}(tl,b,sf) \quad I_1(p)=(b',p_a,p_h) \quad \Gamma\vdash(p_a,(v_1,I_1))\xrightarrow{e}_{exS}((v_2,I_2),\top)}{\Gamma\vdash(p,(v_1,I_1))\xrightarrow{e}_{exC}((v_2,I_4),\top)}\text{ exO}$$

The semantics of entering states and compositions is more complicated with some extra tasks. The event and time valuations for a state need to be reset at activation. For entry into a composition, if it is part of performing a supertransition where which substate should be entered is known, the given substate is entered. Otherwise, the substate to be entered is determined by the default transitions or the history junction if present. In the rules below, recall the parameter h in the context indicates the path from current state to the eventual target of entry when performing a supertransition.

When state p is entered (rule enS): (1) the event and time valuations of p are reset to 0; (2) the state p becomes active, and it becomes the active substate of the parent of p; (3) the entry action a_i of p executes; (4) the composition C is entered, where the path from C to the target becomes the tail of the input path h, i.e. $\mathsf{tail}(h)$.

$$\frac{\begin{array}{c}v_2=v_1[\_,p\mapsto\lambda ev.0,p\mapsto0,\_] \quad I_2=I_1[p\mapsto(\top,\_,\_),\mathsf{parent}(p)\mapsto(\_,p,\_)]\\ \mathsf{state}(\Gamma,p)=(p,a_i,a_d,a_e,tl_i,tl_o,C)\\ \Gamma,p\vdash(a_i,(v_2,I_2))\xrightarrow{e}_a(\alpha_3,\top) \quad \Gamma,\mathsf{tail}(h)\vdash(p,\alpha_3)\xrightarrow{e}_{enC}(\alpha_4,b)\end{array}}{\Gamma,h\vdash(p,(v_1,I_1))\xrightarrow{e}_{enS}(\alpha_4,b)}\text{ enS}$$

For entry into an Or-composition, there are three different cases depending on whether h is empty: if h is not empty, then the first substate recorded in path h is entered (rule enO1); if h is empty, and if the composition has stored a previously active substate p_h, then p_h is entered (rule enO2); otherwise, the default transition list tl will execute and then the target reached by tl, that is ts, is chosen to be entered (rule enO3).

$$\frac{\mathsf{comp}(\Gamma,p) = \mathsf{Or}(tl,b,sf) \quad h \neq \varepsilon \quad \Gamma,h \vdash (p.\mathsf{head}(h),\alpha_1) \xrightarrow{e}_{enS} (\alpha_2,b_1)}{\Gamma,h \vdash (p,\alpha_1) \xrightarrow{e}_{enC} (\alpha_2,b_1)} \text{ enO1}$$

$$\frac{\mathsf{comp}(\Gamma,p) = \mathsf{Or}(tl,b,sf) \quad h = \varepsilon \quad b = \top}{I_1(p) = (b',p_a,p_h) \quad p_h \neq \varepsilon \quad \Gamma,h \vdash (p_h,(v_1,I_1)) \xrightarrow{e}_{enS} (\alpha_2,b_1)} \text{ enO2} \atop {\Gamma,h \vdash (p,(v_1,I_1)) \xrightarrow{e}_{enC} (\alpha_2,b_1)}$$

$$\frac{\mathsf{comp}(\Gamma,p) = \mathsf{Or}(tl,b,sf) \quad h = \varepsilon \quad (b = \top \wedge I_1(p) = (b',p_a,p_h) \wedge p_h = \varepsilon) \vee b = \bot}{\Gamma,p \vdash (tl,(v_1,I_1)) \xrightarrow{e}_{tl} (\alpha_2,\_,\top,a_t,ts,\_) \quad \Gamma,p \vdash (a_t,\alpha_2) \xrightarrow{e}_{a} (\alpha_3,\top)} \atop {\Gamma,ts \backslash p \vdash (ts,\alpha_3) \xrightarrow{e}_{enS} (\alpha_4,b_1)} \text{ enO3} \atop {\Gamma,h \vdash (p,(v_1,I_1)) \xrightarrow{e}_{enC} (\alpha_4,b_1)}$$

Exit from an And-composition consists of exiting from the substates in the reverse priority order and then setting the composition to be inactive. Entry into an And-composition consists of first setting the composition to be active, and then entering the substates in priority order.

Example 3. We use the washing machine example to demonstrate the exit and entry of states and compositions. Suppose state *On* and its substate *Washing* are active, and event *SWITCH* occurs. Then transition 2 from *On* to *Pending* executes. According to the rules, the following entry and exit actions are taken in sequence: (1) state *Washing* exits; (2) state *On* exits; (3) state *Off* is entered using (rule enO1) with h being *Off.Pending*; (4) state *Pending* is entered using (rule enO1) with h being *Pending*.

If another *SWITCH* occurs, transition 1 starting from *Pending* is executed, reaching target state *On*. Then state *On* is entered, followed by entering state *Washing* using (rule enO2) since *Washing* is recorded as the previously active substate.

If event *STOP* occurs while in state *On*, then transition 1 from *On* to *Off* is executed. This causes entry of state *Off* and then state *Sleep* by the default transition, using (rule enO3).

Semantics of State Execution. Execution of a state consists of the following steps: the event and time valuations of the state are updated, taking note of the parameter is. Then the outer transitions are tried in priority order. If no outer transition succeeds, the during action of the state executes, and then the inner transitions are tried in priority order. If no inner transition succeeds, then the active substates of the state are executed. Rule runS defines the first case: (1) occurrences of event e at state p increases by 1, and the execution time of p increases by 1 if it is not in the context of event handling; (2)

the outer transition list tl_o executes successfully, reaching the target state ts, with hp being the lowest common ancestor during the whole transition path; (3) determine the path exS of the state composition to exit, which is the parent of source state p if the transition is from p to itself, otherwise the lowest common ancestor of p and hp, then exit the corresponding composition exS, followed by the execution of the transition actions a_t; (4) determine the path of the target composition enS to enter, and the path h from the composition to the target state, and finally enter enS.

$$
\frac{
\begin{array}{c}
v_2.ev = v_1.ev[(p, e) \mapsto v_1.ev(p, e) + 1] \\
v_3 = \textbf{if } is \textbf{ then } v_2 \textbf{ else } v_2.tv[p \mapsto v_2.tv(p) + 1] \\
\text{state}(\Gamma, p) = (p, a_i, a_d, a_e, tl_i, tl_o, C) \quad \Gamma, p \vdash (tl_o, (v_3, I_1)) \xrightarrow{e}_{tl} (\alpha_2, 1, \top, a_t, ts, hp) \\
exS = \textbf{if } (p = ts = hp) \textbf{ then } \text{parent}(p) \textbf{ else } \text{lca}(p, hp) \\
\Gamma \vdash (exS, \alpha_2) \xrightarrow{e}_{exC} (\alpha_3, \top) \quad \Gamma, p \vdash (a_t, \alpha_3) \xrightarrow{e}_{a} (\alpha_4, \top) \\
enS = \textbf{if } (p = ts = hp) \textbf{ then } \text{parent}(ts) \textbf{ else } \text{lca}(hp, ts) \\
h = \textbf{if } (p = ts = hp) \textbf{ then } [\text{last}(ts)] \textbf{ else } ts \backslash hp \quad \Gamma, h \vdash (enS, \alpha_4) \xrightarrow{e}_{enC} (\alpha_5, b)
\end{array}
}{
\Gamma, is \vdash (p, (v_1, I_1)) \xrightarrow{e}_{runS} (\alpha_5, b)
} \text{ runS}
$$

Rule (runO) defines the execution of an Or-composition. It first extracts the active substate of the composition via the context I_1 and then executes that substate. The execution of an And-composition executes all substates in priority order.

$$
\frac{
\text{comp}(\Gamma, p) = \text{Or}(tl, b, sf) \quad I_1(p) = (b', p_a, p_h) \quad \Gamma, is \vdash (p_a, (v_1, I_1)) \xrightarrow{e}_{runS} (\alpha_2, b)
}{
\Gamma, is \vdash (p, (v_1, I_1)) \xrightarrow{e}_{runC} (\alpha_2, b)
} \text{ runO}
$$

Semantics of a Stateflow Chart. Execution of a Stateflow chart is equivalent to execution of its top-most state composition. Given a sequence of input events $[e_1, \cdots, e_n]$, e_i the trigger event at i-th round, the execution of a Stateflow chart for n rounds is represented by $\Gamma \vdash \alpha_1 \xrightarrow{[e_1, \cdots, e_n]}_{Ch} \alpha_2$. The rule for zero round is $\Gamma \vdash \alpha \xrightarrow{[\,]}_{Ch} \alpha$. Otherwise, the rule for $n > 0$ rounds is as follows.

$$
\frac{
\Gamma, 0 \vdash (root, \alpha_1) \xrightarrow{e_1}_{runC} (\alpha_2, \top) \quad \Gamma \vdash \alpha_2 \xrightarrow{[e_2, \cdots, e_n]}_{Ch} \alpha_3
}{
\Gamma \vdash \alpha_1 \xrightarrow{[e_1, \cdots, e_n]}_{Ch} \alpha_3
}
$$

3.4   Determinism of the Semantics

We prove that the above operational semantics is deterministic, as expected. The theorem in Isabelle/HOL stating determinism of semantics is given as follows. Here predicate *state_exec* corresponds to the semantic relation $\xrightarrow{e}_{runS}$ defined above. The theorem states that given static environment Γ, path p, event e, event handling flag is, and starting dynamic environment $\alpha = (v, I)$, if it is possible to reach dynamic environment $\alpha_1 = (v_1, I_1)$ and early return flag b_1, as well as $\alpha_2 = (v_2, I_2)$ and b_2, then $v_1 = v_2 \wedge I_1 = I_2 \wedge b_1 = b_2$.

theorem *deterministic_state:*
$\forall st1\ b1\ st2\ b2.\ state\_exec\ senv\ p\ e\ is\ v\ I\ v1\ I1\ b1 \longrightarrow$
$\qquad\qquad state\_exec\ senv\ p\ e\ is\ v\ I\ v2\ I2\ b2 \longrightarrow v1 = v2 \wedge I1 = I2 \wedge b1 = b2$

The proof of this theorem mostly consists of analyzing the different cases in the operational semantics, such as actions, outer and inner transitions, state entry and exit, and so on. The full proof is over 3000 lines long.

Due to the existence of junction loops and event broadcasts, termination is not guaranteed for execution of Stateflow charts. This is also one motivation for defining our semantics as relations rather than functions.

4   Automatic Execution of Stateflow Charts

In this section, we present a tool for automatically executing Stateflow charts in Isabelle/HOL. This allows us to validate our semantics by testing on a large number of Stateflow charts. The automatic execution tool consists of two parts: a tactic executing the semantics in Isabelle, and a translation tool from Stateflow charts to their Isabelle representations.

Executable semantics in Isabelle/ML. Automatic execution of Stateflow semantics is implemented as a tactic by writing ML code in Isabelle. Given the Stateflow chart, initial values, and a sequence of input events, it constructs an Isabelle theorem stating the result of execution according to the operational semantics. The tactic consists of functions for constructing each of the arrows in the semantics. For each arrow, the following steps are taken: first necessary inputs are collected, from which it is decided which rule should be used. Then, all premises of the rule are constructed recursively, and the rule is applied to obtain the result. These two steps are explained in detail in the report [20].

We implemented ML functions for automatic execution of all semantic rules. This produces a final theorem corresponding to execution of a chart $\xrightarrow{el}_{Ch}$:

schematic_goal *Ch senv el denv1 ?denv*

Here *senv* and *el* are the static environment and event list. *denv1* is the initial value of dynamic environment, and *?denv* represents the dynamic environment after execution, which will be constructed automatically by the tactic. For a concrete model, this goal would be solved by first expanding the definitions in the statement, followed by the tactic *stateflow_execution.*

Several optimizations in the ML code are needed to reduce its running time. First, there are several places where the same theorem need to be used multiple times. We make sure to save and reuse such theorems. Second, many steps in the derivation require simplification. Rather than using the general simplifier in Isabelle, which may be slow on large inputs, we design simplification methods that are specialized to our needs, e.g. focusing on simplification of functions and arithmetic only.

Translator from Stateflow to Isabelle In previous work, we implemented a translator from Simulink/Stateflow to representations in Python. Based on this work, our translator reads a Simulink/Stateflow model in XML format. Then, after calling the translator from Simulink/Stateflow to Python, it traverses the resulting Python objects of the Stateflow chart and constructs the chart according to the syntax defined in Isabelle.

The overall architecture is shown below. The input consists of an XML file containing the Stateflow chart, and a JSON file containing execution periods, input trigger events, and expected print outputs during execution. After translation to Isabelle/HOL, the semantics is executed automatically and a theorem is produced, from which it is checked whether the output sequence is as expected.

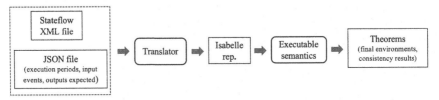

5   Experimental Results

We now discuss experiments conducted to validate our semantics, by comparing the execution results in Isabelle/HOL with simulation results in Simulink for a range of examples. We use examples from [15, Appendix B], as well as the benchmark examples in [5], and some new examples designed specifically for clarifying the semantics. Over a hundred examples are tested in total. They cover all the features introduced in Sect. 2, and their execution based on our semantics is consistent with simulation.

In addition, we test the stop-watch example from [6,7] and the washing machine example in Fig. 1. For the washing machine, in order to compare the orders of execution, we insert output messages in key entry actions and transitions. Given input events *START*, *SWITCH*, ε (10 times), *SWITCH*, *SWITCH*, ε (33 times), where ε corresponds to the cycles with no input event, the resulting theorem shows the output "Init $\to$ Add Water$\to$ Washing $\to$ Pending $\to$ Washing $\to$ Add Water $\to$ Washing $\to$ Add Water $\to$ Washing $\to$ Washing Completed". This is the expected washing cycle interrupted by one switch to *Pending* state.

Apart from correctness, we also test the efficiency of execution within Isabelle. The test environment is a Macbook Pro 2018, with a 2.3 GHz Intel Core i5 processor and 8GB memory. Most of the examples take 0.5s–5s for one simulation step (the washing machine example takes 3.5s for one simulation step), and a few of them with both And-compositions and local event broadcasts take over 10s for one step. As expected, the efficiency of execution in Isabelle is lower than Matlab/Simulink, since formal theorems must be constructed explicitly for each step taken.

6   Conclusion

In this paper, we defined a formal semantics of a large subset of Stateflow that covers many of its complex features, and formalized the semantics in Isabelle/HOL. Furthermore, we implemented a tool for automatic execution of the semantics starting from the Stateflow models. We validated our semantics on a number of Stateflow examples that contain various features we consider. The mechanization of the semantics and the consistency of execution results with Simulink provide strong justification for the correctness of the semantics.

The formal semantics can be used as a foundation for proving correctness of model transformations from Stateflow to other formal models. Hence, for future work, we will consider integrating this work into our model-based design framework on modelling, verification and code generation of embedded systems, from Simulink/Stateflow and AADL combined graphical models to HCSP formal models, and to implementations in SystemC or other low-level programming languages. This semantics is intended to be used in a machine-checked proof for correctness of translation between Stateflow and HCSP programs, which when combined with techniques for verifying HCSP programs, allows to formally verify correctness and safety properties of Stateflow models.

Acknowledgements. This work is supported in part by the NSFC under grants No. 61972385, 62032024, 62192732, 62192730 and 61732001.

References

1. Bourbouh, H., Garoche, P., Garion, C., Gurfinkel, A., Kahsai, T., Thirioux, X.: Automated analysis of Stateflow models. In: LPAR-21. EPiC Series in Computing, vol. 46, pp. 144–161. EasyChair (2017)
2. Cavalcanti, A.: Stateflow diagrams in Circus. Electron. Notes Theor. Comput. Sci. **240**, 23–41 (2009)
3. Chen, C., Sun, J., Liu, Y., Dong, J., Zheng, M.: Formal modeling and validation of Stateflow diagrams. Int. J. Softw. Tools Technol. Transf. **14**(6), 653–671 (2012)
4. Eshuis, R.: Reconciling Statechart semantics. Sci. Comput. Program. **74**(3), 65–99 (2009)
5. Guo, P., Zhan, B., Xu, X., Wang, S., Sun, W.: Translating a large subset of Stateflow to hybrid CSP with code optimization. In: Qin, S., Woodcock, J., Zhang, W. (eds.) SETTA 2021. LNCS, vol. 13071, pp. 3–21. Springer, Cham (2021). https://doi.org/10.1007/978-3-030-91265-9_1
6. Hamon, G.: A denotational semantics for Stateflow. In: EMSOFT 2005, pp. 164–172. ACM (2005)
7. Hamon, G., Rushby, J.: An operational semantics for Stateflow. Int. J. Softw. Tools Technol. Transf. **9**(5–6), 447–456 (2007)
8. Harel, D.: Statecharts: a visual formalism for complex systems. Sci. Comput. Program. **8**(3), 231–274 (1987)
9. Harel, D., Naamad, A.: The STATEMATE semantics of Statecharts. ACM Trans. Softw. Eng. Methodol. **5**(4), 293–333 (1996)
10. He, J.: From CSP to hybrid systems. In: A Classical Mind, Essays in Honour of C.A.R. Hoare, pp. 171–189. Prentice Hall International (UK) Ltd. (1994)
11. Helke, S., Kammüller, F.: Formalizing Statecharts using hierarchical automata. Arch. Formal Proofs (2010)
12. Izerrouken, N., Pantel, M., Thirioux, X.: Machine-checked sequencer for critical embedded code generator. In: Breitman, K., Cavalcanti, A. (eds.) ICFEM 2009. LNCS, vol. 5885, pp. 521–540. Springer, Heidelberg (2009). https://doi.org/10.1007/978-3-642-10373-5_27
13. Jiang, Y., et al.: Dependable model-driven development of CPS: from Stateflow simulation to verified implementation. ACM Trans. Cyber Phys. Syst. **3**(1), 12:1–12:31 (2019)

14. MathWorks: Simulink® User's Guide (2018a). http://www.mathworks.com/help/pdf_doc/simulink/sl_using.pdf

15. MathWorks: Stateflow® User's Guide (2019a). http://www.mathworks.com/help/pdf_doc/stateflow/sf_ug.pdf

16. Mikk, E., Lakhnechi, Y., Siegel, M.: Hierarchical automata as model for Statecharts. In: Shyamasundar, R.K., Ueda, K. (eds.) ASIAN 1997. LNCS, vol. 1345, pp. 181–196. Springer, Heidelberg (1997). https://doi.org/10.1007/3-540-63875-X_52

17. Scaife, N., Sofronis, C., Caspi, P., Tripakis, S., Maraninchi, F.: Defining and translating a "safe" subset of Simulink/Stateflow into Lustre. In: EMSOFT 2004, pp. 259–268. ACM (2004)

18. Xu, X., Wang, S., Zhan, B., Jin, X., Talpin, J., Zhan, N.: Unified graphical co-modeling, analysis and verification of cyber-physical systems by combining AADL and Simulink/Stateflow. Theoret. Comput. Sci. **903**, 1–25 (2022)

19. Yan, G., Jiao, L., Wang, S., Wang, L., Zhan, N.: Automatically generating systemC code from HCSP formal models. ACM Trans. Softw. Eng. Methodol. **29**(1), 4:1–4:39 (2020)

20. Yi, S., Wang, S., Zhan, B., Zhan, N.: Machine-checked executable semantics of Stateflow. CoRR abs/2207.11965 (2022). https://arxiv.org/abs/2207.11965

21. Zhan, N., Wang, S., Zhao, H.: Formal Verification of Simulink/Stateflow Diagrams, A Deductive Approach. Springer, Cham (2017)

22. Chaochen, Z., Ji, W., Ravn, A.P.: A formal description of hybrid systems. In: Alur, R., Henzinger, T.A., Sontag, E.D. (eds.) HS 1995. LNCS, vol. 1066, pp. 511–530. Springer, Heidelberg (1996). https://doi.org/10.1007/BFb0020972

23. Zou, L., Zhan, N., Wang, S., Fränzle, M.: Formal verification of Simulink/Stateflow diagrams. In: Finkbeiner, B., Pu, G., Zhang, L. (eds.) ATVA 2015. LNCS, vol. 9364, pp. 464–481. Springer, Cham (2015). https://doi.org/10.1007/978-3-319-24953-7_33

Correction to: On How to Not Prove Faulty Controllers Safe in Differential Dynamic Logic

Yuvaraj Selvaraj⬤, Jonas Krook⬤, Wolfgang Ahrendt⬤, and Martin Fabian⬤

Correction to:
Chapter "On How to Not Prove Faulty Controllers Safe
in Differential Dynamic Logic" in: A. Riesco and M. Zhang
(Eds.): *Formal Methods and Software Engineering,*
LNCS 13478, https://doi.org/10.1007/978-3-031-17244-1_17

The original version of this paper contains errors in many tables and equations mistakes and has been submitted by mistake. This has been corrected.

The updated original version of this chapter can be found at
https://doi.org/10.1007/978-3-031-17244-1_17

© Springer Nature Switzerland AG 2023
A. Riesco and M. Zhang (Eds.): ICFEM 2022, LNCS 13478, p. C1, 2023.
https://doi.org/10.1007/978-3-031-17244-1_26

Author Index

Printed in the United States
by Baker & Taylor Publisher Services